Brecht and Company

Elisabeth Hauptmann in her early twenties

The proletarian poet, dramatist, and singer
Margarete Steffin, 1934

Ruth Berlau in the role of Miss Julie in
August Strindberg's play of that name, 1930

Brecht stands with a skull under each arm,
1917.

Brecht and Company

Sex, Politics, and the Making of the Modern Drama

John Fuegi

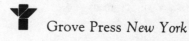 Grove Press *New York*

Published simultaneously in Canada
Printed in the United States of America

FIRST EDITION

Library of Congress Cataloging-in-Publication Data

Fuegi, John.
    Brecht and company: sex, politics, and the making of the modern drama / John Fuegi.—
    1st ed.
    Includes bibliographical references and index.
    ISBN 0-8021-1529-2
    1. Brecht, Bertolt, 1898–1956.   2. Brecht, Bertolt, 1898–1956—
Friends and associates. 3. Authors, German—20th century—
Biography.   I. Title.   II. Title: Brecht and company.   III. Title:
Brecht and company.
PT2603.R397Z61928   1994   832'.912—dc20   93-23051

DESIGN BY LAURA HOUGH

Grove Press
841 Broadway
New York, NY 10003

10 9 8 7 6 5 4 3 2 1

For Jo Francis

Contents

Preface

ESTRAGON: All the dead voices.
VLADIMIR: To be dead is not enough for them.
—Beckett, *Waiting for Godot*

This book is a frank account of those who spent much of their lives in the magnetic orbit of the playwright, poet, director, and hard-driving literary entrepreneur Bertolt Brecht (1898–1956). They lived under the shadow of Hitler, Stalin, and Walter Ulbricht, the first leader of the German Democratic Republic (GDR). It has often been the case throughout this century that those in the most danger have also been the most fearful and have dared least to cry out for help. Their signals of anguish are often so small that they are easily missed. When Maxim Gorky toured one of the earliest Soviet concentration camps in the 1920s, the guards spruced up the camp and put tablecloths and flowers on the tables in the room where the prisoners ate. To show how intellectually free prisoners were, they added the latest newspapers. For the few days of Gorky's visit, the death camp was to look like a model of open-minded penal reform.

In this fake setting, the prisoners did not dare to speak openly to their visitor either individually or en masse. Nevertheless, several decided that when Gorky walked through they would hold their newspapers upside down as a kind of international distress signal. They hoped that Gorky would notice and that a real investigation of their situation would follow that might save their lives. Gorky did not notice the signal. Believing the facade to be reality, he wrote a positive report on the treatment of prisoners. Under the aegis of the Gorky report began the cancerous growth of a system where, according to some estimates, more people died than in Hitler's camps.

Later, whether or not influenced by Stalin's practices, a similar system to disguise death camps would work well for Hitler. As the first waves of the condemned reached the German camps, reassuring postcards were received by those back home, postcards written and signed by the first groups of prisoners. The postcards lured others into following quietly and not disturbing the production plans of the SS. The pretty and wholly fake railway station at Treblinka, the sign over the camp ARBEIT MACHT FREI (Work makes you free), the fake "Red Cross" stations at the various camps where those needing immediate medical help were shot, and the fake "showers" that delivered the deadly fumes of Zyklon-B were essential parts of the death machine.

In a century where deliberate lies and theatrical facades have hidden the most deadly realities, it should not surprise us that many people discussed in this book sent signals of their plight but remained unnoticed and died unrecognized. Deceived and brutalized by both "friends" and enemies, many of these people fell into the hands of the NKVD (later known as the KGB) or the Gestapo, or were hounded by the secret police of the countries to which they fled. Behind the facade of self-serving accounts by Stalin, Brecht, and the East German government, I have looked for many different kinds of upside-down newspapers, the silent signals of those who would speak but, for many reasons, could not or would not at the time.

I first visited Berlin in 1965, four years after the building of the Berlin Wall and nine years after Brecht's death. His widow, Helene Weigel, and his close co-workers such as Elisabeth Hauptmann and Marieluise Fleisser were still alive and willing to talk with me. I worked for two years at the Bertolt Brecht Archive and at the key Brecht theater in the GDR, the Schiffbauerdamm Theater. I had no suspicion in 1965 that a great deal of the texts that I admired then and admire now were not written by Brecht. Only gradually, and in the face of steadily mounting evidence, did it begin to occur to me that it was possible that a number of Brecht's collaborators—usually, but not always, women—had often allowed their work to be published as his.

Finding out what had really happened was a nightmare in the old GDR. Brecht had been elevated to the level of socialist icon. His work was cited in support of policies that had led to the building of the Berlin Wall and a system of spying on citizenry that the East German secret police had modeled on the KGB. It was a world that carefully prescribed what was "history" or "truth." Scholars were allowed access only to Brecht materials that supported those views of Brecht the state wished to promote. Anything deemed either "politisch" or "privat" was strictly off-limits, and so marked in the "Findbuch" or catalogue of Brecht manuscript holdings at the Brecht Archive. Applied to a man who maintained a half dozen or so sexual relationships at any given time and consistently played off one political system against another, this meant thousands of documents could not be seen in Berlin.

Such tight controls created enormous obstacles to understanding how the world-famous plays had been written. When I became interested, for instance, in Brecht's adaptation of Molière's *Don Juan*, I was puzzled that there was almost no manuscript evidence at the Brecht Archive to show he had worked on it. I knew also it was generally agreed among those who had known Brecht that he had only a smattering of French, far too little to do a translation of a complex seventeenth-century text. As I looked carefully at Brecht Archive manuscripts, it gradually dawned on me that the written evidence of authorship of the German version of Don Juan pointed to a former lover of Brecht's, Elisabeth Hauptmann, and a French-Swiss director, Benno Besson.

I went to Hauptmann's East Berlin apartment on October 21, 1966, to ask about this. Then sixty-nine, still active in Communist party affairs (since 1929), she was gracious but evasive when I suggested that Brecht could not have written the German adaptation of Don Juan. When I pointed to the manuscript evidence of her contributions, she said only she knew French quite well. As a child she had had, she said, "a very good French and English teacher." Later, thawing out just a bit, she told me her mother had grown up in Brooklyn and had spoken English regularly with her while she was growing up. She also told me that the original idea of doing a German adaptation of Don Juan had come from Besson.

Besson was known to be unusually outspoken for that time and in that place. With his Swiss passport, he could leave the GDR at will despite the Berlin Wall. When I met with Besson at the Deutsches Theater on November 28, 1966, he told me bluntly that he and Hauptmann had written the German Don Juan and that Brecht had "sich kaum eingemischt" (hardly interfered at all). Besson then added that Don Juan was not the exception but the rule. Brecht had had even less to do with other plays. This was a shocking allegation.

Besson spoke openly of what had happened in the last years of Brecht's life. Elisabeth Hauptmann spoke at first reluctantly and then more openly about her massive contribution to "Brecht" plays in early years, before Hitler came to power. I began to ask if there were others who had written things for Brecht. The names of Margarete Steffin, Ruth Berlau, Ernst Ottwalt, and Martin Pohl were cautiously mentioned. There was reason for caution. In East Germany and the Soviet Union, Ottwalt had been made a nonperson, "an enemy of the people," and had died in the gulag. Martin Pohl had been arrested by the East German secret police, the Stasi, and forced to sign a made-up "confession" that he was a spy for "American imperialists." Steffin, I was to discover, had been left behind by Brecht in Moscow, where she died after having her work used by him for years and neglecting her own mental and physical health. Berlau's work had also apparently been stolen by Brecht, or so she had loudly claimed before she died in a fire in an East Berlin hospital.

The evidence I was turning up in the mid-sixties in the GDR had dangerous implications. Therefore, in the dissertation I completed in 1967 and the book I published from it, I did not discuss what I already strongly suspected about Hauptmann, Besson, Steffin, Pohl, and Berlau. In order to give me an opportunity to dig further, I confined myself at first to discussing the relationship of the plays to traditional sources; the Oriental theatre; the theatre of Sophocles, Shakespeare, and Marlowe; and the novels of Maxim Gorky and Jaroslav Hasek, the great comic novelist of Czechoslovakia.

At the same time, I was working with leading Brecht experts in Europe and America to create the International Brecht Society (IBS) and its annual research volume, *The Brecht Yearbook*. To Helene Weigel's annoyance, which she expressed directly to me, I insisted on maintaining editorial freedom by basing the International Brecht Society outside the GDR. The IBS, under my managing editorship, published fourteen volumes of scholarship between 1971 and 1989, after which I left the journal.

In 1970, I had returned to Berlin to speak with Elisabeth Hauptmann. She had just recovered from a life-threatening illness and now insisted on telling me some of what she claimed to have contributed to the work the world knew as by Brecht. She was one of those who had held a newspaper upside down, and her silence had taken a terrible toll on her. She seemed relieved to tell me at least a little of what had really happened over the years. She said much of the "Brecht" work of the Weimar years, poems and plays, was hers. If anything, from what I now know, I would say that what she told me in 1970 was understated.

In 1974, I published my first findings questioning Brecht's authorship of *Don Juan*. These conclusions have remained unchallenged to this day. My search for evidence about the real authors of other plays, poems, and short stories supposedly by Brecht spread to other countries and involved interviews in places as far-flung as Hong Kong, Paris Cairo, Moscow, Leningrad, and Copenhagen. Hans Bunge, origin head of the Brecht Archive and later a leading dissident in the GDR, kindly made available to me the tapes of the many hours of interviews he had conducted with Ruth Berlau, who had worked very closely with Brecht from 1933 until 1956. In Copenhagen, Rudy Hassing shared with me the material he had gathered both on Ruth Berlau, a native of Copenhagen, and on Margarete Steffin who, fleeing from Hitler, had taken Danish nationality. Hassing had interviewed people who had known Berlau, and had uncovered Steffin letters, diaries, and family photographs. These permitted me to trace what had happened to Steffin in the years of exile that followed the collapse of the Weimar state in 1933, up to her untimely death in Moscow in 1941.

By the early 1970s, the trails I was following led toward Moscow. It was there, from the headquarters of the Comintern, that decisions of the nominally independent German Communist party had been made since the founding of the German party in 1919. I went to Moscow in late 1973 to look at files and to visit Lev Kopelev, expert both on Brecht and on the relations of the Soviet Union toward Germany, and a longtime prisoner in the gulag with Alexander Solzhenitsyn. When I arrived at his ground-floor flat, Kopelev insisted, though it was a bitter winter day, on keeping the window open. Although we both knew that we were certain to be under KGB surveillance, he laughed and his voice boomed: "Who else is going to educate them [the KGB]?" Despite my own fear, the window remained open. Kopelev was one of those souls who had realized that holding a newspaper upside down was not enough. One needed to speak and speak loudly, even if one risked one's life in doing so. Two decades later, another Moscow source grasped my arm so tightly that his nails went through the sleeve of my jacket, and gasped the word *"Strakh"*—"fear," before forcing himself to speak of those years when Stalin had decimated the ranks of Lenin's closest associates and had launched an overtly anti-Semitic campaign against innocent Jewish doctors.

Coincidentally, around the time I did my first Moscow interviews, there was a noticeable tightening in the already severe restrictions on access to unpublished Brecht materials in East Berlin. After Weigel's death in 1973, the Bertolt Brecht Archive in East Berlin came under the control of the official Academy of Arts. Sometimes seemingly on a personal whim, Weigel had occasionally allowed me access to very sensitive items concerning the Soviet Union. After her death, it was clear I would no longer be able to see much that was useful at the Brecht Archive. As a kind of metaphysics of absence, I decided to write down the file numbers of everything I was not allowed to see, everything that was labeled either *"privat"* or *"politisch."* As it happened, almost immediately after, I found out that Harvard University's Houghton Library held a duplicate set of the Berlin Brecht files. Brecht's son, Stefan, an American citizen and a Harvard graduate, had given them to Harvard. With my Berlin list of the *"politisch"* and *"privat"* as guide, I asked Stefan Brecht for permission to see the Harvard files. To his credit, he declared no item off-limits.

While teaching at Harvard in the summer of 1974, I began to work my way through the thousands of pages that were off-limits in East Berlin. At Harvard, I found that the "poor Bert Brecht" of so many published poems had been, as I could clearly see from his bank accounts and contracts, a millionaire. The clothes that made him look poor had been expensively tailored to obtain that special Brechtian, down-at-heel look. The person who declared himself on the side of workers cheated those who worked most closely with him, lying to them and regularly stealing their work and money. Supposedly on the side of workers' theaters, he had promoted commercial undertakings, crossing the United States twice in Charles Laughton's chauffeured limousine. The person who was praised by Ulbricht and his successors for his commitment to Moscow and the GDR had repeatedly but privately hedged his bets. At the time of his sudden death in August 1956, he was preparing to leave for medical treatment in West Germany and to buy a house in Switzerland, using his large hard-currency accounts held there.

The Harvard files led me to other sources in the United States, both Germanies, Holland, France, Scandinavia, and the Soviet Union. With grants from the Rockefeller, Guggenheim, and Kurt Weill Foundations, I conducted a global search for the information that had been so carefully hidden by Brecht, Ulbricht, and his successor, Erich Honecker. I published *Bertolt Brecht: Chaos, According to Plan*, a book on Brecht's world-class work as a stage director. While crediting Brecht with tremendous powers as a director, I outlined some of the evidence that the written work Brecht claimed as his was often primarily the work of others, most notably: Elisabeth Hauptmann, Margarete Steffin, and Ruth Berlau.

Among those who have assisted me over the years were, in Berlin, Elisabeth Hauptmann, Herta Hanisch, Marieluise Fleisser, Käthe Reichel, Käthe Rülicke-Weiler, Isot Kilian, Steffi Spira, Benno Besson, Helene Weigel, Manfred Wekwerth, Ernst Schuhmacher, Martin Pohl, and Hans and Gudrun Bunge. In Moscow, I was helped by Lev Kopelev, Maria Goldovskaya, Masha Maretskaya, Dmitri Shestakov, Boris Singermann, Edward Manukian, Georgi Zaitzev, Arkady Vaksberg, Tatiana Tretiakova, and Yuri Okljanskij. Without them, and without the encouragement of Western colleagues such as David Pike, Eric Bentley, and James Lyon, I would not have dared go further into what was at the time a deadly labyrinth.

The "evidence" one finds in such labyrinths has, one must understand, often been doctored. Books, magazines, and photographs have been slashed or retouched in an attempt to discredit someone, to throw them down the "memory hole," to hide evidence, or to inflate the role of a Stalin or other icons. This tampering was widely practiced on both sides of the Iron Curtain, and both before and after the cold war. In the United States, despite the good intentions behind the Freedom of Information Act, there have been decades of arbitrary blocking, censoring, and illicit use of FBI and other secret files, making reconstruction of events by legitimate scholars needlessly difficult.

I had to memorize and later write down what I was told in the GDR and the Soviet Union. Many of the people I spoke with or whose diaries I have obtained were, like Kopelev and Pohl, camp survivors and/or torture victims. Others had been driven to repeated suicide attempts as a result of decades of mental cruelty or undergone repeated electroshock "treatments." Others, like Steffin, were terminally ill but had been pressured to forgo treatment.

What I have been given by my many deeply scarred witnesses has always been checked against whatever other sources have fortuitously survived: diaries left with friends in the West, letters that escaped the police, the Harvard copy of the Berlin files, tape recordings made semi-officially within East Germany by dissident Brecht scholar Hans Bunge, hospital records, secret-police reports, and documents confiscated or copied by the various secret services of both East and West. Since 1989, I finally had access to the records of top-level secret meetings during the cold war years in Moscow and Berlin.

I hope that in the future other scholars will be permitted to examine the terrain I have covered under vastly improved circumstances. New copies of the original Berlin Brecht and Hauptmann files need to be made immediately to replace fading old ones. More important, new questions need to be asked. So far only a small handful of scholars have begun to go behind the facade of the officially sanitized Bertolt Brecht. My own work is, in a sense, only provisional. It can, in the future, be improved upon. When Brecht's daughter, Mari Barbara Brecht-Schall, has complained to me about the conclusions she knows I have reached about her father, I have often told her that if she can provide facts to contradict my conclusions (many of which have now been in print for two decades), I will welcome them. So far, she has provided none. For future editions, I would be grateful for any corrections that readers can provide.

This book looks at a world beyond death camps dressed up to suggest normalcy, beyond forced confessions, forced silences, and upside-down newspapers. The people heard here often speak out of the shadows. Whenever possible their stories are from their perspective and in their words. Their voices are from Arctic Circle death camps, from the ashes of Treblinka and Auschwitz, and from cemeteries from Berlin to Beverly Hills. This is an account of what can still be heard among all the dead voices.

After those of Shakespeare, the plays published under Brecht's name compete year after year with Chekhov and Molière for greatest number of global performances. It was, we know, The Threepenny Opera that first established and has maintained Brecht's name in the popular imagination. It now seems indisputable that at least 80 percent of that play was written by Elisabeth Hauptmann. If she wrote so much of the most famous of all the plays, it seems fair to ask about other works, poems, short stories, and plays less famous but of even greater stature in the history of world drama. If others wrote much of this work now recognized as of world stature, included in all the major anthologies, why have people such as Hauptmann, Ruth Berlau, and Margarete Steffin and Martin Pohl remained hidden, allowing his name to be placed on their work?

Once upon a Time in Bavaria
(1898–1914)

In 1899, a photographer whose work proudly bears the coat of arms of the Royal Bavarian Court in Munich captured a small fragment of that world of long ago. Echoing formal court portraits, the photograph shows a middle-class child wearing a starched, lace-trimmed, white dress, his boots polished to a mirror gleam. The child's face is half in darkness, half in light. On his head is a wide-brimmed straw hat, a strap digging into his chubby neck. He stands on a bench, feet planted firmly far apart. In one hand he holds a brightly polished toy trumpet. Around the tiny Bertolt Brecht are typical props of photographers' studios of the time: a litter of dusty plants, a tiny hobby horse, and a whip big enough for a real horse.

The proud parents of the child in the photograph were Berthold Friedrich Brecht, born in 1869, and Sophie Brecht, born Wilhelmine Friederike Sophie Brezing in 1871, subjects of the king of Bavaria and the emperor of Germany. Both parents traced their ancestry to the sixteenth century. Both families had produced a steady stream of independent craftspeople and petty officials, with an occasional, adventuresome family member leaving to seek fame and fortune in distant, exotic America. When Sophie and Berthold had met, he was a salesman with Haindl Brothers, a local paper factory. Sophie Brezing's family was Protestant and Berthold Brecht's was Catholic; but in a city known for its association with Martin Luther and its contribution to the establishment of Protestantism with the Augsburg Confession, there was enough religious tolerance to allow an interfaith marriage. When the couple was married on May 15, 1897, the ceremony was a Protestant one, he being less attached to his religion than she to hers.

In Augsburg, on February 10, 1898, at 4:30 in the morning, with the midwife Anna Vogl in attendance, their first child was born at home, 7 Auf dem Rain. On March 20, the child was baptized Eugen Berthold Friedrich Brecht. The parents would always call him Eugen, "wellborn."

Home for the new family with its still modest income was a loud and unsatisfactory place. Their flat was over a toolmaker's small factory where metal was pounded from dawn to dusk. A few months after Eugen's baptism, a quieter place was found in a lodging house in a street called Bei den sieben Kindeln (street of the seven children). The black water of an ancient canal rushed past the house. A plaque on the wall of the new Brecht home commemorated seven children who drowned there when imperial Rome ruled the city.

A second son was born on June 29, 1900, and was baptized Walter Brecht. That September, the family moved just outside the medieval city wall to a house overlooking the old city moat. Two Bleichstrasse (bleach street) was part of a row of four houses known locally as "the Colony," which was financed by Haindl Brothers. The move marked Berthold Brecht's rise in stature following his promotion to the managerial rank of *Prokurist*. Herr Brecht was responsible for buying raw materials for the firm and finding markets for its products. Obviously liked by the Catholic Haindl brothers despite his mixed marriage, the newly named manager was also placed in charge of the Colony. The family occupied the entire second floor at 2 Bleichstrasse, and had two bedrooms and attic space under the sloping roof of the third floor, thus having six bedrooms in all.

Though the Colony was just outside the old city wall, other members of the extended Brecht-Brezing family still lived within easy walking distance. Berthold's brother, Karl, a printer, lived on the Wintergasse in a fourth floor apartment that overlooked Augsburg's main thoroughfare, the Maximilianstrasse. Here the whole clan, including grandparents on the Brezing side, gathered to view the military parades that regularly marked the calendar. On birthdays of the regent, king, and emperor, marching bands led the Augsburg-based Royal Regiments proudly through the center of the old German city. In colorful uniforms of the previous century, with their shiny, pointed helmets and glinting buttons, officers strode with flashing swords drawn, as the hooves of cavalry and heavy artillery clattered on the cobblestones. Such parades were a stirring patriotic sight. The Brechts and Brezings watched closely for the Haindl brothers, Clemens and Friedrich, both honorary cavalry officers. Walter and Eugen, dressed in tiny versions of the uniform of the rapidly growing Imperial German Navy, would be, as Walter Brecht remembered in his memoir, caught in the spirit of the parade below.[1]

These parades with their male, military, and imperial focus reflected the central preoccupations of a *Reich* growing daily as an intellectual, military, and industrial power. The often wildly intemperate speeches of the young Kaiser Wilhelm II made plain that since crushing France in 1871, Germany was preparing to challenge the empires of Ottoman Turkey, Russia, Britain, and Japan. A stream of brilliant

German technological breakthroughs and ever-larger military expenditures on land and sea gave concrete force to the kaiser's dream of expanding his empire. Alert to new opportunities for conquest, in 1900 German forces joined the other major powers in sending colonializing forces to a weak China. The kaiser told his troops to emulate the ancient Huns and to "take no prisoners."[2] Parliamentary efforts to restrain the ruler usually foundered when the flag of nationalism was waved as justification for his demands for larger military expenditures.

The model set by the kaiser within his own family, where he was often brutal, and in his relationship to his ministers, where he was often contemptuous, would be repeated at each subunit of the empire down to the schools, churches, universities, and even to individual families. Since women had few rights, the dominance of fathers and husbands was confirmed by the laws of the state.

The Brecht family followed the typical pattern. At work, Berthold Brecht was part of a structure requiring unquestioned obedience to those above him while giving him virtually unlimited authority over those below. Firmly on the side of the managerial class to which he had just been elevated, he vigorously opposed union organizing and developed a reputation for contemptuous behavior toward union representatives.

At home, Herr Brecht was, if anything, more gracious to his wife than was the norm. He gave his wife a household allowance. But, according to Walter Brecht, the category that his wife labeled "miscellaneous" was a regular source of friction. Fiscal interrogations were a monthly ordeal. As Walter remembered the sessions, his mother's answers about the "miscellaneous" would become more and more frightened until his father would smash his fist upon the table and Sophie Brecht would break into tears.[3] Walter saw nothing odd in his father's behavior.

Within the Colony, the Brecht family was the focal point of community life. The Herr Direktor was in charge of supplies of coal and potatoes bought for the firm at wholesale prices, and was the final arbiter of disputes. Since Berthold Brecht earned considerably more than anyone else in the Colony, his family lived appreciably better than its neighbors. The Brechts could now afford an essential perquisite of the middle class of that era, live-in family servants. The first servant we know anything about was called Fanny. She came with excellent references from the local convent that had trained her as a servant. For some years she was exemplary, on duty seven days a week, virtually twenty-four hours a day, to her small charges and her mistress and master. But when Eugen was about seven and his brother five, she began to rebel, insisting on a life of her own outside the Brecht household. This was not tolerated. She was dismissed. The impact of this on the children is difficult to gauge. In later life, whenever a woman, for any reason, seemed about to leave him, Brecht would show extraordinary fear of being what he called "abandoned." He would always try and hang on to a relationship, denying any loss.

Though we do not know exactly what prompted Fanny's departure, we do know that female servants like Fanny often occupied a deeply ambiguous role in turn-of-the-century, middle- and upper-class households. Often wearing the cast-off clothing of the mistress, these women were and were not the mother. Servants were often required to meet the sexual demands of the master of the house.[4] Further, sexually starved or sexually abused themselves, often they would introduce their small charges to sex. In the virtually universal scheme of that period, it was understood that one bought-and-paid-for female providing "service" of all sorts could be, and often was, replaced by another at the whim of the master. All we know in the case of Fanny is that her needs and those of her employers were different and that was sufficient for her dismissal.

The servant who replaced Fanny was Marie Miller. At twenty-two, she was, according to Walter Brecht, short but strong, loving but not particularly intelligent. Because of her wiry black hair, the family called her "Black Marie." She provided the single-minded devotion that Fanny had refused but at a price. On warm evenings when the windows were open, the Brecht boys noticed Marie sitting at an open window enviously watching young women sitting and giggling with their beaus on park benches on the street below. When Marie would dress or undress the boys, she would sometimes hide objects in her underclothes for them to find. Eugen claimed later that he loved to look for a hidden eraser in its secret hiding places between Marie's breasts or thighs.[5] When Walter, quite innocently, told his mother of these groping games, Black Marie was given a stern lecture. Herr Brecht said privately that he traced Marie's moral lapses to her lower-class origins, but Marie was not dismissed.

The sexual initiation and abuse of children by servants and relatives in turn-of-the-century households was not something that could be openly discussed.[6] Even Freud largely skirted the subject or tended to dismiss such things as fantasy, though many of his female subjects repeatedly spoke of illicit sexual behavior as part of their childhood. Except in the famous "Wolfman" case, Freud is largely silent on the subject of the real, rather than merely fantasized, sexual initiation of children within the family. Rather than recognize widespread "perversion" (even, apparently, within his own family), Freud fantasized and suppressed it. In the Brecht family, the boys were left in Marie's "care." She worked around the clock for the typical salary of twelve marks a month, room and board, and hand-me-down clothes.

Black Marie was up each day well before the family. Leaving her attic room, she would begin her work in the family quarters by six. Winter and summer, the stoves used both for heating and cooking would need to be cleaned and a new fire lit. The unpasteurized milk was set to boil, as was water for coffee, tea, and washing up. With Frau Brecht still asleep in her separate bedroom, Marie would set the table for breakfast for the father and two children. Meanwhile, the local barber would arrive to give the Herr Direktor his daily shave.

After Herr Brecht had put on his high, stiff collar and left to walk the few blocks to the Haindl factory, Marie would get the children ready to go to school. In their early years, the boys attended a school that had originally been run by mendicant friars but had long since become a Protestant institution. The "Barefoot School," as it was called, was also within walking distance. In winter, the boys would be dressed in high-topped, handmade boots, fur hats, and the thick sweaters that Grandma Brezing knit for them. Whenever there was snow on the ground, Marie covered the boys in a large fur wrap and loaded them, school satchels in their laps, into their elegant bright red sled with upholstered arms and backrests.[7] She then harnessed herself to the sled and pulled them along. She knew she had to stop just before getting in sight of the school. Here Eugen would always insist on climbing out. He was happy to be brought to school in a sled dragged by Marie, but he was not happy to have other students see how he got there. At school, in his early years, he was a solid student, able to memorize lessons very quickly.

Sometimes, after Marie had cooked and served supper in the evening, Sophie Brecht would sit in her big, upholstered chair and read poems to the boys or tell them stories, something for which she, like her own mother, had a special talent. She loved also to explain the biblical stories that were both dear to her and a part of her children's lessons at their Protestant school.

Brecht senior often went out in the evening to bowl, or to sing and drink with a local singing group. When they would go to local beer halls and order food, Herr Brecht saved his money, preferring to eat more cheaply at home. He hated to spend money when it was not absolutely necessary. Though not many details of his evening activities are known, a number of Haindl workers would claim that their Herr Direktor's life was not a model of moral behavior. What this probably meant is that he, as did males of all classes at this time, frequented Augsburg's openly tolerated, though decried, bordellos.

Sometimes Father would bring some of his singing companions home. A favorite of the children was Theodor Helm, who would often be asked to accompany himself on the guitar and sing one of his repertoire of folksongs known as Moritaten in that part of Germany. One favorite went:

> When the executioner saw her lovely face
> He cried out loud in pain.
> Then he hurried her off to eternity
> The lovely Queen Jane Grey.[8]

When the boys were still small and Marie would put them to bed, she would light a tiny night-light for Eugen. Without it, the frequently nervous child could not sleep. She slept in an attic bedroom where clothes were hung to dry in rainy weather. During the night, if there was a thunderstorm, or if anything disturbed the children's or her own sleep, she would come running downstairs in her long, white Mother Hubbard nightgown to comfort them or herself. She was mortally afraid of thunderstorms.

Despite the extra work, Marie loved the Christmas season. Walter recalled her sitting with a large clay mixing bowl resting on her flour-smudged apron between her widespread knees as she stirred a mixture of eggs, butter, sugar, flour, almonds, hazelnuts, and cinnamon. The boys would be permitted to taste the mixture from time to time, dipping their little fingers into the big bowl.

On Christmas Eve, excitement was feverish. Everyone dressed formally, Marie wearing one of Mother's high-necked, lace-trimmed black dresses. Dinner included both ham and duck with all the trimmings. While Marie cleared the table, Mother would disappear into the formal living room on a mysterious errand. She would light the real candles on the small Christmas tree and turn the handle of the music box, which would then begin to play Christmas music. Then she came out to get the boys, and they would stand at the door as close to paradise as they would ever get.

The air would be redolent with the scent of the pine tree itself, the smell of candles, and the aroma of baskets of fruit and candy, and of Marie's cookies of every shape and description. The gold angel at the top of the tree and the glass balls hanging from its branches glimmered in the soft light of the oil lamp with its fringed Victorian shade. Small and colorful figures of shepherds and kings bowing reverently to the Christ child were set up in a brightly painted wooden box on a polished side table. The music box tinkled out "Silent Night, Holy Night." Once the music ended, Mother would take her place on the plush Victorian couch and open her family Bible; in her quiet, melodious voice, she would read aloud the story of Christ's birth. The boys were given brightly painted lead soldiers, cannons that fired a small real gunpowder charge, toy steam engines, and books. Eugen particularly liked Karl May's exotic wild West adventure stories about Old Shatterhand, a German adventurer in America, and his trusty Indian partner, Winnetou, which were printed and reprinted in popular editions.

One Christmas, an elegant tricycle for little Walter was among the gifts in the Brecht household. Overwhelmed at his good fortune, he simply stood there and gaped at it. Eugen, not hesitating at all, climbed onto the velvet seat at once and tried to ride it out into the hall. But, as he crossed the threshold, the bike, too small for him, collapsed completely. Both Marie, who had carried it up from its hiding place in the cellar, and little Walter were inconsolable. In later years, in a childishly cruel prank, Eugen would "help" Walter to learn to ride a two-wheel bicycle, inviting disaster by sending him down a hill without telling him how to use the brakes.

Little disturbed the comfortable seasonal routines of the Brecht family. Most summers the Brecht parents would go alone for four weeks on an island vacation off the North Sea coast. Sometimes, while the parents were away, the boys would lodge with a forester named Knörzinger not far from Augsburg. After Herr Knörzinger shot a deer and dragged it home, he sang as he cut it up:

> *Heinrich lay next to his bride*
> *An heiress of the Rhine.*
> *But the poisonous snakes that*
> *Plagued him did not*
> *Lead to sleep divine.*[9]

Several decades later, the "Heiress of the Rhine" *Moritat*, like much else in young Eugen's and Walter's early life, would show up in Brecht's work, placed in a new era but with the basic fabric and violent tone of the song intact.[10]

The boys spent other summers with the paternal grandparents, Karoline and Stephan Brecht, who lived above a flourishing printing shop in the lovely town of Achern in the Black Forest region, only eighteen miles from the border with Alsace-Lorraine. After the death of Grandfather Brecht in 1910, the boys still loved to visit their Grandma, whose cooking they particularly enjoyed.

During the school year, the boys would spend many after-school hours in the open area behind the four Colony houses. Both boys loved to play cowboys and indians and imagine themselves in the exotic, free

America of Karl May. One year, some of the Brecht relatives who had emigrated to New York in the mid-nineteenth century brought them a wonderfully colorful play wigwam where the boys spent long periods with Joanna Dreissinger, a neighbor's child. She was told when she first asked to join the tribe that Eugen was chief and that as a squaw she could only expect menial assignments. She was put in charge of house-keeping but was also sent off on intelligence missions, gathering infor-mation on rival tribes. Apparently quite fearless and enterprising, despite her long dress, she could do everything the boys could. But her squaw status remained unaltered.

Battles between armies of lead soldiers were set up in the grass behind the Colony in good weather and in Eugen's bedroom in bad. Eugen derived his battle plans from real strategies conceived by Napo-léon or Frederick the Great. "He alone," remembered one friend, "de-termined the game. We were his generals and did what he ordered. . . . He was always lordly and imperious towards his playmates."[11] Battles could drag on for days as his generals moved Marshal Eugen's lead soldiers and artillery pieces while he shouted out the orders and natu-rally always won.[12]

Eugen's responses to the most humdrum events of childhood were not quite the expected ones. One day, as the other children stood around and laughed at a little boy called Anton who had made a mess in his pants, Eugen spontaneously yelled: "Antonius of Padua merrily shits in his Wada rah."[13] Without attaching too much meaning to the line, it is in fact a tiny poem that does what Brecht would often do later. He turns a everyday incident in Augsburg into something slightly learned yet playful, exotic, clearly irreverent, and frankly scatological, adding just a touch of nonsense in its made-up rhyme ending.

Spring and fall fairs brought a snake lady to Augsburg and a heady stream of Gypsies, jugglers, magicians, trick cyclists, tightrope walkers, brightly painted wagons, colorful tents, and barkers who would set up carousels and creaky, canvas-hooded swings. Amidst the general ca-cophony, a tall, black-hatted, pale-faced, one-legged man from Ham-burg played a street organ and sang his own lugubrious *Moritaten*. A typical song spoke darkly of "enslaved Germans in foreign parts." The singer prefaced this and his other ballads with the admonition: "Now, people, hear this story. It happened recently. I'll report it true and draw a moral from it." Then, slowly turning the handle of his organ, in his high voice, with a rasp that could cut metal, he sang:

> *My greatest dream, my only wish*
> *Was to sail the seas to*
> *Africa's strand.*

There came a prince
From foreign parts.
He bought me
And six Germans besides.[14]

Always, when he reached the words "foreign parts," the singer would contemptuously spit a stream of tobacco juice. Marking particularly significant points in his ballad, he used an enormously long stick like a billiard cue to point to huge and garish posters mounted behind him, depicting graphic episodes from what he called his "gruesome and lamentable histories." He sang of murders; rape; abductions of children, women, and men; and of attacks by pirates and giant birds.

Sometimes in the spring and fall when the wind was strong, Brecht Senior and Herr Dietz, the Colony handyman, would help the children make long dragon kites in wonderfully bright colors despite Mama's protests at glue spilled on the spotless kitchen table. The kites would share the Augsburg sky with the huge military balloons of Augsburg's Riedinger Balloon Factory as they drifted, with baskets of human freight, on test runs over nearby small communities such as Ingolstadt and dreamily beautiful Dachau.

One year, a rich uncle of the Brecht family caused a bit of a local stir. Josef Wurzler, whose parents had fled to America in 1848 and who had become very wealthy with deals in Brooklyn real estate, came over to visit his relatives. He brought with him an enormous Cadillac and his liveried black chauffeur. He was the living embodiment of the dream of opportunity and great wealth in distant America.

Despite the rapid growth of German industry, as even a small city like Augsburg rapidly became a center for military manufacturing, little seemed to change in the life of the Brechts. But in 1906, Frau Brecht had to go away for a month of medical treatment. Though both boys had been spared the grimmer, often lethal, childhood diseases such as diphtheria, tuberculosis, and scarlet fever, the following year, Eugen's health also caused concern. His general nervousness now took the form of a grimace that sometimes froze the left side of his face. There was also some talk of a heart condition that might have been congenital.[15] Dr. Renner, the family physician, prescribed a water cure at spas in the nearby Black Forest, after which Eugen's facial tic became less pronounced. His mother's health showed no improvement, though she still found time to be disturbed by her child's almost total aversion to soap and water.

On September 18, 1908, Eugen made the shift from the combined primary and middle school to the German gymnasium or high school. For a fee of forty-five marks a year, his parents enrolled him in Augsburg's Royal Bavarian Gymnasium, the school attended by most of Augsburg's middle-class boys. Of the sixty-eight children enrolled in Brecht's class, slightly over half were Catholic. The rest were Protestants, and two boys were listed as "Israelites." The figures reflect the religious pattern in the population of southern Germany at the time.

The curriculum was made up of Protestant religious instruction, with close readings of the Bible combined with a historical exposition of the development of Protestantism (with Jews routinely referred to as *Christ Mördern* [killers of Christ]); German; Latin grammar; geography, with particular emphasis on Bavaria and the Second Reich as a whole; and physical education. In the second year of physical education, the boys marched in drills with wooden staffs.

While Eugen and Walter both made good progress in school, between 1909 and 1910 their home situation changed. Sophie Brecht was found to have breast cancer and had the first of several unsuccessful operations. With Frau Brecht now needing nursing care, Black Marie could no longer carry the work in the household. Fortunately, Herr Brecht's salary was enough to support another servant. The highly intelligent twenty-five-year-old Marie Roecker was engaged and given a room on the same floor as the semi-invalid. That meant that twelve-year-old Eugen had to give up his room near his parents and move upstairs to the mansard area across from Black Marie.

Upstairs, he had all the benefits of home but little supervision and no household responsibilities. His room was cleaned by Black Marie, and he would drop in downstairs for his meals prepared by Marie Roecker. This pattern of being part of a family and yet having a physically separate place proved to be so congenial to him that it was one he would seek to duplicate for the rest of his life.

In 1911, Eugen suffered what a later account described as a "heart shock," his symptoms palpitations and sweats, and was permanently freed from physical education and the school's premilitary training organization, the Defense Society. Instead of joining any of the existing clubs at school, he helped organize his own unauthorized chess club. The group met at the Brecht apartment and published its own newsletter. Sometimes, Father Brecht would also play. He was a rather bad loser; but when Eugen lost a game, any game, in the eyes of his playmates and his brother Walter, he was the worst loser one could imagine.[16]

When Brecht's teacher happened to see a copy of the chess newsletter, the unauthorized club was ended but not Brecht's nonconformist ways. His excellent memory and gift for the German language earned him top marks, but his captiousness would sometimes get him into trouble. Asked to write a brief essay on the conventional subject "what draws us to the mountains," Brecht's answer, "a ski lift," did not sit at all well with Professor Ledermann who gave him an F. When the boy produced a four-line satire, instead of writing a serious essay, on the war in Libya between the fading Turkish Empire and the resurgent Italians, Professor Ledermann said derisively, "We've got a would-be poet here."[17]

He was indeed a would-be poet and was constantly exploring the work of other poets, novelists, and dramatists. He found he particularly liked the earthy formulations of the Luther Bible. His enthusiasm for the Bible was a source of pleasure to his sick mother as was his willing participation in confirmation instruction. On March 29, 1912, Eugen stood before the altar in his best clothes and was formally confirmed in the Protestant faith.

Eugen's mother was not pleased by the lack of effect of his confirmation on his everyday practices. When his nightshirt was put in the wash, she sniffed the front of it and determined that the formal acceptance of religion imposed no restraint on the sexual self-explorations of her son. As Brecht himself put it in a later poem:

> *I couldn't stop*
> *I did it twice a day.*

When he was advised to have minor genital surgery that same year, he commemorated this in a bleak poem that runs in part:

> *My mother didn't want it, the cow,*
> *Because the genitals are so delicate.*
> *My mother said, it's all so ugly*
> *And every fourth dame is a sink of infection anyway.*[18]

At school, the problem of "sinks of infection" would not be addressed until two years later when Dr. Frickinger gave an address on veneral disease.

For the teachers at his school, Eugen's behavior was frustrating. Professor Bernhard could hardly have wanted or expected to hear Eugen turn an assigned impromptu speech on "The Ruling Houses of Germany" into a discourse on the sexual aberrations of these families. Brecht read widely, but his reading included translations of risqué foreign authors such as Verlaine, Rimbaud, Villon and, a little later, Kipling and Whitman. After his father gave him the complete works of Munich playwright and poet Frank Wedekind for Christmas, he devoured this sexually frank author also. Modeling himself on such authors and snitching lines from them whenever the fancy took him, he was writing more and more himself. "Ich muss dichten," he wrote, "I have to write poems." But, in a piece of sober and accurate self-analysis, he also observed, "I do not yet have the strength to write plays."[19] He felt himself to be, and this feeling would persist into adulthood, primarily and rather effortlessly a poet, and only secondarily and by dint of enormous effort, a playwright also.

From his own notebooks and from recollections of various friends of the time, we know that the young poet was spending lots of time with classmates Heinrich Scheuffelhut and Rudolf Hartmann. The boys would walk to and from school together, ogling girls. After school, the three would sit on a bench together under the chestnut trees along the moat to do their homework. Heinrich and Rudolf quickly discovered, however, that sharing homework was a one-way street. Though Eugen borrowed freely from them, it was dangerous for them to borrow from him as his formulations were often too striking to be passed off as their own.

The boys were delighted to be able to buy a second-hand puppet theater, complete with a number of five-inch-high paper-mache puppets. Rudolf's parents allowed the theater to be installed in their apartment. Rudolf's cousin, Ernestine Müller, was drafted to sew costumes and to speak the female parts in a repertoire chosen by Eugen. The program included scenes from Goethe's *Faust*, Shakespeare's *Hamlet*, and lots of Wedekind. The audience was made up of parents of the children. The price of the tickets, two marks for an adult, was relatively high. This was the equivalent of almost half a day's work for a manual laborer or a sixth of Black Marie's income for a month.

As if the puppet theater and his ever-longer efforts at poetry were not enough, the fifteen-year-old now helped found an official school literary magazine, *The Harvest*. As a member of the editorial board, he selected some of his own writings. One of his first published pieces was a precocious parable owing something to the style of Luther's Bible.[20] Slightly more than one hundred words, the piece begins: "A sick old man went walking in the country. He was attacked by four boys who took away his goods." As in almost all his writing of this period, there is a brooding sense of violence, unease, fears of death, and accounts of fiery catastrophes. From the title of the piece, "The Balkan War," and the formulation the "sick old man," it was obvious to Brecht's readers that the old man was the Turkish Empire and that the four boys were the belligerent and rising powers of Greece, Montenegro, Bulgaria, and Serbia. In Brecht's story, it is the old man rather than his attackers who is arrested. "The wise and just judge" who heard the case said the arrest was essential or otherwise "these young fellows would be capable of sowing unrest throughout the land." The irony of arresting the one who was attacked did not prevent the story from being printed. All too clearly, the "young fellows" might well sow a great deal of unrest as a nervous Russia on one side and an Austro-Hungarian Empire on the other fretted about the "young fellows" and signed a series of alliances in the event of open war in that region.

On June 14, 1913, Eugen's school staged a festival to mark the anniversary of the German Wars of Liberation of 1813–15, that is to say, liberation from post-Napoleonic France. The rather typical program began with Haydn's *Military Symphony*, followed by a recitation of "The Battle of Leipzig" and "General Blücher at the Rhine." Later in the month this indoor program was followed by outdoor exercises designed by local regiments to build up "the defense capability of school-age youths." Pleading ill health, Brecht avoided all such exercises. He was nervous and anxious both about his own health and whether he really had friends. On the night of May 18, his heart pounded so violently that he could not get to sleep until eleven. At midnight he was awake again and went downstairs to be comforted by his mother. Another time he asked his father to come up and sit by his bed until he could fall asleep.

In addition to the health problems of Eugen and his mother, in mid-December 1913, the Herr Direktor himself had to submit to a stomach operation at a clinic in Munich. Just before leaving, although in pain, Father put together a billiard table for the boys. Throughout his Munich stay, he was careful to send reassuring messages. One surviving note to Sophie Brecht refers to her as "my sensible wifey" and "Mein lieber guter Schatz" (my dear, good treasure).[21]

Eugen wondered in his diary if his father too had cancer. But Herr Brecht's condition proved to be benign, and at Christmas the boys were permitted to visit him. While sitting in the waiting room, Eugen dashed off several brief poems. But the poems were not centered on a sick father, but instead on the murder of some young boys by brutal older men. The subject matter seems perverse, but this perversity is a central characteristic of Brecht's personal poetry for the rest of his life. In poems ostensibly concerned with the illness, death, or departure of those closest to him, Brecht will usually see injury or "abandonment" to himself or figures like himself.

In some eighty or so poems of late 1913 and early 1914, images of death and abandonment hover everywhere. His contributions to *The Harvest* describe a harvest of destruction. A playlet called *The Bible*, for instance, deals with a beleagued city where most of the defenders are already dead or dying. As a firestorm begins in this play, a young woman (clearly derived from Brecht's intensive reading of the Bible) is urged by her brother to sacrifice herself to the lust of the besieging commander. As she hastens off to make the sacrifice, the curtain closes over flames and carnage.

In the months that followed the creation of Brecht's fictional nightmare of war, Europe lurched closer to real war. At an assembly in June, Brecht's German teacher, Professor Ledermann, ringingly declaimed a poem of his own composition entitled "School Loyalty." The poem ran:

> All Germany arose for this holy battle. . . .
> The sweet fight on God's behalf and for the earth of
> This our homeland.[22]

This declaration was followed by group singing of "Deutschland, Deutschland über Alles."

On June 28, in Sarajevo, Serbian nationalists assassinated the heir to the throne of the Austro-Hungarian Empire. Ultimatums flew throughout July as the great powers examined their options in light of encumbering alliances and existing battle plans.

Everywhere, so it seemed, enthusiasm for war exceeded any restraining force. Austria, with reassurances in early July that Germany had given her absolute support, declared war on tiny Serbia on July 28, and the powder train of linked treaties began to hiss across all of Europe, even involving distant Japan.[23] Germany, having sent an ultimatum to Russia that was ignored, was now at war with her huge neighbor to the east. Hoping to knock France out of the fray by a strike from an unexpected quarter, Germany prepared to violate neighboring Belgium.

In countries like Germany and France where socialist parties had entered parliament and were committed to evolutionary rather than revolutionary change, internal, national political concerns overrode the concerns of the international proletariat. The parliamentarians of the left generally seemed to hope that by backing the war, they would gain adherents and would be able to increase the pace of evolutionary change toward greater levels of social justice in their own countries. Only a handful of socialist leaders, generally not members of any parliament, dared to speak out vigorously against the war. Among the loudest nay-sayers were: Karl Liebknecht in Germany, Lenin in Zurich, and the brilliant Polish-born Marxist theorist Rosa Luxemburg.

A photo of a huge rally in Bavaria addressed by the Wittelsbach ruler, Ludwig III, on August 1, 1914, gives some sense of the universal enthusiasm that marked those days. One of the faces in this photograph is of a nattily dressed young Austrian artist called Adolf Hitler. He stands, his mouth half open, his eyes glowing with enthusiasm, his fashionable hat held shyly aloft. By August 4, with Britain now formally at war with Germany, mobilization efforts were frantic. Within days and despite his Austrian citizenship, Hitler had enlisted in a Bavarian regiment to be shipped, ready or not, to the western front.

Eugen was swept up in the general enthusiasm and firmly believed that right was on the side of Germany. He described Kaiser Wilhelm as:

> *Towering. Loyal. Unbending. Proud. Upright.*
> *King of the country of*
> *Immanuel Kant. . . .*
> *Defiant in the face of the world, he holds to peace*
> *And carries the greatest burden.*[24]

In Augsburg, Walter Brecht heard people in the crowd, echoing what was being published in all the German newspapers, saying of their departing menfolk: "Oh, Ludwig will be home again in a couple of weeks. This war's going to be won fast. It'll all be over before the fall begins."[25] On the sides of the freight cars carrying the troops away to the front, the Augsburgers wrote in chalk: "Many enemies, much honor"; "Every shot, a Russian"; and "Every bayonet lunge a Frenchman." How could they have known that before the fall rains washed their chalk slogans away, hundreds of thousands from many nations, including Germans, would already be dead in the mud of nearby France and distant Russia?

2

"Sweet and Proper Death" (1914–17)

In the heady weeks at the outbreak of war, all over Europe, youths eighteen and older rushed forward in the hundreds of thousands to put on bright uniforms and be shipped to the great and patriotic adventure at the front. Those too young to serve, like the sixteen-year-old Brecht, had to content themselves with less glamorous supporting roles. Eugen was allowed to become one of the first to enlist as an aircraft spotter. He did his first tour of duty on the night of August 7, 1914. At midnight, Eugen and a school friend who had enlisted with him made their way toward one of the medieval towers that were part of the ancient fortifications of the city. Here, an old watchman handed over the keys to the boys. "Just make sure," said the watchman, "you don't fall off the tower."

Eugen wrote of his experience that night: "It was wonderfully lovely up there on the high tower in the middle of the night. Every now and again a train would roll out of the station—a train full of soldiers pulling out at night to an uncertain destiny, perhaps never to return. . . . Often we also heard songs in the quiet night. In the Ratskeller they were singing patriotic songs. Powerfully, the sounds of 'Watch on the Rhine' rose up to us."[1]

This account, written for the *Augsburger Neusten Nachrichten (Newest Reports)*, was published on August 8. The editor of the paper, Herr Brüstle, was sufficiently impressed by Brecht as a reporter that he encouraged him to write more "Augsburg Letters on the War," which became a regular feature and was also picked up by the larger circulation *München-Augsburger Abendzeitung (Evening Paper)*.

Like the nation itself, the "letters" glowed with fervor and compassion for German sacrifices. Brecht described soldiers marching willingly, "with firm and quiet tread" to board trains for the front. This was, said Eugen, "a people's war," a war that represented the "resurrection of the nation." Signing his pieces "Berthold Eugen," he urged his readers "to make sacrifices, even when these sacrifices should demand much blood." In late August, the first of the wounded and dead arrived back into Augsburg. "We saw," Berthold Eugen reported, "the ruins of young men as they were carried past us on that gray day. One had lost both legs. Another an arm. Another, pale as wax, stared up to heaven." His report to his readers ended: "And the great single thing that we Germans want is: To guard our honor. To guard our freedom, to guard ourselves. And that is worth every sacrifice."[2]

The child writing these reports knew as little as the rest of the German population, and his own views were based on radically skewed information. Reporting on the war on every side was massively biased, with defeats ignored and victories blown out of all proportion. German reporting was, if anything, outdone by British writing. Tales of atrocities committed by "the other side" made compromise appear unthinkable.

Though the general propaganda line everywhere was that this was a battle for God, the good, the true, and the beautiful, behind the scenes a different battle was being fought. Ludwig III informed the Prussian chargé d'affaires in Munich on August 14 that Bavaria, as the price for her support of the war effort, expected to emerge from it with control of large portions of Alsace-Lorraine, sections of Belgium and the Netherlands, and the throne of Poland. Similar ambitions were expressed by the king of Saxony and the duke of Württemberg. The Prussians planned annexation of the Baltic and Slavic-held lands to the east.[3]

In fact, Germany had little hope of breaking the British blockade of her ports, nor of winning a vastly overextended two-front war. Reality was not to be found in the vast dreams of empire or in the biased reporting on the war, but in the hundreds of thousands of privately placed death announcements in the German papers. As the torrent of deaths rose, on the streets of Augsburg papers were sold with the hawker's cry: "Get forty thousand Frenchmen for just five pfennig."[4]

At Eugen's school, ten teachers enlisted immediately, and thirty-eight students old enough to serve dropped out of school to be quickly trained and sent to the front. One of these voluntary enlistees was Caspar Neher, whom Eugen had known as a fairly casual school friend since 1911. Born on April 11, 1897, Rudolf Ludwig Caspar Neher was a year older than Brecht. But Cas, as he was known, was slower in most school subjects than his younger friend, though he did show from very early childhood on great gifts in drawing. Neher's father, a stern and rigid gymnasium teacher, made no bones about his disappointment at his son's slowness. Though Herr Neher recognized his son's talent as an artist, he reacted strongly against it as a way of making a living. In 1914, however, he allowed Cas to transfer from the Augsburg Gymnasium to an applied art school in nearby Munich. From there, after his eighteenth birthday, he was enrolled in the Fourth Bavarian Field Artillery unit. Neher's service at the front in various combat units involved thirty-two separate battles. His regiments, like the Sixteenth Bavarian in which Adolf Hitler served, sometimes lost half their members in individual battles. On his short leaves in Augsburg, Cas always spent time with Eugen. From his friend, Brecht began to hear about the realities of trench warfare.

Beginning in 1915, Brecht's writing shifted away from wholly romanticized views of fighting and dying. In a poem called "The Flag Cadet" (the rank of most of Brecht's young friends in the army), he speaks of a young man whose face is pale but his eyes "ablaze with the flame of sacrifice." With the short sword issued to junior officers, the cadet kills five of the enemy, but the poem ends with the cadet, mortally wounded, "screaming with mad, scared eyes."[5]

When the losses at the front became a deluge, standards of physical fitness were lowered both for enlistment and for service in the Defense Society at Eugen's school. By faking his father's signature, he continued to get waivers. His aircraft spotting enthusiasm had sunk, and his contribution to the war effort was now exclusively through his pen. He now had a regular small income from his writing.

Whatever the horrors were for those at the front and for those in the factories working with inadequate safety precautions, income, clothes, and nourishment, material conditions for the Brecht family were, if anything, better than before. The Haindl brothers were often away with their regiments, leaving Herr Brecht greater responsibilities and a larger income. The Brechts, unlike most Germans, were well supplied with food, clothing, and coal to heat their large apartment. And war or no war, service to the family members was provided not only by Black Marie and Marie Roecker but, beginning in 1916, by fourteen-year-old Mari Hold. As Frau Brecht's cancer advanced, she became more of an invalid, requiring a third servant to maintain a proper standard of service for the ever-busier Herr Direktor, his business guests, his ill wife, and two growing boys.

In the culture in which she was slowly dying, Sophie Brecht could expect no open affection to be shown toward her. Of his father's attitude toward his mother, Walter would write later: "No doubt he was filled with love for her, but the demands for sober, dispassionate behavior that everyday life requires stood in the way."[6] The fact that Walter himself felt that such behavior was required explains perhaps why neither he nor his brother expressed in direct physical or verbal ways any of the love they felt for her. In the world of the Brecht household, as in the culture at large, men were supposed to keep physical and emotional distance even from those supposedly closest to them.

According to Eugen's notes, in the winter of 1914–15, around the time of his seventeenth birthday, he began to widen his sexual horizons.

At the municipal ice rink, he met a girl of "advanced ripeness" who not only invited him to kiss her but also made it plain to him that she wanted more. But Eugen did not know how to proceed exactly. He decided therefore to first visit a local brothel. Having been introduced for a fee to the basics, he returned to the eager young lady of the ice rink.[7]

Written decades after these events are supposed to have happened, several of Brecht's notes speak of heterosexual experiences; however, these notes make no mention at all of the homosexuality that had so preoccupied him earlier. The letters, poems, stories, and diaries of his late teens and the first half of his twenties speak of an omnivorous sexuality seeking any outlet or inlet, male or female, young or old. At his attic apartment at the Colony, amidst a litter of paper on every horizontal surface, various musical instruments, and pictures of Napoléon and Nietzsche, Eugen and his friends would read their frequently erotic compositions to each other, sometimes singing them to tunes of their own composition. From his numerous pockets, Eugen would pull slips of paper covered in his execrable handwriting, and would read or sing of real or imagined sexual exploits. As with his homework assignments, the sovereign Eugen would borrow from friends, absorbing their creative work into his own compositions.

He created a Möbius strip of life and poetry. His poems helped his seductions. The seductions became central to the poems. His friends, caught up by his personal magnetism, usually allowed him to take over their work without asking for any recognition. Among the inner circle at this time, those with the requisite energy, talent, time, and necessary selflessness were his brother Walter, a gifted amateur musician who helped his brother to come up with tunes suitable for the guitar; Cas, who remained useful even while he was away at the front, sending back, upon Brecht's request, drawings that Brecht then used as gifts in his seduction campaigns; Georg Pfanzelt, nicknamed Orge, a saturnine young man, a few years older than the rest of the group but saved from military service by his obvious clubfoot, a fine musician, an inventive poet, and absolutely smitten by Brecht's charms; Rudolf Hartmann, who was particularly helpful with the puppet-theater project; Ludwig Prestel, who was sweating out the draft but meanwhile advised Brecht on classical music; and Max Hohenester, Georg Geyer, and Fritz Schreier. An occasional visitor was a girl whose name we do not know who was studying Classical Greek at her gymnasium. She was useful for her ability to read Homer aloud and do sight translations of the original Greek metrics.

For hour after hour, Orge would explain and play Beethoven sonatas for his friend, while Brecht could often be seen carrying a volume with Beethoven's name conspicuously displayed on the cover. Geyer played and explained the works of Bach, Haydn, and Mozart. Brecht's own musical accomplishments were meager but adequate to his purposes. He could pick out tunes with one finger on the piano, strum a guitar well enough to accompany himself in a loud and enthusiastic way, and knew an elementary form of musical notation so that he could jot down the rough outlines of tunes that he thought he might be able to use. Drawing freely on his many talented friends for musical ideas and lines and verses of poems, and borrowing just as freely from the published poems of Rimbaud, Villon, and Kipling in German transla-tion, as well as from the performance works of Frank Wedekind, he would sing to his friends in a voice that was high, driving, and com-pletely untrained.

The effect of his singing was electric. He sang, as Hohenester put it, "with sweeping passion, drunk from his own verses . . . and those who heard him became drunk also."[8] At first in private, and later in settings like restaurants, bars, and brothels, he noticed not only how his audiences were swept away, but that this could easily lead to sexual enthrallment also. Somehow it did not seem to matter that he was not conventionally handsome and none too clean, that his teeth were al-ready rotting and that his breath stank, and that his unmatched, though expensive, clothes looked as if he slept in them; it all was part of his charm, a link to tough poetic models like the poet-murderer Villon or the poet lovers Verlaine and Rimbaud.

But though Eugen had now mastered the role and dress of the bohemian, this was a costume that he could put on or take off at will. During the war years, he dressed appropriately on family occasions in suit, tie, and formal hat. When Herr Clemens Haindl, for instance, would return from the front and invite his top employees over to his villa to give an after-dinner recital on his enormous, built-in house organ, Eugen attended the recital and, signing his work "Berthold Eugen," sent Herr Haindl a poem in which he said the organ playing had evoked images of regiments crossing open fields in battle.[9] This January 1916 poem is conventional in both form and content, replete with "eternal and infinite heaven" and "eternal love."

By the midpoint of the Great War, while still attending events at Herr Haindl's villa, Brecht had begun to doubt many hallowed conven-tions of middle-class propriety. Knowing that as long as he was enrolled in the gymnasium and did not voluntarily enlist he was safe from military service, he still attended school but had drifted further and further away from everything it represented. The subjects he now stud-ied assiduously were love and how to avoid war. At the Augsburg fair, or in the bars, brothels, and back alleys of wartime Augsburg, or in the city's many churches or art galleries, or in the municipal or commercial libraries, including the erotic library in a basement on the Königsplatz, he would cover scraps of paper with scribbled notes for later use in poems growing in length and complexity.

As the war ground on, with the newer technologies of tanks and machine guns and the use of airplanes increasing the death rate, Brecht's poetry reflected deepening despair. He is constantly, not only in imagination but in fact, abandoned as those closest to him leave for almost certain death. Near his eighteenth birthday, that watershed point making him eligible for the draft, he wrote "Soldier's Grave." A soldier-poet stands on the edge of a mass grave desperately seeking to maintain some physical and emotional distance as he contemplates the death of someone to whom he had felt close. Looking at a mass of jumbled bodies, the poet avers:

> *With the soldiers down there*
> *My friend is also there.*
> *But I can't find him.*
> *It's all the same, anyway.*[10]

He signed the poem "Berthold Eugen." It would be the last time he would use this nom de plume but not the last time he would try through poetry to distance himself from both psychological and physical death.

That spring of 1916, Brecht's Latin teacher, Dr. Gebhard, asked the class to prepare an essay on Horace's famous line: "Dulce et decorum est pro patria mori" (it is sweet and proper to die for your fatherland). The next day, the fifteen students now left in a class that had begun with sixty-eight filed into the classroom to await Dr. Gebhard. Eugen took his customary place at the back of the room. When Dr. Gebhard entered, it was clear something was seriously wrong. Brecht was sitting with his head bowed when he heard his name angrily called. He stood up, as required, at attention. Gebhard, in a voice breaking with anger, demanded to know how anyone, least of all a person who was himself a poet, could write something like this about Horace! For Eugen had turned in the following essay:

> The saying that it is sweet and proper to die for one's fatherland can be seen only as crass propaganda. It is always difficult to give up one's life whether in bed or on the field of battle, particularly when, as so often, it is young men who die, young men in the flower of their years. Only those whose own heads are completely hollow could carry barefaced trickery so far as to speak of a gentle jump through the doors of darkness. And even they

would speak that way only as long as they felt nowhere near their own last hour on earth. But, if the grim reaper were to approach them, then they would put their shields on their backs and slink away like the emperor's fat fool at the Battle of Philippi, the fat fool who first dreamed up this saying.[11]

The outraged Dr. Gebhard said that he would demand that the faculty council expel Brecht immediately. Fortunately, however, Brecht's French teacher, a young Benedictine monk and family friend named Father Sauer, argued before the council that the lapse was nothing more serious than an expression "of a schoolboy brain confused by the war."[12] Swayed by Father Sauer, the council agreed to let Brecht remain in school though his record would carry the permanent notation of his "failure to abide by the rules of the school." It had been a close call. If he had been expelled at eighteen, the odds were that he would have been immediately drafted and shipped to a front that was a shell-pocked landscape of the unburied dead, and of tank and air assaults, under constant threat of poison gas attacks.

Outside school, with an appealing mixture of shyness and boldness, he was carrying on several affairs at once and initiating others. Bright, bold, and delicate in his appreciation of the arts, while being at the same time apparently helpless in doing everyday tasks, he appealed to both young men and young women. By the spring of 1916, he was pursuing affairs with Ernestine Müller, Sofie Renner, and Lilly Krause, while having his eye on a certain Therese Ostheimer and a beautiful, dark-haired fifteen-year-old schoolgirl, Paula "Bie" Banholzer. Then he also happened to see still another attractive schoolgirl, the dark-haired Marie Aman, in an Augsburg ice-cream shop.

To bring these affairs to the point where he could begin sleeping with all these young women required careful organization and the regular use of deception. When Marie Aman, perhaps having heard of Brecht's various other dalliances in that small-town community, told him that her pastor had warned her about nonserious relationships, Brecht was indignant. He hurried to see her pastor and assured him that his intentions were strictly honorable and that he intended to marry her as soon as this could be suitably arranged. Both the pastor and Marie were reassured. What Brecht had not said was that his intentions were equally firm with all the young women he was pursuing.

With each object of his attentions assured individually of the honesty of his goals, he made progress on various fronts. Walking one day by a canal, Eugen suddenly grabbed Marie and kissed her. She was shocked and told him that she did not know what consequences a kiss might bring. "My dear child," said the eighteen-year-old Brecht, "you must go to your mother and ask her to enlighten you. That's not my job."[13] Soon he took Marie home to meet his invalid mother. And soon Marie even ventured up to the top floor where Brecht had his bedroom. Frau Brecht was not well enough to intervene and Fräulein Roecker, though nominally in charge of running the household, could only cluck and complain. She had no power to prevent the young master from doing whatever he wanted; and the boy's father seemed more delighted than dismayed at what his son was doing.

Soon dreadful rumors circulated. Marie Aman was told that Eugen had burnt a Bible and a catechism! Yet Brecht's intentions toward Marie seemed honorable. Why else would he have taken her home to meet his mother? Why else would he talk with her about his strict ideas on marriage and family budgets? He was quite explicit in saying that she would get a new hat and a new baby from him in each of the next seven years. And he showed devotion by writing lovely verses in her family album.

Looking at the surviving verses in this and other albums and letters, it is clear that, though often conventional in tone, the verses are consistent in quality. Brecht was distributing them rather evenly among Marie, Bie, Ernestine, Lilly, and Therese. Furthermore, the verses were often effective. Bie Banholzer, to whom he sometimes gave the alternative nickname of "Paul," had also consented to walk with Eugen along the canals. And, one windy autumn day, he seized her and kissed her. She too was frightened by the consequences of a kiss and told him she would never see him again. But after marching up and down under her windows at set hours for several days, looking suitably penitent, he whistled up, and she finally came shyly down. Soon she went home with him and visited his invalid mother. And soon she too was visiting him upstairs in his bedroom. Shortly afterward, Bie invited him to tea at her own home to meet her father, the respectable Dr. Banholzer.[14] While things moved forward nicely now with Bie, though her father remained dubious about this rather ill-kempt young man, Brecht was trying to guide other affairs toward a horizontal goal.

A long letter written to Therese Ostheimer in July 1916 and a fragment of a diary from the fall of the same year give a sense of the mixture of cold self-reflection and burning intensity with which his affairs were usually conducted. Four pages long, using a mixture of formality, shyness, and self-aggrandizement, the eighteen-year-old "artist" Brecht begs an "audience" with eighteen-year-old Therese. In his diary he noted that Therese's eyes were beautiful and intelligent, and that he was reflected in them "as a tiger."[15]

The choice of imagery used here, the boy as tiger reflected in a young woman's eyes, seems almost random, but it reflects a pattern.

Therese Ostheimer is turned into a mirror in which he thinks he sees himself not as a mere, sick schoolboy, but a strong, wild, dominant animal. As one critic who has examined this passage notes, "At the time that a mirror was still water, the name of the one who used it was Narcissus."[16]

In cold, rainy mid-October, following doctor's orders, the "tiger" was at home suffering "heart cramps." But despite the doctor, he felt he must get out in order to see "little Ostheimer or her quiet eyes."[17] But he somehow missed her on her regular route home from school. His heart "very rebellious," he crept back to his attic room. Here, aloud to himself, he read Nietzsche, Spinoza, and the Bible; this last he found "incomparably beautiful, powerful, but an evil book," a book full of "deep cunning," the best possible model he thought for his own writing.

After two weeks of sickness at home, he was anxious to return to school. "I want," he wrote in his diary, "to work again with my head and my limbs, become rich, exert influence, play chess with people." Then he boasts, comparing himself to two successful German playwrights: "I can write, I can write plays better than [Friedrich] Hebbel and wilder than Wedekind." But he also notes, listing preoccupations of which most will remain with him for the rest of his life: "I am lazy. I'm unable to become famous. If I do, I'll go to America and become a cowboy, ride all day long, look at the sky, talk with the bulls, and stare at the grass. Now I'm becoming healthier. . . . It is lovely to be alive." The next day, he says: "No. It is senseless to be alive. Last night I had such a heart cramp that I was astonished; this time the devil is doing a first-class job." His thoughts return to Therese and the different parts of her anatomy. "A man needs something to attach him to the earth," he wrote, "a lap in which to lay his tired head; he needs soft hands, naturalness, lovingness, purity." But it was not just his head that he wished to place in natural, soft, loving laps and hands. Nor did he confine himself to thoughts of female laps and hands.

On July 13, 1916, dropping his old pseudonym of Berthold Eugen and adopting instead the snappier, somewhat American-sounding name of Bert Brecht, he published a long poem in the *Augsburger Neuesten Nachrichten*. "Song of the Fort Donald Railroad Gang" strikes several notes not clearly heard in Brecht's poetry before, but which will be central to most of his verse for almost a decade. Again and again, like his poetic models of Wedekind, Villon, Rimbaud, and Kipling, he will write of violent, amoral, love-hate relationships among men, animals, and women in exotic, wildly improbable locales.

The men of the "Fort Donald" poem exist in a world of fantasized American fragments, a Karl May universe with the technology of trains added. The men of Fort Donald exist without women. Before dawn, they die mysteriously alongside railroad tracks in a pine forest, which somehow also seems to be almost a rain forest next to an overflowing Lake Erie. In the first version of the "Fort Donald" poem, the drowning men sing the hymn supposedly played on the deck of the sinking *Titanic*, "Nearer, My God, to Thee." In later versions (those which Brecht allowed to be published), as the wet men go under, groping together in the dark, they sing a ballad to an obviously much-missed and much-loved "Johnny over the Sea."

In Brecht's poetic universe, groups like the Fort Donald Gang will appear and reappear with interchangeable names in interchangeable locations. Men and dominated, controlled, victimized women (when they are allowed to appear) will be swept away by the forces of nature and technology. Again and again, it is water that draws men and women to it. Water and boats are the scene of bisexual desire and death.

For all of Brecht's pursuit of young women as sexual partners, there is about this almost automatic exercise a pervasive sense of dread, dirt, violation, danger, the loss of self, and the loss of control. When they speak of women, the poems and diaries, and later the short stories and plays, are usually contemptuous and degrading. Women are useful as sexual partners, but the texts make plain that sex with women does not equal love. Love is something between men. And it is of such love that he sang to the young, slightly dandified men that he gathered about him in his bedroom, or swam with in the river Lech, or spent time with in restaurants, beer halls, and brothels.

Many evenings, the Brecht gang could be seen together at Gabler's Tavern. There, amidst the stuffed animal heads on the walls, they would sing, drink, and swap stories. The Gablers pampered their schoolboy customers, serving them bread topped with sliced radishes, despite the rationing. Sometimes the boys would take their guitars, violins, and lanterns, and march through the streets of Augsburg to sing under the windows of one of the young women Brecht was pursuing or go together to one of Augsburg's several whorehouses to sing, drink more, and try to forget death between the hospitable sheets. Following the more popular misogynists of the time, Brecht would speak airily of the need to keep women in their place. Following his beloved Nietzsche, Brecht felt that women should be made to respond to their master's whip. By late 1916, he would now often be seen walking along slapping a whip against a handsome pair of riding boots.

He had also now developed a passion for theater. One school friend, Franz Feuchtmayr, remembers attending the theater as many as forty times with Brecht in the fall of 1916.[18] When Brecht would return from the theater late at night, the light would still be burning in his mother's room. She could not sleep until he returned home; therefore, before going to his attic room, Eugen would stop at her room to say goodnight.

On New Year's Eve, the Feast of Saint Sylvester as this night is known in Germany, the Brecht clique marked the last day of 1916, as they had in previous years, with an all-male sledding party. At midnight, as they all sat around a roaring bonfire, Brecht was heard to say: "The fire would be even lovelier if a naked whore were jumping over it."[19]

That same winter, Brecht would often meet Bie Banholzer at the municipal ice rink. Her parents had bought her a five-mark season ticket that gave her access to the reserved section of the rink. Brecht had no such ticket but was able on one occasion to borrow a season pass from a friend. Bie noticed that while showing the pass to the guard at the rink, Brecht asked the guard how he recognized cardholders so easily that he often did not ask to see their pass. It was easy said the guard. Though he did not have a good memory, he knew at once from the relative shyness or boldness of the person coming to the gate whether that person really had a pass. On Brecht's next visit to the rink, without the borrowed pass this time, he simply waved boldly at the guard and joined Bie in the privileged section.[20] It was about this time that he gave Bie a cheap ring as a symbol of his affection.

At the end of March 1917, Brecht and the five remaining students in an original class of sixty-eight passed a specially formulated wartime version of the school exit exam. Technically, Brecht should have been immediately drafted. With behind-the-scenes help from his father, however, he was assigned a job "helping the war effort" as a clerk at Augsburg's city hall. His middle-class friends Georg Geyer and Rudolf Hartmann, who had graduated with him, were able to get similar assignments. Though every young male in Germany was technically equal in terms of the draft, some were more equal than others.

Soon Brecht was able to quit the city hall job and become instead the private tutor of the fourteen-year-old son of Herr Conrad Kopp, a doctor. Brecht was engaged to tutor young Kopp at the doctor's estate on beautiful, nearby Lake Tegern. Brecht arrived for his job wearing plus fours with a sports cap atop his unruly hair. A modest suggestion of scholarly endeavor was provided by some wire-frame glasses and a copy of Schopenhauer tucked underneath his arm. Mornings were spent over books; afternoons were free for boating and swimming. On weekends, Brecht returned to Augsburg to carouse with friends. The clique was joined suddenly by a dog that came up and adopted Brecht one day. Ina, as the dog was called, was jealous of other companions and put her muzzle between him and anyone else unless she was shooed away. Caspar Neher was part of the group, on leave after barely surviving burial alive in an artillery explosion on the western front.

At the time that Cas was in Augsburg with fresh news of the front, Brecht was delighted to find an article on possible draft deferments for university medical students in the June 1 edition of the local paper. Though he had shown little prior interest in the subject, Brecht lost no time notifying the University of Munich that he would be enrolling there in the fall as a student of medicine. As one simply chose one's own field at this time in German universities, enrollment required no demonstration of special promise in the selected field of study. His leave having expired in August, Neher returned to his regiment dug in at Verdun.[21]

With the university due to open in October, Brecht took the forty-minute train ride to Munich. With a generous allowance from his father, he would have money enough to return home on weekends and during the long university holidays. He was and was not leaving home.

3

"The World Has Laws Only to Be Trampled On" (1917–18)

Though Munich was only forty miles from Augsburg, it was a world on a different scale. Augsburg's years of glory as a magnet of European culture and banking had all but ended by the seventeenth century, while Munich rapidly expanded as the ruling Wittelsbachs made it a center from which to control the surrounding region. Enormously wealthy from the conquest of a large swathe of southern Germany, the Wittelsbachs indulged a boundless passion for art and artists. By the nineteenth century, "Mad" King Ludwig's passion for extravagant architecture and for Richard Wagner nearly bankrupted the state but made the city something of a Paris of the German-speaking world. In the early twentieth century, Munich attracted artists as successful as Kandinsky and as obscure as the water-colorist Hitler. In politics it was home both to monarchists and to implacable revolutionaries such as Karl Radek and Vladimir Ilyich Lenin, who had edited there his aptly named journal, *Iskra* (The spark). With a population of over 600,000, 85 percent of whom were Catholic, and an illegitimate birthrate of one in three, the city Brecht found was a volatile mixture of the archest nationalist conservatism and cosmopolitan bohemianism.

Despite the tremendous human cost of World War I, the Wittelsbachs and the upper-class of Munich and other German cities maintained the appearance of power and prosperity. Though by the winter of 1917, the general population was freezing and close to starvation, Munich, Berlin, Augsburg, and Vienna kept their theaters open and continued to encourage the licensed madness of the Oktoberfest.[1] The pageantry of royal power was likewise maintained as it had been for almost the last millennium. The Royal Cavalry clattered through the city's center several times a day, changing the guard at the numerous Wittelsbach palaces. After nightfall, however, long columns of pale, undernourished recruits were marched to the train stations to be shipped to France, while ambulances and hearses discreetly picked up those who had returned dead or more or less alive.

At first Brecht lived in Munich with an aunt of Caspar Neher. In an area where dialect differences are strong, he was pleased she was used to his Augsburg or Suabian dialect with its markedly rolling r's. His ties to Augsburg remained close. His father, promoted on May 1, 1917, to director of purchasing, was still in charge of purchasing supplies for the Colony. By siphoning off some of these goods, he provided not only Brecht but some of his student friends in Munich with increasingly scarce coal, tea, and potatoes. On weekends Brecht usually returned home to promote his Augsburg affairs and to enjoy ample meals.

Brecht was restless in Munich, moving frequently from one apartment to another. He frequently tacked admonitions on the outside of the door of his flat, often slight changes of proverbs. Playing with the German slang for horse droppings, he turned "the apple does not fall far from the tree" into "the apple does not fall far from the horse." He had a taste for the scatological twist and deliberately unconventional ideas of morality and good taste, which was also the fashion in artistic circles in Munich and nearby Zurich, home of the early Dadaists. Brecht would also have known the Munich cabaret artists Liesl Karlstadt and Karl Valentin who, together with Frank Wedekind, had been attacking convention for years. Brecht loved this kind of humor, not only writing such things himself but all his life being a marvelous audience for it, bellowing with laughter till his sides ached.

In a near constant state of arousal and without a woman in Munich, Brecht invited Bie for a visit. By this time, Bie knew that she was in love with Brecht. She was fascinated by his humor and dazzled by his use of language. She was ready not only to overlook but even to be excited by his filthy fingernails and sloppy dress. Inexperienced as she was, she took his invitation to come to Munich romantically, not sexually. In her touching memoir written in her sixties, Bie Banholzer recalled telling her middle-class parents that she was going for a couple of days to distant farms to do some black-market shopping for food, a common practice among the upper- and middle-class families who could afford black-market prices in days of great scarcity. Her parents allowed her to go. But having planned this closely with Brecht, Bie arranged to complete her black-market run in just one day.

When she reached Munich, there was Brecht beaming in anticipation. After a walking tour of the city, Bie began to worry about where she would stay. But Brecht had made a reservation for adjacent rooms at a second-class hotel next to the train station. Tired by a full day, Bie was amenable when Brecht proposed they go immediately to bed. He stressed that he just wanted to be next to her, fully clothed. Before long, however, he began "to make tender advances." Bie told him she had no idea about what was going on. Without proceeding to consummation that night, he told her what was involved. Grateful for that innocent and enlightening first night, unaware that she had been lied to about his own inexperience, years later Bie wrote: "I believe that it is a rare thing when a young girl is introduced to growing up in such a delicate and inventive way."[2]

Next morning they again walked around downtown Munich. When Bie developed a headache during the afternoon, they went back to the hotel. She was tired and climbed into bed. "As I lay there dozing," she noted in her memoirs, "he literally fell on top of me without seeming to know what he was doing." Later he swore to her that he "had never been with another woman before." Bie returned to Augsburg not telling her parents anything. Brecht remained in Munich but sent her a letter almost daily. At times it was literally that: one letter of the alphabet, his own initial "B" or a big "D" for *Dein* (yours). He also arranged to have friends in Augsburg spy on her and report back to him any signs of her developing an interest in other men. He gave her to understand that she was now his property, his to shape, as he put it, as though she were "dough that responded to every press of the finger."[3]

What happened with Bie began a lifetime pattern for Brecht. During courting he would always be funny yet serious, telling his object that he or she was really the only one and that nobody else really mattered. As a sexual partner, he would seem, at first, considerate, attentive to his partner's pleasure as much as his own. Later, the lover would discover that she or he was one of many. Even when he admitted this, he would claim the other relationships meant nothing in comparison. Each partner was told to remain faithful and obedient to him alone. To remain psychologically present with one while he was off with others, he would send almost daily notes and make frequent telephone calls. If he got any word that the other person was seeing someone else, he would drop everything for as long as it took him to extract a new vow of exclusiveness from the errant partner. With the wanderer back in the fold, he then left to resume his tightly scheduled round of other affairs.

Closeness to Bert Brecht would always be in direct proportion to a very precise distance. Only if he felt threatened with "abandonment," would he be sure to turn up. Only when the partner could no longer be won over by these on-again, off-again appearances would he finally, very reluctantly, drift away, asserting that the other person was at fault. Always, he would blame the end of the relationship on the other person. This system permitted him to avoid decisions about his relationships, while his undeniable charisma provided a constantly fresh crop of willing partners, often eager to outdo the others in dedication and subservience.

Despite Brecht having received his military deferment to study medicine, one classmate observed, "in fact he never studied medicine."[4]

He would enroll for an excessive number of classes (twenty-four credits in his first semester, for instance), have his father-pay for them, then drop many, and have the fees returned to him. The trick provided him with extra pocket money. The only courses that interested him were those involving the Bible or the theater. He attended a course called "Research on the Life of Christ" and one on the modern playwrights Ibsen, Bjørnson, and Strindberg. But he devoted his greatest efforts to a course taught by Professor Artur Kutscher entitled "Practical Theater Criticism." Kutscher was virtually unique in Germany at that time in considering practical work in theater a suitable subject for a university course. He was unusual also for his day in being directly involved with theater artists. He was the close friend, for instance, of Frank Wedekind and brought out the collected works of this poet, playwright, actor, and cabaret performer.

Wedekind was a familiar figure on the streets and stages of Munich, known for having been arrested briefly in 1899 for insulting the Wittelsbachs. His work and life were a standing affront to conventional morality. He wrote and sang openly about what others did and hid. "Grab sin boldly," he wrote, "for with sin enjoyment grows,"[5] and "The world has laws only to be trampled on." His heroes speak of a world where people "dance artfully and gaily over graves," and move in a space amoral and dreamlike, reflecting the excesses of the Expressionists and anticipating the logical nonlogic of the later Theater of the Absurd. He loved con artists and thieves, anyone who combined sex with violence. The line between his work as a poet, playwright, and performer and his "real" life was always shadowy. He wrote a play around Jack the Ripper, played the role of the serial killer himself, and married one of the actresses whom he had murdered on stage.

A number of Wedekind's performance pieces were, for that distant day, daringly sexually ambiguous or homoerotic. Setting his poems to simple folk tunes and accompanying himself on a guitar, he sang of androgynous figures, boys on the edge of puberty dressed in black silk stockings, or of a woman whose breasts were so small that when she turned sideways she looked to him like a boy.[6] "There he stood," wrote Brecht, remembering a typical Wedekind performance, "ugly, brutal, dangerous, with close-cropped red hair, his hands in his trouser pockets, and one felt that the devil himself could not shift him. He came before the curtain as ringmaster in a red tailcoat, carrying a whip and a revolver, and no one could forget that hard, dry, metallic voice, that brazen faun's head with 'eyes like a gloomy owl' set in immobile features."[7] With his casual, American-sounding, and wholly apt first name of Frank, he was and would remain a model for Brecht's own life and style of poetry and theatrical performance.[8]

When he first arrived in Munich, Brecht decided to change his appearance. The old idea that outward appearance could reveal character and intelligence was being given pseudoscientific underpinnings by writers such as Cesare Lombroso, who held, for instance, that a high forehead was a sure mark of high intelligence. Dismayed at his low brow, Brecht shaved an inch from his hairline. But all too soon stubble made it clear what he had done; as he did want to go to the trouble of shaving too often, Brecht took to wearing a cloth cap that, unlike the stiff-brimmed hats of the middle-class that he had worn up until this point, could be pulled down to cover his stubbly forehead. Despite the fact that all his clothes were hand-tailored and always of the best materials, his habits of infrequent washing and shaving, and always looking as though he slept in his clothes lent him the air of being close to the underworld of pimps, murderers, and thieves, like his beloved model Villon.

One poem of late 1917 ties several of these preoccupations together. He flirted with a very young, very blond girl at the Augsburg fair. When she rejected his advances, in revenge, he wrote up the incident and published it in the local paper. This poem, for which he received five marks, not only deals with foreheads and reflects the fashionable misogyny of the day, but also anticipates one of Brecht's most famous later creations, the character of Mack the Knife. The central character of the poem is a man who wears elegant gray gloves and only gives his naked hand "to animals and women." Describing this character's taste, we learn:

> Worth more to him than a broad forehead
> Was a head of golden hair.[9]

That a broad forehead is unnecessary for a sex object is made explicit when the poet asks:

> What do whores need with broad foreheads
> It's far better if their hips are broad.
> More comes out of it that way, and more goes in
> And that increases the pleasure.[10]

Virtually all of Brecht's poems of this period mirror the physiognomic and misogynist commonplaces of centuries of "love" verse and what passed for religious wisdom. To give but one example that may serve for many in German intellectual history, in his Table Talk, Luther tells his listeners: "Men have broad shoulders and narrow hips, and accordingly they possess intelligence." In contrast, says Luther, "women ought to stay at home; the way they were created indicates this, for they have broad hips and a wide fundament to sit upon (to keep house and bear and raise children)."

What Brecht wrote, both at this time and for decades to come, is consistent with the intellectual tradition he had grown up with, where the denigration of women is deemed wholly natural. In a rather typical poem (mirroring perhaps Robert Herrick's "Upon Julia's Clothes"), Brecht writes:

> *Oh you can't imagine what I suffer*
> *When I see a lovely woman*
> *Whose ass in yellow silk*
> *Twitches in the heavenly blue of evening.*[11]

The conventionality of this kind of writing is confirmed by the fact that poems like this were readily sold to and printed by a local paper. The stance is one of aggressive misogyny, where a woman's buttocks lead men astray. Intelligence, real love, and real beauty are only found in males.

The attitudes of Munich residents Heinrich Mann and his brother, the more famous and more decorous Thomas Mann, were fairly typical of what appears to be pervasive at every level of society. Heinrich Mann, for example, wrote a novel about a seemingly very proper professor who is sexually obsessed with a chanteuse. This 1905 novel later became famous as the film *The Blue Angel*, with Marlene Dietrich playing the temptress who lures an intelligent man to his doom. In 1912 Thomas Mann completed *Death in Venice* in which a respected author is swept off his feet by a beautiful boy. The Mann brothers constantly probed that ostensibly forbidden area where representatives of middle-class values move into ostensibly criminal and forbidden, but actually widely practiced, areas of "aberrant" sexuality. In Kutscher's seminar, such themes were a regular part of class discussions. One of the young women in Kutscher's class wrote a very fine seminar paper on Heinrich Mann. Both Kutscher and Brecht were impressed and Brecht arranged to have himself formally introduced. The young woman's name was Hedda Kuhn.

Hedda Kuhn could never have studied at a German university before the Great War. Nowhere in the German-speaking world, except Switzerland, had women been permitted to enter universities. Nor had they been able to complete the prepatory work for the university as the public gymnasia had not accepted female students. During the war, with so many young men away at the front, all this changed; women like Kuhn explored various areas of study, including medicine and sexually explicit plays and novels. Kuhn prided herself on her work as a poet and on being sexually liberated. She was happy to sleep with Brecht but claimed a right to have other lovers—over Brecht's strenuous objections.

However, she found she was not able to maintain her own freedom and productivity as a writer in Brecht's company. He complained that though her poems were musical, he did not understand them.[12] He asked her instead to work on his poetry, to help him with metrics in particular. He knew that he could never seem to get things like rhyme and meter to work for him on his own. Hedda soon got bored with anonymous patchings of his poetry; and getting no encouragement for her own work, she gradually stopped writing poetry altogether.

The affair limped along. Brecht took her for the visit to his parents that was a routine part of his seductions. Frau Brecht was really too ill and too heavily drugged to talk with the visitor at any length. Herr Brecht hoped that because Hedda Kuhn really was a student of medicine, she might keep Eugen on track in his medical studies and thus out of the army. Kuhn did not dare take Brecht home to meet her father in nearby Rastatt. She knew he would object to Brecht's filthy collars and the dirt under his fingernails.

During a weekend visit to Augsburg in the late fall of 1917, a sixteen-year-old would-be poet by the name of Hans Otto Münsterer arranged to have himself introduced to Brecht. After a few minutes of conversation at that first meeting, Brecht told him to come around to the Bleichstrasse for a rendezvous Sunday morning at eleven. Years later Münsterer remembered getting ready in his uncle's elegant flat. He put on his best suit, tied his best cravat in a knot of "unbeatable beauty," and then pulled on a fine pair of gray kid gloves. He considered, but then rejected, wearing a formal top hat. On his way to Brecht's, he saw city crews washing chalk messages off the walls so that they would not provoke workers in the city's mustard gas and munitions factories. One read:

> We're not fighting for the sake of the fatherland,
> And we're not fighting for the sake of God.
> We're fighting for rich folks,
> And we're killing the poor.[13]

At the Brecht family door in the Bleichstrasse, one of the servants pointed Münsterer upstairs. On the third floor the gray-gloved young man faced a door inscribed with ten commandments as formulated in

Nietzsche's *Thus Spake Zarathustra*. Beyond this door "a very different world began." Brecht's bed, a daybed, and a small table were covered with a chaotic jumble of books and papers. The sloping ceiling was decorated with startling pictures drawn by Caspar Neher. Even more startling at that early hour on a Sunday morning was the poised, dark, beautiful Bie Banholzer. True to Nietzsche's admonishment, a whip hung on the bedframe.

The overdressed Hans Otto, thankful he had not brought his top hat, recited a few of his poems. Brecht, the regal bohemian, took notes on the ones he liked. Then, Brecht took up his guitar and, to tunes of his, his brother Walter, and Ludwig Prestel, gave a high-pitched but wholly mesmeric recital of some of his own recently composed poems. In the first of these, a young, innocent, golden-haired woman by the name of Evlyn Roe boards a sailing vessel heading, supposedly, for the Holy Land. The voyage goes on for months and she is regularly raped by the entire crew. Finally, one January, driven mad, she "gave herself to the dark waves." Her body (echoing one of the more gruesome passages in *The Iliad*, where Achilles tosses the body of one of his victims into a river "among the fish who will lick the blood away" and "will feed upon the shining fat of Lykaon")[14] will be eaten by fish large and small. Though she is the repeated victim of gang rape during a holy pilgrimage, she is spurned at heaven's gate by Saint Peter.[15]

Another song sung to Hans Otto that first day was "The Adventurers." Anticipating the work of Beckett just as clearly as it reflects a perennial concern of Brecht, the poem asks: "Why did you not stay in your mother's womb, / Where it was still and where one slept and was simply there?" Next, in the song about Brecht's close friend Georg Pfanzelt, or "Orge," Orge "takes a shit into his own hand" so that he can fondle it before, "full up to his throat in disgust and hate, probably casually, without a grimace, cuts his own throat." The songs had their desired effect. Hans Otto left the flat, enthralled, never to be free of Brecht again.

The scene in the attic room that Sunday morning, with the young dandy arriving for a rendezvous only to find a young woman there before him, is typical of Brecht. Unless hundreds of poems, stories, letters, and diary entries bear no direct relation to his own sexual activities, it is clear that, for many years, he was attracted to both sexes for sex but really preferred the company of men. He liked to have about him, as Klaus Völker discreetly puts it, "dandified men of the Oscar Wilde and Rimbaud type."[16] In his biography of Brecht, one of the best in existence, Völker frequently hints at Brecht's male attachments. Besides the "dandified" men that Völker mentions in his coded reference to homosexuality, Brecht was also clearly drawn to a tough, "rough-trade" kind of man, represented in real life by the whip- and pistol-toting Wedekind. The combination of these two archetypes of male desire would produce the typical Brechtian male vamp, irresistible to women and wholly contemptuous of them.

The teenage student poet who gave erotic recitals to swooning male dandies and compliant female visitors, and who then turned these events into poems, was doing so with no fear of real interference either in Munich or Augsburg. In the Bleichstrasse he had his own complete world with its separate entrance, maid service, and his own books and games, including a billiard set. Downstairs, his father was largely absent on business of the Haindl firm, and his mother was too ill and weak to do anything except occasionally complain about his casual use of "pornographic" words or the fact that he sometimes pissed in the baskets of clean laundry upstairs rather than bothering to go down to the ground-level toilet. "In the laundry, that's sick, only a pornographer would do that," says a mother to her son in one Brecht poem. And in the poem the son replies: "But it's natural. . . . every dog does it," at which point the mother finds no words but simply breaks into tears.[17]

The poet himself firmly believed that his own genius placed him beyond "good" and "evil," and that he could live as loudly and as unconventionally as he desired, regardless of what pain this might cause others. In a universe operating by the rules written on his apartment door, he was the master and beyond bourgeois conventions. As the incarnation also of Schopenhauer's view of the world as will and idea, he would demand that others respond "to every press of his finger." Friends soon discovered that they were allowed to remain in his circle only by recognizing his authority and helping him achieve his ends. Like the interchangeable family maids all conveniently named Marie, they too were interchangeable. He remained the armature upon which their lives were built. They might desire the same from him but could never expect it.

For Cas, almost literally buried alive as he was for years in trenches under almost-constant enemy bombardment, letters from Brecht were a lifeline. Full of conscious or unconscious homoerotic banter, Brecht would sign his letters with words such as "your most submissive belly dancer" or "from the one who loves you." While declaring his love, he also asks Cas to send back sketches to be used as part of the next seduction campaign. He wishes, he says, to seduce the milkmaid's daughter, Sofie Renner. To accomplish this, he wants Cas to do a Brecht portrait where he is to be represented as "big, immoral, extraordinary, ironic, etc.," but not wholly "naked."[18] Perennially jealous, Cas chafed at helping his friend seduce someone else. But at least such involvement meant he was not forgotten.

With his new Munich sophistication, Brecht was now appalled at what he saw on the stage in Augsburg. He told Neher "the Augsburg Municipal theater ought to be closed, on artistic grounds." Brecht was equally vehement in expressing his opinions to Orge, with whom he would spend hours, his friend clumping along on his clubfoot, walking up and down by the city moat. Whenever Orge would disagree with one of Brecht's internally inconsistent but passionately held opinions, Brecht would stamp his foot and yell, "No, I'm right about that," or "Whoever can't comprehend that, can't possibly understand me at all."[19] While reluctantly accepting such reproofs, the always-insecure Orge would jealously complain about Brecht spending time with women.

He did but not always happily. Marie Aman, whose pastor had been assured of Brecht's honorable intentions, was expressing her own sexual ideas to Brecht and he was alarmed. He told Cas that Marie seemed to him "to set out to be seduced, like a bitch in heat." She had even told Brecht that she now reserved the right to take other lovers. He began to suspect her of "a mania to propagate."[20] Simultaneously attracted and repulsed, he described Marie to Cas on December 18, 1917, in mixed terms: "Her eyes are horribly empty, wicked little devouring whirlpools; she has a snub nose that is too broad; her mouth is too big, red, and thick. The lines of her little neck are not pure, she carries herself like a cretin, her walk is slovenly, her stomach protrudes." "But," he concludes, "I am fond of her."[21]

A number of familiar notes are sounded in this letter written to a man who loved Brecht. Marie's sexuality, Brecht claims to Cas, sets a trap. Marie's eyes, "devouring whirlpools" (so unlike the enhancing mirror eyes of Therese Ostheimer), threaten to suck him in and drown him. In this imagery, she becomes the one in control. With a final twist, that he cares for Marie anyway, Brecht thanks Cas for a picture he has sent entitled "The Eternal Kiss," and promises not to kiss Marie while Cas is home for Christmas.

With increasing frequency, the new poems speak of escape to distant parts. Mysterious sailing ships of the sort used earlier in the "Ballad of Evlyn Roe" turn up repeatedly. By the shabbiness of their sails and by the holes in their hulls through which sharks can swim, the ships serve as surrogates for the poet himself. An explicitly loving poem was completed for Cas. In it, Cas is painting a sailing ship in three colors, a motif that is taken, as Michael Morley points out, directly from Kipling's "The Light That Failed." A series of these leaky, or colorful, or black ships with powerful cannon, or ships trailed by long white sharks will haunt the poems for years to come.

The general mood at home was somber as 1917 ended. Not only

was Frau Brecht, despite the morphine, in obvious pain, but Walter, unprotected by "medical studies" was about to be drafted. Three other young men of the circle of carousers, Ludwig Wiedemann, Walter Fikentscher, and Otto Müller—all declared their wish to go and serve the fatherland, though they knew that this probably meant a speedy death. In fact, the New Year would begin with a summons to Brecht, his "medical studies" and "heart cramps" notwithstanding, to report for military duty. However, the influential Herr Direktor Brecht was able to intervene with the local board and postpone disaster for at least a few more months.

For all the young men, death seemed ever close, and they fended it off by making the the attic apartment in the Bleichstrasse boom. In the midst of the din, Brecht tried lines out and modified them with the help of his various friends, borrowed from translations of foreign poets, assembled into composite "Brecht" poems, and set to rudimentary music. A fragmentary notebook of 1918 reflects the fact that the work was a group composition: "Songs for Guitar by Bert Brecht and His Friends."[22]

When Brecht returned to Munich in early 1918, Georg Geyer, a genuine student of medicine, urged him to really sign up for and attend some medical courses. Brecht hoped, and wrote as much to Cas, that the war would be over soon. It looked as though the Russian front would collapse completely in Germany's favor as the czar had been forced to abdicate and maneuvering had begun to get Russia wholly out of the war. Meanwhile, however much against his will, Brecht attended some medical classes. But he often played hookey and continued to spend most of his time in the Kutscher seminar or working on his own love life and related poems.

In January 1918 Brecht was delighted when Kutscher brought Frank Wedekind to class, and when Wedekind suddenly died on March 9, Brecht was devastated. He had lost his closest model of what a poet-playwright-performer could be. In an obituary for Wedekind that was as much a portrait of Brecht as it was of the dead singer, he wrote: "He sang his songs to guitar accompaniment in a brittle voice, slightly monotonous and quite untrained. No singer ever gave me such a shock, such a thrill."[23] With the death of Wedekind and the war in the west still grinding on, Brecht moved restlessly from one rented room in Munich to another. But wherever he was, his pattern of work and play remained the same. He would get up at 6 A.M. and work intensively for several hours on his various literary projects. Later, he would drop in on Hedda Kuhn, or perhaps attend a lecture or two at the university. He only seemed interested in medical lectures when information was given regarding veneral diseases, a subject in which he had more than a passing interest.

Time spared from tiresome lectures was taken up by visits to the theater, the newly emerging cinema, political cabarets such as those where Wedekind had performed, and the Kutscher seminar. One day Brecht gave a talk on the playwright Hanns Johst, another of Kutscher's many literary friends. Removing his cloth cap to reveal his badly shaved forehead, never looking at his audience, with a mixture of arrogance and shyness, he read his lecture in a grating but clearly articulated voice, his Augsburg dialect heightened by his rolling r's. Brecht compared Hanns Johst to a long jumper who starts his approach so far back that he collapses before he reaches the jump-off point. As Brecht spoke, his audience both hissed and applauded. At the end, Kutscher was livid. He denounced Brecht as a "flagellant" and, worse, noting Brecht's cloth cap, as a "proletarian," and demanded that he leave the room.

Brecht, remaining cool under Kutscher's fire, decided to do some fence-mending with Johst himself who had invited him to his house on Lake Starnberg. Though Hedda Kuhn was also invited, Brecht disinvited her. He said: "Johst is a nationalist. Things are going to get hot out there. That's not for you."[24] Before his visit was over, Brecht had charmed his way into the graces of the playwright. He would correspond with Johst, his letters often couched in a sycophantic tone, and become a frequent visitor at a house that was also becoming a haven for Adolf Hitler.[25] By attacking Johst in one forum and then turning all his charm on the man in another, Brecht had things both ways: winning friends among those who recognized that Johst was a miserable playwright as well as an extremely dangerous and influential supporter of nationalist causes, while at the same time keeping links with Johst in case support was ever needed from that quarter.

When, soon after Wedekind's death, Johst came out with a new play, Brecht was horrified at its success. To Kutscher's fury, the "proletarian flagellant" attacked Johst's new play, *The Lonely One*. Not only did he dismiss Johst's work with the phrase "expressionism is frightful," but he boasted he could write a better play in three days. In a matter of at least five weeks (rather than the few days he later liked to claim it had taken), stitching it together mainly from his growing portfolio of violent poems, many of which were slightly modified versions of poems by François Villon, with help from Augsburg friends, he did create a dark, brilliant, misogynist, violent, homoerotic, extended poem of a play, very much in the style of Wedekind. Set in the bars and woods of southern Germany it was supposedly based on "a masculine vamp by the name of K. from Pfersee near Augsburg."[26] In fact, he drew

on incidents from the violent homosexual affair of Rimbaud and Verlaine. Finally, he named his highly stylized self-portrait of a play and its
bisexual hero for the ancient Syrian deity Baal.[27]

While Brecht worked on *Baal*, the military draft caught up with
several members of the Brecht circle, including his now eighteen-year-
old brother, Ludwig Prestel, and Ludwig Wiedemann. At the front,
Wiedemann had not yet been issued a gas mask when the first attack
came. Only the efforts of a friend who tore one from a corpse saved
him. He remembered with horror the essays he had written in school
saying the conventional things about how sweet it was to die for the
fatherland. Only in the face of death did he grasp the import of Brecht's
response to the same ode.[28]

Despite Brecht's boast of needing only three days to write a better play than Johst, *Baal* dragged on for several months before even
the first version was ready for typing. The writing and rewriting of the
play, which would become a regular pattern for Brecht, involved various friends. By the second half of May, it was far enough along that
Herr Direktor Brecht could tell one of his secretaries at the Haindl
paperworks, Fräulein Pauline Israng, to type a clean copy of the frequently unconventional verses. Over the weekend of May 18, 1918,
with Brecht either too shy or too lazy to do it himself, another of
Brecht's friends Otto Bezold, dictated the manuscript to the reluctant
typist. As Otto dictated the highly erotic text with its explicitly sexual
language and its scenes of multiple seductions, murders, and suicides,
Fräulein Israng's typing speed increased dramatically especially in the
passage where Baal brings two sisters up to his attic apartment to
relish fucking both before he casts them aside. Much speed was also
required by Fräulein Israng in scenes where Baal seduces the female
lover of his best friend, Johann, then seduces Johann. Abandoning the
woman to drown herself in the river, Baal first declares his love for
Johann, then murders him in a bar brawl. At the play's close, Baal
feigns death, and grabs and consumes the vulture that has descended
to feed on him. By Monday, May 20, Fräulein Israng and Otto Bezold
were done and eight carbon copies, on scarce paper provided by his
father, were handed to the proud author.

Written partly in reaction to Johst's picture of a rather dull and
decorous figure of a nineteenth-century poet in *The Lonely One*, *Baal*
pays homage to the sexually frank dramas of Wedekind and to Georg
Büchner, the early nineteenth-century author of the play *Woyzeck*. But
Baal is less a play than a flood of individual poems and songs. *Baal* is
long on poetry (often of brilliant effectiveness) and short on dramatic
structure (as one might expect in a first effort). John Willett sees the
work as a "transference" of Brecht's "poetic activity to the stage."[29]

One clearly hears the poetry of Villon, Rimbaud, Verlaine (quoted, in what would be a typical pattern for Brecht, without acknowledgment in the text), and more distant echoes of the homoerotic from Walt Whitman, whose work he would have known in translation.

Above everything else, *Baal* is startlingly modern in its sexual daring and frankness. Contemporary artists such as David Bowie and Rainer Werner Fassbinder have been strongly drawn to the role of this bisexual poet-singer-murderer. Bowie's Berlin-made recording of the songs from *Baal* (arranged by Dominic Muldowney for the BBC television version of the play), give a strong sense of the raging, seductive power of this work in performance.

With *Baal* completed, Brecht felt he had earned a break. He spent part of July on Lake Starnberg with Bie, near King Ludwig II's castle, Neuschwanstein, a model for the castle at Disneyland. That same summer he made a trip with his father to Stuttgart where his father had Haindl Company business to complete. Brecht was supposed to return alone and bring back one of his father's suitcases filled with clothes. He forgot the suitcase on the train. His father was very angry, but the son dismissed his complaints. He told his father the lost items could easily be replaced. This was at a point in the war where most of the German population was in rags.

That same summer, echoing the travels of Baal with Johann, and ignoring the "heart ailment" that mysteriously would come and go throughout Brecht's life, he went off on a vagabond tour of the Black Forest area with Fritz Gehweyer. They earned their meals and lodging by singing and dancing at forest inns. Sometimes they would hike all night and greet the dawn on top of one of Bavaria's small mountains. On August 10, while Fritz was away on an errand, Brecht wrote a seven-page letter to Bie. "Now things are wonderful," he wrote. "A strong wind is blowing across the summit. Down below, gray forested peaks and the moon sinking behind them, an orange lantern veiled in silk." The letter ended: "Many, many kisses, your Bert Brecht."[30]

When the young men returned to Augsburg, they were greeted by draft notices. Not even Herr Direktor Brecht could get more than a six-week delay for his son this time, and Brecht was ordered to report for garrison duty on October 1. But even that might have saved the life of Fritz Gehweyer. Less than six weeks later, Brecht's hiking companion was killed in France. After listening to Georg Geyer before his departure play Mozart's sonata "Death in the Forest" (K. 280), Brecht came over to the piano and scribbled in the margin of Geyer's music:

And he breathed into his hand
And smelled his own breath and it

Smelled foul. And he thought to himself
I'll die soon.[31]

In the Möbius strip that Brecht constantly wove between life and
art, Brecht and Geyer had become very close. Now, the title of the
Mozart sonata played by Geyer and the Brecht poem to accompany it
would be inserted into *Baal* to be sung by Baal to Ekart, one of his male
lovers. The dream light and gloom of the ancient Teutonic forests, the
world captured in the paintings of Caspar David Friedrich, is in the
song.

In late 1918, with war as the background, the poetry that the
Brecht group was creating entwines death with eroticism. The dream
life of a group of "sea robbers" on what might be called a "drunken
boat" is described in ways reflecting Brecht's steady preoccupation with
wombs and water. Moving in a dream world of ballad, Bible, and fairy
story, as well as the real world of the street named for the seven
drowned children, he does what he will so frequently do, using the
traditionally magical number seven. Also, deeply characteristic is the
confusion in this world of "man" and "beast." His men are also composite mythic images, bulls that have the eyes of wolves:

> *They live beautifully, like noble animals*
> *In the soft wind, in the drunken blue!*
> *And often seven bulls mount*
> *A foreign woman they have stolen.*

In another verse we are told:

> *They gaze like wolves between the spars*
> *And, eyes gleaming, they commit murder*
> *In order to not become stiff*
> *Drumming like children while they shit.*[32]

Murder has become tantamount to taking a shit. Women, usually faceless, are objects to be stolen, mounted, usually from behind, and word-
lessly discarded by "noble animals."

With the army but weeks away for the twenty-year-old, the world
of the Augsburg River and the Augsburg fair absorbed him and his male
and female companions in the fall of 1918. He both loved and was
frightened by the big, canvas-covered boat swings at the fair. He would
say later that swinging at the fair with his companions was "as good as
going to bed with them." Mercifully, the fair would close at midnight,
because, as Brecht said, "God needed his own turn on the boat
swings."[33] While God took his turn and Bie went home, Brecht headed

for the bars and brothels with his male companions or would swim or lounge along the river with Cas when he was home briefly on leave. Cas's mother was appalled. She saw Brecht as a bad influence on her son.[34] The closeness of the two young men was painfully obvious to her. "It," Brecht would write ambiguously of his time with Cas, "was better with a friend than with women."[35]

On one wall in Brecht's rooms in the Bleichstrasse hung Cas's brooding, powerful portrait of the brutal but charming God-man Baal. Brecht would stare at it fixedly, hypnotizing himself, as he told Hedda, into a mood for writing. On one table was a recently acquired human skull, one of two stolen, at Brecht's request, by the compliant Bezold. Facing the real skulls was a skull-like life mask that Brecht had had fashioned for him the previous spring. In one corner of the room was a music stand with the open score of Wagner's *Tristan*. Next to the stand was a baton for Brecht to conduct his imaginary orchestra. The central prop of the room was a bed displaying, despite the efforts of the three maids to keep the place tidy, decorative stains of sperm and blood. Hanging from the bedframe was a whip and an elegant guitar, the latter borrowed without asking from Walter, already away at the front.

Here, with lordly grace and brutality, he received a stream of visitors. One day Orge came by, bringing with him Friedrich Mayer, a mutual friend. Brecht already had two visitors. One was Cas and the other was a young woman from the nearby Saint Anna's Gymnasium. The young woman, impressed by the fact that Brecht knew the world of the Munich theater, had come to ask the worldly wise Brecht how she might become an actress. He had her read aloud, but she never seemed able to do exactly what he peremptorily demanded. Finally, she lost her nerve and bolted, forgetting her script in her haste. Brecht picked up the loose-leaf text, shouted at the young woman on the street below and then scattered her papers out of the window, laughing and openly enjoying himself in the face of her obvious discomfiture.[36] Here, and repeatedly later with lovers and acquaintances who fail to follow his lordly directions, he seems to have felt no empathy toward the pain of others, arrogantly certain that what he recommends is right, so they deserve their pain if they, unaccountably, fail to take direction from him.

But though he could impose his will on most of those he dealt with face-to-face, it was more difficult when he had only a bureaucracy as his opponent. In a note to Hedda Kuhn in the fall of 1918, he reveals his fear as his induction date approaches. On that day, so he tells Hedda, "I will be buried."[37] But his luck was actually holding very well. While one part of the German army was preparing Brecht's induction, on September 29 the head of the armed forces, General Ludendorff, communicated to the German emperor the conviction that they must imme-

diately sue for an armistice. As the war lurched to an end, Dr. Raff, a
friend of Brecht's father, managed to get the "medical student" Bert
Brecht assigned to his unit, a clinic for patients with veneral disease,
right up the street from the Colony. The clinic was so conveniently
located that Brecht was able to continue living at home with no inter-
ruption in his various assignations. Instead of having to submit to the
inconvenience of regularly wearing a scratchy military uniform, he was
permitted to create his own.

He was now sometimes seen in sporty jodhpurs, with riding boots
and a horsewhip. None of this had any bearing whatsoever on military
matters. He had bought all this gear in order to further his courtship of
Caspar Neher's sister, Marietta. As she rode like a "young panther,"
Brecht thought it wise to take some riding lessons. Wearing either
jodhpurs or crumpled corduroy pants, he combined them with riding
boots or wildly incongruous yellow shoes. Often he added a yellow
sweater. Sometimes he was bareheaded but at other times wore a military cap.

Though Brecht was interested in quizzing soldiers at the clinic as
to exactly how they had contracted their diseases, he spent as little time
there as possible. He was so lax that instead of coming to the clinic to
sign the duty roster, he began sending it in with one of the family maids
so that he could stay at home making love and poems rather than
devoting himself to the dying war.

Less than a month after Brecht was first enlisted and began his
desultory "military service," shock waves of revolution threatened to
end the war. Czech exiles in Paris called for the immediate abdication
of the emperor of Austria-Hungary. Sailors in Kiel called for the kaiser
to abdicate. In Munich, on November 3, the socialist Kurt Eisner addressed an enormous crowd and rejected belated Wittelsbach offers of
limited democratization. On November 7, virtually without opposition, the army barracks in Munich were handed over to the revolutionaries, and red posters were put up throughout the city announcing the
establishment of the Bavarian Republic. With no fanfare, the eight-
hundred-year rule of the Wittelsbachs ended as several members of the
royal family entered a horse-drawn carriage and clattered away. On
November 9, the kaiser abdicated and fled to Holland.

The war had been waged by thirty nations. Thirty million people
had been captured, wounded, or were still missing. At least nine million
had died. Caspar Neher and Walter Brecht, like hundreds of thousands
of others, bewildered at the sudden end of a war that the German
newspapers had said until the bitter end was almost won, marched
through a shattered Belgium and France back toward what was left of
"home."

"In the Most Significant Moments of the Revolution This Renowned 'Organizational Talent' Is the First to Fail" (1918–19)

At Brecht's "clap hospital" in Augsburg, there was immediate talk both of raising a red flag and of simply going home. Brecht was virtually unique in the ranks of the military; he had never left home. The issues facing the quickly formed soldiers' and workers' councils were being discussed throughout Germany. Those seeking the most radical and fundamental change would take as their model the Russia of Lenin and the Bolsheviks, a model that was precisely what both moderates and the German right wing most feared. The center, including the less radical wings of the various socialist parties, would seek a form of parliamentary political power that rejected the more extreme elements of the Russian revolutionary model.

In Munich, the new socialist prime minister, Kurt Eisner, his flaming and symbolic red beard notwithstanding, followed a moderate path. Unlike Lenin, he advocated freedom of the press, protection of civil liberties, and the development of competing political parties. Tellingly, instead of calling Munich a "soviet," the government chose the less radical appellation of "Republic." Many elements of the old order were kept in place. When the handsome papal legate to Munich, the future pope Eugenio Pacelli, anxiously inquired as to whether the Eisner government planned to abolish the Vatican representative's special butter ration, he was pleased to learn it would be continued.

The overwhelmingly moderate "revolution" of Munich spread to Augsburg. The workers' and soldiers' council formed there was chaired by the editor of the *Schwäbischer Volkszeitung* (the *Suabian People's Paper*), Ernst Niekisch. Brecht would claim later (though the claim has never been independently confirmed) that the soldiers on his ward made him their representative to the council. It was not at all atypical of the period that soldiers elected the least doctrinaire of their junior officers as their representatives. "I got a whole lot of work piled on me," Brecht said, "but I managed to get relieved of it very soon."[1] The apparent brevity and reluctance of Brecht's service on the council, if he served at all, may explain why Niekisch had no recollection of Brecht's contribution when he was asked about it almost half a century later. On

November 9, 1918, Niekisch distributed the manifesto of the workers' and soldiers' council. "Power is in our hands," he wrote, "quiet and order are assured. Under no circumstances will riots be allowed. Stiff penalties will be leveled against those who steal or plunder. The security of persons is assured."[2]

In Berlin, center of an empire that had suddenly collapsed, rival forces rushed to fill a vacuum of both power and moral authority. A curious sort of "revolutionary government" was formed. Wilhelm II had left power in the hands of Prince Maximilian von Baden. The prince saw no better alternative than to entrust the formation of a popular government to Friedrich Ebert, a middle-of-the-road representative of the large and powerful Social Democratic party. The prince's move, as things would turn out, had been a canny one.

Within hours of being handed power, Ebert spoke secretly with the Supreme Army Command under the direct control of General Wilhelm Groener. Groener agreed to back Ebert in order, in Groener's words, to achieve what he saw as "the complete suppression (restlose Bekämpfung) of the Revolution."[3] Having been assured support of the leaders of the army to put down revolutionary activity, Ebert next turned his attention to winning the support of the Berlin workers' and soldiers' council, which turned out to be a moderate body, as were its counterparts elsewhere in Germany.

With the secret backing of the old military caste and an open endorsement of moderation on the part of the workers' and soldiers' council, Ebert then pushed through two other conservative pacts. Negotiating through Herr Direktor Wolfgang Kapp, representative of the virtually feudal Prussian estate owners, the owners agreed to back Ebert as long as he made no move to socialize the land. With the frequently overlapping army and Prussian aristocracy in line, Ebert was next able to have the judges who had administered the imperial system of justice reconfirmed. By maintaining the three key pillars of the old society— the military, the landowners, and the judges—while nominally also serving the interests of the workers' and soldiers' councils, Ebert was helping to ensure not only his own survival as a politician but the survival of the profoundly autocratic, antidemocratic, and militaristic core of the old society itself.

By the time the leading theorist of revolution in Germany, Rosa Luxemburg, reached Berlin, Ebert had already consolidated his own revolutionary position. If Luxemburg wanted to push for more radical change, she would have to try to work with a splinter group of her old party, the Social Democrats. But, as she soon discovered, even the splinter group the Independent Social Democrats seemed to have little stomach for real revolution. Luxemburg's position, together with that of her old comrade the fiery Karl Liebknecht, would become increasingly isolated and desperate in the weeks ahead. A specific issue behind the general one of revolution in Germany, symbolized in the role that would be played by Luxemburg, was the whole question of what position women would occupy in postwar society. "Regardless of party," writes Gordon A. Craig of the prewar period in Germany, "most German males seemed to find the thought of their wives and daughters becoming emancipated and politically informed both alarming and repellant."[4]

In Augsburg, as in Berlin, women now attempted to be heard as an equal voice in determining Germany's future course. One of the most active was the Augsburger eighteen-year-old Lilly Krause, a woman unique in the Reich. During the war she had managed to take and pass a proficiency exam to become a brush-maker's apprentice and thus have some chance at earning an independent living. The beautiful Krause had long been an object of Brecht's attention, and he was still in hot pursuit. He pursued her even when she married a bank clerk by the name of Georg Prem, a fellow revolutionary.

A passionate public speaker on behalf of women's rights, Krause stated at a public gathering: "We want to be and to remain free human beings. Let us close our ranks and unite, and fight for our holy cause at the side of our men!"[5] She pointed out that women had been given full seats and full votes within the Augsburg Workers' council. It was a heady time for independently minded women in Germany during those last few weeks of 1918, with genuine equality seeming within reach.

By January 9, 1919, using pull to jump the queue of those waiting to be discharged, Brecht had himself freed from all further "military service." If he had served at all on the soldiers' and workers' councils in Augsburg, this may have been the moment he chose to free himself of that responsibility as well. When he was seen now in Augsburg at revolutionary meetings, it was not as a participant but either to ogle Lilly Krause or to sit and take notes at the back of the room. The nineteen-year-old Emmi Lauermann, a committed revolutionary, saw Brecht, son of the Haindl Direktor Berthold Brecht, at one such meeting and wondered aloud if he was not a spy.[6] Brecht convinced her that he was there as a poet and playwright, and had no darker motive. He also invited Lauermann to visit him sometime at his apartment. Aware of Brecht's reputation, Lauermann declined.

As the Augsburg revolution inched along, in January, Bie Banholzer told Brecht and her parents that she was pregnant. Her parents said marriage with someone like Brecht was out of the question. They suggested an old Bavarian solution. She would have her child in the country and a foster parent would be found, so that the mother could resume her life in proper middle-class society and later find a more suitable husband. Arrangements were made to send Bie off to the nearby village of Kimratshofen. Brecht revealed nothing as yet to his own parents about his impending fatherhood. He was rather desperate, however, to try and make some extra money. He planned, he told Cas, to write a novel that would earn him ten thousand marks and help him deal with the situation of the woman that the two men now called (using the Greek term for a courtesan) "the hetaera Bie."[7]

On January 1, 1919, in Berlin, Rosa Luxemburg and Karl Lieb-knecht, formally turned their followers into an entity called the Communist Party of Germany (CPG). They also gave themselves the name the Spartacists in commemoration of a famous slave rebellion in ancient Rome. At the outset, the CPG numbered a mere eight hundred, but though small in numbers, it hoped to make up for its smallness by its revolutionary élan. But though the central working group of the CPG was small, it still was not able to coordinate its revolutionary purpose. Jakob Walcher, a close friend of Luxemburg who would become a friend of Brecht years later, observed the confusion. When tens of thousands gathered in Berlin's Siegesallee on January 6, the CPG leadership could not agree as to what the crowd should be told. Toward evening, "freezing, weary, and disappointed," the crowd drifted away. Luxemburg, observing the failure, said of the famed German capacity for organization: "In the most significant moments of the revolution this renowned 'organizational talent' is the first to fail in the most deplorable way."[8]

Adding to the disarray of the CPG, the radical right now openly urged the murder of "Karl, Radek, Rosa, and Company" and put a price of 100,000 marks on their heads.[9] "Red Rosa,"—a Communist, a liberated woman, a Jew who did not know her place but headed a political movement—was the ultimate horror for the right, which called her "ein Teufelsweib"—"a she-devil."[10] In posters, her sometime-lover Karl Liebknecht was accused of being a Soviet agent. Behind the scenes, guided by a certain Captain Pabst and Lieutenant Captain Canaris, the assassination of the CPG leaders and the capture of Radek was being actively planned, with State Attorney Weissmann serving as intermediary between the Ebert government and the paramilitary forces.

The right hoped for a provocation, and the Spartacist rank and file obliged. They seized the newspaper district of Berlin and won some dissident army units over to their side. This gave Ebert and his police chief, Gustav Noske, an opportunity to act. Army units loyal to the generals were marched into Berlin with orders to shoot any Spartacist who dared to resist. One of the units was the Ehrhardt Brigade, fresh from service on the Baltic, their dapper caps bearing the proud symbol of the swastika.

In the face of the approaching storm, Luxemburg, Liebknecht and the other leaders went underground. Though repeatedly warned that she was in extreme danger of betrayal, Luxemburg refused to leave the city. She apparently told her student Jakob Walcher that "she must seal her commitment to the cause with her own blood."[11] On January 15, a paramilitary unit found the three CPG leaders. Luxemburg was loaded into a staff car where an officer fired a bullet into her skull at point-blank range. At the Landwehr Canal, her body was thrown into the water. Liebknecht met a similar fate.[12]

Brecht continued to maintain his distance from revolutionary activity except insofar as it could provide material for his writing. When the news reached Augsburg that Luxemburg and Liebknecht had been "killed while trying to escape," Brecht and Cas were spending the snowy evening of January 19 at Gabler's Tavern. The bar was full of drunken soldiers. Also at Gabler's that evening were two supporters of the Spartacist movement, Lilly Krause-Prem, called by Brecht "Hell's Lilly," and her husband Georg. Neher observed the company in order to do sketches for *Baal*. Brecht sang "The Legend of the Dead Soldier," a song in which the kaiser's military recruiters dig up a buried and decomposing soldier, fill him with schnapps, and march him off to war. He also sang his "Song of the Soldier of the Red Army," in which the army talks about freedom but, as the song avers, "freedom, my children, never came."[13] The army marches behind what the song refers to as "the red, inhuman flag," and with "bloodstained empty hands," the soldiers of the song come "grinning into your paradise." Later, this song was one that Brecht often felt should be suppressed, but it is a candid appraisal of what his feelings really were in early 1919. When Lilly Krause-Prem and her husband, hardly examples of blood-thirstiness or inhumanity, argued with Brecht of the need to make a political commitment, Brecht would not commit himself even to the Independent Social Democrats, claiming that he was an "independent Independent."

Cas was working with Brecht on revisions of *Baal* when the news reached them that Kurt Eisner had been killed by Count Arco-Valley. Neher wrote in his diary: "Blood, blood, blood."[14] Cas and Brecht now began to talk of making a failed revolution the centerpiece of a new play. In its early drafts, it was to be called *Spartacus* but was later renamed *Drums in the Night*. Set in a typical lower-middle-class German bedroom on a November evening in 1918, the play opens with a half-clad Herr Balicke shaving himself while arguing with his wife about their daughter, Anna. He argues that their daughter ought to give up hope of her wartime sweetheart, Andreas Kragler, ever returning from his duty station in Africa. She should go ahead and marry a rich associate of Balicke, a man called Murk who has made his money during the war by arranging shady deals in military supplies and black-market goods. Is she "waiting to marry the pope or a nigger?" bellows Balicke. When it turns out that Anna is pregnant by Murk, both her parents pressure her to marry him and she reluctantly agrees. Just as the engagement party is about to leave for the Piccadilly Bar, there appears a wreck of a man burned black by the African sun. He wears a dark blue artillery uniform and has a stubby pipe clenched in his teeth. As the first act of the play closes with the appearance, as if from the dead, of Kragler a voice booms out at the end of the second act: "The masses are rising. Spartacus is attacking. Murder marches on."

For Brecht and Neher to have a character state baldly that "Spartacus is attacking" or to suggest that the Spartacists were murderers was to grossly distort what had been a complex revolutionary situation. But the primary concern was not to present a fair appraisal of both sides in a dispute but to express its most dramatic aspects in the bluntest language. As with *Baal*, woven into *Spartacus* were several of the songs that Brecht himself was performing at this time. A pub owner called Glubb sings to his own guitar accompaniment "The Legend of the Dead Soldier." Through the haze of smoke and the din of drunks at Glubb's bar, a woman comes in selling newspapers and shouting "Spartacus in newspaper district! Red Rosa addresses open-air meeting in Tierpark! How long will mob disorder be tolerated?" In the last act, the revolutionaries beg the artillerist to put his skills at the service of the revolution. Kragler turns to Anna and asks rhetorically: "Do they want my flesh to rot in the gutter so that their ideas can win out?" He and Anna, already pregnant by Murk, exit to go home to a "white, wide bed." Like *Baal* the new play relied heavily on the poetry his friends were constantly writing. But, unlike *Baal*, the new play not only had a fairly clear-cut dramatic structure but also began to explore social situations and geographical settings less clearly like those in which Neher and Brecht had grown up.

Written in haste on a burningly topical theme, Brecht and Neher were extremely anxious to get this play and the already completed *Baal* staged as quickly as possible. Brecht with his contacts in the Kutscher seminar and Neher from his work at the Munich Art Academy had some contacts in the Munich theater and a few ideas as to how to get some attention for the new plays. They knew that the Cafe Stephanie was a hangout for theater people and so they went there to try their luck. At one table sat the prominent Munich actor Arnold Marle. Brecht went over to the actor and tried to show him the scripts. But Marle waved him off saying, "Go to Dr. Feuchtwanger."[15]

Marle's advice was sound. Dr. Lion Feuchtwanger and his wife, Marta, were known to be very open to new developments in the arts.

Lion Feuchtwanger, from a recently assimilated old Jewish family in southern Germany, was a prolific playwright and a major figure in Munich theatrical life. Immensely knowledgeable about the history of the theater, including the theater of India, and a topflight translator and adaptor of foreign plays into German, Feuchtwanger had provided the German stage with a steady stream of eminently playable works. In early 1919 he was the person who could open the way for new talent in the Munich theater.

Years later Feuchtwanger would remember Brecht appearing at his apartment door in the Georgenstrasse.[16] Brecht was thin, badly shaven, and shabbily dressed, with his speech marked by a strong Augsburg accent. Inside the rather opulent apartment, the strange young man stayed close to the walls and walked about rather shyly. But when he handed the manuscript of the just-completed *Spartacus* to Feuchtwanger, instead of doing the usual thing, saying he had torn the play from his own bleeding heart, he claimed he had written the piece in order to make money. Feuchtwanger, intrigued by this highly unusual young man, promised to read it.

Used to plays with the emotional outbursts and high sentiments that characterized the "Oh, Mensch" style of the then-dominant Expressionist drama, Feuchtwanger was struck by the down-to-earth language of *Spartacus*. Feuchtwanger liked it and called Brecht to ask him why he had lied to him by saying that he had merely written the play for money. Brecht was indignant and shouted that the play had in fact been written for money. However, he did add that he had another play to show Feuchtwanger, a better one, called *Baal*. He would bring that one over.

Feuchtwanger, a serious student of the near and far East, saw that the title character Baal had little but his name in common with the Syrian god. But Feuchtwanger also saw that the play with its wild and chaotic string of erotic incidents was "a very fine affair." He also liked the drawings that Neher had done as preliminary sketches for staging the play. Feuchtwanger decided to do everything he could to help this promising young playwright and his equally talented artist friend.

While Feuchtwanger began to look around for opportunities for his two newest protégés, Neher and Brecht were trying to avoid the competing political pulls of both right and left. The two young men were together as often as the increasingly jealous Cas could make that happen. All too often, from Cas's point of view, Brecht went off with other intimate friends, both male and female. At one time in the spring of 1919, they quarreled bitterly and parted. But Cas found that he preferred to have at least a part of Brecht's company to none at all. Now, as in years to come, he would drift back into Brecht's orbit, admire and work with him intensely for awhile, and then, his jealousy and pride in his own work overwhelming him again, he would move away to work on his own independent career.

Typically, disaffected members of the Brecht clique would stay psychologically close to Brecht by becoming involved with someone with whom Brecht was involved. In Neher's case, in early 1919, he was drawn to Georg Geyer. After Geyer, an excellent pianist, had performed some Bach works for him, Cas was so smitten that he proposed they bring out an illustrated Bach edition together. As they worked on this project, they found an adagio that would be an excellent introduction, they felt, not to Bach but to *Baal!*

When Neher, in that spring of 1919, attempted to widen his horizons with some women dancers he had met, he found Brecht deliberately luring him back. Brecht effortlessly drew him close again by giving him a private recital of his best pornographic songs, many of which were explicitly homosexual. Cas (whose interest in women was never strong) found himself again working with and for Brecht. The latest theater projects were a play featuring a bisexual biblical David singing seductively to an admiring King Saul and another work called *Summer Symphony* which featured, in Brecht's own description, "hotturd" prose. But Neher was not allowed to simply return to the fold. He had strayed, and Brecht, doing what he always did with runaways, gave him a very stern lecture on faults of character. Above all, claimed Brecht, Neher must get rid of his "Spiessbürger" (petit bourgeois) qualities. He must give up listening to flatterers. "You must know," said Brecht, "that nobody tells you the truth. Everyone has [his] own angle."[17]

Having brought Neher back to the fold, Brecht would be off to see Georg Geyer, Hedda Kuhn, the now very obviously pregnant Bie at Kimratshofen, or to visit the House of the Seven Bunnies, one of Augsburg's brothels. One evening, a scantily clad "bunny" stood on a table to sing and act out a song with the refrain: "I've got a bushel of hair on my belly, I think I am an ape."[18] After the "bunny's" suggestive recital, Brecht grabbed a guitar and jumped up to sing one of his own erotic ballads, his adaptation of Goethe's poem about an Indian temple prostitute, "God and the Temple Dancer." At the end of his recital, the audience swarmed over him as a bystander passed around a hat.

On one spring Sunday outing, the Feuchtwangers saw played out a drama that might be entitled "First Comes Food, Then, Possibly, Comes Morality." They were sitting on a park bench in one of the nationalized Wittelsbach palaces, the lovely Nymphenburg Schloss, watching the swans on the lake.[19] They then saw a formally dressed man approach the lake carrying a paper bag. To the Feuchtwangers' horror in these times of near starvation in Munich, the man threw crusts of bread from the bag to the swans. As one of the swans swam close, the man grabbed it and stuffed it under his morning coat. As he hurried by, the Feuchtwangers recognized the Wittelsbach prince, Ludwig Ferdinand, hurrying home with his still-struggling Sunday dinner.

Around the time that Feuchtwanger was promoting Brecht and Neher, one day while sitting at their favorite outdoor café the Hofgarten, the Feuchtwangers had put their coats over the backs of their chairs because the weather was so warm.[20] When they rose to leave, a "silly-looking young man" hurried over to help Dr. Feuchtwanger into his coat. The young man then tried to interest him in a portfolio of sketches. Unimpressed with the sketches, Feuchtwanger declined to help. The name of the artist manqué was Adolf Hitler.

5

"Cold as a Dog, a Great Being with No Human Feeling" (1919–20)

Despite Ernest Niekisch's efforts to have "revolution" stay within boundaries, Kurt Eisner's murder triggered protests throughout Bavaria. There was some looting of shops in Augsburg, and a detachment of the Augsburg workers' and soldiers' council marched out to restore law and order. Three people were killed in sporadic exchanges of gunfire. Those inclined to follow the example of Lenin—who had declared the necessity of open and bloody class warfare—now urged seizing power in Germany. Lenin himself was very much concerned about the need to establish soviets in as many other countries as possible to provide allies for Russia. In the first week of March 1919, he organized the Comintern, designed to coordinate global revolution. The immediate results were encouraging to the Russians. On March 21, a soviet was established in Hungary with Béla Kun as premier and Georg Lukács as deputy commissioner for education. Germany seemed ready to follow. On April 7, Munich was declared to be a "Soviet Republic," and power passed into several odd pairs of hands. Dr. Franz Lipp, now foreign minister, addressed the pope in a rambling but official telegram as "Comrade Pope." Equally unlikely government leaders were anarchist philosopher Gustav Landauer, Expressionist playwright Ernst Toller, and poet Erich Mühsam. So inept was this group that the Berlin leaders of the Communist party ordered Eugene Leviné to take over the government of Bavaria.

On April 13, Leviné declared a dictatorship of the proletariat and began to recruit a Red Army. A Jewish Russian in command of a Munich soviet sent shock waves throughout the openly anti-Semitic German right. Just as the Spartacists' street fighting in Berlin had given Ebert an excuse for wiping out his opponents, troops could now be turned loose on Munich. Radical remnants of the German Army hastily dug up their stockpiled arms and pointed them toward Munich.

The radical right, the Whites, were enflamed by reports of "Red" atrocities of the kind Brecht described in his "Song of the Red Army Soldier." Lost in the uproar against supposed Red bloodthirstiness was

the agenda of people like Lilly Krause-Prem who hoped that a government of the left would establish basic rights for women and proper care
for children. In an address to the "Women of Augsburg" published in
the *Augsburger Neueste Nachrichten* on April 9, 1919, she had called for
nothing more radical than equal voting rights for women, free doctors,
free prescription medicines, and free use of public bathing facilities for
the needy.[1]

On Easter Sunday, April 20, 1919, Augsburg woke to find itself
occupied by two thousand members of General Franz Ritter von Epp's
White Army, which, together with Captain Ernst Röhm, attempted to
destroy the Bavarian soviet. Augsburg's own rather mild version of a
soviet government had gone into hiding. Georg Prem hid in Brecht's
apartment for two nights before being spirited across the nearby Swiss
border. Brecht was able to use his connections with both left and right
to get a permit for a simply frightened Marie Aman to leave Augsburg
for a safer place in the country.

While Georg Prem was hiding upstairs, Walter Brecht was getting
into uniform to march with von Epp's forces. Young men were promised a special emergency graduation from the gymnasium if they would
serve, and were issued a handsome and massive handgun. The mood of
the predominantly middle- and upper-class young men, many of them
junior ex-officers, was jubilant as they set off to crush the "Red menace." Otto Müller left the *Baal* collective to join Walter Brecht and von
Epp. Caspar Neher's still sternly nationalist father wanted his son to
join too, but Cas, with twenty-two battles behind him, now wanted
nothing further to do with war. His diary entry for April 22, 1919,
reads: "Further work on *Baal*."[2] Neher's diary now explicitly refers to
the much-revised play as "his and my *Baal*."

Brecht was not too busy to give up his pursuit of the lovely
horsewoman Caspar's sister Marietta. At what seems like a wildly improbable time, with civil war running through the Brecht clique itself,
he had again begun taking riding lessons in order to chase Marietta. A
mild fall from his horse on April 26 stopped him from riding, but he
continued to wear his jodhpurs and riding boots. Slapping his whip
against the side of his boot and quoting Nietszche, he would declare:
"Wenn du zum Weibe gehst, vergiss die Peitsche nicht" (when you go
to a woman, don't forget to take a whip).[3] "Weibe," as used in Nietszche, is perhaps most faithfully rendered in English as *broads* or *whores*.

These fashionable male sentiments were so ubiquitous, it is not
surprising that misogyny and sadomasochistic whips appear both in
Brecht's everyday life as well as the poems. In one called "On Vitality,"
we find the line:

Women lie all clumped up in a ball
Take your whip to bed with them![4]

He writes of how easy it is, if one has enough Baal-like vitality, to get angels (whose gender is not specified) to lie down on their stomachs to be mounted from behind as they "beg for the final things." In poems and short stories, as well as his letters and diaries, parade ruthless, black-booted, whip-bearing males, often aroused by murder, rape, and other forms of sadomasochism.

One of Brecht's favorite images, the male rider and the female horse, is a recurrent one in classical and modern erotica.[5] In Zola's novel *Nana*, the protagonist (a prostitute who is frequently mounted by men for money) watches a horse race in which a filly called Nana is ridden by a jockey called Price. As both Coral Lansbury and Louise DeSalvo have convincingly shown, women as horses have long served as stock figures for male fantasies of domination, rape, and the general denigration of women.[6] In such works, women are "repeatedly subdued and tied down so they can be 'mounted' more easily, and they always end up as grateful victims, trained to enjoy the whip and the straps, proud to provide pleasure for their masters."[7] Both the classical centaur and an ostensibly modern work such as *Equus* express the dream of doing away with women altogether.

In one of Brecht's many contributions to this genre, Paula Banholzer is given the male form of her name:

There are many, Paul, who need a horse
In order to find a rider.[8]

Similarly, in a poem addressed to the independently minded Hedda Kuhn (addressed by Brecht in English as "He"), the poet speaks of "confused riders" who insist on "carrying the horse." In contrast to "He," not content to be merely ridden, Bie is often praised as being "plantlike" in her devotion. When they are not tractable yet spirited horses, or angels of ambiguous gender to be sodomized, female sexual partners are characterized as "bitches," "tender lambs," or "grass" to be trampled and consumed by "noble bulls."

Men in these poems often satisfy themselves sexually and intellectually with one another, as they have been intellectually admonished to do in literature from Plato to Nietzsche. But, like his literary forebears, Brecht not only celebrates homoerotic sex but also links it with the dehumanization or brutalization of women: the removal of the woman's face, the confusion of her with nonhuman species, her multiple rape and/or murder or suicide. This, of course, neither began with Brecht nor ended with him. We see the persistence of these forms to this day in film, television, and the macho bravado of American pilots who, in their own words, "strap their asses to a piece of flaming metal" in order "to asshole those fuckers," the deliberately faceless and dehumanized Russians and Iranians.[9] This is not violence confined to conventional political description of either the "left" or the "right." This is "natural," sociopathic male violence as still found across the entire political spectrum and among virtually all socioeconomic and ethnic groups.

Deliberately telescoping life and poetry as he plays with the pornographic images of degradation, Brecht often appears in the poems either as himself, or as a character whose name has been formed from the letters of his first and last names, pronounced "bébé" (as is the word for baby in German), or as "Bidi," one of the nicknames to which he now began to answer. In a poem with the title "Anna Speaks Badly of Bidi," the central character is portrayed as "cold as a dog, a great being / With no human feeling."[10] Brecht's descriptions of himself here, and frequently elsewhere, are eerily similar to those the psychologist Eugen Kahn would use in 1931 in his *Psychopathic Personalities.* Kahn analyzes people he calls the "affectively cold" or "active, cold autists, strong in impulse," whose coldness and lack of "affective resonance" permit them to act ruthlessly in the midst of what they see as an "enemy society."[11] Able to either ignore the pain of others or to relish it, Brecht lived in a universe that reflected his own values on a cosmic scale. In one poem, the poet dreams approvingly of his own tombstone: "Here lies B.B. / PURE, LUCID, EVIL."[12] If such language had not been mixed with a deliberate irony, these poems might have been intolerable to those around him and to later literary critics. But because his self-portraits are usually so exaggerated or so downright funny, they remain unchallenged. In a good and a bad sense, there is a childlike quality about his self-descriptions, engaging enough that he could maintain that the universe should turn only around this perpetual "bébé."

In late April 1919, Cas and his Bébé moved rhythmically back and forth in the privacy of the covered swings at the Augsburg fair, clinging "like ticks" to the bucking "animal." Cas saw a red glow in the night sky as the White forces fired on Munich. Above the cacophony of the "nigger music" of the fair (as Brecht described it), they could hear the distant roar of von Epp's cannon as he took Munich.

Walter Brecht described in detail the atrocities committed by the White forces in which he had served.[13] We know that Gustav Landauer, Eugene Leviné, and Kurt Eglhofer of the revolutionary leadership were beaten to death or immediately shot.[14] In a frenzy where Eros was often not distinguishable from Thanatos, those shot were often then mutilated genitally. Walter Brecht saw naked and sexually mutilated bodies of Red prisoners tossed on the back of military trucks to be buried in a mass grave on the outskirts of Munich. Hardly anyone openly associated with the Reds escaped. Only the intervention of some friendly White officers who apparently knew him saved Adolf Hitler. With no means of support as yet (his attempt at becoming a theater designer having failed), at the time of von Epp's arrival at the Red Army barracks, Hitler was living there and wearing a Red Army armband. In the victory parade, cheers roared from the upper- and middle-class apartments along the Ludwigstrasse as "sternly erect, faultlessly in step" von Epp's Free Corps and the Ehrhardt Brigade marched smartly by in review.[15]

The elation of the proud, conservative, openly anti-Semitic forces that took Berlin, Munich, and other German cities out of the hands of the various soviets was suddenly dampened in May when they saw the terms of the Versailles Treaty. The treaty admitted German guilt for the war, put the industrial Ruhr under French supervision, disbanded German armed forces, gave up Germany's hard-won colonies, and exacted massive annual reparations. It was a final indignity for the many who like von Epp and Röhm believed that but for betrayal by their leaders in November, they could have determined the terms of peace and plunder.

In Augsburg, the week after the signing of the Versailles Treaty, most of the usual crowd was gathered at Gabler's. Brecht was in good voice as he sang his latest song, the strongly Kiplingesque "Larry's Ballad of Mama the Army." Like his model, the "poet of empire," Rudyard Kipling, whose work had been available in German translation since 1910 as *Soldatenlieder*, Brecht's own soldiers take pleasure in the murder of opponents while convinced of their own superiority. In Brecht's poem about an army of colonial adventurers, burned black by the Far Eastern sun, each stanza ends with the refrain: "At night there's a din and the enemy's there, Mama! Music plays. One can drink. One can shoot, and the enemy's there, Mama!"

Singing such songs at Gabler's and whorehouses, the Brecht group ate and drank and slept together both indoors and out as the weather turned warmer. The dynamics of the group would change as Brecht would favor this or that admirer, playing one against another. Entire lives revolved around their idol. The young man who had been born with the very ordinary name of Otto Müller became, at Brecht's suggestion, the more distinguished-sounding Otto Müllereisert.

One May night Brecht sat on a bench with Hans Otto Münsterer, a favorite of that moment, the dandy who had visited Brecht one Sunday morning wearing those very elegant gray gloves. As Münsterer remembered this event decades later, they sat in the dripping rain next to the rushing black water of the canal near the Bei den sieben Kindeln. Near the bench, under the chestnut trees, was a sarcophagus with a depiction of the death of the Roman children. Brecht teased Hans Otto (as he had Cas) about "Spiessigkeit," (petit bourgeois propriety) and "made an awful mess of my clothes. I held his hand in mine for a long time."[16] They agreed from now on to use the more informal "Du" rather than the more distant "Sie." The ambiguity of this relationship would echo down the decades. In memoirs published in 1963, after his friend Brecht had been dead for seven years, he claimed that nothing homosexual should be read into the relationship but added also that the relationship was comparable to that of Goethe and Lotte, or Rimbaud and Verlaine.

That summer, among many another explicitly homosexual poems, plays, and letters, Brecht wrote:

> *In July I have an affair with the sky,*
> *I call him Little Boy*
> *Blue, glorious, violet, he loves me.*
> *It's male love.*[17]

The same emphasis on self-reflexive male love, already outlined in *Baal*, was often joined with clear hostility to women. Baal says to his friend Eckart not only, "Ich liebe dich," but adds, "ich mag kein Weib mehr" (I don't care for any bitches anymore). In the world of Baal that Neher and Brecht created, homosexual love blends with misogyny, and "love" itself blends with death in the timeless dance of Eros with Thanatos: "When Baal only saw corpses around him / His lust grew twice as strong." Although Baal's lust for women sometimes overwhelms him, "if a bitch gives you everything, says Baal / Let it go, for she hasn't got anything else."

The twenty-one-year-old Brecht's priorities were clear: emptying his gonads in varied paid and unpaid ways, getting his own work (all mixed up with the work of others) published and being paid for it. Brecht was interested in becoming famous, getting his own car, and possibly getting some money to Bie. Though Bie was now in her eighth month, Brecht had not yet told his parents of his imminent fatherhood. Since she remained decorously away in Kimratshofen, Augsburg's polite society was spared daily reminders of what young Fräulein Banholzer and young Herr Brecht had wrought. Even if Bie had remained in Augsburg, it is doubtful whether Eugen's mother would have registered what had happened. Sophie Brecht was now regularly given massive doses of morphine to try to counter the ever-greater pain of her inoperable cancer.

With the Red Republic bloodily eradicated by mid-June, the Munich authorities welcomed back the students who had been released to the effort. Brecht again signed up for Kutscher's useful seminar. But much of his time was now spent with the childless Feuchtwangers, who had taken him in. Feuchtwanger was working hard to help both Neher and Brecht break into the Munich theater. In fact, Lion Feuchtwanger was so fascinated with Brecht that he wrote a novel about him called, in its first version, *Thomas Brecht*. In it, Brecht is presented as a mechanic, somebody who takes apart and puts together inanimate but powerful artifacts.

A young director named Jacob Geis was another of those completely fascinated by Brecht. Geis promoted Brecht so fanatically that he was soon fired from his first theater job, but he would remain a lifetime supporter. Brecht had also managed to get himself involved with the cabaret artists Liesl Karlstadt and Karl Valentin, who both liked him enough to include him in some of their madcap routines. Brecht's penchant for exaggeration fit well with a cabaret that depended on satiric excess.

Having been unsuccessful in breaking into theater, Adolf Hitler had been newly recruited by the triumphant nationalists in Munich. They wanted him particularly to speak out against the Versailles Treaty. His poison gas–scarred vocal cords gave his voice a mesmerizing timbre that electrified audiences. He told his listeners to open their eyes, to see around them "signs of decay of a slowly ebbing world."[18] The decay that Hitler spoke of so forcefully struck a responsive chord in Munich. Oswald Spengler, another Munich resident, had given the general idea academic respectability with *Die Untergang des Abendlandes*, or *The Decline of the West*, published in Munich between 1918–22. In nearby Vienna, the same vocabulary was being used by the influential Karl Kraus, who warned darkly of a "flood of advertising" that would swamp mankind.[19] Decades later, Brecht said of this period, "All one saw were a few islands even as they were being eaten away by the waves."[20]

The formal establishment of the Weimar Republic was a very mixed bag. The right dominated the judiciary and private landholding. The left managed to push through the enfranchisement of women. As soon as they did, however, all parties on the left soon bowed to their male constituents and played down so-called women's issues. In 1920, the Comintern would officially decree that "women's issues" were to be subordinated to the general goal of revolution. Once revolution was achieved, the directive implied, women would enjoy full equality. Until then, women should not make a fuss within party ranks, argued Lenin as this might alienate male constituents.[21]

In Kimratshofen on July 30, 1919, Bie gave birth to a healthy little boy. In memory of Wedekind, the child was given the name of Frank. The whole Brecht clique came to Kimratshofen for the christening party. Orge played the organ, as Brecht sang "Baal's Chorale" and "Lucifer's Song of Evening." When Brecht's father finally heard about Frank, he refused his son's request to take the child in. Fräulein Roecker was strongly opposed to the idea. Bringing an illegitimate child into the Herr Direktor's home was unthinkable while Frau Brecht was slowly dying and was not seriously considered by anyone but Eugen himself. Bie's parents were emphatically unwilling to take the child, and Bie and Bert seem never to have seriously considered looking after Frank themselves. The redheaded infant was put in the care of the wife of a country-road mender. The child would never have a real home.

As Bie recovered her strength and figure, Brecht returned to his affairs in Augsburg and Munich. Having had some success with occasional journalism, Brecht now applied for a part-time job as theater and opera critic for the small Augsburg paper of the independent wing of the Social Democratic party *Volkswille*. The paper, and its Marxist editor Wendelin Thomas, survived because of a basic anomaly in post–World War I German political life: that the pragmatic Social Democrats had helped smash the Spartacists gave the party a substantial, though mild, presence. In hiring Bert Brecht, son of Herr Direktor Brecht and brother of the soldier Walter Brecht, Wendelin Thomas was not making a radical choice. If Brecht was political at all, it was mainly as a gadfly with a natural talent "pour épater les bourgeois."

One evening the new critic was bowled over by a dark-haired singer with a fine mezzo-soprano voice, and a face and body to match. At the first intermission, Brecht hurried to Marianne Zoff's dressing-room door. Zoff, as she recalled years later, was astounded at Brecht, who was quite unlike the usual debonair stage-door johnny or formal music critic.[22] She saw a young man thin as a rail, wearing a worn-looking leather jacket, rumpled and worn corduroy trousers, carrying a shabby cap. He praised Marianne's singing and everything about her performance. The more he talked, the more fascinating she found him, as though he were some kind of exotic animal in a zoo. She found his closely cropped, ascetic head appealing and was struck by his eyes, dark and small like buttons, his ever-moving thin lips, and his small hands as graceful as those of a pianist. Somehow it did not seem to matter that his none-too-clean underwear showed above his shabby corduroy pants, that dried tobacco caked the corner of his mouth, that his tongue was lilac from licking his pen, and that his hair was unwashed. Zoff stared at him, thinking, "He's quite mad." Suddenly he asked, "May I smoke?" Without thinking of her voice she nodded assent. When she began to cough violently, he stared in disbelief at his acrid cigar as though it could not possibly be the cause of her distress. When the show was over, he was back. He did not propose that they go for a drink but took her on such a long walking tour of Augsburg that her feet ached.

It was a heady time for Marianne Zoff. Her career in provincial Augsburg was successful in a way that would have been harder to achieve in Vienna, Berlin, or Munich. At her Augsburg debut on September 23, 1919, she was a gypsy in *Carmen*. The next month she was Venus in Offenbach's *Orpheus in the Underworld* and Lola in *Cavalleria Rusticana*. In the following year and a half, she would sing Agnes in Smetana's *The Bartered Bride*, Magdalena in Jacques Halévys' *Goldsmith of Toledo*, the Countess in Verdi's *Rigoletto* and Emilia in his *Otello*, an aristocratic boy in Wagner's *Lohengrin*, and her final appearance in Augsburg would be in Wagner's *Walküre*.

As often as his own busy schedule permitted, Brecht would wait for her after her performances. He learned something of her background: Born in Austria in 1893, she was five years older than he. Her father had served as an officer in the Imperial Viennese forces. Her mother was descended from a long line of Sephardic Jews. Soon Marianne was taken to meet his parents in the Bleichstrasse. With her exotic beauty and Viennese graciousness, she charmed even the dying Frau Brecht.

Well-groomed and elegant, Marianne made some efforts to clean him up. He stripped down enough to allow her to wash his ears and neck, which would lead to erotic play. But even with the lure of the erotic, he tried to avoid washing. Marianne wrote a note to herself: "Bert Brecht does not wash himself. . . . One tries everything. But then, he is so witty that finally one laughs and he has escaped again. This filth costs a lot, a great deal, because one then requires the costliest, loveliest-smelling things in order to overcome the bad air in the room, and this is not so simple."[23] He had, she thought, few friends, and she mused whether it was his bad odor or his lies that finally drove people away. Odors and lies notwithstanding, she could not escape her fascination with him. He was a genius, and she wondered at first if that did not give him a right to lie.

When he sang to her, shivers ran down her spine. When they became lovers, she apparently knew nothing of his numerous other affairs, and he perhaps did not know that she had led a less than sheltered life. Since 1917, she had shared an apartment in Munich with a tiny, wealthy Jewish admirer, Oskar Camillus Recht. He manufactured playing cards, and when business was bad, which was often, Recht would apparently rob his own company's till. With his jealous hysteria and his sword stick, he looked like the knave of hearts on one of his own playing cards. When Recht would later learn of Brecht and Brecht of Recht, the offstage scenes would rival what Marianne was doing onstage in productions of Verdi and Wagner.

In October 1919, Brecht published his first theater review. It was a solid and balanced piece on an Augsburg performance of Ibsen's rather daring play *Ghosts*. Perhaps partly because the play's real subject was venereal disease combined with a cover-up of an extramarital affair with a maid, Ibsen came off rather well in Brecht's review. So also did a film on venereal disease and prostitution reviewed two weeks later. "If," warned Brecht, "cinemas are allowed to continue to present such dirty stuff as this, soon nobody will bother to go to regular theaters."[24] He rushed to see all the newest films, including Chaplin's, which had started to flood Germany.

But his early stabs at film writing, like the still unstaged *Baal* and *Spartacus*, still brought in nothing. He decided to try short stories. In one of these called "Bargan Lets It Happen, a Pirate Story," Bargan falls head over heels in love with a fellow pirate, a filthy and treacherous man, clubfooted like Brecht's close friend Orge.[25] Bargan is wasting away from a probably venereal ailment called by Brecht simply the "American Disease." Croze—"The Clubfoot of Saint Marie"—and Bargan storm ashore to plunge into the Chilean jungle at the "Gulf of Marie." The women of the city stand shivering in flimsy slips waiting to be divided among the conquerors. Bargan selects a young woman but his possession of her is disputed by the madly jealous Croze, who takes the woman away with him. She is found in his tent the next morning with her throat slit from ear to ear. On the "evening of the third day," Bargan orders the slaughter of the seventy remaining inhabitants, loads their goods on ox carts, and sets the city to the torch. The rape of a city and the jealousy among men over a disputed captive echo scenes from the *Iliad*. Other parts of the story echo the Roman author Tacitus, familiar to Brecht from his gymnasium studies.

The pirates leave the burning city to make their way back to their ship, led by Bargan mounted on a black stallion, who guides the troops into a deadly trap. Thinking they are in a dry streambed, they find they are in a rapidly filling tidal estuary. "The flooding waters," reports an unnamed narrator, "looked like an eye that grew darker and darker, the way it happens in lovemaking when one is swept away by the drug of ecstasy." Saving himself, Bargan makes it back to the ship where he joins Croze. When the other sailors reach the vessel, they find Croze below decks, somewhat "bleich" or "pale" and shivering but grinning all over his ugly face while Bargan stares at him longingly. Seeing their leader so far gone in love, the sailors load the lovers into the ship's longboat to send them off to live or die together so that the rest can return to some serious piracy.

In a fragment called "Bargan's Youth," we learn that the dark-skinned Bargan grew up in another of Brecht's "dark forests."[26] Like Brecht and Baal, Bargan becomes a poet, singing his ballads to music of his own composition and with his own guitar accompaniment. Fatally attractive to women, he prefers men. Another man, also a poet, follows Bargan into the woods and grabs at his crotch. Later, after setting fire to the plantation where they both work, the second poet and another male lover are found lying together in the bushes watching the flames while "taking pleasure in one another." As the plantation burns, Bargan swings through the trees to jump on a stolen horse and gallop away.

Though set in a made-up "Chile," on leaky sailing ships, or in a Kiplingesque India, these stories and poems use building blocks from Brecht's own far more mundane experience. Like many of his fictional heroes, he could seduce almost anyone at will. As Cas had long since seen, his friend's songs, particularly when he performed them himself, had "power, power, totally uncanny power." There was a chain reaction in everything he did. Sexual experience was poured into passionate, violent stories and poems. These in turn brought him more admirers in a perpetual cycle of sex for text and vice versa.

In secretary or business tycoon, male or female, knees weakened and inhibitions slipped away as Brecht, in his favorite performing stance, stood above them on a table at bars, brothels, or fashionable apartments such as that of the Feuchtwangers. With his feet spread apart, guitar pressed close to his crotch, almost concave belly thrust forward, he made the animal-gut strings howl to back up his high, scratchy voice. People came and saw and heard and were conquered. One December evening in 1919, in a typical rough bar near Augsburg, "a thin-lipped young gent with a coolly ironic look" heard Brecht perform.[27] His coolness slipped away as he was drawn to the power that Cas had heard and felt. This particular young man, Peter Suhrkamp by name, would become one of the most powerful publishers in Germany in this century, and his career would be built in large part by his association with Brecht.

While Brecht kept in the public eye as a seductive performer, Lion Feuchtwanger's efforts on behalf of his young protégé continued. On one occasion, he received Brecht's father who wanted to know what promise his son might have as a writer. "I am usually not of the opinion," Dr. Feuchtwanger said, "that one should encourage a young person to become a writer. However, if Brecht does not become a writer—he is a genius—then that would be a sin."[28] The Herr Direktor was impressed. "Fine," he said to Dr. Feuchtwanger, "I'm going to continue to send him his checks." With this support in hand, Brecht was able to drop all pretense of attending the university and now worked toward being recognized as a professional writer.

Though Feuchtwanger made a strong case for *Baal* at the well-established Musarion Verlag, it was turned down. He next took *Baal*, together with Neher's brooding and powerful sketches, to the Georg-Müller Verlag. That firm, though apparently having some reservations about it in the increasingly conservative climate of Munich, went ahead anyway and began to set the type for *Baal*. Finally, a breakthrough seemed near. Wanting to ride its momentum, Brecht immediately began to think of conquering the acknowledged center of German cultural life, the old imperial capital Berlin.

In planning a move to Berlin, he was as careful as he had been before. When embracing the new, he would always hold on to the old, for safety's sake. For all the wild extravagance of his poetry, he was far too cautious a person to move rashly. He spoke and wrote of excess but practiced rigorous control, determined that he would be the hammer rather than the anvil, the rider rather than the horse. Relationships—whether to various lovers, philosophies, theories, other poets, cities, or apartments—would always be cumulative. In adding Marianne, Hedda, or Müllereisert to his intimate circle, he never had any intention of giving up Cas, Bie, or Marie Aman. Similarly, though he was willing, indeed eager, to flirt with Berlin, he did not propose to give up Munich and Augsburg.

6

"Why Can't the Jews Be Got out of the Way?" (1920–21)

On February 21, 1920, with only typescripts in hand as printer's proofs for *Baal* were not yet ready, Brecht headed for Berlin. As the train steamed north, he worked on a poem that he titled "Sentimental Song #1004." The number suggests the continuation of a vast series, a prodigious sexual boast. This specific number tells cognoscenti that the twenty-two-year-old Brecht has already outdone by one the number of seductions claimed by Casanova in his entire lifetime and the number of Spanish conquests of Don Juan.

Simple in language and seemingly simple in content, the poem, retitled by Brecht before publication "Remembering Marie A.," recounts a seduction. The poet remembers the setting more than the woman herself. She was "pale and silent" like a "lofty dream" as he held her in his arms under a "slender plum tree" one "blue September." Above the man and the woman, a cloud drifts by and passes out of sight. Then, with an almost cinematic cut, the poem jumps forward to a time when the poet muses to an unseen and unheard companion that by now the slender plum tree may not only have grown but may been chopped down for firewood. The woman, the poet says in the third and concluding stanza, may now have had her seventh child. What remains in the poet's mind is the dream of that cloud passing briefly by:

> *And even the kiss I would have long forgotten*
> *If that cloud had not been there*
> *That I still know and I will always know*
> *It was very white and came there from on high.*[1]

My English rendition (like that of John Willett) does not give a sense of the complexity of this kind of simplicity in German, with its pun on the two meanings of "weiss," *to know* and *white*. Knowledge and the cloud are linguistically telescoped. This deceptively simple poem, easy to remember and later made easy to sing when it was set to a French turn-of-the century popular tune, is a staple of the German literary repertoire.

Twenty years later, though Brecht would speak of a "dehumanized situation" in Wordsworth when Wordsworth writes of "a lovely Apparition, sent / To be a moment's ornament," he did not submit his own poetry to similar evaluation.[2] "Poetry," he observes in his musings on Wordsworth, "is never mere expression. Reading a poem is of the same order as seeing and hearing, that is, something a great deal less passive."

In Brecht's "Ballad of the Death of Anna Cloudface," written in the same period as "Marie A," we encounter the same themes that Brecht would later find in Wordsworth. John Willett assumes from a contextual reference that the "Anna" of the Brecht poem may be a real person called Anna Gewölke, or Anna Cloudy.[3] If so, then again a person is displaced by a cloud. The first two lines repeat the formulaic seven, the mythic number of childhood at 7 Auf dem Rain or Bei den sieben Kindeln (street of the seven children).

> *Seven years went by. With kirschwasser and whiskey*
> *He washed her face out of his brain.*

The poem ends with the lines:

> *With the white winds of wild April*
> *His pale wishes fly like the clouds:*
> *A face disappears. And a mouth is stilled.*[4]

We move again from wind and clouds to facelessness. Though scores of examples of such treatment of women occur, the "Ballad of the Secrets of Any Man at All" provides a direct comparative treatment of the sexes. We are told in this August 1920 poem:

> *Everyone knows what a man is. He has a name.*
> *He walks along the street. He sits at the bar.*
> *You can see his face, you can hear his voice*
> *And a woman washed his shirt, and a woman combed his hair.*[5]

This "any man at all," whose face you can see and whose voice you can hear, is tended, almost as if a baby, by unnamed, silent, faceless women.

The male-oriented world of "Any Man at All," is part of a "great chain of being," a universe where the smallest part is directly linked to the entire universe.[6] In a poem written between 1918–20, called originally in badly spelled German "Gottes Liblingskoral" or "God's Favorite Chorale," a connection is directly made between the small unit, Brecht, and the ruler of the universe, God the Father. We know exactly what God's concerns are: "When the blue wind of evening wakes God the Father, he sees the heaven above him turn pale and it pleases him. Then his ears are quickened by the great cosmic chorale and he abandons himself to it."[7] God's attention turns to "the frightened prayers of mothers of great men," and to:

> The great words of great men.
> And the wonderful songs of Bert Brecht, for whom
>   things are going badly.

But not all badly, not when God the Father listens to your "wonderful songs," and when those songs nestle up against the "great words of great men."

Women are heard by this God but only in their capacity as frightened beings who happen also to be the "mothers of great men." "Sinful" women are rejected in heaven. When Evlyn Roe, who has been repeatedly raped on her way to the Holy Land, finally commits suicide, Saint Peter slams shut the gates of heaven in her face, saying "God has said he will not have the whore Evlyn Roe." In contrast, the various male sinners are well received in heaven. In the world of Brecht's poetry, God maintains a double standard.

As Brecht himself sometimes recognizes and self-mockingly admits, such things are the stuff of his own fantasies. He tells us he chooses the words in his poems as one might mix an exotic cocktail. What he wants are "sentences that can be flung out, the crazy enjoyment of the flesh of words," or words that will "knock out the listener's teeth."[8] It is verse designed for performance, verse of passion, power, and naked brutality. It just happened also to have been verse that in its male-oriented sex and violence catered directly to the predominant market taste of the various publishing outlets he wished to deal with in Berlin.[9]

It was cold in late February in Berlin. The address of his admirer Frank Warschauer, 13 Eislebenstrasse (ice life street), helped reinforce the poetically useful idea of Berlin as a cold place. But the apartment of the wealthy Warschauer was safe and warm. Six years Brecht's senior, and already well connected to Berlin's theater, film, and literary circles, Warschauer introduced Brecht to Berlin's makers and breakers in publishing and the arts. He was impressed with what he saw. "Boy," Brecht wrote to Cas, "everything is horribly overfilled with tasteless things, but on what a scale."[10]

In early March, there was a masked ball at Berlin's arts and crafts museum. He attended in the costume of a monk. Spotting a fetching young woman in blackface dressed as a hula dancer, he asked her to dance. He said he was not very good at dancing. After he had trodden on Dora Mannheim's bare feet a few times with his "makeshift" dancing, she asked if it would not be better to sit down and talk. This was more Brecht's element, and talk they did until the early hours of the next morning when Brecht then walked Mannheim home through the Tiergarten. The relationship flourished, even though Fräulein Do, as he half-formally, half-jokingly called her, allowed nothing physical yet, not even a kiss. But she was willing to continue to see and guide him around Berlin. She took him to the popular Café des Westens where Rosa Valetti had established a cabaret. Brecht had no idea as yet as to how to get tickets to the café cum cabaret; this was left to Mannheim.

On March 13, the budding relationship of monk and hula dancer was interrupted. Shots were fired in the Tiergarten. The radical right that had helped Ebert kill the Spartacists the year before now threatened to seize power from him. When Ebert asked the commander of the government forces, General Hans von Seeckt, to defend the capital, he was told the army would not fire on its own comrades. With no backing from that vital quarter, Ebert fled and the Ehrhardt Brigade, with its swastika-bedecked helmets, marched triumphantly into Berlin to set up a new "government" headed by Wolfgang Kapp, a man with a long record of contempt for democracy.[11]

Brecht also fled. He was, he assured Fräulein Do, leaving only to rescue his father in case of riots in Augsburg. But when Brecht got out of the train in Munich fifteen hours later, he had completely forgotten his cover story. As he admitted in a letter to Fräulein Do, he dropped his things off at his pension and went off at once to see the latest madcap comedy routines of his friends Valentin and Karlstadt.[12] When Fräulein Do failed to respond to this letter, he sent her another telling her how desperate he was without her. With her still ignoring him, he wrote to say he "felt an animal drive" come over him, and this could result "in a daily urge to run to the bars to lose my virginity."[13] She was intrigued by and wary of this odd young man from the provinces with his gift of gab but general awkwardness. She took him under her wing, helping him build a widening circle of useful people.

Despite von Seeckt's refusal to use the army to oppose Ehrhardt's renegade brigade, the unarmed workers of Berlin refused to deal with Kapp and halted all public services. In the face of the workers' intransigence and depite a pusillanimous government, the putsch ended on March 17 and Ebert was able to return. He dared make no attempt, however, to remove von Seeckt. No Weimar politician would prove courageous or dextrous enough to bring the army or von Seeckt to heel.

Ebert would not last long. Neither the workers nor the army trusted the government. In the Reichstag elections of June 1920, Ebert's centrist Social Democratic party (SDP) lost almost half its supporters, with parties to the right and left benefiting from its losses.[14] Though still the majority party in terms of total votes, the SDP would never again be the decisive force in a fractionalized and radicalized Weimar state.

Brecht continued to be oblivious of politics. As late as March 1921, he would say: "Meanwhile, I just trot indifferently along, with an unruffled expression, appreciative and irresponsible in bed, deceitful maybe, capable of transcending my own situation, pretty cold, wholly unpolitical."[15] In April 1920, in Augsburg, he wrote a rather complex review of Schiller's play *Don Carlos*, saying that he had loved this play for years.[16] But he added that his readers should also turn their attention to films such as the newly released French film *Bread*, and to novels such as Upton Sinclair's *The Jungle*. Brecht had been swept away by Sinclair's brutal account of conditions in the Chicago slaughterhouses at the turn of the century, and the novel would have a permanent effect on his work as he would dip into it again and again. Similarly useful was a Danish novel by Johannes Vilhelm Jensen called *Hjulet (The Wheel)*, which appeared in German translation in 1921.[17] Though Jensen would receive the Nobel Prize for literature in 1944, in 1921 he was little known and Brecht could still take things from his work without immediate notice and condemnation. He had now begun to connect the idea of "cold" Berlin with the idea of Berlin as a "jungle." He would telescope his own feelings about Berlin with Sinclair's description of Chicago and combine that with the erotic-intellectual interaction of the characters Evanston and Lee in *The Wheel*. In this, he had the makings of his next play.

Full of enthusiasm for the foreign, American, French, Danish, and British, he was not impressed when Thomas Mann read in Augsburg from his work-in-progress *The Magic Mountain*. Always jealous of Mann's stature in the world of letters, Brecht conducted guerrilla warfare with the novelist throughout his life. With no thought of fairness, Brecht derided Mann as a writer, human being, and political thinker. On April 26, 1920, he dismissed Mann's profound novel on the crippled condition of Europe as merely a description "of a couple of dozen lung patients who are conducting a kind of naive guerrilla war against death."[18]

In the Bleichstrasse, Dr. Renner was conducting a real-life battle against death. The doctor knew things were hopeless, but he told his patient the conventional lie that she was getting better. Herr Direktor Brecht was told, however, that her death was only a matter of time and that all that could be done was to continue to alleviate her pain with morphine.

At the end of April, the weather was warm enough for her window to be opened. When the chestnut tree before her window burst into blossom, she was pleased both by the sight of the blossoms and by their rich scent. But during the night of May 1, after falling asleep, she slipped quietly away. The next morning, the Herr Direktor was bowed by grief. Eugen looked at his brother, approached him, and made a tiny adjustment to Walter's collar. The gesture was a small but caring one, and Walter saw it as his mother's last gift being passed on to him. She had always cared about proper dress for all members of her family.

That evening, as the open coffin of Wilhemine Friederike Sophie Brezing Brecht lay in the parlor and Walter and his father kept pious watch, they heard the sounds of a raucous party above in Eugen's apartment. "Who knows why he did this in his mourning," wrote Walter years later. "We others who lived in the house were dumb with pain."[19]

Caspar Neher had seen many dead men during the war but never a dead woman. He seemed fascinated by Frau Brecht's corpse and began a few sketches.[20] While people were still coming to see the body, Brecht stood outside the house for hours staring into the black water of the city moat. As so often when under stress, he channeled his feelings into a poem. In "Song about My Mother," he observes: "I no longer remember her face as it was before she had the pain." He then asks: "Oh, why do we not say that which is important, it would have been / So easy and yet we will be damned because of it." The poem ends: "She cannot be dug out again with the fingernails."[21] The emotion is expressed in phrases that he would recycle in a variety of contexts. Not having shared with his mother "that which was important" is repeated in a poem on masturbation. The image of "fingernails" is used again in the poem in which he talks of pissing in the laundry and where his mother says that this will drive her to her grave.

The day he wrote "Song about My Mother" he also wrote "The Insulted." Instead of being the epicenter of "God's Favorite Chorale," here "clouds gesture dismissively" as "giant black dogs appear at every corner":

> *Nobody loves me. I can die like a dog . . .*
> *at the whim of the planet,*
> *the Earth turning in cold space,*
> *in a system I have not approved of.*[22]

Though the newly dead mother briefly appears in it, the poem begins and ends with the "insulted one," the unloved survivor, in a cold universe that he neither controls nor of which he approves.

His various forms of expression are so entwined that a division of them into fiction and fact is often arbitrary, notably in the diaries from Brecht's early years. Professor Renate Voris's excellent analysis sees them as examples of "staged honesty."[23] Less charitably, German scholar Klaus Theweleit sees Brecht's fantasies reflected in a generation of German men who were almost ubiquitously protofascist and misogynist.[24]

One set of extraordinary diaries that run from June 15, 1920 (six weeks after the death of his mother), and then break off in February 1922 records the same recurrent dreams and nightmares that pervade virtually all of Brecht's early poems and plays. Here also are Brecht's fears of being unloved; of impotence, tuberculosis, or heart failure; of powerlessness; of abandonment on a planet turning in cold space; of old age, death, and burial itself. He is both godlike creator and the helpless, powerless, so often abandoned Bébé. The world of humans and other animals is entwined as he laboriously examines a public coupling of his bitch, Ina, or speaks of his own couplings with the "leaky pot Marianne" as conducted "like horses."[25] The line between homosexual and heterosexual activity is blurred when he "takes" the excessively independent "He" or Bie/Paul. On one occasion, immediately after he has said that Cas often looks like a "bumfucker," there is a snippet of verse where a large worm crawls out of the anus of a woman who has turned her back toward him. He is frightened when the worm "wanted to shake my hand."[26]

The image of the worm-hand that comes out to grasp him echoes the other fears of independent, active women that haunt Brecht's verse and, Theweleit points out, much of the writing of this generation of men. The worm-hand, like the whirlpool eyes of Marie Aman, is deeply threatening. This fear of women's active sexuality or of any form of independent activity by women was, as Theweleit shows, widespread among men of the generation who lived before, during, and after World War I.[27] Theweleit provides overwhelming evidence of male fixations on an interchangeable repertoire of mindless whores, maids, nurses, and mothers; or figures of terror: "unnatural women" like the classical Medusa, or revolutionaries like the "Teufelsweib"—"the Devil's Woman,"—Rosa Luxemburg.

Theweleit attempts to show that a willingness to dismiss, systematically denigrate, and violate women helped prepare the way for the fundamental intolerance that was the hallmark of various totalitarian states. In the homes of the patriarchs, said Virginia Woolf in 1938, "we have in embryo the creature, Dictator as we call him when he is Italian or German, who believes that he has the right, whether given by God, Nature, sex or race is immaterial, to dictate to other human beings how they shall live; what they shall do."[28]

In Brecht's reflexive world of fantasy his shifts from fact to fiction or fiction to fact are almost too fast for his eyes, or ours, to catch. He had, as Marianne Zoff had noticed, virtually no awareness of such distinctions. He begins one sentence with the assertion, "I create the story," but ends it with, "or rather it creates me."[29] "Sentences come thrusting up straight from my breast," he writes, "I just copy them down."[30] Making a virtue of intellectual limitations, he notes: "I don't think I could ever have as grown-up a philosophy as Goethe or Hebbel, who, as far as ideas are concerned, must have had the memories of tram conductors. I keep forgetting my own opinions and can't make up my mind to learn them by heart. Even cities, adventures, faces, disappear in the wrinkles of my brain faster than the life of grass."[31]

Unsure of what his own opinions are and what his own history has been, part seriously, part ironically, he will declare: "When things get so murky and involved, then you have to help yourself out with papers; and that's security. Papers are something secure, writing is more than doing; there is a space between writing and doing; paper duplicates, simplifies."[32] But he is equally unsure of the source of the writing. He takes enormous pride in his written world; he is, after all, absolutely convinced of his own genius. But he also takes no responsibility for the various opinions and counteropinions that well up in his mouth or from his pen. If paper (the material, of course, that his father manufactures and from which the family lives) is a source of some security in a fleeting, cold, and hostile world, the words that go down on that paper are rebellious things. For words to be useful to him, they must be brought under control. "Words have their own intelligence," he notes, "some need to be shot; martial law must be declared, so that anyone may gun them down wherever they have been placed: particularly those that have entered racially mixed marriages or who keep bad company or who resist being buried as long as they still have admirers."[33]

Dreams of shooting miscegenational words; fucking, taming, or killing rebellious women-runaway horses; lounging in the rocking womb of ships; or long, white sharks nuzzling the bodies of women who have been raped or murdered, or who have committed suicide—these fantasies veer suddenly to fears of drowning and impotence. He will speak of being a "golden demigod for a while, grinning above the tribes of monkeys." But the "demigod" is also a drunk writer who is entwined with Orge Pfanzelt and Müllereisert under a concealing table. But later he will rail: "My father always abandons me in times of peril."[34] Imagining himself in peril and abandoned in Augsburg, he dreams of absinthe seas, America, Timbuktu, Tahiti; of wigwams, grass huts, a kraal; of American Indians, Maori, Malays; and of a big, agile soldier viewed from the rear in a jungle[35] or a bullfighter whose "elegant neck and bum" Brecht admires in a film as the man slides his hissing weapon into the thick body of the bull.[36] Or he will dream he can "exercise power," becoming one of the colonial masters about whom he has read. "As he, the master," writes Brecht in a diary entry of May 30, 1921, "strides through the liana forest, he ought to treat men like plants, mowing them down with his sickle, or like niggers with incomprehensible gurgling noises in their larynxes, understanding nothing but the whip."[37]

Attacks on women easily become racial attacks. When Marianne-Mar-Ma does not do what he wants, she is characterized as being "as jealous as a negress." These "Weiber-Frauen," are to be handled with whips, so Brecht recommends, like the "niggers." "Women," he says, "never reach further than their bed" and "can't be sharply distinguished from one another." Furthermore, a "woman has no kind of imagination" and "leads no kind of intellectual life."[38]

He doth protest too much. Everything must turn around a male figure, the colonial master, with his whip and his whistling-in-the-dark belief in his own power and centrality. But the same master is nagged by dread, a haunting, childlike fear of entrapment, abandonment, and powerlessness in swamp or jungle or in the eyes, anuses, or wombs of women, or the holds of leaky ships. "Love" blends with "death" as forcefully as it ever does in Wagner's "Liebestod."

His mother dead but not yet buried, he fled Augsburg, not saying where he was going but noting in his diary in the distancing third person: "They were bones that they laid in the shroud. He left before the earth blanketed her. Why look on [. . .] the obvious?"[39] There are, of course, answers to this rhetorical question. Though he can kill off other women at a great rate in his world of metaphor and can allude to her death in the "Song about My Mother," his mother is left psychically unburied; perhaps thereby she remains unlost.

In the poem whose writing immediately precedes the "Song about My Mother," a woman becomes immortal by being trampled and consumed by a man. Again the poet is an old man looking back:

> I had a woman who was stronger than I was,
> The way grass is stronger than the bull:
> It stands itself up again.
> She saw that I was evil, and loved me.[40]

The woman who is consumed is, at least in the world of an oft-repeated Brechtian metaphor, the stronger one, for the grass will stand again after being trampled by the bull. The bull blends with the poet-diarist as he says he is as "tough as a bull's balls."[41] In the dream space-time of poetry and diary, the bull-poet can trample, consume, and eject whatever is left of vegetal women from both ends of his alimentary canal.

But he will find he has problems with "leftovers," fragments consumed but not fully digested, or buried but not yet decayed. Hedda

Kuhn, whom he sometimes calls "the Jewess of Rastatt"[42] or "the Jewess of Berlin," and the half-Jewish, dark-skinned "Maori" or "Gauguin" woman Marianne and her lover Recht, who is also Jewish, are "leftovers." Brecht sees "a pogrom coming up."[43] "One sees what is dangerous, that which is leftover, the undeveloped, the undigested, the leavings that one can no longer control. Slowly we are constipated by unresolved affairs, by half-chewed events. We are poisoned by that which is not wholly consumed."[44] From things that are terrifying because "one can no longer control" them to "unresolved affairs" to an expected pogrom to "blockages" and "poisonings" in his own life caused, in his view, primarily by Kuhn and Recht, he moves on to consider the world as body, and the Jews as an entity that constipate and poison that body. Brecht writes, "Whatever has been buried sleeps poorly. The earth, which is supposed to help us by digesting it, spews it out." Groping then within his labored metaphorical construct, he asks: "Why can't the Jews be got out of the way?"[45] Answering his own question he concludes: "The spit gives out before the Jews do."

The largest "leftover" for Brecht, apart from the psychically unburied, polluting mother, remained Hedda Kuhn. The violent anti-Semitism of Munich had led her to transfer her medical studies to nearby, less violent Freiburg. From there she would move to Berlin, and send Brecht invitations and money to visit her. Though obviously taken with Brecht, she valued her independence and sexual freedom, and set her own schedule of visits. In one Brecht poem of this period called simply "Of He," the poet announces that "He" (Hedda) is to be dismissed for cause:

> She knew what a woman is with her brain,
> But did not know it
> In her knees, when it was light she knew the way
> with her eyes,
> But when it was dark she did not know it. . . .
> She wasn't wise like Bie the lovable, Bie the plant,
> She was always running around elsewhere
> And her heart was thoughtless.[46]

"He" is dismissed as the servant Fanny had been by his parents when she failed to devote all her energies to the family, replaced by a devoted group of servants all named Marie. "He," like Fanny, lacked the plant-like virtue of staying put, being immediately accessible when wanted. Brecht now declares that "He" is dead. Then, shifting the image from earth to sky, he declares that she is to be "completely gone, like a cloud, of which it can be said: it never was."

But, sometimes Hedda would turn up and stay when Brecht had

other plans. "So she stayed," he writes indignantly on one occasion when she visited him briefly in Augsburg. "She did not notice my face, which was far from patient, she just stayed. I walked along beside her like a stranger in my clean shirt, profoundly disappointed. I wanted to be lying in bed on my own, diagonally across it, with a newspaper and a looking glass."[47] Here in bed he could show himself "a film version of my rise to fame."[48]

But when Hedda did leave to return to Berlin, he went not home to bed but swimming with Ludwig "Lud" Prestel. They had written some poetry together, including the song included in *Baal* "If a Woman's Hips Be Ample."[49] Lud not only made contributions to the poems but often came up with suitable tunes to accompany them. For all his usefulness, Lud had to share Brecht with many others, male and female. Brecht, Cas, and Otto left on a hiking tour, swimming together every day, buying bread, stealing potatoes, and performing in country inns in the towns of Ehingen, Unter-Marchtal, Beuron, and Möhringen. Returning to Augsburg, Brecht and his friends worked on a play about David and Solomon where Solomon is both "loved by a hundred broads" and is God's "Minion."[50]

Galgei, the play about Solomon, and the letters to "Do" and "He" in a Berlin now called "Babel" are filled with sex, death, and "drifters," who explore every nook and cranny of "die Welt" (the world, which is female in German), seeking every kind of pleasure and indulging in frequent violence. The drifter, an often-bisexual man who is nowhere at home, loving men and fucking, often from the rear, faceless and nameless women, begins to have in tow a bloody and violent companion, Brecht's white, savage, and most Freudian shark. In July, in the "Ballad on Many Ships," Brecht writes of a man:

> Hatless and naked and with his own sharks in tow.
> He knows his world. He has seen her.
> He has a lust in him to be drowned
> And he has a lust to not go down to death.[51]

The poems and the diary explore a sexual boundary at the juncture of life and death, where death is enjoyed yet avoided. Brecht mused: "I'm beginning to feel a faint prejudice against binary divisions (strong-weak, big-small, happy-unhappy, ideal-not ideal). It only happens because people are unable to think of more than two things at once. That's all that will fit in a sparrow-sized brain. But the soundest policy," as he says, returning to a nautical metaphor, "is just to keep tacking." The best course is not to make choices between options but to grab both: "Klein oder Gross! Beides!"—"Small or large! Both!"[52]

Acceptance of multiple things is especially useful in the world of theory. He declares: "A man with only one theory is lost. He must have several, four, many! He must stuff his pockets with them as if they were newspapers, always the latest, one can live well between the theories, one can be comfortably housed between theories."[53] Later, applying this idea of choosing "both" in his own real life situation, he notes: "Of course I want Timbuktu and a child and a house and no doors and to be alone in bed and to have a woman in bed, the apple off the tree and the timber too, and not to wield the axe and to have the tree complete with blossom, apples, and foliage, all in close-up outside my window. Plus a servant to dig in manure."[54]

In many ways the dream of having the best of both sides of everything was realized. Even if it was somewhat grudgingly given, he had his father's support and a place where he could do exactly what he liked. The traffic of visitors of both sexes at all hours at the Bleichstrasse continued briskly. Loud were the wails some nights as Ma (Marianne) complained about the knave of hearts having practiced "perversions on her." Between Ma's visits, he pushed other sexual dalliances along. With the youngest maid in the household, the now eighteen-year-old Mari Hold, the young master sometimes had special things in mind. He had her strip off her maid's uniform and dress in drag, putting on Brecht's clothes while he took photographs of her.[55]

On September 5, there was an orgy of sorts at Otto's place involving Cas, Otto, Bert, and four "girls." During the afternoon there was lots of drinking and then "jokes were made not with words but with hands."[56] Brecht had come with "that Mülleger girl" but had not spoken to her at the party, and she sat, as Brecht put it, with the arm of a "slimy fat Jew" around her. Brecht sang for a while but then threw down his guitar to grab a young woman by the name of Hansi Haase out of Otto's arms. Otto tried to fight him, and Bert fought "like a negro" while Haase's head was banged against a chair, a cupboard, and a wooden partition. Brecht then kissed her bruises and wrestled with her, but "she [didn't] want it." Someone had a motion picture camera and shot what was happening. Brecht started to write out a monologue for a play he was working on but was interrupted when Cas grabbed Hansi and "flung her against the wall." But Cas looked "like a pansy" who "hasn't got his mind on the job." Meanwhile, Otto was now "lying half-drunk behind the desk with a girl, working away."

On September 9, after a stroll with Hansi Haase, Brecht mused that women such as Haase had "a certain drive in their blood for negroes possibly." What he wanted of women, however, he now wrote, was "to bottle them and preserve them and caress them and make do with those solid clouds, with whatever's crooked, tangled, misplaced;

want to be able to beat them up, knock sense into them, love them down and joke with my thighs. Better to stuff some old virgin with skin like a dog than poke around in everybody's pet little hole."[57]

On September 12, he wrote: "I sit in the Kindl Beer Cellar and listen to Herr Goldschmidt talk about the economic situation in Russia, a bunch of abstract stuff about unions and control systems. I didn't stay long. I am frightened not by the disorder of the place but by the order they would like to achieve. I am now very much against Bolshevism. . . . I say, thanks for the fruit and now I ask for a car."[58]

Brecht was getting more and more fed up with Augsburg and Munich. And there were now unmistakable signs that not only many of his friends but also the increasingly conservative Augsburg authorities were getting fed up with him. His first review in the *Volkswille* had been temperate and well informed, but his later reviews became idiosyncratic and gratuitously insulting. After one biting review of the farce *Old Heidelberg* in October 1920, the Stadttheater attempted to cut off complimentary tickets to the *Volkswille*. The paper, which had declared itself as of December 1, 1920, to be a publication of the Unified Communist Party of Germany, vigorously protested that such tickets were given to the bourgeois press but not to its staff. The privilege was restored briefly until the paper itself closed down in January 1921.

Brecht returned to the play about God's "boyfriend," but again words rebelled. Reality, he felt, had become "encrusted with words" that had "become hard, hurt when you throw them around, lie around dead." "One doesn't have his own words," he rails. "In the beginning was not the word, the word is at the end. It is the corpse of the thing." Having dismissed words, he then continues: "What an extraordinary creature the human being is. . . . The way he takes things into his body, runs around in rain and wind, makes young small humans out of humans by sticking himself into them and filling them full of fluids while crying out in pleasure. Dear God, let me see through the crust, let me cut through it."[59]

He filled so many people with fluids on a schedule so complex that the mere organizing of it required the skill of a virtuoso. The schedule also meant his lying all the time to those closest to him. He now began to discover that he had worn thin the patience of those he had deceived most often. By the end of 1920, he had begun to think about finding a new crop of people to dazzle and beguile.

"The Still Recognized Führer . . . in His Augsburg Headquarters" (1921–22)

Caspar Neher's biographer, Max Högel, describes Brecht as exerting the same kind of magnetism that Hitler exercised over his followers. Högel says that Brecht was "Führer" of a group that met at Brecht's "Hauptquartier."[1] But, as Högel notes, Brecht was beginning to have trouble keeping his followers. "Even from the beginning of 1920," says Högel, "a great unease . . . hung over the entire clique."[2] A year later, when Münsterer visited the "Hauptquartier," he saw a man no longer as certain of his future as before.

In early 1921, Brecht managed to get himself into serious and very public trouble. Still reviewing periodically for the *Volkswille*, his "work" was now both idiosyncratic and, so said some, libelous. Though many critics insist on seeing Brecht's work for this Communist party paper as an early sign of his commitment to communism, rather his reviews seem another example, like *Baal*, *Spartacus*, and his poetry, of his advancing his own kind of guerrilla theater, his own anarchic egocentricity, and lampooning the values of the bourgeoisie, of which his own family and the families of all his friends were part. By early 1921, reviewing for Brecht had become, and would remain, a kind of machine-gunning of the opposition, clearing the stage for the production of his own work.

If Brecht had been committed to communism or the *Volkswille*, surely he would not have behaved as he did. According to one observer, when Brecht attended the last performance that he was to review for the *Volkswille*, he went out of his way to be obnoxious.[3] The play staged on the evening of January 8, 1921, was Friedrich Hebbel's biblical tragedy *Judith*, completed in 1840. It was precisely the kind of drama that Brecht wished to displace. Not content to wait until he could write a savage review, Brecht upstaged the Hebbel play even during its performance. He laughed openly at the tragedy and got up after every scene, climbing over the legs of five or six neighbors to do so, then returning well after the next scene had begun. This open contempt for the feelings of others is hardly likely to have helped the cause of the *Volkswille*, though it did promote his own well-established notoriety.

Brecht's *Volkswille* review attacked Hebbel, the theater management, and the talents of eighteen-year-old Vera-Maria Eberle, whom he deemed to be a "swine" and a "shamelessly ambitious, small, inconsequential player, who is not up to her role." On the very day of Brecht's inflammatory review, the *Volkswille* was closed down by the government authorities, leaving Augsburg with no voice of opposition.[4] Four days later, Brecht was sued. Months later, Brecht, who had no real defense for having called Eberle names, lost his case and signed a consent agreement that involved payment and a published apology. He then refused to carry out the terms to which he had agreed. He claimed what was flatly untrue: that the attorney who had handled the case had exceeded his authority. In September 1921, he was hauled into court once again. This time he was sued by the attorney who had defended Vera-Maria Eberle, as well as the actress herself; he lost both cases. His combined fines plus the cost of an apology in three separate newspapers now ran to several hundred marks, and if he had not found a way to get these paid, he would have had to serve a twenty-five-day jail sentence.[5] His father, as usual, rescued him.

Brecht was now facing open rebellion among those he had previously dominated and whose own creative efforts he had regularly claimed as his own. By 1921, the members of his circle were being drawn away by forces not even Brecht could control. The women, whose jobs were given to returning veterans, needed to find husbands if they were not to be literally out on the street. The men, whatever they might want to do sexually in private, needed a public image that provided some protection, as Oscar Wilde's marriage and children had done for him in England. Moreover, unlike Brecht, they needed to support themselves. In October, nearing his twenty-fourth birthday and still comfortably supported by his father, Brecht could say of his writing: "Well, I don't need to make a living from it. It would be unseemly for me to strain myself."[6] In part, this was whistling in the dark since Brecht had failed to make a living from his writing, but it was also true that his father seemed willing to support him almost indefinitely.

Cas was being nagged to start selling his pictures and to get away from Brecht. Inflation had so gutted the Neher accounts that the family had to sell their house and move to a much smaller one.[7] Cas was studying painting with the aristocratic Professor Ludwig Ritter von Herterich, and serving as assistant to Leo Pasetti, a stage designer. Pasetti managed to get him a small job painting some sets at Bavaria Film Studios. He soon began to get nibbles for set-design work both in Munich and Berlin.

As Cas began to establish his independence, Brecht attacked him for "selfishness." In a poem, Brecht declared Cas to be dead and "ready for the worms."[8] Still the lure of Brecht remained strong. Cas adopted the cheap-looking but expensive wire-frame glasses that Brecht now favored. And though he was just as pinchpenny as Brecht and hated to spend money on clothes, Cas adopted the lifelong habit of wearing expensive silk shirts. Whenever Brecht deigned to spend time with him, Cas hung onto Brecht's every word, loving his humor, despairing whenever Brecht was unkind, and boundlessly elated when Brecht would suggest, as he often did, that they could share an apartment together.

Like Cas, Orge remained attracted but had doubts about going on with Brecht. He tried to convince Brecht that the two of them should live together and that he should be given credit for his years of making contributions to "Brecht's" work. As Brecht told a confidant and as she put it into verse: "He shamelessly demanded / That I now pay him back for his friendship." What seems clear is that Orge wanted either to be really close to Brecht or, if that was not possible, to break with him and enter a conventional profession and marriage.

In an earlier portion of his diary, he had said of Orge and Buschiri (Otto Müllereisert):

> When Georgie and Buschiri and their friends are drunk
> Then they lazily, adoringly, put their arms around one another
> Quietly under the table.[9]

In another contemporaneous poem, two men drift down a river together:

> Though their love was with averted eye
> They remained as one many nights together
> And also: when the sun was high.[10]

But where in a poem young men might love even when the sun was high, in the real life of young adults, more circumspection was necessary, as Hans Otto Münsterer demonstrated for decades.[11]

Otto Müllereisert, who had changed his name at Brecht's behest, appeared by early 1921 to have less time for Bébé. Otto was trying to finish up his medical studies and would then move to Berlin. Even Walter—a talented singer, writer, and composer—was no longer at the disposal of his ever-demanding brother. Following in his father's footsteps, he completed the paper technology course at the Technical Institute in Darmstadt and then visited the United States to look at the most advanced technologies. He married and went to work with his father at the Haindl plant. By 1926, he would become a managing director there; and in 1931, though he was just thirty-one years old, he was named to the chair of professor of Paper Technology at Darmstadt.

As the ties that had previously bound his immediate circle began to unravel, Brecht complained in a diary entry of September 24, 1920: "I have no power over anybody."[12] That day, he had failed to persuade Orge to do yet another rewrite of a scene in *Baal*. Brecht had arranged a working meeting, but when Orge arrived, Otto Müllereisert came by and "chattered nonsensically on with a dog whip." Brecht said to himself at this: "It's ludicrous. Just because of literature, I debased myself, and I had no power. I am nothing. I am ashamed of myself."

He was also having trouble with women. For years he had had one friend spy on another to let him know of any signs of other liaisons. Whenever he got such news, he would demand that these be broken off. He said of this: "From time to time I shoot at birds who try to get away and gobble them up again."[13]

Bie Banholzer was one of whom Brecht was demanding faithfulness, even as he was living on and off with Ma. Moreover, he was telling her she had to do more for three-year-old Frank. It was unseemly, Brecht told Bie, for a mother who had a young son to go dancing and spend time with other men! She was angry at these attempts to control her through their son, and accepted a job as a kind of au pair in Nuremberg. There, very much on the rebound, Bie became engaged to a young man who lived in the house where she worked. She wrote to Brecht about the engagement, and he immediately turned up on the doorstep. Bie happened to be sick, but Brecht used this to his advantage. He sat on her bed and could not be budged, despite the presence of her hapless fiancé. Using all his charm, Brecht won over Bie's landlady-employer, who began to prepare special meals for him. He remained for five days, staying around the clock, using the time when his rival went off to work with particular effectiveness. Finally he convinced Bie that he would remain true to her and that she must immediately break off the engagement.

That done, Brecht hurried off to Marianne while writing to and arranging visits with Hedda, and continuing his periodic erotic encounters with Marie Aman. Hedda, as usual, was insisting on having her own life and this was a problem.

Ma now developed a curious plan. She would, she declared, marry Recht but have all her children by Brecht. Furious, but not daring yet to enter marriage himself, Brecht was not sure how he could stop this other match. When Ma found she was pregnant, he hoped that she would bear a number of what he had begun to refer to as "little Brechts." Ma should stick with him, he thought, as he had been "the first to satisfy her sexually." On May 9, Brecht was walking toward the Augsburg railway station when Recht, "white as a wall," grabbed his elbow.[14] He announced that a Dr. W. had happened to be visiting just when Ma began to lose a serious amount of blood and, with it, the baby. This same doctor, Brecht knew, had performed an earlier abortion on her. Staggering home, Brecht wrote: "And this is the leaky pot, with every man's discharges trickling into it, that I wanted to install in my rooms. . . . Out! Out! Now let her be used as a whore, thrown to other men, left for R. to have. . . . Henceforth, she can cruise the oceans as she likes. . . . In the evening I walked by the Lech, smoked and pulled myself together. I thought about *Galgei*, and all the rest, about Frank too. At night I've been sleeping badly as though I'd committed a murder." He visited Ma at the Munich clinic where she was recovering and "cruelly" showed her pictures of young Frank. Leaving the clinic, he dropped in on Bie who, so he says, "is good again and in love, as am I."

But on May 18, Ma sent one of her servants to announce her arrival. Shortly after, she stood in Brecht's doorway, pale as a corpse, unsteady on her feet, and smelling of powder. Brecht wondered if she was not worried about her healthy rival, Bie, mother of his first child. He proposed to Ma that she take little Frank into her care at least for the summer, and she did not turn him down flat. He was soon writing poems about her again, saying "she looked like burned grass in the throes of passion."[15] Soon they were off together to the village of Possenhofen. He now writes: "She is like the sea, always changing according to the light, even and strong."

"As I ate cherries in front of the mirror today," Brecht wrote in June, "I saw my idiotic face. With these self-contained black bullets disappearing into my mouth, it looked less tied, more lascivious and contradictory. It has elements of brutality, stillness, looseness, canniness and cowardice, but only as elements, and it is more changeable and characterless than a landscape under drifting clouds. That's why so many people can't keep track of my face ('you've too many of them,' says Hedda)."[16] The same diary entry continues: "I observe that I am beginning to become a classic."

He was now convinced that his work with all its various characters and points of view will survive through the ages. This attitude, he felt, absolved him of responsibility for any of the "Brechts" who happened to show up on any given occasion. In creating other personae, he distanced himself from his own. As "genius" and as "classic author" he could, therefore, enter any agreement and later disown it. To Ma, he wrote, "A contract is a good thing, one can always break it."[17] Praising Shakespeare's *Merchant of Venice*, he opines: "A man is more than a contract, than ships or money or happiness." The "man" referred to is Shylock, but there is no line between a play and life in Brecht's thinking and writing. People he knows are described as characters in plays or

short stories. He sees his own life in stage terms, looking for the denoue-
ment or noting as a difficulty approaches: "The fourth act curtain is
about to go up!"[18]

The multiple characters he assumed, and for whom he was responsible only when he said so, enabled him to exist outside any external
system of law or moral standards. In his self-created universe of "Wille
und Vorstellung" (will and imagination), he could perpetually remain
both dependent and independent, an advocate of liberty and a practitioner of tyranny, a person who tied down others by promises and
contracts while breaking them himself at will.

By mid-August, Ma had been persuaded to break with Recht,
though this meant a loss of income and that she would have to take a
singing job offered to her in Wiesbaden. Brecht saw her off. Through
the train window, her face looked to him "like a blossom, smiling."[19]
Though he had enough money for himself from his father, he felt
pressure from Bie to use some in support of their child. Brecht tried to
persuade his father to take over responsibility for Frank; but when he
refused, Brecht believed it was the housekeeper, Fräulein Roecker, who
was preventing his father from taking in the boy as this would mean less
"Bequemlichkeit" (comfort) for her.[20]

Persuading Orge, Cas, and Lud to work with him, if only briefly,
he made some progress on a play about a fat bisexual character called
Galgei, who sails with a crew of "niggers."[21] Besides the contributions
of his friends, Brecht notes: "I riffle through the Rimbaud volume and
make certain borrowings."[22] He was plagiarizing copyrighted material,
but he saw it as his for the taking. It was a habit he would keep for the
rest of his life.

He was intrigued by the nineteenth-century German revolutionary and playwright Georg Büchner. He described Büchner's powerful
play on the French Revolution, *Danton*, as "an ecstatic sequence of
scenes."[23] In another diary note, he dismisses Gerhart Hauptmann,
declaring loftily: "Yes, there was something petty about the Hauptmann
era."[24] His dismissal of Hauptmann, who had received the Nobel Prize
for Literature only a decade before, is as arrogant as it is farsighted:
Hauptmann is only rarely played now.

Baal was still not in print by the fall, even though Brecht had read
what were supposed to be final proofs in July. In fact, the publisher,
fearing a lawsuit with such a sexually explicit work, had decided not to
bring it out at all.[25] His Munich film agent, an avaricious soul by the
name of Dr. Werner Klette, always seemed on the brink of selling
something, but somehow the sale and the money always disappeared.

On a happier note, Brecht learned that his story "Bargan" had
been accepted for the November-December issue of the prestigious

national journal *Der Neue Merkur*.[26] Brecht hoped that now, almost two years after his aborted first visit, the publication of the sensational story of the pirate Bargan's relationship with Croze would help him establish a beachhead in Berlin. As the old year turned to the new, an abandoned "Führer," whom nobody in Augsburg seemed willing to obey anymore, looked to Berlin for a new "Hauptquartier" where he might find others not yet disenchanted with him, more willing to do his bidding.

Thinking now more and more of Berlin and rejecting those who had rejected him in southern Germany, he attacked everyone and everything. "The Oktoberfest is here now," he wrote in an entry dripping with contempt for what he had previously so extravagantly loved. "How boring it all is. What faces, tiles in a urinal! What voices, like domestic animals."[27] Neither the play called *Galgei* nor the one called *Jungle* made much progress without helpers. To add to his misery, the court case around his *Volkswille* reviews had exposed him to public disgrace. It was time to get away. Gathering up just published copies of "Bargan" to take with him, he would made his way north by stages.

Brecht was happy to accept an invitation from Frank Warschauer to stay with him again at the Eislebenstrasse flat in Berlin. Hedda had also written in October to ask: "If you're coming to Berlin to see me shall I get you a room? As your wife?"[28] Insisting as usual on independence, Hedda added that she had been "breaking her marriage vows." Brecht wrote back, not answering her wry question, simply telling her to line up a room for him. It would be useful to have more than one in Berlin.

He decided to combine the Berlin trip with stopovers: first in Nuremberg to see Bie, whom he still declared periodically he loved above anyone else; and then in Wiesbaden to see Ma and to declare there the uniqueness of his love. Before leaving, perhaps believing fictions of atrocities by "black" French troops in the occupied territories he would be passing through, he bought an illegal pistol to take with him. Wanting to make a particularly good impression in Berlin, he borrowed a natty hat and shoes from the elegant, gray-gloved Hans Otto Münsterer.

The visit to Nuremberg to see Bie, apparently currently not involved with anyone else, could be brief. After a few intensive hours, he boarded the Wiesbaden train at 1:30 in the morning. Unable to sleep, and terrified that he might be searched and his pistol found, he tried to mail it back home from an intervening station. But the post office was not open at that hour. He then tried to hide it in the train toilet but found no place to put it. Fortunately, he arrived in Wiesbaden, "the whore's city"[29] as he called it, with the pistol undiscovered.

He gave Marianne a book of homoerotic bent called *Knabenbriefe*

(Boys' letters).[30] Marianne's flat in Weisbaden consisted of one small room with a hard bed. Hard or not, they spent a great deal of time there. She got up late to go to the opera house where she was appearing in *Madame Butterfly*. Brecht thought she was as bad as the production generally, all part of what he called "a Negro theater!" But if Puccini was bad, Wagner was awful. "I barely lasted through *Rheingold*" he wrote. "The little gods declaim amidst careful copies of Jurassic rocks, and the steam from the laundry where they wash lord Wotan's underwear makes you sick."[31]

The next day, he was swept away by Chaplin's *The Face on the Barroom Floor*. Noting the audience's enjoyment, he wrote: "The film owes at least part of its effectiveness to the brutality of the audience."[32] The next diary entry turns inward. Thinking ahead to Berlin, now routinely referred to as "Chicago," he writes: "The great fear of cold Chicago!" He goes on to worry about inflation, and there was good reason to worry. From the end of 1921 when the mark traded at less than two hundred to the dollar, by the end of 1923 it ballooned to 4.2 billion to the dollar. Making his first attempt at understanding a basic economic question, Brecht notes that men are "hung out to dry on the basis of a tiny change in the exchange rate, payment, chance, the way a complicated and expensive organism can be ruined because of some barely measurable change in the air, a trick of the wind, sacrificed without either a worshipper or a god. The question arises whether one can break out of the dismal law of causal necessity that is within mankind. . . . Is there no mercy, no credit given, is there nobody who does not believe we are sinners, nobody who thinks better of us than we do ourselves."[33] Suddenly there is a note of real powerlessness. This is too real to joke about, too concrete to be ignored or ever again forgotten. If economics cannot be understood and controlled, all his other systems of control and subjugation can be rendered worthless.

Brecht saw Wiesbaden as a "shop window city" where everything was for sale for the right price in the right currency. On November 7, he took the cheap night train for Berlin. He could hardly sleep at all, and drank and smoked most of the night. It was chilly and rainy when he arrived in Berlin on the morning of November 8. With his two suitcases, he went to the lodgings Hedda had booked; but he found the room had not been prepared. The place struck him as being "dark, cold, frightening." Nor was Hedda warm to him. She introduced him to her current flame, "a young man," according to Brecht, "with a thick head, rather a brutal face, slow, tough, bourgeois."[34] Brecht was furious. She had always offered him warmth and "comradely support," but it was not enough for Brecht. "She did not possess," writes Werner Mittenzwei, "the unconditional dependency that Brecht demanded of others, but did not provide himself."[35]

A letter from Bie awaited Brecht at Hedda's. She wrote she had been pregnant now for two months. Her letter was full of "composure and love, without a single murmur of complaint," Brecht said. But he was "frightened beyond measure" at the news. He sent her small sums of money, which she promptly returned. He complained about this and ended one letter: "You are my little wife and you must be 'obedient' otherwise I will beat you, yes."[36] At the same time, he wrote a quick note to Ma, claiming his Berlin situation was both cold and lonely, "ich habe niemand hier"—"I don't have anyone here."[37] He lied to her, saying that when he had telephoned Hedda about mail for him, but "there was nothing there." He begged Ma to write often, though she should not, he said, expect much from him. He also wrote to Otto Müllereisert, who was now completing his medical studies, asking his help in advising Bie on how to abort the child.

Always worried about money, he nevertheless arranged to pay someone take dictation from him. With introductions arranged by Hermann Kasack, Warschauer, and Fräulein Do, he seemed to meet everyone in the world of publishing, theater, and political cabaret. At Änne Maenz's Künstlerlokal he dropped off some of his film scripts for Olga Tschechowa, a visiting Russian film actress. Kasack had him meet the dramatist Heinrich Eduard Jacob and took him to the Kiepenheuer Verlag in Potsdam to meet Oskar Loerke, then chief reader at the large S. Fischer Verlag. Brecht hated the pictures of hunger that he saw at the Secession show organized by Max Liebermann. He dismissed not only the Secessionists but "those compassionate dramatists (Hauptmann, Ibsen), the beginning of the end! All this yields is flat plays (that is to say, one cannot walk around these figures)."[38] Only a passionless theater was left, from which people left the cheap seats to go to brothels and films. He liked little of what he saw on stage, from Dumas's play about Kean at the Deutsches Theater with Albert Bassermann to Goethe's *Götz von Berlichingen* with Eugen Klöpfer in the title role. The one bright spot was Jessner's production of *Othello* with Fritz Kortner, Johanna Hofer, and Albert Steinrück. Steinrück, Brecht thought, was "brilliant, thin humorless, . . . a graphic artist."

At an artist's hangout, the Romanisches Café, he arranged to meet a poet and cabaret singer in the tradition of Wedekind, the painfully thin but fiery Klabund. Klabund introduced Brecht to "a young Hebrew," who told him to be at Erich Reiss Verlag at noon the next day to discuss a possible contract. Taking up Warschauer's offer of hospitality, he temporarily left his rented room. At supper one evening at Warschauers' he met the actor Alexander Granach, who introduced him to Herr Goldberg of the Tribune Theater, who gave Brecht some paid readings there. He collected three hundred marks from the *Der Neue Merkur*.

All in all, he was making a fair amount of money for someone still largely unknown. Despite this and the warmth of Warschauer's hospitality, he felt lonely, cold, abused. "I am in a ghetto here," he wrote to Ma, "and it snows within oneself."[39] He complained that Ma was not writing enough but did not, of course, tell her he was worried about Bie's pregnancy. Loving letters from the still vaguely attached Cas and Otto helped some, but not enough. Moodily looking at the Warschauer's maid, he briefly identified with her: she "lives and works in a hole, is consumptive, has no home, no man, never says a word for days on end." He concluded, however: "I am far removed from pity, all I mean is: how poor we are, how apelike and prone to being abused, poor, hungry, patient."[40] The next day, he wrote: "Nausea and doubt. That is the coldness that man finds in his heart. One can laugh, one can mock it, but it is there in the laughter and further fuels the mockery."

A few days later, things seemed a bit better. He saw and liked Werner Krauss in Max Reinhardt's production of Strindberg's *Dream Play*. He generally approved of Strindberg, declaring him to be "that campaigner for men's rights."[41] Warschauer had arranged that Brecht be given a boost at Oswald Films, and the head of Kiepenheuer Verlag arranged an introduction at Terra Films. He was invited to all the parties, and his mesmeric charm as a singer seemed to work as well in Berlin as it had in Augsburg and Munich. He and Klabund sang what Brecht characterized as "the first crude, barbaric songs of the new age, an age forged in iron." Brecht was well received, even if Heinrich Eduard Jacob did combine his help with a parody to Brecht's face of the visitor's rolling Augsburg r's.

Otto Zarek, Max Reinhardt's assistant and former dramaturge at the Munich Kammerspiel, was also helping. In Munich, Brecht had characterized Zarek as "male midwife of the Kammerspiel, minion of that rubber merchant (Neuhofer) who uses a condom to masturbate."[42] But in Berlin, Zarek had the right contacts. Zarek took him around to audition at the "Weiber-Kabaretts," the brilliant, innovative, women-owned and -managed (hence their title) political cabarets of Berlin.

Brecht gravitated almost immediately to Trude Hesterberg's cabaret, The Wild Stage. Here, a typical act was introduced by the elderly Herr Schäfer, who brought on the hermaphroditic Wilhelm Bendow, who appeared in an extravagantly female paper-mache body with mysterious drawings and writing all over it. Herr Bendow, also known as Lydia Smith or Magnesia the Tattoooed Lady, wore a flaming red wig and a skimpy two-piece bathing suit. "Good evening, gentlemen," he would announce, "welcome to my establishment. . . . Here at my rear, a part of me that has attracted the particular interest of a high official in the Ministry for Arts and Letters, I cannot show you absolutely everything as certain parts of my behind are under police edict. But over here you can see a picture depicting 'the decline of the west' and over here, on my other thigh, is a celebration of the ritual of circumcision being performed on General Ludendorff."[43] Alfred Beierle, his face daubed dead white and in a bright red wig, presented texts of Brecht's Munich idol, Wedekind. To a lugubrious street organ accompaniment, Kate Kühl performed a medley of tough *Moritaten* where the murder of women seemed almost routine.

Hesterberg's cabaret seemed made to measure for the violent and still sexually ambiguous Bert Brecht. One gray Sunday morning in November, he auditioned at her Berlin apartment. This veteran of political satire was jolted awake by Brecht's electric rendition of the "Song of the Dead Soldier," polished at Gabler's and innumerable whorehouses and bars. His singing, thought Hesterberg, had about it a "touch of the demonic."[44] She engaged him for six days for the princely sum of five hundred marks. He was worth it. "His voice," said the playwright Zuckmayer, "floated with emotional vibratos," and he sang with "something approaching beauty."[45] Thrilled by his reception, as both men and women tended to swoon, Brecht wrote to Ma: "Berlin is now captured in my arms."[46]

In December, Otto Zarek invited the rising star to a private party at Zarek's parents' home. Long after Brecht had arrived and while he was preparing to perform, a young man by the name of Arnolt Bronnen, another one of Zarek's guests, was still trying to find the place. Recently arrived from Vienna and not very secure in his geography of Berlin, Bronnen was, as usual, somewhat late and broke. Stick thin, he froze as he walked along looking for the Zareks' address. Over a threadbare suit saved from his prewar days in Vienna, he wore an equally threadbare military overcoat given to him upon his discharge from an Italian prisoner-of-war camp. The overcoat was buttoned to the neck, concealing a scar on his throat, a war wound that even now left him unable to control the pitch of his voice. For all his shabbiness of dress, the monocle clamped in Bronnen's eye hinted at his wish to be taken in by the high society of Prussian Berlin. Now twenty-six years old, he had come to Berlin the year before as a protégé of the writer, editor, and crusading pedophile Gustav Wyneken.[47] Wyneken had lined him up a job as a gofer at Berlin's biggest department store, while Bronnen waited to get his wildly erotic plays staged.

Bronnen checked the house numbers, looking for the brass plate announcing Herr Direktor Zarek. When he finally found the name and rang the bell, there was no answer for a long time. He rang the bell again, and finally a maid opened the door to show him upstairs to a large, opulent apartment filled wall-to-wall with plump, well-dressed, important-looking people. Among all these Berlin entrepreneurs who looked as if they had stepped out of one of Georg Grosz's etchings, Bronnen felt wholly out of place, slinking around the edge of the room listening to conversations that all seemed to turn around how to trade in marks.[48] Finally he was spotted by Frau Direktor Zarek who hastened over to him, grasping at once what was wrong. "Ach, the young gentleman is here to see Otto? He's never here with us! He's with his friends in the back room." She rang the servant's bell. "Erna, take the gentleman back to join the young people."

Erna conducted the gentleman to a door that opened onto a barely lit room, thick with smoke, furnished in pure bohemian. As Bronnen entered, somebody got up, put down a wet cigar, took up a guitar, and began to sing. Bronnen heard a voice that was scratchy, with a marked provincial accent, and driven by savage rhythms. The voice sang:

> And that woman has had her seventh child
> And yet that cloud that had only bloomed for a moment
> When I looked up it had vanished in the air.

Bronnen felt himself being swept away and thought: "Love, great love in the world, give him to me as my friend." When Otto Zarek introduced Brecht and Bronnen, the two young men began at once to compare notes on their completed but unstaged plays, *Excess* and *Parricide*, and *Baal* and *Spartacus*. Bronnen was a man who fell in love suddenly, more often with men than women. He had been introduced to heterosexuality by his family's "fat Bohemian cook" but otherwise had little experience with women.[49] Later, serving as a private tutor, Bronnen seduced the prettier boys placed in his charge.[50]

He had written his play *Excess* just before the war and had sent it to Wyneken, whom he had met in Vienna. At that time, Wyneken was running camps for adolescent boys where what he frankly called "a Socratic approach to Eros" was practiced. Though Wyneken wrote to say he loved *Excess*, Bronnen's timing was awful. The war broke out, halting publication. This did not dampen Bronnen's enthusiasm for the war itself. He rushed off to serve and was wounded on the Italian front and placed in a prisoner-of-war camp in Sicily. Men in the camp looked at him, so he thought, "the way one looks at the wares in a brothel."[51] After the war, he had managed (with Wyneken's help) to get his next play, *Parricide*, published but not produced.

Brecht's explicitly homosexual short story "Bargan Lets It Happen" and the bisexuality in *Baal*, which Brecht showed him in manuscript, clearly suggested the possibility of a love affair to Bronnen. For Brecht, personally and professionally, the meeting with Bronnen was only another in a string of opportunities that were presenting themselves.

Just before Christmas, Brecht's father came to Berlin on business. "My father was here," Brecht wrote. "We sat opposite one another in a bar, two people who belong together in a vague sort of way, which is quite a lot among our kind! He was interested in me in a careful sort of way, gave me 1,000 marks, spoke about his business affairs, did not ask about where things stood with Marianne, said there would be ham and duck at Christmas and that I would be sent some. That pleased me."[52]

Soon after, Ma arrived from Wiesbaden. It was cold and wet, but the pension where they were staying was cozy and warm. She sang some Mahler for him, but he had to dash off, he said, to deal with some film business. Unbeknownst to Ma, he had arranged that Bronnen should come by for a tête-à-tête one Sunday morning. By design or accident, he was dealing with one or another of his affairs when the smitten Arnolt arrived at the pension. Bronnen's knock was answered by a young, beautiful woman clearly very much at home. In his own Viennese dialect, Marianne Zoff told the crushed Bronnen: "Bert isn't even here." No she did not know when he would be back. He was off seeing some publisher; he might even stay away for lunch.

Suddenly Brecht returned. For Bronnen the arrival "was like a sunrise, one forgot the night."[53] Almost without the two men noticing it, they slipped over to the "Du" form of address, an unusually swift shift to intimacy, as Marianne well knew. Brecht had a plan ready for the two of them: they would conquer the Berlin theater together. He was in fine form: his humor, his ideas, his way of seeing the world and expressing himself—all dazzled Bronnen. Afternoon slipped into late evening. There was not much to eat in the place. Ma opened a can of sardines, and they passed around their one fork until the small can was empty.

On December 24, Brecht signed a remunerative deal with the Erich Reiss Verlag.[54] The contract contained an escape clause for Brecht in the event that Reiss failed to print a play that had been sold to a major theater. It was almost immediately invoked. Though he did not have a firm deal with a major theater for *Baal* in 1922, he claimed he did and took the play to Kiepenheuer Verlag where he collected more money.

Brecht and Ma moved to Warschauer's apartment. Here, Brecht declared to his Jewish host and his fiancée, the "hospitality is Asiatic." Brecht and his Jewish companion were given their own Christmas tree. The holiday was slightly marred by a notice from Wiesbaden saying that Marianne, who had left without obtaining leave, probably would not be rehired. On New Year's Eve, Ma and Brecht went with the Warschauers to see Reinhardt's production of *Orpheus in the Under-*

world. The show was followed by a champagne supper and the telling of fortunes. Marianne stayed for another week before returning to try to save her job in Wiesbaden.

Soon after Ma left, Brecht moved out of the Warschauers and took a room in a red-light district. With Ma's departure, he had more time to spend with the adoring Arnolt Bronnen, who now bent almost all his efforts to help his Augsburg friend's career. Bronnen believed that Brecht was also helping him. Years later he would write: "Brecht was a friend who went to bat in a tough, stubborn way for those he thought worthy of his friendship."[55]

Various deals began to come together. Brecht's diary entry for January 7 reads: "Paddling with my hands and feet. First of all dealing with publishers: Reiss offered 750 marks, Kiepenheuer 800. Both want stage rights too. I've already signed up with Reiss but took the contract back to show it to Kasack. I also had to talk to Dreimasken [another publisher]. It seemed a good idea to ask them for 1,000 a month for one year. On top of that, I got Kiepenheuer to leave Dreimasken the stage rights for my next plays. Dreimasken wavered, offered 5,000. I hadn't brought *Garga* [the name he was currently using for the play that would become *In the Jungle of Cities*] with me as I did not want to let them have it. But stuck out anyway for the 1,000." The diary entry ends on a note of triumph: "Finally they agreed after I had talked them into a stupor."[56]

These business negotiations deserve close examination. He had signed a contract with Reiss on December 24 that specified that the firm would pay him 750 marks a month for "all rights to all works that Brecht writes between 1/1/22 and 31/12/24."[57] Within a week of that contract supposedly taking effect, Brecht was back in the marketplace. He would soon have not only the contract with Reiss for the dramatic edition rights but had also sold the book publication rights to Kiepenheuer for 1,000 marks, while reserving the rights to future plays such as *Garga* to Dreimasken for an additional 1,000 marks a month. He also kept the rights to his poetry and short stories. With his sly skill and total lack of scruple, the publishers no more had him on an exclusive basis than did any of his lovers.

As his successes in business mounted, his confidence increased. He was, as Bronnen saw to his sorrow, able to seduce business and sexual partners almost completely at will, singing and sleeping his way toward the top of the Berlin heap. One evening the two of them went over to Kasack's in Potsdam where Brecht, as usual, worked his charms. Even with the highly sophisticated crowd who came to such literary evenings in Berlin, Brecht's singing put "people under a magic spell." His audience became, as Bronnen noted, "like lemurs and he alone remained a human being."[58] Brecht was everywhere in demand to sing, to seduce, to be seduced, and to enjoy the awesome power his poetry and sexuality gave him over almost everyone he met.

Moving briskly from bed to bed in Berlin, at the end of January he suddenly noticed that he had begun to "piss blood." When he disappeared for two days, an anxious Hedda came by with Bronnen to find out what was happening. He looked ill enough that they thought it best to get him to a hospital. Another one of the tough young men that Hedda was now interested in was an intern at Berlin's sprawling Charité Hospital. Dr. Wollheim, Hedda's friend and future husband, agreed to get Brecht admitted but only on the condition Hedda would not visit him at the hospital! Brecht's complaint was pyelonephritis,[59] though he later claimed he had been admitted for the more romantic malady of malnutrition. He called Wiesbaden demanding that Ma come immediately.

When Ma got to Berlin and came to the Charité, she found Arnolt there already. Ma and Arnolt sat on opposite sides of the bed, attempting to outdo each other in helping the patient. Brecht proposed that Arnolt invent an ailment so he could join him day and night on the ward. As Bert chattered about having Arnolt in the bed next to him, the jealous Marianne glowered. Arnolt was happy at the idea: he was a veteran of all-male wards and barracks, and he knew what could be done there.

The standoff between Arnolt and Marianne lasted three days, until Ma happened to see letters from the pregnant Bie. She fell ill from shock and took to bed at the Warschauers, leaving the field to Arnolt. He took it as a sign of the deepest intimacy that his friend decided to adopt the final syllable of Arnolt's first name. He would now call himself Bertolt rather than the Berthold that he had inherited from his father. For Bronnen it was a form of marriage. For the new Bertolt, all it meant was a somewhat less aristocratic-sounding name and perhaps nothing more.

There was nothing that Arnolt was not now prepared to do for his beloved Bertolt. He worried that Brecht did not have enough money and decided, encouraged by Brecht, to steal a bit on the side from his department-store employer. Though *Parricide* was already in print, it brought in next to nothing. His regular salary was 850 marks a month at Wertheim, less than a third of what Brecht would receive from his contracts. One of the jobs Bronnen did for his employer was to sell theater tickets to porters at the big Berlin hotels, who in turn sold them to foreigners for hard currency. He sold some tickets and kept the money to give to Bert. He was found out and almost fired.[60]

Brecht, despite a stream of visitors and with ample time to work on his plays, became bored and concerned about missing opportunities. Getting himself discharged, he raced around Berlin with the doting Arnolt, who introduced Bertolt to Herbert Ihering, one of Berlin's most influential drama critics. The three began discussing the Kleist Prize, an award given by a different critic each year to a new German writer of particular promise. This year Ihering would award the prize. Bronnen said he should consider giving it to Brecht. Ihering promised to take a look at some of Brecht's work.

After this encounter, the two friends were approached by another of the major figures of Berlin theater. Amidst a crowd of blond men, Bronnen noticed "the brunette Dr. Moritz Seeler." Seeler, who already had met Brecht, was now introduced to Bronnen. Seeler had read and liked Bronnen's *Parricide*. He declared that he was going to open the Junge Bühne (young stage), a new experimental theater, and wanted to open it with *Parricide*. Bronnen was struck speechless. "It's alright, Arnolt," declared Brecht. "Let him have the play. Just one condition. I'll have to direct it." On the sidewalk, the deal was struck. The one hook in the agreement was that Seeler had already lined up the actors for the main roles.

The play seemed almost made to measure for Brecht's directorial debut. With murder shading over imperceptibly into the kinkily erotic, and misogyny interwoven with homosexuality, the play might easily have been one of Brecht's early plays. Bronnen's play takes place in a German-speaking city in the midst of a war. The play centers on a family called Fessel, meaning *chains* or *handcuffs*. The "chained" family sublets a room to two young women who use it to ply their trade as prostitutes. The family also gets income from "Jews," but they do not pay enough for the family to live at the level it would like. Walter Fessel wants to become a farmer, but his father insists that his son become an attorney. Preoccupied with his sexual identity and the family's hold on him, Walter has trouble studying anything.

Walter's lover Edmund says to him, "You, you, I always want to hold you."[61] After Walter's halfhearted "No," Edmund goes on passionately: "And your lap and such lips and such hands." Walter again says, "No," but as they head for bed, Walter's buxom mother bustles in from the next room. She replaces Edmund as Walter's seducer, stripping in front of the moonlit window and beckoning her eighteen-year-old son to her bed. They are interrupted by Herr Fessel who comes in brandishing a revolver. After wrestling the gun away and strangling his father, Walter declares to his mother, who is still beckoning him to her bed, that she is too old for him. The play ends with an ecstatic Walter declaring all the fathers of the "Vaterland" now metaphorically dead.

Seeler had cast Heinrich George, a well-known actor, as the father. In rehearsal, a tug-of-war began between the 130-pound Brecht and George, who weighed twice as much. Brecht subjected George to "sadistic tongue lashings" and told him "everything you are doing is shit." In the back row of the theater sat the hapless author of the play. Too much in love with Brecht to object, Bronnen watched his play and the actors being torn to pieces by his idol. Finally, George chucked his script in a great arc into the fifteenth row of seats. Brecht was too much the dramatist to let the moment pass. Brecht "cleared his throat loudly, slammed shut his copy of the script, switched off the small rehearsal light, said 'Good day,' and turned to look for Bronnen."[62] Bronnen saw an air of triumph, a satanic gleam in his eye.

All was not lost. Seeler managed to replace Brecht with Dr. Berthold Viertel, a young and talented Viennese. With the other cast estranged, Viertel found the up-and-coming Alexander Granach to play the father and Elisabeth Bergner, then emerging as a star in the androgynous "girl-boy" roles that were then popular. Bronnen accepted this salvaging of his work, but it was bittersweet; he did not want his play to succeed at the price of his friend's failure, but Seeler insisted. So while Viertel rehearsed the play with the new cast, Brecht and Bronnen stayed away, spending their days at the movies, including the German classics *The Cabinet of Dr. Caligari* and *The Golem*, and two famous American films *Orphans in the Storm* and *Birth of a Nation*.

That spring Bronnen was invited to visit the film producer Stephan Grossmann at his country home outside Berlin. He persuaded Brecht to go along. There they made the acquaintance of publisher Ernst Rowohlt, and film writer and producer Henrik Galeen, known for *The Golem* and *Nosferatu*. When Brecht spoke excitedly about Galeen's films, Grossmann told the two friends about a film competition that had not yet been announced. Oswald Films was going to offer a prize of 100,000 now rapidly depreciating paper marks to encourage young writers to produce the "best and most modern exposé" (or "treatment" as we would say now). In what Bronnen took to be a spirit of "good-hearted corruption," Grossmann told them that as he was on the jury, he could guarantee them the prize.[63]

Bronnen was not really interested in film writing, but Brecht got very excited. On the way home, he began to rough out a treatment that he wanted to call *The Second Flood*, but that Bronnen felt would be better named *Robinson on Asunción*. Their theme was a "gruesome catastrophe," a super civilization throwing itself into an ever-deeper abyss of barbarism. After two days of work, the project was still far from complete. Even with later revisions, however, it was to remain a piece of makeshift work unworthy of either of the two writers.

When Brecht had not been with Bronnen going to movies or parties or working on the film treatment, he had been pouring his feelings into revisions of a play that was still being called *Garga* although it would be retitled *In the Jungle of Cities*. Set in a mythical Chicago, it tells the wildly improbable story of a sadomasochistic love-hate relationship between two men. But though the story is improbable (as in most of Brecht), the power and passion of its language are more than sufficient to maintain its momentum as a dramatic piece.

The core of the play is an exchange that resonates with power similar to soliloquies in Shakespeare's *Macbeth* or Beckett's *Godot*. In a desolate spot outside Chicago, Shlink declares to Garga, the man he loves and for whom he is willing to sacrifice everything: "The infinite isolation of man makes even enmity an unreachable goal. Understanding, even with animals, is not possible."[64] Garga replies: "Language is not sufficient to achieve understanding."

> SHLINK: "I have observed the animals. Love, warmth from the closeness of bodies, is our only blessing in the darkness! But this union of the organs is unique and does not bridge the chasm of language. That is why they come together to breed beings that they hope, in their hopeless isolation, will stand by them. And these generations then stare coldly into one another's eyes. If you stuffed a ship full to bursting with human bodies, there would be such loneliness in it that they all would freeze. Are you listening, Garga? Yes, so great is the isolation that there is not even a fight. The forest! That's where mankind comes from. Hairy, with the jaw of apes, good animals that knew how to live. Everything was so easy. They simply tore the flesh off one another. I see them clearly: how they with trembling flanks stared into the whites of one another's eyes, biting into necks, rolling down, and the bloody one down among the roots was the conquered one, and the one that had trampled down the most forest was the winner!"[65]

But Garga has hardly listened to his lover-enemy. He is, he feels, the future, the winner of this particular struggle. Here he launches into his own soliloquy, almost wholly drawn, as Eric Bentley has pointed out, from Rimbaud, a speech full of references to gold, iron, rage, and ruthlessness, and of the inevitable triumph of the young (Garga) over the old (Shlink). He will, says Garga, here significantly varying from Rimbaud, "mingle with life." What Rimbaud had proposed is "mingle with politics."[66]

The darkness and horror of this play, with its eerie flashes of illumination, was inspired by Verlaine's affair with Rimbaud (whose poetry is cited without acknowledgment), and by Jensen's *The Wheel* and Sinclair's *The Jungle*.[67] It draws some of its bizarre economics from the now largely forgotten American author G. H. Lorimer's 1902 *Letters from a Self-Made Merchant to His Son*.[68] It was also, as he saw it, to be a kind of oppositional piece to one of Friedrich Schiller's most famous works, *The Robbers*.[69] Also echoed in the play are sentiments found in the homoerotic *Knabenbriefe*, the book Brecht gave to Marianne. Bronnen did not know about these sources when he first was given the play to read. He saw the character of Garga as obviously Brecht. But who, Bronnen asked, was Garga's mysterious opponent/lover, a bisexual Malay lumber merchant who is about to be lynched as the play ends? Brecht did not answer Bronnen's question directly but said that the meaning of the play was in Garga's line: "The Chaos is all used up. It was the best of times?" On another occasion, Bronnen declared that the play with its other characters called George, Maë, and Marie was really "the family tree of the Brechts."[70] Though he was perhaps right about it being autobiographical, the play remained deeply mysterious to him.

With the film treatment unfinished, his own work not yet staged, and his debut as a director aborted, Brecht was feeling unappreciated on several fronts. He was not sure of Bie, who had finally written to say that her pregnancy was over without saying how it had ended. Hedda was off with her doctor lover. Ma, all too aware of Brecht's other affairs though she tried to ignore them, would sometimes write letters that made him fear she would finally leave him. She had lost her job as a result of dashing back and forth between Wiesbaden and Berlin, but when she would return to Berlin in response to his calls, he had little time for her. So she would leave again, often returning now to her parents' home in Austria where she could live rent free. By the spring of 1922, she was ill and in a hospital. Instead of rushing to see her, Brecht offered excuses why he could not get away.

At times the desperate, infantile Brecht displaces Brecht the all-powerful genius-master. He writes on one occasion: "Dear Marianne, i cannot write well, i know that i haven't been good, i also lied and messed up my face, but i beg you dear Marianne to stay with me. i am going to try to do something about my laziness and weaknesses, i've also lied a lot, but i love only you." The letter ends with the cry "help me, i care for you. Dear Marianne!"[71] Usually, the cries of a helpless Bébé brought Ma running, but now that she was ill, he was no longer absolutely sure this particular trick would work with her.

He also felt abandoned and outdone by Bronnen, who seemed to be becoming the success that Brecht so desperately needed to be. Bronnen's *Parricide* was chosen in the spring of 1922 for staging in Frankfurt am Main. Bronnen left Berlin briefly to attend the dress rehearsal.

When he got back, he found Brecht gone. A tiny note said only "extremely urgent business" had called him away.[72]

On April 26, Brecht left Berlin to head south, back to Munich and Augsburg. On the train he scribbled in his notebook his most famous, later much-revised poem, "On Poor BB," a self-portrait as well as a hymn to and epitaph on the modern city. The "Poor BB"—pronounced "bébé"—exists somewhere between "a black forest" of Teutonic folklore and the buildings of a Manhattan after some undefined collapse. It begins:

> I, Bertolt Brecht, come out of the black forests.
> As I lay in the womb my mother carried me
> Into the cities. The cold of the forests will
> Remain with me till I die.

One of the original stanzas written on the train stresses an imaginary and wholly parallel situation to Bébé now seen as an adult:

> Maybe, I think, I have been carried off to paper and women
> And I shall never again emerge from the asphalt city.

When he revised this poem for publication three years later, the then twenty-seven-year-old Bébé assigned a passive role to women and a controlling role to himself. In a cold and brutal universe, women are the only force he feels he can continue to subject to his own power:

> In my empty rocking chairs before noon
> I will sit down a pair of women
> And look at them without a care and say to them
> In me you have someone on whom you cannot build.

In all the versions, women are plural, nameless, faceless, and interchangeable. All are expected to care for Bébé though he goes out of his way to show how little he cares for them and how little they can rely on him.

But like Brecht himself, the world is not a safe place on which to build. The tall, thin antennae of the buildings on Manhattan's island were built "as though they were indestructible," but the poem claims:

> Of these cities will remain only that which blows through
> The wind.

The bitter and revelatory final stanza (now with an American cigar added as a prop in the revised version) describes:

During the earthquakes that will come, I hopefully
Will not, through bitterness, allow my Virginia cigar to go out
I, Bertolt Brecht, thrown off course into the asphalt city
From the black forests inside my mother in an earlier time.

First written on the train back to Munich after his failure as a director of Bronnen's *Parricide*, revised in late 1924 after his fame had begun to spread throughout the German-speaking world, this is a poem of the ilk of other twentieth-century prophecies of the final collapse of a decaying world: Eliot's *Wasteland*, Spengler's *Decline of the West*, Beckett's *Endgame*, Conrad's *Heart of Darkness*, and Sylvia Plath's final poems. It is also clear that Bébé, like Nero, will survive to observe its passing.

8

"Down with the Goddamned Jewish Sow, Murder Walther Rathenau" (1922)

The tremors that Brecht registered in "Poor BB" did not prompt him to examine the pillars of the state. He paid little attention to politics and the fearsome, apparently inexplicable field of economics, and bridled if anyone brought up topics of social concern. He showed no understanding of the Zionism of Jewish friends, and it would be several years before he began to interest himself in communism, which so many other intellectuals and artists of the 1920s saw as the only viable path to the amelioration of poverty, racism, and discrimination against women.

As the mark declined, and Wall Street rapidly bought up pieces of the German wreck at knockdown prices, Brecht made his own clever deals to profit from rising inflation. By the middle of 1923, one dollar would buy half the best seats in an entire theater.[1] The dollar was the measure of German existence. American food, advertising, the Barnum and Bailey Circus, films, jazz musicians, dances and dancers, and boxers flooded Germany. Everywhere there were songs like "Yes, We Have No Bananas" and "My Parrot Eats No Hard-Boiled Eggs," and music groups with made-up American names.

At the same time, through the Comintern and other front agencies, a countertide of Soviet "advisors" (including hit squads), Soviet literature, theatrical touring companies, composers, and the brilliant films of a new generation of Soviet film makers swept over the country. By hook or by crook, the Soviet Union still hoped to add Germany to the ranks of Sovietized states. As the Soviets came west, a steady stream of German Communist party officials spent time in Moscow desperately seeking guidance as to how to apply Russian revolutionary methods back home.

The American and Soviet cultural invasions provided grist for the nationalist and anti-Semitic mill in Germany. The "Jews of Wall Street" or the "Jews of the Kremlin" were presumed hostile to anything truly German. In Munich, such sentiments helped the spectacular growth of the tiny, virulent Deutsche Arbeiterpartei (DAP) that saw "the Jewish race as corrupters of the world."[2] This was the party that Adolf Hitler (after being turned down as a set designer by Lion Feuchtwanger) joined in late 1919. Supposedly, Hitler was the 555th member of the Deutsche Arbeiterpartei—actually the numbers were inflated by giving the first card issued the number five hundred. But Hitler wanted more than just any number. He demanded the membership number seven to give himself, as Fest points out, "the nimbus of a magic number."[3]

As Hitler's influence on the DAP grew, he could insist on more changes than his own party number. He demanded a change in the party's name, making it the National Socialist German Worker's party (Die Nationalsozialistische Deutsche Arbeiterpartei). The move opened the party to nominal socialists while maintaining a determinedly nationalistic and explicitly anti-Semitic bias. When challenged about this, Hitler replied: "They say we're a bunch of anti-Semitic rowdies. . . . But if we save Germany, we'll have carried out the greatest deed in the world."[4] Fueled by prejudice and a middle class reduced by inflation and desperately fearful of the Communists, the NSDAP would grow at cancerous rates and begin to contemplate a national and international role.

Brecht's own horizon remained the same: to advance his career without getting smashed in a collision of satellites that orbited around him. Bronnen's addition to the throng of admirers inevitably meant that Cas would be jealous and need periodic soothing. Ma had to be won back, and Bie needed at least some attention. Fortunately, Bronnen was distracted much of the time by a huge surge of interest in his own work. Suddenly, everyone was talking about *Parricide*. It opened both in Frankfurt and in Hamburg (where it was performed in a boxing ring), and would open in Berlin on May 14. "I found my own work to be a tiger," Bronnen wrote later, "restlessly striding up and down behind bars that were much too flimsy. The stage was a cage for humans. It would be something horrible if they were ever to break out."[5] But the break that Bronnen clearly feared and desired came at the opening matinee in Berlin. It took half an hour of tumult and the intervention of the Berlin police to clear the theater after the performance.

Ernst Rowohlt was waiting for Bronnen outside. He gave him a huge hug and asked: "Will you become my author and give me everything you write? I'm offering you a year's contract for 50,000 marks."[6] As this was four times his income from his department store job, Bronnen did not stop to think. Had he done so, he might have been able to hedge an income of 50,000 rapidly shrinking paper marks by asking to get some portion of this money either in dollars or in inflation-proof gold marks.

With what looked at first like a very lucrative deal done, Bronnen was happy. He would now have Rowohlt's advertising department behind him to help his career. He would be discussed in the national press, though, as Bronnen himself noted, the leading political paper in Germany, the *Frankfurter Allgemeine Zeitung*, saw his work as endorsing the kind of violence increasingly practiced by the radical and anti-Semitic right.[7] Bronnen's breakthrough to fame was so sudden he had no idea how to handle it. The film producer and political activist Stephan Grossmann invited him to his luxurious flat that looked out over the lion cages of the Berlin zoo.[8] Grossmann offered him coffee and the young actress Annie Mewes, so it seemed to Bronnen, who began a halfhearted affair with her at Grossmann's behest. Women only seemed to work for Bronnen when combined with simultaneous affairs with men, preferably men that the woman was also involved with sexually.

At the Frankfurt opening of *Parricide*, he was impressed with two of the actresses. Helene Weigel was, like himself, a product of Vienna's Jewish middle class and someone who seemed to exist between the sexes. The other woman, somewhat older, but also a rising star in the German theater was Gerda Müller, who had come originally from the German-Polish border. She moved, both onstage and off, "like a panther." Müller's interest in Bronnen was strong enough that they soon began an affair, and his interest was sufficiently weak that it soon ended. "I was," he wrote later, "at the most basic level of sexuality; orgasm was like death to me and death itself an orgasm."[9] His sexual confusion was interwoven with familial and religious confusion about his Jewish father and his non-Jewish mother. He recognized that he had a burning hatred both of his one brother and his father. In a Vienna where anti-Semitism was pervasive, he had persistently dreamed he was not a Jew, not the child of his Jewish father. He had changed his name slightly from his father's, Bronner, to Bronnen to establish some distance.

Two days after the successful *Parricide* premiere in Berlin, a letter reached Bronnen from Brecht. If he had heard of his friend's success, he did not congratulate him. The letter, though beginning with "Lieber Arnolt" and ending with the phrase "I embrace you," was largely a business letter describing the various jobs that Bronnen was to do for him. Enclosed with the letter was a draft of the film treatment that they had been urged to enter into the rigged competition. Bronnen, said Brecht, should rework the piece giving some depth to the characters while typing up the text. The rest of the letter was devoted to Brecht's detailed instructions about the Kleist Prize. Bronnen was to immediately send Brecht's plays to Herbert Ihering and to impress upon him the absolute necessity of not dividing the prize. Ideally, wrote Brecht, both men should receive the prize, one after another. The passage giving Bronnen these instructions is heavily underlined. Bronnen is also asked

to pick up a Brecht manuscript from Heinrich Eduard Jacob, and remind him about Brecht's honorarium check.

As Bronnen noted when this letter was followed by others with all
kinds of assignments, he had his hands full now with his own plays and
so running around Berlin on Brecht's behalf was "a thorn in the sole."[10]
But still Bronnen did not turn his importunate friend down. He explained why he did this by saying Brecht always "peppered his assignments with jokes." It also mattered very much to Bronnen that Brecht
included sentiments like "I wait with longing for your letters" or would
speak of Bronnen as "my dear swan" or "my little pigeon" or say "I
take you in my arms." All this helped to offset the various business
errands requested and periodic references to Marianne. Bronnen continued, despite his own growing fame, to be willing to be Brecht's gofer
in Berlin theater circles. The exchanges of professional favors between
the friends still seemed fair enough as the middle of 1922 approached.
Brecht, for instance, put in a word for *Parricide* in Munich, and Otto
Falckenberg of the Munich Kammerspiel had written to inquire about
putting on the play there and having Bronnen come down for the
Munich premiere.

Brecht then wrote to say that during Bronnen's visit south the two
of them could stay together at his flat in the Bleichstrasse and commute
from there to Munich. Bronnen was ecstatic, but no sooner was the
invitation extended than it was withdrawn, apparently at Ma's insistence. Brecht said only that "machine guns have been set up"[11] and
Bronnen could be caught in their crossfire. "It is depressing for me,"
continued Brecht, "and we must think about where else we could
manage to meet." Not waiting for anything more specific from Brecht,
Bronnen headed for Munich and went straight to the theater as the
curtain rose on his play. "After the curtain fell on *Vatermord* [*Parricide*]
in the Kammerspiel in Munich," wrote Bronnen in the third person,
"with a sigh of relief he allowed himself to be be taken into the arms of
the other, the loved one."[12]

That night there was no time or place for them to spend more time
in one another's arms as they both attended an all-night party. The next
morning, Bronnen discovered that the lodging Brecht had found for
him was a tiny hole of a room that he was to share with the giant Cas
in the run-down apartment of "a horribly stinking little woman." As
both Cas and Bronnen wanted Brecht alone, this arrangement was a
disaster for them but ideal protection for Brecht as neither of them had
a private place to which to invite him.

The hostility between "Tiger Cas" and "Panther Bronnen," as
Brecht now called the odd couple, was palpable. A savagely drawn
Neher sketch gives a sense of Neher's horror. Bronnen and Brecht stand

closely together, each with an arm around the other's shoulder. Brecht's face, a moon over his shoulder, is almost a death's head. With what is perhaps an animal or human bone, he strikes a drum with blurring speed. Above both heads is a strange squawking bird that almost has Brecht's hair in its talons. A sun blazes over Bronnen and fireworks explode next to him. He holds a whip emblazoned with the word "Vatermord." The two men stand on a pedestal behind what appear to be the spear points of an iron fence. At their feet is a bottle and jagged houses familiar to us from German Expressionist film. On the pedestal is written Nicht Berühren (do not touch).

Around the end of June, Cas's hatred had almost fatal consequences for Bronnen. Both were invited to a party at the Feuchtwangers. As Bronnen sat listening to Frau Feuchtwanger gush enthusiastically about events in Moscow, Lion saw Cas raising a large bottle of French champagne to bring it down on Bronnen's head. Neher was drunk and intent on doing in his unwelcome roommate and a competitor for Brecht's love. At the last instant, Lion was able to grab the bottle and send Neher home to sleep things off. After Cas left, Lion said to Arnolt: "I was only just able to prevent it. He would certainly have got you and then I would have been jailed; as far as the *Miesbacher Anzeiger* and the *Völkischen Beobachter* [two Nazi-owned newspapers], I'm capable of anything."[13] The subject of Nazi attitudes toward Feuchtwanger was then dropped for that evening. A couple of days later, Feuchtwanger recounted that during the previous week young thugs had come by each evening to throw gravel at his window. "We won't be able to stay much longer in Munich," he concluded. Bronnen, knowing Feuchtwanger's stature in the community, was skeptical. His host smiled and said: "It is you who doubt that? Your *Vatermord* is the starter's gun for such youths who at first throw stones or hit one with bottles."[14]

Almost the following day, on June 24, a clique of young right-wing ex-military officers in Berlin organized and carried out the assassination of the foreign minister of the Weimar state, Walther Rathenau. Before his death, hecklers had chanted at his public appearances, "Down with the goddamned Jewish sow, murder Walther Rathenau."

It was clearly a time for violence on and off the stage. Brecht, like Bronnen, began to be swamped with offers. At the Kammerspiel, Otto Falckenberg announced that he would direct the play *Spartacus*, now given at Marta Feuchtwanger's suggestion the evocative title *Drums in the Night*. The Bavarian State Theater hired Erich Engel to direct *In the Jungle of Cities*. And Seeler, though he had had such a bad experience with Brecht directing *Parricide*, announced that Brecht would direct *Baal* for the Junge Bühne.

Seeler's announcement proved premature. Brecht's star was beginning to rise and with it his price tag. For all the later legends that developed about Brecht's interest in avant-garde and politically charged theater, throughout his life he would always be willing to dump an experimental and/or political production for a major commercial theater with major stars. A telegram on behalf of Felix Holländer of the prestigious Deutsches Theater offering thirty thousand marks, cash up front, for *Baal* put Seeler's relatively penurious operation out of the running.[15] Only when Brecht was unable to close a big-time commercial deal for a play would he think of returning to Seeler. Unlike other beginning playwrights, he could afford to be tough in all his negotiations. He knew he could always fall back on his father's money if his bluff for ever-larger sums was called.

By the second half of 1922, Brecht, like Bronnen, was pursued by theater managers, publishers, directors, and actors and actresses eager for roles in the plays he had written with Caspar Neher. As with Bronnen and Feuchtwanger, the casting couch began to play a large role in Brecht's already very active life, as Marianne soon suspected. During that hot, intense summer in Munich, Ma discovered she was again pregnant. Trying perhaps to create some sense of family, she decided to fetch Frank, now three, from his foster family in Kimratshofen to have him stay with her for the summer.

These efforts at domesticity did not attract Brecht, who spent much of his time back in Augsburg where he again occasionally got Orge to work for him. He wrote to Ma that he had made a sign to remind him to work harder. Stuck to his armoire door with a dagger, it said simply: M + F. And work hard he did, in his own manner. He auditioned (and more) young actresses such as Blandine Ebinger (married at the time to the composer Friedrich Holländer) and Carola Neher (no relation to Caspar Neher).[16]

Bronnen—like Cas, Marianne, Bie, Orge, and others—was finding it difficult to see Brecht privately or even work with him in a mutually helpful way. "His brain," Bronnen noted of Brecht, "seemed to be a monstrous sucking organ that could envelop any material with its many arms." Bronnen began to see his own material disappear into a one-way vacuum created by Brecht's "very underground lust for power" ("eine sehr untergründige Herrschsucht").[17]

Bronnen began to recognize that Brecht "collected acquaintances, and he knew that this was the best time for doing it, like the season for gathering mushrooms. He took Bronnen along on his collecting trips, using him like a shield to ward off spears." Brecht's appetite for help and new people made Bronnen feel ill, and he took a brief but unsatisfactory vacation with the "sex-drenched" Gerda Müller. But Müller (as

Bronnen recognized), "existed mainly as a fantasy of Brecht,"[18] and she soon left Bronnen to move to Berlin. Bronnen went back to Munich, but Brecht was in the middle of affairs conducted in connection with rehearsals for *Drums*. Arnolt realized that he had to get back to his typewriter in Berlin where he could work for himself. The parting was brief: "I'll come right after *Drums*," said Brecht. "Get an apartment for us."[19] Unbeknownst to Arnolt, Cas had been given the same instruction, as he was also now planning to move to Berlin.

Brecht was trying to get Herbert Ihering to come down for the premiere scheduled for September 29. As Brecht knew, Ihering was now in the final stages of making the decision on the Kleist Prize and was rumored to be thinking of giving it to Bronnen for *Parricide*.

Also lined up to attend the opening were Brecht's own family and Bie, who thought herself soon to become a member of the family. Soon after Brecht's last visit to her in Nuremberg to bring her back into the fold, Bie had had to return to Augsburg to help her mother nurse her dying father, taking a job at a bank there to support herself. Meanwhile, Bert Brecht assured her, all appearances to the contrary, that she was his one and only love. When Bie's father died, Brecht convinced her mother of his honest intentions. Bie found herself back in his magic circle. But Brecht had a logistical problem. In order to be able to invite Bie and also keep her in the dark about Ma, Brecht had to persuade the pregnant Ma to stay home. Fortunately, Bronnen was kept busy in Berlin, where Gerda Müller had summoned him to her premiere there. Bronnen obediently stayed but sent Brecht a telegram on the day of the premiere telling the man he loved of his own "deepest wishes."

On the evening of September 29, directed by Otto Falckenberg, *Drums* opened in Munich with marvelously skewed sets by Otto Reigbert. (Brecht had not persuaded the theater to engage the untried Caspar Neher.) The play, with its rolling drums and its endorsement of the defeat of the Spartacists, was a palpable hit with the opening night audience. Bie was a bit disappointed that Brecht was too busy afterward to see her and that she was sent back to Augsburg right away. On the way she worried about his faithfulness.

On this occasion Bert had had a good professional excuse for not being with her. The next day was to be the opening of a comedy revue in which he was heavily involved both as its inspiration and as a performer. He wanted also, of course, to spend every possible minute with Ihering, who had come such a long way to see Brecht's work. It was essential that Ihering have a chance to hear him perform with a guitar, which Brecht knew was most seductive.

The show he had organized for September 30 at the Kammerspiel was a relatively light comedy program under the title of one of the bars in the play *Drums*, "Die rote Zibebe" (The red raisin). Not only was Brecht featured in the performance but he also had brought in the Munich comedy team of Liesl Karlstadt and Karl Valentin, and the cabaret performer–poet Klabund. For the first time ever, the hallowed Kammerspiel opened its doors to a program not devoted to high culture. In one skit the lanky Valentin, perched atop a penny-farthing bicycle rode around the stage as though he were in a circus ring. The audience was told that on his third circuit he would ride through darkness and mist. A strip on which was written "darkness and mist" was solemnly stretched across the stage. After wobbly starts in the wrong direction, Valentin rode through the tape triumphantly. The evening was a great success, and Ihering returned to Berlin visibly delighted.

In a letter to Bronnen written entirely in Bronnen's own lowercase style, Brecht now thanked his lover for the telegram he had sent for the *Drums* premiere. Of the show itself he said self-deprecatingly, "it went well, it did not rain in the theater."[20] He asked if the apartment Bronnen had found was warm. He had a dozen or so errands for Bronnen to do—all couched in terms of violence, fire, earthquakes, the eradication of vermin. Clearly playing on Bronnen's desires, he said he would be coming to Berlin soon, bringing a "fig leaf and a bowler hat" and "a lantern as part of the trousseau, the guitar, the typewriter."

In mid-October, after whipping up press interest in the anticipated violence and seeking to extend his sway, Hitler went with his own special train carrying eight hundred paramilitary supporters with their own marching band to the small city of Coburg. When the city fathers met the train and asked Hitler not to march, he defied them and his troops strutted through the city with drums rolling. The police stood passively as violence broke out. This march through provincial Coburg was upstaged that month by Mussolini's taking of Rome with his Fascio di Combattimento numbering four million members by the end of 1922.

As parts of Europe began their headlong lurch to the right, cultural life moved forward with its own momentum and preoccupations. Ihering's review of the Munich production of *Drums in the Night* appeared in Berlin on November 5. "The twenty-four-year-old poet Bert Brecht," wrote Ihering in the paper the *Berliner Börsen-Courier*, "has altered the literary face of Germany overnight." Not only was the review extraordinary in its praise but, in light of the upcoming decision on the Kleist Prize, Brecht was gratified that Ihering asked that Brecht send him a brief biographical statement. That seemed like a good indication that he might receive the prize rather than his rival Bronnen.

At the beginning of the second week of October, there was mix-up between Bronnen and Brecht. Without telling Brecht and perhaps not knowing that Brecht, in his severely regulated world of relationships, hated someone else taking the initiative, the always impulsive Bronnen headed south. But at the same time Brecht was heading north to put the final push on Ihering and to try to line up some firm dates and advance money for premieres of his work in Berlin. Bronnen arrived in Augsburg with Brecht's bed still warm. Brecht's father was cordial and invited him to stay. The author of *Parricide* was not impressed by Brecht's father, nor did he like Fraülein Roecker, who ran what seemed to Bronnen a "dry puritanical household." Bronnen stayed for two days, making an expedition to Munich to see *Drums*. Finally, he decided to try and meet Brecht in Berlin; that same day Brecht left to go back to Munich.

Bronnen was disappointed but still encouraged by Brecht's earlier request that he should begin looking for a room for them together. Rooms had become particularly expensive and hard to get because the city was overrun by a flood of White Russians fleeing Lenin. Bronnen ran into Cas, and they discovered to their horror that Brecht had told each separately that he planned to live with him. Though they did not particularly care for one another, they shared similar woes and interests, and decided to move in together. "It almost looked," Bronnen said, "like a marriage of two abandoned brides."[21] Their problems were compounded by the sinking mark. In November 1922, it took three hundred paper marks to buy one stable gold mark. Three months later, the ratio would be twenty thousand to one. Those who could renegotiated contracts so that a portion of their income came either in dollars or in gold marks, but neither Bronnen nor Neher had quite enough stature yet to achieve this miraculous transformation.

The "brides" took over their new apartment on November 1. They were forbidden by their new landlady to rearrange the furniture, so they slept side by side in two single beds. Tellingly, considering what his and Cas's attitude now was toward Brecht, Bronnen began work on a script that he gave the title *Verrat*, or *Treason*. When Brecht realized they had moved in together, he wrote to Arnolt: "Be nice to cas and show him cold chikago rub snow into him when he freezes and when he finds he is wounded in the evening rub salt into his wounds. . . . in short baptize him with piss into the mysteries of cold chikago and wipe his little ass with a rasp so that he really notices but absolve me in that it is you who are the sinner."[22]

Meanwhile, another Brecht drama was developing in Munich. The sword-stick–carrying Herr Recht had still not given up hopes of winning the lovely Marianne though she had told him she was pregnant with Brecht's child. Recht decided to try to play off Bie against Ma in the hopes of forcing Brecht to drop Ma. He visited Bie[23] and told her of Ma's pregnancy. As both Bie and Ma believed they were to marry Brecht, Recht convinced the women they should confront Brecht together and force him to make a decision.

When Bie and Recht arrived in Munich from Augsburg, Ma greeted them at the station, and the odd trio took a cab to look for Brecht. They found him at the Kammerspiel and demanded that he meet them in a café in the Maximilianstrasse. While Recht stayed across the street, Marianne, the senior of the two women, made a speech to Brecht that boiled down to the question: which of us do you really want to marry? He replied, with a cynical but engaging grin, "Both!" At this, very much the grand opera performer, Marianne swept out of the café.

With hardly a glance at the departing diva, Brecht reached his hands to Bie, but she drew back, saying "No, Bert, I'm not going to marry you anymore." Then Bie swept out of the café and returned to the station. But no sooner had the train left than she saw Bert in the train corridor signaling her to come out to talk with him. She begged him to leave her alone, but he insisted on seizing her hand. Within an hour they were not only reconciled but had set a date for their marriage. There would, however, have to be a brief delay. Meanwhile, said Brecht, just to give the child a name, he would marry Marianne. But he would then divorce Ma after the child was born and promptly marry Bie. Brecht wrote all this up in the form of an agreement. He also agreed to spend weekends with Bie in Augsburg.

These engagements with Bie were hard to keep as he had so much else to juggle. In October, he was negotiating a contract with the Munich Kammerspiel to become a dramaturge or drama consultant, director, and in-house playwright for them. Egged on by Feuchtwanger, one of its leading dramatists, the Kammerspiel agreed to Brecht's appointment and to peg his earnings to the gold mark. For Brecht, it was an enormous windfall. The theater was taking a stunning risk.

Not content to confine his activities to Munich even though they were paying him very handsomely, Brecht was also working to influence the casting and directing of *Drums*, which was now being scheduled for its all-important Berlin premiere. And not at all willing to lose track of Bronnen, he was writing to him asking him rather desperately to provide any ideas he might have for a new play that Brecht had no idea how to complete but which he had already promised to the Deutsches Theater. The new piece had been triggered by a performance in Munich of *Hannibal* written by the nineteenth-century anti-Semite and great-man cultist Christian Dietrich Grabbe.

In the midst of all this activity and with the Kleist Prize question still unresolved, on November 3, 1922, in a ceremony that he kept as quiet as possible, Brecht married the five-months' pregnant Marianne Zoff. Only the Feuchtwangers and Otto Müllereisert were in attendance. Wanting to have at least a two-day honeymoon with one bride, Brecht lied to Bie about the date of the wedding.[24] November 6, the day he claimed the wedding took place, he turned up briefly to give his second bride a part of his affection.

On November 13, 1922, the big news broke in Berlin. Ihering had decided to give Brecht, not Bronnen, the Kleist Prize. Ihering's encomium, published in the *Berliner Börsen-Courier*, ran:

> In his first play, *Drums in the Night*, Bert Brecht has given artistic form to contemporary events that were previously only talked about. The real event is that our times are the background here, the atmosphere, even in those plays [of his] that are in no way contemporary in their theme. Brecht's nerves, Brecht's blood is filled with the horror of our times . . . [and] Brecht physically feels the chaos and putrefaction. This is the reason for the unparalleled pictorial power of his use of language. This is a language you feel on your tongue, on your palette, in your ears and on your spine.[25]

Praise like this from one of the leading drama critics in Germany created a great rush to put work of the rising star on stage and in print. The same day, the same newspaper published a scene from Brecht's version of *Hannibal*. Brecht's general is almost as down-to-earth as his Kragler "burned black by the African sun" or his tough fighters Bargan or Croze. Again, as with Garga and Shlink in *Jungle*, language proves not to be the best means of communication as Hannibal's soldiers stumble and curse through swamps at the foot of the Alps. The commander is a rough, powerful black man from North Africa, with, as Brecht puts it, the organizational skills of a Rockefeller, a man who has charisma and organizational skills enough to keep a polyglot army together while fighting the combined might of Rome for three decades. The power of his portrait of the black general makes it particularly regrettable that this was one of the many plays that Brecht was never able to complete.

In direct contrast to the brilliant fragment of *Hannibal* was Brecht's and Bronnen's prize-winning filmscript *Robinson on Asunción*, which appeared in the *Berliner Börsen-Courier* on November 26, 1922.[26] Done for money, for a prize that was guaranteed to them before a word had been written, the script shows how little the two writers cared. With the exception perhaps of one or two good sentences, it is a mishmash of every cliché about jungles, technology, volcanoes, islands, and women that both writers were working with from 1921–22. But, with the stock of Bronnen and Brecht extremely bullish, it was an ideal time for the film company that had bought it sight unseen to toss it onto the market.

Kiepenheuer Verlag brought out an eight-hundred-copy edition of the long-delayed *Baal*. With the interest generated by the Kleist Prize announcement, they rapidly printed a far-larger second edition. Theaters had an equally strong interest in getting the rights to these plays. In negotiating, Brecht tried in every case to be taken on as a director. Not only did he feel he knew exactly how these plays should be staged but he also wanted to receive the fees and the acknowledgment as a director so that he would have more than one string to his theatrical bow.

The Deutsches Theater, recalling the *Parricide* incident, was adamant about not allowing him to direct *Drums*. Finally, as Brecht wanted at least the large advance he was offered, he allowed the play to be directed instead by his friend who had directed it in Munich, Otto Falckenberg. The cast was first-rate, including the rising star Alexander Granach as Kragler, the Brecht admirer Blandine Ebinger as Anna, and Brecht's opponent from *Parricide*, Heinrich George, as Anna's blustering and brutal father. But opening as it did on December 20, just before Christmas and at a time when many of the wealthy had left Berlin for winter sports resorts, it closed after a short, unprofitable run. But because Brecht had insisted on being paid up front, he still did well financially.

Brecht's year ended both with the coveted Kleist Prize and considerable financial security from the Deutsches Theater and his gold mark salary in Munich. Bronnen had fared nowhere near as well. His contracts yielded only paper money whose worth disappeared faster than one could run to the bank. His successes as a published author and oft-produced playwright were considerable, but as a manipulator of money, contracts, and people like Herbert Ihering, he was in no way cool or ruthless enough to be any real competition to the man he still so extravagantly loved.

9

"What Concern Is It of Yours That People Are Starving?" (1923–24)

Nineteen twenty-two was ending with Brecht's horizons expanding. The newly married, now unemployed and seven months' pregnant, Marianne, however, felt less and less happy. Brecht might be married to her in a technical sense but he was hardly ever home. When she sought solace from Marta Feuchtwanger, she was told: "When one is married to a genius, one has to be able to get by without lots of things." But Marianne replied, "I don't want a genius, I simply want a husband who loves me."[1]

Living on and off on Akademiestrasse (academy street), Brecht dreamed more and more of moving to Berlin. Meanwhile, not only did he go around the corner to the Feuchtwangers for relief, but he also rented a second place in the same Munich district of Starnberg, where he could have privacy to conduct his affairs. But these were temporary expedients. Berlin remained his ultimate goal. He wrote to Ihering, "One can't even turn around in this town, and the people are so stupid here that one needs to expend so much humor that one is left in a bad mood."[2] In a letter to Bronnen in Berlin, Brecht described Munich as comprising "cavalcades of dreary dog turds and hitler on Monopteros shitting on moses igelstein." In the same violent, part-playful–part-serious letter, Brecht said he and Bronnen should get together to talk about Bronnen's newest play *Treason*. Using Bronnen's own lowercase style, Brecht said, "i take you in my arms your b."[3] But he also told the jealous Bronnen that he hoped to get Neher back to Munich to do the sets for the upcoming production of *Jungle*.

Neher was again trying to establish his own personal and professional life apart from Brecht. In January 1923, with Jürgen Fehling as director, he designed a well-received production of Heinrich von Kleist's play *Kätchen von Heilbronn* at the Berlin Staatstheater. He had met the sister of a fellow set designer and had become engaged to the lovely, lively Erika Tornquist. An August marriage was planned in her home city of Graz in Austria. Brecht, of course, felt abandoned and wanted to find a way to get Neher back to Munich again.

To Bronnen's surprise and joy, Brecht suddenly turned up in

Berlin and "was wonderful, witty, in the best of spirits." It turned out he was in Berlin to persuade Cas to come to Munich to do the set designs for *Jungle*. With Brecht focusing all his charm, Neher capitulated. "Tiger Cas," noted Bronnen jealously, "had been captured again and sat in his cage at the Residenz Theater painting the set for *Jungle*. The black panther Bronnen, responding to the hypnotizing voice of the controller of the beasts of prey, gave birth to ideas for staging and 'provided details.' "[4]

With the Neher mission accomplished, Brecht left without any thanks or goodbye to Bronnen. The first Bronnen knew of his departure was a letter postmarked "Munich." Without reading it, he first tore it up and then burned the pieces. However, when another Brecht letter arrived ten days later, he could not resist opening it. The letter revealed to Bronnen what Brecht said was a "trade secret." The "secret" was that "it is only by means of literature that this world can be populated." He then added, "As soon as Marianne has given birth I'll come up to see you perhaps for a couple of weeks." Meanwhile, wondered Brecht, "couldn't you come for a couple of days?"[5] But the invitation was nonspecific, and Bronnen knew by now that such invitations from Brecht were not invitations at all.

Marianne gave birth to a healthy baby girl on March 12, and the couple named the baby Hanne. Brecht did not go to Berlin, but as he had done when Frank was born, he developed a new relationship. At the Feuchtwangers he had met Marieluise Fleisser, a young woman who was studying at the University of Munich. She came from the same kind of small-town and family milieu as Brecht, growing up in nearby Ingolstadt. Like Brecht, she had come to Lion Feuchtwanger to ask him to help establish herself as a prose writer and playwright. Before actually meeting Brecht, she had read his plays and been overwhelmed. When she then met him at the Feuchtwangers' in early 1923, she knew at once she wanted to spend every minute of the day and night with him.

It seemed he was everywhere except at home with Marianne and the new baby. His usual excuse was that he needed to make money for the family. But, in fact, in what would be a lifetime practice, when he made money he concealed it, keeping most of it for his own use. Like his father, he kept total control, providing as little as he could get away with for household expenses. His checks home were always "in the mail." But as Ma and anyone else having financial dealings with Brecht knew, you did not hold your breath waiting for these checks to arrive.

For all his continued pleading to Marianne that they were poor, his Berlin and Munich contracts yielded him a regular income and left him free to take on any other assignment that struck his fancy. In early 1923, after long efforts to sell some work to the cinema, he was taken on to provide a story outline for a short silent film called *Mysteries of a Barber Shop*. The film involves a series of gags where customers are sliced up while being shaved or getting their hair cut. Valentin in the role of the barber played his brilliant comedic self.

From the film studio, Brecht dashed off to the Residenz Theater to see how Cas was doing with the sets of *Jungle* and how the play's director, Erich Engel, was dealing with the lovers-enemies Garga and Shlink. Engel was glad to see him as he was clearly modeling Garga on Brecht himself. He tried to have Garga (played in the production by Erwin Faber) carry his head at the same odd protruding angle as Brecht. Faber was also to use typical Brecht gestures: "a nervous flying movement of the head" and "grimacing grins, tortured animation of the whole body, the hysteria, the strange graphic mimicry."[6]

Marianne was growing desperate. She had found one of Bert's letters to Bie and had contrasted the "love and tenderness" expressed in that letter with the way she was being treated. She had enough insight into the realities of her situation to draft a letter to Bie saying that she wanted to give Bert his freedom so that he could marry Bie.[7] What Ma did not seem to recognize was that Brecht's "love and tenderness" only increased when he was in danger of losing a lover.

That spring, when Brecht failed to appear, Bronnen began to try to abandon not only the idea of a relationship with Brecht but the very idea of theater itself. He was now beginning to make a name for himself as a novelist, publishing in 1923 a novel of most explicit bisexuality called *Die Septembernovelle*.[8] As he became both very famous and notorious for his sexual frankness in his life and writing, tempting offers were made to him by the huge Ufa firm where Erich Pommer was anxious to engage him to work on the famous F. W. Murnau's new films. But Bronnen, unclear about his relationship both with Brecht and the theater and the openly homosexual Murnau, found he could not make up his mind. Murnau told Bronnen, whose looks Murnau much admired, he might have a future as a film actor. "What would Brecht say," Bronnen wondered, "or more, what would Brecht not say?"[9] Suddenly, there was a special delivery postcard from Brecht on May 5, 1923, saying that had he but known the date of the premiere of *Jungle* (set in Munich for May 8), he would have invited Bronnen. But, Brecht asked, could he come anyway even at short notice? The time left was too short and Bronnen stayed in Berlin.

Though Bronnen had not been told in time about the premiere, Bie had been. She had a ravishing, skin-tight dress made in gleaming black silk. Not wanting to travel from Augsburg in this revealing dress, she changed into it at her aunt's apartment in Munich, where she had to put up with her aunt's chatter about her admiration for a new

Munich orator, Herr Hitler. Bie arrived at the theater somewhat late and breathless. Brecht was waiting for her outside. He ushered her to her seat and then signaled for the performance of *Jungle* to begin.

Jungle elicited a similar reaction in Munich as *Parricide* had at its Berlin premiere. The obvious homosexuality of Garga's relationship with the Malay Shlink, the brutal treatment of women, the explicit racism, and the love-death scene of Shlink's farewell to Garga as the long knives of a racist, lynch-minded mob slit the canvas of the tent in which they have been lying together echoed scenes in Bronnen's play. Garga was, in Brecht's words, a portrait of Rimbaud, and the play included a number of passages taken verbatim from Rimbaud though the program made no note of this fact. The text, as he noted later, also contained "autobiographical elements."[10]

The Munich audience was divided into those who loved the play and considered it to be the new path for German theater, and those who considered it to be an insult to the German state theater apparatus. As the violently aroused audience finally began to file out of the theater, Bert told Bie that they could now go off alone together at least for a time, and she hobbled through the street in her tight dress. Brecht did not propose that they take a taxi to their destination, the Café Fahrig. Brecht had brought along a bottle of now-warm champagne that he had been given earlier by one of his admirers. He was incensed when the waiter charged a corking fee. They sat for two hours over the bottle, and then Brecht accompanied Bie on the long hobble back to her aunt's in the Schwanthalerstrasse. He dropped her off and was gone.

The next day Bie returned alone to Augsburg as sure as she could ever be of Bert's love. But there had been no talk recently of Brecht's promise to divorce Ma so he could marry Bie. Bie began to worry at Brecht's silence and decided to take her marriage-cum-divorce "contract" to a lawyer, who took one look and declared it to be unenforceable and an affront to public morality.[11] Bie now started to take dancing lessons in Augsburg and began meeting other young men. "The magnetism that Brecht exerted on me," she wrote later, "which made me obey him, began to be relaxed. Distance is a great help in this regard."[12] But when Brecht heard Bie had taken up with a young man, he returned and demanded she break it off. In Bie's presence, he declared to the somewhat tongue-tied Gross, "She knows that I'm getting divorced in order to marry her, then she'll be my bride."[13] Bie was persuaded to send Gross packing. At this Brecht returned to Berlin. As Bie said, "He'd carried out his mission." Soon Bie learned, however, that Brecht now "had another iron in the fire." In fact there were several irons both in Berlin and in Munich, and some hot and cooling fires.

On May 29, now sensing Bronnen's disaffection, Brecht became solicitous. He sent him an express postcard. "You anishole," he wrote; couldn't he "come with the very next train you scum i take you in my arms biddi bert plan on a long stay jungle early june?"[14] Bronnen's hopes were rekindled. He decided to go to Munich both to see Brecht and, on the side, to investigate the phenomenon of Hitler. "I heard Hitler for the first time on the radio," he wrote. "I was overwhelmed by the similarity of the two phenomena. Hitler drew his undeniable power suggestively, like the radio and film, not from the human but from the technical."[15] "Could a person such as I was," he asked rhetorically, "with the forms of expression I was used to using, withstand this power at all?"

When Bronnen arrived in Munich on June 2, he was met by Brecht. The two men shook hands and shyly put their arms around one another. The men went off together to the Zirkus-Krone to hear one of Herr Hitler's widely advertised speeches. As the event was organized partly like a modern rock performance and partly like an entrance of a Roman emperor, Hitler was preceded by other speakers, an introductory roll of drums, and a blast of trumpets. Only then did he strut to the front to stare hypnotically at the crowd until it quieted down for him to launch into his performance. "Wolf" Hitler, as he was known to his intimates, would describe a "jungle"[16] world that had to be fought for and controlled by the pure Aryan West. This would be difficult, he acknowledged, because everywhere there were "signs of decay of a slowly ebbing world,"[17] a world in which the body of the Aryan West was threatened by waves of racially inferior microbes. Hackneyed though the themes were, it was the performance that mattered. Kurt Luedecke, a previously uncommitted businessman who attended one such speech noted: "Presently, my critical faculty was swept away. . . . I forgot everything but the man; then, glancing round, I saw that his magnetism was holding these thousands as one. . . . I experienced an exaltation that could only be likened to religious conversion."[18]

Bronnen, though he had been swept away previously by hearing Hitler on the radio, seems to have been somewhat less impressed by Hitler in person, perhaps reacting partly to the venue, the Zirkus-Krone, where the great Barnum and Bailey Circus had appeared to great acclaim, he saw Hitler's presentation as "a sickening trapeze act." The orator released, Bronnen noted, "brutal animal instincts" in the crowd, reactions which he guided like a "Viehentfessler" (a person who unchains wild animals). But though Bronnen saw through the act, he was not immune to the allure of the setting. Hitler's world of barked orders, wolves and whips, guns and drums, a world largely without any active roles for women—this was a world where Bronnen felt at home.

With Marianne and the baby in the next room at the Akademie-strasse apartment, and with four other people dropping by and failing to leave, sleep and sex were out of the question. Bronnen and Brecht spent much of the night talking about what they had just seen. Despite having been warned by his Jewish friends Lion Feuchtwanger and Arnold Zweig that Hitler was extremely dangerous, Brecht said approvingly of Hitler's staging, "He has the advantage of a man who has always seen the theater from the cheapest gallery."[19]

Though he rarely saw Brecht alone, Bronnen stayed in Munich for a month amidst the sea of brown uniforms, swastikas and placards announcing an unending stream of Hitler appearances. Bronnen heard how the Jewish members of Munich's cultural circle felt less and less comfortable. They, together with the non-Jewish Brecht, often spoke longingly of the more liberal atmosphere they believed prevailed in Berlin. Speaking of Hitler's brown-uniformed people as inhabitants of a mythical kingdom called "Mahagonni," Brecht said to Bronnen that he now definitely wished to move to Berlin. He had only a few things to finish up in Munich, he said, "then I'll be in Berlin. Then I have an idea for the two of us."[20] In July, he sent another note to Bronnen. Brecht styled himself now as "The Lord of the South Sea" while Bronnen was "The Lord of the North Sea." Brecht longed, he wrote, "to look into your aryan face. the way it was in may."[21]

Unable to make progress on his own that summer, Brecht was functioning as a kind of surgeon working on unwieldy plays by other people. He put in a lot of work on a very wooden adaptation of Selma Lagerlöf's play *Gösta Berling*, only to find out later the publishing company holding the German rights would not release them to him. Brecht next became involved in doing some surgery on a play Bronnen was directing in Berlin, an ecstatic, erotic piece called *Pastor Ephraim Magnus* by the young Hanns Henny Jahnn. The play was a timely potpourri of madness, bestiality, flaming poetry, blood, and cruelty. Without having consulted the original author, Brecht started to carve it up.

It was a time of particular horror in Berlin. Inflation had so decimated the economy that Germany had long since fallen behind on her reparation payments to France. France sent in armed forces to occupy the mines and factories of the Ruhr, furthering the decline of the German economy as products now flowed directly to France. Prohibited from maintaining armed forces, Germany could offer no official resistance to the French. Resistance, when it happened at all in the Ruhr, came from unofficial groups from the radical right and left.

By the summer of 1923, Germany resembled a vast fire sale of disposable assets. Berlin was full of those left homeless from the economic wars and the maimed from World War I. Seeing misery on his way to and from the theater, Bronnen wondered what could be done. He felt "that there in the East a new, perhaps the new, world was coming into being."[22] Soviet representatives asked him to become Berlin correspondent for *Nakanunje* (The overnight dispatch) and for *Isvestia*, one of the two key official Soviet papers. Bronnen asked Brecht for advice about taking on an assignment from Moscow. Brecht said, his voice cracking with anger, "What concern is it of yours if people are starving?"[23] Brecht's recommendation was as clear as Kragler's rejection of the Spartacists in *Drums in the Night*: "One has to reach the top, establish oneself, have one's own theater, stage one's own plays. Then one will be able to see further, and get further."

Bronnen dropped the idea of writing for Moscow and returned to the Jahnn play. The rehearsals limped forward with Brecht chopping Jahnn's play down from its original three hundred pages to a more playable two hours. When it opened on August 23, it aroused the rage of virtually all including the original author. He remarked that his play had been lost, but no decent Brecht play had been found. When Brecht tried to cash his check for the adaptation, it bounced.

Meanwhile, the now twenty-six-year-old Caspar Neher had married the nineteen-year-old Erika Tornquist. It would prove a difficult marriage for Erika, with Cas often away with close male friends. Erika particularly hated when he was off with Brecht. She trusted Brecht no more than had Caspar Neher's mother. But, periodically, marriage or no marriage, Neher would be drawn back, although the relationship would never again be what it once had been. For Brecht, his friends' marriages were a form of abandonment that he would never really forgive.

At around the time of Neher's treasonous marriage, a somewhat disconsolate Brecht dropped by Bronnen's sublet room at 3 Nürnberger Platz. Trying to get a bit of evening breeze, both men stood close together at Bronnen's narrow window looking down on the Nürnberger Platz. Bronnen was mainly silent, simply enjoying Brecht's physical closeness, remembering fondly the time of their first meeting, the tremendous excitement he had felt on seeing and hearing Brecht for the first time. It had been a time, as he remembered, of "gegenseitiger Befruchtung"—"impregnation of each by the other." But this had faded and could not be brought back. For Brecht, as Bronnen now saw, "the question of [Brecht's] friendship with Bronnen was not at all a question of constancy but, at best, a question of usefulness, of intensity."[24]

In the midst of separate reveries, Brecht suddenly spoke out. "What one needs," said Brecht, "is an actress." Bronnen was deeply agitated and asked himself why Brecht needed an actress. He felt so hurt by Brecht's remark that he wanted to jump out of the window or, better yet, jump out with Brecht. As the light faded in the square below, Bronnen noticed a light go on across the square in the window of Helene Weigel, an actress acquaintance from the Frankfurt *Parricide*. He had later visited her in Berlin, where she had rather mothered him. He felt very much at home with her familiar Viennese accent and dinners. Bronnen gestured toward Weigel's window and said: "Over there is where Helene Weigel lives. You know, the one who was in Frankfurt. Now she is engaged by [Leopold] Jessner. I think she would like it if you went to her." Brecht stepped back from the window and grasped the lapels of Bronnen's jacket. Bronnen said, "I'll call her up and tell her you're coming."[25] When he returned from making the call, the man he loved was already walking across the Nürnberger Platz toward the lighted skylight on the other side.

Weigel did not fit any conventional image of an actress. Barely five feet tall, slender as a boy, she had her hair cut very short, revealing ears that seemed too large for her face. But her unusually deep voice could shake an audience with the tiniest whisper or an ear-shattering bellow. Her voice, figure, clothes, and walk combined to present very much the kind of androgyny to which Brecht, like Wedekind, was strongly drawn.

Weigel had been born on May 12, 1900, to an assimilated Jewish family in Vienna. Her mother owned and managed a toy store. Her father, like Brecht's, managed a factory. Helene Weigel and her one sister were brought up with the standard complement of servants. With regular paths to higher education blocked for girls, Weigel was sent to a *Mädchen-Lyzeum*, where two-thirds of the girls were upper crust and Jewish. Anti-Semitic behavior, widely prevalent in Viennese circles, could not establish a hold at this particular school. Moreover, the school's director told her charges that given the appropriate opportunities, girls could achieve at the same level as boys in all fields of endeavor; and she brought a stream of successful professional women to the school for her pupils to emulate. For Helene Weigel, the visits of the actress Lia Rosen and the internationally famous writer Karin Michaëlis were to determine the course of her life. Michaëlis, both famous and infamous throughout Europe for her book *The Dangerous Age*, spoke and wrote frankly of women's sexual needs.

Inspired by Michaëlis and Rosen, the teenage Helene Weigel determined to break out of the mold for women of her class by entering what her worried parents saw as the morally dubious and uncertain world of the theater. Totally committed to her objective, she stole the money for her first acting lessons from her father's trouser pockets. In the last year of the war, as the ancient Austro-Hungarian Empire neared final collapse, she left school, where she was bored and barely able to scrape by. Nobody could talk her out of the idea of trying to make her way in the theater, despite her absence of conventional good looks. Her one major supporter at the time was Karin Michaëlis. Weigel was finally allowed to audition for the famous Viennese director Arthur Rundt in December 1917. Michaëlis went along to provide moral support as Weigel gave her rendition of J. G. Herder's ballad "Edward." Michaëlis wrote later that she heard in Weigel's voice at this audition "the tones of a pipe organ, the rattle of death, the cries of women giving birth, and the joy of love's ecstasy."[26] Rundt was equally impressed, according to Michaëlis, exclaiming that Weigel was "one of the greatest dramatic geniuses ever born."

Soon Weigel found herself, as she wrote to Michaëlis back in Denmark, "hotly loving" Dr. Rundt, who petitioned his wife for divorce while giving private lessons to his eighteen-year-old protégée. In the midst of this dangerous, but by no means unusual, telescoping of the personal and the professional, Weigel began to make tiny stage appearances in the Vienna area. In early 1919, she joined the Neue (New) Theater in Frankfurt. As she made progress in her career, she continued to write to Michaëlis. She longs, she says, to talk directly with Michaëlis rather than having to write; unfortunately for history, for her writing was not a favorite form of expression. Apart from a few deeply personal letters to Michaëlis, Weigel would leave few written traces of her own life in all its personal, professional, and, later, political complexity.

In Frankfurt, opposite the great Albert Steinrück, she played the untrue Marie, victim of her murderous but mad and misused lover, in Büchner's *Woyzeck*; she was the prostitute Anna in Johst's play *The King*; and she played an old woman in Georg Kaiser's Expressionist play *Gas II*. Reviewers particularly noticed her voice, with its "hard tone of conscious eccentricity."[27] Even in the small part in *Gas II*, her "sonorous organ marked by deep sensitivity of feeling" brought her attention.[28] But her voice was not always positively reviewed. One critic wrote of her in January 1921: "Yelling is her normal tone of voice."[29] As late as 1928, a Berlin critic would write of her: "The talented Fräulein Weigel seems to place worth on being the noisiest actress in Berlin, her horrible yells should be stilled as quickly as possible."[30] But she could not be ignored. Though not pretty in any conventional sense, she was thought suitable to play ingenues, as well as boy-girl and older women's roles.

By mid-October 1919, her letters to Michaëlis spoke of her love for the director of the New Theatre, Privy Councillor Zeiss, and of her three-year contract for 5,400, 7,000, and 9,000 marks, respectively, for each year. Whatever successes she achieved professionally, she always needed, she told Michaëlis, "tenderness and love."

After her move to Berlin to work with the fabled director Jessner, Weigel was again back to small roles when she met Brecht. In the Weimar years, she never achieved in Berlin the recognition that had come so swiftly in Frankfurt. But she did temporarily find "tenderness and love." After an affair with the obscure actor Friedrich Gnass, an affair had begun with the up-and-coming actor Alexander Granach. Like herself and Bronnen, Granach was an assimilated Jew who had come to Berlin from the former Austro-Hungarian Empire. As it happened, among Granach's earliest important roles in Berlin had been those in Bronnen's *Parricide* and Brecht's *Jungle*. These connections, plus the Kleist Prize, meant that Bertolt Brecht was a familiar name to Helene Weigel.

Apparently, she did not hesitate to invite Brecht into her atelier at 16 Spichernstrasse when he appeared on her doorstep on that late summer evening of 1923. As it got later and later and it was clear he had no intention of leaving, the question of sleeping arrangements came up. Brecht was dismayed when Weigel matter-of-factly made up the sofa in her living room for him and then retired to her own bedroom. During the night there came a knock at her bedroom door. Though it was late August, Brecht told Weigel that he was cold and wanted to join her in her bed. Instead, Weigel handed him another blanket and sent him back to the sofa. When she got up the next morning, he had already left.

Not having been allowed into Weigel's bed that first night and the check for the work on the Jahnn play having bounced, Brecht decided to head back to Munich. He had good reason to leave urgently. He had learned from his frequent hostess in Berlin, Esther Warschauer, that Marianne had written that she was so fed up with the marriage that she intended to move back to her parents' place in Pichling, Austria. Brecht, with his time-tested mixture of carrot and stick, had tried to persuade her from moving out. He told her he loved her, claimed he was sleeping alone, and then openly threatened that if she once left, she would never be allowed back.[31]

But when he got back to Munich, Ma and the baby were gone. At once, he fired off a fierce note, "I am going to file for divorce on grounds of [your] infidelity," ending the letter, "you can really go to the devil."[32] After a few more weeks, he decided he wanted to see no more of Ma or their daughter, Hanne. He wrote to Marianne: "Your things are here to be picked up. I'm going to let the girl go. You can go to hell."[33] Then, in a typically sudden shift, shortly thereafter he suggested they make a trip to Capri together in the coming summer.

10

"Jabyourknifeintohimjackhiphiphurrah" (1923–24)

In 1923, inflation ran faster than new prices could be put on anything offered for sale. At this time, the Munich Kammerspiel failed to produce a play it had contracted with Feuchtwanger. In recognizing the error, Rudolf Frank, one of the managers, said, "Dear Doctor, you are, I'm sure, no Shylock."[1] But in correcting the original error, the theater created a disaster for themselves and a gold mine for Brecht. Feuchtwanger, now concentrating on novels, did not want to do another play anyway, so he pushed Brecht forward to co-write a play with him.

Frank hoped the two would do a simple remounting of Shakespeare's *Macbeth* as the theater urgently needed a relatively cheap boxoffice success. Brecht and Feuchtwanger proposed instead Christopher Marlowe's *Edward II*, a lesser-known play of the Elizabethan era. This play could be tinkered with without arousing the kind of criticism that an altered *Macbeth* would have generated. The two authors were to adapt the text and Brecht was to direct it. The time of the premiere was left open, and Brecht was given a free hand as to casting, set designer, and personnel.

Meanwhile, Brecht was working behind the scenes to try to stop a rival production of the play in Berlin that involved Weigel's lover Alexander Granach. Brecht begged Granach to leave the Berlin *Edward II* for his own. If the Munich production went well, wrote Brecht, then this version could be played in Berlin later. Combining a polite request with a direct threat, Brecht said that his new version would "push your old translation up against the wall."[2] Nevertheless, Granach did one Berlin performance of *Edward II* on November 2, using the translation of A. R. Meyer.

At the same time, Brecht was hustling Weigel. Within weeks of his first visit to her atelier, Brecht was writing letters to her using the "Du" form and calling her by the nickname "Helletier" (Animal Helli).[3] Despite having told Bronnen that "what one needs is an actress," he would not propose any stage work to her for years. Weigel claimed that Brecht thought very little of her as an actress until he worked with her in 1929, six years after meeting her.[4] At least one critic sees this as an example of Brecht's prevailing narcissism. "For the person who only seeks himself, the 'usefulness' of a woman is," writes Fritz Raddatz, "most perfectly manifested in an actress (actors are apes said Brecht on one occasion). For Brecht, the actress is . . . an extension of the self."[5]

Pursuing Weigel relentlessly, he invited her to visit him in Munich. He also proposed that they might take a trip together to Paris for a few days and that later they could go to Italy. He evidently did not tell her that the scheduling would be tight. He had also invited the newly married Cas and the now frequently disaffected Ma to join him at slightly different times in Italy.

Where Brecht had warned Granach about using existing German translations of *Edward II*, Brecht (whose English was rudimentary), was relying heavily both on the Meyer text and on a 1912 Walter Heymel translation. As he was directly infringing copyright, Brecht did not mention the translators, though the final Feuchtwanger-Brecht text lifts at least one line in six directly from Heymel.[6] The new version was certainly different in tone, but Brecht felt no compunction in stealing copyrighted material, even though he was risking his own, Feuchtwanger's, and the Kammerspiel's financially endangered neck.

For those familiar with Brecht's earlier work—*Baal, Jungle* and "Bargan" (all having enthusiastic and often murderous bisexual activities at their core)—the Brecht-Feuchtwanger version of Marlowe's 1591–92 chronicle play treads familiar ground: an unhappily married monarch who takes up publicly with Gaveston, the son of a butcher. The queen, called Isabella in Marlowe and Anna in Brecht-Feuchtwanger, takes up with Edward's rival, Mortimer. But Mortimer barks at her: "With knees spread wide and eyes closed, you snap at everything and cannot be satisfied, Anna."

Mortimer's weariness and bitterness sound the basic tenor of the play and capture the mood in Munich at the time. Gaveston, like the other characters in the adaptation, lives in the worst of all possible worlds. Because of his uncontrollable and objectively inexplicable passion, the king is crushed by the turning wheel of "the slut Fortune." Like Garga and Shlink in *Jungle*, and Croze and Bargan in the Bargan stories, the characters in the reworked *Edward II* are locked aesthetically, physically and linguistically in the close embrace of lovers-enemies. The king, Gaveston, the queen, and Mortimer move swiftly and knowingly to their violent, erotic ends.

The changes wrought are often achieved with great economy of means. In Marlowe, Young Mortimer contemplates his end as follows:

Base Fortune, now I see, that in the wheel
There is a point, to which when men aspire,

> *They tumble headlong down: that point I touched,*
> *And, seeing there was no place to mount up higher,*
> *Why should I grieve at my declining fall.*

Mortimer sees himself as having made a choice by aspiring to fortune. When he sees his end, he does not grieve at the choice he made. He strides from life with his head held high. In Brecht-Feuchtwanger, Mortimer says:

> *There is, my boy, a wheel that the*
> *Slut Fortune turns. It forces you with it upwards.*
> *Upwards and upwards. You hold on tight. Upwards.*
> *There comes a point, the highest. From there you see*
> *There is no ladder. It forces you downwards.*
> *Because it's round. He who has seen this, is he forced*
> *To fall, my boy, or does he let himself fall? The question's*
> *A joke. Relish it!*

The person on this wheel (echoing both the medieval torture instrument—the wheel on which heretics, among others, were broken—and the great carrousels and swings that both frightened and excited Brecht at the Augsburg fair) is passive; the person is forced both upwards and then downwards. In this universe, human activities and desires are not guided by their own free will but are a metaphysical "joke."

While Brecht rehearsed, efforts to topple the German government were intense on both the left and the right. In Soviet circles, with Lenin struggling with an illness that would kill him within a few months, a tremendous push was being made to try to send Germany over the revolutionary brink. On October 23, the government of Saxony was deposed by Communist forces led by activists from Moscow. At the same time, a Moscow-backed uprising began in the vital port city of Hamburg. Moscow set November 7, anniversary of the Soviet Union's own successful revolution, as a date for upheaval throughout Germany.

At the same time, Russia laid the groundwork for her own later invasion by Germany when she entered into a secret manufacturing and military alliance with representatives of the old German military establishment. In direct violation of the Versailles Treaty, a "private firm," funded at seventy-five million marks by the Weimar government and with the full complicity of Lenin's government, commenced planning for a Junker factory near Moscow, with a production target of six hundred aircraft a year. With the cooperation of the general staff of both countries, German factories for the manufacture of poison gas and of three hundred thousand shells a year were established on Russian soil. The moving force in making these arrangements for Russia was Karl Radek. The key German negotiator was World War I officer and Ehrhardt Brigade supporter General Hans von Seeckt. Von Seeckt's objective was to prepare a blueprint for an offensive war: "The existence of Poland is intolerable and incompatible with Germany's vital interests. . . ." he wrote. "Poland is more intolerable for Russia than for ourselves."[7] Together, Russia and Germany should destroy Poland, said von Seeckt; then Germany could wheel west to defeat France. Here von Seeckt outlines clearly the later Hitler/Stalin Pact.

While the Weimar government and the Wehrmacht made their secret deals, Hitler, Ernst Röhm, and their ever-growing number of violent adherents were preparing a coup against the Weimar state. The right was stockpiling weapons, forbidden under the Versailles Treaty and the laws of Weimar. As it had when von Epp and the Ehrhardt Brigade had seized the city before, the right transformed the area immediately surrounding Munich into what Joachim Fest calls "a bivouac of brutish soldiery."[8]

For the general populace, life seemed to go its normal way. Theaters continued to function. People continued to stroll in Munich's many lovely parks. One typical fall evening in one of Munich's loveliest and most peaceful parks, Brecht's fellow dramaturge and immediate boss, Bernhard Reich, sat with Soviet actress and director Asja Lazis. Lazis had no papers permitting her to work in Germany; she was not married to Reich but was living with him. In increasingly xenophobic Bavaria, she could be deported at any moment. She had already been arrested once in Berlin after directing a revolutionary piece for five thousand spectators. Reich, the son of a wealthy grain dealer in the small Czech-German border town of Olmütz, was suspect by association. The revolutionary couple noticed Brecht out for a stroll with the lovely Marianne. Ma was in Munich for one of her infrequent visits. Introductions were made all around.

Brecht listened as the strikingly beautiful Lazis, in her heavily accented German, spoke of revolutionary theater in her native Latvia and the Russian revolutionary theater in Petrograd and Moscow. She had worked with Sergei Eisenstein, the revolutionary poet Mayakovsky, and the somewhat older director Vsevolod Meyerhold, who were rendering familiar objects strange by placing them in new, revolutionary contexts. The younger members of the group had published in 1922 an aptly named "Eccentric Manifesto," which advocated borrowing techniques from everyday life as well as from cabaret singers, jazz bands, boxing, street performers, and the circus and cinema. "We prefer," as one advocate put it, "Charlie's arse to Eleonora Duse's hands."[9] Brecht was so impressed with Lazis that he proposed to her that she become his directorial assistant on the production of *Edward II*. Through her, Brecht would add to his production many of the latest techniques of the Soviet revolutionary theater, a theater well ahead of anywhere else in the world at that time. For the politically threatened Lazis, the chance to work at a state theater could not have come at a better time.

Reich, imbued as he was with revolutionary morality that put the cause before personal feelings, did not react in a "bourgeois" way to Brecht's obvious interest in his wife in all but name. In fact, Reich found himself being swept away by Brecht. He was overwhelmed by the raw poetic force of the *Edward* script and did not object when Brecht declared himself casually "the heir of Gerhart Hauptmann."[10]

Equally smitten, both romantically and artistically, was another of Feuchtwanger's protégés, the young writer Marieluise Fleisser, now attending the *Edward* rehearsals. Somewhat plain and rather shy, she had lovely blond hair cut in a fashionable pageboy and (according to no less a connoisseur in such matters than the Don Juan of Munich poets, Bruno Frank) "the best boobs in middle Europe."[11] Learning that she was a student at the University of Munich but wanted to become a writer, Brecht had asked, "What did she need a Ph.D. for?" Taking the hint, she dropped her studies. She completed some fine short stories that Feuchtwanger arranged to have published and began work on a play about her hometown, Ingolstadt. When her father learned she had abandoned the possibility of a safe future as a teacher for the risky business of becoming a writer, he immediately stopped her allowance and ordered her home. Temporarily, the budding affair with Brecht was broken up.

Though most people reacted as Fleisser did to Brecht's charm, a few people resisted it. Rudolf Frank, the man responsible for Brecht's gold mark contract, looked with an unusually sober eye at the artistic chaos he saw Brecht creating at the Kammerspiel. Frank decided he had better try to present this chaos in the best possible light. One day he advised Brecht, "Invent a theory, my dear Brecht! When one presents Germans with a theory, they are willing to swallow anything."[12] This was music to Brecht's ears. He would develop in the years to come an immense body of critical writing. Brecht was a person who really believed that "a man with only one theory was lost."[13] From now on, he would remain ready to generate theories, frequently contradictory ones, for all theatrical occasions. What began as a cover-up for a contract mistake in Munich in 1923 would eventually, as we shall see, turn into the most influential body of critical writing on theater that the twentieth century would produce.

As rehearsals moved forward under the direction of the new theorist and "heir of Hauptmann," November 7, the day dreaded by the Weimar government as the anniversary of the Russian revolution, came and went. To the relief of the German government, Soviet backing was insufficient to tip the revolutionary scales. The next day, however, the anniversary of the fall of the House of Hohenzollern in 1918, a blow was struck from the radical right. Hitler fired his pistol into the air at the Bürgerbräukeller on the evening of November 8 and forced the Munich government to throw in its hand and march with him on that "Babylon" of a city, Berlin.

Though more politically alert people like the Feuchtwangers were made aware that night of the danger, Brecht, Lazis, and Reich missed the fact that a right-wing coup had taken place on their doorstep. According to Reich's account, when they arrived at the Kammerspiel as usual shortly before ten on November 9, 1923, they were surprised to see the *Edward* cast standing outside the theater reading a shared newspaper. Without glancing at the paper, Reich and Brecht said, "Let's get started if you please."[14] But one of the actors said, "Read this first," and handed them a special edition of one of Hitler's two Munich papers. When Brecht realized that the city was under martial law, the rehearsal was canceled for the day.

Hitler had ordered a massive demonstration on November 9. He declared to his followers, "If it comes off, all's well, if not, we'll hang ourselves."[15] Adolf Hitler, General Ludendorff, Max Erwin von Scheubner-Richter, and Hermann Göring strode along, their troops sixteen abreast, toward the Rathaus where troops loyal to the government had taken up their defensive positions. The first shot fired by the defenders killed von Scheubner-Richter and he held on to Hitler so forcefully as to drag him down, wrenching his arm out of joint as he did so. While General Ludendorff stalked haughtily forward, bullets or no, Hitler fled in an ambulance. He had himself taken to the lovely nearby village of Utting, where his aide Ernst "Putzi" Hanfstaengl had a country estate. Here Hitler was found and taken into custody two days later.

The putsch leaders arrested, Munich returned to the hallucinatory state that passed for normalcy. Rehearsals of *Edward II* started again. With no contractual restrictions placed upon him, Brecht spared no expense. If he did not like a set, he ordered it completely rebuilt, no matter how much had been spent on it. Reich recalled that Brecht the director was "absolutely categorical. He did not argue with replies, he swept them away. He made it clear to his interlocutors that he regarded all resistance as hopeless and they should not waste time but should immediately capitulate to him."[16]

"Was this attitude cunning, a pose, youthful presumption, or had he an inner right to it?" asked Reich many years later. The question takes us, I believe, to the heart of a problem central to the members of the Brecht circle, both on the left and the right. Though Reich had personally seen Hitler's first attempt to seize totalitarian powers, and though both Reich and Lazis had subsequently been victims of Stalin's "illegal repressions," and though by 1956 the scale of Stalin's crimes had been revealed by Khrushchev, Reich still accepted in 1957 the idea that there are individuals with "an inner right" to act in an absolutely categorical manner. The ubiquitousness of the idea of granting limitless power to "genius" indicates why Reich, and millions like him, had no viable defense against Stalin and Hitler. The idea, like theater itself, has no logical boundaries.

It is one thing at this distant remove to point out Reich's inability to resist the call of "genius," but to understand this century at all, it is essential to recognize the wholly irrational power these figures—whether Hitler, Stalin, or Brecht—exerted when they were encountered in person. Brecht is very much a part of this century of the charismatic, irrational yet effective Pied Piper powers that could, in the case of both Hitler and Stalin, lure tens of millions of supposedly intelligent beings to embrace their butchers.

David Bowie has spoken of Hitler as the first rock star. If we would understand the power that either Hitler or Brecht exerted on audiences in Munich in the early 1920s, Bowie's observation gives us a clue as to how supposedly rational beings can be turned to putty in the hands of immensely skilled performers. That this happened regularly at Hitler's performances is now perfectly obvious. However, in much of the writing done on Brecht, perhaps because of his later, at least theoretical insistence on the cool and rational in performance, surprisingly little attention has been paid to him as utterly mesmeric performer able to seduce both men and women at will. But, again and again, we have instances of this happening, and Bernhard Reich is simply part of the kind of hysteric acceptance that was ubiquitous when Brecht performed or turned his full charm on another person. Not just the young, but cynical and seasoned performers and analysts of performance found themselves regularly swept away by Brecht. Typical, in the fall of 1923 in Munich, was the reaction of the cabaret performer Carl Zuckmayer who, for the first time, heard Brecht sing at a Munich party in mid-October. "When he reached for the guitar," wrote Zuckmayer of Brecht that evening, the noisy hum of conversations turned to silence, the steps of the dancers doing the tango in dark corners of the room stopped and everyone sat on the floor around him caught up in his magic spell." That evening, Brecht sang the "Ballad of the Pirates," with its men who murder and rape as casually as they shit; the "Remembering Marie A," with its kitschy, totally gripping French chanson tune. He sang the "Ballad of the Drowned Girl," who, rejected by her "lover," drifts downstream with water rats playing in her hair, and the gruesome *Moritat* of "Jakob Apfelböck," who murders his parents and has them molder in a cupboard in the home where he continues to live. Hearing the slender Brecht, with his guitar clutched against his stomach, render these songs in a voice that was "raw and cutting," Zuckmayer says of himself that he was "totally caught up, moved, caught in the magic, painfully stirred."[17]

By the time Zuckmayer heard him perform, Brecht had become an almost totally irresistible seductive force. He could now usually impose his own will on virtually anybody, and was so gifted with an ability to shape and turn any contract to his own advantage that stopping him from having his will became well-nigh impossible. At the Munich Kammerspiel, a lordly Brecht decided that Lazis would be not only his assistant director for *Edward II* but would also play the "trouser" role of the king's son. Rudolf Frank remonstrated with Brecht in vain, telling him that Lazis was not an actress, spoke incomprehensible German, and was totally unsuited for the part. Frank even told Lazis to her face that she was a "cow," a "catastrophe," and "the ruin of the Kammerspiel." Both Brecht and Lazis ignored him. The rehearsal pace was leisurely and regal. Faced with a calamity that they had managed themselves into, management remembered that Karl Valentin and Liesl Karlstadt had been well received with their "Red Raisin" cabaret show in September 1922. In a highly unusual move, the Kammerspiel now brought them back night after night to try to have their brilliant comedy keep the Kammerspiel afloat amidst the red ink of Brecht's endless rehearsals of *Edward*.

Munich rehearsals were interrupted in December as Brecht left to earn more money by helping to supervise a *Baal* production in Leipzig under the direction of Alwin Kronacher. Both Brecht and his play were to be carefully staged sensations in Leipzig. The young playwright had spared no effort or expense to look the part of the poor but tough young poet. He slouched around Leipzig unwashed and unshaved, smelly, shabby, in a worn-looking but carefully hand-tailored leather jacket cut large to make him look bigger, from which his thin neck stuck out at an odd angle. He wore rumpled but expensive corduroy trousers from which poked his clearly none-too-clean "November gray underwear." A sporting cap suitable for ringside or racetrack was pulled down over his forehead. On one hand was a blue signet ring. On his nose perched round, wire-frame glasses looking like the sort that charities issued to the unemployed. Brecht's glasses, however, were made of platinum. For all this careful costuming, he needed a setting. This was a suite (paid for by the Leipzig theater) at the Fürstenhof Hotel, a bastion of feudal magnificence.

At *Baal* rehearsals, chaos seemed to reign. Lothar Körner, in the title role, raged at the young, arrogant Brecht and stormed off. Margarete Anton, playing the female lead, fainted under the pressure and was carried off as Brecht wondered aloud about the color of her underwear. On the day of the opening, Körner croaked that his voice could stand no more of Baal's bellowing. Anton had barely recovered from her fainting fit. Dr. Kronacher, the nominal director of the piece, was a nervous wreck as he looked at what had apparently become with Brecht's expensive "help," a chaotic jumble. At the eye of the hurricane, Brecht stayed calm. He was still revising the text even before the actors had mastered what he had already written. In the audience that evening would be critics from all over Germany, including the two main Berlin critics, Ihering and his rival Alfred Kerr.

Chaotic rehearsals or no, the performance went well. Afterward, amidst the noise of whistles, boos, and applause, "there appeared on stage," wrote Hans Netonek in his review, "a shy, pale, slender youth, the poet Bertolt Brecht."[18] The look on the youth's face seemed to the reviewer to say, "My God, what have I done?" The national reviews the following day were mixed. Ihering, as usual, was full of praise. Kerr, equally predictably (he usually damned out of hand that which Ihering had praised), wrote of the show, "Liquor, liquor, liquor, naked, naked, naked women." Even as the shabby figure in the sporting cap had checked out of the Fürstenhof Hotel and was on his way back to Munich to commit further public indiscretions, the mayor of Leipzig insisted on having *Baal* removed from the repertoire.

To further ensure notoriety at this time, Brecht's various publications were issued with dedications to various lovers. The poems themselves were also designed to shock. In one poem dedicated to Gerda Müller (with whom he had taken up when Bronnen had left), he wrote, "One takes a s—— . . . One makes a poem."[19] Having poked cloacal fun at poetry itself, he went on to praise "the heavenly fruit of a nonimmaculate conception!"

Ever surer of the techniques useful in maintaining control of his entourage, he mixed and matched liaisons with the flair of the virtuoso, often using one lover to help him with problems with another. When he heard that Bie was engaged to someone else once again, he instructed Helene Weigel to take care of her. Just beginning a pregnancy with the latest little Brecht, Weigel found Bie an apartment and a job in Berlin, and called to persuade her to move there. Not waiting for an answer, Weigel hung up. When Bie despite this peremptory summons did not arrive, Weigel made a special trip to Augsburg. Bie remembered asking how Brecht was doing, to which Weigel said only that Brecht "couldn't leave Berlin on such short notice and so that's why he had sent her."[20] In his stead, Weigel spoke long and earnestly as to why Bie should move to Berlin. Perhaps because her heart was not completely in it, Weigel got nowhere. On March 1, Bie married the jealous Herrmann Gross. Gross refused to have anything to do with Frank, the child Bie had had with Brecht. Since Ma now had her hands full with Hanne, Frank would be passed from pillar to post. Weigel tried to take care of the unwanted child, persuading distant relatives in Austria to take care of him periodically.

Nineteen twenty-four began with Brecht busy in his usual tangle of affairs, while Reich and Lazis were trying to glean from the anti-Soviet Munich and other German papers what was really going on in the Soviet Union. They learned that on January 11, the Comintern had announced that the Social Democratic party in Germany was merely "a section of German fascism in disguise." This was a binding directive that would radically split the left, forcing the German Communist party to work against the other parliamentary socialists. In the years immediately ahead, the decision would have catastrophic consequences. Many German Communists, including those at the top level such as Ruth Fischer and Jakob Walcher, began to wonder if the Comintern grasped the specifics of the German situation. Was not the splitting of the left manna for the radical right? Increasingly, it seemed to the best-informed observers that Comintern decisions were directed by internal Russian party politics rather than the good of the revolutionary cause in other countries. When Lenin died some ten days later with his successor unclear, socialism in the Soviet Union and abroad was left in disarray.

As the Soviet Union would be involved in internal problems over Lenin's succession for the next several years, the Western powers, including the United States, made massive efforts to try to stabilize Germany. Backed by the United States, the Weimar leaders invalidated the old and now wholly worthless paper marks and issued new currency valued at the prewar rate of 4.2 marks to the dollar. Passive resistance to French occupation of the Ruhr was declared contrary to national interest as well as illegal so that the factories and mines could run again. These measures were backed by the Dawes Plan of the United States, which called for the French to leave the Ruhr and a rescheduling of the payments for which the Versailles Treaty had called.

The Dawes Plan gave the political centrists a tool to slow crippling inflation in 1924 and thereby to undercut the hopes of both right and left. The plan was, of course, called a sellout to American commercial interests, but this seemed to the centrists a price worth paying. It would give Weimar time at least to make an attempt to stabilize itself and establish viable democratic institutions.

The global events that were of such direct concern to politically concerned Europeans seem to have been almost wholly ignored by

Brecht. When a fellow dramaturge insisted on loaning him books by Georg Lukács and Johannes R. Becher dealing with revolution and the arts, he returned them with a recommendation to read that chronicler of empire Rudyard Kipling.

After Brecht's return from Leipzig in late 1923, it would take him four more months of rehearsals with full cast and full stage crew to get *Edward II* ready. The expense was colossal and kept climbing when he insisted on borrowing the great actor Erwin Faber from Munich's Residenz Theater. Reich recalls that if a certain scene did not work in rehearsal, the "nervous director Brecht" would so berate "the incompetent dramatist Brecht" that finally, "after a lot of pushing and shoving, the dramatist would scribble a sensible version." Very often, after Brecht had worked on verses for the piece, Feuchtwanger would have to redo them so they matched the gritty, irregular rhythm of the production.[21] Rehearsal scenes of masses of soldiers were left in Asja Lazis's highly competent hands. She worked with the actors to induce the kind of mechanical or puppetlike style that she had seen Meyerhold use so effectively in Moscow.

What was emerging in these complex rehearsals was a dearly won simplicity. It was, Fleisser noted, "*Moritaten* singer–like theater," in which Brecht used "disconcertingly simple and at the same time easily perceptible means that quietly sawed on one's nerves."[22] Here was theater for the senses as well as for the mind. Particularly powerful in Fleisser's recollection was the scene where the king was made to stand endlessly in a dungeon that doubled as the castle's sewage system. Between the theater audience and the caged king, Neher had hung a metal net. Each time Edward would lunge at this net as though pursuing his tormentors, he would then instantly leap back as though the net were electrified.

At various points, a singer would comment on what was going on in the life of the infatuated monarch. One song ran, "Eddy's whore has hair on his chest, pray for us, pray for us, pray for us." But the king, Bargan-like, ignored all warnings and declared to his lover, "Like that triangle of storks in the heavens that seem to stand still while flying, so there remains in us thy picture, undisturbed by time." Failing to convince the king to give up either his lover or his crown, his rival Mortimer has the king brutally assassinated.

The homosexual king's life, loves, and death in *Edward* would mark an end to this subject matter in the plays that Brecht would, with considerable help from others, complete in the years to come. Hereafter, it became exceedingly rare that Brecht's published work dealt with homosexuality in the ecstatic way it had previously. Both personally and professionally, he began, publicly at least, to distance himself from the homoerotic, though the magnetism he exerted on homosexual men never seems to have abated. However, a general shift in the treatment of sexuality itself was starting to take place even in *Edward*. The sexual drive was beginning to be seen as perhaps something that might need careful bridling if wholesale destruction (such as that of the entire kingdom of Britain in *Edward*) was to be avoided. The male sex drive would no longer be seen as the wholly positive, Dionysian life force portrayed, for instance, in *Baal*. In the years ahead, the male figures learn to control and use sex to their advantage rather than allowing it to run free and bring about their own destruction.

For all of the meticulousness and enormous cost of the months of rehearsals of *Edward*, on its opening night of March 18, 1924, not everything ran smoothly. Brecht was suspected of having provided liquor at intermission to Oskar Homolka, cast as the brutal Mortimer.[23] Homolka sat like a drunken zombie throughout the second half of the play. Lazis, as predicted, created a problem with her heavy accent. At the play's close, she was supposed to denounce Mortimer, her former lover and now murderer of her husband, by crying out "Mörder" in German. But the word that came out was closer to the French word "merde" (shit) than to "Mörder"!

At the party that followed at the Feuchtwangers', the hulking Homolka sat in a corner, where he was ignored. Leopold Jessner, who had come down to Munich specially for the performance, ate his dish of Bavarian swine's head with great relish. He was, as it turned out, so impressed with the play that he would schedule it at his own theater for next season in Berlin. Ihering was, as always, full of praise for his protégé. The descendant of the duke of Saxe-Meiningen, who had developed ensemble playing in Germany, turned up at the party. Marta Feuchtwanger noticed that while one group of young people rolled up the Feuchtwangers' big Oriental rug in their living room so dancing could begin, in a side room a lovely blond woman began to strip for Caspar Neher until he rudely turned her away.[24]

The play was generally a success with the more avant-garde critics, but with this limited support it would play only for a few days, leaving the Kammerspiel without the box-office returns it so critically needed. Brecht, however, had established his own personal style as a director. By stressing the chronicle-play style of the late sixteenth century, Brecht led the modern theater backwards toward the future. A direct presentational style of acting stripped away years of what he called contemptuously "the plaster monument style" of German stage production of the classics. For audiences, the result was electric. For the Kammerspiel, the result was near bankruptcy.

With his labors complete at the Kammerspiel, Brecht borrowed money from the Feuchtwangers and took off with Ma in mid-April for Capri. No sooner did they get there than Caspar Neher, minus his new wife, turned up. In a note to Weigel, Brecht mentioned that Cas had arrived. "Tomorrow I'm going off with him to Naples," he wrote, "where there are drinks, music, and syphilis."[25] Asja Lazis was in Naples without Bernhard Reich. In a note to Weigel, Brecht said that Marianne and "her child" (as he called his daughter, Hanne) would soon be joining Ma's mother in Austria to spend the rest of the summer. Of the child that Weigel was carrying, whom they had decided to call Pietro, he wrote, "I'm extraordinarily happy about you and Pietro. Will he be big and fat and funny? Will he sing, 'I have no bananas?' "

Leaving Ma on Capri, Bert and Cas crossed to the mainland to enjoy the pleasures of the harbor dives of Positano, where the lovely Asja Lazis was staying. With Lazis also being wooed by another importunate German the then largely unknown Walter Benjamin, Brecht met Helene Weigel and "Pietro" in Florence. From here, she went to Berlin to prepare for the birth of the baby and Brecht to Augsburg to try to write a new play for the fall season in Berlin.

That summer, Munich had been following the "trial" of Adolf Hitler and General Ludendorff for their part in the November 9 coup attempt. But as the trial had developed, the "defendant" Hitler put his accusers on trial for not doing enough for the *Vaterland*. In his theatrical closing oration, Hitler declaimed, "May you declare us guilty a thousand times; the goddess of the eternal court will smile and gently tear in two the brief of the State Prosecutor and the verdict of the court; for she aquits [sic] us."[26] The court largely agreed with Hitler. Ludendorff was acquitted altogether. Hitler, having instigated an interchange that led to the deaths of at least seventeen and to the wounding of numerous others on November 8 and 9, was given a maximum sentence of five years but declared eligible for parole after six months.

Hitler served his sentence only until December 20, 1924, in kingly splendor at the fortress of Landsberg, in one of the loveliest landscapes in all Germany. He took his meals at the head of a kind of English university–style high table, decorated always with a swastika flag, while fellow prisoners cleaned his room. He was allowed to receive countless visitors and had leisure enough to write *Mein Kampf*, a book drenched in "images of puberty: copulation, sodomy, perversion, rape, contamination of the blood."[27]

Hitler was released from jail the next year with a new book and a new, less radical image fostered by his supporters. He quickly established his own nattily attired bodyguard, or *Schutzstaffel*, called the SS for short. Others might laugh at such pretentiousness, but Hitler was fully aware of the increased theatrical effectiveness of his arrivals and

departures in a large Mercedes, with black-clad, jackbooted men surrounding him. Image, as he had seen from Mussolini, and from Barnum
and Bailey on their European tours, was 90 percent of the battle.

After a spring holiday with her husband in deceptively calm Italy,
Marianne was erroneously convinced she would be moving to Berlin
with Bert and their child. She asked for Gustav Kiepenheuer's help in
finding a suitable flat, "a four- or five-room place, preferably unfur-
nished, on the first floor, sunny and dry, with a bath and a separate
kitchen."[28] The rent, she said, should not be more than one hundred
marks. Frau Brecht-Zoff's letter put Herr Kiepenheuer and his staff in a
most awkward position. Weigel, growing large with Pietro, made it
appear that Brecht might be making different arrangements than those
his legal wife was contemplating. Kiepenheuer, who had been paying
Brecht regularly despite the playwright's other sources of income, was
not interested in discussing Brecht's living arrangements. He wanted to
know when Brecht would deliver the long overdue poetry manuscripts
called for in his contract. When the inflation had been at its worst,
Kiepenheuer had paid Brecht what was then a fortune in Germany,
twenty American dollars. Even so, as Kiepenheuer wrote to his second
in command, Brecht's friend Hermann Kasack, "Brecht hasn't sent
anything yet; I'm involved in looking for an apartment for the two of
them."

Brecht was no more working on the poetry volume than he was
seriously interested in sharing an apartment with Hanne and Ma in
Berlin. He had returned to a draft of something called *Galgei*, which he
first worked on with Orge Pfanzelt in 1918. *Galgei* had originally been
set in Augsburg but became more exotic over the years. A man with the
name of Brown appeared together with "beasts of prey." Brown then
murdered a man called Matti as "God left for Chicago" while the sky
above (originally merely "violet" in 1918) displayed "the cruel constel-
lations." Brecht had been reading German translations of Kipling, Jensen, and Chesterton's Father Brown detective stories. By 1924, the
character of galgei (lowercase now as Brecht had adopted Bronnen's
orthography) was hanging out in Saipong, a vaguely Anglo-Indian setting based on German translations of Kipling's stories about "Mama,"
Kipling's nickname for the British Army in India.

In a discarded early version of this play, a character called bak asks
galgei, "have you ever handled a woman with paprika i'll never forget
how a woman once bit me on the tit because i didn't beat her long
enough." To which galgei replies, "she liked your beating did she?"

BAK: that's not so uncommon but don't put on an act with me i
bet you're just as ready to give your flesh its head in that sort of

situation don't tell me a man with a face like yours isn't sensitive to the impressions one can pick up in gents' urinals say.

GALGEI: i must tell you that in the circumstances i find it difficult to put up with your remarks.

BAK: take a good look at your innermost self do you feel any impulse say to hit me in the face?

GALGEI: just a fleeting one.

BAK: look the other way i get too excited when you look at me excuse me.

We are also told that "every spring blood has to flow," and one character urges: "jabyourknifeintohimjackhiphiphurrah."[29] As Brecht knew, and so described the work, *Galgei* was "a sex murder story." It was also a rough-trade sex murder story of an explicit kind. As in other plays written while he was part of a male clique, there is the explicit excitement of the homoerotic. Again, women are marginalized, brutalized, and made to appear to enjoy male brutality toward them.

In late August, Brecht wrote to Helene Weigel in Berlin, complaining that she had not written enough to him. He felt very much alone. He had roughed out, he claimed, four acts of *Galgei*. "What I have is satisfying, some of it good,"[30] he wrote. In fact, he could not complete it on his own at all, and the Augsburg friends he had always counted on to help him with his writing were no longer available. By the summer of 1924, he did manage to line up a new position in Berlin when he was offered a year's contract as dramaturge with the world-famous director Max Reinhardt.

Though Brecht was now finally moving to Berlin, he still had his place in Augsburg, where his father could afford to keep an apartment and servants always ready for the visits of his famous son in the years to come. To further ease his transition to "cold Chicago," he persuaded the youngest maid in his father's household, the pert, pretty Mari Hold, to join him there to run his household exactly as he wanted it, keeping strictly to the Augsburg model of his childhood and youth.

"A Woman Must Give Up a Lot"
(1924–25)

The move to Berlin had been prepared with Brecht's usual mixture of boldness and wariness. He was shedding much of the baggage of earlier days, silently dropping Marianne, the new baby, and "family life," but still very much hoping to keep Ma available as at least an occasional sexual partner. Gone now too was Bie. He had told Ma, falsely, that it was his wish, not Bie's, that she marry someone else. Little Frank would be shunted from one foster home to another until his teens. Gone also was Orge, who had had the temerity to ask that Brecht recognize his love and his contributions to "Brecht's" poetry. But while shedding some leftovers, there would be much that he kept as he made his circumspect move to the northern city: his parental home would remain as a refuge, and his father's money would continue to be available.

Brecht established himself in a kind of small south German enclave in the middle of cold Berlin, surrounding himself wherever possible with friends and acquaintances from Augsburg, Munich, and Austria. Cas was now in Berlin full-time, though he was rarely available to help Brecht with writing new plays. Cas had his hands full with productions at major theaters throughout Germany and Austria. Similarly, Bronnen was very busy with his new work and unwilling to be at Brecht's beck and call twenty-four hours a day. Feuchtwanger had largely abandoned writing plays in favor of a series of best-selling historical novels.

Helene Weigel, now very round with "Pietro," had virtually no ability as a writer. Even her letters usually have a wooden, wholly unimaginative quality about them. But she was determined to make herself invaluable to Brecht in other ways. Unlike Marianne, Weigel sensed that establishing distance from Brecht might be the best means of keeping him close. She gave him her Spichernstrasse flat to save him the trouble of looking for his own, something he had never been able to do. With its slanting ceilings, the Spichernstrasse flat echoed the Bleichstrasse. Weigel, always immensely practical, found herself another place nearby at 52 Babelsbergerstrasse. Brecht could come and go at Weigel's on his own schedule. There he could relax amidst Biedermeier furniture similar to that with which he had grown up and could rely on getting good Viennese cooking.

Brecht's pretty maid, Mari "Peppi" Hold, repeated the rituals she had first learned as a fourteen-year-old in the Brecht household, even dressing in his clothes for him at his request. Before the master was up, she took out the ashes and relit the stoves, brought in the milk and the newspaper, and put on water to boil for his tea. She brought him the newspaper in his bedroom, opened the drapes, and every few days, brought him hot shaving water. For breakfast, there would be the hot porridge that only she could successfully make, together with a steaming cup of tea. As he was very finicky about cold, she had to light the stove in his study as early as possible so that he would feel warm when he sat down at his desk for his customary few hours of morning work. Visitors of both sexes would come by in the course of the day, occasionally asking "who is that lovely girl?" and he would proudly reply that she, like him, came from Bavaria. Late at night, Mari would serve the visitors sandwiches and drinks, and keep the ashtrays from overflowing. When the last guest was gone and Brecht was back in bed and she had closed his drapes, she aired out the other rooms for the next day.[1]

With Mari Hold's and Helene Weigel's assistance, Brecht remained, as Klaus Völker has aptly described his lifelong living arrangements, "bound to Augsburg and his parents' home."[2] He even found a tailor who had moved to Berlin from Augsburg, a man who was delighted to outfit Brecht and his various mistresses at special rates. He would hand make "self-consciously ordinary and shabby-looking" clothes for Brecht.[3] For the mistresses, he made up a special overcoat of merino wool. What was true for daytime wear also applied to sleepwear. Brecht required that women acquire a supply of the long, white Mother Hubbard nightgowns that the maids and his mother had worn in Augsburg.

Brecht's new job at Max Reinhardt's Deutsches Theater proved ideal for his purposes. He met the leading personalities in the Berlin theater and read all the scripts with all the new ideas. The job also gave him access to Reinhardt's various theaters, where experiments were being conducted not only with the more modern texts but also with staging techniques for mass spectacles of epic proportions.

His fellow dramaturge was the playwright and cabaret performer Carl Zuckmayer. Zuckmayer would arrive at the Deutsches Theater in the morning with the day's newspapers and a large empty briefcase. He would wrap up the coal briquettes placed there to heat his office and exit. Brecht appeared less often than the coal-carrying Zuckmayer. When Brecht did come, he looked in his oversize leather jacket, Zuckmayer noted, "like a cross between a truck driver and a Jesuit seminarian." Brecht demanded that all powers be transferred to him "so that he could mould the repertoire entirely according to his own ideas." When Reinhardt rejected his demand, Brecht "confined his activity to occasional appearances to collect his salary."[4]

Brecht was free to pursue his own projects and make all kinds of subsidiary income-producing deals. Not having written the volume of poems that he had already been paid a fortune for, he got Kiepenheuer to accept *Edward II* as a kind of temporary substitute. This had required some fast semilegal footwork. His coauthor, Feuchtwanger, was under contract to another publisher. For Brecht to meet his obligation to his publisher and for Feuchtwanger to avoid his obligation to his, it was agreed that only Brecht's name would appear on the cover of the book. Buried inside, in small letters that might be easily overlooked, was the acknowledgment: "I wrote this play with Lion Feuchtwanger." No mention was made of "borrowings" from Heymel's translation. Pleading poverty and claiming he was contributing toward the support of several households, Brecht persuaded Feuchtwanger, who had but one wife and no children, to waive his royalties.

Knowledgeable people were aware of the sleight of hand that had been involved in removing Feuchtwanger's name, but it was not a sufficiently important matter for anyone to get excited. Jessner, having seen and liked the play in Munich, decided to put it on in Berlin but was not willing to engage the slow, expensive, gifted, and demanding Brecht as the director. Instead, Jessner used Jürgen Fehling, his own reliable, talented staff person. Erwin Faber, who had played the title role under Brecht's direction, was hired. Brecht attended Fehling's rehearsals but shouted that everything was "Scheisse [shit]!" Fehling retorted that Brecht was the apostle of "Dünnschisstheater"—"diarrhea theater."[5] With Fehling and Brecht at scatological odds, Feuchtwanger was asked to tame his coauthor. "Do you always have to say *Scheisse?*" Feuchtwanger asked. "Couldn't you perhaps say instead: That is too stylized?"[6] Brecht soon was shouting that everything was too stylized. Fehling barred both authors from rehearsals. The show closed rapidly, the fate of virtually all Brecht productions until *The Threepenny Opera* in 1928.

Toward the end of 1924, Erich Engel, who had directed *Jungle* in Munich, was asked to direct its Berlin premiere for the Deutsches Theater. Engel was happy to have Brecht attend rehearsals and become essentially his co-director. The two would often co-direct productions of Brecht plays from now on, frequently using set designs by Caspar Neher. *Jungle* opened on October 29. As usual, Ihering was full of praise. Kerr dismissed it as "wholly worthless junk" and charged Brecht with plagiarism.[7] Garga, he pointed out, spoke passage after passage taken from a German translation of Rimbaud. In his guarded reply to this most serious charge, Brecht claimed that performance provided no opportunity for quotation marks. Fortunately for him, the play was not yet in print, and so his argument was accepted. If the Berlin critics now began to recognize he had stolen from copyrighted sources, he would either have to pay for the "borrowings" or find a less obvious way to lift things from foreign sources.

On November 3 (an unfortunate date, the second anniversary of Brecht's marriage to Zoff), Weigel gave birth to a baby boy. With Brecht still married to Ma, the child was given the name Stefan Sebastian Weigel. Brecht had no more time for this child than for the others. He would visit, and he would play rather nicely with the child for a brief time but then disappear again.

By late 1924, most of the old Munich crowd of cultural figures had moved to Berlin, hoping to get away from the brownshirts, swastikas, and open anti-Semitism in Munich. When the Feuchtwangers moved to Berlin, Brecht could again hang out at their apartment. He also spent time exploring Berlin's lively and varied brothel life, and went to lots of parties with the literary and theatrical crowd. Since his first visit to Berlin, he had continued his pursuit of Dora Mannheim, the "hula dancer" whom he had first met in 1919. At her flat, a group of literary folk would sometimes gather, and she liked to have Brecht over as one of Berlin's emerging stars. Shortly after the birth of Stefan, Brecht attended a party at Mannheim's flat. Among her other guests that particular evening was a twenty-seven-year-old writer and translator by the name of Elisabeth Hauptmann, a highly intelligent woman, strikingly lovely and beautifully dressed, with enormous brown eyes and glossy, short, beautifully waved brown hair.

Elisabeth Hauptmann, though having arrived fairly recently in Berlin from a tiny town in Westphalia, had about her a cosmopolitan elegance. Her father had held the title of *Hofrat* (privy councillor) at the Prussian court, and her mother, Josephine Diestelhorst, was a former concert pianist who had grown up in the bilingual setting of an Austrian immigrant family in Brooklyn. In the early 1890s, she came to Europe and met and married her distant cousin, Privy Councillor Clemens Hauptmann. They settled in the tiny town of Peckelsheim where the *Hofrat* took over his father's medical practice. The three children of this marriage grew up amidst the values and practices of the prewar Prussian nobility. As at the imperial court itself, the children were expected to be proficient in English, German, and French. They also learned a very great deal about music, playing regularly, and learning standard musical notation. Until the war broke out in 1914, the children spent each summer on the Isle of Wight, where they spoke only English.

Elisabeth had shown great creativity and aptitude for study. Her mother encouraged her, but her father did not. Though the one boy in the family flunked out of the gymnasium, ran up gambling debts, and showed far more interest in hunting and fraternity life than study; nevertheless, he was the only one sent on to the university, while receiving brutal beatings from his father along the way. With an understatement that she seemed to have learned along with her beautiful English, Hauptmann observed of the mixture of brutality and discrimination with which she had grown up: "It was all not very nice."[8]

At the end of World War I, Bess (as she was called at home) got jobs as a private tutor on the local landed estates. Irma, her sister, married and moved to America. Elisabeth also tried to leave. She desperately wanted to be allowed to study and to become a writer, preferably in Berlin. But her father did not approve of such ideas for women.

She went to Berlin anyway in 1922, financing her education and starting her career largely on her own. Her mother had only a little of her own money to provide help to her daughter. The only jobs offered to Hauptmann in Berlin were secretarial, tutorial, and dead-end translation jobs. She found that her income from these bits and pieces was not enough to support her in her studies. Alone and lonely at first in Berlin, she gradually began to make friends among other young women in similar positions, such as Dora Mannheim.

At Dora Manheim's party, Hauptmann reacted to Brecht as so many other men and women had. He was famous, charismatic, sexy, and deeply interested in literature—particularly the American, British, and French literature she knew best. And despite his mistress and new baby in Berlin, his largely abandoned wife and baby, as well as another mistress and baby in south Germany, he was very much available for a new relationship. He could receive visitors at any time of the day or night without having to explain anything to Weigel, Marianne, or anyone else.

Bess Hauptmann and Bert Brecht, with their Americanized first names, became a curious couple with as many divergent interests and attitudes as shared ones. She was well dressed, obviously cultured, soft spoken, and well organized. He, despite a decent income from his own earnings and from his family, and with the daily ministrations of Mari Hold, dressed and acted tough, and appeared to be in a continual state of chaos. Under her tutelage, though he did not get rid of his leather and corduroy outfits, he did buy a number of winter and summer suits, a fashionable trilby, a regular overcoat to go with the new hat, and a supply of silk shirts and ties. Topping off this impression of elegance, instead of always smoking a stinking cigar, he was now sometimes seen extracting a cigarette from an engraved silver cigarette case she had given him. His whiskey came from a small silver hip flask. They addressed one another using expressions from Karl May known to every German child. She became the "chief's girl," while he was the "chief." Over the winter of 1924–25, the "chief" had used his personal magnetism almost magically to assemble an entire tribe who dropped in at his apartment in much the same way he had gathered the youth of Augsburg around him in years past. Among those seen frequently at the Spichernstrasse flat were the writer and boxer Emil Hesse Burri, whom Brecht had first met in Munich. Burri introduced Brecht to the national light-heavyweight champion, Paul Samson-Körner, who became a regular source of inside information on boxing. Like the Berlin wine salesman Joachim von Ribbentrop, Brecht was now part of the tough world of professional fighters. Caspar Neher occasionally stopped by the Spichernstrasse, though most of his increasingly successful work was now with other writers and directors. Bernhard Reich and Asja Lazis came too, bringing a whiff of the tough world of Soviet artists and agents of the Comintern.

After a few hours of work with Hauptmann at his apartment each morning, Brecht left to pursue his other affairs. Hauptmann often continued until very late at night, finding new material and turning the bits and pieces produced during the morning into a coherent whole. She kept her own apartment but had a special phone installed as an answering service for him. He seemed to her to be in need of a kind of mother-wife. He was inept in dealing with the demands of everyday domestic life. He was terrified of doctors and would not even go to a dentist without someone to accompany him. When ill, usually with a flare-up of the kidney trouble that had landed him in the Charité, she prepared a sitz bath for him and stayed with him as he soaked.

Seeing him daily, Hauptmann saw how difficult it was for Brecht to complete anything, particularly if it was longer than about twenty lines of verse. Poetry came naturally, but plays usually came only very slowly and with vast amounts of help from friends. Years later, he would tell both Eric Bentley and James Schevill that he really was a poet not a playwright.[9] He often had good ideas for plays, but somehow, as in the case of Hannibal and Galgei, after a fine start, he would be unable to complete the work. The loss of Orge and Lud, and Cas's distance had disrupted his working rhythm, and he had not yet reestablished it in Berlin. Except for the Edward II adaptation done with Feuchtwanger, he had not finished a play in three years. But he remained as brash as ever, declaring himself the one true hope of the German stage and disparaging established writers.

Like a conjurer leading his audience to concentrate on his right hand while the trick was being done with the left, Brecht was able to convince the general public that he was writing. He could not fool Hauptmann. With love and despair, she observed in her diary in 1926: "If I could get Brecht to do what I wanted, then I would first ensure that he become 1 cm fatter all around. That, second, he get a different, less provisional apartment. I would also like to get him to work on something proper, something longer—not just on essays and so on, short things, scraps, the half-finished."[10] But when he continued to work on essays and "scraps," Hauptmann found herself writing things almost wholly on her own and then, with Brecht's wholehearted approval, sending these items to theaters and publishers as genuine "Brecht" products.

After Brecht met Hauptmann, the British critic John Willett notes a tremendous improvement in the skill with which English language sources are used in work published under Brecht's name. Speaking of work derived from English-language sources (though this, in my opinion, is far too restrictive, as Hauptmann was similarly involved with French-language originals), Willett notes that from late 1924 on, "after Hauptmann met Brecht, it is often difficult to know who wrote exactly what."[11] Sometimes, very rarely and very privately, Brecht himself admits that his own role in the creation of a work was not central. As John Willett has noted, in late 1925, Brecht sent Hauptmann the bound typescript of the play *A Man's a Man* that they had worked on together throughout 1925. Brecht said in his cover note: "It was a troublesome play, and even piecing the manuscript together from 20 lb of paper was heavy work; it took me 2 days, ½ a bottle of brandy, 4 bottles of soda water, 8–10 cigars and a lot of patience, and it was the only part I did on my own."[12] Characteristically, though he admitted privately his own work had mainly been editorial, the note was not published.

Close examination of the manuscript trail makes it clear that by 1925 the work of Hauptmann and Brecht had become totally intertwined, and he regularly took over her work as his own. For instance, a short, and subsequently very famous, piece, "The Benares Song," is written in Brecht's hand but underneath Hauptmann wrote at the time, "By Hauptmann. Brecht's handwriting."[13] Likewise, the equally well-known "Alabama Song" is in Hauptmann's hand and notated "English by Hauptmann." These handwritten notations raise a fundamental problem with identification of texts of which Brecht may be assumed to be the author. If, as in the case of "The Benares Song," a work can be in Brecht's hand and yet still be "by Hauptmann," as Hauptmann herself originally claimed and as John Willett agrees, then handwriting per se is not enough to define a text as being by one person or by the other. If this is true of handwritten work, what is then to be done with typewritten texts? Even though we know there are ways of telling from the strike pattern whether it was Hauptmann, Brecht, or a third party who did the actual typing, that does not rule out the possibility that one person dictated it to the other seated at the typewriter. In light of all this, and after examining tens of thousand of pages of material from the Brecht workshop at different stages of his life, it is my carefully considered opinion that we need to pay attention not only to the handwriting or strike pattern in typewritten texts but to a whole array of other markers in the texts, as well as to external markers such as whether he was physically present when much of the work was being done.

Given the basic fact that much published as Brecht over the years is clearly based on materials drawn from other languages, one of the most obvious questions always will be whether it was Brecht or someone else who had the linguistic skills necessary to do the work from originals in other languages. As we have already seen, and as we shall see again and again, usually Brecht was not the person with the requisite knowledge of original languages. Another important internal clue as to probable authorship of any given text is, I believe, the thematic orientation of the work. Hauptmann and her female successors in years to come will, as we shall see, consistently build around a central woman in virtually all work published under their own names. Equally consistently, when Brecht is alone and writes poems or drafts sections of play texts on his own, he usually gravitates toward material that has a central and often violent, misogynist male figure like (as we have seen) Baal, Bargan, or (as we shall see later) Mack the Knife of *The Threepenny Opera*, or, in Brecht's last years, the rapist Garbe in the incomplete play of that name.

I believe that the best plays published under the Brecht label in the years ahead combine the talents of the primary writers in a dramatically effective playing off of one point of view against the other. It is this internal contrast and conflict, I believe, that often raises the work to an entirely new level of universality. Plays they do together, almost as parents jointly conceiving a child, are, in my view, at a level well above that of Brecht working alone, or of Hauptmann alone or each of her successors alone.

If Hauptmann's hand is found frequently in "Brecht" plays, poems, and songs from early 1925 on, her contribution to Brecht short stories in the Berlin years also seems astonishingly large. After examining the original manuscripts of "Brecht" short stories of the 1920s, John Willett conservatively notes, "The major responsibility was quite likely to be Hauptmann's."[14] The original manuscripts, notes Willett, often show few or "no marks of Brecht's hand." Willett thinks it likely that at least seven of the eleven short stories that comprise what he still calls "Brecht's Berlin stories" are Hauptmann's. What is true of "Brecht's

Berlin stories" applies also to a number of "Brecht" poems from late 1924 on.

Later in the twenties, as we shall see, huge sections of some of the most famous "Brecht" plays and large sections of new dramaturgical theories are clearly written by Hauptmann. The body of work known as the *Lehrstücke*—"learning" or "teaching plays"—is unthinkable without her, as are major texts such as *Saint Joan of the Stockyards* and, as noted, the final form of *A Man's a Man*. Indeed, the manuscript and biographical evidence strongly indicates, as we will see later, that even the most famous text of them all (and certainly the biggest money-maker), *The Threepenny Opera*, is overwhelmingly her work. After World War II, most of the play adaptations done in Berlin are over-whelmingly Hauptmann's work, with Brecht's participation in the writing marginal at best.

Unless one was physically present, of course, it is difficult to say with total certainty who did what many years ago in the Brecht collective. But the surviving body of manuscript and internal thematic evidence of plays, poems, and short stories written between early 1925 and the fall of Weimar in early 1933 and published as Brecht texts, and scores of eyewitness accounts and contemporaneous documents such as diaries and contracts show clear evidence of Hauptmann's role in creating works published to this day as authentic "Brecht." And, as we will see, the shift in "Brecht's" treatment of women from early 1925 on is exactly congruent with the themes central to those works Hauptmann would insist on publishing under her own name.

Hauptmann herself, with her usual classical, almost British, under-statement, would sometimes admit to what she had done in creating "Brecht" texts. Driven to a suicide attempt in the 1950s by statements by Brecht that she knew to be "wrong from the ground up," she would note: "Up until thirty-three I either wrote or wrote down most of the poems. There was hardly anyone else there who wrote. Hardly anyone to provide material, no one else from January '25 on."[15] For once partially dropping her protective stance toward Brecht as playwright, she said in a Berlin interview in 1970 that her contributions to some of the *Lehrstücke* was as high as 80 percent.[16] Astounding though this claim appeared at the time, I believe that manuscript and other written and oral evidence of the period shows that in her interviews with me she radically understated the scope and magnitude of her contributions.

Unless one has the actual drafts of poems and plays, it is difficult to reconstruct the creation process for work produced many years ago. But despite the havoc of years of war and exile, and the radical censor-ship that marked attempts at real scholarship in the German Demo-cratic Republic, ample evidence has survived to show Hauptmann's contribution to a large number of works published under Brecht's name. In 1925, for instance, we can clearly trace how she began to turn out a series of beautiful renderings of some of Kipling's most difficult dialect verse. This would not have been possible for Brecht, whose knowledge of English was, as his close friend Hans Otto Münsterer pointed out, "next to nothing."[17] Hauptmann, however, with a mother raised in Brooklyn, had spoken English often while growing up and thereby acquired a fine grasp of the nuances of English.[18] Another clear indication of Hauptmann's role in translating Kipling is the type of material selected. Brecht seems consistently drawn to those Kipling poems that are dominated by what one critic has called "a gospel of violence [that] leads nowhere except to more violence."[19] Hauptmann, the surviving evidence indicates, gravitated toward those that show compassion for women in a violent, male-dominated world.

Professor James K. Lyon, an authority on Brecht's poetry, notes of Hauptmann's renditions of Kipling: "Brecht liked her translations."[20] "In fact," Lyon continues, "[Brecht] made relatively few changes in her texts of 'The Ladies,' 'Cholera Camp,' or 'Mary, Pity Women,' the only ones where her preliminary translations are available for comparison."[21] Though Hauptmann must be credited with fully 80 to 90 percent of the text of the Kipling adaptations, "The Ladies" came out in the magazine Die Dame in 1927 under Brecht's name. List Verlag did the same with "Cholera Camp" and "Mary, Pity Women." When Lyon asked Hauptmann why she had allowed this, she said, "she intentionally omitted her name because Brecht's alone carried more weight."[22]

That Hauptmann, very much in love with Brecht and hoping to marry him, wrote a staggeringly large quantity of what was sold as though Brecht were the primary author might seem an aberration in literary history, but it may not be as exceptional as it first appears. There are, for instance, at least two striking and well-documented parallels from the same general period of American literature. Several critics have argued that credit for the famous Little House on the Prairie book series should be shared by the ostensible author, Laura Ingalls Wilder, and her largely forgotten daughter, Rose Wilder Lane. We also know that at least one of F. Scott Fitzgerald's most typical short stories, a piece called "The Millionaire's Girl," was actually written in 1929 by the now largely forgotten Zelda Fitzgerald. Though Fitzgerald's literary agent, Harold Ober, learned the story was by Zelda,[23] he still recommended publishing it as an F. Scott piece in The Saturday Evening Post. His reasons were simple enough. As usual, F. Scott Fitzgerald owed him money and sent him more excuses than work to be sold. The Post, Ober knew, would pay $4,000 (a fortune in the wreck of the economy after the Wall Street collapse), for one F. Scott story. However, if the same piece appeared in the journal *College Humor* where Ober had been selling Zelda's work (sometimes retouched by F. Scott) under the byline "By F. Scott and Zelda Fitzgerald," the going price would be $800. Under these circumstances, Zelda went along with the deception. Delighted with this source of income, F. Scott boasted to Hemingway that he, the "old whore," was being paid "4,000 a screw" by the *Post*.[24] He added in another note, "My mind is the loose cunt of a whore, to fit all genitals."[25] More accurately perhaps, he might have described himself as literary pimp, living off his wife's $4,000 "screw."

Within months of the agreement to have her story appear in the *Post* under her husband's name (the most egregious of a whole series of deceptions concerning her authorship of stories about various women and their difficulties),[26] Zelda Fitzgerald began to exhibit the signs of extraordinary mental distress that would lead to her incarceration and eventual death in an institution. Zelda Fitzgerald allowing her own creative efforts to be published under her more-famous husband's name precisely parallels what happened to Hauptmann. Brecht, like F. Scott Fitzgerald, was having trouble finishing work, and Hauptmann, like Zelda Fitzgerald, knew that the fees paid would be considerably higher if she allowed Brecht to publish her work under his more famous name. In Rose Wilder Lane's case, as she initially viewed her mother's work as juvenilia that might possibly damage her own reputation as an author of adult works; and as the books were published as though they were authentic accounts of her mother's childhood, the daughter's position in not wanting her ghostwriting to be recognized is perhaps readily understandable.

In all these cases, which I would subsume under the heading "The Zelda Syndrome," the literary establishment turned a blind eye to what was widespread deception. Such marketing practices, often—but not always—involving a woman who was then promptly forgotten, would be as readily practiced in prewar New York as in Paris or Berlin or nominally socialist Moscow and the postwar German Democratic Republic.[27]

From late 1924 on, Brecht was delighted to have someone who provided both sex and text, especially since her salary was paid by Kiepenheuer. Hauptmann, in the first flush of artistic and sexual excitement, saw it all as more pleasure than work. In his atelier, she was at the center of the Berlin literary life that she had yearned to enter. Though there were other lovers—Caspar Neher, Helene Weigel, Gerda Müller, Asja Lazis, and Arnolt Bronnen (to name only the most enduring ones)—Hauptmann felt she was the real center of both his personal and professional life. Brecht, a virtuoso of such arrangements, encouraged her to think so, pointing to the unhappiness of his marriage with Ma and his efforts to end it. He would declare he would never marry Weigel. Playing an even older card in his increasingly dog-eared deck, he took Hauptmann home the next summer to meet his father. Surely that meant his intentions toward her were honorable and serious? He wrote her private notes expressing his deep appreciation of her work as a writer, admitting privately that he often contributed the lesser part to work published under his name. Hauptmann, now twenty-eight, hoped that after his divorce from Ma they could marry and together reshape modern poetry and the theater.

But with Brecht's constant stream of other affairs and his inability to finish "a long, real piece of work," Hauptmann lived constantly with what she called in 1926 "fear in the belly." He continued to be superb with small items, the striking and brutal individual scene of a *Hannibal* or *Galgei*, or the very singable songs that could be added to a play to give it greater zest. But for the first four years in Berlin, no really new Brecht plays would be completed. For almost the entire period Brecht spent in Berlin before Hitler would come to full power in early 1933, the plays he was most interested in—*Joe Fleischhacker*, which, though often promised to producers, would remain little more than a sketch; a similarly incomplete play about international deals in wheat called *Weizen*, the fragment *Der Brotladen* (The breadshop); and, finally, the several hundred inchoate pages of the violent *Fatzer*, whose title hero in the 1930 version would still pursue a woman as a "hairy hole"—would never be finished.

It was fortunate for Brecht that, immediately after Hauptmann's arrival, the plays, poems and short stories that she worked on did get finished. At the same time, there was (as we see over and over again) a steady transformation of the content and range of what was completed in the workshop. Her choice of specific Kipling poems dealing with women is symptomatic of a general shift in "Brecht." Women's roles become steadily richer, positive, and three-dimensional. And, at the same time, we begin to see sovereign, wholly assured adaptations of English language originals (and, to a somewhat lesser extent, French also), which reveal someone who so deeply understands the original language that she can create a similarly nuanced German adaptation.

While Hauptmann took on more of the writing, Brecht saw himself as fighting a desperate battle against the older, more entrenched members of the literary establishment. Trying to even up the odds a bit, Brecht got together in 1925 with a group of other young men (no women were enlisted) who were trying to make it in Berlin publishing and theater. The group called themselves simply Group 1925. It included Expressionist poet Johannes R. Becher; poet, cabaret performer, and playwright Klabund; novelist and physician Alfred Döblin; satirist Kurt Tucholsky; novelist Egon Kisch; and former Spartacist Rudolf Leonhard. Carl Zuckmayer was asked to join, but he declined, telling Brecht: "For you, a collective is a group of intelligent people who contribute that which one person wants, namely you." Brecht chuckled and agreed.[28]

Brecht's first year in Berlin was not bad financially. Besides his stipend from Reinhardt's theater organization, he managed to continue to string Kiepenheuer along. But that deal became shakier and shakier as he sold short workshop artifacts to other publishers but still failed to deliver the work he owed to Kiepenheuer. By mid-1925, he was negotiating a new deal. He managed to persuade the giant publisher Ullstein to buy up both the Kiepenheuer and the equally overdue Dreimasken contract. He claimed that he was leaving Kiepenheuer because one of the firm's backers was attempting to censor a volume of Brecht's poetry. However, the archives of the Kiepenheuer firm show Brecht's story was a lie.

By leaving Kiepenheuer, Brecht cut off Hauptmann's only regular source of income and made her directly dependent on him, a practice he followed with collaborators, usually women, throughout his life. Frequently, he gave Hauptmann little or nothing from earnings now more and more often derived from works of which she was the principal author. She was forced to borrow from Lion Feuchtwanger.

Brecht bragged to Helene Weigel about his new deal. Not only had he managed to get Ullstein to agree to pay him five hundred marks a month, but he also managed to exclude from the deal plays that he "wrote with others." Consequently, Elisabeth Hauptmann's name (though in very small letters) would begin to appear on some of the works. His new deal was, as Brecht boasted, "a rare instance of an author exploiting Ullstein."[29] For Ullstein (publishers of a string of sleazy magazines, among other things), support of the Kleist Prize winner was a public relations move that made sound business sense. For Hauptmann, credit for published work, even in tiny letters at first, gave her hope of later breaking into Berlin publishing in her own right.

Perhaps because she was becoming so valuable, Brecht both praised and denigrated her. Typical of this mixed feeling is a short piece called "Fat Ham," published in mid-1925. Brecht authority Klaus Völker claims the "Fat Ham" story "described the appearance and physical characteristics of his faithful assistant but also paid tribute to her indispensable help in difficult times."[30] Ham's role aboard the ark in the story is to use his fat rear end to plug leaks that he had left in the craft at the time it was built.[31] Ham is also compared to an ass. Almost certainly conflating "Maultier" (mule) and the separate breed "Esel" (ass), Brecht says an ass plugs a gap left in creation. What this slender, intelligent, creative woman thought of this portrait is not known. Quite apart from its concealed misogyny (one needs Völker's key to the story to see the male Ham as the female Hauptmann), the story is sympto-matic of Brecht's need to denigrate people.[32] He does this throughout his life, behind the backs of friends, lovers, and colleagues, and through demeaning parable and metaphor. To Weigel, he denigrates Zoff. To Zoff, he denigrates Weigel. When Hauptmann enters the picture and she becomes essential in that previously exclusively male domain, the creation of the texts, a new need arises in him. Though he may grudg-ingly acknowledge that the ship of the texts would neither exist nor stay afloat without her, there are great dangers to him should she choose to move from her position.

As Hauptmann's role in Brecht's personal and professional life grew, so did Marianne's concern about it. Ma, like Hauptmann herself, assumed Brecht was planning to make Hauptmann his wife. When Ma wrote to complain about this new woman, Brecht complained about her letter, saying it was "unintelligent and unfriendly."[33] He went on to say he was no more involved with Elisabeth Hauptmann than he was with Gustav Kiepenheuer. Given Brecht's past history of bisexuality even this may have been true, but it was a wholly inadequate response to Ma's legitimate concern.

Ma had grown more skilled in spotting his lies and now set down a general evaluation of him. "When I experience something bitter," she wrote to herself, "I always think, now that's the worst, but it is never the worst. Always there is more to be angry about. That Brecht is half-mad and a half-fool is bad. Worse is people's talk as they joke about him, 'He doesn't seem to have anything else in his head than filling new books and new women, never two children from one. From each one, one, that's funny.' I think to myself, what will my daughter say to that when she is more grown up and hears such things."[34] Noting how far she has declined in her own estimation, she takes hold of her self, concluding: "But this much I know, I will work day and night in order not to have to take anything from a man who is suddenly more a stranger to me than anybody else, from a fool with whom I still have some sympathy because his star is starting to sink."

As Marianne now "began to take my hand away from his, but with tears on my face," she began to restart her career. In 1925, she got a singing engagement for the fall in the town of Münster, about six hours by train from Berlin. It would pay her a monthly salary of 550 marks. Frantic at signs of incipient mutiny, Brecht wrote his usual letters mixing attack with blandishment. He denied his relationship with Wei-gel was of importance and that the existence of the baby Stefan took anything away from Hanne. While demanding that Ma write often, he claimed her letters were "slovenly, ill considered, and complaining, and written only when you want money. . . . If I get three more letters like your last ones, I will begin to wonder if you have lost your reason."[35] Then he turned around and begged her at least to let them get together for part of the summer. Despite the stream of insults and her own intuition, Marianne agreed.

In June, after a series of delays caused, he said, by his contract negotiations to leave Kiepenheuer for Ullstein, he left Berlin with Hauptmann in what was to be a typically tightly scheduled round of affairs. Weigel, perhaps knowing he planned to take Hauptmann with him to Augsburg, had gone to Munich for a guest engagement as Marie in Büchner's *Woyzeck*. Hauptmann and Brecht stopped briefly in Augsburg to meet his father. With Brecht's marriage to Zoff in seemingly final disarray, Hauptmann had reason to think that meeting Brecht's father was a prelude to Brecht's marrying her. Meanwhile, living openly together in Augsburg, they worked on *Galgei*.

In a letter to Weigel (whom he did not visit though she was on his doorstep in Munich), Brecht said he had only been able to finish a few sonnets in Augsburg. His letter ended, "If I had two selves, I would murder one of them."[36] In another letter, he asks Weigel: "Am I being lost to you??? Are you being reserved with men and proper both early and late??? I don't want to hear anything about such things." He adds, "You must not worry about the winter. One way or another things will work out, Helli."[37]

While Hauptmann went back to Berlin to work on *Galgei*, Brecht was off to meet Ma and Hanne at Baden near Vienna. In a reassuring note to Weigel, he told her how "unusually boring" things were for him. He claimed to be living by himself in a "lonely room." But when he left his "lonely room" in July (leaving his bill unpaid), Ma was again pregnant with a little Brecht. Ma knew she could not appear in Münster in the fall growing rounder from day to day and expect her engagement there to last.

When Ma told Brecht of the pregnancy, he asked Dr. Otto Müllereisert either to provide something Ma could take herself or for him to arrange for an abortionist. A note to Marianne ran: "If you want the child, have it. If not (and it would be smarter to wait as otherwise it will cost 6,000 marks and your stage career for ever and in spring you can have twins). . . . Otto is now in Munich, in order to speak with those people we have talked about—to cover all possibilities! Don't do anything before you get my next letter!"[38] In letters that followed, Brecht made excuses about having no money to send her, but included directions as to what she should buy in order to induce an abortion. Finally, he sent the tablets that Otto, risking his medical career for his friend, had helped provide. They did not have the desired effect. Marianne left with Hanne for Münster, still pregnant and still arguing with Brecht about the money he had promised. When she complained about the debts he had left behind in Austria, he replied: "Please don't write me at all when you can't write five lines without subaltern hints and ironies and cannot write a letter at all without concealed attacks in it."[39]

Ma's pregnancy was terminated somehow around the time that she made her first appearances on the Münster stage in the fall, to good notices, in Strauss's *Ariadne auf Naxos* and Albert Lortzning's *Casanova*.

At the end of the summer of 1925, Brecht set down some thoughts on how human relationships should be established in contractual terms. He had reached a conclusion that "one must make a special contract with every single person."[40] Astoundingly, by this he often literally meant a written contract. From his general premise, he then goes on in this short essay to consider the special domain of contracts between men and women. Here he states as a given that "a man through the power of his contract can demand a great deal." In contrast, however, "a woman must give up a lot." Any elasticity built into a contract usually has to then be absorbed by the female partner. Though a woman may seek, he acknowledges, to modify such clearly unequal agreements, "there is a great deal that a woman must accept as unchangeable." His own concern remained not how things actually were for those bound by his cleverly framed, wholly one-sided deals, but how they appeared externally. Brecht understood as well as perhaps anyone in the doomed state of Weimar that it was not so much what one did as what the media reported that controlled "reality." In both the public and the private spheres, lies told often enough and loudly enough displaced "truth."

"The Corpses That Fell around Him
Did Not Bother Him" (1925–26)

With no really new work coming together satisfactorily, Brecht would try with the help of Hauptmann and others to turn the fragmentary *Galgei* script into something usable. The various versions of the play almost constitute an archaeological dig. The bottom layer was the work of the male collective in Augsburg and reflects the attitudes that were current among the group. The next layer reveals in almost every line the very different perspective of Elisabeth Hauptmann.

The original *Galgei* was now retitled *Mann ist Mann*. The German, usually rendered in English as *A Man's a Man*, has an untranslatable twist. When spoken, the verb can be understood either as "ist" (is) or "isst" (eats), suggesting that man is a cannibal. Joining the rewrite team whenever their busy schedules permitted were Bernhard Reich, Caspar Neher, and the tough-looking boxer-journalist Emil Burri. With Hauptmann always present, a loosely knit group would gather at Brecht's apartment on weekday mornings. When the group broke up around noon, with Brecht off to Weigel's for lunch and a postprandial nap, Hauptmann worked on, making sense of the various ideas that had been put forward that morning.

The play was shifting toward the material she had been working on most intensely, her brilliant translations of Kipling's difficult dialect verse. "With [Hauptmann's] arrival," says Willett, "the Kipling ties become more authentic. Nothing perhaps is more amazing to the English reader today than the quality of the soldiers' language."[1] Equally amazing, in my view, is a radical shift in the orientation of the relationship of men to women. Where *Galgei* had turned around homoerotic encounters in urinals and had marginalized and brutalized faceless women, *A Man's a Man* (despite its title) centers on the business dealings of a remarkable woman named Widow Begbick. Here, for the first time in a "Brecht" play, we see events from the point of view of a woman.[2] Not only this, but the men in the piece are as interchangeable, as faceless and brainless, as women had been in earlier Brecht work written with his previously all-male clique. Much of the hostility toward women and the homoeroticism that marked the earlier version was removed in the rewrite. The intelligent, tough Begbick runs rings around the men in the play, using their uncontrollable drives for drink and sex to drive her own shrewd bargains and build her own business. Her business is a supply wagon-cum-brothel that is essential to the men who serve "Mama," the slang name for the British Army in a kind of composite India and other vague but exotic places in Kipling's fabled East.

Begbick is not only central to A Man's a Man but, in various incarnations, will become the fulcrum of at least two other important "Brecht" plays. In a mythical Alaska-cum-Miami, Begbick will be the central figure in the Mahagonny opera. Later, rebaptized as Mother Courage in the play of that name, she will become a wanderer through-out Europe and will pull her stage supply wagon to world fame.

As Brecht's first full year of working with Hauptmann drew to a close, he sent her a letter and made her a present. The present was the much marked-up typescript of A Man's a Man bound in red leather, of which the assembling was the only part he had done alone.[3] When A Man's a Man was published in 1926, Hauptmann's name was missing, and she got no royalties. After Brecht's death when Brecht's letters were published, his note acknowledging Hauptmann's central role in creating A Man's a Man was left out, like well over a thousand similarly reveal-ing items.

Though A Man's a Man had already been declared finished by the end of 1925, the group would again rework it in the spring of 1926. But not until early 1928 would it be performed, outside of a radio version in 1927. An ecstatic though anonymous reviewer of this version de-clared it "the most powerful and original stage play of our time."[4] Because the play was introduced on the air by Brecht and the book version bore only his name, the reviewer did not know that it was overwhelmingly the work of Elisabeth Hauptmann.

During this time, Brecht worked fitfully on a new project about the American figure Dan Drew with Emil Burri. Burri's own play, American Youth, was finished that same spring. Dr. Seeler, the producer of Parricide, returned in 1926 looking for scripts for his experimental Junge Bühne (Young Stage). Rather than give him a Berlin premiere of A Man's a Man, Hauptmann and Brecht decided to retool Baal. As theatrical fashion had moved away now from the ecstatic Expressionism of 1918, they turned to the 1926 buzzword in the arts "neue Sachlich-keit"—"New Objectivity." To make Baal look as if based in the objec-tive world, Hauptmann came up with a fake newspaper article about an Augsburg mechanic named Joseph K.[5] A mechanic was one of the alter egos Brecht liked to play with for himself, and the one Feuchtwanger had chosen to portray Brecht in the novel Thomas Wendt.[6]

Seeler agreed to put on the reworked *Baal* for one day on February 14. The successful and expensive Caspar Neher was willing to do the sets cheaply. Weigel, Blandine Ebinger, Gerda Müller, and Oskar Homolka agreed to perform. Despite Seeler's misgivings, perhaps because he was too broke to engage anyone else, Brecht was permitted to direct. To Seeler's horror, it seemed the show would go the way of *Parricide*. This time, however, Brecht was able to avoid an open break with the actors. The new *Baal* was supposedly set in the semi-industrialized world of the early automobile, but the photos of Neher's sets, simple drawings done on what appear to be huge rolls of unbleached muslin, do not reflect this.

Industrialized or not, the play was violent. Hanns Henny Jahnn, there at Brecht's invitation, remembered that even before the play started, "The atmosphere was charged with tension and impatience, already poisoned. It was hot. It was abnormal."[7] In one of the bar scenes, Jahnn was convinced the audience was about to panic and trample him. The show ended amid deafening shouts but without the audience coming to blows. One-day matinees did not a career make. But what might have looked like a failure for the playwright Bertolt Brecht was declared by the theorist Brecht to be the fault of a theater that did not give itself unreservedly to his ideas.[8] Ihering continued to support his protégé and arranged to publish a stream of Brecht's short pieces in the *Berliner Börsen-Courier*. Some of these short works advanced theories of the theater, and others were journalism on whatever the newest theme of the day might be.

In his more serious work from around 1925 to about 1930, Brecht advanced the main outlines of what the world has come to know as "epic theater." Though John Willett speaks of epic theater as "a high-sounding phrase of the 1920s made to embrace any kind of play that Brecht wrote—taut or loose, realistic or fantastic, didactic or amusing—and some quite ephemeral mannerisms as well," the term has proven to be so flexible that it has inspired much of the most dynamic work of the modern stage.[9] Peter Brook, for instance, has declared unequivocally: "Brecht is the key figure of our time, and all theatre work today at some point starts or returns to his statements and achievement."[10] The impulse that had such an extraordinary effect on Peter Brook can also be detected in works as diverse as Weiss's *Marat/Sade*, Schaeffer's *Equus*, and the brilliant stage adaptation of Dickens's "epic" novel *Nicholas Nickleby*.

In a diary entry of March 23, 1926, Elisabeth Hauptmann noted the genesis of "epic theater": "Brecht finds the formula for 'epic theater': playing as though by memory (citing gestures and attitudes)." Brecht tended to treat the term as though it were his invention, but it had a prior history.[11] Thomas Hardy labeled his 1909 work *The Dynasts* "an epic drama." Brecht's and Bronnen's friend Otto Zarek had applied the term "epic theater" to Bronnen's *Excess;* and the producer Jo Lherman had spoken of Bronnen's *Battle of Catalonia* as "epic theater."[12] The term was also used in 1924 to describe Piscator's production of Alfons Paquet's play *Flags.*

Instead of following the relatively tight structure of classical drama, Hardy, Bronnen, Paquet, and Piscator took over the episodic structure of epic poetry in order to create the mixed genre form "epic theater." But where earlier German theorists and practitioners had borrowed epic elements to structure their new plays, Brecht drew attention to the way epics were actually performed. In the classical epic, one performer represented all the characters. As one person could not really be all these characters, Brecht felt a distance would be maintained between the performer and the various roles being presented. The "epic" actor, therefore, would remain cool rather than being wholly caught up in the role of an Oedipus or Hamlet or Lear.

In arguing in early 1926 for this approach to acting, Brecht was directly following principles that the Soviet director Vsevolod Meyerhold had been advocating for two decades.[13] These principles were thoroughly known to Asja Lazis in 1923 when she worked on *Edward II.* Meyerhold had written in 1907 that the first principle of the modern actor's diction was that "the words must be coldly 'coined.' "[14] Using the term "stylized theater," Meyerhold had observed (when Brecht was nine years old), the essence of human relationships should be presented on stage through "gestures, poses, glances, and silences." But where Meyerhold assumed, I believe correctly, that cold acting elicits hot responses in spectators, Brecht assumed the opposite: that the epic spectator observing cool performances would retain a cool distance from what was presented on stage.

As far as "epic" acting is concerned, what Brecht was calling for was a simpler, more direct style, something different from the then-current style in some more backward German theaters, something he denounced variously as "unnatural, cramped, and outdated."[15] Basically, his "epic theater" rested on three pillars: new forms and content emphasizing the contemporary and the technological; a new style of acting and directing that would de-emphasize emotion; and a new spectator who was supposed to both enjoy and be instructed by what happened on the brilliantly lit stage. In developing these various ideas, the real difficulty was that what he was proposing never hung together in actual plays. When he tried to build plays around what he called the "big subjects," deals in wheat and changes in technology, he was never able to complete them.

While Brecht theorized, Bronnen became the hottest ticket in the Weimar theater. His *Battle of Catalonia* enraged World War I German officers with its frank depiction of homosexuality in the trenches, practices made explicit by Caspar Neher's projected drawings. Then, Bronnen's *Rebels of the Rhineland* included a striking scene of lesbian incest. And as though this were not enough, one day when Bronnen dropped in on a Jessner rehearsal of *Rebels*, he was astounded to see not the flag of Weimar draped across the stage but, most provocatively and opportunistically, a huge nationalist flag of old Imperial Germany. "This flag," Jessner assured the playwright, "will ensure our success."[16] Jessner was right. The flag, though no part of Bronnen's original conception, became a rallying point for a radical right that rather improbably saw Bronnen as a spokesperson for nationalism. And Bronnen, prompted by sudden adulation on the right, would increasingly move in rightist circles and write about rightist subjects.

Through most of the twenties, Brecht had nothing with which to counter Bronnen's box-office success but managed to remain in the public eye nevertheless. *Baal* was performed in Vienna with an introduction by Austrian poet Hugo von Hoffmannsthal, who used the play to pose the question of whether "personality" was real or something that could be modified at will, as American behaviorist John B. Watson argued.[17] Hoffmannsthal claimed: "Our time is unredeemed; and do you know what it wants to be redeemed from? . . . The individual. . . . Our age groans too heavily under the weight of this child of the sixteenth century that the nineteenth fed to monstrous proportions. . . . We are anonymous forces. Potentialities of the soul. Individuality is an arabesque we have thrown away. . . ." He summed up as follows: "I would go far as to claim that all the ominous events we have been witnessing in the last twelve years [that is, since the start of World War I] are nothing but a very awkward and long, drawn-out way of burying the concept of the European individual in the grave it has dug for itself."[18] Though such responses to a refurbished play were gratifying, Brecht still did not have a new play.

Brecht's theoretical and journalistic pieces found a ready sale in the popular press, particularly in the partly serious, partly sleazy Ullstein magazines *Uhu* and *Querschnitt* (Cross section). These magazines made money the time-honored way: they mixed sports with sex and violence, and attacked all those who disagreed with their point of view. Werner Mittenzwei accurately observes that no other magazine "had such an intensive influence on [Brecht's] development" than *Querschnitt*.[19] The magazine built its profitable readership not so much on its cultural articles on Picasso or Léger but on its short pieces on boxing, "Americanism"—then very much in vogue—guest contributions by

Ernest Hemingway, pieces on "dance girls," articles by Bronnen on the importance of film; and lots of pieces on car racing and jazz. Like contemporary tabloids, the photos were big attractions. There one found pictures of the American dancer Josephine Baker dressed only in a skirt made of bananas. Women could enter the magazine's Venus de Milo competition with revealing pictures of their anatomy. The judges included Carola Neher, one of Brecht's current mistresses. Both intellectual and anti-intellectual, like Brecht himself, the magazine argued for sports and detective fiction, and claimed that famous writers such as Gerhart Hauptmann and Thomas Mann were, as Mittenzwei puts it, "bourgeois chatterboxes alien and distant from the present." *Querschnitt*, always fashionably on the side of the popular, argued, "the new generation loves dance, sports, to travel and to make money in ingenious ways."[20]

Following a trend that saw the hard-boiled detective story as the best thing in contemporary literature, in the spring of 1926, Brecht joined that bandwagon. And when he saw Alfred Flechtheim's essay advancing the idea that boxing was displacing theater and Franz Bleis's similarly oriented essay "Remarks on the Theater"[21] in *Querschnitt* in January 1926, a month later, in Ihering's *Berliner Börsen-Courier*, Brecht published a piece called "More Good Sport" advancing the same arguments.[22] Since Brecht's strident views closely coincided with those of the Ullstein editors, and since he was virtually irresistible in person, almost anything he sent was assured of publication and a handsome honorarium even if it was very similar to a previous article.

Bringing his diverse interests together, Brecht began to argue that spectators in the "epic theater" should coolly contemplate stage action in the same informed manner as spectators at boxing matches. As Mittenzwei points out, this wholly ignores the passion and blood that are a standard feature at boxing matches. When Brecht hung around the Berlin boxing crowd and wrote about it, he was endorsing an activity distinguished not by the triumph of reason but the alliance of technical skill with force in a sport clearly marked at the time by widespread corruption and explicit racism.

At the end of February 1926, Brecht was shocked to discover that his wife, Marianne Zoff, had taken up with a fellow actor by the name of Theo Lingen, a man ten years younger than she. Though he had seen neither Zoff nor his daughter regularly, Brecht now claimed that Lingen was sexually abusing little Hanne. Whether he really believed this or was making the claim in order to try to break up Marianne's relationship is not clear. The claim was followed by a declaration that he would now stop paying the irregular amount he had been sending as child support. A few days later, he wrote to say he was going to leave Germany. In the same letter he claimed, though he was now living with Hauptmann, Weigel, and Mari Hold, that he had no relationship with any other woman.[23]

When the threat of leaving Germany failed to work, he declared he would have Hanne removed from her mother if she continued to live with that "boy." In a lordly note, he observed: "I am willing to let you have her as within the marriage, *as long as I will decide*, as within a marriage, the most important things" (italics added).[24] Harping on the claim that Theo Lingen was abusing Hanne, Brecht kept up his epistolary and legal pressure. Marianne refused to break off the relationship with the man she was now determined to marry as soon as possible, but Brecht would delay her for more than two years as he maneuvered to reduce his own financial liabilities. Meanwhile, he wanted their difficulties to be kept out of public sight, begging Marianne at one point, "Please, when you can, don't talk about the two of us with anyone else." At the same time, using his usual techniques, he continued to threaten, cajole, and insult her in letters. "Are you really," he wrote in April, "going to move about with this comedian who is ten years younger. . . ?"[25]

He still dreamed of immortality. In a fragment, he wrote: "One can only become immortal when one has a name. How does one get a name? Through the mistakes that one makes."[26] Revelling in inconsistency, he made one pronouncement after another. He declared of the old theater that it "was not planned to be a theater for men. It was a theater thought up for women." Indeed, it was a theater "for old women."[27] He would, he said, rectify this.

After *Baal*, Brecht had nothing new to offer Seeler. He suggested that the work of his admirer Marieluise Fleisser might serve. She had continued to work with Feuchtwanger and had published several fine short stories and one play that Feuchtwanger felt was very good. Brecht convinced Seeler that the Junge Bühne should do Fleisser's play, its Christ motif in the title *The Foot Washing*. Seeler was not at all sure about it. The title was bad, he thought, and he changed it to reflect the play's setting, Fleisser's hometown of Ingolstadt. He telegraphed her the new title *Purgatory in Ingolstadt*; and thinking she had no say in the matter, Fleisser agreed. When the Berlin cast first read the handwritten text (Fleisser did not yet own a typewriter and could not afford a secretary), they were entranced. "The cast," wrote Seeler to Fleisser, "sat there breathless, completely swept up by the play." Among them was Helene Weigel.

In late April, Fleisser left Ingolstadt for Berlin. She hoped to see Brecht and to attend the last weeks of rehearsal of her play. On the train, she was so nervous that she ran a fever and vomited throughout the trip. She was met in Berlin by Dr. Seeler, who took one look at her provincial clothes and wondered aloud where she had left her hat. Fleisser did not own one.

At the theater, she was caught in cross fire. The nominal director of the play, Paul Bildt, had one idea about the play, Seeler had another, and Brecht had yet a third. She found herself again overwhelmed by Brecht. Brecht, she saw, expected to command, to crack a whip and demand immediate obedience. Still ill from her train journey, she found herself agreeing with Brecht's interpretation. Seeler "looked at me from a distance as though I had fallen into a pit of snakes."[28] The poisonous atmosphere was exacerbated by Brecht's interest in Fleisser. Both Weigel and Hauptmann noticed.

Despite the personal and professional infighting behind the scenes, the one-day performance of the play on April 25, 1926, was greeted with a storm of applause. The next day, both Ihering and Kerr agreed that the play was an unusually fine piece of work—an unprecedented situation—though Kerr did wonder in print if she had really written it or was merely a front for Bert Brecht. If anything, thought Kerr, the play was better than Brecht's usual standard.[29] Seeler took Fleisser and Brecht to lunch that day but spoke almost exclusively with her. As Fleisser remembered the scene, Brecht got redder and redder in the face. Finally, he unscrewed the top from the salt shaker and flung the contents in Seeler's face.[30]

Fleisser, hat or no, was suddenly all the fashion in Berlin. Brecht turned on all the charm that she was by no means disposed to resist. There was talk of putting on another Ingolstadt play of hers in the fall if she could complete it in time. Ullstein, perhaps with prompting from Feuchtwanger and Brecht, gave her a small monthly stipend for a year.

Brecht made a trip to Cologne to see Lothar Müthel perform the title role in *Edward II*. The show closed after only nine performances, but Brecht praised Müthel extravagantly. In a note to Ihering, he stated in italics, "*Müthel totally astonishing, really something for you.*"[31] In a more detailed note included with the letter, Brecht stated, "the eminent meaning of the actor Lothar Müthel for contemporary dramaturgy was clearly visible." Either damning or praising other theater figures vigorously, Brecht would make tremendous efforts to ensure that Ihering would see things his way. The technique was effective. Ihering regularly tended to say things in his own theater pieces that were consistent with whatever Brecht's current views happened to be.

In Cologne, Brecht met Ma, who told him she definitely wanted a divorce. "Don't get divorced," Brecht said. "We can continue to live separately. I have my work, you have Theo Lingen, my income is going up, I can pay for you and Hanne. I must continue to be your husband; otherwise I will have to marry XY, and that I don't want to do."[32] But when Marianne would not agree to his plan to maintain a wholly fictional marriage, he suddenly reversed his field. He filed for divorce himself. This gave him the legal advantage as plaintiff. His brief stated: "The plaintiff files for divorce and asks that the marriage be ended and that the defendant be declared to be the sole guilty party. As support he maintains that the defendant had sexual intercourse with the actor Theo Lingen in 1926."[33] "The defendant" countered with a similar argument that "the plaintiff is alone responsible as the plaintiff has had intercourse with the actress Helene Weigel, and has lived with her for years, and has had a child by her." This charge and countercharge would go on from 1926 to 1928 with Hanne in the middle.

If he had failed with Ma, his luck was better with Ullstein Verlag. He was able to persuade them to renew his contract despite not delivering new plays. Though he had repeatedly insulted Leopold Jessner the previous spring in various publications, in a letter Brecht now expressed surprise that he would not even meet with him to talk about doing a production of *Mann ist Mann*. For all Brecht's public brashness, a note of despair appears in his private letters to Ihering. "The air," he wrote, "is thin these years around my affairs."[34] He urged Ihering to be hostile to Jessner because the war should be a total one as there was nothing to save in the contemporary theater.

He took another look at Frank Norris's novel *The Pit*, with its stirring scenes of the "bulls" and "bears" of the Chicago and New York stock exchanges. He hoped to turn this into a play called *Joe Fleischhacker* (Joe the meat chopper) for Piscator's radically left-wing stage. But he hedged his bets, hoping to also get something produced by the two other biggest and most influential of the Berlin producers, Jessner and Reinhardt. He would keep pressure on Jessner to do *A Man's a Man*; while for Reinhardt, he planned, though never completed, a loose group of scenes of American life as a fast-moving revue. The indefatigable Hauptmann canvassed her American relatives and got material from her mother, and used this to prepare draft treatments of these various American subjects. Neither play went anywhere, and again he turned to mainly short poems, journalism, and short stories. Occasionally, in Hauptmann's unpublished diary, there is a clear view of how they worked together. They stayed home, keeping the drapes drawn to discourage visitors, working under the light of a red-shaded lamp, stoking themselves with whiskey and tobacco.[35] To raise much-needed funds, the two toyed with the idea of selling pornographic sonnets to rich women. Hauptmann would head off to see if she could extract yet another advance from a publisher. They did apparently still have enough money on hand at this time to buy Brecht a new, gray summer suit, an elegant cap, and some ties.

One "Brecht" story completed during 1926 is called "North Sea

Crabs." It is a piece about the wrecking of an elegant apartment by the apartment owner's former buddies who had served with him in a machine-gun unit on the western front. A can of crabs is chopped open on top of a Bechstein piano and doused with tomatoes and whiskey. Bottles are opened by smashing their necks against the mahogany furniture. The resulting disorder, declare the guests, is what makes an apartment really an apartment. The story was sold to a newspaper in Munich but with only Brecht's name signed to it though the manuscript, as John Willett notes, is mainly Hauptmann's work.[36]

As spring turned to summer in 1926, Brecht planned his yearly escape from Berlin. His sexual interest in Hauptmann now waning as it often did after two or so years of a liaison, he did not propose she join him. Generally speaking, from now on he would often sexually ignore Hauptmann. The sexual magnetism he could exert at will would now usually be used only when it was necessary to bring her back when she showed signs of being fed up, and ready to leave him and set herself up as a writer in her own right.

Brecht left for Paris for a brief holiday with Caspar Neher. Later, it was on to Vienna to check on the workings of the Viennese Stock Exchange. But he could make neither head nor tail of the goings-on there despite speaking to one of the leading experts. It is not known whether he was too busy to visit little Frank Banholzer who was now staying with relatives of Helene Weigel near Vienna. Little Frank was a leftover that for whom Weigel had had to take over responsibility as Brecht was usually too busy or claimed to be too broke to do anything to help. He was treating Hanne and Ma by this time much the same way, claiming he could not meet their expenses and often failing to pay child support for Hanne.

He was now telling Ma that his income was going up. But he also told her that he was flat broke. But even as he claimed he was broke, he was arranging to buy a large car. Knowing nothing about cars, he persuaded his old Augsburg friend Otto Müllereisert to get one for him. This proved to be a nightmare for Otto. The money to pay for the car was supposed to be in the mail, but somehow it was always delayed. Brecht said he was getting the money from Weigel. Otto went ahead and bought a car, a huge, secondhand, British-made Daimler, but then found he could not get the full purchase price refunded by Brecht. It was bad enough having Brecht owe him the enormous sum of sixteen hundred marks, but then the stately foreign car broke down. It turned out that very few repair shops in Germany were equipped to repair the British-made car. Making things worse for Otto, not only had Brecht failed to pay fully for the car, but he now declared that any repairs would be Otto's responsibility. He sent Otto a peremptory telegram

saying only: "Wann kommt auto—Brecht"—"When is car coming—
Brecht."[37] In his bitter reply to this telegram, Otto said their old friendship was being ruined by "your unreliability and failure to keep
agreements."[38] Finally, though she was broke herself, Weigel had to
step in and contribute to the car fund. Otto wrote to Brecht (alluding
in his letter to the Italian fascist adventurer and writer D'Annunzio),
saying "I'm not going along anymore with your D'Annunzio allure."[39]
Faced with potential mutiny, Brecht again, and with predictable results,
turned his full "D'Annunzio allure" on Otto.

At the end of July 1926, Brecht briefly visited Weigel and little
Stefan who were vacationing in Brecht's favorite kind of country setting, at lovely Kochelsee, about fifty miles from Munich. From there he
hurried to Augsburg for an assignation with Marieluise Fleisser. From
the open windows of the attic apartment in the Bleichstrasse, her laughter was now heard. She did not know what her status was, she wrote
later, friend or wife, co-worker or lover.[40] He told her, as he had told
so many, she was to become his wife. With the wind blowing through
the open window, he would lean back on his bed and sing, as he had to
Caspar Neher, Otto, Orge, Bie, Hauptmann, and so many others, his
erotic "Achilles Verses."

With Fleisser, he moved back and forth between the roles of
master and child. Demonstrating mastery over them, he would yell for
one of the family maids to open and then close a window. Sometimes
he would put on a bowler hat like the one Baal wore in Caspar Neher's
drawing pinned over the bed. The hat, he claimed in a beguiling, almost
childlike manner, helped him to think. Then, coming over from his
narrow bed to hers, he, in her words, "made her happy."

Fleisser spoke with him one day about some materials that might
be used in her next play. She had noticed that a group of army engineers
in her hometown had been busy building a bridge over the city's medieval moat. She had noticed also the flirtations of the soldiers with the
young women of the town. Brecht got excited and soon was sketching
a complete play and urging her to write it at once. She knew she could
not work that way. She needed time to think and let the theme mature.
He seemed surprised that she did not immediately do what he had told
her to do. Fleisser, using the same vocabulary that Bronnen had applied
both to Brecht and Hitler, felt that Brecht was an "animal trainer."
And, even more strongly, she wrote, "The corpses that fell around him
did not bother him."[41]

Though Fleisser was still very anxious to please him that summer,
she still could not carry out his order as to how she should write. She
thought the problem lay in the fact that their approaches to writing were
different. But difficulties went away whenever he was beautiful and

awake with her. "Forceful and delicate and rapid like a bird," as she described the sex that summer, he would make her happy again. But, after he was asleep, she found herself lying awake, her fists tightly clenched.

Brecht dreamed different dreams. The Daimler, he now concluded, should become Weigel's car. He dreamed of something newer, possibly one of the big American cars. Hauptmann boldly proposed to several companies the exchange of a new car for a Brecht advertising jingle. Most of the car companies, including Ford and Dodge, turned the idea down. But the Steyr Company in Austria, which made weapons as well as cars, agreed to the arrangement. Brecht's "poem" in payment included:

> We were bred
> In a weapons factory.
> Our little brother is the Manlicher Carbine.

Other lines run:

> Our motor is
> A piece of thinking ore.

This motor is so silent, so say the poem's last two lines:

> That you will think
> That you are driving the shadow of your car.

Using the poem, Steyr ran an ad campaign about their deal with Brecht in the Ullstein chain of magazines. The deal itself gives us a sense of what the Brecht name was worth at this time and further helps explain why Hauptmann often published under Brecht's name rather than her own. The sheer doggerel quality of this crashingly bad "poem" also helps us understand that if such nonsense as this was accepted as genuine Brecht, how easy it really was to establish lots of other poems, vastly superior to this one, but by other hands, as genuine "Brecht." Brecht at his best, is a world-class poet. But Brecht at his worst is a horrible hack.

Except for the business with the car, Brecht had not communicated much with the "chief girl," Elisabeth Hauptmann, during the summer. She, however, had kept working to meet Brecht's publishing deadlines. But between writing things to be published under his high-priced name, she wanted also to complete something not to be given to him. Using material her brother-in-law had gathered for her in

Chicago and from her American mother's memories of the stock exchange in New York, Hauptmann wrote her material in two distinctly
different ways. In one, she roughed out a plan for the Joe Fleischhacker
piece done in the Brechtian, generally macho style with women having
only subsidiary roles. This she would give to the "chief." Then, quite
separately, she presented the material from an opposing viewpoint. In
her story, the central figure, Mabel Tarkington, is a strong, independent
woman who secretly becomes a highly successful trader on the Chicago
exchange. She reads sexually frank books, determines what she wants
to do with her body, drives and fixes her own car (an obvious dig at
Brecht's incapacity in this regard), and says she will determine whom
she will marry. The problem with all this is that potential husbands are
terrified of her courage and independent ways, and run away. Hauptmann (like her heroine whose deals are submitted to the exchange under
an assumed name) did not sign her own name to her sexually frank
work. Hauptmann took the pseudonym Catherine Ux. "Juliet without
Romeo," as the piece was called, was accepted by the Leipzig journal
Das Leben (Life) and published in the August issue where it was almost
completely ignored.[42]

In the "Juliet" story, as usually but not always in surviving
"Brecht" texts where the physical evidence shows Hauptmann's hand
to be dominant, one finds precisely this same concern for the plight of
the helpless and the appearance of a strong, central female character.
However, throughout the twenties and early thirties, when the surviving manuscripts show evidence of Brecht's hand as the dominant one,
we continue to find a stream of male-oriented, overwhelmingly violent
texts of which the following is typical:

> When I come again
> Under a moon even more raw, my dears
> Then I will come with a tank
> I will speak to you with a cannon
> And wipe you out.[43]

But in longer works, Brecht's violent, male-oriented contributions are
interwoven with the very different concerns of Hauptmann. One of the
earliest and clearest examples of this, of course, is *A Man's a Man*.
Here, male adventurers familiar to us from Brecht's earlier work are
offset by the Widow Begbick, the kind of strong woman who shows up
regularly in Hauptmann's writing.

At the end of the summer of 1926, Brecht went to Darmstadt to
work with his old Munich disciple Jacob Geis who was directing a
production of *A Man's a Man* there. The work as revised by Brecht and

Hauptmann from the original *Galgei* material remained, as Lion Feucht-wanger saw at once when he read the play, a "rather childish derivation from Kipling." True though this observation is, the text turned out to be one of remarkable power when staged. And it is clear from contemporary accounts that it was staged with remarkable brilliance in Darmstadt with Ernst Legal in the lead role and with a Neher set that John Willett describes as "paper-thin, elegant, brilliantly lit with whites and khakis predominating."[44] This would also be, as Willett notes, the first time that the half-height curtain we have grown to associate with Brecht productions was used by Caspar Neher.

The 1926 version of the play owed a particular debt to Kipling's collection of stories called *Soldiers Three,* written in various dialects of the British Isles and set in India at the time of the Raj. A machine-gun unit, all the while speaking Hauptmann's brilliant rendering of Kipling, shoots up and robs the Pagoda of the Yellow God. This pagoda is a place run for profit by a mysterious Mr. Wang who is clearly a refugee from *In the Jungle of Cities.* In attacking the pagoda, however, the unit loses one of its number. Declaring that one man is exactly like another, hence the title of the play, the remaining three persuade a mild-mannered local porter called Galy Gay (held over obviously from the original *Galgei*) to dress up as their bloodthirsty comrade. They are assisted in recruiting Galy Gay by Leokadia Begbick, the owner of a perambulating brothel-cum-canteen. Begbick comes forward in the play to announce the transformation of the mild-mannered Galy Gay into "the human typhoon" Jeriah Jip: "Tonight you will see a man reassembled like a car." This widow wanders through an ostensible India of 1925, but with Victoria still on her throne, accompanied by her three nubile daughters who, conveniently enough for the Darmstadt production, can also form themselves into a small jazz band. A character called Bloody Five, who had gained his name by shooting five "Shiks" at the Battle of Dschadseefluss, is attacked by uncontrollable sexual urges whenever it rains. Desperate to retake control of his own life rather than having to periodically return to Begbick's ministrations every time it rains, he goes off into the bush, as he says, to "shoot off my cock" with his army pistol and returns, his voice several octaves higher. With lines such as these, one can imagine what might have happened in Hauptmann's hometown of Peckelsheim had her name been displayed as coauthor.

The text is an eerie evocation of what can happen to a reasonable human being when threatened, as Galy Gay is in the play, with torture or death. The work dramatizes a great truth of this or other centuries, that virtually anyone can be turned into a killer if the temptation is great enough or the circumstances are inhumane enough. In one published version, one scene is headed: "The Demonstrability of Any Conceivable Assertion." In the first edition of the play, inside the front cover are photos of a mass of virtually identical men, while inside the back cover is a photo of a mass of virtually identical cars. One man is indeed like another in the way that one car is like another. Within the text, two men dressed in a blanket are then sold as an "army elephant" at a cut-rate price to the gullible Galy Gay who, expecting to make a huge profit on the deal, manages to overlook the fact that the elephant is no elephant and that if it were, the deal is illegal. Once the deal has been made, those who have set him up will sentence him to death for his crime. After he is placed before a firing squad and faces death, he is more than willing to take up the offer to live on with the new personality of the murderous Jip.

The line between the human and the mechanical-technical, as well as the line between the human and the animal, was often now erased. Given this scheme of things—which owes a great deal to the American behaviorist school and Hofmannsthal's observations, crossed with some apparent knowledge of Pavlovian behavior modification techniques in the Soviet Union, and under the shadow of Lang's film *Metropolis*—personality is not something fixed, holy, immutable, but something that can be molded like the parts that make up a car or any other kind of machine. The "new man" of the Brecht-Hauptmann play is himself a patchwork created by trickery, threats of death, and by dreams of glory as a conqueror. He achieves on stage a gigantic public orgasm of brutality as he forces, with obvious Freudian overtones, the cannon of his unit into the narrow defile that guards the entrance to "Tibet." The "hero" feels "the desire to sink my teeth into the enemy's throat . . . to carry out the conqueror's mission."

Form echoing content, the play itself looks as though its various bits and pieces could be reassembled in a variety of different formats. In this regard, the play as a structural unit has obvious parallels to montage theory as expounded by the Soviet materialist aesthetician Sergei Eisenstein. It is the sequencing of montage elements in Eisenstein's films that yields the meaning. The building blocks of the montage sequence do not have much meaning in themselves.

Hauptmann, working perhaps from one of those editions of Kipling that are adorned with the ancient Indian symbol of the swastika, needed only to render Kipling into lively and accurate German in order to have the new text be drenched in casual murder and outright racism. The men of the play kill and curse casually while getting, as had Baal, sexual kicks by doing so. Stoking the killers between the battles is the person who shows Galy Gay how to feed the cannon, Widow Begbick.

For all its sex, violence, and technical brilliance, the Geis production of the play in Darmstadt did not bring with it the Berlin offers for which Brecht still hoped. But several technical elements that Neher had come up with would live on and become hallmarks of what was now being gathered together to constitute the "Brecht style."[45] The bright white light Neher used here to replace traditional "mood lighting" would be used by Brecht as a kind of signature for most of the productions with which he would be associated. The use of jazz and other forms of "American" music would also now regularly reappear. Likewise, Neher's linen half-curtain would become almost obligatory. Audiences would expect to see a lightweight curtain whisked across the stage from side to side rather than the traditional ponderous curtain lowered from above. This half-height curtain permitted the audience to see over it so that scene changes between acts would be partially visible. And, as Neher saw with later productions, this plain white curtain could also serve as a kind of screen on which words or images could be projected or drawn. With this development, most of the elements we have come to know as the Brecht theater have been pulled together. And though, as can be seen, most of the individual elements and even the combination of elements of this theater should be credited to people other than Brecht, it will be under his name, and as a result of his advocacy, that they will advance to reshape the modern theater.

"Let the Tips of Your Fingers Stroke the Tips of Her Breasts" (1926–27)

Brecht's statements about the barrenness of contemporary theater in Germany, together with his interest in popular culture and of the world of mechanical objects, made him an obvious candidate for a move to the popular, mechanical medium of film. But though many of his friends had done this, most of his own efforts in this direction went nowhere. Other than the script he had done with Bronnen and the barbershop piece he had done with Valentin in Munich, he was unable to break into this new medium.

Once he found he had failed in it, he began to sneer at the medium, despite his admiration for the power of films like Chaplin's *Face on the Barroom Floor* and *Goldrush*. He now declared that unlike the many theater people he knew who were moving over to film, he would prefer to go down with the ship of the drama, "farting in its sails" if necessary to move it forward. "The film," he now wrote, "takes no responsibility, it doesn't need to extend itself. Dramaturgically it has remained so simple because all film is, is a couple of kilometers of celluloid in a lead box. One does not expect," he grumpily concluded, "fugues from a saw bent across someone's knee."[1]

From what was going on in the film world at the time, Brecht's comment can be seen as reactionary in the extreme. This was the year that Vertov finished his revolutionary *A Sixth of the World* and Pudovkin, *Mechanics of the Brain*. In Berlin, it was the year of the release of Chaplin's *Goldrush*, Fritz Lang's *Metropolis*, as well as Eisenstein's *Battleship Potemkin*. But despite the advanced artistic and political level reached in film by 1926, Brecht made no sustained effort to understand it.

In contrast to Brecht's peeved "saw bent across the knee" reaction to film, Lion Feuchtwanger saw Soviet films such as *Potemkin* as revolutionary bombs that could be flung again and again into the various centers of the bourgeois world. There is a marvelous scene that opens the second volume of Feuchtwanger's 1930 novel *Success*, which describes the impact of *Potemkin* on the reactionary minister Klenk in Berlin in 1926. In the real world, as well as in Feuchtwanger's novel, the

Berlin authorities were shaken by *Potemkin* and managed to ban it for much of July 1926. Brecht's shrill argument against film is revealing. When fighting any rival, be it Thomas Mann, Gerhart Hauptmann, Richard Wagner, or Ma and her lover, Theo Lingen, he would attack with any weapon he could lay his hands on, including deliberate lies.

At the same time as he was unfairly attacking film in the mid-twenties, Brecht also came very close to attacking homosexuals. Where in work done within the male collective of Orge, Cas, and Otto, homosexual experiences were everywhere and were treated sympathetically, now that the real-life models of these stage characters had established lives largely outside Brecht's orbit, he attacked homosexuality. Speaking of the great poet Rilke, he said his way of dealing with God "is wholly faggot."[2] The word Brecht used was "schwul," then as now, a far from neutral term.[3] He also denounced the work of the more or less openly (for that time) homosexual group of poets that formed the Stefan George circle. As Bronnen was widely known to be bisexual, such attacks spilled over to Bronnen as well as to other prominent targets. Though some of Brecht's attacks might have simply been seen as denouncements of the kind of precious poetry that he felt should be done away with as soon as possible and replaced, there is an explicit homophobic undercurrent to much of what he now did.[4] Trying, for instance, to undercut Thomas Mann, he would go so far as to circulate homosexual sonnets he had written to which he signed Thomas Mann's name. As Mann was rumored to be homosexual and was, in fact, bisexual, Brecht's vicious attacks could hardly fail to hit their mark.

By the middle of 1926, another change was that Brecht had begun to realize that if he was indeed going to write about the "big subjects," he needed far more grounding in economics. Not knowing how the stock or commodity markets worked, he had found that writing a play on the international sale of wheat, for instance, was beyond his capacity. While on one of his customary summer visits to Augsburg, he wrote to ask Hauptmann for some recommended readings. She supplied him with a list, including Marx's *Das Kapital*. On July 26, 1926, Hauptmann notes (with just a touch of venom) that such things were new discoveries, "at least for him."

It was one thing for Hauptmann to send him basic books on complicated subjects and another for him to read them. He apparently wrote to Hauptmann in the fall: "I am now stuck eight feet deep in *Kapital*."[5] The surviving copy of *Das Kapital* from Brecht's library is almost completely lacking in marginalia and other typical signs of use. Years later, Brecht's friend the composer Hanns Eisler would say that he doubted that Brecht had read the whole work. But whether or not he read Marx thoroughly, Brecht soon was declaring enthusiastically that "this man Marx was the only audience for my plays that I had come across."[6] Here, Marx is the audience looking at Brecht.

The general intemperateness that marked Brecht's dealings both with people and with ideas was a great help in facilitating his turn toward Marxism, for it clearly echoes Marx's own behavior. As Karl Jaspers has long since pointed out of Marx's writings, Marx "does not quote examples or adduce facts which run counter to his own theory but only those which clearly support or confirm that which he considers the ultimate truth."[7] For instance, instead of grasping the basic fact that the new industrialists could and would make extensive ameliorative efforts with regard to the work force precisely in order to head off the ultimate uprising and overthrow of capitalism, Marx ignored the available evidence, such as the Factory Act of 1833, that suggested the exact opposite and that has held true until the present. Like Brecht, we know Marx was given to outbursts of verbal violence and character assassination of those who did not slavishly follow him and his ideas. Marx would stoop even to violently racist and anti-Semitic attacks such as the one on his rival in the international socialist movement Ferdinand Lasalle, whom Marx characterized as a "Jewish Nigger." But it is the violently apocalyptic, the "I am sure I am always rightness" of Marx that seems to speak most directly to Brecht and to confirm his own correctness in the use of similar tactics in his own professional and personal life. Like Marx, while Brecht might begin to develop theories about a world of equality, this would never cause him to change his own strictly patriarchal domestic arrangements in the slightest.

Even with the volumes of Marx at his elbow that summer, when Brecht returned to Berlin in the fall, he had not, to Piscator's dismay, finished the play about deals in wheat. Brecht's first encounter with Marx came just before he happened to meet one of Germany's leading Marxist economists. One evening in the winter of 1926–27 Brecht was having supper at a restaurant called Schlichter's, a place named for its right-wing owner. The owner's brother was the now largely forgotten artist Rudolf Schlichter, whose rather wooden portraits hung in the restaurant and in Brecht's and Helene Weigel's apartments. On the evening in question, Rudolf Schlichter dined at the restaurant with Dr. Fritz Sternberg, author of the newly published tome *Imperialism*. Sternberg could not take his eyes off a man at a nearby table. The man had, noted Sternberg, something "extraordinary, unforgettable" about him.[8]

After being introduced to Sternberg, Brecht made his usual hyperbolic pronouncements with which he usually managed to steamroller new acquaintances, but Sternberg calmly pointed out the obvious holes in them. When Sternberg made the observation that he thought that

Baal (the only work of Brecht that he knew at that time) was not as good a play as the very earliest work of Wedekind (surely an accurate assessment), the atmosphere became tense. Brecht turned to Schlichter and asked in a pseudopolite tone: "Tell me, didn't you say that Herr Sternberg completed his doctorate in economics? Why don't you ask him if he could help me with the buying of a suit. Perhaps I could do that more economically with his help."[9] That was the low point of the evening. Later, speaking of *Drums in the Night*, Brecht said, "Since I wrote that play, it has not been possible for me to find a vision strong enough in the relationship of a man to a woman that would be able to sustain an entire play." "That is the first not only interesting but progressive sentence that you have spoken," responded Sternberg. With a vehemence that made Brecht's entire body shake, noted Sternberg, he asked why Sternberg thought this such a progressive idea.

Beginning with Plato's *Symposium*, Sternberg now gave Brecht a "masculinist" interpretation to his review in a nutshell of literature, which was in explicit opposition to "feminist" interpretations. "For Plato," Sternberg opined, "making a woman the center of man's life did not even come into question." He went on, "In the *Thousand and One Nights*, women were interchangeable." Then, with some fast footwork, the role of Beatrice in Dante's *Divine Comedy* was dismissed. According to Sternberg, the poem is wholly about Dante himself. Further, in a dazzling example of tunnel vision, "Tristan and Isolde" was not, according to Sternberg, a tale about two lovers but really "an illustration of the medieval principle of the vassal Tristan's obligations to his liege lord."

Brecht was fascinated by Sternberg's dismissal of the importance of women both in world literature and in the thinking of so important a figure as Plato. By this time, he was in a deeply compromised psychological position. The indications are legion that he still had and would continue to have what one future lover called an "Abneigung gegen die Frauen" (aversion to women).[10] Sternberg seemed to show that women had no importance in the great tradition, which reinforced Brecht's own deeply divided attitude toward women, evidenced by his simultaneous praise and dismissal of Hauptmann as "Ham." In the world of metaphor, and we have seen this earlier with his treatment of women, Jews, and "niggers," Brecht could articulate views that would have made at least some people's hair stand on end if he had stated them directly rather than, as he does here and later, clothing them in beguiling metaphor.

Sternberg's classically "grounded" misogyny or "masculinism" was useful to Brecht, but Sternberg had the further virtue of making himself available as a kind of in-house expert on world economics from a Marxist perspective. Sternberg recognized quickly that Brecht was incapable of "systematic thinking."[11] In his memoirs, he notes that Brecht's train of thought did not follow a logical sequence, but his thoughts moved like knights on a chess board, straight for a short distance, then turning radically to the right or the left. Brecht's "weakness" in this formulation became a "strength." In a presentation copy of *A Man's a Man*, Brecht wrote admiringly for Sternberg, "To my first teacher."

Though a Marxist, Brecht's "teacher" was not a member of the CPG. Sternberg felt that the CPG reflected the battlefield of the Soviet Union where after Lenin's death in 1924, one faction savagely fought another. According to this view, the CPG, directed as it was by the Moscow-based and -controlled Comintern, was not a party capable of solving German problems. As Brecht had declared himself years ago to be an "independent independent," Sternberg's position was very good news. It permitted him to continue to have Marx as audience, but he did not need to tie his own hands by joining the German Communist party and having to submit to its discipline.

At about this same time, Brecht met other independent Marxist thinkers, among them Jakob Walcher, Hertha Gordon, and Karl Korsch. Walcher, who had been a student of Rosa Luxemburg who had also opposed Leninist domination of the newly founded CPG, would bounce in and out of the party. Though he had participated in a number of meetings with Lenin, he often disagreed with the course the Russian and German Communist parties were taking. Hertha Gordon was also a direct link to an independent strand in Marxist thinking. She had served as a courier between Lenin and Klara Zetkin, the prominent CPG functionary and early fighter for women's rights. Karl Korsch, like Sternberg, operated largely outside the CPG.

The fact Brecht had embraced Marxism and now moved increasingly among Marxist friends had no discernible effect on the pattern of his daily life. He continued to maintain ties to Bronnen and the circle of nationalist friends with whom his former lover was now involved. His daily routine continued to follow, in the smallest detail, the pattern of life as it had been lived in the imperial era in Augsburg by his father, Herr Direktor Brecht. What was true of Brecht's household was also true of his business arrangements. Before and after his discovery of Marx, he continued to use Elisabeth Hauptmann's or anyone else's work with minimum, if any, acknowledgment. Neither now nor later would he make an effort to change his lucrative publishing arrangements with capitalist publishing concerns.

Similarly, and not surprisingly with someone like Sternberg as teacher, his view of "love" did not change with Marxism. In a poem written in his fifties, the poet will still take for granted an absolute need for one person to be dominated and the other to dominate. Within a relationship, says this poem, always "one reaps balsam and the other reaps blows."[12] There is no doubt of the gender of the one who gets the balsam and the one who gets the blows. The final lines say, "Pass the knife to him whom you love and he will kill. If he knows you love him, he will cut you up."

Though Brecht would now speak a great deal about changing his plays to include more explicit Marxism and to show the increasing importance in the world of modern technology, these remained mainly theoretical concerns. The fact is that in all the years to come, only two plays (*The Measures Taken* and *Mother*—both based on Hauptmann's dramaturgy and beliefs) are clear-cut in their endorsement of communism. And, for all the talk about the importance of technology for the new drama, there is no major play of any period in Brecht's life that requires anything more sophisticated in the way of modern technology than a slide projector or a conventional turntable stage. Brecht would remain true to a kind of drama similar to the classical Greek theater and Shakespeare's chronicle plays. In his theater, he would reintroduce verse into drama and the use of a chorus, music, masks, and the kind of commentator on events used by Shakespeare in the Henry plays. Unlike the Russians and Piscator, who would often overwhelm the stage and the verbal text with gigantic new stage machines, the theatrical future for Brecht lay in the far simpler past. And instead of replacing the towering central figure of classical drama with the mass hero that socialist theory seemed to demand, Brecht consistently returned both as dramatist and as director to towering, often violent, central figures.

Before being introduced to Marxism in late 1926, Brecht had, as we know, written with obvious relish of murderers slogging through jungles, of sailors on rotting hulks sailing shark-infested waters gangbanging and then tossing aside "foreign" women, of Jewish "leftovers," of men routinely enjoying the rape and killing of people of various other colors as they "take" a fortress in Tibet or raze a city in Chile. Now his heroes, often no less bloody and no less colonial, will march with merciless tread in pursuit of their messianic Marxist purpose. Conspiratorial, vengeful, convinced utterly of their own correctness, and willing to lie, steal, and murder for their cause, they will push deeply into the terrain that the Kipling-fathered *Galgei* mastered in earlier articulations of the Brechtian world view. These "new" figures would exhibit the intolerance that characterized Karl Marx himself in his personal relations and that "furious and ruthless energy" that Lenin personally recommended for his own instrument of state power the dreaded Cheka, the forerunner of the NKVD—Norodnyj Kommissariat Vnutrennykh Del, or People's Commissariat for Internal Affairs.

(This book will use NKVD as the general term for this many-named organization until it becomes the KGB in 1956.) We now know as a result of glasnost that in the personal written instructions of Lenin, the Cheka was told to practice such cruelty toward enemies "that they will not forget it for decades." Those who were not to be immediately killed were to be sent to what Lenin called (perhaps borrowing the term from British usage during the Boer War) "concentration camps."[13]

Brecht now identified with these purposeful, murdering, always correct commissars and Comintern agents. A poem representative of the "new" orientation of the Brecht-Hauptmann workshop appeared in the *Berliner Börsen-Courier* on November 7, 1926 (the anniversary, of course, of the Russian Revolution). Brecht's poem bears the title "Verwisch die Spuren!" (Wipe out your tracks!)[14] The poem gives a series of instructions to go undercover, and to hide one's face and tracks. Agents are to avoid arrest. They must be stern enough to hide from their own parents, to slam the door on their own comrades, to sign nothing, and keep moving, changing houses all the time.

Another poem clearly stating the violent, profoundly amoral themes Brecht continually articulates is called "To Kronos." Here a group has decided, with no specific reason given, to get rid of a companion. They tell their victim, "You have to go, like the smoke to heaven that nobody holds back." The last stanza states:

> *You we want to kill*
> *You must not live.*
> *Whatever lies we may have to believe:*
> *You must never have existed.*[15]

What I find striking here is the continuity between the violence in earlier works such as *Baal,* and the murderous Garga and ruthless pirates who murder and rape as easily as they "take a shit," and the doctrine articulated in the "Wipe out Your Tracks!" and "To Kronos" poems.

Brecht's "new" view, supposedly now grounded in Marx and in the various other Communist classics he was dipping into under the influence of his many friends on the left, is wholly congruent not only with the "leftovers" imagery of earlier Brecht poems and diary entries but also with the widely known and cited 1869 "Catechism of a Revolutionist." The "Catechism" was the work of the older Mikhail Bakunin and the young, deadly Nechaev, two men who related to one another in ways that Edmund Wilson has directly compared to Verlaine's violent, homoerotic relationship with Rimbaud.[16] The heroes of the "Catechism" are men who have deliberately "broken with all the laws and codes of morals of the educated world." With Lenin's blessing, the original Soviet secret-police mechanism took over most elements of the "Catechism," and these doctrines were then exported for use within foreign Communist parties including the CPG.

Later, in one of those multiple mirrorings in the relationship of Marxism to nazism, seeing how efficacious the devices of the "Catechism" were in Lenin's hands, Hitler would adopt them as part of the basic structure of nazism.[17] As early as 1920, after the Munich Marxists had shown compassion toward others and then been murdered for their pains, Hitler stated, "National Socialism is what Marxism [in Germany] could have been had it freed itself from the absurd, artificial link with a democratic system."[18]

The "Catechism," Mein Kampf, and Brecht's poem "To Kronos" represent extremes, but they are extremes that flow directly into one another. Each work elevates an "Übermensch" to a position where he can casually arrange the death of anyone deemed literally or figuratively an "Untermensch." Each advocates acting outside the law to achieve some "higher good." Each supports cheating or killing to achieve a "higher" aim. This embracing of extremes that are wholly outside democratic systems of law, morality, or social or psychological restraint was, I believe, an essential feature on both the radical left and right of the Weimar years.

The writer Hans Sahl, who met Brecht in Berlin around this time, has noted the use of coldness in Brecht's personal life as well as in his writing. "The question arises," writes Sahl of Brecht, "whether with this doing away with compassion [Mitleid] as a spontaneous attitude for inter-human relations, the ground is not being prepared for exactly that kind of totalitarianism in which there are only supposed to be controlled emotions, and where compassion is only to be allowed in those instances where, in the view of those in power, [it] is historically 'correct.' The cold exclusion of emotions and this freezing of inter-human relations in both Stalinism and Naziism, this viewing of human beings from outside, simply as mere material to be used in making history, all of this . . . is in a certain sense anticipated poetically by Brecht and thus made fit for introduction to polite society."[19] And this polite society seemed very ready to embrace the doctrine of coldness. As Klaus Theweleit's detailed studies of male fantasies in the Weimar era so clearly show, cold dreams of murder, of violent but "good" acts against the hated, "immoral other"—whether a father who "sold out" at Versailles, a woman, a Jew, a Frenchman, or a "nigger"—were ubiquitous.

It should perhaps not surprise us that, from its first day, state-sanctioned or -tolerated violence arced across the poles of Weimar. The murder of Rosa Luxemburg was "justified" by direct state involvement in the act itself and by the judiciary giving the perpetrators of the crime ludicrously mild sentences. Gradually, on the other side, murder would be condoned as Moscow-directed hit squads would be sent to Germany. Both extremes—each blaming, of course, the hated other—came to subscribe to the same ruthless code. Both sides claimed superior wisdom and historical justification for their actions. Both believed in reducing the hated other to "thingness." Each could declare of enemies, as Brecht put it, and Hitler or Eichmann or the NKVD head, Lavrenty Beria, could not have framed it better, "You have to go, like the smoke to heaven."

It is all too clear that the brutality and misogyny that marked Brecht's pre-Marxist universe does not abate with his discovery of Marx nor with his continued close cooperation with Elisabeth Hauptmann. His encounter with Marxism, as practiced by the heirs of Bakunin, was not a doctrine that asked Brecht either to reject the pleasure he had always taken either in seeing people in pain or abate his fantasies of violence. The Marxism that Brecht was now becoming involved with justified violence on the grandest scale. But the violence now, so it was argued, was to ensure that future generations could enjoy a world free of violence, free of the brutality of capitalism at its worst. When Brecht, with his own violent orientation, said upon first encountering Marx that he was the best spectator for his plays, this is an exaggeration that is both playful and serious. Without the playfulness, it would be unacceptable in its arrogance; but it remains arrogant nevertheless. What is done here is similar to what he had done in the pre-Marxist Brecht universe, where Brecht made himself the epicenter. In "God's Favorite Chorale," we may recall, the universe had sung to God the Father of "the great words of great men. And the wonderful songs of Bert Brecht."[20]

Descriptions of a universe centered around Brecht and the phallus are intertwined with opposite images, signaling fear of abandonment and loss of control. He is terrified of any force that can overwhelm him, be it the flood that threatens the last small islands in his early poetry and plays, the hurricanes that loom on the horizon in later ones, or the inexplicable economic forces that can suddenly wipe a person out, or the fear of uncontrolled giving way to sexual urges that leads Bloody Five to the radical measure of "shooting off his cock."

We have seen earlier in his diary how Brecht, with the galloping inflation of 1921, telescoped metaphysics and economics.[21] As he saw it, men like himself were "hung out to dry on the basis of a tiny change in the exchange rate, payment, chance, the way a complicated and expensive organism can be ruined because of some barely measurable change in the air, a trick of the wind, sacrificed without either a worshiper or a god." "The question arises," he had said, "whether one can break out of the dismal law of causal necessity that is within mankind." In encountering Marx in 1926, Brecht finally found someone who argued not only that "the dismal law of causal necessity" could be broken but went further to assert as scientific fact that it would be broken.

At the level of Brecht's deepest psychic economy, his need always to feel in control and to be central to the world scheme, Marx provided a cosmic answer. Marx had apparently seen a way to end that desperate metaphysical situation where human beings were made the sacrificial victims of economic forces. Suddenly, here was a bearded, almost god-like patriarch, an all-powerful savior, the supposed discoverer of "laws" of economics as fixed as the law of gravity, who now had his eye on the erstwhile poor Bert Brecht.

Brecht's discovery of Marx had come at a most apposite time. Daily, the Soviet Union seemed to consolidate its position, while a sick if not dying capitalism was racked by crisis after crisis. Marxism had about it an air of the inevitable. It claimed to be a cold, rational, scientific doctrine smashing its way toward a new era of peace and plenty. From Brecht's perspective, either he was going to ride this wave of history or to be smashed by it. In typical Brecht fashion, he would subscribe to a doctrine but not be tied to it. Though married to Marxism, it would be a marriage permitting him a variety of affairs on the side.

In 1926, the year of his discovery of Marx, Brecht ended the year with a kind of summing-up letter to the long-suffering Helene Weigel. "I think," he wrote, "that you are a bit down because there is nothing going on in the theater, but I believe that you know that I value you enormously much, even when I seldom or never say it." "Dear Helli," the letter concludes, I kiss you."[22] As with his mother, he did not speak of love. In his pampered tough-guy world, there was no room for the personal warmth that Weigel craved nor the equality of which Weigel, Hauptmann, and Fleisser dreamed. It is difficult to find evidence that would permit arguing against Marieluise Fleisser's assessment of Brecht: "In the final goal he wanted to help human beings. But in daily practice he was a despiser of humankind."[23]

Secure in his domination of the domestic space created for him by Hold, Hauptmann, and Weigel, and financially supported by his father and by contracts extracted under false pretenses from Ullstein and others, Brecht was making violent Oedipal capital of *Das Kapital*, while Hauptmann finished up some "Brecht" work on the long-overdue Ullstein account. In early 1927, the book of poems Brecht had been paid for long before by Kiepenheuer was published by Ullstein. It was called *Die Hauspostille*, or *Manual of Piety*. With dozens of sexually explicit poems, this was not a conventional manual of piety.[24] Rather, the text shows a clear affiliation with a text Hauptmann and Brecht would surely have known at this time, the then-famous Walter Mehring's dazzlingly antireligious book of poems *Das Ketzenbrevier* (The heretics' breviary).[25]

At one extreme in *Manual of Piety* are the older, sometimes explicitly antirevolutionary articulations of violence that had been written with Orge and other lovers in the Augsburg years. Despite his recent exposure to *Das Kapital*, Brecht still included in the volume his 1919 poem about the Red Army marching into "paradise" with "blood-stained empty hands." But at the other extreme are a couple of newer, vaguely Marxist, still very violent texts generated by Hauptmann under the sign of Rudyard Kipling. The fourth section of the *Manual of Piety* consists of five poems under the heading "Songs of Mahagonny." Of these, two are new. Both are in English. One is titled "The Alabama Song," and the other, "The Benares Song." Both, we now know, were written by Hauptmann.

In "The Benares Song," men find themselves lost in a dark world devastated by earthquake, on a planet "on which there is not much fun" and where "there is no door that is ajar." Here men seek a haven where there are welcoming women (metaphorical doors that are ajar) and where their thirst will be satisfied. The world of these two poems is very close to that of Widow Begbick's canteen-cum-brothel that is the center of *A Man's a Man*. For all of Brecht's discussions with Sternberg about how silly it is to organize works of art around the attraction of women for men, this is what the Mahagonny poems and *A Man's a Man* articulate. Indeed, it is clear from the time that Hauptmann had begun to work with him in late 1924 that women, who had been marginalized as mindless and faceless objects in virtually all Brecht's previous work, will rapidly become central, beings who control as much by what is between their ears as what is between their legs.

In the clear-cut instance of the Mahagonny poems, we have what appears at first to be the unmistakable "voice" of Brecht. But we are mistaken. John Willett, arguably the leading authority on the poetry of Brecht, notes matter-of-factly: "Elisabeth Hauptmann . . . wrote him the two English-language 'Mahagonny Songs' which have ever since figured among his poems."[26] In an interview with James Lyon, Hauptmann said it was "self-evident' that she had written a poem such as "The Alabama Song."[27] As confirmation of this, the two songs are marked in the archival copies in Hauptmann's hand: "English by Hauptmann" on one and "By Hauptmann. Brecht's handwriting" on the other.[28]

If Willett and Lyon are correct, as I believe they are, about the real authorship of such quintessentially "Brechtian" artifacts as the stream of Kipling poems and the English songs about Mahagonny, then we must recognize that what we have supposed to be a genuinely "Brecht-ian" voice can be by another person, a person with a very different world view from that articulated by Bertolt Brecht throughout his life. Hauptmann may speak in what we choose to recognize as "his" voice, but what she says in that voice is very much hers.

With the book of poems finally out, Hauptmann went on to produce a publishable text of *Jungle* and *A Man's a Man*. Brecht, meanwhile, stayed in the public eye, behaving as outrageously as he knew how in judging a poetry contest. Rejecting all the entries in the contest, he violated all the rules and submitted on his own some dog-gerel verses written by the bicycle racer Hannes Küpper. Küpper's verses carried the fashionable, tough American-English title: "He! He! The Iron Man!" Brecht gave the prize to the cyclist, saying he could not give it to a representative of "the sensitive part of a used-up bourgeoisie that I don't want to have anything to do with!"[29] It was a fashionable thing to attack the bourgeoisie. In fact, half the old bourgeoisie seemed to be doing it now. Adolf Hitler and Arnolt Bronnen, for instance, declared that the German bourgeoisie was incapable of digging Ger-many out of the pit she had been left in by the Versailles Treaty.

Using any rostrum, Hitler and Bronnen could be counted on for mounting attacks on all kinds of classes and institutions. When Brecht, Bronnen, and their friend novelist Alfred Döblin were invited together to Dresden in March 1926, Bronnen ensured a scandal with a speech in which he violently abused the Dresden directors.[30] Brecht was meek-ness itself by comparison. He read aloud a small parable mildly rebuk-ing the festival authorities for not greeting "three gods" at the gate of their city. His poem was applauded by the formally clad festival goers.

The behavior of Brecht and Bronnen at Dresden marked one of the basic differences between these two men. Bronnen was literally of the avant-garde; he was a man of real if shifting passions. He would always be found among those who rushed into any fray, whatever the cost might be to him personally. But, as Bronnen had discovered, Brecht operated on almost exactly the opposite basis. While giving an appearance of intemperateness, he hedged all his bets, both personal and political. In all relationships, he would maintain a certain unbreach-able distance. It was a distance that retained for him the greatest possi-ble flexibility, while demanding the greatest possible commitment from others. Sexually and politically, and at the intersection of the two, Brecht's relationships exist in a dramatic balance of desire and repul-sion, magnetism and distance, passion and coldness, commitment and aversion.

A wholly spontaneous act was rare in Brecht's life. Whatever passion Brecht brought to any kind of alliance, he simultaneously maintained a sense of distance. Although winds might blow strongly from either the West or East, as either American capital or Soviet ideology seemed at times to gain the upper hand, Brecht would always be positioned in such a way that he could make progress with or against either wind. He would support Marxism but not join a party. He would attack ideas of property but hold on to his own. Arguing for marriage, he would live outside it. Arguing for the new, he would cling to the old. Attacking the bourgeoisie, he would live a life that his later friend Eric Bentley would describe as "bottomlessly bourgeois."[31] He lived his earlier fantastic dream of enjoying the blossoms of a tree while, at the same moment, burning the logs of that tree.

Both Bronnen and Brecht, though, as we repeatedly see, in psychologically very different ways, continued to push the brash, the new, the technical. In the second half of the twenties, both began to be interested in the financial, political, and aesthetic possibilities of the new medium of radio. Though he was the most-produced dramatist in Berlin, Bronnen had begun to wonder if any kind of change could really be brought about through the old means of the theater. Prey as always to his enthusiasms and hoping to change the world, Bronnen threw himself into radio. With the head of Berlin radio, Alfred Braun, Bronnen did a radio version of Schiller's Wallenstein trilogy. It was the first literary play done for this medium.

Besides radio, Bronnen was now interested in the whole question of women's rights and women's feelings. His eye was caught by an obituary of the American film star Barbara La Marr, dead in the dream factory at age thirty. Bronnen experienced what he called "a writing orgasm" in setting down her story. The serial rights were quickly sold to the magazine *Die Dame* for twelve thousand gold marks. Bronnen was ecstatic. Finally he was able to buy a car and become "a tiger in the asphalt jungle."[32] Swinging violently from incipient feminism, the "tiger" began to write for the male-oriented paper *Sport im Bilder (Sport in Pictures)*. He also began to move in circles where anti-Semitism was explicit. Reshaping his own history in terms of his current enthusiasms, he was delighted when he was told by his mother that he was not the son of his hated Jewish, professor father but the result of her affair with a gentile.

Sailing now in ever-deeper nationalist waters, Bronnen began work on a novel on the German province of Ober-Schlesien. As background, he read the novels of the radically right-wing intellectual Ernst Jünger. He wrote a note to Jünger and arranged a meeting. "Nationalism," said the men in the Jünger circle, "is not interested in tolerance as life itself is intolerant. It is fanatical and unjust, because everything that comes from blood is fanatical and unjust. It does not bother to justify itself scientifically because science weakens life."[33] For Bronnen, such calls were what he longed for, and he now longed for Jünger as he had longed five years earlier for Brecht.

As Bronnen took up with Jünger, Marieluise Fleisser returned to Berlin in the late fall of 1926 in hopes of working with Feuchtwanger and seeing Brecht. With her small income from Ullstein, she thought she would have some measure of professional independence as a writer. As Julius Elias, the Ullstein editor responsible for their young writers, had put it, "They are our race horses, we simply let them run."[34] But Fleisser was not allowed to run in races of her own choosing or at the speed that she knew was best for her. Elias wanted her to produce a novel rather than to continue to work in the short story and dramatic forms where she felt most at home.[35] She was asked to produce something on a salable subject provided by Elias, the story of an American accused of the bloody murder of a schoolchild. But Fleisser wanted nothing to do with such subjects, although they were a staple of Ullstein enterprises.

Fleisser's personal life was also not moving in the direction she wanted. Smitten with Brecht, she wanted him to follow through on his various hints to her of marriage. But she saw him rarely and strictly on his schedule. One day Brecht heard about a whorehouse featuring very young prostitutes. He decided to visit there and invited Fleisser along. "We're going to drive north to the whores in a dive," he told her over the phone. "Come along with us, it won't harm you to know about things like this."[36] At this brothel, with its "bonbon green" lighting and a host of pale young women, one person turned to her and said, "You are like a flower in a swamp." Brecht was pleased by the comment, and they stayed at the place for an hour and a half. On another such expedition, Brecht drew her attention to a fat pimp sending one of his stable out on her nightly patrol. The pimp called out after his "Schützling," or "tiny charge," as Fleisser puts it, using the vocabulary of that milieu, "Erika, swing that purse more." To Brecht's evident satisfaction, Erika seemed to grow in stature and swung her lacquered handbag "optimistically." "Such details," said Fleisser, "made him [Brecht] happy."[37] She should, he said, observe such things and write about them. But she knew that this was as wrong for her as the American child-murderer idea had been.

She did not dare tell Brecht her real feelings about his suggestions because she saw him as a "Dompteur," (breaker of wild beasts).[38] He was, she knew, a man who was used to getting totally his own way, to shouting at, cajoling, flattering, and sleeping with people until they did exactly what he wanted. She still loved him and did not dare to say anything that might drive him away. She knew, however, that "destruction was lodged inside" her, and she also knew it could not remain that way. "He had been riding her," she realized, "as though she were his sled."[39]

But even as she recognized his behavior patterns, her desire for him was still there. She would put up with a great deal more before really trying to break away. Not content with the way she dressed, he sent her to the place he sent all "his" women, the tailor from Augsburg whom he had met. Brecht even told her how to wear the stock overcoat of black merino wool, "unbuttoned, held together by one's elbow across the stomach."[40] Fleisser met some of the other coat wearers. She began to understand something of the life of Helene Weigel and Elisabeth Hauptmann. Almost against her will, she found herself liking both these women. They helped her and they understood both her poverty and her infatuation with Brecht. Weigel would allow her to bathe at her place and loaned her some of her own clothes. Sometimes she would meet Brecht at Weigel's place as he had now made it a habit to come by at least at mealtimes. But whether he was really there or not, Brecht was always a presence for Weigel. Not only were there the button eyes of his son, Stefan, but also Caspar Neher's big mural of him painted on one of Weigel's walls.

Weigel told Fleisser that she had been rather rebellious until she had met Brecht. She intimated that she had picked Brecht as father of her child for his intelligence. But the child seemed to have inherited another characteristic. Fleisser frequently found herself being attacked by Stefan as he tried to burrow "like a tick" and grab under her skirts. When Weigel made no effort to stop him, Fleisser asked, "Is that also supposed to be a sign of genius?" Weigel only laughed. When the two women talked together about men, Weigel was blunt. "Give up men," she said. "They're all bad." And indeed, it seems that Weigel followed her own advice. Often left entirely alone by Brecht when he was off with various other long- or short-term lovers, and knowing how brutally Brecht would react if she spent time with other men, Weigel favored the company of women, often actresses who, like herself, played the androgynous roles much favored on stage and in film.

Seeing the pattern of Brecht's behavior, the stream of other merino-coated women, Fleisser was becoming aware that all Brecht's talk of marriage last summer had probably been just talk. She tried to lead things away from the personal back to a professional level, to talk about writing. Reluctantly, she showed him the beginning of her new play. But glancing at it, he gave her an unhappy look. "So," he said, "you're being rebellious again! We'll just let it lie around a while."

She decided to leave before being directly rejected. He saw her off cheerfully, almost certainly expecting she would return. Back in Ingolstadt, however, she not only now managed to make progress with her play, but she also took up with another man, Josef "Bepp" Haindl. If Haindl's correspondence is a reliable guide, he was not very bright and barely literate. A local swimming champion, he had great legs and a body as dark and hairy as an otter, which were his main attraction for her. He doted on her and seemed to have no interest in other women, but he was also a violently jealous man with eyes that had a kind of yellow fog around the pupils. She would literally have to fear for her life if she ever attempted to break with him. When he took over his parents' small tobacco and spirits shop in Ingolstadt, he expected her to look after it and fit her writing in between selling cigars and schnapps. She did. During 1927, although working slowly, she was able to finish and publish several excellent short stories as well as the complete text of a new play about Ingolstadt, which she would begin to circulate in early 1928.

Brecht was becoming involved in some remunerative work for Berlin radio. Alfred Braun asked Brecht about a radio production of *A Man's a Man*. Since Brecht had not managed to get a stage production of the play in Berlin, the radio seemed a good substitute. Brecht negotiated a contract that gave him all of the author's receipts and did not mention his privately acknowledged coauthor of the play, Elisabeth Hauptmann. The female lead was given to Helene Weigel, who needed the money. Though she and her son, Stefan, lived with their own maid and still had the Daimler, Weigel's cash situation in early 1927 was dire enough that she twice failed to pay her insurance premiums.[41]

Brecht's new contacts with the emerging medium of radio began to pay off in many ways. Of particular value were those he made through radio in the worlds of popular and avant-garde musical composition in Berlin. The broadcast of *A Man's a Man* was accompanied by the work of the composer Edmund Meisel who had done the famous music for Eisenstein's film *Battleship Potemkin*. Brecht also met the young composer Franz Servatius Bruinier, only twenty-one years old at the time.[42] Bruinier worked with Brecht on the music printed in the text of the *Manual of Piety*. Like Hauptmann, he received no acknowledgment in the text though, as Fritz Hennenberg has shown, the music is in Bruinier's careful musical script. The music was built upon popular North and South American music—jazz, blues, and the music for the shimmy, the Charleston, the tango, and the fox-trot—all forms used at this time by Bruinier in his performances as a cabaret artist and composer.

In 1927, at Bruinier's Monday Evening Club, the music ranged from the most popular American forms as played by native German groups who gave themselves American-sounding names such as Sid

Kay's Fellows and the Weintraub Syncopators to the Leninist and musically avant-garde version of Ivan Goll's play *Paris Is Burning*. Brecht regularly attended the club and even sometimes performed with Bruinier in 1926 and early 1927. For all Bruinier's importance in developing Brecht's knowledge of various strands of modern popular music and his writing of music for many of the early songs, he remains almost completely forgotten now. Life was most unkind to Bruinier. Not only was his work stolen, but he also contracted tuberculosis in the summer of 1927 and died within a year at age twenty-three.

At the same time that Brecht was still working with Bruinier, he was introduced to the young avant-garde composer Kurt Weill. Weill had been gaining a name for himself by his work with two of the leading dramatists of the day Ivan Goll and Georg Kaiser, and had also begun to be recognized for his practical and theoretical contributions to radio music. As a reviewer for the magazine *Der deutsche Rundfunk* since early 1925, he had established a reputation as one of the sharpest and most creative minds working in the new medium. He was equally well known in theater and opera. His work had been produced all over Germany before he met Brecht. Given Weill's reputation both as a composer and as a critic, for him to call the March 1927 radio production of *A Man's a Man* "the most novel and powerful play of our time" was a tremendous feather in Brecht's cap.[43] Weill was sufficiently impressed that he arranged to meet Brecht. Soon, Weill and his wife, dancer Lotte Lenya, became part of the inner Brecht circle. It would be a relationship that would bring Lenya and Weill both great fame and great pain.

Lenya and Weill were a curious couple. Born on March 2, 1900, to an old and quite well-off Jewish family in Leipzig, he had grown up as the son of the cantor at Leipzig's palatial new and thriving synagogue. Kurt Weill was not religious himself but had "naturally" adopted the habits of Jewish households of that day where the male expected privacy for study and creativity, while women were supposed to play supporting roles. Lenya had no interest in the traditional wifely pursuits of cooking and cleaning, but was determined to have her own career as a performer. Born Karoline Blamauer on October 18, 1898, in a working-class district of Vienna, where her father worked as a coachman and her mother as a laundress, she grew up sleeping on the lid of a coal bin; and in her early teens, she did acrobatic and high-wire turns in a local circus. After finishing secondary school in Vienna, she persuaded an aunt in Zurich to take her in. She apparently worked part-time as a teenage prostitute while studying ballet. Despite her late start as a ballerina and rather homely looks, here she managed to get a few tiny roles as a dancer. In 1920, she moved to Berlin to work with a struggling acting company that played only Shakespeare. In 1922, she successfully auditioned for Georg Kaiser, who then introduced her to the young, ascending Kurt Weill. Soon, to the horror of his rather snobbish parents, Weill married this homely gentile woman with a past, on January 28, 1926, in a civil ceremony.

Lenya and Weill lived in a third-floor flat in Berlin's Pension Hassforth. Then as now the place was decorated in a style more apt for a funeral parlor than a home. Weill's grand piano was pitch black, and here he sat all day long as happy as a child, playing and composing. Lenya was not happy. One day she told him: "This is a horrible life for me. I only see you at mealtimes." Peering at her through his thick glasses, he replied: "But Lenya, you know you come right after my music."[44] With her physical and emotional needs largely ignored within her marriage, Lenya would more or less openly conduct affairs with men and women. Weill seems to have been quite relaxed about her affairs as he spoke about them openly in at least one newspaper interview.[45]

Soon after Weill met Brecht, they talked of working together. Weill was eager to have something performed at the prestigious German Chamber Music Festival. Originally under the patronage of Prince von Fürstenberg at Donaueschingen, each summer the festival featured the very best of the new, daring modern composers including Arnold Schönberg, Darius Milhaud, Paul Hindemith, and Igor Stravinsky. In the summer of 1927, the festival was moved to the fashionable spa of Baden-Baden, where it was sponsored by Prince Heinrich XIV, remaining both experimental and cosmopolitan.

Casting about for something that could be used as a compositional base for the festival, Weill turned to the Mahagonny poems from the *Manual of Piety*. Weill was overwhelmed by their power, not knowing then or ever that at least half of them were Hauptmann's work and that other material was based on Villon and Kipling. As Weill had used, as Willett notes, "texts by Kipling and Villon for his pantomime *Zaubermacht of 1923*," the *Manual of Piety* was familiar ground.[46] Weill suggested to the collective that these poems could form a base for a loosely constructed "Songspiel" on a mythical "Mahagonny." A fabric was now stitched together with threads from the rough, exotic world of Jack London's Yukon short stories, Charlie Chaplin's *Gold Rush*, and as Michael Feingold pointed out to me, with verbatim phrases from the "gold rush" poems of Robert W. Service, to which Hauptmann would have had direct access in their original English. Weill would have been familiar with a tune popular since early 1922 and repeatedly reissued by record companies in Berlin and Vienna: a so-called Afrikanischer Shimmy titled "Komm nach Mahagonne."[47] The song was by the well-known Berlin cabaret performer O. A. Alberts and was replete with the "frustrated eroticism" that was his trademark. The music for "Komm nach Mahagonne," or "Come to Mahagonne," was by Leopold Krauss-Elka, writer of innumerable hit tunes. In the Mahagonny lyrics, the play with the word "Zi-zi-zi-zi-zivilis" echoes the "Zi-Zi-Zi-Zi-Ziehhar-monika" found in the original song.

Though basic tunes for a number of the individual poems had already been provided by Krauss-Elka and Bruinier, these were only a jump-off point for Weill. His concern was with writing music that would turn these individual, very different pieces into a performable whole. In doing so, he would change the prior work of the Brecht workshop in a fundamental way. Music would no longer be fragmentary, a primitive, usually borrowed accompaniment for an individual cabaret song. Nor would it be a mere insertion as in *Baal, Drums,* and *A Man's a Man.*

In the future, Lenya and Weill would also insist on other changes, demanding work that contained more substantial roles for women than had been produced in the Brecht workshop thus far despite Hauptmann's beginning efforts in that direction. For the workshop, Weill's skills and energy, combined with the performance skills of Lenya, would prove to be manna from heaven. Where the new type of play that Brecht had dreamed of with a violent World War I piece called *Fatzer* had not come together, and would never come together, it was Weill's use of a linked, sophisticated fabric that would magically transform a series of fragments into a coherent and performable whole. Since Weill was spending more and more time now working with Brecht and Hauptmann, his contribution to the festival program in 1927 would read "A Songspiel after Texts by Bert Brecht by Kurt Weill."

Works such as this, as performed more often than not by Lenya, would have a savage, lascivious edge echoing Lenya's real life history as circus performer and teenage prostitute. Weill was working now both with and against musical convention in a style at times serious and then suddenly mocking and bitingly ironic. What began to emerge would be a kind of mock cantata for four male and two female voices. As the *Mahagonny Songspiel* (as the work would be called) began to take shape, Lenya, anxious to get to work as a performer and to get out of the confines of the Pension Hassforth, was delighted that Kurt composed some of the pieces in a range that she, as an untrained singer, could perform.

Brecht was apparently dubious when the idea of Lenya first came up. But he agreed to come by the pension to hear her audition one of the "zonks" as they pronounced such creations. On the audition day, banging and shouting were heard downstairs. Herr Hassforth had taken one look at the deliberately disreputable-looking Bertolt Brecht and slammed the door yelling, "We're not giving anything." Only over Herr Hassforth's protests was Brecht admitted and shown upstairs. Lenya totally mangled the words of Hauptmann's "Alabama Song," but that didn't trouble Brecht. He had no more idea how to pronounce them properly than did Lenya. With great courtesy, Lenya recalled years later, he adjusted the way she held her arm as she sang about the moon over Alabama. "Not quite so Egyptian,"[48] he said. Lenya passed the test, and Brecht now insisted to his Baden-Baden co-director Walter Brügmann that Lenya be given a key part in the production.

Brecht also was able to persuade Caspar Neher to work on this avant-garde piece. When blown up on the huge screen he had installed, Neher's pictures of provocatively posed and near-naked prostitutes would be sure to cause a fuss in Baden-Baden. Neher also designed a boxing ring to be used as the center of the action, the same device used in 1922 in Bronnen's *Parricide* and by Piscator in one of his 1924 Communist party productions.

The text being created in the Brecht-Hauptmann-Weill workshop, with elements from the *Manual of Piety* and *A Man's a Man*, was even by today's standards astounding in its sexual frankness—though Brecht's idea of having Lenya and Irene Eden appear as though they were in the Garden of Eden before the Fall was turned down by the festival management. It was already bad enough that a certain Madame Begbick (taken from the Hauptmann-Brecht reworking of *A Man's a Man*) was to give the following bilingual foreplay instructions to the whorehouse customers, "Let the tips of your fingers / Stroke the tips of her breasts / And wait for the quivering of her flesh," and then, intoned rather improbably in Latin, "Introducto pene frontem in fronte ponens requiescat."[49]

The 1927 Baden-Baden festival began in a decorous way. The cosmopolitan audience in high-fashion summer dresses, white summer suits, and straw hats listened to "atonal cello sonatas and settings of Petrarchan sonnets for string trio, voice, and solo oboe."[50] Then on July 17 a pistol shot signaled the opening of *Mahagonny* and introduced a parody of a utopia set somewhere in "America." Four men, with the American-sounding names of Jim, Jake, Bill, and Joe have chopped down trees for seven years and are now ready to spend their earnings in pursuit of some serious pleasure. Begbick, in front of a place called the Here-You-May-Do-Anything Inn, paraded her wares, seven women in advanced stages of undress.[51] After haggling, Jim selected a woman called Jenny and retired with her for some vigorous sex behind a semi-transparent screen at center stage. Then, in a staged prize fight, Trinity Moses killed Alaska-Wolf-Joe. Next, a barely clothed Lenya sashayed through her "zonks" "in a hoarse voice with lascivious inflections."[52]

Brecht stood at one corner of the ring as if he might be a gentleman second or a customer of Begbick.

The audience, like the reviewers later, was very much divided, and the performers left the concert area not really knowing whether their work had been a success. Later, back at the bar of the festival hotel, the conductor Otto Klemperer, the new head of the famous Kroll Opera in Berlin, slapped Lenya on the back and, with a booming laugh, quoted the pidgin English of Hauptmann's "Benares Song": "Is here no telephone?" At this, the whole bar crowd launched into the song. Clearly, the show had been a hit with some of the most experimental people of German cultural life. For Lenya, that Baden-Baden performance would serve as the launching pad for an international career as a singer. For Weill, *Mahagonny* marked a transition from the strictly avant-garde to the more popular. For Brecht, who had never had a popular success before, *Mahagonny* would point toward works in which music, both serious and popular, is central.

But despite the success of *Mahagonny*, Hauptmann remained as obscure as ever. The reasons behind this can only partially be accounted for. Obviously, the sexual explicitness of *Mahagonny* would have been problematic both for her and her parents back in provincial Peckelsheim. With the marriage with Zoff inching toward formal dissolution, Hauptmann hoped marriage with Brecht would come soon and that she could remain in the background. Only when that dream was smashed later would she suddenly, but even then only briefly, demand direct recognition for her primary role in texts produced in the Brecht factory.

14

"The Pawnbroker . . . Took Anything That Might Be Useful to Him from Right and Left" (1927–28)

While the *Mahagonny Songspiel* shock waves continued to spread, Brecht returned to Augsburg. He was alone. By the middle of 1927, the sexual relationships with Fleisser and Hauptmann had lost much of their intensity for him. But just as he had done with others, he wanted them not to enter other alliances and to continue to provide him with writing help and sex whenever he needed it.

It was now becoming obvious to Hauptmann that her friend the actress Carola Neher was having an intense affair with Brecht. Brecht had first met Carola Neher in Munich in 1922. She had left a convent school at age fourteen and spent some time in Baden-Baden, Munich, and Nuremberg. While she was still in her early teens, she met and married the playwright, poet, and cabaret performer the then thirty-four-year-old Klabund. A remarkable man, he had suffered from pulmonary tuberculosis since he was seventeen but had continued to perform and write, living whatever life he had with extraordinary passion. Confident in his beloved's great talent, Klabund cast her in major roles in his own plays, especially in the boy-girl roles. In 1925, Klabund gave Neher the female lead in his highly successful adaptation of the classical Chinese play *The Chalk Circle* and in 1926, in his play *Burning Earth*, both of which would prove useful later as the basis of "Brecht" plays.

Though some dismissed Neher as simply a sexpot, she was a richly sensitive woman who herself wrote poetry and was genuinely interested in trying to help alleviate the social problems facing Germany and the world. Where others would merely theorize about helping the proletariat, Carola Neher would join the CPG and give up the style of life available to her as one of Weimar's biggest stars of stage and screen.

When Neher got her first major role in Berlin in 1927, she dazzled even the most hardened critics. Stephan Grossmann wrote that her mere appearance "produced mass intoxication in the theater."[1] She radiated such liveliness "that everything that was not young, should and must slink away." Brecht was not about to slink away. But the relationship had not reached the point by the middle of 1927 where Brecht could get Neher to join him in Augsburg.

As was virtually always the case when he was alone, Brecht was having difficulty writing drama. Only half-jokingly, he would tell Alfred Döblin around this time that "my poetry is the strongest argument against my play writing."[2] Though the remark has something about it of Brecht's typical hyperbole, it also has a kernel of truth. He was always most comfortable when he could provide poems set to music for plays, and then get others like Caspar Neher or Elisabeth Hauptmann to do much of the structural work needed to change the poems into a play. Generally, poems flowed naturally from him. Coming relatively easily, poetry constituted what John Willett has aptly called "a dangerously seductive distraction," taking him away from what was for Brecht "the tougher and less natural job" of writing plays.[3]

Failing with his play projects in the summer of 1927, he caught up with some business correspondence, including letters to Weigel charging her with various tasks. One wholly typical letter to her contains a long list of errands she is to carry out for him, among them to send him as much Marxist literature as possible, and ends simply with "I kiss you."[4] He still maintained his connections with the increasingly right-wing Bronnen and his nationalist friends, and with the German aristocracy. He wrote a thank-you note to the crown prince of Reuss, Prince Heinrich XIV, his host at the Baden-Baden festival. He sent a threatening note to a functionary in Essen demanding a royalty check for a play on problems in the Ruhr that Brecht had not completed; and a letter to Felix Gasbarra, a member of Piscator's theater collective in Berlin, complaining about the subsidiary role Brecht was apparently to be given in the collective. In another note, this one directly to Piscator, he sought to define his role in the collective as one where he would be willing to take political guidance but would maintain his own dramaturgical independence. From Piscator's perspective, however, what Brecht was proposing made no sense in a collective, and the two would never be able to see eye to eye.

Piscator's theater made dramaturgy (here including both the content and the construction of plays) dependent on whatever political issue his Communist party–oriented theater was currently supporting. Where Brecht as an author believed in the primacy of a written text for theatrical use, Piscator treated the written word as gunpowder to be loaded into political fireworks; the gunpowder per se interested him not at all; it was the explosion that counted.[5] Piscator also believed in collective work, which he wanted immediately available to other revolutionaries. He did not want outdated royalty concerns to inhibit such use.

When Brecht tried to be "revolutionary" and produce something to Piscator's liking, it did not work. Despite all Hauptmann did to get him materials on the Chicago wheat exchange from her American relatives, he made little progress with his play on that subject, *Joe Fleisch-hacker*. He next turned to *Fatzer*, a story of four deserters from a German tank regiment at the end of World War I. But this material, some 550 chaotic pages of which have survived, began to look more and more like a restatement of the fantastic adventures of the four comrades in *A Man's a Man* and less and less like something suitable for Pisca-tor's stage. With neither *Fleischhacker* nor *Fatzer* working out, Brecht then worked for part of the summer trying, without Hauptmann there to help him, to translate a ballad of Upton Sinclair for Piscator's use. But after eight attempts, he saw the work was a failure. In a letter to Piscator, Brecht blamed Sinclair.[6]

Unable to progress on things for Piscator, he had turned to some more private projects. At the photo studio at 24 Bahnhofstrasse where his parents had had his baby pictures made, he arranged with the noted photographer Konrad Ressler to do a portfolio of portraits. This set of thirty-two glass negatives survived World War II, and was finally found and published sixty years after they were made. In the photographs, he is clean shaven for once and without his cheap-looking glasses; wholly at ease with the photographer, his head is shorn like a convict or a monk, and he wears a huge, full-length leather overcoat, a leather vest poking out from underneath, his leather belt knotted as casually around his waist as the leather tie around his thin neck; in most, he holds a wet stump of a cigar either in his hand or his mouth, sometimes a book and a pen. He stares or smiles out of the photos, variously tough, gentle, boyish, prematurely old, formal, totally casual. He would be com-pletely at home in the punk or art scene of London, Berlin, or any other major capital today. From these pictures, one senses the magnetism that Brecht knew he could exert over virtually anyone, male or female, young or old.

That same summer, he also arranged to have pornographic son-nets, which he had been writing since his teenage days, privately printed.[7] These included poems with lines such as: "she hoped to enter paradise with the cocks of twenty sailors in her hand"; "An old cunt instructs a young one"; "before I finally have you bent over a chair, I hope you'll be wetter than the last one I loved"; and "lie to her my son, tell her yours is bigger than anyone else's."

While he busied himself in Augsburg with personal portraits, pornography, and an occasional new poem, his associates in Berlin had begun work on a new round of "Brecht" projects. Weill took Brecht's early poem "Death in the Forest" and composed for it a haunting score for ten wind instruments and a single bass voice. Weill now declared to his publisher, Universal Edition of Vienna, that he planned a full-scale opera version of *Mahagonny*. The head of Universal Edition, Emil Hertzka, was alarmed at what he saw as a too-narrow focus developing in Weill's work. But Weill argued that "[the work] is directed to a different and much larger audience . . . [and its] appeal will be unusually broad."[8] Finally Hertzka agreed to back Weill and to double the composer's modest monthly advance of two hundred marks.

Feeling personally abandoned as Brecht's affair with Carola Neher had heated up, Hauptmann was busy trying to create a follow-up to the success of *Mahagonny*. In the winter of 1927–28, friends in England sent her a copy of John Gay's *Beggar's Opera*, the 1728 parody of corrupt London society and of that society's favorite composer, Handel. Hauptmann was immediately fascinated with the work of John Gay on account of its sympathy for London's exploited poor; its savage satire on the behavior of British society; and its emphasis both in *The Beggar's Opera* and in *Polly*, its even more radical successor, on strong females trying to assert themselves despite a clearly male-dominated society.

The Beggar's Opera itself is a play within a play. Prisoners at London's infamous Newgate prison stage a play about a receiver of stolen goods and police informer called Peachum, his wife, and his lovely, smart, highly independent daughter, Polly. Other characters are the Newgate warden, Lockit, and his daughter, Lucy. Rounding out the cast is Macheath, a highwayman that women (including both Polly and Lucy) find irresistible. When Peachum has Macheath sent to Newgate, a duet is sung between the two lovers of Macheath, who wishes, Brecht-like, that he could keep both lovely ladies. Lucy, despite her jealousy toward her rival Polly and under the nose of her father, gets the prisoner freed. In the continuation of the story as presented in the 1729 opera *Polly* (a work deemed so radical that the lord chamberlain promptly had it banned from the stage though it circulated in printed form), Macheath has been sent in a prison convoy to the West Indies. The valiant Polly follows him there and has to fight off the unwelcome attentions of a planter called Ducat. Polly is smarter and more valiant than anyone else in the play. She escapes from Ducat, disguises herself as a man, and fights against and defeats a bunch of pirates. She is too late, however, to save Macheath from execution. After Macheath's well-deserved death, rather than returning to corrupt England, Polly remains in the West Indies and marries a presumably less corrupt native prince.

Hauptmann was immediately taken with Gay's bold heroine and her problems with the womanizer Macheath, a man obviously akin to Brecht. She began work at once on a new version of *The Beggar's Opera* designed to fit Berlin. Brecht, however, showed scant enthusiasm for the project.[9] Not only did he not have enough English, as we know, to read this complex early eighteenth-century work in the original, but he was also too busy with the interminable *Fatzer* and *Joe Fleischhacker* to bother with what Hauptmann was doing.

Fleischhacker was long overdue. Piscator had announced *Fleisch-*

hacker (under the title *Weizen,* or *Wheat*) for the 1927–28 season, but Brecht turned up empty-handed. He did work for a time with Felix Gasbarra, Leo Lania, and Piscator on ambitious plays that were completed and staged such as *Rasputin, The Romanovs, The War* and *The People That Stood up against Them,* and the dramatization of the Czech novelist Jaroslav Hasek's *Adventures of the Good Soldier Schweik;* but we know from both Piscator and Brecht that the alliance was always uneasy. *Wheat* was never finished.

Brecht was out hustling slightly modified versions of old works. In October 1927, he was involved in a Radio Berlin broadcast of *Macbeth,* to which he contributed an introduction. In December, he partially supervised a reworked version of his early play *Jungle* as directed in Darmstadt by Carl Ebert. And in early January 1928, he worked with Erich Engel as the older man directed the Berlin stage premiere of *A Man's a Man.* In the cast was Brecht's old enemy from the *Parricide* debacle, the massive and plausibly brutal Heinrich George. Weigel, in jackboots and trousers, played Begbick. None of these works survived for more than a handful of performances. As the actors who played in them knew, one did Brecht productions in those days for love, not money.

By the spring of 1928, Piscator was sure that Brecht really was not capable of working with contemporary themes. Brecht always seemed more comfortable when a play dealt either with other countries, often exotic, or other times, often erotic. In unpublished jottings about Brecht left to the Academy of Arts in Berlin, we find Piscator remembering riding on the top level of an omnibus with Brecht at around the time Brecht was stopping work with Piscator's company. Piscator asked Brecht about current projects. Brecht is supposed to have said: "Da schreibt Frau H. über eine 3 penny opera" (Well, Frau H. is writing about a three penny opera). All winter, Brecht had shown scant interest in Hauptmann's *Beggar's Opera* project. But this was to suddenly change in the late spring of 1928 when an opportunity came along to sell it. Ernst Josef Aufricht, a new theatrical entrepreneur in Berlin, had been given a sum of 100,000 marks by his father, a wealthy Jewish entrepreneur from Ober-Schlesien. Aufricht used this sum to lease the turn-of-the-century Schiffbauerdamm Theater, an old-fashioned place full of velvet plush, brass, and mahogany. Fritz Wreede, head of the Felix Bloch Erben Company, the biggest and most prestigious of the theatrical agencies, offered Aufricht the then-famous Hermann Sudermann's newest play. Glancing at it, Aufricht threw it away. He next paid some option money for a play called *Mississippi* by the fashionable Georg Kaiser, but it did not get finished. A little desperate by now, Aufricht decided to make the rounds of the various artists hangouts to see what he might be able to find.

One day in the second half of April, Brecht was sitting at his usual place at Schlichter's restaurant with cigar and newspaper when Aufricht came in with his young assistant, Heinrich Fischer, in tow.[10] Though Aufricht had not met Brecht, he knew him by description. Spotting him at his usual place wearing his usual tough-guy costume, Aufricht found him exuding charm. Brecht eagerly began to talk about *Fleischhacker*. He did not mention it was already promised to Piscator. But Fischer and Aufricht did not like the sound of *Fleischhacker* anyway. As the impresarios got up to leave, Brecht suddenly said: "Then I've got something on the side. You could look at six or seven scenes from it tomorrow. It's an adaptation of John Gay's *Beggar's Opera*."[11]

The next day Aufricht and Fischer got their first look at the play.[12] They were immediately taken with the "insolence and dry wit," as they put it, of the text and determined to grab it at once. They were convinced by the biting style of the piece that they were reading authentic Brecht. The mistake was understandable for, of course, they were reading a text just as authentic as a number of other texts primarily prepared by Hauptmann but attributed to Brecht. Swept away by Hauptmann's superb work, Aufricht called Brecht to make a deal. But Brecht wanted to attach a condition. He wanted to bring Kurt Weill into the project to do the music. As Fischer and Aufricht had read the work as a rather funny, literary operetta, they were not sure Weill was the best choice for the music. Thus, while agreeing to take a look at Weill, they engaged the Berlin operetta director Theo Mackeben to do a version of J. C. Pepusch's original score. To direct, they engaged the experienced Erich Engel.

As Aufricht and Fischer worked to open the Schiffbauerdamm Theater with *Beggar's* on Aufricht's birthday, August 31, Brecht was busy making deals. As he well knew, having put the clause in himself, his contract with the Ullstein concern excluded operas. This meant he could sell it elsewhere rather than giving it up to Ullstein for the advance money he had been receiving. He decided to take *Beggar's* to Fritz Wreede.

A contract was drafted at Brecht's direction, and arrangements made to sign it at the Felix Bloch Erben offices on April 26.[13] Brecht invited Weill to go along to the signing but did not include Hauptmann, even though the text delivered to Felix Bloch Erben was clearly hers. Felix Bloch Erben's original hectographically reproduced version of this text has survived. It is currently part of the holdings of the old East Berlin Academy of Arts, where it is still treated as though it were a Brecht text.[14] But when American scholar Ronald K. Shull and East German scholar Joachim Lucchesi took a close look at the original typescript, they saw it "relied heavily on Gay's original piece including the retention of a number of song texts of Gay in Hauptmann's translation."[15]

Given the existence of this text, plus the fact that Hauptmann was the only person in the workshop who had the necessary skills to render such complex English into equally complex German, there can be little doubt that *at least* 80 percent of the fabric of the work that Felix Bloch Erben would soon globally market was hers. Both in a published article and in a recent interview with me, Klaus Völker, one of the most knowledgeable people in the world on the Brecht circle, told me it was his view that "Elisabeth Hauptmann was responsible for as much as 80 or even 90 percent of the published text of *The Threepenny Opera*."[16] Though, later, Brecht would put in work on the text and contribute songs taken primarily from other authors, though the lyrics of the song "Mack the Knife" are almost certainly wholly his, the fact remains that the text bought by Aufricht and later sold to Felix Bloch Erben was almost exclusively written by Elisabeth Hauptmann.

Despite the fact that it was clearly Hauptmann's work being sold, outside the Felix Bloch Erben offices on the Nikolsburger Platz in late April 1928, Brecht sat Weill down on a bench to outline the deal he would be asked to sign. Though Weill was used to getting 50 percent or even two-thirds of the income from projects that he had done with major playwrights like Ivan Goll and Georg Kaiser, this was not what Brecht had in mind.[17] Weill told Lenya later that he had been presented with a strictly take-it-or-leave-it deal. Brecht declared the division would be: Hauptmann would get 12.5 percent; Weill, 25 percent; and Brecht, the remaining 62.5 percent. Brecht claimed that Aufricht did not really need Weill at all as he could use the original eighteenth-century score. The question that day was simple: did Weill want 25 percent of something, or would he prefer 100 percent of nothing? When Brecht took Weill upstairs to meet Herr Wreede, there it was in black and white: "Bert Brecht, Berlin W. 50, Spichernstrasse 16, and Kurt Weill, Charlottenburg, Luisenplatz 3," agree with Felix Bloch Erben to "jointly exploit the intellectual property of the revised work with music: *The Beggar's Opera*." The division of royalties was just as Brecht had outlined it. There was 12.5 percent for "Frau Elisabeth Hauptmann who," as the contract says, with massive understatement, "is assisting on the book." As Hauptmann's name had not appeared at all on any of the earlier work she had done that had been published under Brecht's name, 12.5 percent was certainly better than nothing but failed to recognize that the work sold that day was virtually 100 percent her writing.[18]

That April day in 1928, Herr Wreede had no idea of the extent of Hauptmann's work. What Wreede did know was that Brecht had a well-earned reputation for not completing contractual work anywhere near on time. Therefore, Wreede had insisted on putting a number of cautious provisions into the firm's agreement with "the author." The contract would go into effect only when the following had taken place: a production contract was signed with the Schiffbauerdamm Theater; Brecht delivered the finished libretto in a timely way; and six weeks after the libretto was completed, Herr Weill delivered the completed score.

It was a solid piece of business done by Brecht that day, one that he and his heirs would earn millions by and that would advance him, a person still almost completely unknown outside Germany, to world fame. Even to this day, for the person on the street, if Brecht's name is known at all, it is usually as the author of the ever-popular *Threepenny Opera*, rather than the author of other, more highbrow texts. On April 30, 1928, four days after making the *Beggar's* deal that would make him rich, he wrote a little handwritten note on the borrowed stationery of Berlin's grand Fürstenhof Hotel. This was something that he had chosen, for whatever reason, not to have done by Hauptmann. The note confirmed to Universal Edition in Vienna the receipt of a three-thousand-mark check. This was, as the note makes clear, a down payment for the expanded version of *Mahagonny* that Weill, again using Hauptmann's original English language poems, was working to complete.

While Brecht quietly resold *Mahagonny* and presented Hauptmann's *Beggar's Opera* as his work, she published a fine short story in *Uhu* in April 1928. Published under her own name, the story is set in San Francisco at the time of the earthquake of 1906. "Bessie Soundso" (an echo of Bess, the short form of her own first name used in her private circle) tells of the heroism and leadership of the young woman of the story's title. Stressing her identification with Bessie, the story was printed with a photo of Hauptmann in a Salvation Army uniform.

Bessie, leader of a small Salvation Army group, spends the evening before the earthquake singing before a hostile crowd in a San Francisco bar. When the earthquake begins, she is in the street with a male Salvation Army colleague who tires to lecture the onlookers on religion. The narrow street in which they stand is blocked by a large car; and Bessie realizes they must push the car out of the way if the street is to be cleared or everybody will be killed by falling debris. Bessie puts practicality ahead of religion and orders her colleagues (in the slightly nonidiomatic English of the original story): "Stop that nonsense! Get the car away! Get out of the town!"[19] The car is moved and the crowd is saved. Though the style of this piece sounds very like what is usually thought to be the Brecht "voice," what the voice says is radically different from that of works written by Brecht. Poems and songs that he wrote alone never have the feminist signature of the "Bessie Soundso" story. Bess gets things done while men theorize.

With the *Beggar's Opera* deal requiring that the work be completed, Brecht began to meet with his old friend Erich Engel, the play's director, to line up parts for Helene Weigel and Carola Neher. Neher was to get the role of Polly, while Weigel—aptly enough, for this was what she was often forced to do in real life with Brecht—was to play the role of the madame, an older woman who caters to the gangster chief's taste for younger women. Caspar Neher was to design the sets and costumes.

Despite Brecht's interest in the casting of the new show, he had little time to spare to get it written. He was still dunning the theater management in the provincial town of Essen for work he claimed to have done. As usual, he threatened legal action if his conditions were not met. He was also corresponding with Ferdinand Reyher, an American writer who he hoped could promote his affairs in America. Reyher had just visited Berlin where he had hoped to have his own plays, in Elisabeth Hauptmann's translations, staged. Brecht said he hoped Reyher could return to Berlin to work with Hauptmann so that Reyher's play could be "quickly and reliably completed."[20] Included with Brecht's letter was Hauptmann's version of Reyher's play.

By May 10, with the show scheduled to open in late August, neither libretto nor score were really complete. Engel, Brecht, Hauptmann, Weill, and Lenya decided to go to Le Lavandou, a small village in the south of France, to work together. However, in July, Brecht told Weigel he had finished work on the play he was still calling *The Beggar's Opera*.[21] Actually, it would not be finished at the time the curtain was scheduled to rise in late August. To Hauptmann's despair, Brecht dashed back to Berlin to spend two weeks looking in on *Warren Hastings*, a play in which he had a financial interest with Lion Feuchtwanger. He thought the production itself awful but noted it was doing well at the box office. Next, he dashed to Heidelberg to check on a revival of *In the Jungle of Cities*. From there, it was on to Homburg to visit Fritz Sternberg and then to the Bavarian village of Utting, writing an occasional letter from a house overlooking the Ammersee, one of his favorite lakes. He did not get to Berlin from Utting until August 20. Rehearsals had begun at the Schiffbauerdamm Theater on August 1, using of necessity what the other collaborators had produced in the south of France.[22] Some of Hauptmann's free renderings of Kipling ballads, including the "Cannon Song" (used earlier in the 1928 Berlin *A Man's a Man*), had been inserted. The surviving manuscripts, and the tone of the works themselves, indicate that Hauptmann was responsible for the songs that tell a story from a woman's point of view. One of these, "The Song of

Pirate Jenny," reveals Hauptmann's knowledge of Gay's later play *Polly* where the heroine bravely battles pirates. Another Hauptmann song appears to be the now very famous "Barbara Song." Finally, the "Jealousy Duet" is Hauptmann's near-verbatim rendering of Gay's original words.

Though by the time of Brecht's arrival on August 20 the work was reasonably complete, we know that Brecht did put in several things. Most of these were not his but four Villon ballads taken virtually verbatim from an early twentieth-century volume of translations by K. L. Ammer, including what would become several of the most prominent songs in the play.[23] The "Ballad of a Pleasant Life" contains one of the most famous lines in "Brecht," "Nur wer im Wohlstand Lebt, lebt angenehm" (Only he who lives well, lives pleasantly).[24] The "Ballad of the Pimp" is also straight Villon-Ammer, as is the "Ballad of the Famous" that was used here and then again in *Mother Courage.* The others saw these pieces as typical Brecht songs. They were. He had been using Ammer's translations from the time of *Baal* and *In the Jungle of Cities.*

Unaware of where the "Brecht" songs were coming from, Weill created a highly original score for the emerging piece. Following Berlin fashion, he worked in a number of tunes based on North and South American popular songs and on American jazz. When Weill performed a piano reduction of the score, Aufricht realized at once that the music was at least as good as the rather makeshift but lively libretto. Plans to use the eighteenth-century Pepusch score were now dropped, and Aufricht engaged a small Berlin jazz group with the fashionably American-sounding name of the Lewis Ruth Band. The music was to be conducted by Theo Mackeben. Weill now convinced Aufricht and Engel that after Lenya's popular success in Baden-Baden with *Mahagonny,* she should be given a singing role as one of the numerous whores in the piece. For Lenya, the transition was an easy one. Several scenes and songs familiar to her from *A Man's a Man,* which had been revised in *Mahagonny,* were recycled for this production. Brecht returned from Utting after missing three of four weeks of rehearsals. Both major and minor casting and most of the blocking of the show had been done by Aufricht and Engel.

Late that August, half of Berlin seemed involved in the troubles of the show. At rehearsals, familiar faces like Lion Feuchtwanger, Georg Grosz, and Austrian playwright and satirist Karl Kraus could be seen in the semidarkness, together with Kraus's protégé, the unknown Elias Canetti. Later, cast, authors, composer, band, and kibitzers would adjourn to Schlichter's Café to debate what should happen next. At one session, Feuchtwanger, who was good with titles, finally came up with

"The Threepenny Opera," and this was jotted down by Brecht and given to the press. In the babble and smoke of Schlichter's, Kraus would write lines for the show and pass them to Brecht, who would cheerfully accept what he happened to like. Canetti saw that Kraus, like everyone else it seemed, was completely overwhelmed.

Away from the restaurant table, sitting quietly at home reading Brecht's *Manual of Piety*, Canetti was himself so overwhelmed with the power of this book of poems that this future Nobel Prize winner in literature said later: "My own writings crumbled into dust. It would be too much to say that I was ashamed of them; they simply no longer existed; nothing was left of them, not even shame."[25] At this same time, the poet and songwriter, Kurt Tucholsky was similarly dazzled by Brecht as a poet, comparing him in 1928 to Gottfried Benn, one of the greatest masters of German poetry of the twentieth century.

Overwhelmed as they were by Brecht's poetry, both Tucholsky and Canetti were less enthusiastic about Brecht as a person and as a playwright. As Canetti saw the way *Threepenny* was done, his horror grew. The Peachums in the play deal in fake costumes, and Canetti thought Brecht himself wore a "proletarian disguise." Canetti did not see in Brecht a handsome, rakish figure with nose and hair reminiscent of busts of ancient Roman emperors that others sometimes seemed to see but a startlingly thin man whose words came out in a choppy, wooden way, and "when he gazed at you," as Canetti noted, "you felt like an object of value that he, the pawnbroker, with his piercing black eyes, was appraising as something that had no value." The "pawnbroker," Canetti saw, "took anything that might be useful to him from right and left, from behind and in front of him." "He did not care for people, Canetti surmised, "but he put up with them," and "he respected those who were persistently useful to him." Lotte Lenya, a similarly close observer, noted, "Back of all his maneuvers, back of all the charm, a gnawing concern for his own myth, and forever assessing people for what they could contribute to him (and invariably getting it)."[26]

Soon after rehearsals began, Carola Neher, cast as Polly, had been called away to what would prove to be her husband's deathbed in Davos. Twice a day, the frantic Aufricht called to get bulletins on the dying poet. After Klabund died in mid-August, Neher returned to Berlin only to discover that during her absence many of her best lines had been reassigned. She complained to Brecht when he got back to Berlin at the end of the third week in August. Much taken with the fetching young widow, he hastened to beef up her role by recycling lines from other characters. To Aufricht's horror, Brecht had a table brought out on stage, and here Brecht and Carola Neher huddled together. This stopped rehearsals completely, and there was much muttering among the other cast members. Finally, at five o'clock one morning, Aufricht asked whether instead of blocking the stage, Neher and Brecht might not go off together to his private office. Neher was incensed. She threw her script at Aufricht's feet and told him to play the part himself. The next day Brecht recommended that Engel and Aufricht "go to Neher's apartment with a bouquet of roses and the bride's dress of Polly." But though the roses were accepted, the maid came out to inform them that "the honorable lady is not receiving today."[27]

With Neher refusing to continue, a frantic scramble ensued. Not only was Neher now out, but suddenly Weigel was rushed off to have her appendix removed. It was a difficult situation in every way. At this late date, almost everyone of any stature was already tied up for the start of the new Berlin season and the Aufricht show was due to open in a week. Though he was not the director of record for the show, Brecht was known to be a holy terror at rehearsals. He was also thought to be commercial poison as nothing with his name on it had ever played more than a few days.

Aufricht was finally able to replace Carola Neher with the blond, blue-eyed, consummately professional Roma Bahn. Speedily, Bahn mastered the ever-changing lines and the show's complex musical cues. Weigel was replaced by the cabaret artist Rosa Valetti. Though hardened as a performer at Berlin's very raunchy cabarets, Valetti refused to sing the "Song of Sexual Dependency," which recalls Brecht's pornographic sonnets. To Brecht's dismay, the song then had to be dropped. But always the literary ecologist, a firm believer in literary recycling, Brecht saved it for later use. Brecht wanted to drop some of Hauptmann's Kipling translations, but she fought to keep in "Mary, Pity Women!" one of her special favorites. Finally, it was agreed it would be kept as the refrain for the song sung by Polly when Mack the Knife flees on their wedding day, as well as the "Cannon Song," with its echoes of the "Barrack-Room Ballads."[28]

It had become a show that was now well beyond any single person's control, taking whatever shape it had from a wild and wide variety of suggestions, and built on the debris of multiple crises. Brecht constantly argued with the director of the show Erich Engel and wanted, in the "epic" manner, to mark the beginning of each song by lowering oil lamps. Engel thought the idea contrived and said it would be better to cut the music altogether. This brought an irate Weill into the fray. But then Brecht himself began to slash away at some of the songs, dropping the Solomon "zonk"[29] that Lenya was to have sung. He shortened Erich Ponto's part as Peachum so much that Ponto now threatened to leave. Aufricht said the show's final chorus was so much "like Bach" that it would have to go. Caspar Neher, however, came down on the side of the final chorale and said he would never work with Weill again if the composer did not insist to Aufricht that the chorus be kept. Finally, the mechanical horse that was supposed to bring in the melodramatic messenger announcing the highwayman, rapist, multiple murderer Macheath's improbable pardon could not be gotten out of the starting gate. "No horse, no play," announced Brecht but was overruled by the increasingly more desperate Aufricht.

As though none of this were enough, Harold Paulsen, the great operetta star who was to play Mack the Knife, threatened to leave unless he had the last say about his costume. Whereas the rest of the cast had had to make do with some leftover costumes that Aufricht had snapped up cheaply, Paulsen had gone to Berlin's most expensive tailor for a double-breasted black suit, which he wore with gleaming laquered black shoes, blinding white spats, a sword cane tucked underneath his arm, an expensive black bowler rakishly askew on his immaculately coiffed head, and a stiff standing collar—all this topped off by a flowing, sky blue cravat matching the color of Paulsen's eyes. Aufricht was appalled. This was the typical elegant evening dress of stylish and upper-middle-class Berlin, the people who would be sitting in the opening night audience. Paulsen remained adamant. Either he kept the costume or he would leave the show. "Let him keep it," said Brecht. "Weill and I will introduce him with a Moritat that will describe his crimes, and that way he will appear even more frightening with that blue necktie."

Though several legends conflict, it seems Brecht and Weill set down the words and music that night to what they called simply "The Moritat of Mack the Knife." For years to come, arguments would rage as to which of the two was really responsible for the song. In fact (like so much of the work published under Brecht's name), it would be more honest to think of at least two people as having been parents to the song. The song's strictly male orientation and its casual violence toward women and anyone who gets in Mackie's wholly egocentric way is quintessential Brecht, although the deliberate confusion of sharks with human beings is an echo of the same theme treated in a famous Georg Grosz drawing of 1921, with its three typical Grosz denizens of Berlin brothels, called simply Haifische (Sharks). The seeming simplicity of the music of the eminently singable and danceable "Moritat of Mack the Knife" conceals its complexity, the artful interweaving of dance elements from the blues tradition; even the seeming repetition of its sixteen-measure melody is deceptive, as Kowalke points out, for "each stanza after the first two is clothed in new musical attire pieced together from altered instrumentation, rhythmic patterns, countermelodies, and dynamics."[30]

Of the work as a whole, it is my view that none of the various "parents" could have produced the work without the others. Most of the basic fabric of the play, including several of the songs, was clearly Hauptmann's. The sophisticated score was overwhelmingly Weill. The visual feel of the production from scenic projections to the half-height curtain was vintage Caspar Neher. Mackie's costume (virtually obligatory since in all productions) was the invention of Harold Paulsen. The title, so legend has it, came from Lion Feuchtwanger. The crowd scenes, particularly the march of the beggars, seem to be taken from Piscator's January 1928 *Schweik* production. Several key songs were the work of the fifteenth-century French murderer, thief, and poet Villon as translated into German by K. L. Ammer. Others are Kipling reworked by Hauptmann and sometimes reworked again by Brecht. Finally, at least the lyrics of "Mack the Knife," together with some rewriting of the "Cannon Song" and nips and tucks, and small insertions and large redistributions (giving, for instance, songs or other lines to a performer other than the one Weill or Hauptmann had originally had in mind) were, as far as I can determine, the vital contribution Bertolt Brecht made to the work.

Changes, mainly cuts rather than the writing of new material, continued right up to August 30. Weill noticed at the last moment that Lenya's name was not in the program, and he furiously announced his plans to withdraw at once. Lenya quieted him down, sure that her performance would be one that would not be overlooked even without her name in the program. When the cast and management finally got to bed on the morning of August 31, the script still looked like a series of fragments. To Aufricht, with a large piece of his father's fortune at stake, the way to bankruptcy looked fully paved. It would not have helped his nerves to know that Rosa Valetti had signed a contract with Berlin's Comics' Cabaret to appear there if *Threepenny*, as was widely expected, opened and closed on the same day.

15

"A Robot That Stood There, Used to Coldness of the Emotions" (1928–29)

Caspar Neher's white curtain with the words "Die 3 Groschenoper" in black letters swished open on the night of August 31, 1928. Kurt Gerron, in the role of ballad singer, cranked the handle of a hand organ and sang the "*Moritat* of Mack the Knife," while Paulsen, with the lethal glide of a black panther, crossed the stage. To everyone's horror, the hand organ failed to work. Only with the second verse of the lugubrious song did the leader of the Lewis Ruth Band spring to the rescue. Scantily clad whores stared as Paulsen glided by, and Lenya rasped, "That was Mack the Knife."

Then Erich Ponto as Peachum explained how he outfitted "beggars" to look poor and needy, and gave them quotes from the Bible to try to wring some change out of passers-by. The scene ended without applause. Now, to rhythms pitched between a French chanson and a death march, the chambermaid Jenny, one of Hauptmann's many abandoned women in this work, sang her fantasy of future power, asking "Who shall we kill?" and answering "All of them." Not even this thawed the first-night audience.

Next came the scene of one of Mack the Knife's oft-repeated "weddings." To Aufricht's horror, none of what he thought were the funny lines got a laugh. After the entrance of Mackie's old army comrade and possible lover, Tiger Brown, now the police chief of London, Mackie's gang and Tiger Brown faced an audience sitting in stone-faced silence. Three golden lights were lowered as the words "The Cannon Song" were projected on a screen above the stage. Now Mackie and Brown, with the Lewis Ruth Band playing away at a fox-trot tempo, launched into their song about having served together in the British Army in India. They sang lustily of shooting up "new races" and (rhyming neatly, even in German, with "Cutch Behar") turning people into "beefsteak tartare." The gang stomped out the refrain in their heavy army boots. At this, the audience did not just thaw, it boiled over, not allowing the show to continue until a "beefsteak tartare" encore was served up.

The next day, and for months after, the show was always sold out.

Even Brecht's old nemesis Alfred Kerr seemed to like much of it, singling out Lenya for special praise and predicting future stardom for her. When the man-about-town and playwright-libretticist Count Kessler went to see *Threepenny* a few days later, he went in the company of an ambassador and a bank director. He describes in his diary how the work was seen by those well versed in the Berlin theater scene, "Gripping production, Piscatoresque, primitive and proletarian."[1] Shortly after, Kessler attended a party given by Piscator at his "lovely light apartment decorated by Gropius. Met Brecht. Strikingly decadent head, almost a classical criminal physiognomy, very dark, black hair, black eyes, dark skin, a singularly threatening facial expression, almost the typical thug. But when one talks with him he thaws out, becomes almost naive."[2]

All Europe now began to sing the songs of *Threepenny*. It was two years since Brecht had first read Marx and rather longer since Hauptmann had first begun to study the Marxist classics, but in *Threepenny* as a whole, the level of general social analysis is well behind that of John Gay. The poor in Gay are really poor, not merely disguised as such. But with Gay's framing tale of genuine prisoners performing a play missing from *Threepenny*, what we see are Peachum's cleverly outfitted and rehearsed fakes rather than the genuinely poor. The presentation of blind people who turn out to see perfectly well and of "cripples" who are actually sound of limb is deeply reactionary, particularly against the real-life backdrop of Berlin's vast army of the poor, homeless, crippled, and chronically undernourished. Noting such deficiencies in *Threepenny*, the official CPG paper, *Die Rote Fahne* (The red flag), declared that the adaptation "contained not a trace of modern social or political satire." Max Brod, noting the emphasis on tough males in the work, predicted that this kind of orientation, which he saw as widespread in the new drama, was helping to prepare the ground for a new and perhaps more terrible war than the last.[3]

It is often overlooked that *Threepenny* sympathetically highlights prostitutes, chambermaids, and other women. Polly, for instance, takes over the gang and runs it well after Mackie is jailed. Also of importance from a feminist perspective is Polly's song "Pirate Jenny," which plots revenge against those who plague her in the present. The philosopher Ernst Bloch, however, mused darkly that he heard in this song, " 'Evil,' the subterranean element of woman, her secret complicity with undermining things."[4]

At the core of *The Threepenny Opera* is the opposition between Hauptmann's women tired of being kicked around by ruthless and egocentric men, and these Brechtian men themselves, men sometimes of Brecht's creation and at other times (still reflecting his own proclivities), fantasies taken from Kipling, "poet of Empire," and the murderer-poet Villon. Typical of these men is the police chief who dreams his homo-erotically tinged dreams of the old days in India with his beloved Mackie. Equally representative of Brecht's personal concerns is the cold yet priapic Mackie, who is, like Blody (*sic*) Five in *A Man's a Man*, a prisoner of sexual desire, driven by his whorehouse schedule, "this is Thursday, it must be Turnbridge."

Change—if it is to come at all into the fetishistic world of the sword-stick-carrying Mackie and the posturing, ineffective police chief—arises from the initiative taken by the deeply divided Jenny or the intelligent, determined, sexy Polly. With her eyes open (as her song about her lack of interest in other, more proper lovers makes plain), Polly enters into a "marriage" with Mackie. From this base, she will make her move both to control the gang and Macheath himself. At the same time, the singer of the song of "Pirate Jenny" (at first sight just another typical maid-prostitute of the Brechtian universe) dreams a savage dream of a time when her ship will come in, loaded with Freudian cannon, and a time when women will determine who dies and who lives.

The drama at the center of *The Threepenny Opera* can be seen as the drama of Brecht and Hauptmann themselves, of a woman's dream of either equality or, failing that, of seizing power herself, and a man's dream of infinite prolongation of the days of shooting other races, of unpunished rape and murder, of a world of buying and selling the bodies of women. At the deepest level, *Threepenny* strikes ancient chords of violent male fantasy with which one group of audience members readily identifies. Equally present is always that chord that Ernst Bloch heard and feared and that Hauptmann, Lenya, and Carola Neher would incorporate both onstage and off: Polly and Jenny dream of a world where they can have power or share power, a world where they can express their own sexual desires freely and not serve at the beck and call of fathers, husbands, and the customers at Turnbridge. In Hauptmann's brilliant articulation of one deep, enduring stream of desire and in Brecht's expression of the very opposite, both given wings by the music of Weill, *Threepenny* mirrors our own deepest and most violent wishes and fears. It is what Weill, Hauptmann, and Brecht achieved together that lifts the work to a virtually mythic level and accounts, so I believe, for its enduring and deserved success.

Brecht's theories of epic distance notwithstanding, the virulence of *Threepenny* fever increased. Feet tapped to the beguiling rhythms of Mackie's tale of multiple murders and rape, the gang's chopping of native races into "beefsteak tartare," and Jenny's dream of turning the cannon on her foes. Felix Bloch Erben moved to license foreign translations and productions, and this brought in a flood of additional income. Brecht took the position with regard to Hauptmann that she should have no contractual share in the money from foreign translations. Her responsibility, so he claimed, had been solely for doing a German version.[5]

Within weeks of *Threepenny*'s opening, Brecht and Weill were the toast of Europe. In London, even the staid *Times* (reviewing the Berlin production) had good things to say, even if it did, with inadvertent insight, telescope names and credit the show to "Kurt Brecht," who had been influenced, thought the *Times*, by the "Communistic Herr Piscator." Within five years, the work was translated into eighteen languages and performed more than ten thousand times. When *Threepenny* opened in Paris, not only did it do splendidly at the box office, but it also won the endorsement of both the young Jean-Paul Sartre and Simone de Beauvoir, with Sartre (whose life is strikingly similar to that of Brecht) learning the catchy tunes by heart.

The flood of Brecht's foreign income was mainly deposited in Switzerland hidden from tax authorities.[6] But before this big flood of money had really begun, Brecht's divorce case with Marianne Zoff lurched to a final decision. On September 16, 1928, the Berlin court ruled: "The marriage of the parties is ended on the basis of claim and counterclaim. Both parties carry the blame for the separation. Neither is entitled to costs from the other."[7] On November 2, Marianne Zoff was finally able to marry Theo Lingen, who had been for years her real husband and father to little Hanne, now five and a half years old. For years, the marriage had been a fiction, but it had been a useful fiction for Brecht. It had protected him from others—Hauptmann, Weigel, Fleisser, Neher—who were all encouraged to think they would marry him once his divorce was final.

As income from *Threepenny* grew, even with their smaller portion of it, Weill and Lenya began to enjoy a new life. They bought their first car, a large and handsome Graham-Page, and left the Pension Hassforth to buy their own place in Kleinmachnow, the artist's colony area of Berlin. Brecht also moved.

After spending much of September and all of October in Augsburg where, without Hauptmann, he tinkered away interminably at the violent and misogynist *Fatzer* but made little progress, he returned to Berlin in November. With his maid, Mari Hold, he now moved into a far more spacious place than the old Spichernstrasse flat. The new place was off the fashionable Kurfürstendamm, at 19 Hardenbergstrasse. From the windows of their fifth floor apartment, they could look down on the roofs and lights of the central section of Berlin.

Brecht was much in demand. Papers asked his opinion on all

subjects, and he provided shocking responses. When *Die Dame* asked him what had provided "the strongest influence" on his writing, he replied, "You'll laugh: the Bible." Everyone clamored to print what they thought was his newest work. *Uhu* published and gave a short-story prize to a piece called "Die Bestie" (The beast). John Willett observes, with his customary understatement, that there are only a few marks in Brecht's hand on the original manuscript of "Die Bestie," and that Hauptmann's marks on the group of stories of which "Die Bestie" is a part "by contrast are frequent."[8] The "beast" story deals with a vicious, anti-Semitic bureaucrat who when he tries to play himself in a film fails and is then replaced by an actor who seems more authentic in the role than the original person. In another of the stories of this period (again, almost certainly by Hauptmann but published under Brecht's name), the title character, "Barbara," is almost killed by the mad automobile driver and woman hater of a man with whom she painfully finds herself associated.

Clearly enjoying the fame brought to him through such works as *Threepenny* and the prizewinning "Die Bestie," still Brecht had not managed to complete anything for Berlin's most serious stage, Piscator's. Repeatedly failing to deliver anything suitably revolutionary, Brecht asked Ihering to intercede to have Piscator consider *Drums in the Night*, one of Brecht's very oldest plays.[9] Brecht, Piscator, and Sternberg talked at length in November about the possibility of Piscator doing *Drums*.[10] But for all of Brecht's new fame, Piscator was not to be swayed from his revolutionary purpose. He tried to make plain to Brecht that the Kragler who had turned his back on the Spartacus-led revolution in Brecht's play of 1919 would now have to either reverse his position or the play would have to show how wrong his position had been. But though Brecht talked endlessly about introducing new material, in fact he would never be able to revise the play in the manner Piscator required. For all their surface similarity, there was an unbridgeable gap between what Brecht and Piscator wanted. For Piscator, revolution was primary, and the theater was the conveyor belt to help bring revolution closer. Though Brecht had argued for years that the very stuff of revolution should be central to the new "epic theater," Brecht did one of his 180-degree turns when Piscator pointed out that history was almost wholly lacking in *Drums in the Night*. Brecht claimed, "The minute I have places for dramatic action that do not coincide with reality, things go well for me." Brecht preferred the playwright's imagination to reality, returning to the most ancient roots of imaginative storytelling. The road to Brecht's, as distinct from Piscator's, "epic theater," would increasingly lie in the past. But though he would often go further and further back in time, both for his subjects and for the form in which those subjects were presented, he would still argue that this was the theater of the future. Paradoxically, he was to be proven correct, but he could not himself openly admit it until decades later.

The deep ambivalence he felt toward the dramaturgy of the past is seen most clearly in the polar swings of his comments on Shakespeare.[11] For instance, when Brecht was involved in October 1927 in the broadcast of a workshop adaptation of *Macbeth*,[12] he declared that Shakespearean dramaturgy was most useful for modern playwrights.[13] A year later, after Sternberg had pointed out to him that Shakespeare's heroes represented a late-medieval rather than a modern point of view, Brecht went on the attack, saying that "later times will call this drama a drama for cannibals."[14] Both in form and in content, Shakespeare and the classics generally were "too limited; they do not show the world, rather simply themselves. Showcase personalities. Words used as jewels or ornaments. Small horizons, bourgeois."[15] Years later, finally rather coyly aware that his own plays were often amazingly similar in their "chronicle" structure to those of Shakespeare, Brecht again reversed himself and declared, "In order to treat of great actions, we need to study the structure of the classics, particularly that of Shakespeare."[16]

A close observer of Brecht over several decades, Sternberg saw clearly in the late 1920s that Brecht's penchant for radical shifts in point of view was fundamental both to his stage work and his everyday life. He noticed Brecht doing this repeatedly in conversations. When Sternberg asked about this, Brecht nonchalantly admitted it. He said that when he was among "four to ten men," what he said "had as little to do with his own opinion as anything said by one of his stage characters."[17] He had adopted for everyday discussion an attitude that permitted him to expound and attack a variety of incongruent points of view. For Brecht, "reality"—like "epic theater," "marriage," or "truth"— was whatever he said it was at any given moment.

Perhaps, along with the poet Gottfried Benn, Brecht really believed that reality was simply a bourgeois construction.[18] Whether based on Marx or any other theory, Brecht's shifting point of view enabled him to organize his life, his work, and his concepts of morality around himself. But this egocentrism was tempered by enormous personal magnetism, sexual charm, a kind of naiveté, and an often zany humor that was, as Bronnen saw, almost childlike. He beguiled virtually everyone, eliciting self-effacing loyalty to his various conflicting causes even from the most gifted people he encountered. His very need for help was obviously a key part of the magnetism he exerted on someone like Elisabeth Hauptmann. In his presence, one could be useful. There can be no serious doubt that right up until his death, Brecht's charmed circle was a place where greatness gathered and where the lightning of extraordinary creativity very frequently struck.

By early 1929, a number of new and brilliant projects moved

forward in the charmed circle. While at the same time completing incidental music for works of Piscator, Jessner, Bronnen, and Kaiser, Kurt Weill was working with Hauptmann and Brecht on a cantata on Lindbergh's epochal crossing of the Atlantic in May 1927. According to Dr. Paula Hanssen, who told me this in a private letter, the early drafts of the Lindbergh material are in Hauptmann's handwriting. This is consistent with her work on material from English sources both in British and in American English. Another version of the Lindbergh material was prepared in the workshop in April–May, with Hanns Eisler now involved in what proved to be an unsuccessful effort to try to turn the material into agitprop so that Eisler could compose suitably rousing music. The project was taken up in its final form in the spring of 1929 for the 1929 Baden-Baden summer festival. For some reason, Eisler was dropped and Paul Hindemith came in to do parts of the score. Also planned for Baden-Baden, with a score by Hindemith, was a piece on the crash of four flyers called *The Baden-Baden Cantata of Acquiescence*. It would have a film insert and a small circuslike prologue.

As though all this were not enough for the spring, Brecht and Weill were also being nagged by Aufricht to produce other works for the Schiffbauerdamm Theater. In a complex business deal, Aufricht had moved *Threepenny* to a second theater where it continued to sell every seat. This left the Schiffbauerdamm open for new experimental work, and Aufricht decided to stage a politically radical play called *Poison Gas over Berlin* by Peter Martin Lampel. The play exposed the Reichswehr's illegal experiments with poison gas (manufactured, as we know, in the Soviet Union!) and inadvertent killing of several German civilians. Key figures in the play were the chief of the German Army, the Reichswehr, General Hans von Seeckt, and his closest associate, General Kurt von Schleicher, both of whom were anxious to cover up what the army was doing. When word got around that Aufricht was planning to put on *Poison Gas*, he was threatened with a change of tax status, which would effectively close his theater.

Aufricht did not want to give in to censorship and agreed to one, essentially closed performance for the authorities. Nor did he want further trouble, so he was horrified when he discovered that Brecht was writing deliberately provocative new material for an actor to read in front of the curtain on the opening night of *Poison Gas*. Aufricht grabbed Brecht's new text and tore it up. The show got a lukewarm critical reception, giving Aufricht an opportunity to close it on account of its artistic failure, not because of censorship.

Despite the problems with *Poison Gas*, Aufricht asked Brecht what new piece he might have. He wanted something to fill the spring gap immediately, as well as a kind of *Threepenny* clone, something equally popular that could open on the play's first anniversary, August 31, 1929. Brecht did what he had done when Moritz Seeler had asked a couple of years before for something new for his Junge Bühne. Partly to thwart Seeler (with whom he had been at odds since the salt-throwing episode in April 1926), he urged Ihering to offer Fleisser's newest work, which had premiered in Dresden in March 1928 to a glowing review by Ihering. This still left the more difficult assignment, coming up with a work with the impact of *Threepenny*. Again, Bess Hauptmann tried to fill the bill, this time with a play to be called, with deliberate irony, *Happy End*.

Margot and Ernst Josef Aufricht prepared to stage Fleisser's newest play. They chose as director Jacob Geis, best known for his work on various Brecht productions and his slavish personal adherence to Brecht. This meant Brecht was free to take over. He gave both Helene Weigel and Carola Neher major roles. In addition, he recommended Peter Lorre, a still-unknown actor, a tiny man with bulging eyes. Caspar Neher was to do sets and costumes. After all this was in place, Brecht telegrammed Fleisser. She wrote later, referring to herself in the third person: "His telegram frightened her, that she was being ordered to go to the big city, in a great rush she had to be there. The poet was her fixed point, he only had to wave to her. She left everything where it was and got onto the train."[19] Leaving her jealous, uncomprehending, violent fiancé, Bepp Haindl, behind, she hoped for Brecht's attention again in Berlin; but she found that he had little interest in her personally. She had to fend for herself amid an atmosphere at rehearsals that was poisonous.

Brecht was directing the play to be far more sexually suggestive in performance than it was in the written text. After his recent scare with *Poison Gas*, Aufricht was alarmed; but Brecht was not going to be gainsaid by anybody. Fleisser was beyond opposing the "Dompteur" Brecht on questions of staging. He demanded that she rewrite the play at rehearsal, but she found that she could not write under such pressure and stayed away from rehearsals. "That was open rebellion," Fleisser observed, "and at an inappropriate moment against an Almighty, against her personal Lord, if not her actual Creator."[20]

Fleisser had seen her play as a simple story. A group of army engineers come to Ingolstadt to build a bridge. The soldiers flirt with the young women of the town and discreet allusions are made to what goes on between them. The bridge is then finished, the soldiers leave, and the small town returns to its everyday life. But in the eyes of Brecht, the opportunity to have the play carry very risqué implications proved irresistible. Fleisser's lines, innocent enough when spoken in a neutral setting, sounded like something straight out of *Mahagonny* when Lenya said them or when Carola Neher delivered her lines from inside a covered swing that just happened, as she spoke, to move to the rhythm and loud sounds of sexual intercourse.

Predictably, the conservative forces who had objected to *Poison Gas* now denounced Fleisser as "worse than a Josephine Baker of the white race." Throughout Germany, the radical right rallied to denounce what a Jewish producer was doing in Berlin with the cooperation of a decadent German woman. In Ingolstadt itself, reviewers said Fleisser had turned the city into "the deepest, most sexual and primitive ape forest." Both the mayor and Fleisser's own father were appalled at what Marieluise had done. Neither they nor anyone else in Ingolstadt knew it had not been her doing at all. But she was still too loyal to Brecht to tell anyone. Apparently, one reviewer who knew the original play asked her directly if he could not talk about this in his paper. She said no, she was "not going to attack anyone from the rear."[21]

While the storm was breaking, she got a phone call. It was Brecht. "A whole stack of letters are lying here for you,"[22] he said in a voice that sounded "thin like a whip" to her. At his new Hardenbergstrasse apartment, she read through the pile of what was mainly hate mail and hate press clippings, "a horrible flood of stinking slime." Her father and her lover, Bepp Haindl, wondered if it would be safe for her to return to Ingolstadt. As she read, she was aware of Brecht's pocket watch, hung on a nail from the ceiling, ticking away next to her ear.

Suddenly, she became aware that Brecht was staring at her, his "eyes full with a satanic gleam." The letters were bad enough, but this look from the man she still loved was worse. "Was he enjoying her pain?" and "what chief devil was riding him?" she wondered. Years later, she recalled those terrible moments: "His look was a knife, it killed something within her at that critical moment." She hoped he would speak, "that it was not a robot that stood there, used to coldness of the emotions." But he remained silent. She felt more dead than alive but determined not to give him the satisfaction of seeing her break down and cry. Neither of them spoke a word as she left.

Ill with horror at the coolness of his emotions in the face of her pain, only days later Fleisser was struck another terrible blow. On April 10, 1929, she opened the paper to find a picture of Weigel and a story of Weigel's marriage that day in a small civil ceremony to Bert Brecht. Fleisser suddenly found both her professional and personal lives in shambles. The news caught her at the lowest ebb. Thinking life no longer worth living, she made a serious attempt to open her veins.

Brecht's marriage was at least as terrible for Hauptmann. She had given years of her creative life and virtually all the credit and income from her work to a man that she had been encouraged to think she would eventually marry.[23] Desperate, she now also attempted suicide;

but like Fleisser, she too would be found and dragged reluctantly back to life. While she was recovering, needing some support consistent with her deeply held beliefs, she joined the CPG.

On the day of his wedding, Brecht had left immediately after the ceremony to hurry to the train station to meet Carola Neher. As she got off the train, Brecht was there clutching a bunch of flowers. He said he had just gotten married, but "it did not mean a thing." Neher threw the bouquet at his feet and left.

None of these developments seems to have disturbed Brecht's equilibrium or to have permanently undone his alliances. He continued to live his life exactly as he had before marrying Weigel. Fleisser said in 1973: "Brecht hesitated a long while before deciding between Carola Neher and Helene Weigel. He thought Helene Weigel would be more useful to his career. He made absolutely plain to her that both he and his work could not get along without other women."[24] Brecht was chronically jealous, and Carola Neher, both extremely lovely and determinedly liberated. Weigel's lack of conventional beauty, her tolerance of his multiple liaisons, and her willingness as an actress to do his bidding may have governed his choice.

The marriage gave Brecht, now thirty-one and enormously wealthy, a close approximation of the physical and psychological freedoms and maternal sheltering he had enjoyed in childhood and youth. With Weigel, he had all the benefits of a home, but with few of the responsibilities of an adult or a father. Years later, Eric Bentley (who had countless opportunities to observe Brecht in "home" situations from 1942 to 1956) would tell me that he never knew anyone more "mothered" than Brecht.

The line between Weigel's everyday life and her stage life would be hazy. He cast her as a mother or a wife or, in the role so frequently combined in Brecht's mind, of mother and whore, such as the madame in *Threepenny* or Begbick in *A Man's a Man*. From the time he pressed her into service to try to bring Bie to Berlin, she had basically agreed to mother him and his other women, and to pimp for him. Since Weigel was willing to play the largely asexual roles of mother and madame, he would always want to return to her. With her, he was and was not married. The marriage did, and did not, "mean a thing."

Elisabeth Hauptmann was fully aware of the implications of the legal union with Weigel. Were Brecht now to die without a will, the money earned from "intellectual property," such as the fortune represented by *Threepenny*, would go to his legal wife. Hauptmann, suddenly having no hope of becoming his wife, would have to find other ways to protect her legal status with texts including the ones on which she was currently working.

Hauptmann's disaffection was so great after his marriage to Weigel that he had to find ways to lure her back. An undated letter to "Liebe Bess"[25] (couched in the distancing "Sie" form that she insisted on after his marriage) says, "It occurred to me today that you might want to get in on the Massary deal." The Massary deal apparently involved the Berlin film and operetta star Fritzi Massary.[26] She was the highest-paid star of the time, the "nightingale" in a stream of shallow film and stage hits involving crooks and diamond-bedecked molls. At her Berlin premieres, the Rolls-Royces, Lincolns, Mercedeses, and Cadillacs were parked as far as the eye could see. Brecht proposed, for ten thousand marks, that Hauptmann take some Chicago and Salvation Army elements, and "hammer them together into a small play." "I am giving you," he wrote, "a plot outline." But the sketchy plot description he "gave" her was, in terms of content, not tone, a pastiche of Hauptmann's own short stories set in Chicago and in Salvation Army settings.

Brecht says Hauptmann should write "something moving and funny." His treatment of the central figure, clearly linked to Bess Hauptmann through the name "Mimosa Bess," was demeaning. In a joking aside, he wrote, "You can't get into a Mimosa's panties."[27] The choice of the plant name Mimosa suggests a return to "plantlike" women who are trampled by bulls. But Hauptmann was not about to create plantlike women in something "moving and funny." Her women would be the dominant forces in a dream-nightmare vision of brutal, gangland "Chicago."

Hauptmann would allow Brecht to keep her hidden with her new play. As John Willett notes that *Happy End* "was put together in the summer of 1929 *much as [The Threepenny Opera] had been a year earlier. That is to say there would be a basic script written by Hauptmann for which Brecht would write songs to be set by Weill*" (italics added to emphasize Willett's observation that Hauptmann was as responsible for the "basic script" of *The Threepenny Opera* as she was for *Happy End*).[28]

In the unhappy creative course of *Happy End* and the Brecht scam that lay behind it, Brecht represented himself originally as the author of *Happy End*. He said he had worked with Hauptmann on the text and claimed that the new play was based on the work of an American author called Dorothy Lane. Hauptmann went directly to Felix Bloch Erben and showed them her text of *Happy End*. They were convinced it was hers and wrote a contract with her on the standard printed form that presupposed that all playwrights were male: "Herr [sic] Fräulein Hauptmann of Berlin W. 50, Spichernstrasse 16" would market her "intellectual property," a work called "Happy End" and written under "the pseudonym of Dorothy Lane," with Felix Bloch Erben. Hauptmann left with her very own check for five thousand marks in hand. Next, she defined Brecht's role in the creation of the new work. On April 26, 1929 (that is, within a week of Brecht's marriage to Weigel), she wrote the following unpublished memo to Brecht: "I have written a play that will appear under the pseudonym Dorothy Lane and that has already been accepted for production at the Theater am Schiffbauerdamm in Berlin. The work is appearing through the stage publisher Felix Bloch Erben. You have obligated yourself to me to write the lyrics for the songs for this piece. I have informed Felix Bloch Erben of this, and you have acknowledged the existence of my contract with Felix Bloch Erben. I, on my side, have informed Felix Bloch Erben that you reserve the right to use the texts of your songs in separate book publication and in cabaret appearances."[29] Fearing an open break with a newly assertive Hauptmann, Brecht wrote back: "I have declared myself ready to write the songs of the piece. I may use these songs, following the terms of the contract with Felix Bloch Erben, for cabaret etc., etc."

The deal Hauptmann very privately struck in late April 1929 was a complicated one legally and psychologically. To maintain the parallel to *The Threepenny Opera*, it had to appear that an English predecessor for *Happy End* existed. As nothing was available to be appropriated other than Hauptmann's own short stories, the pseudonymous "Dorothy Lane" had been cooked up. From the language of Hauptmann's contract, we can see that Felix Bloch Erben knew that this was an invention; but neither Margot nor Ernst Josef Aufricht nor Kurt Weill were told either by Fritz Wreede, Hauptmann, or Brecht what was happening. Second, the work was to be presented to the public as though Brecht's role was as important in this show as it had been to *Threepenny*. It was but not in the way the Aufrichts and almost everyone else thought at the time.[30]

Hauptmann's behind-the-scenes revolt against Brecht's deceptive and exploitative business practices was happening in a Berlin that was racked by explosive political tension as right, left, and middle literally fought for the streets of the city. The Communist paramilitary group, the Red Fighting Front (RFF) of Berlin, was planning its annual May Day rally. But workers who had rallied to the banners of the nationalists were known to be planning a counterrally. Caught in the middle was the Social Democrat police chief of Berlin Karl Zörrgiebel, who had tried to stop Aufricht from staging *Poison Gas*. Fearing violence, Zörrgiebel banned all street demonstrations scheduled for May 1. The RFF announced it would march anyway, and the right responded predictably. Anticipating what would happen, Brecht asked Fritz Sternberg if he could visit him at his apartment overlooking the CPG headquarters, the Karl-Liebknecht-Haus. On May 1, the two men watched police shoot and kill unarmed workers. Brecht turned as pale as Sternberg had ever seen him. Though only a small number were killed that day in Berlin, the fact that a Social Democratic government force had fired on Communist workers, as they had done in late 1918 and early 1919, would make any subsequent alliance between the two big parties of the left, the SDP and the CPG, virtually impossible. With the left divided, the door was open for the rise of the combined right and the takeover of Germany a few years later by Hitler's thugs.

If the killing made Brecht's face pale, a controversy in the Berlin newspapers made it red. Alfred Kerr declared in the *Berliner Tagblatt* that Brecht had plagiarized a German translation of Villon in *The Threepenny Opera*. The satirist Kurt Tucholsky, noting also the large number of thefts from Rudyard Kipling, began in his comedy routines to refer to a certain "Rudyard Brecht" and to mock *Threepenny* as "literature which can't do harm, or cause the capitalists alarm."[31] The controversy spread to the streets of Berlin as a Tucholsky cabaret skit began to circulate and eventually appeared in print. In the skit, one person asks another: "Who is the play by?" The other person replies, "Brecht." At which the first asks again, "Then who's the play by?"[32]

On May 6, in Ihering's hospitable *Berliner Börsen-Courier*, Brecht replied to Kerr's allegation. It was true, he wrote, that he had forgotten to include the name of the Villon translator, but that was because he had "a fundamental laxity in questions of literary property." He also denied the work included any Kipling. He may even have believed this claim and been unaware of how much Kipling Hauptmann had kept in it. Brecht's riposte about his own contempt for intellectual property, particularly when published in Berlin's equivalent of *The Wall Street Journal*, made Kerr look old-fashioned in worrying about such things. Brecht opined in the *Film-Kurier*, "Literary property is an item that should be classed with allotment gardens and such things."[33]

However, while airily deriding such things in public, privately Brecht was busy cultivating his own intellectual property garden and negotiating ever-bigger new deals. He increased Weill's ire about the original inequity of the *Threepenny* deal by demanding that Weill's publisher give Brecht a larger portion of Weill's earnings from music sales. And on May 17, 1929, in a spectacular private coup, Brecht was able to sign a new "general contract" with Felix Bloch Erben. Fritz Wreede committed the firm to pay Brecht a staggering one thousand gold marks a month for seven years. Though the gold mark was not in general circulation, Brecht insisted on this provision so that he would have a hedge if the German paper mark should ever decline again in the way it had in 1922–23. Brecht's obligation, according to this contract, was to provide a minimum of three plays to the firm. Significantly, the deal was to include plays "written in cooperation with one or more other authors." Having just signed a contract with Hauptmann for her *Happy End*, Wreede now knew of Hauptmann's contribution to work marketed under the Brecht label. However, though Wreede thought he was a model of foresight, Brecht inserted a loophole: the "general contract" was to cover only plays, not operas.

Brecht was counting on Fritz Wreede not to reveal that the Brecht who had a fundamental laxity in questions of intellectual property was selling the commodities of the Brecht factory at the highest possible price. Incredibly, while he was dividing and subdividing, selling and reselling the rights to his intellectual property, the myth Brecht shamelessly promoted of his own progressiveness with regard to questions of property seems to have been widely believed. It would persist even though Piscator pointed out in 1929 in his book *The Political Theater* that Brecht had shouted at the Piscator collective, "My name is a brand name, and whoever uses this brand name has to pay for it."[34] Despite observations and suspicions voiced by Tucholsky about whether Brecht was really writing his own plays, Brecht was lucky that Hauptmann, still waiting for him to provide the lyrics for *Happy End*, did not come forward to reveal the truth about what had been going on for years.

With a torrent of income from *Threepenny* productions in other countries flowing free and untaxed into a Swiss account, and with the secret gold mark deal in place, Brecht finished up a few odds and ends but showed no concern for getting *Happy End* finished. Instead, he looked up Asja Lazis, who was in Berlin on Soviet assignment. He saw her at the Pension Voss, where he met her German friend and sometime lover the scholar-critic Walter Benjamin. Benjamin had firsthand knowledge of conditions of artistic production in the Soviet Union and was one of the Weimar era's most brilliant and prolific writers on the interaction of "high" and "low" culture, as well as of pedagogy and the uses of radio to educate children. Somehow, despite their range of similar interests, the two men did not hit it off at first. Brecht seemed withdrawn at the first meeting. But, later, he returned to see Benjamin and to sing him the most "pornographic" of his verses, and Benjamin came under Brecht's spell. Benjamin's friend the film critic Siegfried Kracauer warned Benjamin that his behavior with Brecht was "slavish-masochistic."[35] The warning had no discernible effect.

By the second half of May, Brecht wanted to leave Berlin and its troubles behind. He was booked for his usual holiday in the south of France, where he could be far away from blood spilled in the streets by the Berlin police; from the suicide attempts of various lovers; from the plagiarism attacks made on him in the papers, in cabarets, and openly on the streets; from the quiet but determined and dangerous rebellion of Hauptmann on the *Happy End* deal; and (with the impresario still unaware of Brecht's relatively minor role in this and other plays' creation) from Aufricht's nagging to complete *Happy End*.

On May 20, Brecht was off at his usual high speed in the "singing

Steyr," heading south. He took with him several works that Hauptmann had completed the previous winter and spring. The archsalesman and showman, Bertolt Brecht would personally present these works as his in July at the Baden-Baden music festival.

"His Pain at His Weakness, His Inability to Systematize Anything, Was Almost Physical" (1928–29)

The work Brecht took with him when he left Berlin marked an unusually sharp shift in the workshop's orientation. Elisabeth Hauptmann remembered this change beginning about the time of the first success of *Threepenny* in the fall of 1928. One of her old and close friends, Bianka Mynat-Mynotti (who would later call herself Margaret Mynatt), had brought her a copy of Arthur Waley's English versions of *The No Plays of Japan.* "I was," Hauptmann told me, "overwhelmed by Waley." Enchanted by the austere beauty of these fourteenth- and fifteenth-century plays, she began to translate several of them. The project, she told one interviewer, was strictly her own, and she did not show it to Brecht.[1]

As always, there was little time for her own work. She worried constantly about delivering new "Brecht" products to deadlines set by Brecht but never kept by him. There was particularly strong pressure to do something new with Kurt Weill. An expansion of the original, rather short *Mahagonny*, which Weill now wanted to do, was moving slowly with Brecht showing little interest. At the same time, the Baden-Baden organizers were asking for something new for the 1929 summer festival. This year, under the direction of Weill's friend Paul Hindemith, the festival would be devoted to didactic applications of modern music.

At the time the Baden-Baden request for something didactic came in, Hauptmann was busy with her translations of Waley. Aware that Waley had taken liberties with the original, she found native speakers of Japanese to help her improve the texts. Though Brecht still had nothing to do with this work,[2] Kurt Weill happened to see her translation of the play *Taniko* and got so excited he showed it to Brecht. Brecht immediately began to treat it as his own, taking over virtually 100 percent of her work word for word.

In the comparatist Peter Szondi's 1966 volume on *Der Jasager* or *He Who Says Yes* and its genesis, we are shown exactly how Waley's English-language text of *Taniko* or *The Valley Hurling*, becomes in Hauptmann's version (which she published under her own name in 1930) *Taniko oder der Wurf ins Tal,* and how this, with additions I will

discuss below, was taken over word for word by what was published in
1931 with Brecht given as the primary author, as *Der Jasager*. One does
not need to know German in order to see how Hauptmann became
"Brecht."[3]

Hauptmann Version:

Ich bin der Lehrer. Ich habe eine Schule in einem Tempel in der
Stadt. Ich habe einen Schüler, dessen Vater tot ist. Er hat nur
seine Mutter, die für ihn sorgt. Ich will jetzt zu ihnen gehen und
ihnen Lebewohl sagen, denn ich begebe mich in Kürze auf eine
Reise in die Berge. *Er klopft an die Tür des Hauses.* Darf ich
eintreten?

Brecht Version:

Ich bin der Lehrer. Ich habe eine Schule in der Stadt und habe
einen Schüler, dessen Vater tot ist. Er hat nur mehr seine Mutter, die für ihn sorgt. Jetzt will ich zu ihnen gehen und ihnen
Lebewohl sagen, denn ich begebe mich in Kürze auf eine Reise
in die Berge. *Er klopft an die Tür.* Darf ich eintreten?

In terms of content, the deletion of reference to the fact that the
school where the teacher works is in a temple is the sole change here.
This will then be followed up on in the remaining text to make the
play less religious, more secular. Whether Brecht made these "secularizing" changes, or whether these came either from Hauptmann or
from the other worker on the text, Kurt Weill, cannot be determined
at this time. Whether the secularization constitutes an improvement,
or whether this makes the act of hurling the child over the cliff late in
the play even more barbaric if it is unsupported by an ancient system
of religious belief, is debatable. What is not debatable is that Hauptmann's original text, except for the brief secularizing insertions made
by an unknown hand, is, from first to last, the fabric of the entire
play. Here first is Hauptmann's moving rendition of Waley's rather
wooden version of the original Japanese play's conclusion, followed
by the "Brecht" version:

Hauptmann:

Fuss an Fuss standen sie zusammengedrängt
An dem Rande des Abgrunds
Und warfen ihn hinab mit geschlossenen Augen
Keiner schuldiger als sein Nachbar
Und warfen Erdklumpen

Und flache Steine
Hinterher.

"Brecht":

Fuss an Fuss standen sie zusammengedrängt
An dem Rande des Abgrunds
Und warfen ihn hinab mit geschlossenen Augen
Keiner schuldiger als sein Nachbar
Und warfen Erdklumpen
Und flache Steine
Hinterher.

If we did not have the original version of this play as published by Hauptmann under her own name, and as here reproduced from Szondi's superb 1966 comparative edition, we would not be able to see how a typical "Brecht" text of the late 1920s was created, a text virtually identical in its genesis as most other plays of this period, including, of course, the most famous and remunerative one of them all, *The Three-penny Opera*.

The discovery of the Japanese drama by Hauptmann in 1928–29 (after her earlier finding of crucial English-language texts such as those of John Gay and Rudyard Kipling) was crucial to the next phase of works that the world thinks of as quintessentially Brechtian. For years now, despite his constant blustering and sloganeering, and the almost accidental commercial success of the "knocked-together" *Threepenny*, he had had continuous difficulties in completing a new play. Since moving to Berlin, he had largely been coasting on rewrites of the earliest plays. Though he was now increasingly presenting himself as a close reader of Marx and as a playwright whose work reflected both modern technology and the realities of modern political life, he was unable to complete plays on modern subjects or in what he was calling the "epic" vein. When he had tried new things, as in the case of the "epics" *Fatzer* and *Fleischhacker,* he found he could not complete them, though the macho brutality of these fragments still draws admirers. (Most notable among these is the contemporary playwright Heiner Müller, who thinks, perhaps correctly, that *Fatzer* is one of the two best things Brecht ever wrote.)[4]

Despite his rapidly growing bank accounts from the clever contractual deal he had made for himself the year before on Hauptmann's *Threepenny Opera* and the new gold mark deal with Felix Bloch Erben, by the spring of 1929, there was in a psychological sense a real "poor Bert Brecht." Many years later, when the poet and critic Ernest Bornemann would point out to him parallels between Brecht and Ernest Hemingway (another man whom we now know was deeply troubled beneath all the masculine bluster), Brecht was furious and threw Bornemann out.[5] Werner Mittenzwei writes of Brecht's situation in the 1920s, "His pain at his weakness, his inability to systematize anything, was almost physical."[6]

One of the things he was constantly trying to systematize was the whole idea of "epic theater." It is a term that is constantly twisted and reshaped by Brecht as he tries to generate a consistent theory to explain what he was attempting. But what happened was that "epic" became what John Willett has aptly called "a high-sounding phrase of the 1920s made to embrace any kind of play that Brecht wrote—taut or loose, realistic or fantastic, didactic or amusing—and some quite ephemeral mannerisms as well."[7] Rather than being a reliable guide to the work, his theory was a patchwork used to cover up his consistent failure to get an "epic" work on a modern subject to hang together in a satisfying way.

It was in the winter of 1928–29, after years of continual creative crisis, that Brecht took over Hauptmann's versions of the Japanese plays and the dramaturgical ideas that lay behind the plays. Neither the plays nor the medieval Japanese playwright Seami's fifteenth-century writings on theater were, to say the very least, exactly modern, but at least it seemed to Brecht as to Hauptmann before him that from a structural perspective they could be deemed "epic." At once, with characteristic vehemence, and with a buyer in clear sight in Baden-Baden, rather like Galy Gay selling the fake "army elephant" in A Man's a Man, Brecht declared his commitment to Lehrstücke, or "didactic plays," and started to theorize about them.

Felix Bloch Erben saw this turn in the products of the Brecht workshop as a full-fledged disaster. These were decidedly not works that could be sold to regular theaters to amortize the enormous gold mark investments the firm was making each month. Furthermore, as all the new work involved music, they all slid through the loophole that Brecht had inserted into the gold mark contract. Brecht, of course, knew the workshop was shifting to primarily musical works before signing the gold mark agreement in the spring of 1929.

Throughout the winter of 1928–29, between the time when Brecht's divorce from Marianne Zoff had finally come through in the fall and before the sudden marriage to Weigel that had so devastated Fleisser and Hauptmann, the workshop hummed with this strange but beguiling new product line: Lehrstücke. Script sessions usually took place each morning from nine to one at Brecht's apartment in the Hardenbergstrasse. Hauptmann and Brecht would be joined by Weill,

or Hindemith, or by old friends from the Munich days such as Bernhard Reich and Asja Lazis, or by new friends and collaborators such as
the film maker Slatan Dudow or the brilliant yet "slavish-masochistic"
Walter Benjamin. Sandwiches, coffee, and stronger drinks would be
served by the pretty maid, Mari Hold. Brecht, a creature of the most
rigid habit in his daily and weekly schedule, followed these morning
sessions with a hearty lunch and a postprandial nap under his own
portrait on the wall at Weigel's. Then it was on to nurture his stream
of new personal and/or business affairs and to do repair work on old
ones.

In the March 1929 issue of *Uhu*, Hauptmann published a revealing
novella with the biblical title "And He Shall Be Thy Lord." As is true
of most of her other pieces published in the Weimar years, it has
slightly disguised autobiographical references in it. She tells the story of
a man and wife who had met, like Hauptmann and Brecht, five years
before. The couple in the story has a small workshop for repairing and
selling secondhand motorcycles. The man in the story does little work,
preferring to spend most of his time smoking and talking, or lying in
bed and having things brought to him there, or off on other affairs. The
story makes clear that virtually none of the income from the shop
derives from his handiwork except when he is brought in to close a deal
that his wife has arranged; but he insists on being acknowledged as
"Herr" or "lord," hence the title of the story.

To ensure that the autobiographical element was not overlooked,
Hauptmann published the story with a photo of herself dressed in
grubby workclothes, standing in front of a motorcycle repair shop. But
despite all the signals she was sending, I know of no one at that time,
other than Marieluise Fleisser, who caught on to what Hauptmann was
repeatedly saying about conditions inside the Brecht workshop. Hauptmann remained, and has remained to this day, the female equivalent of
what Ralph Ellison calls "the invisible man."

For the firm of "Brecht & Co." to operate, Hauptmann had to
continuously both identify original subjects to be translated and/or
adapted from English and French (her two main working languages
other than German) and then guide the works to completion. She could
not count on his reading, mostly one detective story after another, to
turn up very much. But Brecht, like the "lord" of the secondhand
motorcycle shop, was dynamite in the theory, public relations, and sales
departments, pushing workshop wares all over Germany and into several foreign countries.

Like his successful salesman-manager father, the younger Herr
Brecht—rash, bullying, unscrupulous, and charming—was a marketing
manager and one-man publicity band of enormous energy and talent.

He nagged critics and publishers constantly, both personally and by letter. Everything coming from the factory got reviewed and paid for, often several times over and with the lion's share of fame and fortune going directly to him. The profits from *Threepenny* productions were making him increasingly wealthy, but his appetite seemed to increase with feeding. More requests came in for "his work," and the workshop was hard-pressed to meet demand and find suitable new subjects for sale on what was now a broad international market. Hauptmann, with her grasp of several foreign languages, was constantly looking out for new subjects suitable for adaptation and international sale.

In the middle of 1927, all Europe had been electrified at the first successful transatlantic flight as Charles Lindbergh piloted his tiny plane, *The Spirit of St. Louis*, from New York to Paris. Later that year, Lindbergh published an enthralling account of his life and that of his airplane called simply *We*. It was translated rapidly into German and became a publishing sensation. The involvement of the Brecht workshop for the last several years with American themes and Brecht's theoretical hymns to technology made the Lindbergh story a natural for adaptation. The *Lindberghflug* (Lindbergh flight), as the workshop adaptation would be called, used several small but direct borrowings from Lindbergh's own book, but it was to take its formal structure from the Japanese models with which Hauptmann was working. An early draft of the relatively short text of this very fine piece of work was published, with only Brecht's name on it, in the April issue of *Uhu*, one month after Hauptmann's revelatory piece in the same magazine.

The play about Lindbergh is sufficiently simple in structure that John Willett has described it in four sentences: "A flier (Lindbergh) describes his preparations for his solo flight of 1927 across the Atlantic. His enemies—Fog, Snowstorm, Sleep—express their determination to beat him; ships at sea and both continents make reports: all through the mouth of the chorus. Against this he repeats his aim (to overcome the primitive) and also his fears. He lands, and the work ends in praise of man's achievement of flying."[8] The play echoes both in content and in formal structure the medieval *Everyman* where that figure is caught between those luring him to Heaven or to Hell, as well as the use of the classical chorus in the works of Aeschylus and Sophocles. The use of choral figures was most welcome to Kurt Weill, giving him a central, internally determined rationale for music with the grand sweep of the adventure of humankind itself. As the work shaped up, it looked so interesting that Hindemith, head of the Baden-Baden festival, decided to compose music for sections of this same text.

The *Lindberghflug* being relatively short, a search began for something to fill out the Baden-Baden program. Again, work that Hauptmann had done on her own would be used. This time it was the plays of Seami and his son-in-law Zenchiku. These plays were mined to create a stark drama set in the modern world. Four airmen have crash-landed and are shown deciding to do away with one of their number. The title of this grim piece was to be *The Baden-Baden Cantata of Acquiescence*. In addition, working this time from a French translation of a classical Chinese play titled *Ho-Han Chan*, Hauptmann wrote the basic text of a play titled *Die Ausnahme und die Regel*, or *The Exception and the Rule*.[9] From surviving typescripts, we can also see that she mined an adjacent vein, creating German versions of a number of Chinese poems found in Waley's English translation.[10]

By the late twenties, the theoretical statements on drama made by the Japanese and Chinese authors Hauptmann had discovered and translated constituted a mine of new thinking on the phenomenon we call the didactic play, or *Lehrstück*. Of this large and important body of work, as John Willett has since pointed out, "there is no good evidence that it was ever, as so often assumed his [Brecht's] particular invention."[11] For Willett, the evidence of origin points rather more clearly to Hauptmann and Hindemith. The role of Hindemith is not really disputed, and the surviving typescripts of Hauptmann that I have managed to see, despite the blocking efforts of the East German authorities, support Willett's view of Hauptmann's role.[12]

As the work on the *Lindberghflug* already made plain, the way "forward" to the "new" drama lay hundreds of years backwards in the world of hierarchical, ritualistic, deeply religious fourteenth- and fifteenth-century China and Japan. Of particular value in formal terms for Hauptmann was the speed with which her Japanese models simply narrated sections of the story. Hauptmann found here a device that enabled her to get around what she saw as the usual "artificially constructed, time-consuming structure"[13] that was common in the nineteenth- and early twentieth-century European theater. This feature now became a vital one not only for all the *Lehrstücke* but for other plays written and published under the Brecht label. The adaptation the following year of Gorky's *Mother* would be (at Hauptmann's suggestion) built around this formal device, and it would be essential to one of the most famous of the later plays *The Good Woman of Setzuan*. These "Brechtian" techniques would serve as models for later works like *A Chorus Line* and the stage version of *Nicholas Nickleby*. From these examples, it is clear that Elisabeth Hauptmann's discoveries in Far Eastern theater have immeasurably enriched world theater practice in the modern era.

In late May 1929, leaving Hauptmann to try to finish up the *Happy End* project that Weill and the Aufrichts were waiting for, Brecht had headed off for some vacation time in Marseilles. About a hundred and fifty miles out of Berlin, in the mountainous region near the town of Fulda, he became involved in a serious accident. Driving at his usual reckless speed, he had to swerve off the road in order to avoid a head-on collision with a truck. He ended up with his radiator wrapped around a tree. Though the car was totaled, he walked away virtually unscathed. He then arranged to have photos taken of him standing next to the wreck. *Uhu* ran a story on the famous Ullstein author with the pictures, which Hauptmann then used, joined by an endorsement from Brecht, to get a new car from the manufacturer.[14]

While the article for *Uhu* was being prepared and Hauptmann was lining up a new car for him, Brecht was secretly dealing with problems growing out of his plagiarisms in *The Threepenny Opera*. The news of Brecht's theft had reached K. L. Ammer, the author of the German translations of Villon that Brecht had taken. A former officer in the Austro-Hungarian imperial forces, Ammer wondered how to get redress. Preparing for battle, Ammer asked the advice of Baron Seiller, president of the reactionary and explicitly anti-Semitic Retired Officer's Club of the former Hapsburg empire. Ammer told the baron that though under his pen name Klammer, he had worked closely years before with Stefan Zweig, he had now broken with Zweig "on racial grounds."[15] He then asked advice on how to deal with "the murderous Bolshevik Bert Brecht."

Next, Ammer wrote to Felix Bloch Erben demanding money. The firm advised Brecht to quietly settle as not only would Ammer be sure to win in court, but the attendant publicity would do neither Felix Bloch Erben nor Brecht any good. Brecht agreed to give the ex-officer 2.5 percent of his own 62.5 percent. In a curious and still not fully explained sidelight on this matter, Ammer never seems to have pursued the question of other borrowings from him. As early as the first Berlin production of *Jungle*, Herwarth Walden had pointed out the Verlaine and Rimbaud plagiarisms in the play.[16] Had Ammer tracked this down, he could have extracted even more money from "the murderous Bolshevik."

While Brecht was making his arrangements with Ammer, he made little effort to help Hauptmann "hammer together" *Happy End*. With the contract for that play in Hauptmann's name and the advance check in her hands, Brecht had little interest in delivering. Weill, who needed texts to have any chance of completing his music on time, had to reach back to previously written work or create new songs, rather than waiting for new song texts from Brecht.

Though *Happy End* was only partly done, the team faced an even tighter deadline for the didactic pieces due to be presented at Baden-

Baden on July 25 and 28. Not only was a text about four downed aviators nowhere near finished (though Hindemith was clamoring for it to complete the score),[17] but the writing team had also decided that they wanted to preface this incomplete program with a "clown show" that still needed to be written.[18] Finally, the film maker Carl Koch was racing to finish a small film on the theme of death to be projected at Baden-Baden to accompany the work on the four downed flyers. The film featured a dancer friend of Brecht, the sex sensation of the German dance scene at the time Valeska Gert.[19]

Not only were Hindemith and Weill jockeying for Brecht's attention, but now a third composer turned up. Hanns Eisler—part of that remarkable Viennese family that produced such top CPG functionaries as Gerhart Eisler and their sister, Ruth Fischer—was now popping in and out.[20] For Brecht, the more composers there were, the more secure he felt. Meanwhile, however, Hauptmann and Aufricht were being driven to distraction as the work on *Happy End* got the shortest possible shrift. Just as with *Threepenny*, neither the script nor the songs for *Happy End* were complete when Brecht left in mid-July, this year for Baden-Baden.

There Brecht joined Weill, Hindemith, and Hanns Eisler. Caspar Neher came too to do sets, overhead projections, and costumes. Finally, Koch's film also arrived. All the makings were there for Brecht's usual scandal. Brecht personally invited the dean of German drama, Gerhart Hauptmann, to attend the show. Also in the audience were André Gide and dozens of the major drama and music critics of Europe and America.

The *Lindberghflug* itself seems to have gone off without untoward incident; and it would get solid reviews both in the German and international press, and be staged on both sides of the Atlantic. But *The Baden-Baden Cantata of Acquiescence*, the accompanying Valeska Gert film, and the short "Clown Show" stirred up an enormous fuss. When the film of death elicited loud objections from the audience, Brecht apparently yelled to the projectionist, "Show again the ill-received portrait of death." But if the twice-repeated portrayal of death was ill received, the "Clown Show" brought worse.

Keeping things in the extended family, Brecht had lined up Theo Lingen, Marianne Zoff's new husband, to play the role of a gigantic clown who lurched about the stage on wooden stilts with his arms lengthened by attached broomsticks. Lingen was outfitted with a bladder full of blood and a huge paper-mache head. As he would complain about pain in this or that part of his anatomy, Lingen's two clown companions would saw off his limbs and head as blood squirted everywhere. Though the limbs and head of the clown were transparently fake, the mere acting out of the sawing up of a human being was enough to elicit horror and fear in the audience.

Gerhart Hauptmann, Brecht's invited guest, stalked out during the performance. Hanns Eisler, observing the audience's reaction very closely, noted later what he had seen when Lingen's extremities were sawed off. "These feet," said Eisler, "were obviously made of chunks of wood. This crude byplay disturbed a number of spectators. Several fainted even though it was clear that only wood was being sawed and that this was certainly not a naturalistic production."[21] In fact, the music critic sitting right next to Eisler was so overwhelmed that Eisler had to help him out of his seat and take him outside to revive him with a glass of water. The now headless Lingen, peering through his fake chest, saw the audience go wild, and as he wrote to Elisabeth Hauptmann later, anything not tied down in the theater was thrown at the stage.[22]

In many ways, the film of the always sensational Valeska Gert and the "Clown Show" had upstaged the longer works on the program. But this was just as well; it kept people from noticing that the Baden-Baden Cantata was unfinished. Further, it meant that not as much time would be spent on the critical analysis of the dubious central thesis of the uncompleted work: that there are cases where a person should acquiesce (hence the title of the piece) if some other, presumably higher, authority decides that one should die.

The theme of agreeing to be killed, with a sadomasochistic undercurrent, was something Brecht had played with in Baal, Jungle, and with Hauptmann in A Man's a Man. Hauptmann, herself a master at self-effacement and the recipient of a stream of insults and psychological blows from Brecht, found the theme of slavish subservience in various medieval Japanese plays an apt one to work and rework. Over a period of several years, the workshop, which was itself organized around a supreme master with a stream of self-effacing servants, would produce a gallery of the helpless, of clowns, of young and inexperienced androgynous figures, and of women or children who submit to dismemberment or being shot or flung over cliffs at the behest of powerful, usually male, authority figures.

Though the style of several of these new works was narrative or "epic," what such sadomasochistic subjects were supposed to have to do with theories of "epic" detachment has never been explained. After the "Clown Show" in Baden-Baden, Hanns Eisler tried to tell Brecht that the newly minted theories of the "distanced" spectator simply did not work. Obviously, said Eisler, audiences were as emotionally involved in these new works as they ever had been in earlier theater. Brecht dismissed Eisler's observation about the critic who had fainted and asked derisively if the same man was able to stand other music performances, why not this one? Fascinated as he was with his own idea of performance as something an audience could view with more intelligence than consuming passion, he was not prepared to hear that this was not so. To him, it all looked plain enough. Under his guidance, actors should follow his directions and give cool, fragmented performances. Audiences should then react coolly and with intelligence. In fact, as is abundantly clear from hundreds of eye-witness records, emotion and near riot greeted virtually everything Brecht had so far done or would ever do in the theater. But it would be twenty years before Brecht could finally recognize this himself. To this day, it is doubtful that most Brecht critics have done so.

There was, I believe, a basic psychological non sequitur built into Brecht's Rube Goldbergian theories of "cool," non-naturalistic performance. E. H. Gombrich has reexamined the basis of much of the classical audience response theory that Brecht, like many others, took for granted. Drawing on the scientific experiments that have been done to measure responses in the animal kingdom, Gombrich has pointed out that primary responses of fish, flies, and large animals seem to be triggered by what he calls a "minimum image." As he points out, "Birds will open their beaks when they see the feeding parent approaching the nest, but they will also do so when they are shown two darkish roundels of different size, the silhouette of the head and body of the bird 'represented' in its most 'generalized' form."[23] These forms are, as Gombrich concludes, "keys which happen to fit into biological or psychological locks, or counterfeit coins which make the machine work when dropped into the slot." Gombrich's minimal function hypothesis can be applied, I believe, to virtually any form of play performance. Whether we look at Punch and Judy shows done with hand puppets in a park, or Javanese shadow plays, or the medieval Japanese plays of Seami, or the stylized performances of classical Athens, audiences are clearly swept up emotionally. This seems to be particularly true when the stage action is accompanied and reinforced by music. Then the eye and the ear, both independently and together, are bombarded by more than enough emotion-triggering signals.

After the furor in Baden-Baden, the local authorities there would successfully lobby to have the festival moved out of that city. Meanwhile, Brecht was back in Augsburg. As he had done the year before with *Threepenny* when he had missed three of the four weeks of rehearsals, in the summer of 1929 he ignored all requests to come to Berlin to work on the upcoming *Happy End* production now only a month away. Everyone else had already assembled. Carola Neher was to play the female lead; Helene Weigel was cast as a rival gang leader, the formidable "Lady in Gray"; and Peter Lorre was to play an exotic, heavily accented, "American" gangster of Asian origin. Weill's music was based, it now appears likely, both on new lyrics by Hauptmann and older poems of Hauptmann-Brecht.[24] Aufricht (unaware of the true author of the lyrics) thought them as brilliant as anything in *The Threepenny Opera*. But still Brecht did not arrive, and the third act still existed only in outline form.

Unaware that Hauptmann was the main author and that she was the one needing the encouragement to finish off the third act, Margot and Ernst Josef Aufricht still thought the problem lay with Brecht. In desperation, with much of his and his wife's joint fortune sunk into a still partially unwritten show, Herr Aufricht sent off a telegram demanding to know when Brecht planned to arrive. Brecht promptly declared to Caspar Neher that he had been insulted by Aufricht and would not return unless the producer came down to Augsburg to offer his personal apologies. Kurt Weill advised Aufricht to call Brecht's bluff and send him another telegram, this one saying simply "Play canceled, going on vacation." The trick worked, within two days Brecht appeared in Berlin and seemed ready at last to go to work.

But now, instead of trying everything in his power to help Hauptmann succeed with her play, he seemed determined to sabotage it. It was as if he knew that if this particular show was to become a great success, a kind of second *Threepenny Opera*, Hauptmann's role would finally be recognized by Fritz Wreede at Felix Bloch Erben, and Hauptmann would be wealthy enough to break with him and sell her work for its full worth. His long years of serving as a kind of literary pimp for her might suddenly end and, even more disturbingly, questions might begin to be asked about who had really written much of the earlier work.

Instead of helping Hauptmann to complete the still-sketchy third act, he slashed and rearranged the completed portions of her text while acting, as he had with Fleisser's work, as though she had no real say. He took away many lines from the gangster chief, played by Heinrich George—Brecht's old enemy from the *Parricide* in 1922—and gave them to Helene Weigel. George quit, not wanting to play an "amputated" role. This then enabled Brecht to bring in the more tractable, though sometimes roaringly drunk on stage, Oskar Homolka.

But now problems erupted with the show's nominal director. Erich Engel was furious that they were rehearsing a play that Brecht made no effort to complete. Brecht was delighted when Engel quit. He told Aufricht that Engel was no loss as he was "a worn-out sort of man anyway."[25] With Engel gone, Brecht brought in as "play doctors" other friends from the Munich days, Asja Lazis and Bernhard Reich. He cut to ribbons the role of one of the gangsters played by Kurt Gerron.

When Gerron, on the night of the dress rehearsal, had the temerity to complain about his now skeletal role, Brecht blew up and shouted at him: "You fat-ass comedian, you abortion! If you were to lose weight tomorrow, you'd be out of a job." Gerron replied, "You would have been better off writing a play instead of coming up here and shitting on the stage."[26]

All this seemed sufficiently reminiscent of the final rehearsal of *The Threepenny Opera* that the Aufrichts, who had sunk their personal fortunes in it, still hoped the show would turn out fine. With six of Hauptmann's and Weill's most brilliant songs in hand, Aufricht still had every hope for a happy outcome with *Happy End*. Not even Brecht trying to back out of the production and his contract with Hauptmann altogether (he was stopped by an indignant Weill) managed to stop the production completely.

The program of the ever-changing show was finally sent to the printers. It was consciously designed to look very similar in most particulars to that of *Threepenny*. Caspar Neher designed the sets. There was music by Kurt Weill. Carola Neher, who had missed the *Threepenny* opening and lived to regret it, was here to play one of the two female leads, Lilian Holliday, also known as "Halleluja Lilian." Weigel played the other female lead, The Fly. The Lewis Ruth Band had again been engaged and, as with *Threepenny*, was to be directed by Theo Mackeben. The program gave directing credit to Erich Engel and Brecht. The work, said the program, was based on a "Magazine Story by Dorothy Lane" though, as Wreede knew, no such story and no Dorothy Lane existed. The big change, however, was that with *Threepenny*, Brecht had claimed credit for the adaptation of Gay's original opera, while the *Happy End* program read: "German Adaptation: Elisabeth Hauptmann." Apparently, only Wreede, Hauptmann, and Brecht knew the work was not an adaptation but strictly a Hauptmann original. Weill and Brecht were credited with the songs, though several of them bear the usual traces of being more Hauptmann than Brecht texts.[27]

"We'll Have to Get Rid of Them" (1929–30)

To Margot and Ernst Josef Aufricht's delight, despite the direct political tone of the play, so deftly had Hauptmann presented the story that the first two acts of Happy End got off to a far better start with the opening-night audience than Threepenny the year before. The story followed the adventures of the dazzlingly beautiful Carola Neher in the role of Lieutenant Lilian Holliday of the Salvation Army. Lilian and her gangster-lover, Bill Cracker, rocket around "Chicago," trying to stay out of the clutches of Dr. Nakamura, a mysterious Asian gangster, played by Peter Lorre, and the Lady in Gray, a rival gang leader, played by Weigel. While in Threepenny the police chief of London worked with the gangster chief, Mackie, in this play the Salvation Army was joined in dubious alliance with gangland Chicago. By the end of Act Two, the Aufrichts had begun to congratulate themselves on having backed another big winner.

With Act Three, the ironic "happy end" was now supposed to heave into sight. But, to the horror of the Aufrichts, Weigel came to the front of the stage and, stepping out of her part altogether, read aloud from a Communist party brochure. The bandleader, Theo Mackeben, valiantly tried to sing the show's scheduled finale to try and drown out Weigel; but nobody could ever drown out Weigel. She read on and on as the audience booed, whistled, and stomped for the show to close.

The reviews the next day were generally bad. Weigel's provocation of the audience was deemed offensive and not in keeping with the bright, bitter, self-consciously ironic tenor set by the work as a whole. But however good the show was as a whole (and it has been revived in recent years with conspicuous success), the opening-night sabotage and the bad reviews caused it to close within a week. The Aufrichts, out 130,000 marks, decided to do no more "Brecht" for awhile. The closing destroyed Hauptmann's best hope of ever gaining professional independence from Bert Brecht.

It is clearer to us than it was to virtually anyone at the time what Hauptmann had achieved despite the psychological obstacles Brecht constantly created for her. Until Weigel-Brecht's sabotage at the end, she had come very close to competing head-on with *Threepenny*, one of the greatest theatrical successes of all time. She had achieved this without using largely cliché roles for women, and her text far more determinedly explored the burgher as crook. Further, *Happy End* clearly anticipated the horror of what lay immediately ahead for Germany, a state run by criminals. The most obvious example of her extraordinary historical foresight is her scene where the criminals are about to execute one of their number while the police turn and walk away.

Most of the songs are taken from work she did with Brecht in earlier years and set in an exotic Kiplingesque, racist never-never land where women still follow tough, unfaithful cigar-smoking men to the ends of the earth, while the men urge one another to fire their Brownings through whorehouse doors to hurry up busy customers.[1] One of the songs was the "Ballad of Hell's Lilly," which Brecht wrote in 1919 before meeting Hauptmann. Here, he had presented a belittling view of the Augsburg Communist women's rights leader Lilly Krause-Prem. If not for Weill's music, the content of the older songs would have been all too obviously at variance with the social questions posed by Hauptmann's text. But Weill's music for "Surabaya Johnny," for instance, though it quotes the first four distinctive tones from the "*Moritat* of Mack the Knife," here signals the danger that Johnny, for all his charm, represents. The same refrain in the original "Mack the Knife" had permitted and encouraged audiences to sing along with Mack and identify with him. Similarly, in the *Threepenny* "Cannon Song," the music invited the audience to stomp out the refrain themselves. Weill would no longer permit this in *Happy End*. Weill undercut the hardened "Hell's Lilly" with savage musical irony. Similarly, the classical, "angel-pure" soprano tones of the Salvation Army songs demand that the listener register the incongruency of deeply amoral lyrics and their supposed lofty, religious intent.

Like Hauptmann, Weill was now distancing himself both from Brecht and what Brecht represented. He no longer simply accepted Brecht's extravagant theoretical postulates. He told one person in 1929 that he considered there to be nothing new about Brecht's insistence on the separation between a spoken text in a musical play and the actor's switching to the song form.[2] Weill also claimed—correctly, I think—that Brecht himself did not really take his theories that seriously. The point Weill makes here may seem small, but it points to something far more fundamental. No longer would he accept Brecht's tyranny and unmoderated machismo.

Married to a woman who was unusually liberated for that day, Weill is consistently considerate of the difficult role of women in male-dominated societies. Even before meeting Lenya, women often played a positive and central role in Weill's musical world. His 1923 *Frauen-tanz, Sieben Gedichte des Mittelalters,* or *Women's Dance, Seven Poems of the Middle Ages,* is clearly sympathetic to the situation of women in the medieval period. Women also play central roles in his 1925 *Der Protago-nist* and his 1926 *Royal Palace.* And the head of the photo studio in the 1927 *The Tsar Has Himself Photographed* is a woman. Later, his first major work after he went into exile in America, the extraordinarily successful *Street Scene,* would be appropriately called "in some ways a feminist tract."[3] Far more progressive in the politics of the personal than Brecht would ever be, the distance between the two of them would soon become impossible to bridge.

However, Weill and Hauptmann were faced with a box-office failure, and their work had been undercut by Brecht and Weigel. After Brecht's high-handedness with *Threepenny,* their bitterness was so strong that it would never fade away. But Brecht was too powerful and vindictive for them to risk challenging him openly as they attempted to establish personal and professional lives less dependent on him. This would be difficult, however, because as soon as anyone tried to leave Brecht, he would "shoot" as "one of the birds attempts to fly away."

Hauptmann could have explained to the newspapers what had happened behind the scenes in creating both *Threepenny* and *Happy End,* but she, like Fleisser, hesitated to publicly attack the man whom she had loved and to whom she had given so much. Unlike Fleisser, Hauptmann did not fail to point out to Brecht privately her anger at his duplicity with regard to his marriage to Weigel and his failure to follow through on his professional obligations. He listened and then, in one of the "poem weapons" that mark his relationships throughout his life, lashed out at her, yet praising the importance of her work. This untitled poem—written in the peeved, patronizing style that marks Brecht's poems urging submission to his will—was published in the *Collected Works* with no reference to its real-life addressee.[4] The poem begins, "You, the essential one," but it ends with the threat, "Do not put yourself on the never-to-be-torn-up list of those who have fallen away."[5]

Between the warm beginning and the semi-religious "fallen away" end, Brecht admits to Hauptmann that she had "escaped notice as very familiar things do." From her, says he, "special insight is required. Those who stand closest to the work, the cooks in the kitchen, eat last." She should forget her "couple of scars." Switching then to self-praise, he states, "Think of it, the blows that you have dealt out have been accepted without complaint." He does not ask whether her complaints have justification. Poetically, he places her in the posture of sinner, reserving for himself the role of hero of forbearance.

Brecht followed up the poem by attempting to resume both sexual and professional relations. He proposed to Hauptmann that they go off to Augsburg to stay there together as they had when their relationship was young. He was worried about losing "the useful one." But it would be October before she was persuaded to go to Augsburg with him. It would be announced to Weigel as a working trip. In Brecht's old apartment in the Bleichstrasse, Hauptmann began to rough out *Die heilige Johanne der Schlachthöfe* or *Saint Joan of the Stockyards*—a reworking of the "Chicago" of *Happy End*, this time in a deeply tragic key that would involve the physical destruction of her protagonist. A modern restatement of Joan's military gifts, not to be tolerated in a woman, Hauptmann's play was largely modeled on Shaw's enormously successful play of 1924, *Saint Joan*.

It is possible at this time, though her diary makes no mention of it, that Hauptmann saw Virginia Woolf's *A Room of One's Own*, published in 1929. Whether or not Hauptmann saw the text, it is startling how closely Brecht and Hauptmann were actually living the life that Virginia Woolf dreamed of for the mythical sister she created for William Shakespeare. Woolf's imaginative version of the Shakespeare household at Stratford, "Shakespeare's Sister," adds a gifted sister called Judith. The boy, William, is sent to the local grammar school, an opportunity denied to Judith though she is "wonderfully gifted" in poetry. William proves to be a somewhat wayward lad, "a wild boy who poached rabbits, perhaps shot a deer, and had, rather sooner than he should have done, to marry a woman in the neighbourhood, who bore him a child rather quicker than was right."[6]

William leaves for London where his own poetic talent is swiftly recognized, and he becomes a major part of the theatrical scene. Unwilling to marry someone local as her parents wish, Judith determines to head for the big city on her own. She, however, is given no real encouragement for a talent that is no less than his. Woolf writes, "[S]he found herself with child . . . and so—who shall measure the heat and violence of the poet's heart when caught and tangled in a woman's body?—killed herself one winter's night and lies buried at some cross-roads where the omnibuses now stop outside the Elephant and Castle."[7] The situation of Will and Judith parallels the situation of Bess and Bert in 1929. Bess Hauptmann too had enormous difficulty getting her own poetic gift recognized. She too had been driven to a suicide attempt the previous spring while struggling to complete *Happy End*.

When we turn to details of the kind of upbringing Woolf imagines for her Judith and Will, they live out exactly what actually happened to Bess and Bert hundreds of years later in Germany. Unlike her brother, known in Peckelsheim as a not very bright rake, Elisabeth Hauptmann

was not encouraged to advance her education. While Bess Hauptmann
was strongly musical and had "a gift . . . for the tune of words," her gifts
were deliberately suppressed by her father (though quietly and somewhat fearfully encouraged by her mother). In contrast, Bertolt Brecht
had been sent to the local grammar school and encouraged by his father
to go on to the university though he was something of a "wild boy" in
Augsburg, repeating several times over Shakespeare's fathering a child
"rather quicker than was right."

Hauptmann's arrival in Berlin is strikingly like that of Judith in
London in the late sixteenth century. Hauptmann was not supported by
her parents at first (though her mother later would arrange that her own
modest inheritance go to her gifted daughter). Hauptmann did not have
enough money to study at the university. She had immediately to earn
her own way, taking whatever ill-paid odd jobs she could as an English
and French teacher, and as translator and editor, learning by helping
others the art and craft of writing. After two years of this, when she was
twenty-seven, the charismatic twenty-six-year-old Brecht entered her
life.

Elisabeth Hauptmann continued to be generally silent about what
happened to her in the Brecht workshop. But Marieluise Fleisser was
eager to make a final break with her former lover and to expose Brecht's
exploitative working methods. Her life had become a nightmare after
her Schiffbauerdamm fiasco. When she had tried to end her engagement
to Bepp Haindl, he had come to Berlin and held a knife to her throat
until she "agreed" to sex and to wear his engagement ring. After that
violent "lover" returned to Ingolstadt, she sought protection from the
Prussian radical nationalist and sworn enemy of Brecht Hellmut Draws-
Tychsen, one of the oddest and most vicious writers of the Weimar era.
To her horror, she found she had stepped out of the frying pan and into
the fire. Draws-Tychsen was "her protector toward the outside world
but a rapist inside her world."[8]

Trying to describe her own real-life world of robbery and rape,
Fleisser began in late 1929 to write what she called a "psychodrama,"
a slightly fictionalized account of recent experiences. She called it *Tiefseefisch* or *Deepseafish*, and likened it to Brecht's *In the Jungle of Cities*,
which Bronnen had thought autobiographical.[9] The work has some of
the explosive power rather of Strindberg's *Miss Julie*. In her play,
Fleisser takes her characters to places so brutal that suicide seems the
only way out. And indeed, for the rest of Fleisser's own life, she often
found herself close to suicide and to complete mental breakdowns
while dealing daily with the tyranny of the various violent males in her
life.

In Fleisser's play, Tütü (who speaks the kind of lines that would have been immediately recognizable in the Berlin of that day as Brecht) has set up a drama and short-story assembly line. In choosing the name Tütü, Fleisser may have wished to draw attention to the bisexuality that Brecht was now at pains to play down. The great homosexual comic of Weimar, Wilhelm Bendow, famous for the homosexually suggestive skit "The Tattooed Lady," ran his Berlin cabaret for a time under the name the tü tü. The Tütü-Napoléon of literature signs contracts with a number of young people including a young woman called Gesine. In a factorylike setting women like Gesine provide Tütü-Napoléon, also known as "the Chief," with work that he then signs before it leaves the factory. Fleisser took the play to Ernst Josef Aufricht who was still fuming about what Brecht had done with Fleisser's play and *Happy End*. Aufricht wanted to put it on right away. But his second-in-command, Heinrich Fischer, leaked the news of this to Brecht. Clearly realizing what a danger it represented, Brecht sent back the order, "Withdraw this play." The message was clear: if Aufricht and Fleisser dared to put on this work, they would become Brecht's permanent enemies. Aufricht bowed to what he saw as necessity, but Fleisser did not wholly drop the subject. In February 1930, she gave a reading of part of the play at a celebration marking the one-thousandth anniversary of the German playwright Roswitha von Gandersheim.[10] She even published a section of it on May 18 in her mentor Herbert Ihering's *Berliner Börsen-Courier*. But her insights were ignored for decades.

In the face of cowardice, indifference, and vindictiveness, Fleisser and Hauptmann were fighting a losing battle. Like characters in an Artaud production, they repeatedly "signaled through the flames" to draw attention to their own condition but remained almost completely ignored. But they did not give up even as the decade would end with the world economy worsening and with women being told that they they should know their place, give up the gains they had made in the immediate postwar years, and return home to where they really belonged, back to *Kinder, Küche, und Kirche*—children, kitchen, and church. Reflecting the general attitude in Germany as elsewhere, a group portrait of the International, done by Otto Griebel of the Comintern-funded German Revolutionary Artists' Association, depicts only men as workers. On what was supposedly "the other" political flank, the radical right, Nazi portraits are similar to those of Griebel, overwhelmingly depicting either males in heroic attitudes or women in traditionally subservient ones.

Neither in industry, politics, nor the arts, with few exceptions, were gifted women of the late 1920s recognized by males, who were themselves anxious to secure their own primacy and aggrandizement. Virginia Woolf observed in *A Room of One's Own*: "Whatever may be their use in civilised societies, mirrors are essential to all violent and heroic action. That is why Napoléon and Mussolini both insist so emphatically upon the inferiority of women, for if they were not inferior, they would cease to enlarge."[11] Later, as the world lurched ever closer to war, Woolf noted that unchallenged male rule of the household, the essential building block of dictatorship, was alive and well not only in Italy under Mussolini and in Germany under Hitler but "in the heart of England."[12] Even in the Soviet Union, with its theoretical commitment to gender equality, women in powerful positions in Soviet society under Stalin became ever fewer in the 1930s, though jobs as physicians and engineers continued to remain open for some years to come in that country. For Elisabeth Hauptmann and Helene Weigel (though not for Woolf or Fleisser), the program of the left seemed to offer hope. Increasingly, Hauptmann and Weigel would move in that direction, joining the Communist party in 1929. If equality was ever to come, this was the direction from where they believed it most likely to come.

In the chaotic winter of 1929–30, the shock of the Wall Street crash hit Europe. German firms owned or controlled by American companies—such as Opel, the electrical trust AEG, and the film companies Tobis and Nero—scrambled to stay afloat as banks fearful for money in these and similar enterprises attempted to call in loans.[13] By December, German welfare rolls were rising rapidly. At this turning point, the president of the Reichsbank, the arrogant and extremely ambitious Hjalmar Schacht, issued on December 6 a manifesto "accusing the government of fiscal irresponsibility." Joining the attack, and doing so in direct alliance with Hitler, was Alfred Hugenberg, the most powerful industrialist and media baron in Germany.[14] Hugenberg wrote to three thousand American business leaders urging them not to grant credits to the German government.[15]

With the government weakened by intensive attacks from within, and after intense lobbying by the military for him to do something about it, the crusty, eighty-three-year-old President Paul von Hindenburg, a veteran field marshal, summoned the centrist politician Heinrich Brüning and told him to form a cabinet that would rule by decree. At one stroke, parliamentary democracy in the state of Weimar was dissolved. The final slide to totalitarianism had begun.

While the Weimar state floundered from crisis to crisis, Brecht, if his underlinings and marginalia are a true guide, was drawn in the fall of 1929 to the journal with the rather ponderous title Unter dem Banner des Marxismus.[16] An essay in that journal is underlined by Brecht at points where the relationship of "contradictions" to the "dialectical process" is discussed. This term "contradictions" struck a responsive chord. He had yearned in his earlier diaries[17] for a world where he could take both sides on all issues. Here in the world of Lenin, Marx (however little he had read of him), and Hegel, he had found a clear-cut endorsement for the simultaneous acceptance of opposites within the dialectical process.[18] Furthermore, this clash of the dialectic could serve as the underpinning of the newest plays and his theories of drama.

With the backdrop of Wall Street's fall, the Marxist-Hegelian-Leninist classics rapidly gained further credence and their methods, widespread endorsement. Following the Soviet model, violence was now deemed to be fully admissible in Germany in order, so it was said, to do away permanently with capitalism and with violence itself. The proletariat was, as the poet Johannes R. Becher would claim in one poem, a "fire-toothed! Iron-beaked slashbird!"[19]

By the spring of 1930, German capital was desperately seeking to hedge its bets, backing radical nationalists who might form some kind of bulwark against any attempt at a "slashbird" Communist coup, but at the same time, in a virtually schizoid move that reflected Germany at large, the biggest firms, including Krupp, Thyssen, and the American-owned AEG trust, were encouraged by the Soviet Union to send large delegations there to deepen existing industrial and trade ties. It was an idea that brought apparent benefits to the Soviet Union with a flood of the best German technology in armaments, chemicals, and so on; and it was a good idea for the German side in that this expanded market could take up some of the slack caused by the general collapse of the American economy.

In simultaneously pursuing an alliance with the nationalists and the Soviets, the industrialists were following the same policy as the armed forces. As early as 1924, General von Seeckt had written a memo for the Weimar government saying frankly that a future Germany, working with Russia, would have an obligation to swallow Poland between them. The same von Seeckt pushed successfully in 1930 for the militarization of economic policy of the Reich and the selection of prototypes of poison gas, tanks, guns, and planes to be developed in the Soviet Union and later mass produced for what he saw as an inevitable war. So successful was this, that in 1941, Major Wurmsiedler of the German General Staff stated correctly, "When Hitler came to power in 1933, he found all the technical preparations for rearmament ready, thanks to the Reichswehr."[20]

The duplicitous activities occurring at the very highest levels of industry, the military, and government were matched in the cultural sphere with heavy dependence on state funds for radio, opera and theater, and on increasingly conservative or increasingly Sovietized capital for the publication of books, magazines, and newspapers. The line between politics and culture would become increasingly blurred with Alfred Hugenberg owning one huge press empire, American capital still directing the film industry, political appointees rife in the radio network, and the Soviets building up a huge media apparatus in Germany through efforts of the press genius Willi Münzenberg.

In the thick of this was Arnolt Bronnen. In late 1929, addressing a national meeting of radio executives, he said they paid too little attention to their listeners, "Das Volk."[21] Bronnen's speech was interpreted by the parties from the center to the left as a call for nationalist involvement in broadcasting. Bronnen, however, said he was only arguing that people be given more involvement in program planning. He argued that debate on such vital issues as the restrictions proposed at the time on abortion laws should be discussed on the air with interactive feedback via the telephone.

The debate moving forward in a crumbling Weimar concerning the role of the state in the creation and dissemination of cultural artifacts had its counterpart in the Soviet Union. When the radical revolutionary poet Mayakovsky, working closely with the innovative director Meyerhold, had the temerity in the spring of 1930 to stage *The Bedbug*, a brilliant satire on the concentration of power and wealth in the hands of Soviet bureaucrats, he was reprimanded in *Pravda*. On April 14, the poet was found hanging in a Leningrad hotel room, having kicked, so said the official account, a chair from underneath himself. Once dead, however, Mayakovsky was now posthumously declared to have been a strong supporter of the revolution.

Mayakovsky's death, however it may have really occurred, sent an important signal to the Soviet intelligentsia about the dangers of dissent. And given the all too close connections that existed between the Soviet Union and the CPG, more and more German artists who were CPG members would be pressured only to create art deemed consistent with whatever party policy demanded at any given moment.

After tense negotiations and with many cuts of the more sexually explicit pieces, the large-scale version of *Mahagonny* that had been in the works for well over a year was to open in Leipzig in March 1930 as the national cabinet was tottering. The production was prepared mainly by Kurt Weill and Caspar Neher, with Brecht paying little attention. Brecht, with his contract with Felix Bloch Erben providing him with a one thousand gold marks a month that climbed in value in direct proportion to the fall in value of the paper mark, had no incentive to earn mere paper from the Leipzig production. But neither Kurt Weill nor Caspar Neher had a financial safety net under them. By early 1930, working with Brecht was a luxury and a pain that they could not often afford, and they turned elsewhere for work. In 1929, Neher did twenty-nine productions all over Germany with top directors: Max Reinhardt, Leopold Jessner, Erwin Piscator, and Erich Engel. Neher was no longer wholly under Brecht's spell. He had now established an intimate personal and professional relationship with the composer Rudolf Wagner-Régeny. Neher also had begun regularly working with the increasingly disaffected Kurt Weill.

For Weill, the work with the gifted, reliable Neher was a great pleasure and a real contrast to work with Brecht. For years, Brecht had either delivered texts late, in fragmentary shape, or not at all, and then altered them at will, regardless of the impact that obviously had on their congruency with Weill's music.[22] For Weill, Brecht was professionally irresponsible and personally offensive. The work in Leipzig on *Mahagonny* was done using sets by Neher. There was, as Weill and Lenya noted, "a strange and ugly atmosphere"[23] when finally *Mahagonny* was ready to open. Outside marched nationalists denouncing the Jew Kurt Weill. Before the final scene could begin, "fist fights had broken out in the aisles." Soon "the theater was a screaming mass of people."

For other opera houses contemplating putting on *Mahagonny*, the theater riot in Leipzig was a warning. With a collapsing economy and with Nazis now beginning to make inroads into some state governments,[24] state-supported cultural enterprises knew that if they dared continue to stage works like *Mahagonny*, Nazis would campaign against them for their support of what the Nazis were calling obscene and decadent "Jewish" art.

But however clear the threat was becoming from the right, the left had not managed to form a united opposition. It tended to flirt more often with the violent right (just as the Soviet Union was doing in allowing German weapons to be tested and built on its territory) rather than seriously consider uniting with more moderate elements on the left. Germany's 1929 Nobel Prize winner in literature, Thomas Mann, was appalled at this development, as were many others urging Germans to unite behind a non-Nazi and nontotalitarian agenda of any sort. When the SDP, in fact, made a concerted attempt to organize a joint activity at the cavernous Berlin Sportpalast, over half a million Berlin workers, far more than could be admitted to the arena, turned out in support of the event. However, as Sternberg told Brecht at the time, he was sure that the CPG would not enter an alliance unless it was allowed to dominate it.[25] This proved to be true. The CPG, guided from Stalin's Moscow, not only maintained its position that the SDP was "social-fascist" but also decided to set up a rival system of "Red" unions.[26]

From a mere dozen seats in the Reichstag at the time of the Wall

Street collapse, with the left ever more fragmented, Hitler parlayed his position in 1930 to 107 seats, making his NSDAP the second largest party in Germany. As Count Kessler, one of the most seasoned political observers of the Weimar period, observed of Hitler's triumph: "Opening of the Reichstag. All afternoon and all evening massive Nazi demonstrations. In Leipzigstrasse they smashed in the windows of the [Jewish-owned] Wertheim and Grünfeld department stores. In the evening they assembled on the Potsdamer Platz yelling 'Germany Awake' and 'Jews Croak' and 'Heil, heil.' Periodically, the police would chase the groups and drive them off, but they would then reassemble."[27]

Not many people in Berlin had taken Hitler very seriously before this. Now, Herr H. von Wedderkopp, the editor of *Querschnitt*, wanted to get someone to write a piece on "the new man." Wedderkopp asked Arnolt Bronnen to do a piece on Hitler. But Bronnen said he had not yet met him. Wedderkopp asked if Bronnen could do a story on some other National Socialist figure? Having heard glowing reports on the intelligence, charm, and literacy of a certain young (then thirty-two years old), still rather obscure Joseph Goebbels who had completed a doctorate in philology at Heidelberg in 1921 and who had been made gauleiter or party head of Berlin for the NSDAP in 1926, Bronnen suggested that by using his nationalist connections, he could try to meet Dr. Goebbels. Goebbels already had the high-sounding title of gauleiter and held a Nazi seat in the Reichstag, but he still had no car and lived in a one-room place far from the center of Berlin.

Bronnen immediately became smitten and took to making his car available so he could spend more time with the charming Goebbels. Generous as Bronnen always was in friendship, he promoted his new friend's career. Bronnen proposed to his boss, Alfred Braun at Berlin Radio, that they now do what Bronnen had spoken of for a long time, produce a radio debate on abortion. Goebbels and Piscator would oppose one another on the air. Both accepted Bronnen's invitation and attended a planning session at Berlin radio headquarters in the Masurenallee.[28] It was Goebbels first visit there. In a map-bedecked room, the Nazi leader spoke of the need to get rid of abortion so that an expanded German race would then spread German culture to the East. Piscator pointed out that Slavic peoples had been in this geographical area virtually since time immemorial. Goebbels limped over to the wall map, pointed, and said: "We'll have to move them, we'll have to get rid of them."[29]

The debate was interrupted as a messenger came in to ask if Herr Dr. Goebbels would be kind enough to join Herr Dr. Flesch and Herr Dr. Braun for lunch? "Are they Jews?" asked Goebbels. Bronnen was embarrassed, admitting that Herr Dr. Flesch was a Jew. Goebbels cut him off: "Then it is out of the question." Goebbels turned to the Aryan Piscator, asking him to lunch. Piscator brusquely declined. Later, when the Social Democratic management of the station saw the kind of material that would be produced as part of this debate, they got very cold feet and canceled the debate.

As it turned out, the gauleiter was attracted to more than Bronnen himself. Bronnen's newest fiancée, a lovely young Russian emigré actress by the name of Olga Scharkina, soon caught the gauleiter's own wandering eye. Time with Arnolt was also time spent with Olga, and soon Olga and Josef were spending their own time together. Bronnen, who remained either oblivious of or condoned what was going on, now proposed marriage to Olga. The wedding reception was booked at the swank Blue White Club of Berlin, a bastion of conservatism. To avoid any possible problem that might arise with the event, Bronnen had his mother now publicly declare that Arnolt was not the child of her husband, the Jewish Professor Bronner. This formal "Aryanization" permitted Goebbels to attend Arnolt's and Olga's wedding. Goebbels appeared and gave Olga a large bouquet of red roses. After the reception, Olga and Arnolt returned to his fashionable apartment in the Helmstedterstrasse. But hardly were they in bed than the phone rang. It was the Berlin headquarters of the Nazi party. Goebbels needed Olga right away. She left and did not return until twenty-four hours later.

Despite the pleasure he seemed to derive from sharing Olga, at times the situation was difficult for Arnolt. When Goebbels, his star rising, moved from his one-room apartment to a one-and-half-room place nearer the city center, Arnolt tried to ignore what he saw as the poor taste with which the new place was decorated. But things got worse when the rather stout Hermann Göring came to the housewarming party and told tasteless jokes.

Brecht, meanwhile, moved between the political fronts, maintaining friendly contacts on both the left and the radical right. His economic position was excellent. The rapid fall of the German economy was having the pleasant effect of enhancing Brecht's personal finances as his gold mark and foreign income soared in value. But wealthy or not, he was open to more and was delighted when Nero Film bought the film rights to *Threepenny*. Hauptmann received nothing from the deal. Brecht signed the contract and collected the forty thousand marks that went with it, but also demanded that he be hired to do the script.

Though continuing to play the role of outsider and to dress as though he were poor, he was in fact part of Weimar's brilliant, tough, arrogant, and wealthy inner circle. His portrait was done by numerous artists. They stressed the scar he had acquired down one cheek (almost certainly from his wrecking of the Steyr the year before) and his Roman nose which, with his hair combed down now over his forehead, gave him the air of an ancient Roman emperor, as seen in the bronze bust by Paul Hamann. He gave a plaster copy of this portrait head to Elisabeth Hauptmann so she would always have at least something of him as a presence in her apartment when he was not there in person.

Hauptmann was often alone with the plaster bust of Brecht-Caesar rather than the man himself. She had none of the adulation or support that Brecht had as a wealthy, powerful, and famous man; only 12.5 percent of the German rights to *Threepenny*; nothing coming in from *Happy End* after its engineered collapse; and no gold mark income; and thus her financial and psychological position was usually precarious. Hauptmann would be helped a little bit in her finances at the beginning of 1930 by a deal signed January 17 with Kiepenheuer Verlag to bring out the collected works of Brecht in a uniform paperback edition. A new editor for the firm was Peter Suhrkamp, a man Brecht had brought into his orbit years before by his singing at a rough Munich bar. Suhrkamp, who had moved from Ullstein, had arranged to publish an open-ended series of Brecht works under the general title *Versuche*, or Essays (in the French sense). What this meant, of course, is that Hauptmann would do all the work to make that possible and could periodically insert, though in very small letters, her own name on some works as a "Mitarbeiter," or "co-worker."[30]

"Evil Ingredients, Very Finely Distributed, of Reactionary Thinking Grounded in Senseless Authority" (1930)

The new work going on at Brecht's Hardenbergstrasse apartment owed its organizational principle to the techniques learned by Hauptmann from the medieval Japanese drama via Arthur Waley. Her version of one short play, called originally *Taniko* and in Waley's version *The Valley Hurling*, was published, as we saw earlier, under her own name. It was ignored. When the "Brecht" version appeared in the *Versuche*, nobody noticed that Hauptmann's previously published version constituted almost 100 percent of the "Brecht" text.[1] Similar silence greeted her broadcast over Berlin radio in 1931 of what was explicitly identified as her version of Seami's *Taniko*.[2] This version has been available in print since 1977 but has been all but ignored by scholars.[3]

Hauptmann was working on, with some help from Brecht and others, the play *Saint Joan of the Stockyards* and a new choral work, similar in many ways to the *Lindberghflug*, that was to be called *Die Massnahme*, or *The Measures Taken*. In terms of formal structure and its theme of acquiescence to authority even when it means death, *Measures* is a direct transposition of the religious and mythic core of *He Who Says Yes* into the contemporary political sphere.[4] So close is the connection that the first draft of *Measures* was actually called *Der Jasager*. Though clearly grounded in medieval Japan, *Measures* is a work that purports to show how Communist revolutionary practice was carried from Moscow to China in this century.[5]

Work on this hybrid play was given a boost by a visit from the great Soviet director Meyerhold's company to Berlin at this time. The company had brought a radically anti-British work called *Roar China!* written by Sergei Tretiakov, a former Soviet professor at the University of Peking. When *Roar China!* was criticized by the Berlin bourgeois press as too harsh a portrait of British imperialism in China, Brecht wrote a note defending it. Unfortunately, Meyerhold's company was not allowed by Soviet authorities to bring another play in their repertoire. Their production of Mayakovsky's satire *The Bedbug* presented a bitter commentary on the privileged among the Soviet intelligentsia. The period of experiment in the arts that had marked the first phase of the Russian Revolution would be displaced in the second half of the 1930s by the kind of old-fashioned naturalist work that Stanislavsky had done well before the revolution.

Not knowing yet the course things were about to take in Moscow, where this style of work would soon be officially denigrated, *Measures* moved forward. Among those who dropped by the workshop to make periodical contributions to *Measures* were Slatan Dudow, a Bulgarian with a strong interest in cinema, the playwright Emil Burri, and the composer Hanns Eisler, who had worked on *The Baden-Baden Cantata of Acquiescence*. Just a few months younger than Brecht, Eisler was born to Jewish university professors in Austria, where he had known Arnolt Bronnen and the Bronner family. Eisler had begun his study of music in Vienna, and had gone later to Holland and Berlin where he studied with such giants of the avant-garde as Arnold Schönberg and Anton von Webern. He had begun to investigate the teachings of the CPG and had sought to join in 1926, but his application seems to have never been processed, perhaps because of his sister, Elfriede (born in 1895). Under the name Ruth Fischer (Fischer was her mother's maiden name), she had risen to extremely high rank in the CPG after Rosa Luxemburg's death in 1919. However, when the Comintern sought to dictate German policy after Lenin's death, she dared to openly oppose Kremlin policy. She was expelled in August 1926.

Hanns Eisler did not follow his sister's "renegade" path.[6] After Wall Street's Black Friday, Hanns Eisler felt he was ready for a greater commitment to CPG causes.[7] He was following very much in the footsteps of his older brother, Gerhart Eisler (born in 1887). Gerhart Eisler had apparently shared in 1926 some of his sister's reservations, and Moscow had reassigned him outside Germany. After a period of indoctrination in Moscow, from 1929–31 (bracketing the time that *The Measures Taken* was being written), Gerhart Eisler was serving in China at the highest level as a representative of the Moscow-based Executive Committee of the Comintern.

For Brecht, Eisler had happened along at the right moment. Weill had become less and less willing to put up with Brecht, and Paul Hindemith had been so fed up with his experiences at the festival that he didn't want to work with Brecht anymore. Brecht had been delighted to welcome the committed Communist Eisler to the working group. By the time Hanns Eisler became a member of the Brecht circle, he was not only well known as a composer but as a critic. He wrote regularly for the CPG journal, *Die Rote Fahne*, where he published reviews as bitingly polemical as the best of Brecht.[8] Roly-poly, bald since his early twenties, very fond of food and good living generally, with a large cigar usually tucked in his small mouth, Eisler shared many of Brecht's interests and attitudes. He had left a wife and infant son behind in Vienna, and was a regular patron of prostitutes.

While Eisler now had almost daily contact with Brecht and Hauptmann, his published reminiscences are almost wholly silent about her very existence.[9] From hundreds of pages of his remarks, one would not know that Hauptmann worked on *The Measures Taken* project.[10] Only in the radio version (not in the book version) of Hans Bunge's interviews with Eisler can be found the following: "I was with Brecht during the work on *Massnahme* and during the work on *Mutter* [one of the next plays produced by the collective] every morning, mainly from nine to one at Brecht's apartment 'Am Knie.' That was a long period. We really worked together those mornings. During this time Hauptmann helped us with irreplaceable services."[11] But except for this one comment, though his path would constantly cross hers for thirty-five years, often on a daily basis, Hauptmann remained as invisible and unheard of to Eisler as she did to most other male members of the Brecht circle.

Measures opens with a group of political agitators (three male and one female) who have just returned from China to Moscow and have sacrificed one of their number to their political mission. They are to explain their actions to a party-appointed Control Chorus. Before the four comrades are allowed to say anything at all in *Measures*, this Control Chorus (backed in ear-drum bursting triple fortissimo by Hanns Eisler's music) declares:

> *Come forward! Your work was successful, in this land also*
> *The Revolution is on the march, and there also are the ordered*
> *ranks of the fighters.*
> *We concur with you.*[12]

Clearly a decision has been made by the Moscow Control Chorus, representing the Comintern, before it hears the evidence.[13]

The agitators, at least three of whom are Caucasian and male, wore masks when they entered China so that they would be thought Chinese. They also swore to speak only Chinese even when they are ill with a fever or asleep. Three of these four were experienced, while the fourth, the Young Comrade, was being sent on what appears to be his first assignment. The four comrades play the role of this inexperienced Young Comrade in turn. Seeing coolies brutally beaten as they try to tug a rice barge upriver, the Young Comrade tries to alleviate their pain rather than waiting until it becomes so unbearable that they rise up against their oppressors. Next, during a strike, the Young Comrade interferes to try to stop a brutal police officer. Then, when sent to ask for money and arms from a wealthy woman who deals in rice, the young comrade's horror is so great that he/she reviles the woman and runs away. Finally, the Young Comrade supports a workers' uprising that the other comrades think is premature.

After each of these "errors," the more experienced comrades try to reason with him/her. Finally, they decide that he/she so threatens their work that he/she must be killed. They explain this to the Young Comrade who (like the child in *He Who Says Yes*) consents to be done away with and dumped into a pit. They then return to Moscow to report their actions to the Control Chorus.

In this barest outline, this short work would seem easily dismissed as crude propaganda. When both *He Who Says Yes* and *Measures* were submitted to Hindemith in the late spring of 1930 for the New Music Festival, the committee wanted nothing to do with either work "because [of]," as they put it, "the formal inferiority of the text." After the furor in Leipzig when *Mahagonny* had been staged there, *Measures* seemed sure to provoke a riot, particularly with Eisler's hard-hitting score.

Brecht, a veteran in such affairs, treated the rejection as a victory. He had forced the reactionaries to show their true colors! This would teach the public something. He now decided he would not only have to put his name on didactic works but actually set up as a teacher.[14] He had a talk about this with Walter Benjamin and proposed that they establish a critical reading society that would meet under their "Führung," or direction.

Brecht was also negotiating with Seymour Nebenzahl, an American producer in Europe, who represented the Berlin-based company Nero Film. With Warner Brothers' backing, Nebenzahl proposed to buy the rights for German and French film versions of *Threepenny*, to be directed by G. W. Pabst, one of the top figures in modern cinema.

Brecht was willing to talk with Nero but set his usual conditions. He would have to write the script. Nebenzahl agreed even though Brecht had almost no experience in film writing and was notorious for not delivering work that had been promised and paid for. Nero agreed in early May to pay Brecht and Weill forty thousand marks each for the screen rights but reserved payment for other work until it became clearer as to what Brecht would deliver. This seemed like a good idea on Nebenzahl's part, but while it was unlikely that Brecht would deliver something he had already been paid for, it was absolutely certain that he would deliver nothing if he was not prepaid.

Soon, both the script for a *Threepenny* film and the critical reading group were pushed aside when Brecht's kidney problem flared up again. For some reason, instead of trying to get treatment in Berlin, he went off to see an old friend from the Munich days, Dr. Schmitt, who had a clinic in Munich. Here, as with many old spas still operating all over

Germany, the doctor apparently used water to treat virtually anything from heart troubles to kidneys. He was known far and wide as "Wasser Schmitt." Whether he was a crank or a fine physician, Schmitt brought Brecht enough relief that he left Munich for the Mediterranean.

From the village of Le Lavandou, Brecht wrote to Eisler that he had "survived Schmitt" but was not making progress on some proposed revisions of *Measures*. He had with him, he said, a copy of Friedrich Engel's work on the dialectic, but it lay on his table under a copy of one of Brecht's favorite authors of detective stories, Edgar Wallace, the author of *Sanders of the River* and *The Hand of Power*. Brecht was joined at Le Lavandou by Elisabeth Hauptmann and Emil Burri, and the trio drove on to Bavaria. At the Villa Mendel in the tiny town of Unterschondorf, they settled down to some long overdue work on the *Saint Joan* project and something tentatively called *The Exception and the Rule*. Most pressing, however, was the film treatment of *Threepenny* promised to Nero for August 3. Even with a personal visit that summer by G. W. Pabst, and the presence of Hauptmann, Burri, Caspar Neher, Slatan Dudow, and Piscator's colleague Leo Lania (engaged by Nero to help the process forward), the filmscript was not completely finished.[15] But a strong woman character very like those found in Hauptmann's *Happy End* was added to the story at this time.

While the filmscript limped along, Fritz Wreede of Felix Bloch Erben was growing ever more furious at paying one thousand gold marks a month while the German economy was collapsing and he was getting no usable plays from Brecht. He also counted on the film to generate publicity to sell other Brecht works. The only thing that was really moving in the workshop was the *Saint Joan of the Stockyards* piece; Hauptmann was unaware of Brecht's gold mark deal and did not therefore share Brecht's desire to finish this quickly for Felix Bloch Erben.

He Who Says Yes was performed at a Berlin high school that summer, and Brecht's old friend Frank Warschauer declared in print that he was appalled at what the play clearly advocated: the murder of a small child because ancient custom required it. His fierce essay, published in the widely read magazine *Die Weltbühne*, was titled "No to the Yes Sayer." In the original Waley version, *The Valley Hurling*, some boys set out on a religious pilgrimage with a revered teacher. Journeying over high mountains, one boy falls ill, making him the bearer of pollution. Custom prescribed he must now be (hence the title of the play) hurled into the valley below. With their murderous deed done, the remaining pilgrims are left "sighing for the sad ways of the world and the bitter ordinances of it." Starkly brutal as well as aesthetically compelling, the Japanese original has some of the power of *Everyman* or *Oedipus the King*.

Although *He Who Says Yes* was written by a group claiming to be atheistic Marxists, both the medieval Japanese text on which it was based and its Western counterparts were undergirded by religious belief. Perhaps anticipating the negative reaction to the play, the writers had introduced one small modification. In the German play, the teacher asks the sick boy whether he is in agreement with what is to happen. Even with its small changes, Hanns Eisler still declared *He Who Says Yes* to be a piece of "imbecilic feudalism."[16]

It is, however, difficult to deny the sheer emotional power of this throwback to medieval and classical dramatic form. Critic Edward Cole has observed, "It has a remarkable dramatic line, its profound tragedy mounting through each of its ten brief numbers with the inevitability of Greek tragedy."[17] Both libretto and score are classically circular in structure. There is no hint here of the kind of musical undercutting of the libretto found in the scores of Weill's *Mahagonny* and *Happy End*. With complete agreement of music and text throughout, *He Who Says Yes* ends where it begins with a haunting "Choral of Acquiescence." The choral theme is stated quietly, almost soothingly, at the opening, but when it returns at the all-important moment that the sick child is asked if he agrees to be killed, the orchestra underlines the question with "a mighty fortissimo."[18] From this moment on, as Jürgen Schebera notes, a stamping, marching rhythm uncannily like that of Eisler's fighting songs drives the work to its end. But if we hear echoes of Eisler here, we are also returned to a world where human sacrifice was a serious alternative, as with Abraham and Isaac, or Oedipus. But in *He Who Says Yes*, the bizarre human sacrifice is actually carried out.

Warschauer did not deny the artistic merits of the work. The problem was that the work argues that "one not think about the ethical shortcomings of it all!" "Here it is much more important," he went on, "to establish that in this school opera, there is artificially and effectively blown into the souls of young people, something that contains the evil ingredients, very finely distributed, of reactionary thinking grounded in senseless authority."[19]

Brecht, with one eye on the similar *Measures*,[20] was not about to back off. He proposed instead that a second version of *He Who Says Yes*, in which the child says no instead of yes and which would be titled *Neinsager*, or *He Who Says No*, be played on the same program. This enabled Brecht to avoid committing himself to one position or the other, as well as to give him royalties from both. As usual, Weill was not asked for his consent in this fundamental shift of what was supposed to have been a joint work.[21] And *He Who Says Yes* (but not *He Who Says No*) was performed in German schools over a hundred times within six months.

Brecht had technically evaded Warschauer's objections by the instant creation of a largely nonperformed *He Who Says No*, but Warschauer's point affected other work being done at the time. A draft called *The Rule and the Exception,* which was to have contained a Communist tribunal similar to *Measures'* and also condoned a murder, was now inverted. It became *The Exception and the Rule.*²² The Communist tribunal was purged and a heinous capitalist court was substituted; otherwise, the plot remained the same. On a journey across a desert, a merchant kills his coolie when that generous person tries to offer him a drink of water. The court agrees that the coolie is guilty of kindness and therefore deserved to die. In the view of Hauptmann-Brecht in the dying years of Weimar, a death sentence is the reward for a kind deed both before a Communist or a capitalist tribunal.

Surviving traces of the play about the kind coolie point again to Hauptmann. In 1929, she discovered a French translation of a Chinese play, which she then translated into German under the title "Die zwei Mantelhälften" (The two pieces of the overcoat).²³ By the winter of 1930–31 (apparently after Hauptmann had shown her work to both Emil Burri and Brecht), this had become nine independent scenes; and by the summer of 1931, these formed the spine of the finished play *The Exception and the Rule.* In my view, the play is as formally brilliant as *Measures* and *He Who Says Yes,* which it resembles so closely. It would first be published in the Soviet Union in 1937 (with all royalties going to Brecht) and first performed (in Hebrew translation and with royalties to Brecht) in Palestine in May 1938.

While work on *Exception* had moved forward in the middle of 1931, little progress was made on the *Threepenny Opera* treatment that Brecht was supposed to deliver to Nero Film. The company was furious when Brecht called on August 3, the due date for the work, and simply read out some notes over the phone. That was bad enough, but the notes themselves, with their new title "Die Beule" (The lump on the head), were very different from the original smash hit to which Nero had bought the rights. Brecht had cut several of Weill's songs altogether and changed the lyrics of others. Nero was appalled and instructed G. W. Pabst to move forward with the project without Brecht, basing his work on the original opera itself. With this, presenting himself as a maligned artist whose work was being appropriated without his approval, Brecht dragooned a reluctant Kurt Weill into a lawsuit against Nero.

Brecht returned to Berlin that fall still with nothing to offer Felix Bloch Erben except promises, with the storm around the *Threepenny* film, with attacks still coming on the reactionary *He Who Says Yes,* and without a venue for *Measures* after its rejection by the Berlin summer festival. Nonetheless, Brecht the teacher-revolutionary now tried to start a journal with Walter Benjamin to be called *Krisis und Kritik.* It never got off the ground.

Amidst much hoopla, the *Threepenny* trial began on October 17.

Each side accused the other of bad faith; probably both were right. Nero's lawyers went for Brecht's jugular, pointing out how bizarre it was that a person who boasted of his "basic laxity with regard to questions of intellectual property" should be asking for protection on just such an issue. Instead of answering the charge, Brecht made a suitably theatrical exit from the courtroom. The judge separated the case of Weill, whose music was in fact being altered by Nero, from Brecht's more ambiguous one. On November 4, the court awarded Weill sixteen thousand marks but gave Brecht nothing. Brecht appealed, and Nero, in order to get him off its back, agreed out of court to pay him sixteen thousand further marks to have him agree not to write the script. Furthermore, Brecht got Nero to release the *Threepenny* film rights back to him in the unusually brief time of two years.

During the courtroom encounter with Nero, Brecht was presented with a daughter. This child, born on October 18, 1930, was given the uncommon first name Mari, the same spelling as used by his longtime maid, Mari Hold. The full name of the new baby was given as Mari Barbara Brecht. This child had, said Brecht, perhaps jokingly, two mothers. One was Mari Hold, who mostly took care of the child, and the other was Brecht's nominal wife, Helene Weigel. The child, said Brecht, had Mari's eyes.[24] Perhaps a certified birth certificate exists that would shed definitive light on who was the child's real mother. My own search, thus far, has been fruitless. Brecht's correspondence with Weigel, always desultory unless he wants a job done or her return, provides nothing for the months prior to the birth of Mari Barbara. If the child was Mari's, it would not be inconsistent with Weigel's behavior to treat the child as her own. She had, after all, repeatedly had to make arrangements for the care of Frank, Brecht's child by Bie Banholzer and was still doing so up to the mid-thirties. If Mari had wished to hide the birth of a child, her mother, a midwife, could have helped arrange it.

With the new baby having two mothers to look after her, there was no difficulty in casting one of them in *Measures*, though it was scheduled to open only a few weeks after Mari Barbara's birth. The Hindemith group had turned the piece down for the Berlin summer festival, but Hanns Eisler's excellent connections with the CPG provided the Grossen Schauspielhaus as well as his friend conductor Karl Rankl. The cast was first-rate. Along with Helene Weigel, there were two of the biggest names in Berlin, Ernst Busch and Alexander Granach. For those sections where an operatically trained voice was needed, they engaged a well-known tenor, Anton Maria Topitz. The actors were directed by Slatan Dudow. The long choral sections were sung by three workers' choruses: the Schubert Choir; the Mixed Choir of Greater Berlin; and the Fichte Choir, all under the general direction of Karl

Rankl, making a total of some four hundred male and female voices.[25] As most of the workers had daytime jobs and these jobs were far away from the Schauspielhaus, rehearsals were held in the late evening. The work opened on December 13, 1930.

If any work bearing Brecht's name deserves the description of tragedy in the ancient Greek sense, it is this one. Where death in Brecht's early work was always egocentric and often entwined with Eros, the later works with or by Hauptmann raise death (particularly in the *Lehrstücke*) to the level of ancient Greek drama. Backed by four hundred and fifty powerful voices and an orchestra dominated by percussion instruments in what one reviewer called "aggressive, hammering, three- or four-quarter time," *Measures* literally overwhelms audiences despite the simplicity of the acting part of the production.[26] Drenched in the religious music tradition of Germany, it mines the "marching-as-to-war" melodies of Luther with the drive of the Salvation Army hymnal and haunting psalmodic elements drawn from the German-Jewish and Catholic traditions.

The score's dependence on old German traditions was matched by key elements in the libretto. One reviewer pointed out that a possible German model for the play was Heinrich von Kleist's *The Prince of Homburg*, where the broken prince submits to the justice of the supreme ruler of the German state who has ordered his death.[27] Set in Prussia or China, argued this reviewer, militarism drives both plays. Other reviewers spoke of the work as a revival of the medieval mystery play and the militant, pedagogical Jesuit drama of the Counter-Reformation.

The point of view expressed in *Measures* put the official CPG press in a very difficult position. If ever a dramatically compelling hymn was written to the theme of the need to be ruthless, the need to suppress humane impulses in order, supposedly, to achieve long-term humane ends, this was it. However, it was one thing to use murder as a method; it was quite another to publicly sanction it. The CPG declared itself to be pleased to see Brecht seeming to commit himself to the Communist cause, but spokesperson Alfred Kurella, in a long, detailed article published both in Germany and Moscow, declared that Brecht still had a great deal to learn about communism and its working methods. Brecht was furious at this. He called Kurella to tell him, "You are no longer my friend."[28]

Angry or not, Brecht did not break with Kurella. Nor did he change either his everyday style of living nor the workshop's writing toward the CPG's position. Instead, he studied the history of Marxism, meeting both with party Communists and with party dissidents, assembling an expensive, if rarely read, library of "Marxist classics." But though he kept his distance from the party and the party, from him, *Measures'* acceptance of the point of view of the Moscow Control Chorus, and of Moscow's need to export revolution, meant that Brecht was popularly seen as having accepted Moscow as his guiding light.

"Should Fascism Come to Power, It Will Ride over Your Skulls and Spines Like a Terrific Tank" (1931)

Under her real name, in January 1931, Hauptmann published a story titled "In Search of Extra Income" in *Uhu*.[1] It chronicled the increasingly desperate circumstances of the young, lovely, rather proper Anna Menken as she is driven by "artistic" men "with fat cigars" toward the world of pornographic photography, "girlie-show dancing," and prostitution. The parallels between the woman writer and the "girlie" subject are too striking to be merely coincidental. For years, Hauptmann's work had been sold by an artistic man with an omnipresent cigar.

As with other forms of prostitution, Hauptmann's knowledge of her exploitation and the ability to break free remained two different things. Now approaching her mid-thirties, she would try over and over again both to be heard as herself and to break away.[2] After Brecht's own sudden marriage to Weigel in 1929, on March 16, 1931, Hauptmann also got married. Little is known of her professional editor husband besides his name, Fritz Hacke. Sensing the possibility of losing her, Brecht immediately followed his usual pattern of suddenly paying intense attention. By March 1932, Hauptmann was divorced and again publishing under Brecht's name. It was a losing battle. She was not the kind of person who would come forward to clearly say exploitation was at the core of the Brecht workshop, as Fleisser had tried to finally do with *Tiefseefisch*.

As the crisis in Germany deepened, the Soviet Union seemed to flourish. A constant stream of announcements from Moscow based on rigged statistics and the widespread use of slave labor declared that the latest five-year plan had been exceeded. Much of what was said was a lie. Both Hitler and Stalin had discovered that lies said often enough and loud enough become accepted truth. As the star of capitalism seemed in terminal decline, the "Red" star drew more and more people toward it.[3] As thousands of artists and critics from all over the world made their way to the Soviet Union, a flood of Soviet artists, critics, and Comintern operatives flowed west as part of a coordinated effort to win ever more foreign adherents to the Soviet cause. Asja Lazis, after years of work in the Soviet theater, was a Soviet emissary to Berlin in 1930.

The former Hungarian aristocrat Gyorgy von Lukács, now plain Georg Lukács, was also sent by the Soviets to promote the Berlin journal *Linkskurve* (Curve to the left). In early 1931, the tall, slender, bald playwright and novelist Sergei Tretiakov with his serviceable German was sent to Berlin to recruit for Moscow. His years of association with leading lights of the Soviet cinema and theater, including Meyerhold and Mayakovsky, made Tretiakov particularly welcome among the left-wing Berlin avant-garde.

At the time of Tretiakov's arrival, Brecht was putting the finishing directorial touches on a new production of *A Man's a Man* at the Prussian Staatstheater. Helene Weigel played the female lead in the bobbed hair favored by liberated women in the postwar period. Peter Lorre as Galy Gay was a parody version of the macho superhero. He had hand grenades and pistols all over him, and a large knife between his teeth. As the vastly popular film M, with Lorre as a sex murderer, had just been released, this gave the role of Galy Gay an added level of both publicity and horror.

Tretiakov attended the play on February 6 (one of the six nights the play was performed) and was impressed as its "giant soldiers, armed to the teeth and wearing jackets caked with lime, blood and excrement stalk about the stage, holding on to wires to keep them from falling off the stilts inside their trouser legs."[4] Tretiakov could see its similarities to the brilliant, formally experimental work done in Russia for decades, borrowed freely and borrowed extremely well. But the similarity to the Russian avant-garde was also obvious to those who wished to attack Russian experiments and to tar Brecht with the same brush.

As became increasingly clear in the thirties, Stalin had only contempt for experimental theater work. Stalin liked Stanislavsky's Moscow Art Theater, with its museumlike productions. Stanislavsky was flattered by the attention and, as the now-published correspondence reveals, showed a sickening sycophancy toward the Soviet ruler.[5] It was a sycophancy well rewarded. The budget of the Moscow Art Theater steadily increased while that of experimental theaters such as those of Alexander Tairov and Meyerhold would be cut to ribbons in the years immediately ahead.

It was not yet wholly clear in 1930 and 1931 that torture and death, not budget cuts, awaited the experimental camp. First would come a seemingly more or less casual remark by Stalin or one of his minions such as Andrei Zhdanov or Andrei Vyshinsky. Then there would be an official statement in a newspaper or journal, deploring this or praising that. Then, like infantry following the tanks, attacks would come from the state controlled journals. Next, came manipulated "public opinion" supporting the attacks. Then the NKVD would make arrests of "elements hostile to Soviet reality." These "elements" would be tortured, forced to sign made-up confessions compromising their comrades, and usually shot after a fifteen-minute "hearing."

In Berlin, in 1931, the effect of Moscow policy became stronger and stronger. Marxist sinologist Karl Wittvogel directly attacked Meyerhold's experimental work dealing with Chinese themes. Sniffing the critical wind, Georg Lukács attacked Tretiakov. Both in the Soviet Union and wherever the Comintern cast its long shadow in the years ahead, the experimenters would be forced to fall silent or join the current line. Tretiakov, who was and would remain a strong supporter of Stalin's foreign and domestic policies in general, had no way of yet knowing that in choosing to continue to speak out on behalf of the experimental in the arts, he was signing his own death warrant.

Drawn to Brecht's circle in 1931, and wanting to promote him as a friend and ally in artistic experimentation within the Communist camp, Tretiakov visited Brecht in Augsburg. Walking through a cemetery they discussed how even in death the class structure of German society remained. The graves of the rich were marked with large, permanent stone grave markers. At the other end of the cemetery were the tiny, often unmarked graves of the destitute.

During one walk together, Brecht told Tretiakov with more drama than truth: "I am a physician by education. As a boy, I was mobilized in the war and placed in a hospital. I dressed wounds, applied iodine, gave enemas, performed blood transfusions. If the doctor ordered me, 'Amputate a leg, Brecht,' I would answer, 'Yes, your excellency,' and cut off the leg. If I was told, 'Make a trepanation,' I opened the man's skull and tinkered with his brains."[6] This fanciful account of Brecht as reluctant surgeon, with all its uses of a subjunctive form in German that Tretiakov never grasped, was followed by a carefully manipulated account of his life in revolutionary Augsburg from late 1918 through early 1919. "I was a member of the Augsburg Revolutionary Committee," Brecht told Tretiakov. "Nearby, in Munich, Leviné raised the banner of Soviet power. Augsburg lived in the reflected glow of Munich. The hospital was the only military unit in the town. It elected me to the Revolutionary Committee." Brecht gave Tretiakov no hint that he had never really studied medicine, had never done brain surgery, had in fact attacked the revolution in his poetry, and had been taking private riding lessons while Munich and Augsburg were attacked by counterrevolutionaries, several of whom were relatives or his closest friends.

After they returned to Berlin, Brecht took Tretiakov to a party at Fritz Sternberg's. Tretiakov was introduced there to a mixture of Communist party members, former party members, and nonmembers, like Brecht and Sternberg. Discussion was lively and unrestrained, including an attack on Stalin's collectivization policy.[7] Tretiakov, a strong advocate of Stalin's policies (which, as he knew, included the outright murder of tens of thousands of kulaks and their families), burst out to Brecht, "Where have you brought me? There are enemies of the party here, enemies of the Soviet Union."[8] "What do you mean?" Brecht replied. "Here, with full justification, so it appears to me, Stalin's collectivization policy is being criticized." Later, visiting the Soviet Union at Tretiakov's invitation, Brecht would give interviews publicly endorsing Stalin's policies.

Before he left Germany to return to the Soviet Union, Tretiakov had to know that as far as party discipline was concerned Brecht was a maverick. Despite this, Brecht was a highly visible and persuasive figure of the sort that the Comintern wanted recruited. In addition, Tretiakov hoped to be produced. He returned to the Soviet Union to promote Brecht's experimental work, so like his own, and he left Brecht with one of his own plays, I Want a Child. Sexually frank, it proposes a system of selective breeding in humans that anticipates features of the breeding system of the SS. Though this translation adaptation could be readily seen to be as much a Brecht play as "his" other adaptations, the very existence of it is often ignored. There is no mention of this dubious work in Jan Knopf's Brecht Handbuch: Theater.

In hoping to get Brecht to openly support the Soviet Union, Tretiakov was following a pattern pursued by the Comintern: Gide and Malraux in France, George Bernard Shaw in England, Karin Michaëlis and Martin Andersen-Nexø in Scandinavia, Feuchtwanger and Brecht in Germany, Hemingway in America, and thousands of other prominent artists were invited to lend their support to Soviet positions. They were to throw their weight behind the three mainstays of Stalin's policy: 1) remaining content for the moment to develop socialism only in the Soviet Union; 2) treating other parties on the left as "fascists in disguise"; and 3) agreeing to the general stategy adopted by the Comintern that fascism was to be treated as a passing, soon to be crushed phenomenon.

These positions were directly opposed by Stalin's former rival Trotsky, who had been forced into exile and who would finally be murdered on Stalin's orders. In 1931, Trotsky warned: "Workers, Communists . . . should fascism come to power it will ride over your skulls and spines like a terrific tank. Your salvation lies in merciless struggle. And only a fighting unity with Social Democratic workers can bring victory. Make haste, you have very little time left."[9] While Trotsky warned of the madness of Stalin's Comintern policy in allowing the German left to remain split, other voices also began to warn of an anti-Semitic streak in Stalin. According to Walter Benjamin, the question was raised in the Brecht circle by the writer Soma Morgen-stern.[10] This was a real issue for Benjamin, himself a Jew, but there is no evidence that Brecht ever recognized this as a problem.

Not surprisingly, Soviet inroads in Germany produced violent reactions on the nationalist right. Arnolt Bronnen, like millions of others, was now urgently trying to find solutions to German problems within Germany. Bronnen saw the future of Germany as socialist but not the kind preached by Hitler's Bavarian branch of the Nazi party. In 1931, Bronnen became involved in plotting to remove Hitler as the head of the National Socialist movement in Germany in order to replace him with Joseph Goebbels.[11] Co-plotters included Dr. Weissauer, chief edi-tor of the Nazi party paper in Berlin *Der Angriff* (The attack); Dr. Otto Strasser; and Captain Walter Stennes, who had been Chiang Kai-shek's secret-police chief in Canton in 1927 when Chiang (strongly supported by Josef Stalin) had slaughtered his former Communist allies by the thousands. With what they felt was the silent assent of Goebbels, they planned a putsch against Hitler's control of the NSDAP.

On April 1, 1931 (an unfortunate choice of day if the coup was to be taken seriously), *Der Angriff* carried banner headlines announcing that Goebbels was to take the helm of a Berlin-controlled Nazi party. But to Stennes' horror, Goebbels was nowhere to be found. He did not even answer his telephone. The plotters sent Bronnen over to investi-gate. Goebbels was "ill in bed." Bronnen told Goebbels he was needed. Goebbels cut him off. He was too sick. Without Goebbels, the revolt collapsed. Hitler flew to Berlin and promoted Goebbels, thanking him for his support of what many now realized was an increasingly unstop-pable führer.

In May 1931, the major bank of Austria, the Kreditanstalt, closed its doors. Other banks failed, factories closed, and millions of jobless and often homeless spilled onto the streets. As Germany sank deeper into chaos that May, Brecht drove south with Hauptmann and Emil Burri through Augsburg, Lausanne, and Marseilles to return to a favor-ite haunt, the seaside resort of Le Lavandou. Also on holiday were Kurt Weill, Lotte Lenya, prominent left-wing newspaper correspondent Ber-nard von Brentano, and Walter Benjamin. In a businesslike letter to Weigel in Berlin, Brecht complained that he was not getting as good service at his Riviera hotel as the year before.[12]

In mid-June, Brecht left Le Lavandou and drove to another favor-ite vacation spot, the Ammersee, an area with spectacular alpine views much favored by upper-class Bavarians as a country retreat. He met briefly Mari Hold, Mari Barbara (now eight months old), Helene Wei-gel, and Stefan (now seven years old). Now wealthy, and with real estate values driven radically down in the depression, Brecht had begun to

think of buying a country house in this lovely region where he had
wandered as a youth. The area was particularly favored by those in
Munich Nazi circles who were closest to Hitler. It was here that Hitler's
adjutant the Harvard-educated Putzi Hanfstaengl had his villa. Here
Hitler had fled after the 1923 Beer Hall Putsch.[13] From here, he had been
taken to the nearby Landsberg fortress where he and his companions
wrote *Mein Kampf*.[14]

Brecht hoped to get help from his father in buying an estate. Joined
in Utting by Elisabeth Hauptmann after Mari Hold and Helene Weigel
had left, Brecht made a trip to talk finances with his father in Augsburg.
The Herr Direktor agreed to help if a suitable estate could be found for
purchase.

From Augsburg, on June 28, Brecht wrote a letter to Hauptmann's
sister in distant Peckelsheim. Apparently, Irma Warmber had come all
the way from Saint Louis, Missouri, to try to help her father after the
death of his wife the year before.[15] Frau Warmber was dismayed that
her sister, who lived far closer, had not come home. The family was also
concerned, of course, that after Brecht's marriage to Weigel in early
1929, Bess's plans to marry Brecht could no longer be used to justify her
periodically living with him. In a letter to Hauptmann's sister, addressed to the "Very Honored, Gracious Lady," Brecht explains that
not only is "Frau Hauptmann's" work too important for her to leave
but that her health also poses problems. "I admit openly," he says in
his letter, "that on these grounds, I have always strongly counseled your
sister against such journeys, and for her to examine in the closest
possible way their necessity." "Hopefully," he goes on, "you will not
assume that I have done this only on egoistic grounds." "I do not
believe," the letter concludes, "that you need have the slightest concern
about your sister's future, as she is talented enough to be able to earn
her daily bread and more, and that her economic situation has permanently improved. It is more her health situation that makes every over-
exertion so decisively dangerous for her."[16]

Most of what Brecht claimed in the letter was a lie or a half-truth.
Hauptmann's financial situation, largely unaffected by the small legacy
she had received from her mother, continued to be bad. Her relatively
steady income from her small percentage of the German *Threepenny* was
steadily falling as fewer German stages dared produce it in the face of
increasing nationalist pressure. With *Happy End*'s prospects ruined by
Brecht and Weigel, Hauptmann was still dependent on handouts from
him or earned from editing "Brecht's" work. Her requests, like those
of others, were usually unsuccessful as well as demeaning since Brecht
persisted in pleading poverty. Brecht always thought her strong enough
to make countless trips with him up and down the length of Germany

and to France. He never seems to have considered that perhaps it was his behavior toward Hauptmann that was as responsible as anything in contributing to her now almost chronic nervousness.

Brecht and Hauptmann returned to Berlin from Augsburg in the fall of 1931. Despite having delivered nothing for two years while receiving one thousand gold marks a month from Felix Bloch Erben, Brecht was still able to talk Fritz Wreede into continuing to pay. Brecht's personality was so strong that Wreede could not say "no" to him in person. Brecht persuaded Wreede that a couple of new plays were soon to be completed. The first of these was *Saint Joan of the Stockyards*, publicly announced in August 1930. Wreede was persuaded that completion was imminent. Then Brecht threw in a bonus, a new version of Shakespeare's *Measure for Measure*.[17]

Instead of working on what he had promised to Wreede, Brecht began other projects. In 1931, the Berlin subscription theater the Volksbühne had staged Maxim Gorky's novel *Mother* in an adaptation by Günther Weisenborn and Günther Stark. Set in Russia in 1902, the novel told of a deeply religious woman who becomes convinced that the only realistic way to carry out the Christian principle of helping the poor was to join the Communist party. Relying on a film adaptation by the great Russian filmmaker Vsevolod Pudovkin, Stark and Weisenborn had boiled the sprawling novel down into a series of short, dramatic scenes in the same naturalist or representational manner as the novel itself. Changing it to a more presentational style, Hauptmann worked with Brecht, Hungarian director Slatan Dudow, and Hanns Eisler, who composed the music.[18] Where the original novel had ended with the unsuccessful uprising of 1905, the new German version brought events to the brink of the successful revolution of 1917. The central character, Pelegea Wlassowa, leads a march against the czarist forces, carrying in her own hand the banner of revolution.

Formally, *Die Mutter*, or *The Mother*, borrows heavily from the stage devices Hauptmann had introduced to the collective from her work with Japanese medieval drama. She told me in 1966 that she suggested opening the play with a direct address to the audience. This was the key to the construction of the whole play as characters come to the stage apron and say who they are and what they are going to do. Again, borrowing from the Japanese choral forms, at crucial points in the text (using words that directly point to Nikolai Bukharin's *The ABCs of Communism*), the ABCs of communism are presented in verse form half-recited, half-sung to Hanns Eisler's stirring music.[19]

While the work on turning *Mother* into a "Brecht" play moved along and Hauptmann's name was dropped as one of its authors, Brecht developed an interest in an experimental film about unemployed Berlin workers. His co-workers on this project were Slatan Dudow and a shadowy, ex-right-wing spy named Ernst Ottwalt.[20] Once a strutting Freikorps member who had helped with the military eradication of the Spartacists in 1919–20, Ottwalt had now taken on similarly sinister tasks on the left. Immediately upon becoming a party member in September 1931, Ottwalt joined a group called the BB-Familie, a military-industrial espionage unit run by Moscow and the CPG. In his role as agent and as part of the Brecht ménage, Ottwalt fit in well.

According to Ilse Bartels and Ernst Busch (who were present), much of the writing of the *Kuhle Wampe* script was done by Ottwalt. Though this was known at the time, for publicity purposes—after all, was Brecht not the famous author of *The Threepenny Opera?*—the work was published as though Brecht were mainly responsible for it. The film was shot at the camp called Kuhle Wampe from which the film took its name. It featured the "Red" campers, people who were out of work and homeless but who had banded together to create a tent community on the shores of a large lake. From here, the unemployed streamed forth daily on bicycles, trying to land any job advertised that day in the newspaper. As part of the "Red" campers' entertainment in real life and in the film, an agitprop group presented skits on problems of the unemployed.

Among the crowds of unemployed workers who participated in the film was twenty-three-year-old Margarete Steffin. At the time she joined the *Kuhle Wampe* project, Steffin had recently been fired from her job as a bookkeeper "because of political interests of a Communist nature."[21] Steffin had contracted tuberculosis not long before but still had attended the Marxist Worker School where Helene Weigel was giving a practicum in stage vocal work. This would bring Steffin into the immediate Brecht circle.

While work on *Kuhle Wampe* moved from the shooting to the editing stage, and the adaptation of Gorky's *Mother* was completed and circulated among potential producers, work moved forward with the *Saint Joan of the Stockyards* project. The surviving records of the play give an unusually clear picture of how it came into being. Jan Knopf, one of the editors of the newest Brecht edition, notes: "From the work materials one can determine that *no small part—including the text—of the preparatory work was provided by Emil Burri and Elisabeth Hauptmann who were also responsible for the plot*; Brecht's work consisted primarily of checking up on suggestions, editing and expanding the text" (italics added).[22] After saying Burri and Hauptmann are responsible for the central elements of the play, however, Knopf does not address the question of authorship itself.[23] Ignoring all the thematically related writings published under Hauptmann's own name, he adds this work to the *Collected Works of Brecht*. Who wrote what is a matter of marginal concern for Knopf.[24] *Saint Joan of the Stockyards* is thought by some critics, who also ignore the question of authorship, to be one of Brecht's best works. One says: "Viewed from an artistic perspective, the play represents a peak in Brecht's achievement."[25]

The play's strength, in my own view, is traceable to two radically different, wholly irreconcilable points of view. Without reducing the play only to reflections of the strong personalities who participated in its creation, there is little doubt that they are reflected here. The central drama of the work (as with *The Threepenny Opera*) is the conflict between the title character, who is a typical Hauptmann creation, and her opponent, the arch-Brechtian figure of Mauler. As we have repeatedly seen, Hauptmann's own work presents strong, independent, intelligent, capable women characters trying to maintain their pride and independence in a world dominated by men. A typical central character in a Hauptmann work cares about other people, puts her own life on the line, and works to change the world for the better. When Brecht writes on his own, or where one finds the clearest traces that his was the primary hand in creating a text, we find figures like Baal, Garga, "poor Bébé," Fatzer, Macheath, or a figure he had now begun to write about, the mysterious and often brutal Herr Keuner. Consistently, his own male characters are arrogant, egocentric, ruthless, charismatic men who boastfully exploit and denigrate anyone unwise enough to enter their powerful orbits.

Nowhere is this clear-cut opposition quite as readily visible as in *Saint Joan of the Stockyards*. In what is basically a return to the devices of the old morality play, the Hauptmann figure, Joan Dark (d'Arc), is an orator and leader, a woman of great courage who uses all her daring, intelligence, and hope to fight against the representative of everything evil, brutal, and cunning. Often alone, but willing like her great historical predecessor to fight anyway, Joan Dark faces off against the quintessential Brecht figure of Pierpoint Mauler.[26]

It is no accident that the most famous single quote from Goethe's *Faust*, "There are two souls in my breast," is omnipresent in semiserious-semiparodic form in the *Saint Joan*. There are two souls in the *Saint Joan* play itself, and they are locked in deadly battle. The split apparent in *Measures* between the Young Comrade and the Moscow Control Chorus is played out in *Saint Joan* in a way that clearly anticipates the divided characters who will appear in many later Brecht plays.

The dramatic opposition of Joan Dark, who tries through direct human persuasion to change humanity for the better, and the clever, vicious Mauler is the greatest strength and most serious weakness of the play today. Joan, carefully and plausibly developed, learns the hard way that in the long run her work with the Salvation Army will not benefit the poor. (It is worth noting that Joan's demonstration that the Salvation Army cannot permanently help the poor is a gloss on Friedrich Engels's classic text on this subject.[27]) So lucid is her final analysis that Mauler must silence her and twist her legacy as quasi-saint to suit his own profoundly amoral and reactionary purposes.

Joan's opponent is so corrupt that even his heart and stomach (as his rival Criddle learns too late) give him guidance as to how to better play the market and extract greater profit. With the arch-villain Mauler representing capitalism, the *Saint Joan* play works only if we find his villainy plausible. In today's mixed, free market–social democratic models that usually attempt to ameliorate at least the most glaring inhumanities toward the poor, Mauler seems more caricature than dramatic character.

Though this play echoes persistent concerns both of Brecht and Hauptmann, there is perhaps another biographical reference in it. The religious, proto-Communist Joan Dark is, at the play's conclusion, "twenty-three years old" and dying from "something wrong with her lungs."[28] Margarete Steffin, who entered the Brecht circle at precisely this time, was twenty-three years old, had tuberculosis, and was a committed Communist who also felt a strong pull toward religion.

This dark, personally revealing work was published by Peter Suhrkamp in the paperback *Versuche* series. However, when it was delivered to Wreede in late 1931, no one dared tackle it on a major stage in Germany. Had it been completed when first proposed in 1929, it would have been both playable and influential. Now it was useless. But astoundingly, again simply overwhelmed by Brecht's personality, Wreede agreed to continue to pay the one thousand gold mark monthly advance. Brecht promised Wreede that a very playable German version of *Measure for Measure* would soon be completed.

"It Was Hitler's Best Time. His Neck Was Still Slender Then and Radiated Sensuality." (1931–32)

By late 1931–32, Hauptmann's high hopes for working with Brecht on a mutually respectful basis and of some personal commitment from him could no longer be reasonably sustained. He had his eye on Steffin and was still trying to hustle Carola Neher, while now married to Weigel. It was now as clear to Hauptmann—as it had earlier become to Bie Banholzer, Orge Pfanzelt, and Marianne Zoff—that Brecht's stream of blandishments, lies, attacks, and his compulsive affairs were a deadly threat to self-esteem. Hauptmann would continue to do some editing—their joint work would be printed in the paperbound *Versuche* series—but she needed separation from Brecht. Hauptmann would have been happy with equal billing rather than primacy, but Brecht could not accept public recognition of Hauptmann's real role in *The Threepenny Opera*, *He Who Said Yes*, *Measures*, and the most recent works, *The Mother* and *Saint Joan of the Stockyards*, as well as innumerable poems and short stories going back to early 1925. As a result, one of the most productive relationships in the history of drama would now more or less peter out.

In late 1931, Hauptmann submitted one of her short stories to the committed left-wing publisher Wieland Herzfelde, for inclusion in a collection to be called *Thirty New Storytellers of the New Germany*. Titled "Gastfeindschaft" (Emnity toward a guest), an obvious play on the German "Gastfreundschaft" (hospitality), her story examines the uneasy dynamics created when the upper-middle-class Streicher (the family name of one of Berlin's most prominent Nazis) family invites an unemployed and homeless man to their Christmas celebration. At the end of the evening, the man prefers going back into the cold, rather than pretending to have anything in common with his hosts. Bitter, accurate, powerful, the story is precisely the kind of work that the popular press had no interest in as Germany slid further toward the abyss.

In the fall of 1931, at Bad Harzburg, under the shadow of the ruined eleventh-century castle of Holy Roman Emperor Henry IV, a meeting was held that would hasten the collapse of Weimar's semidemocratic state. Organized by the powerful press magnate and nationalist leader multimillionaire Alfred Hugenberg, the meeting brought together Hitler, army head General von Seeckt, the leaders of the German Veterans' organization, and the leaders of the paramilitary Stahlhelm (Steel helmet) organization. Among those who attended the meeting at Harzburg, both as Goebbels's close friend and as a journalist, was Arnolt Bronnen. At the Hotel Germania, Bronnen sat near Hitler and observed him closely. "It was," Bronnen wrote later, "Hitler's best time. His neck was still slender then and radiated sensuality like his hands, his hair, and his, for a man, slender chest."[1] However, Hitler radiated not only sensuality but intense charisma offset by no moral scruple.

After Harzburg, Bronnen's bosses at Berlin radio recognized that if the Nazi party entered the government and began to determine budgets of state enterprises, it would be essential to have good relations with the NSDAP. Bronnen was asked to serve as an intermediary. But Bronnen, aware of his strength as a broker, set a condition. His own place in the radio hierarchy would have to be improved if he was to take on assignments like this. He was then promoted to head a department and given a large salary increase.

Reaping the rewards of the charisma he had exercised over the power brokers at Harzburg, Hitler's enormous supercharged Mercedes was now seen parked at the huge, expensive Hotel Kaiserhof directly across from the Berlin chancellery. His own star rising with that of his führer, Goebbels now acquired a large car and moved from his one-and-half-room apartment to a huge place on the Reichskanzlerplatz. Here Hitler often joined him in the evening and they would listen, so they said, to Wagner.

The living standard of the Nazis and other clever speculators climbed with the worsening depression, but Fritz Wreede and Ernst Josef Aufricht found themselves hard-pressed to find plays that would sell well enough to keep their businesses going. Despite his own huge losses in recent years from Brecht, Aufricht was now persuaded by the actress Trude Hesterberg and her banker lover, Fritz Schönherr, to put on a new production of *Mahagonny* with Hesterberg, needless to say, to play Begbick. The offer was an excellent one. Hesterberg, veteran of the Berlin cabaret scene, was one of the best drawing cards in Berlin theater. Accepting the proposal, Aufricht sent his associate Robert Vambery to pick up the money. For some reason, it was handed over in cash rather than by check.

Aufricht spared no expense to reassemble many of the people who had helped make *The Threepenny Opera* so successful in 1928. Caspar Neher would design both sets and costumes and, for the first time, be credited as director of the production. Aufricht signed up Harold

Paulsen (Macheath in the original *Threepenny*) and Lenya, now a major star from her role in newly released *Threepenny* film, to play the whore Jenny. With the two major roles cast, nothing suitable was left for Helene Weigel who had, in Aufricht's view, sabotaged his last big production, *Happy End*.

Rehearsals at the Kürfurstendamm Theater were poisonous. Neither Brecht nor Weigel had any role in the production, but they kibitzed anyway. Brecht, who had treated Weill's work with disrespect for several years, was now barely civil to him in public. When Brecht sought to dictate what tone the production should take, Weill insisted on the importance of his music. Soon, librettist and composer were so alienated that they started to have their lawyers present at rehearsals. In one argument with Weill, Brecht shouted that he was going "to throw this phony Richard Strauss in complete war paint down the stairs."[2]

Aufricht saw he had to get Brecht out of the rehearsals. When he learned that *Mother* was available, Aufricht decided to produce it if this would get Brecht away from the *Mahagonny* rehearsals. Delighted with getting funds for *Mother* (while still being paid royalties for *Mahagonny*), Brecht moved to the unheated cellar of the big theater to begin planning the production. Curiously, given his usual eagerness to direct, that assignment was given to his old ally Emil Burri. The lead was given to Weigel, even though up until this time Brecht had not really had much good to say about her work as an actress.[3] Key male parts were taken by the singer-actor Ernst Busch and by Marianne Zoff's second husband, Theo Lingen. With the trauma of the divorce past, Brecht and Weigel were now reasonably friendly with Zoff and Lingen. The small maid's part was to be played by Margarete Steffin who had been part of the crowd scenes in the *Kuhle Wampe* film.

On the first day of rehearsals, Steffin arrived early.[4] She had been told that Ernst Ottwalt would write some new material for her, and she was anxious to meet Ernst Busch, the handsome male lead, and Burri, the director. She cared less at that time about Brecht's arrival. She knew him largely by reputation, and what she knew did not make him attractive. To her, a dedicated Communist party member, he was the opportunist who had become wealthy from *The Threepenny Opera* play and film. She remembered reading somewhere that he had stolen *Threepenny* "from A to Z." She also knew he had a bad reputation among Berlin workers as a man who spared little time for workers' groups.

Brecht arrived late at the rehearsal of *Mother*. To Steffin, he looked tired, his mind elsewhere. He seemed to be both shy and modest, with an attitude that many would have taken as rude, but which she saw as a lack of self-confidence. If he had made a lot of money from *Threepenny*, it did not look to her as if he had invested any of it into clothes:

his suit was shabby, and his hair poked out from under a cap that he never bothered to take off. No sooner had he arrived than he was gone again.

Later, at those rehearsals when Brecht did bother to turn up, it became obvious to Weigel and others that something was going on between him and Margarete Steffin. He could not seem to see enough of this slender, vivacious, intelligent woman with her blond hair cut in the fashionable bob of the liberated women. He arranged private "working" sessions with her and, despite her objections, tried to grope under her skirt. Steffin was not prudish. She was a Communist who believed in free sexual expression, but she wanted to get to know her partner first.

Born in a loud, filthy, smelly, tiny, damp Berlin slum flat in 1908, Grete Steffin had grown up in a family where both her mother, Johanna, and father, August, were active in the Communist party. Grete was committed to communism but had a low opinion of the CPG itself. Grete's younger sister, Herta, and her fiancé, Herbert Hanisch, were in the anarcho-syndicalist wing of the party. "Things were very poor for us at home," Herta told one interviewer later. "Father drank a lot. Mother had to sew all the time. She sewed trousers for forty-eight pfennig, workers' trousers."[5] But though Johanna Steffin had a full-time job and was often out on party business in the evening and weekends, her husband expected her to do all the housework and serve meals at his convenience.

August Steffin himself was erratically employed in the building trades. He never told his wife what he earned and drank up most of it anyway. Drunk, his behavior to family members was not, said Herta years later, "very nice." When the family was out together, socialism or no socialism, Herr Steffin required his wife and daughters to walk three steps behind him. Whenever he felt his authority as "head of the family" challenged in any way, he became violent, threatening to smash the whole household. His personal hygiene included relieving himself in front of everybody in the kitchen sink.

At a school with eight hundred pupils, Grete established a brilliant academic record. Very religious, and trying hard to combine Christian compassion for the poor with her family's brand of socialism, she established a religious study circle. She bribed kids to attend by completing homework assignments for them. Her creative writing was so good that she won a Berlin-wide competition and was a published author before her teens. She showed such great promise both as a writer and linguist that when she did not have the money to enter gymnasium and prepare for the university, her teachers offered to pay for her; but her father would not allow it. He argued that education would alienate

1. Brecht (born February 10, 1898) photographed in August 1899 in the atelier of the distinguished Augsburg photographer Konrad Ressler

2. Brecht family, 1908. Eugen, Walter, Berthold, and Sophie Brecht (born Wilhelmine Friederike Sophie Brezing).

3. House at 2 Bleichstrasse, 1910. Eugen and Walter are at right-hand window. The houses in the Colony still stand today.

4. "Black Marie," the maid who, according to Brecht, hid small objects between her breasts and thighs for her small charges to find

6. The watercolorist, and future charismatic politician, a rather dapper Adolf Hitler (inset) celebrates the outbreak of "the Great War" in Munich's main square, 1914.

5. One-legged Moritaten singer at Augsburg Fair, with hand organ and visual aids, half sings, half tells tales of murder, rape, exotic foreign parts, and the saving of the helpless by mother love.

7. With Neher away at war, Brecht sings to a doting Otto Müllereisert as an obviously jealous "Orge" Pfanzelt looks on.

8. Brecht lover, Caspar Neher. On April 14, 1917, while serving on the Western Front in France with 28th Bavarian Close Combat Battery, Neher was buried alive and barely survived. Somewhat recovered, he joined the 2nd Battery of the 4th Bavarian Field Artillery Regiment at Verdun, where he served until the war ended in late 1918.

9. *Rosa Luxemburg, Polish-born leader of the Spartacus movement. Opposing Lenin, Luxemburg argued that the German Communist party must not allow itself to be dominated by Moscow through the supra-national organization being planned, the Comintern. Attacked in the right-wing press and in inflammatory posters as "a bride of the devil" and as a Jew, she was murdered by government-backed radical-right forces on January 15, 1919.*

10. *Christening party, July 30, 1919, for Bie Banholzer's and Brecht's child, Frank Banholzer. From left to right: Bie Banholzer, Otto Müllereisert (spy for von Epp's right-wing forces), Caspar Neher, an unknown woman, Orge Pfanzelt, Brecht, and Bie's brother-in-law.*

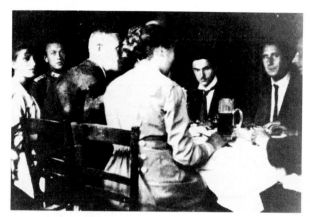

11. *Marie Rose Aman, original subject of "Sentimental Song #1004," later relabeled (the reference to one more seduction than those of Casanova and Don Juan now dropped) as "Remembering Marie A"*

12. *Lilly Krause, revolutionary, argued for equal rights for women. Resisting his sexual advances, she is denigrated by Brecht in the poem "Hell's Lilly."*

13. Frank Banholzer, future Luftwaffe bombardier and part of the Wehrmacht forces that try to overrun the USSR in WWII. Here seen with the first of his many foster parents.

14. Marianne Zoff wearing one of the coats provided by her sword-cane carrying admirer, Recht, manufacturer of playing cards

15. "Do Not Touch" is the admonition on this Neher sketch of Brecht and Bronnen. The drawing of the two figures, here shown as one, depicts Brecht beating a drum with what appears to be perhaps a thigh bone while Bronnen brandishes a whip/banner emblazoned with the title of one of his violent and bisexual plays: Vatermord (Parricide). Neher had come to Munich to meet up with Brecht and to see Drums in the Night.

16. Otto Reigbert's set for the explicitly counterrevolutionary play Drums, as staged in Munich in the summer of 1922. Note Reigbert's use of a visible stage lighting fixture, which will then be picked up by Neher and used for the production of The Three-penny Opera in Berlin in August 1928.

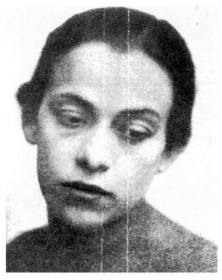

17. *Publicity photo of Helene Weigel done in the mid-1920s*

18. *Announcement of Hitler's 1923 Beer Hall Putsch, which very briefly interrupted rehearsals of* Edward II, *then being conducted a few hundred yards away*

19. *Caspar Neher's steel net separates the openly homosexual and about to be murdered king from the audience in* Edward II, *Munich, 1923.*

20. *The Soviet revolutionary director Asja Lazis, who brought Brecht the latest news of radical Soviet experiments in cold acting and in radical modification of classic texts, ideas incorporated into the production of* Edward II *in Munich in 1923*

21. Mari Hold-Ohm. *After the sudden death of her husband when he apparently discovered pictures of her wearing Brecht's clothes, Mari destroyed the pictures of her early life as Brecht's maid.*

22. *Glamour picture taken of Elisabeth Hauptmann in the mid-1920s, at about the time she met Brecht*

23. *Brecht standing in his Spichernstrasse apartment, mid-1920s. At a time when it was all the rage to be photographed with boxers, we see, at the piano, the boxer Paul Samson-Körner. To the right of Brecht is Samson-Körner's manager, Seelenfrend (wearing boxing gloves); the teacher Hans Borchardt; and the doggerel versifier Hannes Küpper. Elisabeth Hauptmann is marginalized, at the typewriter, ready to take down the words of the group of men and turn them into something publishable.*

24. *Violence of the cool, distant, or "epic" theater. Baal, in Brecht's and Homolka's Junge Bühne staging of the play, Berlin, 1926. Oskar Homolka as Baal has a stranglehold on Paul Bildt, playing Johannes. The impresario of the show, Moritz Seeler, would experience violence firsthand, dying as a slave laborer under the Nazis.*

25. *Marieluise Fleisser, 1927. She wears the coat made on a semi-assembly-line basis by Brecht's Berlin tailor, who expensively outfitted Brecht to look poor and who gave a discount to women ordering "the coat."*

26. Mahagonny, *Baden-Baden, 1927. A fashionable mix of a superb musical score combined with sex, violence, and foreign words ("is here no telephone?"), in the same way as used in Berlin cabaret by Walter Mehring ("my darling girl schenk ein and mix sie"), and the poet/sailor ("gif öss a Whisky, du, ach du!") Joachim Ringelnatz.*

27. *Carola Neher with (left to right) Piscator, Ihering, and Brecht, 1929. Goebbels would promote a cooperative Ihering to head Vienna's Burgtheater during the Third Reich. Piscator would flee the USSR in the mid-30s after recognizing what was happening to those who dissented in any way from Stalin's dictatorship.*

28. Mann ist Mann, 1928. *Weigel as Begbick in jackboots that match those of Hans Leibelt as the priapic, then self-castrated "Blody [sic] Five." Camp follower in the play and real-life intimate of Weigel, Steffi Spira, is center. At Weigel's request, Spira would try in the 1930s to help Weigel leave Brecht.*

29. *Stressing her contribution to* Saint Joan of the Stockyards, *Hauptmann had this picture taken of her in a Salvation Army costume.*

30. *Hauptmann/Weill/Neher/Villon/Klammer/Brecht:* The Threepenny Opera, 1928. *Note Neher's borrowing here of the obvious light source used by Reigbert in the Munich* Drums *production of 1922.*

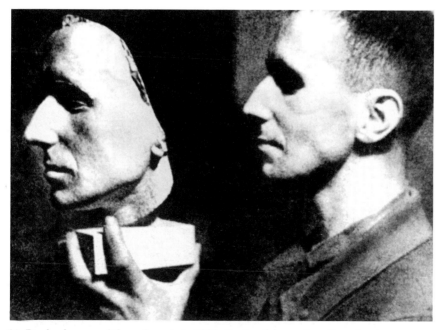

31. *Brecht observes a life mask made in 1931. Copies of the mask and/or other portraits were distributed to various lovers, such as Hauptmann and Weigel, followed by letters and phone calls whenever anyone showed signs of leaving him. Locked from his teen years on into an erotic schedule that required his frequent absence, he sought a stream of devices to help him remain "present" for each lover.*

32. Fleisser's *anti-militarist play*, Sappers of Ingolstadt, *1929, with the emerging stars Peter Lorre and Lotte Lenya. The work was directed by Brecht's slavish admirer Jacob Geis, with sets by Neher. Geis allowed Brecht to turn the play into such a sexually explicit work that attacks on it from the right were inevitable, and Fleisser's career as a Weimar playwright was brutally interrupted. Her efforts to show what Brecht was up to were too bold to be staged by those who, like Aufricht, feared Brecht's revenge.*

33. *Elisabeth Hauptmann in front of a motorcycle shop. The photo was published in* Uhu *in March 1929 under her own name, together with her revealingly autobiographical short story with its biblical title: "And He Shall Be Your Lord."*

34. Cast of Happy End, *1929. Carola Neher (with hat) would die on June 28, 1942, in Stalin's system of concentration camps. Kurt Gerron (behind her, with cigar), the Tiger Brown of the original cast of* The Threepenny Opera, *would die in Hitler's gas chambers in Auschwitz. Weigel's and Brecht's attempt to sabotage Hauptmann's rebellion as an independent playwright was successful, and she was forced back into her usual harness thereafter.*

35. Clown Show, Baden-Baden, 1929. Audience members fainted as the wooden limbs and paper-mache head of the clown (Marianne Zoff's husband, Theo Lingen, in this production) were sawn off.

36. Bronnen's and Olga's close friend, a novelist of limited talent but a propagandist of genius, Dr. Joseph Goebbels

37. Otto Griebel's The International, 1930. Women have been entirely forgotten in a picture that would later hang proudly in the German Democratic Republic's "German Museum" in Berlin until the fall of the Wall.

38. *The Hauptmann/Weill/Brecht school opera,* He Who Says Yes, *1930. Starkly beautiful in form and a radical shift of drama produced in the Brecht workshop. The play was quietly recognized as Hauptmann's by publication in Hannes Küpper's journal,* Scheinwerfer, *in the small city of Essen in the winter issue of 1929/30 before it appeared (in only slightly changed form) under Brecht's name.*

39. *The Hauptmann/Eisler/Brecht* The Measures Taken, *Berlin, 1930. The score begins and ends in triple fortissimo, with the central theme of the work—Moscow knows best— backed by choirs comprising over 400 voices. Again, as with* He Who Says Yes *and* The Clown Show, *despite all the theoretical emphasis on coolness and distance, real audiences were profoundly moved.*

40. *Lorre, dressed to kill:* Mann ist Mann,
*1931. Lorre had just appeared as the psy-
chopathic child murderer in Fritz Lang's international hit* M.

41. Margarete Steffin, 1931

42. *A teenage Steffin performs in chorus.*

41. *Steffin (center, behind table) in* The Mother, *directed by Emil Burri. In the proletarian milieu in which Steffin lived, she reports it was widely believed at the time that Brecht's works such as* The Threepenny Opera *were "stolen from A to Z."*

43. *Program for* The Mother, *1932. Note minuscule cost of admission— and hence virtually nonexistent income for the players. Professionals like Weigel, Lingen, and the singer Ernst Busch had other income. Steffin did not.*

45. *Brecht, posed with the Steyr that Hauptmann had swapped for some of Brecht's most hackneyed "verse" on the relationship between the car and Steyr's other manufacturing branch, automatic weapons*

46. *Adolf Hitler's highly successful election poster of 1932, where he was declared to be "Germany's Last Hope." At the end of 1932 in Brecht's apartment a group of radical right-wingers drank a toast to "a bloodless putsch from the right." Within weeks, Hitler legally would become chancellor.*

47. *Part of a minority in a cabinet that included only two other Nazis, Wilhelm Frick and Hermann Goering, Hitler becomes German chancellor, January 1933. Among those who appointed him was his immediate predecessor, Franz von Papen, who, confident that he and other continuing cabinet members could control Hitler, declared: "we have him framed in."*

48. *The burning Reichstag, the night of February 27, 1933. Hitler used the occasion to "frame in" enemies anywhere on the political spectrum who he thought might block his further progress in bringing Germany totally under his personal command.*

her from her own class and forced her to go to work at age fourteen. She quickly taught herself to become a superb typist and stenographer, and got a secretarial job with a Berlin book publisher. Here she was so outspoken in her Communist beliefs that she was fired and had to then rely on short-term jobs.

Even in her teens, Steffin showed signs of the tuberculosis that would eventually kill her. Often ill by the late 1920s, she remained active in socialist theatrical groups as a singer and narrator. As a teenager, she began to teach herself Russian so she could read Lenin in the original. At eighteen, she began to spend more and more time at the flat of a young male friend. In one of her erotic poems, she recalled lying with her friend on top of her as she wondered, "Ob der Junge nicht bald fertig ist" (Is the kid not finished yet?).[6] The kid did finish, and she soon found herself pregnant. With abortions illegal, she made an expensive deal with a local pharmacist. After twenty hours of excruciating pain, she saw two bloody blobs at her feet.[7] After recovering from this, she volunteered as a singer and narrator in agitprop productions of the kind included in the *Kuhle Wampe* film.

While Burri rehearsed *Mother* with Weigel, Busch, and Steffin, *Mahagonny* rehearsals continued upstairs. The whores' chorus of *Mahagonny* began to be modeled on the shows with high-kicking, scantily clad dancers then popular in Berlin and Paris. Neher created his usual series of sexually frank pictures to be projected over the stage, together with a picture of a moving arrow representing the hurricane that threatened to sweep away the later-day Sodom and Gomorrah Mahagonny. Aufricht liked the pictures and the arrow, but not Neher's use of titles projected between scenes. Aufricht insisted on having these texts read aloud by a master of ceremonies in an evening jacket.

Downstairs, Burri worked on a simple, stark production of *Mother*. The Hauptmann-Brecht adaptation shows a simple Russian woman taking a leadership role, promoting rebellion, and defying the police, finally, at the cost of her life. Here the Communist goal is literally worth any sacrifice, and exerts a force even greater than the bond between any two individuals—including mother and son, or lover and lover. This something-greater-than-both-of-them, their main hope of eventual salvation, is referred to in the text of the play as "The Third Thing,"[8] an echo of the Holy Trinity itself, presented as a holy of holies. Songs such as "Arise, the Party Is in Danger" and "In Praise of Communism" were to be delivered, as Eisler instructed, in a triple fortissimo that shook the rehearsal room.

The final touches were put on *Mahagonny* so it could open to take advantage of Christmas-time business. *Mother* was being readied to open on January 15, the anniversary of Rosa Luxemburg's murder. The two productions precisely reflect Berlin theater in late 1931. Upstairs, scantily clad women kicked in unison while "In Praise of Communism" was sung with passion and conviction in triple fortissimo in the cellar. Outside the theater, armed and uniformed Nazi thugs openly marched with ever-less fear of police reprisals. Franz Pfeffer von Salomon's standing orders to his fighting Nazi detachments read: "The only form in which the SA displays itself to the public must be en masse. This is one of the most powerful forms of propaganda. The sight of a large body of disciplined men, inwardly and outwardly alike, makes the most profound impression upon every German and speaks to his heart in a more convincing and persuasive language than writing and oratory and logic ever can. Calm composure and matter-of-factness emphasizes the impression of the strength of marching columns."[9]

Mahagonny did excellently at the box office, running for fifty performances. Lenya later recalled: "Today, I have but to meet a true Berliner of that time, a survivor of that truly glorious public, to hear him say: 'Yes, yes, *The Threepenny Opera* was wonderful of course, but *Mahagonny*, and there follows a silence, a meaning beyond words that I do understand. There were those who came night after night, *Mahagonny* addicts, who tell me that they would leave the theatre in a kind of trance and walk the streets, Kurt's insidious bittersweet melodies repeating over and over inside their heads."[10]

Aufricht would later remember the *Mahagonny* production as "a Witches' Sabbath of injustice, horror, and brutality, that announced themselves as elements of the approaching future."[11] Night after night, on Neher's huge screen mounted above the stage, a map of Mahagonny was shown. On the screen, a moving arrow marked the advance of an enormous hurricane, as Weill's music thundered and as a "radio announcer" warned constantly of impending doom. Each night, at the last instant, the arrow marking the hurricane on the big screen would miraculously and inexplicably swerve, and each night the city would be spared.

At the progressive Volksbühne, it was a tough time for Weigel. Not only did she have to deal daily with her husband's latest young lover but as a Jewish woman and committed party member, every day she had to face the anti-Semitic thugs outside the theater who constituted a threat to her very life. At the opening, noted Ihering, Weigel was visibly ill at ease at first but settled down later.[12]

Of her rival in the cast of *Mother*, "Steffin was very good," said Weigel of her actress colleague. "She looked marvelous for the part."[13] Every night, Steffin sang of the need for revolution. Later, doctors would tell Steffin that her rehearsals and performances in the winter of 1931–32 in usually unheated theaters had hastened the progress of the tuberculosis that was to kill her at age thirty-two. Some nights, when the show ended, the rich, charismatic director would be waiting for her; and in his large car, he would drive her through the Nazi-patrolled streets to her tiny room in "Red" Wedding. Soon he gave her copies of the "special sonnets," the erotic works he had had privately printed years ago in Augsburg.

What Steffin, the self-educated twenty-three-year-old, wrote in response to Brecht's sonnets is astounding. In content, sexual frankness, and, above all, in quality, much of Steffin's writing so matches his that to this day Brecht experts argue as to what is his and what is hers. With the lower-case style that Brecht had himself taken over from Arnolt Bronnen, a typical poem is addressed to Brecht:

> when you asked me the first time
> whether i was wet, i asked myself, what does that mean?
> when you asked whether you should check to see
> i was ashamed of myself. i was wet.
>
> and when you asked whether i would come
> as you took me the first time.
> i didn't know that i could come.
> but i said nothing and i came, i came, i love you.
>
> i behaved like an inexperienced girl even though i had lived
> with a man for four and a half years.
> but only through you did i become a woman.
>
> i also began through you to love myself
> and i didn't ask anymore: what will come next?
> finally i learned to enjoy the present
> without fear of future changes between us.
>
> when i come to you let it be in such a way
> as if i came to you every day,
> in the few hours i spend with you
> let me have no wishes of my own.
>
> when i am with you you must
> tell me what has been going on for you
> but do not tell me about the other women.
> and may i myself say only: yes.[14]

Her appreciation of Brecht's sexual superiority to the "kid," her earlier sexual partner, explains something of the hold Brecht was taking on Steffin's life. In this poem, Steffin's successful mimicking of the tone of Brechtian verse also shows the immediate influence he had on her as a writer. But though this poem—like other verse, prose, and plays of Steffin—is very similar to Brecht's work, it is also something quite different. Steffin radically inverts Brechtian language. Where he consistently speaks of a brutal world seen from a male perspective, Steffin expresses her own, non- or antimasculine vision of the world. This is, like the achievement of Hauptmann before her, a form of poetic ventriloquism. We hear what seems to be Brecht's voice. But the words spoken in that voice are hers. Steffin neither accepts a male visual or aural perspective unchallenged, nor does she accept a male-oriented system in determining the emotional, social, and ethical value of an event.

In Steffin's writing, as with Hauptmann's, the basic orientation exactly corresponds to what is described by Carol Gilligan in her book *In a Different Voice*.[15] The emphasis is always on maintaining warm social connections rather than on some abstract principle of law or logic. Hers is a world where one person feels responsibility for another, a world at a very far remove from Brecht's "I am a person on whom you cannot rely." Hers is not a world of winner and losers dominated by deception and violence. Steffin's and Hauptmann's writing consistently finds a way to express "a different voice," whereas Brecht's own writing hardly ever does.

Brecht quickly recognized that the voice used by Steffin blended in such a way with his writing that it could be marketed as his own. He welcomed such contributions in the way that Canetti had observed at the time *Threepenny* was being stitched together in late 1928. For the young, largely uneducated Steffin, it was deeply flattering that her work could blend indistinguishably with that of an acknowledged master of modern literature. And, at the practical, everyday level, as Steffin was taken into the collective, she found him and the circles in which he moved irresistible attractions.

After her unheated, tiny tenement, his large apartment was heaven. There she found a warm, dry, well-lit world with a piano and hundreds of books—including his impressive, if little read, volumes of Marxist thought—and a maid to keep everything in order and make sure he was fed his favorite meals. Not only was the place extremely comfortable but it was also exciting, both politically and intellectually. She met there the economist Karl Korsch as he argued passionately that in true communism, unlike what was now being created in the Soviet Union under Stalin, the state would wither away, and personal relations would be sufficiently harmonious that no government as such would be needed. She also met Walter Benjamin and Hanns Eisler, and formed friendships with both of them. And, less happily, she met the stream of other women in his life.

Still, most of Grete's nights in Berlin were apparently spent alone at her tiny flat as Brecht maintained a kind of Mack the Knife routine of going from one partner to another on a schedule that he alone determined. Steffin never knew when he might arrive, and whether he would want immediate sexual gratification or casually declare that he could not function sexually just then as he had come from another partner. She found herself tortured by images of him with other women. The situation was further complicated when she discovered that she was pregnant with Brecht's child. She worried whether she should have the child or again attempt to get an illegal abortion. This, as she knew from her earlier brutal experience, would be hard and expensive to arrange. She had little money of her own since in the low-budget production of *Mother*, often played for the unemployed, the cast was lucky if they took home two marks per night. It was not enough to live on even by herself, and certainly not enough, even if her own health were better, for her to think of trying to feed and clothe a baby also. Despite being a Communist, and supposedly not believing at all in the supernatural, she went to see a fortune teller who told her she would not outlive her thirty-third year. Believing both that she did not have long to live and that she would never be able to count on Brecht, she decided to not have the baby.

21

"Moscow Is Convinced the Road to Soviet Germany Lies through Hitler" (1932)

As Steffin worried about her unwanted pregnancy in early 1932, the film *Kuhle Wampe* was now almost ready for release. After battles with the Berlin censors, who objected to nude scenes in the film and attempted to prevent any Berlin showing, Brecht received an invitation from Tretiakov to bring the film to Moscow for its premiere. Brecht was delighted. He began to plan the trip jointly with Steffin. A visit to the Soviet Union with the man she loved seemed boundlessly attractive to her; and, in addition, she could get a free, legal, and medically reliable abortion there.

In April, Germany went to the polls. Overwhelmingly, voters moved from left to right, casting 19.4 million votes for the World War I commander von Hindenburg; 13.4 million for Hitler; and a only 3.7 million for the Communist candidate, Ernst Thälmann. A prisoner of Moscow policy forbidding cooperation with the still very large SDP, the German Communist party slid further into isolation, losing millions of supporters to nationalist candidates of various stripes. In local elections on April 24, Nazis in Prussia established an absolute majority. The results were similar in the Bavarian local election. As the Nazi juggernaut gathered speed, still Moscow made no move to change Comintern policy.

In the Soviet Union, NKVD victims by the tens of thousands were being shipped from the Ukraine to concentration camps. The whole agricultural infrastructure fell to ruins as Stalin forced collectivization and used famine as a weapon to break the will of the population. Children died of hunger in every village. Those who broke into local homes to take any morsel of food from the inhabitants, enjoyed "white bread, poultry, canned fruit and delicacies, wines and sweets."[1]

In order to have a pliant instrument to destroy one "subclass," another "superclass" was created. The NKVD physically executed Stalin's orders, but they were backed by an intelligentsia who either published glowing accounts of Stalin's genius or kept their mouths shut altogether. Those who cooperated with Stalin joined the privilegentsia.[2] Leading editors, film makers, writers (such as Brecht's host Tretiakov), stage directors, and actors, together with key figures in the Comintern and allied "cultural" organizations—all received special ration cards, housing, travel privileges, medical care, and schooling for their children. The silence of the special new class was monumental. It is now estimated that at least eleven million deaths are directly attributable to the famine policies pursued by Stalin while the privileged members of the intelligentsia stood by.[3]

Early in May, soon after a Berlin radio broadcast of *Saint Joan of the Stockyards*, with Carola Neher in the lead and Helene Weigel in a supporting role, the semisecret lovers Brecht and Steffin left for Moscow with Slatan Dudow.

According to a note made in Brecht's diary, the great Russian film maker Sergei Eisenstein was with them on the train. Eisenstein was being summoned home to Moscow in disgrace for his decadence and formalism. For Brecht, also thought a formalist by the dominant and conservative Moscow critics, Eisenstein's case was a warning of what was to come as the arts were brought under Stalin's steel heel. Since around 1927, one formalist group after another had been broken as Stalin consolidated his conservative, even paranoid, hold on the arts and all other areas of Soviet life. Even as Brecht and Eisenstein now steamed toward Moscow, the major experimental formalist painters— Natan Altman, Pavel Filonov and Kazimir Malevich (accused, quite absurdly, of being a German spy)—were under intensifying attack. With such signs increasing daily, Brecht would have had to have been unusually blind to have not spotted the ever-growing danger.

On the platform in Moscow was Tretiakov with Brecht's other old friends Asja Lazis and Bernhard Reich, the latter now vice-chancellor of the Moscow Acting Institute. Also part of the welcoming committee was Piscator, who, apparently still not seeing fully the dangers he would soon begin to denounce vehemently, was soon telling Brecht about the great opportunities available for work on the Soviet stage and in cinema.

Steffin had her abortion (the first of several she would have during her years with Brecht) but still looked very ill.[4] Not waiting for the *Kuhle Wampe* premiere, she went to a state sanitorium in the Crimea. Here, she began to recover some of her strength, while observing the conditions of women in the Soviet Union and rapidly improving her Russian. She noted that Soviet women had equal rights and control of their own bodies. Abortions were free. Sexual harassment and rape were severely punished. She attended a local tribunal where a husband was tried for insisting on sex against his wife's will. In a letter to Brecht, Grete said the husband was sentenced to five years in prison and thrown out of the party. If Brecht was interested, it was not evident from his replies.

The Moscow screening of *Kuhle Wampe* was a great disappointment for Brecht. He had been caught by a turn of the Soviet tide. The film had montage sequences of the kind that had previously been much praised in Soviet circles. Now, however, Sergei Eisenstein returned from Berlin and Hollywood to find himself attacked for the use of montage. Parallel to Stalin's draconian implementation of collectivization, formal experimentation in the arts was now being eliminated. The screws would be slowly tightened so that by 1937–38, most of the experimentalists would be dead or in the gulag. Meanwhile, Tretiakov's usefulness as a lure for foreign artists like Brecht kept him alive, well paid, and well fed.

The audience at the *Kuhle Wampe* screening was at first merely cool but then turned hostile. The fact that unemployed workers had bicycles was greeted with incomprehension by people who did not expect even employed workers to own such a luxury item. An unemployed worker in the film who also owned a watch was altogether too much for the Soviet audience. The film seemed almost to constitute a provocation, suggesting that the unemployed of the West were better off than employed Soviet citizens!

Brecht tried to make the best of things. Fortunately for him, though he represented the kind of art Stalin wished to see stamped out, his support of communism could be useful for propaganda, as were such Western intellectuals as Malraux, Shaw, and countless others. He was encouraged, therefore, to talk with the Soviet authorities about publishing some of his works in Russian. To show how open the Soviets were, he was taken to see a production of *Threepenny* directed by the experimental Russian director Alexander Tairov. But Brecht was not impressed with the production itself.[5] He rarely approved of other people's productions of his plays.

He was pleased, however, to be introduced to Tretiakov's influential boss Mikhail Koltsov. Brilliant, slightly vain, a womanizer, fluent in several European languages, exactly the same age as Brecht, Koltsov was near the top of the Soviet publishing heap. A tireless propagandist for Stalin as the Georgian marched through the ranks to supreme power in the Soviet state, Koltsov had a direct line to Stalin himself. Koltsov's sponsorship of an artist meant food, money, a fine apartment, and a high position either within the Soviet Union or to coveted posts abroad. Most important, Koltsov could provide not just quantities of nonconvertible paper rubles but also convertible ruble contracts for favored authors willing to turn a blind eye to murderous policies.

Though Grete was still in the hospital in the Crimea, Brecht left to return to Berlin. At the Soviet border, he was stopped by the NKVD, which confiscated a number of papers he was carrying. The NKVD knew he was in contact with Tretiakov, Eisenstein, Tairov, and Meyerhold, against whom the NKVD was busy building cases. Even Koltsov was not beyond their purview. Though he might be riding high now, he too would eventually be charged with trafficking with foreigners and put on the conveyor belt of death. Perhaps unaware of the implications of his brief NKVD encounter, Brecht continued to Berlin.

In Berlin, following the general line set in Moscow, Georg Lukács was now attacking Brecht's associate Ernst Ottwalt for his use of "reportage" and "montage." When *Kuhle Wampe* finally had its Berlin premiere in early summer, it received predictably mixed reviews on the left. Most ironically, however, the "Red" campers featured in the film were the most angry about it. Why had the nonproletarian film makers never asked them for their point of view, they asked in a letter.[6] Where did the film makers get the idea that they had large cars as depicted in the film? Their questions were never answered. For all the brilliance of its montage sequences, the film concentrated on what its middle-class makers saw, quite wrongly, as the point of view of the unemployed. Oddly, considering when it was made, there is hardly a hint in the film of the approaching Nazi hurricane.

Perhaps to make up for the lack of a clear picture of the Nazi menace in *Kuhle Wampe*, in late 1932, Ottwalt would publish perhaps the hardest-hitting anti-Nazi book to come out before Hitler's seizure of power in early 1933. Using the Nazi's own slogan against them, he titled his book *Deutschland Erwache*, or *Germany Awake*. In his opening chapter, he set forth the central importance of anti-Semitism to nazism and traced the virulence of this doctrine back through German history.

Party theorist Georg Lukács now identified Brecht and Ottwalt with "decadent," "Trotskyist" heresies. The charge was extremely dangerous. Either Lukács was naive about this or was lying when he claimed to be taken aback at a party meeting in Berlin where Helene Weigel attacked him for his published views against her husband. Lukács defended himself, saying that as a Hungarian citizen with a limited work permit he was himself in danger. He added that Weigel should go directly to the German police and not just limit her remarks about him to a public meeting.[7]

Steffin was still in the Soviet Union getting treatment for her tuberculosis. She wrote to Walter Benjamin, who had become a close and understanding friend, that she hoped to make a trip to Soviet Georgia. She had become fascinated by stories about the twelfth-century Georgian Queen Tamara, generally thought to be the best and most successful ruler that turbulent region ever had. The queen had ruled in her own name, had taken lovers when she wished, and rejected them when she chose. It was, as Grete wistfully noted in her warm and open letter, a brief golden time in Georgia's history. She wanted to write a book on the subject and was convinced it could become a best-seller.[8]

When she wrote to Brecht, she routinely and honestly declared her own faithfulness and her longing for him. She also occasionally mentioned her own writing, but she wrote that she was ashamed to take up Brecht's valuable time with her work. He was, after all, already the known master. She was a largely uneducated twenty-four-year-old who was wholly unknown. Steffin sent him some of her writing anyway. He said little about it, only occasionally giving encouragement.

In June 1932, the newly promoted Arnolt Bronnen welcomed Goebbels to the radio station in the Masurenallee. Goebbels held forth at length about new elections, Hitler's price for cooperating in any way with the federal government. Echoing the theme plastered on billboards, Goebbels thundered that Hitler was "Germany's last hope." After his radio speech, Goebbels sent a gracious handwritten note to Bronnen, thanking his friend for his "great contribution" to "the Movement."

Hitler, traveling in a chartered plane and accompanied by his personal photographer, spoke at four or five rallies a day, organized with military precision in each of twenty-one German cities. It was not so much what he said but the mesmerizing delivery that mattered. His campaign, as the rock star David Bowie has observed, was accompanied by the kind of frenzy and delirium that is a standard and carefully planned component of the major tours of contemporary rock stars.

When the ballots were counted on July 31, 1932, the new campaigning techniques had proved their worth. Nazis had elected a staggering 230 Reichstag deputies, and the other nationalist parties, 33. The Social Democrats' number had shrunk to 133, and the German Communist party, to 89. The Nazis now demanded of President von Hindenburg that he use his constitutional powers to name a Nazi party deputy as president of the Reichstag. The successful Nazi candidate for this high office was the much-decorated World War I fighter pilot Hermann Göring.

Lion and Marta Feuchtwanger, despairing of Communist party chances in the election, had cast their vote for von Hindenburg in what they saw as an anti-Hitler measure.[9] They had their servants put steel shutters over the windows of their villa with its Oriental carpets, library of incunabula, and Lion's Gothic worktable salvaged from an ancient monastery. They left in their large car, with Marta, as usual, at the wheel, driving through East and West Prussia, through the Polish corridor then dividing Germany, to the Baltic coast near Lithuania. As the disturbing election returns came in, they were settled in the village of Nidden. The weather was glorious, the wild strawberries were at their tastiest. Walking along the dunes, they passed piles of brown and black clothing with the swastika insignia as the owners of these clothes, young male and female Nazis, splashed naked in the surf.[10]

In Berlin, fearing a coup from either the left or the right, Chancellor von Papen had taken all police power into his own hands. When the chancellor banned the wearing of paramilitary uniforms in public, the Nazis defied him. Goebbels limped jauntily into a prominent café on the Potsdamer Platz with fifty Nazi paramilitary, or, as they were called, Sturmabteilungen (SA) leaders in full uniform, while, as his diary triumphantly notes, "the police look stumped and then shamefacedly turn their eyes away."[11] In July alone, eighty-six people died in street fighting in Bavaria and areas to the east and north.

As murder began to rule the streets of major and minor cities, Bert, Helene Weigel, Mari Hold, and the children, Stefan and Mari Barbara, drove south to the beautiful Ammersee region in the two family cars, the Daimler and the Steyr. Arriving there, Brecht bought an estate near the village of Utting from the nobleman and retired Polizei-oberst (police chief) Josef Ritter von Reiss. In a depressed market, Brecht was able to buy it outright, using his gold-mark and *Threepenny* income, plus cash from his father. He was in some danger of becoming what a later Marxist author would call, with more than a hint of malice, an "Erfolgsautor," a term suggesting a kind of "boulevard success." According to this critic, the post World War II German playwright Heiner Müller, "Without Hitler, Brecht would not have become Brecht but rather a kind of boulevard success. *Threepenny Opera, Mahagonny* would have continued brilliantly, but thank God, along came Hitler. Then [Brecht] had time for himself."[12] Malicious and riddled with Oedipal conflict at his father in Marxist dramaturgy, Müller's observation has a disturbing accuracy. From 1928 on, Brecht was a "boulevard success," all his protestations of "poor Bert Brecht" and "Marxist struggle" notwithstanding. In 1932, such was his success that a country estate was virtually an obligation, like a big car, an emphatic and most public confirmation of his status.

The Ritter von Reiss estate comprised thirty-five acres of forest and meadows planted on the model of the English landscape garden, popular in Germany from the late eighteenth century on. In his notes on the property, Brecht said: "The arrangement happily hides its real riches. Though the estate is not particularly large, it gives the impression of being a massive park."[13] Deep in the woods, noted the new purchaser, one came upon a deep, dark pond stocked with delectable carp. The main house on the estate was old and beautifully built. Brecht noted its stairs made from "noble" wood, paneled ceilings, large ovens with iron panels with intricate designs, built-in oak tables and benches in the entranceway, and massive doors with lovely brass handles. As the house was carefully placed on superbly landscaped grounds, views were beautiful and tranquil in all directions.

It seems odd for a self-declared Marxist to be buying a country estate practically next door to Hitler while blood ran in the streets of Germany. Either Brecht had not really noticed how dire the political situation was, or, rather more likely, he had accepted the Soviet position that if Hitler was to come to power, his tenure would be brief and would be followed by the establishment of a real and permanent soviet. If that was Brecht's view, he, like Stalin, had radically miscalculated.

Göring was sworn in as presiding officer of the Reichstag. Reichstag member Klara Zetkin, associate in 1918 and 1919 of Luxemburg and Liebknecht, looked seriously ill as she rose to speak. After following Comintern orders for years, she now urged the left to unite against the fascist threat. Zetkin's words were greeted with open contempt in a Reichstag now dominated by parties of the right. An exultant Göring allowed the storm of "Heils" from the uniformed Nazi deputies that drowned out the end of Zetkin's speech to go on and on. The Third Reich had its first official and legal forum at the national level. It could now ride roughshod over all its enemies.

Weigel, Mari Hold, and the children did not stay long at Utting. Soon after they left, Brecht was joined by Grete Steffin. He had written to her in the Soviet Union inviting her to come to the new estate as soon as he was alone.[14] But he had not offered any money to pay for her long, exhausting trip from Moscow to southern Germany. He told her to try to get some money from Koltsov's associate Comrade H. Diamond or borrow some from Asja Lazis. He also wanted Steffin to recover the papers the NKVD had taken from him, perhaps with the help of a mutual friend of theirs, Otto Katz, who had a position in the Comintern. Whether Steffin was successful in this dangerous assignment is not known, but she did find enough money in Moscow for the trip to Utting.

It was not all pleasure when Steffin, still far from well, arrived. Brecht had to deliver the long-promised adaptation of Shakespeare's *Measure for Measure* by the end of September or, Wreede said, the gold mark payments would finally stop. Though Hauptmann had put in some time on the adaptation, she was so disaffected by Brecht's string of women that she had not completed it. Steffin tried to help with the writing, exactly as Orge had done for seven years in Augsburg and as Hauptmann had begun to do when she took over the rejected Orge's place seven years before. She would put her skills at the disposal of a man she, like her various predecessors and successors, loved not wisely but too well.

In the fall of 1932, with German unemployment figures climbing, the Nazis hoped to build on the mood of growing hopelessness and gain even more power through yet another hastily called election. Hitler resumed his crisscross flights over Germany. Fully aware of the hold he could exert by performance alone, "he was," as Joachim Fest puts it, "with the freedom of a great orator . . . freeing himself more and more from specific content and concrete ideas."[15] The less specific he was, the more people were persuaded. Hitler descended from the clouds in his private airplane to move enormous crowds to what he called "forward-driving hysteria," and what Goebbels characterized, with the hyperbole of a political flack, as "the divine services of our political work."[16] The SDP leadership made desperate efforts to see whether the Communists might finally be willing to join with them to stop him; but after consultations with Moscow, the Soviet attaché in Berlin, Vinogradov, brusquely broke off further negotiations stating: "Moscow is convinced the road to Soviet Germany leads through Hitler."

Brecht and Steffin left Utting in late September to return to Berlin. They brought with them a work that marked a major transition in the life of the collective, a play to which both the exiting Hauptmann and the entering Steffin had contributed. On September 29, the *Measure for Measure* "adaptation" that Wreede had been waiting for, titled *Round Heads, Peak Heads*, was finally delivered to the Felix Bloch Erben offices. After one look at it, Wreede was beside himself. As John Willett correctly says of the play, there runs through it a "profound misconception" that "anti-Semitism was only a political weapon, and that in due course the Nazi leaders and the rich Jews would combine against the working class irrespective of race."[18] Wreede knew as clearly as did Brecht (who had admitted in a private letter to Hanns Eisler that the play was unplayable under these political circumstances) that in the fall of 1932, it would not last through one performance anywhere in the Reich.[19]

Wreede saw he had been had. In the hopes of getting a fairly innocuous Shakespeare adaptation that could be widely played, he had paid advances to Brecht every month, and now Brecht had sent him this! Wreede demanded to talk to Brecht as soon as possible to tell him to his face that he would cut off his checks altogether if a more satisfactory work was not delivered at once. But this was easier said than done. As usual, Brecht was always up to his ears in a host of other affairs. Months would pass as Brecht dodged the irate publisher.

Hauptmann was now attempting to concentrate on writing and publishing under her own name. We know from her later correspondence with Brecht's father that she worked on a film treatment (she provides no details), a radio play on the history of the airplane, and a "reportage" for a fashion magazine.[20] At the same time, despite Brecht's obviously blossoming affair and working relationship with Steffin, Hauptmann was completing the editorial work on the fifth, sixth, and seventh volumes of Brecht's collected works (including much that she had written under his name) in the *Versuche* series.

Besides the plays that Hauptmann and Brecht had written together since late 1924, the *Versuche* contained some of Brecht's theoretical pieces on "epic theater" and a few of his short prose works. One of the most revealing of these was an open-ended series called the Geschichten vom Herrn Keuner, or The Stories of Mr. Keuner. The name Keuner, as spoken by Brecht with his Suabian accent, sounded very like "Keiner," suggesting to the listener that Brecht was talking about a "Mr. Nobody."[21] In "Mr. Keuner on Originality," Keuner states that great works, like great buildings, cannot be constructed by one person. In "Mr. Keuner and the Helpless Boy," a child says he had had two pieces of small change and another boy stole one of them. "Did you yell?" asks Keuner. The boy says yes and gives a demonstration in a very weak voice. At this, stroking the boy's head, Keuner steals the other coin and then "went off unconcernedly."[22]

While maintaining contacts with right-wing friends, Brecht did finally manage to start a "Study Circle of Critical Marxism" organized mainly around party maverick Karl Korsch. The usual members of the Brecht circle would attend the "Critical Marxism" meetings, including party members Helene Weigel and Bess Hauptmann, and (health permitting) Grete Steffin. It met at the spacious Hardenbergstrasse apartment near the fashionable street the Kurfürstendamm. Mari Hold prepared drinks and sandwiches, and cleared up after the "Critical Marxists" left.

These gatherings were sometimes joined by key Soviet officials stationed in or visiting Berlin. Elisabeth Hauptmann had now taken as flat-mates the fine Russian poet Lily Brik and her husband, a Red Army general, one of the many Soviet officers on exchange with the Reichswehr. Anatole Lunacharski, the former commissar for education for all of Russia and Lenin's companion in arms, came with his wife, Natalya Rosenel. When a guest said on one occasion that "there is no room in this Germany for progressive humanist ideas" and urged that preparations be made to emigrate, Lunacharski was indignant. "Fight!" he urged. "Fight to the last breath, each one at his station, each with his own weapon, be it the writing of articles or novels, through architecture, through giving recitations, through staging plays, even, if must be, on the barricades themselves."[23] When the talk again turned to emigration, Lunacharski said: "Think of our own Russian revolutionary history, even in emigration one can contribute to the fight. We knew that we would eventually win." Then, turning to his host, Lunacharski said: "Brecht, you for instance will continue to write your plays even if for the foreseeable future they cannot be played. But there will come a time, of this I have no doubt, when you will have your own theater in Berlin." He then raised his glass "to Brecht's own theater!"

Leaving Brecht's apartment, on the street below, Lunacharski saw faces familiar to him from the drawings of Georg Grosz. These are not the real citizens of Berlin, he remarked to his wife, "this is scum." Privately, the commissar would say later how bad it was that all these intellectuals would endlessly debate in Brecht's apartment high above the fray while below the party was literally being slaughtered.

In late September, the Munich police asked Berlin headquarters to share any information, particularly of a political nature, they might have on "the writer and director Bertold Brecht."[24] The Munich police were aware Brecht was "making a great deal of money" from his writing and that he had bought the Utting estate. In response to the Munich inquiry, the Berlin police noted Brecht's connection with the Communist movement as an "actor and reciter." But as far as actual anti-Nazi activities, the police mentioned nothing. In fact, as the police must have known since they had all major Communist papers and other organizations under steady surveillance, Brecht was notably less active than his closest associates. As John Willett pointed out a number of years ago, there are but "*three* poems about the Nazis which Brecht wrote before January 1933, when Hitler came to power."[25] Once Hitler had come to power, Brecht would rewrite his own history (as he had done with Tretiakov about his supposed revolutionary past in Augsburg) and declare how early he had become a prominent anti-Nazi. With regard to a daily commitment either to an anti-Nazi or a disciplined party position, the Brecht of the last years of Weimar was not as active as, for instance, Carola Neher, Ernst Toller, Ernst Ottwalt, Piscator, George Grosz, or Weigel—all of whom were willing to give up their bourgeois careers or go to jail for their beliefs. Though Brecht had certainly done a number of left-wing productions in the last couple of years, they were more often than not attacked by German party spokesperson Alfred Kurella, Lukács, and the official party press. John Willett correctly points out that "he only marginally contributed to the party press."[26]

Brecht was far more circumspect than most members of his immediate circle. Weigel, Carola Neher, Steffin, or Hauptmann was much more likely to attend party meetings than Brecht himself. At performances of *Mother*, Weigel and Steffin were on stage; and Emil Burri was credited with directing the play and most liable to be arrested on any given evening. Brecht had helped provide the actors with some of the ammunition, but he preferred not to fire it off himself. As police surveillance and intervention intensified in the last months of 1932, Weigel and Steffin, not Brecht, were hustled off briefly for interrogation.

For one last moment in the fall of 1932, it appeared that the Brecht circle's work with the CPG was having some real effect. At the November 6 Reichstag election, the CPG picked up an additional eleven seats while the Nazis lost thirty-four. Many observers hoped Hitler had peaked in popularity and that he would be given only a minority position in the cabinet, which would force him to abide by the law. Others left Berlin to establish new lives abroad. Einstein and Georg Grosz left for America; Piscator was already in Moscow; Carola Neher decided to move with her Communist functionary husband to Prague. But on the surface, life in the Weimar state still showed some signs of normalcy. Konrad Heiden was correcting proofs on his savage, revealing book on Hitler for Rowohlt Verlag. And Ernst Rowohlt, hedging his political bets, hoped to bring out the memoirs of his right-wing friend Ernst von Salamon, known throughout Germany for his part in the assassination of Walter Rathenau, the man the right had decried as "the Jewish sow."

As the old year neared its end, an article in *Uhu* declared the "women's movement" to be clinically dead. Things looked grim for the female members of the Brecht circle. Fleisser's career and mental health had largely collapsed, and Hauptmann's, except for an occasional short story or radio play published under her own name, had never really gotten started. Weigel, exhausted with performing in dangerous and unprofitable plays, was at the end of her tether with Brecht. Steffin, the current favorite, was far from well. A famous surgeon had operated twice, unsuccessfully, on her lungs at Berlin's Charité Hospital. After her release, Weigel's continuing insistence that Steffin could not stay with Brecht left her nearly homeless. She had no income other than her work with Brecht, and he was chary about handing anything over if he could find a way to avoid it. Finally, with a Prussian, state-funded health insurance plan and travel money from Eisler and Brecht, Steffin left in early February 1933 for a tuberculosis clinic at Agra, near Lugano in Switzerland.

As the year 1932 came to a close, Brecht invited a select group to his annual all-male New Year's party. Among these was the independent Marxist Fritz Sternberg, but the rest of the group comprised the intellectual side of Germany's radical right. Arnolt Bronnen brought the convicted plotter in the assassination of Rathenau, Ernst von Salamon and several other rightist friends. Brecht's friend, the painter Rudolf Schlichter, was known to have direct ties through his brother to the right. As midnight approached, a toast was proposed. In his memoirs, Sternberg recalls that those gathered at Brecht's apartment that night clinked glasses and drank "to a successful and bloodless putsch from the right."[27]

I have checked and double-checked this account with the publisher of Sternberg's memoir. Though the story is so radically at variance with Brecht's own accounts of his antinazism, the authenticity of this eyewitness account is unimpeachable. I see no reason why Sternberg would have made it up. It seems to reinforce the possibility that Brecht erroneously believed Stalin's position about Hitler's transience.

Nineteen thirty-three began with Hitler seeing the usefulness of proclaiming his devotion to legal means of gaining power. He danced a decorous minuet, trying to convince the now rather doddering state president, Hindenburg, to admit Nazis to cabinet-level positions in the government. Meanwhile, the Berlin theater sought to find works to suit the times and the tastes of its diverse Berlin public. A playwright friend of Hitler and Brecht, Hanns Johst was very popular. *Having,* a play by a Hungarian Communist friend of Lukács named Julius Hay, featured multiple poisonings by a land-grabbing woman and was doing nicely at the box office.

Arnolt Bronnen now often spent nights in a café with Viktor Lutze, future head of the SA after Hitler would have Ernst Röhm murdered in 1934. Lutze's recommendation for political behavior was: "Tromp the accelerator and straight into the curve."[28] (History best knows Lutze from the famous scene in *Triumph of the Will* where, in a stadium filled with 100,000 dedicated Nazis, three men march alone to the Cenotaph. The three are Himmler, Hitler, and Lutze.)

On January 30, Marta Feuchtwanger learned to her horror that Germany had roared around the final curve to the right. Hindenburg had been prevailed upon to appoint Hitler as chancellor in a cabinet where Nazi members would be a small minority. Papen declared of Hitler, "No danger at all. We've hired him for our act."[29] One member of the hired act was Hermann Göring, now given jurisdiction over the police of Berlin and Prussia.

On the day of Hitler's accession as chancellor, Goebbels, with his great gift for blending the political with the dazzlingly theatrical and pseudoreligious in what he called "divine services," arranged to have twenty-five thousand uniformed Nazis, carrying flickering torches and with accompanying military music, march down Unter den Linden, through the Brandenburg Gate, past the chancellery where Hitler could be seen at a lighted window and past the looming dome of the Reichstag building and the posh Adlon Hotel. As they marched past with an endless stream of swastika-bedecked banners, at a window of the chancellery, the eighty-six-year-old president of the Republic, Hindenburg, was seen looking out, "abstractedly pounding his cane in time to the music of the bands."[30] The parade continued from seven in the evening until midnight. Goebbels summed up his propaganda coup as "this night of the great miracle" that had ended "in an insensate tumult of enthusiasm." Hitler stayed up until dawn and told his closest followers this night marked the start of "the greatest Germanic racial revolution in world history." At dawn, Hitler returned to the grand Hotel Kaiserhof to get some sleep so that he could begin at once what he called the "German Resurrection."[31]

Brecht doggedly went about his business. On February 2, 1933, he and Weill, without Hauptmann, sold the English rights for Threepenny "for valuable consideration." At the same time, Brecht was asked by the Berlin Finance Office for taxes owed from 1931 and 1932. The amounts (measured by Brecht's earnings) were modest, 128 marks for income tax still owed for 1932, and "crisis tax" amounts of 57.90 marks for 1931 and 30.77 marks for 1932. Small or not, Brecht was determined not to pay. He wrote to the Finance Office on February 10, saying the monies he received were not "income" at all but merely advances on future earnings.[32] He took the opposite position with Wreede. If he had admitted to Wreede that he viewed the payments as mere loans, Wreede could then ask for the money back and Brecht had no intention of returning the money.

The air crackled with rumors of plots and counterplots from the left and right. Now apparently worried about his safety, Brecht had several boxes of his things packed and a photo taken. On February 24, Göring pushed legislation through the Reichstag to have SA and SS formations throughout Germany sworn in as auxiliary police units. Showing off his culture by quoting Shakespeare, the parliamentary president boasted, "My measures will not be sicklied o'er by any legal scruples. It's not my business to do justice, it's my business to annihilate and exterminate, that's all!"[33] German Communist party officials, receiving little help from Moscow, moved to hideouts. Just one day before Göring's seizure of police powers, Brecht, claiming to have a problem with his appendix, checked into his friend Dr. Mayer's small private hospital in the Augsburgerstrasse.[34] Licensed to kill, Göring's auxiliaries fanned out throughout the Reich. In one brutal foray, among thousands like it, on February 27, at 3.15 A.M., uniformed SA troopers broke into the apartment of Kurt Löwenstein, a Social Democratic party leader. After firing ten shots and thinking he was dead, they returned to headquarters for further assignments.

That same February 27, Fritz Wreede prepared an irate letter to go by special messenger to Brecht. He complained he had now paid Brecht over forty-four thousand gold marks and had obtained nothing usable in return. He said he would now not only stop the payments of one thousand gold marks a month on Brecht's general contract but would start using the money coming in on Threepenny to pay off advances made under the general contract. Not everything was as dire with Brecht's affairs that day. Hanns Eisler reported that on the previous night's

Vienna opening of *Measures,* two thousand people had applauded the piece. That was good, Brecht said guardedly, but "in these days there were things that could not be talked about on the telephone."

Among Brecht's visitors at Dr. Mayer's clinic was writer Walter Mehring. He told Brecht that a person who worked in the German Foreign Office and was a friend of Mehring's mother had come by to tell her: "Your son feels at his best in Paris. He should go back to Paris again." When she asked how long her son should stay away, the reply was "fifteen years."[35]

On the evening of February 27, Hitler went, so he said later, to Goebbels's new flat to listen to some Wagner. Their quiet cultural evening was interrupted when Hitler's old Munich aide-de-camp, Putzi Hanfstaengl, called to say that the Reichstag building was on fire. Herr Göring was on the scene of the fire immediately. He did not have far to go to get from his neighboring palace through the connecting underground passage to the basement of the main Reichstag building itself. Bronnen, working late on the night of the fire, went up to the roof of the building from where he could see the flames. He said: "First there were rehearsals. Now we have the premiere."[36] Few opponents of the Nazis believed that the Reichstag fire had been set by Van der Lubbe, a Dutch tramp, acting under orders from Moscow, as the Nazis alleged.

All that night, any known or suspected Communist official who had been foolish enough to spend the night in his or her own bed was awakened, savagely beaten, and then taken either to the morgue or into "protective custody." Brecht was out of harm's way. From the clinic the next morning, he made a quick and ineffective call to ask Fritz Wreede to change his mind and not cut off the general contract income. He then called Peter Suhrkamp at Kiepenheuer to ask for help to get out of Berlin that same day. He did not want to risk going back to his apartment before leaving. The jewelry chest he had there would have to remain for now, along with crates of papers, and his books and furniture. He asked Hauptmann to give him any cash she had, and she scraped together four hundred marks.

Joined by Weigel and the now nine-year-old Stefan, Brecht was picked up by Peter Suhrkamp in the publisher's private car. The streets of the city were patrolled by Göring's auxiliaries, with orders to shoot first and ask questions later. The station was under observation as it was an obvious place for people seeking to flee. Mari Hold was in Bavaria with little Mari Barbara. Steffin was at a clinic in Switzerland, and Hauptmann remained behind both to work on CPG business and to try, despite the danger involved, to rescue her joint work with Brecht.

The group heading for the train station in Suhrkamp's car was small. Past the storm troopers, Brecht with wife and little Stefan were allowed to board the through train for Prague. Most of what Brecht and Weigel saw out of the train windows they were seeing for the last time. The hurricane foretold in Trotsky's writings and avoided in *Mahagonny* would now arrive in devastating force. By 1945, hardly a building remained standing.

"Let Us Speak Quite Frankly with One Another, Herr Brecht, You Have Lived a Very Rich Life at My Expense" (1933)

Hitler used the Reichstag fire as an excuse to cut off all political opposition. Communist party leader Ernst Thälmann was found and arrested. The ease of his arrest, and of thousands of others like it, was another example of Moscow's underestimation of Hitler. The CPG was ready neither to fight openly, nor to establish an effective underground resistance movement in the Reich. CPG functionary Wilhelm Pieck shouted at a Comintern meeting some years later that German Communists gave up not out of cowardice, as they were accused of doing, but because "Moscow ordered us to give up."[1] But the problem behind this was that leaders like Pieck, Thälmann, and Ulbricht had followed the "Moscow Control Chorus" for years, even though many, notably Trotsky, thought them absolutely wrong.

In fact, instead of opposing Hitler after the Reichstag burning and Hitler's wholesale murder of German Communists, in 1933 Stalin began immediately to negotiate a rapprochement with Hitler, without any regard for the safety of party members in Germany like Elisabeth Hauptmann.[2] But Hitler was not yet ready to negotiate. First he would consolidate power in his own hands and wriggle out of the restraints with which the power brokers thought they could hold him.

On March 13, Goebbels was officially made minister of propaganda. The first German concentration camp was opened a week later. Working swiftly to create an aura of legitimacy, Goebbels planned a theatrically brilliant, pseudoreligious spectacle for March 23. Distancing themselves from the burned Reichstag building that had served Weimar, a Nazi-dominated parliament opened in the Garrison Church at Potsdam, scene in the past of Germany's greatest imperial triumphs. In this historic church, in full military uniform, Field Marshal von Hindenburg intoned: "May the old spirit of this place of rest infuse the soul of the present generation, may it free us of selfishness and of party strife and in a sense of national self-confidence and spiritual renewal may it bring us together to bless a united, free, and proud Germany!"[3] After a round of applause lead by Hitler, the president concluded, "With these wishes I greet the New Reichstag and now give the floor to the Reich's Chancellor."

On May 10, Goebbels presided over the public burning of books in Berlin and other major cities. Commenting on their authors, Goebbels said, "They may live on for a while, these gentlemen in their emigré cafés in Paris and Prague, but their life cord has already been cut, they are cadavers on leave from death."[4] Goebbels put out a list of authors whose works were to be withdrawn at once from all bookstores and libraries: Lion Feuchtwanger, Ernst Glaeser, Arthur Holitscher, Alfred Kerr, Egon Erwin Kisch, Emil Ludwig, Heinrich Mann, Ernst Ottwalt, Theodor Plievier, Erich Maria Remarque, Kurt Tucholsky, and Arnold Zweig. Notably, Bertolt Brecht was not on this list.

Erika and Klaus Mann and Fritz Sternberg thought that Brecht, like many of their mutual friends, could have returned to Germany.[5] This is not as implausible as it at first sounds. As Elaine S. Hochman has convincingly shown, for the first two years of the Third Reich, Goebbels fought to preserve an open or modernist attitude toward the arts.[6] He actively tried to prevent modernists such as Mies van der Rohe from leaving and to lure other progressive German cultural figures living abroad to return. We tend to now forget that the mishmash title of NSDAP included a socialist component that many people inside the Nazi party took very seriously. I have been told by Herbert Marshall that when he was serving as Piscator's translator in Moscow in 1935, Goebbels invited Piscator to return.[7] If Piscator with his long and distinguished record both of procommunism and antinazism could be invited back, Brecht's return was not inconceivable. Perhaps for that reason, his citizenship would not be taken away until the middle of 1935 and then only after Moscow had pressured Brecht to finally get off the political fence.[8]

A great many of Brecht's closest friends, supporters, and family members remained in the Third Reich, doing well for most of the Nazi years. Brecht's main supporter in the media, Herbert Ihering, stayed at the *Berliner Börsen-Courier*, making the adjustments necessary to accommodate the new regime. So well was Ihering eventually regarded within the Goebbels ministry that he was later put in charge of Vienna's important Burgtheater. Brecht's publisher Peter Suhrkamp, the man who helped Brecht to get away on February 28, would also prosper for most of the years of the Third Reich and would be given control of the Jewish-owned Fischer Verlag when the Fischers were forced to emigrate. Even Erich Engel and Marianne Zoff (though both were half-Jewish and defined by the Nazis as one of mixed race, or a "Mischling") stayed on and did reasonably well. Caspar Neher remained also and, despite selectively applied laws against homosexuals, became the hottest ticket in set design throughout the years of the Third Reich. Most of the friends of Brecht's youth in Augsburg also stayed, as did his younger brother Walter, his father, and his children by Marianne and Bie.

To entice people to stay, Goebbels offered film and theater artists premium wages and even his personal protection against harassment. He approached half-Jewish film director Fritz Lang, but despite Goebbels's blandishments, Lang decided to leave to try his luck in Hollywood.[9] This loss was offset by the return in the late thirties of G. W. Pabst, director of the film version of *The Threepenny Opera* and one of the greatest names in the history of world cinema.[10] The case of Pabst makes plain that those who did not directly attack the Third Reich, even people closely connected to *The Threepenny Opera*, could return right up until the outbreak of World War II. Nor had Brecht burnt his bridges behind him. For several months, the German authorities would be told he was traveling abroad, not in exile.

Once Brecht, Weigel, and little Stefan were beyond the German border, they were joined by three-year-old Mari Barbara and Mari Hold. Why Hold decided to leave her language and country behind to share the uncertain existence of exiles is something of a mystery. Perhaps she was in fact the mother of Mari Barbara, as Brecht seems to hint at times, or perhaps she, like so many others, was sexually attached to her master. Had she wished to stay on in the Third Reich, as the rest of her family did, I know of no reason why she could not have done so.

Soon after, Weigel and the children went on to Austria to stay for a while with Weigel's family in its large apartment in Vienna.[11] Apparently, when Weigel left Vienna later, she took with her enough jewels and cash to support herself and the children for about two years without Brecht's help. Though nominally married to Brecht, she had carefully maintained her own place during the Weimar years, mainly supporting herself. She did not want to be dependent on him with his stream of liaisons, any one of which could suddenly turn serious, leaving her without support.

Fortunately for her, not only did her wealthy parents rally to help but she also got extraordinary help from two friends from her schoolgirl days, writers Karin Michaëlis and Maria Lazar. Lazar and Michaëlis lived on a small island in Denmark about four hours by car and ferry from Copenhagen. Immediately after the Reichstag fire, they tried to help friends threatened by the Nazis. Michaëlis, wealthy from the sale of then famous novels, owned several houses in the village of Thurø. She decided to make these freely available to those threatened by Hitler, including Helene Weigel and members of her family.

At the time Weigel got her invitation to Denmark, Brecht was in Switzerland, where he spent several weeks with people he had known slightly in Berlin, novelist Lisa Tetzner and her husband Kurt Kläber.

From there, he wrote to Margarete Steffin at the nearby Agra Sanitorium, repeatedly cautioning her to be faithful.[12] Away from Brecht, Grete was busy with her own writing, a series of short stories and erotic sonnets far better than could have been expected from a beginning writer. In a stream of letters, Brecht addressed Grete frequently as "liebes altes scheusal" (dear old horror). He signed the letters in a way oddly inconsistent with his Marxist beliefs, using the old south German expression "Grüss gott!" (greetings in the name of God). He sent her a number of incomplete sonnets, which he asked her to finish as he had not found suitable rhymes. He said he would check up on this assignment when he next saw her. Meanwhile, wrote Brecht, using the ambiguity that German permits, she was to remain "meine kleine frau" (my little wife or my little woman).

One letter refers to artists and intellectuals remaining in Berlin (including, of course, Suhrkamp, Ihering, and Neher) as "a nice and sympathetic and careless rabble"; however, "the working class continues to fight on, without means, without any leadership. . . . Nothing was prepared, absolutely nothing."[13]

He said he would arrange to have his father send Grete some money to tide her over, implying that he did not have money enough himself. In fact, he had been depositing funds in a Swiss bank account for years. He also said he would arrange to get her travel documents as he had "mobilized good people in Berlin." The letter ends with a "Grüss gott!"

"I am so glad," he writes in his next letter, "that you are happy sitting up there taking the cure as bravely as before. It must succeed, that is the basis of everything else, the taking over of power!"[14] That Grete's recovery was linked directly to the success of the revolution was praise indeed of her potential as a writer dedicated to the struggle to change the world. A little later, Brecht visited the sanitorium to check on the completion of the erotic sonnets and for some dalliance about which he then wrote in a later sonnet.

After the brief visit to Agra, Brecht made a flying visit to Paris in April, invited there by Kurt Weill. Many of the Unter den Linden crowd had managed by this time to get to France. Anna Seghers, the Communist novelist, and Hanns Eisler both met with Brecht during his April stay. Willi Münzenberg had transferred his Comintern-backed Berlin press to Paris, as had the other major Berlin publisher on the left, Wieland Herzfelde. Both expressed interest in publishing Brecht as soon as possible. Weill, in the middle of an affair with Caspar Neher's wife, Erika, had left Berlin on March 21 to drive to Paris with the Nehers. Lenya arrived in Paris soon after. She had been separated from Weill for the last year, living with an opera singer, Otto von Pasetti, who accompanied her to Paris. Both came to sing in a production that Weill, Caspar Neher, and impresario Edward James were putting together.

In December 1932, Weill had been invited by the Vicomtesse de Noailles and Princess Edmonde de Polignac (both well known as part of the former Proust circle) to present a medley of his works at the Salle Gaveau. Among those attending were Stravinsky, Darius Milhaud, Arthur Honegger, André Gide, Cocteau, Picasso, and Fernand Léger. The reaction both by the public and the press was extraordinary, and it was clear he must be invited back.[15] By late March, he was facing the prospect of having to make a living entirely outside Germany.

After the last years in Weimar when Brecht had been so difficult, even dishonest, he would have preferred not to work with Brecht. Both Weill and Neher had decided to avoid Brecht, Weill collaborating with Georg Kaiser on a work called *Silversea*, or *A Winter's Tale*, and then with Caspar Neher on an opera called *Die Burgschaft*, or *The Agreement*. After the Nazis began openly disrupting shows by Jewish composers, however, Weill's work had no serious chance of enduring success in the closing months of Weimar. When he reached Paris in late March, Weill was approached by his former student Maurice Abravanel, who had himself just fled from Hitler, and by Edward James, the wealthy husband of the dancer Tilly Losch. James was a major backer of the ballet group Les ballets 1933 that included emigré Russians George Balanchine and Boris Kochno.[16] Weill was asked to create a work featuring Losch. Weill proposed Jean Cocteau for the libretto, but Cocteau pleaded too little time. With that, despite having been called a "phony Richard Strauss" by Brecht in Berlin, Weill decided to ask him to write the libretto, with a large dancing role for Tilly Losch and a large singing role for Lenya.

Not having any better offers on the table, Brecht agreed and spent the last two weeks in April working closely with Neher and Weill. As with much of the work of Weill, women's concerns would be central to the work. What began to emerge from the collaborative efforts was a *ballet chanté* built around the biblical seven deadly sins. In a savage rereading of the Bible, a rural family in Louisiana sends their daughter, Anna, to the big city to make a career and to send the money home. The Family was to be played by an all-male quartet in which the Mother was a mustachioed bass. Anna turns out to be two very different people. Anna I is sensible. She is a singer and manages her sister's career. Anna II is a dancer and, like the Young Comrade of *Measures*, gives in to her natural kind impulses. She is warned about this by the stern and disciplined Anna I who serves with the Family as a kind of Control Chorus.

In the scene called "Laziness," Anna II is not sufficiently vicious as a confidence trickster. In "Pride," she does not want to take all her clothes off for a grubby cabaret owner until her sister persuades her this is necessary. The work closes with the sisters returning to Louisiana with Anna I saying proudly "We did it!" But Anna II (in an obvious echo of *He Who Says Yes*) says brokenly, "Yes, Anna." By early May, words and music were sufficiently complete that rehearsals could commence. George Balanchine worked with the dancers, and Maurice Abravanel with the singers; Anna II was played by Tilly Losch, and Lenya sang the role of Anna I. On stage and off, things were torrid. Though continuing to live with her male opera singer companion, Lenya now began an affair with Tilly Losch.[17] Meanwhile, Weill was still involved with Erika Neher, while Caspar Neher was being introduced into a homosexual circle including Edward James, Gide, and Cocteau. Brecht was hustling wives of emigré friends and had taken up with a young Belgian woman he had just met.

Brecht urged Steffin to remain chaste, but fearing that she would act in the same way he did, he went to Agra to try to get her to join him in Paris. His concentrated charm had its usual desired effect, despite the advice of her doctor, H. Alexander, and the logic of her finances, given that her fees at Agra were paid by her German medical insurance. From now on, her medical care was intermittent and inadequate as she was almost always without money, though her work would soon be regularly sold for excellent prices, but under Brecht's name and with the royalty checks usually coming to him.

Most pressing on their arrival in Paris was finishing *The Seven Deadly Sins*. After his many years of dilatoriness and rudeness toward Weill and Neher, Brecht seems to have worked reasonably harmoniously on *Seven Deadly Sins*. But still, even before the premiere, Weill believed Brecht was involved in some shady business.[18] Weill claimed to have proposed a musical version of *Round Heads, Peak Heads* to Brecht but then heard that Brecht was working with Hanns Eisler on the project. The rumors turned out to be true, infuriating Weill once again though he, as usual, remained polite to Brecht in public.

Once the final touches had been put on the libretto of *Seven Deadly Sins* (which he was pointedly not invited to direct), Brecht began work on new publishing contracts to replace the shaky ones with Fritz Wreede. Wreede had written him on February 27 (hours before the Reichstag fire) saying that he intended to stop the one thousand gold marks a month that he was paying Brecht, and then again on April 29 claiming that Brecht owed Felix Bloch Erben over forty-four thousand gold marks. Usually misspelling the firm owner's name as "Wrede," Brecht wrote back arguing it was Felix Bloch Erben who owed him around forty-four thousand gold marks. The exasperated Wreede replied that, first, one needed a law degree to follow the twists and turns of Brecht's arguments, and, second, "let us speak quite frankly with one another, Herr Brecht, you have lived a very rich life at my expense."[19] Alternately threatening and conciliatory as was his wont, Brecht continued to write to "Wrede" for years to come.

In an (unpublished) letter of May 26, 1933, Brecht asked Wreede to block a production of *The Threepenny Opera*. "I have heard," wrote Brecht, "that Aufricht wants to put on a production of *The Threepenny Opera* in Paris for The Committee for Jews Driven out of Germany." Desperate to get the charity production stopped, Brecht telegraphed Felix Bloch Erben, "Prevent Aufricht's Three Penny Opera production in Paris."[20] The effort was successful, and the Jewish rescue committee received nothing. Whether Brecht did not want to be identified too closely with a Jewish committee or whether he hoped to earn more from a more commercial venue in Paris has never been explained.

In those early weeks and months outside Germany, like so many others, Brecht was in a state of shock. He was beyond his depth on many of the most fundamental questions. The ambivalence he had exhibited with his friends on both the radical left and right in the last years, months, and days of Weimar continued. He was not at all sure that he had permanently left—Hauptmann and Brecht's father were desperately trying to keep Brecht's options open in Germany. Despite the danger to herself as a known Communist who could be arrested and tortured by the Gestapo, Hauptmann visited the Berlin tax office to enquire about Brecht's delinquent payments. She was able to arrange to have his overdue bill of 295.25 marks sent to Augsburg. Paying the bill, Herr Direktor Brecht wrote to the tax authorities that his son was "off on a journey."[21]

While Hitler was consolidating power after the Reichstag fire, Stalin and the Soviet Union remained almost wholly silent for a full year while Hitler and Stalin negotiated secretly.[22] Knowing nothing presumably of these behind-the-scenes moves, Brecht wrote (but may not have sent) a note to Tretiakov saying that the Comintern was providing no leadership.[23] But when Brecht met the Soviet newspaper correspondent and novelist Ilya Ehrenburg in Paris, Brecht only "talked about death, about Meyerhold's productions, about agreeable trifles."[24]

Brecht was also negotiating with Moscow; and with the implicit backing of Koltsov, he was soon able to conclude an agreement to supply texts for the Moscow journal *International Literature* and to be paid for them in precious hard currency. In Paris, a Comintern-front press called Editions du Carrefour agreed to publish a book of some earlier songs written with Hanns Eisler. All the real work of assembling the volume and guiding it through the press would be done by Steffin.

Brecht arranged to have his Moscow earnings sent in his name to Steffin's Paris address rather than to Denmark.[25] Next, cashing in on the fame of *Threepenny*, he negotiated a handsome deal with a Dutch firm for something to be called *The Threepenny Novel*, for which a large advance was paid that he had sent to Denmark to await his arrival there.

It was a scheme he had long since developed for concealing income: income from different sources was sent to different addresses or placed directly in a variety of accounts of friends, agents, and so on. Brecht was the only one who knew the total. With his usually upper-middle-class level of earnings a well-kept secret, in clothes that looked the part, he could complain about how poor he was and how careful he had to be in spending money. Steffin and Weigel were kept in constant fear of poverty, which reduced their requests for money, even for something as literally vital as Steffin's desperately needed medical care.

Steffin, like Hauptmann before her, was not deceived by Brecht's scams, even though she allowed them to continue. In the earliest weeks together in Paris, she already suspected him of dishonesty. She was particularly agonized by his sexual duplicity. He expected her to remain faithful (which she was generally happy to be as long as she could spend time with him) while he maintained other liaisons, concealing some and boasting about others. He even seemed to enjoy the pain she obviously felt when he did this. She also suspected he was hiding money. On May 27, she wrote a small parable of two soldiers on a march, one of whom is concealing "cigarettes" and "a couple of onions" from his female companion.[26] When she reveals she has found his cache, he lies about it. She becomes "angry, sad, and quiet" and begins to doubt his ability "to tell the difference between a lie and the truth." The real-life Steffin was now sure Brecht lied to her regularly, but like her fictional counterpart, she remained angry, sad, and quiet. She hoped against hope he would change his habits, knowing "as things went today [the day of the discovery of his lie to her], so they will go tomorrow."

Seven Deadly Sins opened at the Théâtre des Champs-Elysées on June 7. Despite a fine score by Weill to underscore the biting libretto, sets by Caspar Neher, a brilliant performance by Losch, and Lenya's lascivious inflections, neither the general public, nor the press, nor the key members of the old Proust circle were enthusiastic. Serge Lifar said huffily to Count Kessler that the work constituted "de la pourriture de Ballet." The production closed after a few days, though plans were made to move it to London. Caspar and Erika Neher permanently returned to Nazi Germany.

From Brecht's perspective, the most important thing about the production had been that he was paid well. He could also look forward to being paid royalties for the upcoming London production. On June

10, he sent a postcard to Weigel in Denmark saying: "the ballet went quite well, but was, finally, not that important."[27] He also said he hoped to line up some film work for himself and perhaps some roles for her on the Paris emigré stage before leaving for Denmark in eight days or so. He asked if she had lined up a car for them yet.

Brecht had inquired about film work in Paris and talked with Aufricht. Aufricht, whether or not he knew that Brecht had blocked the Jewish benefit performance of *Threepenny*, still wanted to work with him. Aufricht had in mind something he called "The Theater of Judgment," which would "try" Göring and Nero, back-to-back, as arsonists. Brecht backed away from this bold project, an enterprise that would have earned him an honored place on the Nazi assassination list. The next fall, he did not sign a petition against the annexation of the Saar region, though it was signed by numerous close friends such as Lion Feuchtwanger, Johannes R. Becher, and Carola Neher. Later, the legend of Brecht the bold anti-Nazi would be developed, but the sad fact of the years before and after the Nazis came to power is that Brecht consistently maintained but a low anti-Nazi profile.

Back in Berlin, Dr. Peche of the Gestapo was preparing to seize the Weigel and Brecht cars under the act of May 26, 1933, permitting the seizure of Communist property.[28] But though the cars were taken, Brecht's other holdings were not: his estate in Bavaria was not seized, and his apartment in Berlin was not ransacked. Under the nose of the Gestapo, Hauptmann regularly came by his old apartment to pack their joint manuscripts for shipment out of the country.

By about June 19, Brecht was ready to leave for Denmark. Steffin was instructed to stay behind working on Editions du Carrefour and Moscow projects, looking for a house for Brecht, improving her French and Russian, looking for a car for him if Weigel hadn't got one yet, and staying faithful—keeping everything, as Brecht put it, "in Ordnung" (in order). From Steffin's diary and letters, we know her physical and mental health were under severe strain. It was clear that she should not have left the Swiss sanitorium. In July, Dr. Alexander of Agra told her father that she had a large, actively tubercular hole at the top of her right lung.[29] Herr Steffin was warned that his daughter should not delay a further operation on this lung as otherwise the condition would spread. But there was little that her father—a largely unemployed, alcoholic man, under Nazi surveillance as an active Communist—could do to help his daughter in a distant country.

Without money and not knowing what to do next, Steffin wrote to Dr. Alexander to ask whether she could accept an invitation from Anna Seghers to join her on the shores of the North Sea. Alexander urged her to have her operation at once and to stay away from damp sea air. She tried to get the name of a suitable Paris physician from Hanns Eisler, who was rumored to know about such things, but he always seemed too busy with his own affairs to help.[30] Not wanting to ask Brecht for money, Steffin simply worked harder to try to earn enough for her health needs.

Steffin constantly worried how long Brecht might continue his relationship with her. There were clear signs he was involved in several new affairs. One was with Dorothea Borchardt, the wife of his friend Hans Borchardt, and another with a young Dutch woman named Jeanne who boasted to Grete directly of her affair with Brecht. Even before she had left the Agra hospital to come to Paris, Steffin summed up her anguish and her hope: "Dear bidi, mornings, afternoons, evenings, and nights i am always alone here in my present quarters. i am always somewhat fearful of the night. for the last ten years i have become used to dreaming every night. but now, every night, i dream the same dream: i see you with some bunch of women, i get very upset, constantly wake up, screaming, always the same stupid theatrics . . . often i ask myself as i lie here unable to sleep, when your diverse friends will say (as one said to me this week) to another girl like me: 'Yes, it was about that time, it must have been around '32–'33 that he had that girl with him, i think her name was grete steffin, after that she . . .' and then i hear over and over again something that helli said to me in berlin: 'I'm sorry for you my dear child.' at such moments i am sorry for myself but i cannot get back to sleep again."[31] The letter ended with a comment on one of Brecht's erotic sonnets that he had given her to read in his absence. "By the way," writes Steffin, "i don't agree with what you say in sonnet 6":

> men don't like to suffer for passion.
> they like what is freely given but don't like demands.
> of course i give shabby counsel.[32]

The poem was a violent blow to Grete for its commitment to strictly male values that she knew were those of the poet himself.

The poems and letters he sent to Steffin argue for technical proficiency in bed, but desire does not depend *for the male partner* on something as transitory as passion or "possession,"[33] in both senses of the word. In lovemaking, women are to be so "possessed" as to be altered beyond all recognition.[34] Also, as the poet says in "Sonnet 5": "They [women] should show that they do not have any choice. That they are the ones who are chosen. . . . As though there were for her, when he did not speak, simply silence."[35] Women were to live in a silent world waiting for their master's voice. Then, generalizing from women to "the unfortunate," in a still unpublished version of "Sonnet 10," he writes:

"What I don't like to admit is that I myself have contempt for the unfortunate."[36]

Steffin told Brecht in one of her counterpoems: "*I believe in possession.*"[37] In another, she complained directly about his various other partners, saying that she felt herself "beleidigt" (outraged) by his behavior with other women. Yet, even so she still loved him and still fervently believed that the work they could do together would help change the world for the better. In July, she wrote, "I will become healthy again, as long as your love is not withdrawn from me." And later: "The word is for me an embrace, a kiss. That I must wait for you so long, I kiss that word in every one of your letters. And I cry when I read it, because it is then as though you were with me again, and I am the one without any wishes, as though I was sleeping alongside you."[38] In Berlin, she had begged in one of her poems that he not insist on telling her "about the other women," that he be fully with her, for she knew:

> *when you just touch me, i*
> *must lie down at once.*
> *neither shame nor regret can stop me.*[39]

Once he left for Denmark, she needed something of his while he was gone, even if it was only a piece of his underwear.[40] Eventually, Brecht bought her a cheap metal ring, as he had done for Bie Banholzer years ago. Actually, he bought three at once and offered Steffin a choice among them. He did not explain what he would do with the two rings she had not selected. While giving her the cheap ring instead of actually proposing marriage, he claimed that if she were not ill, he would divorce Weigel at once to marry her. But he also gave her too much work and too little money for her to have any serious opportunity for treatment of her tuberculosis. Substituting symbolic action for reality, he gave Steffin a second gift, this one expropriated from heaven: Orion, the constellation of the great hunter who, legend had it, had threatened to kill everything upon the earth. Brecht said that from now on, they could look up at Orion to be joined in the heavens though they might be apart on earth.

23

"There Are Friends One Can Run over with a 1,000-Ton Freight Train" (1933)

Despite her gift from heaven, Steffin's mundane circumstances were decidedly modest. Despite the deals he had closed with Moscow, Amsterdam, Paris, and London, Brecht still plead poverty. He left her at cheap lodgings, with no bathing facilities, at 36, Avenue Morere, Seine-et-Oise, distant from the city, and from friends and working associates.

By June 21, Brecht—together with Weigel, Mari Barbara, Stefan, and Mari Hold—was installed in Denmark in the large, handsomely appointed waterfront house on Karin Michaëlis's estate on the lovely island of Thurø. Other German emigrés occupied the smaller guest houses on the estate. Weigel's childhood friend Maria Lazar was there with her daughter, Judith. Alfred Ostermoor, an obscure and impoverished writer, stayed periodically. Also, there was Brecht's collaborator on *Kuhle Wampe*, Ernst Ottwalt, with his wife, Waltraut Nicolas. The nights at Thurø were often broken by Waltraut Nicholas as she woke, screaming with fear, thinking she was still within reach of the Gestapo.[1]

Indeed, Thurø was being watched by Nazi authorities. Goebbels was interested in the properly "Aryan" author Karin Michaëlis, whose books sold well in Germany. Through Margarete Gärtner, a mutual friend, Goebbels invited Michaëlis to tour the Reich at the government's expense.[2] Though Michaëlis was not willing to go to Germany, she did agree to join the Reich's Union of German Writers. With Michaëlis a member of the Reich's union, her books could continue to sell in Hitler's Reich as long as she was moderate in her public statements about the Reich and its new masters. Goebbels probably hoped that she would exert a moderating influence on her various German guests.

Though pampered by Michaëlis and Weigel, Brecht was not satisfied with the living situation. He was used to having his own place with privacy enough for him to conduct his affairs. Weigel was expected to fend off unwelcome visitors and shield him so that he could either write or be with the people, usually women, with whom he chose to be. Observing Brecht on a daily basis, Alfred Ostermoor told his wife, "What I dislike about him is the manner of his private life, and his neglect of Comrade Helli."³ Weigel was pressed to find something better suited to Brecht's needs. On the nearby mainland, in what was then the small town of Svendborg, Weigel found a fairly large, thatched roof house that they could afford. The house was just outside the town, on a beach called Skovsbostrand. The windows looked over the beautiful sound. Brecht and Weigel decided to buy the house just as soon as they could get that dearest of all things for the political emigré, valid residence papers.⁴

The police could not have been more cooperative when Brecht, accompanied by the famous and wealthy Michaëlis, came on July 20 to present his valid German passport and to ask about a residence permit for such an obviously respectable author, his Jewish wife, and two small children. The officer in charge made the first entry in the file for foreigners, number 36316-57120, in the name of Bertolt Brecht and wife (listed simply as Helene Brecht rather than Helene Weigel) and the two children. Brecht had left Germany, so the police report declared, because Frau Brecht was Jewish. "The applicant declared," stated the report, "that he is in no manner whatsoever active in politics, and that he will attempt in no way to fight either the new system in Germany or any of its individual representatives, nor indeed had any intention to involve himself in political questions either in Germany or anywhere else, but rather would continue as usual his work as a playwright." This view, the officer hastened to report, was also that of Michaëlis who had drawn attention to the Danish Royal Theater's production of *The Threepenny Opera*.

A week after the first police report was written, with no questions asked about the accuracy of Brecht's statements about his own politics, a six-month residence permit was issued. He signed the papers putting up 5,050 kroner of his and Weigel's money toward the seven thousand kroner purchase price of the house. Before the family and Mari Hold moved in, Karin Michaëlis's many friends in Copenhagen were asked if someone could give free advice on the extensive remodeling the Brechts wanted.

Among those in Copenhagen who heard that the famous author Brecht was staying with Michaëlis was the twenty-seven-year-old actress-journalist Ruth Berlau-Lund and the architect Mogens Voltelen. Berlau was anxious to meet Brecht in the hopes of getting from him new anti-fascist texts for the Revolutionary Theater group she had founded in Copenhagen. Voltelen was willing to help the emigrés in remodeling. In early August, Berlau and Voltelen went out to visit Michaëlis and her guests. It would be an encounter that would change the course of Ruth Berlau's life.⁵

Because of her vigorous and generous support of social causes,

Berlau was known in Copenhagen as Red Ruth. Born to Wilhelm and Bianca Berlau in 1906, the second of two girls, the family was moderately wealthy from Wilhelm Berlau's trade with his native Germany, a practice that he continued with great profit throughout World War I. Ruth and her slightly older sister, Edith, attended a private Catholic school. Though outwardly the family appeared a model of upper-middle-class propriety, there are strong hints that Wilhelm Berlau, a heavy drinker, sexually abused his children and beat his wife. When her daughters were still in their early teens, Bianca Berlau made an extremely serious suicide attempt, slitting her wrists deeply as well as turning on the gas. Her daughters found her in a gas-filled room lying in a pool of blood. They got her to the hospital in the nick of time. When Wilhelm Berlau, drunk as usual, heard what his wife had done, his first words were not of concern for her but for himself as he feared a scandal. After this, separating from her husband and taking the children with her, Bianca Berlau established a lingerie shop on her own. Leaving school at fourteen, Ruth also established a business, selling coffee from door-to-door.

Intelligent, imaginative, and always adventuresome, in 1928, Ruth Berlau came up with the idea of making a solo bicycle trip to Paris and writing an account of her adventures for the Danish newspapers. The articles she wrote back to the paper *Extrabladet* were published under her byline and with accompanying photos. On her return, she found she was famous and recognized everywhere. Shortly after, she married a man twenty years her senior, the prominent doctor Robert Lund, and became the stepmother of two of his four children. With the complement of servants that Lund could afford, Berlau was still free to live very much her own life, which she did to the full. She was admitted as a student actress to the Royal Danish Theater and began to play lead roles in Copenhagen in works such as Brecht's *In the Jungle of Cities* and Strindberg's *Miss Julie*.

In 1930, she bicycled to Moscow, again writing for the Danish papers. She was particularly impressed by what she saw in the Soviet Union as equal conditions and opportunities for women. She was also much taken by the Soviet theater, at that time still the place of pilgrimage for theater artists from around the world. For Berlau, the Soviet Union was a "new world," a world unlike the one she had left where women still had only a narrow range of professional opportunities.

More activist than theorist, after her return from Moscow, Ruth immediately began to try to introduce ideas from this "new world" into her Danish homeland. She obtained Danish Communist party membership and established a workers' theater group called the Revolutionary Theater. From now on, she lived a dual life. She was part of the high society world of Lund, living in a large, luxurious apartment overlooking Kongens Have (the garden of the king). At the same time, she was up to her ears in Communist party work. When she met the young architect, designer, and photographer Mogens Voltelen, they began an affair and she recruited him to work in the Revolutionary Theater she had founded.[6]

In early 1933, Red Ruth was invited to bring her theater company to Moscow for a world theater festival. In Moscow, the group did well, winning a prize in competition with the top revolutionary theaters in the world. She had become well known both in Denmark and in international theater circles. Eager to extend her range as an activist for women's rights particularly, Berlau had begun work on a novel about a liberated Russian woman who marries and suffers with her less liberated Danish husband. Berlau seemed to be everywhere. One could hardly miss her. Stunningly beautiful, whether dressed down for her revolutionary activities or dressed up for a high society function, she drove around town in a large Lincoln Continental.

Each summer, the wealthy Berlau-Lunds would tour Germany, Austria, Italy, or the fashionable south of France. In winter, they would be seen on the ski slopes of Norway, Switzerland, Austria, and Italy. He was no prude and apparently was quite tolerant of her work as an actress and as a revolutionary. He turned a more or less blind eye when she was drawn to discreet marital indiscretions. As Lund's photos from this period show, Ruth was certainly no prude herself, often hiking topless or swimming naked in mountain streams.

When Berlau heard in the middle of 1933 that the author of *Drums in the Night* (in which she had played her first lead role) was at Thurø, she determined to meet him.[7] After the four-hour trip from Copenhagen, they met Brecht and Weigel at Michaëlis's waterfront house. Berlau was struck by the air of sovereignty and assurance of both Brecht and Weigel. Brecht was dressed in the one-piece blue overalls with numerous pockets of the sort worn by automobile mechanics and flyers. He wore this suit open at the neck but held together at the waist by a black leather belt. For once, he was not wearing his cheap-looking but actually platinum-framed glasses. Berlau could clearly see his eyes, "clear, dark, saying a great deal, laughing." He greeted her in a way she found unique and inimitable. He seemed simultaneously to step forward and backward as his hand went out to meet hers, determined to maintain distance even as he came close. After she got to know him, she wrote, "Distance, dear God distance! Not only as a director does he require distance, but also in his private life."[8]

The conversation was conducted in German as neither Weigel nor Brecht had learned any Danish. Having grown up with a German father,

Ruth spoke in ungrammatical but readily understandable German. Never having mastered the polite "Sie" form, she went over at once to the familiar "Du" that only a handful of people were allowed to use with Brecht.

At the end of lunch, when a dish of compote was brought to the table for dessert, Brecht picked up his dish and disappeared. Weigel announced to the table at large, "After eating, Brecht always refreshes himself with a nap." After the dessert, Mogens Voltelen went off with Weigel to the nearby mainland to consult with her on the remodeling of the house she and Brecht had bought.

Left to her own devices at Thurø, Ruth was walking about the Michaëlis estate when she suddenly heard a hello. The tone was delicate but questioning. Brecht took Berlau to his workroom. They talked of the theater. He recommended that she buy a slide projector for her workers' theater. She laughed with delight at this as she already had one. He showed her a copy of one of the gray paperbound *Versuche* volumes, a series interrupted since the Reichstag fire. The volume contained the adaptation of Gorky's novel *Mother*. It was, he said, a very scarce copy now, one that he could not loan to her. When he left, she tucked the volume in with her own things.

As Voltelen and Berlau prepared to drive off to return to Copenhagen, Berlau called out to Brecht, "Don't forget my address!" He pointed to the pocket next to his heart and replied, "No, no, this is where it is." Soon Berlau and Voltelen returned so the architect could supervise the remodeling of the house. Berlau drove Brecht and Weigel into Copenhagen to work with Ruth's workers' theater troupe and to introduce the couple to artistic and intellectual circles. One night in Copenhagen, Brecht invited Berlau into his room. Taking up the guitar, he sang to her, to the tune of "Mack the Knife," a *Moritat* he had written on the burning of the Reichstag building. While he was singing, Weigel happened to come in, and Ruth noticed that Brecht's wife glared daggers. Berlau did not understand, but Weigel knew that these private song recitals were a seduction routine polished over the years.

After the recital, when both Brecht and Weigel had left the room, Berlau saw a gray silk shirt of Brecht that looked in need of washing. Impulsively, she picked it up and pressed it to her nose.[9] As she described this later, the shirt had an overwhelming, earthy smell. Her pulse racing and knees feeling weak, she tucked the shirt under her jacket. Later, realizing what she had unconsciously done, she put it back where she had found it.

Steffin's numerous letters to Brecht and his few to her make it clear that she knew nothing about Ruth Berlau or the purchase of the Skovsbostrand house. Despite her illness and her distance from the center of town, Steffin spent most of the summer trying to find a suitable apartment for Brecht. She returned from these trips exhausted but could not really sleep. Her family in Berlin wrote often, but the news was awful. Grete's mother wrote (as Grete now passed on in a letter to Brecht) of "a comrade, who had disappeared without a trace since march, now came to see my sister, he had been in a concentration camp, every part of his body looked terrible, and on top of that, he is almost blind from the many blows they had given to his skull."[10] Despite news such as this, Steffin began to wonder about how to get Brecht's things from his apartment there. She wrote to Brecht: "a suggestion: is Hauptmann still in Berlin? . . . things of yours could be sent this way . . . write to me sometime about this. also, i would be glad to go back there and take care of everything for you."[11] But in response, only an occasional letter would arrive, listing tasks he wanted carried out, including whether she might be able to buy him a car and worrying whether "everything was in order."[12] In this letter he casually mentions buying a house.

He did not respond to her repeated inquiries about Hauptmann (who under the constant threat of Gestapo arrest and torture was taking care of his affairs), or what he really wanted to do about the housing question, or their relationship. He was just as evasive on the question of further publication with the Comintern press. She was trying to develop a project Willi Münzenberg sponsored called DAD. The letters probably stand for "Das andere Deutschland" (the other Germany). Grete did most of the work attempting to gather this collection of essays from prominent exiles. It was a time-consuming project, but if Steffin could establish herself as a kind of party-sponsored free-lance editor, she could perhaps gain independence and take care of her pressing health needs. But Brecht objected to what she was doing. He was jealous, uncomfortable with the fact her work involved getting to know the German emigré Comintern functionaries Otto Katz, Alfred Kurella, and Alfred Kantorowicz.

Despite repeated requests, Brecht failed to help. She wrote: "please, i'm asking this for the ? time, is ottwalt going to send something? will he cooperate? is he coming here? have you written to graf, to feuchtwanger? if not, i can write, perhaps also in your name?"[13] Finally, in a letter dated August 30, 1933, he specifically advised: "Handle everything connected with the society [that is, the Comintern] in a delaying manner and don't let yourself get disturbed. Point out to them your own health and your work for me."[14] For Grete, the committed party member, his urging her to work for him rather than "the society" was strange. It also prevented her from improving either her lot or her health.

But because she loved him, she did not openly challenge him. For her, it was important that he suddenly mentioned in what was essentially a business letter that he wanted her hand on his thigh.[15] But having mentioned this, he veered back to business. He said that he had made a good deal with the Dutch publisher de Lange in Holland. Now, as he put it, "it will be a little time before we starve, old Grete."[16] What he did not yet say was that the money earned from de Lange had gone into the new house where he planned to live not with Steffin but with Weigel. And when Steffin wrote to ask about the new *Threepenny* novel—"what have you said to your partner Weill [about this]?"—she got no reply.[17]

In one letter of this period, Brecht outlined his general working method. "You know my principle," he wrote, "the bridge principle. Bridges can carry so and so much of a load. There are friends one can run over with a 1,000-ton freight train, others that bear the weight of a bus, but most only bear a perambulator. But bridges that only carry a perambulator are still bridges."[18] By reminding her of it, he strongly suggests she use this "principle," but Steffin was unable to turn people into objects.

Steffin mentions in mid-July that her knee had become so swollen for a few days that she had been unable to get around anymore by public transportation to look at houses for Brecht. She joked to Brecht that Dr. Alexander had said the worse it went for her the better, because then "I will get myself operated on as quickly as possible."[19] But despite this broad hint about the urgency of her medical need, she never asked him directly for help, and he, though he had enough to buy a house and a car and to travel all over Europe whenever he felt like it, never volunteered the money. Of the new house and Steffin's possibly living nearby, he said the house was on the sound, not the sea. From a medical perspective, the distinction is a hair-splitting one.

At times, she would shyly mention her own writing and would send him something of hers with a request for his comments. "Dear bidi," she wrote in one such letter, "I am including a story for you, I would like to write a number of such things when I am bored. Do you find them to be fun? Write to me for sure about them."[20] But usually her requests would be ignored as he asked instead for large and small pieces of help with his own writing. On July 24, she wrote: "please bidi start being nice to me again. i always wait for your letters, and would like to write to you every day. denmark is awfully far away, but you should know anyway, I remain the same." The "i remain the same" was a code they had agreed to, which told him that she was faithful. He was supposed to say the same. Steffin's July 24 letter continued: "things cannot go well for me here when i do not know if you will be good to me. don't leave me here, agitated, worrying and imagining things. you write that you want me to busy myself with you, oh bidi, i do that ALWAYS."[21] On September 7, she noted in her diary: "Doesn't write. Is he coming? Alone? To me?" On September 8, having heard he would soon be back, she wrote: "Brecht has written that he doesn't want to be picked up. 1) He wants to be picked up by somebody else. 2) Nothing matters to me anymore."[22]

By this time, dust was flying at the newly purchased house as workers began the remodeling. Voltelen had drawn up plans to change the stable connected to the house into a spacious study for Brecht, with its own toilet, a large supplementary stove, and a private door so that he could receive visitors at any time without their having to go through the main house. The attic of the house, steeply pitched under the dry-thatch roof, a firetrap of a place with two chimneys going through it, could only be reached by a steep ladder drawn up and down by a rope. Weigel was to sleep here, separate from Brecht. Brecht, Mari Hold, and the two children would sleep on the ground floor.

At the time Brecht announced he was to leave alone for Paris, Weigel wanted to get away also. She could not work in a country where she did not know the language and in a village where there was no theater. Weigel wanted to earn her own living and to be active in the anti-Nazi effort. She thought this could best be done from the Soviet Union, where she could do radio readings that would reach Nazi Germany. She was angry about Brecht's departure and had to be aware both of his various affairs and of how little he was doing either against the Nazis or for the Comintern.

Brecht left for Paris despite Weigel's anger, but he was worried that she might leave him permanently. He first wrote Weigel a postcard urging that "the walls [between us] not become a gulf."[23] The next six weeks brought a stream of missives. She did not write enough, he said in one letter and pointed out that Mari Hold was writing to him. As usual, one person was played against another. Besides reestablishing the affair with Steffin and at least two others, Brecht was pleased to meet his old friend, the cultural theorist Walter Benjamin. Benjamin was getting a small stipend from the Frankfurt Institute for Social Research, an independent, Marxist-oriented "think tank," which had now transferred its operations and considerable bank account outside of Germany. Brecht promptly invited Benjamin to come, at his own expense, to Svendborg, where he could stay cheaply. He also borrowed some money from his friend, though Benjamin could barely afford it.

As almost all of fashionable Paris was still away on summer holidays in mid-September, Grete and Bert went to Sanary-sur-Mer on the Riviera, where he had worked in previous summers on *Threepenny* and *Happy End* with Hauptmann, Lenya, and Weill. With Brecht now staying at his old haunt the Hôtel de la Plage, it seemed as though the resort community had become a German cultural colony. The Feuchtwangers were there, installed in the villa they had purchased with the large advance received for a novel called *The Oppenheim Family*. Also at Sanary were other famous figures in German culture, now exiled: Thomas Mann, Ludwig Marcuse, René Schickele, Ernst Toller, Franz Werfel, Friedrich Wolf, and Brecht's old critical nemesis from Berlin Alfred Kerr.

From Sanary, Brecht wrote again to Weigel in Denmark. He asked if she had received the ten thousand French francs (about fifteen hundred marks) he claimed to have sent her from his Swiss account. Needless to say, the money had not arrived. He complained in his letter about what he felt was the excessive emphasis many of the German emigrés in France (many of them Jewish) were placing on the anti-Semitic part of Hitler's policy. He scoffed at old Jewish friends from Germany who were now "investing in land in Zion." If Weigel, with her own Jewish background and most of her family in Austria, ever opposed this point of view, she did not do so in any letter that I have found so far. The same letter to Weigel went on to give her pointers for her upcoming trip to the Soviet Union. She was to invite the highly influential Tretiakov to visit Skovsbostrand. Take fifty marks' worth of Western items along as presents, he urged. "That's the main thing, getting a number of friends, please, don't argue and don't allow yourself to be drawn into any disputes." The letter ended, "Dear Helli, I kiss you b."[24] Before they headed back to Paris in late September, he and Grete began work on the first chapter of *The Threepenny Novel*.

Weigel arrived in Moscow in late September, welcomed by the Tretiakovs. But she immediately came down with what has usually been described as acute appendicitis. As she had supposedly had her appendix out at the time of the *Threepenny Opera*, this may have been, as was frequent at the time, a code word for an abortion.[25] In a telegram to Brecht, she told him that the ten thousand French francs he had promised had never arrived and she needed money.

Ill and without funds in Moscow, Weigel wrote asking him to come to join her. But after having avoided all the Comintern work he could, he now claimed he could not come because of his important Comintern work in Paris—a notion that he surely knew would be well received by the ubiquitous NKVD, which read both domestic and foreign correspondence. He told Weigel he would have liked to have come, "but," as he went on, "I am tying the first thin threads together here." He said (using a primitive code that referred to the party as "the old study society") that the party "has loaded a small but important assignment around my neck." Apparently, a member of Willi Münzenberg's staff, a man newly in from Moscow by the name of Otto Katz (known in France as André Simone), had asked Brecht to work on a treatment about the Reichstag fire trial.[26] Brecht advised Weigel in Moscow, "Have Tretiakov look after you." He also told her to bring back complete editions of Marx and Lenin, and three or four years of issues of the journal *The Marxist Banner*. The letter ended, as usual, with "I kiss you b." He had then added a postscript expressing his concern about her having perhaps gotten thinner as a result of her illness.[27] In his next letter to Weigel in Moscow, he noted, "we are very far apart."

Meanwhile, Brecht and Steffin were staying together, at a rate of 2.20 francs per night, in a room with a telephone and a view over the roofs of Paris at a large hotel on the Boulevard St-Germain.[28] By now, Brecht had numerous sources of income: 1,237.85 francs for *Seven Deadly Sins;* money arriving from Moscow; offers for radio plays coming in from London; a second installment of a large advance about to come in from de Lange; and Brecht's Swiss bank account. But Brecht continued to complain of poverty, and nothing was done to get Steffin the medical help she obviously needed.

Brecht wanted Steffin available to serve his needs twenty-four hours a day, seven days a week. Brecht argued correctly that without her the new novel would not be completed. Wanting to please him, she hid her condition whenever she could, and continued to write for him and to sleep with him whenever he wanted. The couple apparently did not use birth control. Her years with Brecht are marked by several abortions, each of them psychologically and physically draining for a person already dangerously ill from steadily advancing tuberculosis.[29]

In mid-December, Hermann Kesten, the editor who had arranged the *Threepenny Novel* contract for de Lange, got a call from Brecht. Brecht was sick, he told Kesten.[30] According to Kesten's written account, Brecht asked him to come to Brecht's hotel "between the statues of Danton and Diderot." To Kesten's surprise, after they had hardly exchanged a few words about "health, Hitler and the weather," Brecht put down his cigar and said in a simultaneously friendly and threatening way, "You and I are going to make an agreement with one another, an agreement that we will become friends. . . . Our contract," Brecht went on, "shall provide that everywhere you go you will speak well of me and of my work, and I'll do the same for you. I have contracts like this with Lion Feuchtwanger, Arnold Zweig, and Alfred Döblin." Kesten tried to politely and jokingly demur, but Brecht was not to be sidetracked. "I hear from all sides that you laugh at me," declared Brecht. "That," he went on, "cannot continue without consequences. When it is necessary, I'll climb over dead bodies to get my way. In Hessen there was a young director who opposed me. He ended up committing suicide."

Brecht also claimed that Caspar Neher's career depended on him. This was a flat lie. Neher's connections with Brecht and Weill were clear handicaps in the Third Reich. Furthermore, Neher had been at least as useful to Brecht as Brecht had been to him.

The next day, Kesten recapitulated the previous day's conversation in a letter. "By way of shedding light on this comprehensive proposal," he wrote to Brecht, "you explained that you are not primarily a writer or poet but rather 'a teacher of behavior'; that as a Marxist, you are antagonistic to the entire world of the bourgeoisie and are driven and prepared to proceed against your opponents with the most drastic armaments of the capitalists, to which normally you object; that you are driven to destroy by all means you have at hand the economic and literary existence of your opponents and your nonfriends; that you are ready and willing to do this, that indeed, you had already done this in some cases; on the other hand, however, you were prepared to offer your friends every kindness and assistance."[31]

When Brecht got this account, which Kesten said he proposed to send to de Lange in Amsterdam, Brecht got very worried and asked Kesten to meet him at once at a neutral café. There, he claimed the previous day's proposal was merely a joke. He asked that the letter be withdrawn. Kesten, not wanting further trouble, agreed to do so. Brecht now made another offer. Would Kesten like to pay an advance on another new book Brecht was planning, a satiric work to be called the *Tui Novel*, loosely modeled on the members of the Frankfurt Institute for Social Research? Kesten would need to move fast, he said, as Münzenberg was also after it. Kesten did not want *Tui*. As it turned out, neither did Münzenberg. Like almost everything else Brecht was writing at this time, this stylized work was totally unsuited to a Communist campaign. It would have alienated the very people Münzenberg hoped to recruit for the anti-Nazi effort.

So pronounced in fact was Brecht's lack of real antifascist work in 1933 that Sergei Tretiakov wrote to complain. Brecht's reply evaded the issue of why he was doing so little by generalizing and claiming that the time for "glittering declarations, protests etc. is over until further notice."[32] Tretiakov had reason to complain. It was not a question of "glittering declarations" but of direct, open opposition to the Nazis. This Brecht was loath to do. He was still acting as if he was only away from Nazi Germany temporarily, with his father's help.[33] During the first two years of exile, only rarely did Brecht take a clear *public* position on the issues of greatest concern to the emigré community. Though he drafted lots of position papers on the Nazis, almost without exception they would not be published until decades later when it was safe.

In December 1933, however, Brecht did react positively to a request from the left-wing Union of Proletarian-Revolutionary Writers to write an open letter concerning the arrest in Nazi Germany of actor Hans Otto. Addressed to Heinrich George, one of the favorite actors of the Nazi regime, Brecht's letter begged George to intervene on Otto's behalf. The letter spoke unequivocally of the barbarism of the Nazi regime, calling its rulers "butchers."[34] But this open letter remained the exception rather than the rule. Brecht's only other public contribution to the anti-Nazi effort during this period were the poems included in the Comintern volume he would finally bring out with Hanns Eisler in 1934. A number of these either unequivocally denounced Hitler or praised the Communist party.

By the onset of winter in Berlin, the Gestapo net finally tightened around Hauptmann. She was on the CPG list that the Gestapo took from the ransacked CPG headquarters that showed that Hauptmann had been the head of the women's section of her cell. The Gestapo also knew that her flat-mates were a Red Army General (who was working with the Reichswehr under the secret pact of 1922) and his wife. As if this were not enough to attract Gestapo attention, she had carried out occasional party assignments as well as handling Brecht's financial affairs and having been repeatedly seen going in and out of his apartment when rescuing their joint papers. Her flat at 57 Schlüterstrasse was repeatedly searched by the Gestapo.

During the night of November 15, the Gestapo came for Hauptmann. They took her to Gestapo headquarters in the Albrechtstrasse, where people were known to be tortured to death. She did not talk about what she experienced there. Somehow she managed to get released after only a week in solitary confinement at Gestapo headquarters. She was repeatedly questioned about her illegal activities in taking papers and valuables from Brecht's apartment. Daringly, through her friend Margaret Mynatt, who came to visit her at this dangerous time before herself fleeing to England, she managed to get out the last of the papers in Brecht's flat. She carefully packed a suitcase far too large to carry inconspicuously. Leaving it in Berlin, she later sent instructions for Brecht senior to try to pick it up.[35] Though under Gestapo watch, she somehow got herself out of Berlin. It would be interesting to know if perhaps Peter Suhrkamp provided help. We know that Suhrkamp somehow got warnings of impending SS raids.

Hauptmann reached Paris by December 10.[36] There, despite the all too obvious presence of Steffin, Weigel, and several new lovers—as well as his intense interest in Ruth Berlau—Brecht tried to induce Hauptmann to stay on in Europe, and resume their sexual and professional relationship. She declined. Though ill upon her arrival in Paris, Hauptmann was willing, as a disciplined party member, to put in some time on the song volume that Steffin was assembling for Editions du Carrefour, but she knew her time with Brecht had passed. As she had had ample opportunity to observe, he always preferred women far younger than the thirty-seven-year-old Hauptmann. She decided to make her own way to America as soon as her health would permit.[37]

Meanwhile, Weigel had made her way back to Skovsbostrand from Moscow. She was deeply disappointed that Brecht had not come to Moscow while she was ill and that she had been unable to sustain her career from a Moscow base. In late December, even though Hauptmann was still ill, Brecht and Steffin left Paris for Denmark. Reaching Copenhagen, Brecht called to ask Ruth Berlau to house Steffin at her large apartment at 18 Prinsessensgade. He told Berlau only that Steffin was a party member fleeing from Hitler. He did not say she was one of his lovers.

Steffin went to work at once with Berlau on a Copenhagen production of *Mahagonny*, with neither Kurt Weill's consent nor any payment of royalties to him. Not knowing yet that Steffin was Brecht's lover Berlau was happy to help a Communist on the run from Hitler. For years now, she had run a kind of Comintern hotel at her flat. She was quite used to hearing from one of her maids at all hours of the day or night that yet another Comintern agent on assignment needed a place to stay.[38] They were always made welcome both by Ruth herself and by her tolerant husband.

Behind a society facade, Ruth Berlau and Mogens Voltelen were deeply involved in Comintern affairs. After the collapse of the Berlin CPG and the Comintern's center there, its main western operations center was transferred to Copenhagen. Voltelen rented the office space and as cover set up companies such as one called Selvo & Co. Here, Comintern experts provided brilliantly faked documentation; carried out assassinations; set up secret shortwave radio communications; or arranged to disable or sink ships at sea. At Berlau's home in the posh Prinsessensgade, there was a constant stream of agents on their way back to Moscow or on their way out to other assignments around the world.

With arrangements made to lodge one admirer with another, and both of them working on his behalf, Brecht was free to return to the now remodeled house in Skovsbostrand. He and Weigel celebrated their first Christmas out of Germany around a Christmas tree, just as he had done since his Augsburg childhood. His furniture had been shipped to him from Berlin by his childhood friend Dr. Otto Müllereisert. Papers had arrived from Augsburg sent by Orge Pfanzelt.[39] The Berlin manuscripts, smuggled out by Hauptmann, had arrived safely, with the dishes with which they had been packed.

Surrounded by the most familiar things of his youth in Augsburg and of his years spent in Berlin, he would soon begin to describe the Spartan nature of his situation as an exile. His poems speak of a Chinese scroll he had called "The Doubter," which could be rapidly rolled up if instant flight was necessary.[40] He also mentions two carved theatrical masks and a small radio on which he listened to the daily news in German. Finally, he mentions a small black army footlocker. On the footlocker rest his copper smoking utensils, inside the vital manuscripts. His poems stress this handful of objects as though these were all he—the poor, hunted exile—had with him.[41] There is no mention there of the comforts of home brought from Germany, antiques bought by Weigel, his silver cigarette case and whiskey flask, handmade silk shirts, or his extensive library including the rare 1818 Göttingen edition of Vergil and the 1691 Hamburg edition of Terence.

Weigel continued to give Brecht at the Skovsbostrand house the distance he insisted on to conduct his affairs. He insisted on being waited upon hand and foot while also playing the roles of "poor poet," "great master," and sometimes secretive but always compulsive Don Juan. The newly installed stove had to be going full blast so he could have his breakfast served to him and could begin work by 8 A.M. at the latest. His new toilet was a primitive affair that somebody needed to empty daily. Fortunately, for tasks like this, Mari Hold was with the family at Skovsbostrand. Her bedroom was downstairs where she could easily minister to the needs of Brecht and the two children at all hours of the day and night. As in Augsburg and in Berlin, she had to be up very early and go to bed very late. It would be a surprise to Mari Hold when decades later she was shown a poem in which Brecht claimed he had given up servants.

As 1933 ended, he could be assured not only of his own comfort in Skovsbostrand but that in Copenhagen, Steffin and Berlau were busy promoting his business affairs, assisting him with their writing and translating skills, and remaining ready to provide sexual variety for him during his visits there. At the same time, his contracts with Moscow and Western agencies for Brecht items were paying well, and he was able to avoid sharing income with the now distant Hauptmann and Weill. Residence permit in hand, he had easily cleared what was for many the highest hurdle confronting those who had left Germany to try to settle and work abroad.

"You Have Achieved a Masterwork, Old Muck" (1933–35)

Around Christmas 1933, Grete Steffin, lonely and ill in Copenhagen, told Ruth Berlau of her love for Brecht. With this, the atmosphere became oppressive in the Berlau-Lund household. By mid-January, despite being without money, Steffin had moved to a nearby pension. Steffin wrote to Walter Benjamin in Paris, "I have made an agreement with Brecht that I stay here provisionally, and will not go on to Berlin until he has visited here."[1] She quickly proved herself a wizard with languages, learning Danish and improving her French, English, and Russian.[2] She would later add Swedish and Norwegian.

One of the less savory jobs Steffin took on for Brecht was trying to make actual a publicity item that was apparently a pure invention. A local newspaper reported that Weill had heard a Copenhagen broadcast of *Mahagonny* and declared: "The music was exactly as I had imagined it should be. Marvelous artists."[3] Steffin wrote to him, asking for confirmation, but Weill told Lenya: "I had no idea that *Mahagonny* was given there [Copenhagen] and have not sent a telegram either."[4]

Steffin had taken over most of Hauptmann's old roles. As with Hauptmann, Brecht would drop in on Steffin when it suited him sexually to do so but allowed her no equivalent license. Nor, for the most part, would Steffin's role in the creation of new Brecht works be acknowledged in print or the royalty statements. Though Steffin often worked with languages Brecht knew little or not at all, the texts would be published both in Moscow and in the West with his name either alone or listed first. Brecht was still incapable of finishing any large project in the absence of Steffin (as with Hauptmann). The important plays of the period are written only with Steffin's daily work. After Steffin's death, few new plays were completed except for the rewriting of work well begun before she died and the post–World War II plays written by Hauptmann.

Though some of the original manuscripts with Steffin's work have been lost or stolen, it is clear from the clues in the Harvard and Moscow collections and from Steffin family papers that she was directly involved in the creation of all the plays written between late 1933 and the middle of 1941. At least thirty major texts were produced in the Steffin years, including: *The Threepenny Novel*; *Round Heads, Peak Heads*; *Fear and Misery of the Third Reich*; *Señora Carrar's Rifles*; *Galileo*; *Mother Courage*; *Arturo Ui*; the first versions of *The Good Woman of Setzuan* and *The Caucasian Chalk Circle*; *The Trial of Lucullus*; three novellas; one large novel (still unpublished); two volumes of poetry; thousands of pages of translations; at least three one-act plays; two full-length plays; an adaptation of Nordahl Grieg's play *The Defeat*; a large number of parables told in the Chinese manner; a series of "Refugee Conversations" (often taken verbatim by Steffin from friends of Brecht and Steffin). All show hundreds of signs of Steffin's authorship. She also wrote at least six short stories in her own name. The earliest Brecht works where Steffin's input is clearly seen are *The Threepenny Novel*, a revised version of *Round Heads*, and the small, superbly playable *The Horations and the Curations*, a strangely compelling mixture of Chinese stage devices Steffin was now picking up from Arthur Waley and classical Roman history, which had long intrigued Brecht.

In Svendborg, Weigel was trying to help Brecht with his enterprises by learning to type, but she developed tendinitis and her hand was put in a cast. With this, the subject of bringing Steffin to Svendborg was broached. In March, a room was found for her in the rather staid and gloomy Pension Stella Maris, a couple of minutes away from the Brecht-Weigel house. Huge and drafty, overlooking the sound with its frequent fogs and cold wet winter winds, Stella Maris was wholly unsuited for a person with tuberculosis. Weigel, claiming (almost certainly with accuracy) that Steffin's illness was contagious, did not allow her to eat with them. Mari Hold and Weigel would prepare her food, which Brecht would take to her by car and then hurry back to eat with "the family."

When Steffin tried to get a residence permit, the Svendborg police were hostile. The Stella Maris innkeeper told the police Steffin "spent most of her time with Bertold [sic] Brecht, carrying out secretarial assignments or reading proofs."[5] The police did not bother the wealthy and famous author directly, but they grilled Steffin repeatedly as to what she, a person who admitted to having been fired from a job in Berlin because of her Communist sympathies, was really doing in Denmark. Working for Brecht was illegal as Brecht had only a residence permit, not a work permit. On May 15, she told the police that "she had nothing to do with [Brecht's] work." Called back on August 11, she said "that she worked independently and in no way carried out work that could be performed by a Danish national, and also did no secretarial work for foreigners."

Police harassment continued as she corrected proofs on the

Brecht-Eisler song volume for Münzenberg's Comintern press and re-wrote *The Threepenny Novel* throughout to improve its style and focus. Meanwhile, in Amsterdam, the publishers were tearing out their hair that Brecht had not delivered *The Threepenny Novel*. In a stream of letters, they told Brecht it was essential that they publish the book before the German summer tourists (seen as the primary purchasers of the book) returned home.[6] Brecht, with Steffin's help, finally finished the book. Despite all of Steffin's efforts, the result is so wooden and colorless that it is not surprising that Eric Bentley dismisses it when he declares, "Brecht never really succeeded in writing a novel—i.e., never became a fully epic writer."[7]

But there was another problem. The company thought it had the rights to recover some of its now very large investment by selling translation rights. Brecht ignored all requests for clarification of the issue while negotiating the sale of the disputed rights to the Soviet Union and a large firm in Paris, as well as several people in England.[8] Though he had given Hauptmann's longtime friend Margaret Mynatt to understand that she was his sole agent in Britain, she found he had given it to several other people there to sell.[9]

Tretiakov translated a number of plays—*Saint Joan of the Stockyards*, *The Measures Taken*, and *The Mother*—into Russian, which were published in 1934 as *Epicheskie dramy*. However, even as these works were appearing, Stalin's close associate Andrei Zhdanov officially declared that all "formalist" experiments in the arts must stop.[10] Both Tretiakov and Brecht were among the "formalists." Hastily, in a six-page letter that he must have known would be read by the NKVD, Tretiakov wrote to tell Brecht there were problems, but they were ones that would be hard to discuss by mail and needed to be discussed directly.[11]

At the same conference, Zhdanov announced that henceforth the arts would follow socialist realist norms, that is, exclusively positive renditions of socialist "reality," the result of which was predictable. Most of the delegates there owed their careers and privileged life-styles to Joseph Stalin. "A continuous hosanna," wrote one commentator on the conference, "went up from dawn to dusk [to] the 'steel colossus [a play on Stalin's name],' the 'great engineer,' the 'great pilot,' the 'great master . . .' the 'greatest of the theorists,' the 'finest of the Leninists,' and finally the 'greatest of the great.' "[12] The man who had argued against preparing to meet the threat of Hitler was declared incomparably wise.[13]

As Hitler's power increased, so did the call for Stalin to be given total power. The two men seem to mirror one other, while each periodically declared how great the differences were between them. Neither of these desperately insecure men could live in a world where anyone else would be allowed to challenge his authority. To the extent they ever really had friends or lovers, these would be sacrificed as needed. In the middle of 1934 Hitler liquidated one of his closest associates, the homosexual leader of the SA, Ernst Röhm. Similarly, Stalin moved against those who had helped him to power. Soviet historian Roy Medvedev has noted of this era in the Soviet Union: "One after the other Zinoviev, Kamenev, Bukharin, and other opposition leaders published articles confessing again and again that they had erred while the 'great chief of toilers thoughout the whole world,' Comrade Stalin, had always been right."[14] With these "confessions," the slide of Lenin's closest associates to arrest, torture, and death was well on its way.

Tretiakov's alarming letter sparked an idea that perhaps two birds could be killed with one stone. The Russian-speaking Steffin, about to be displaced in Brecht's bed anyway by the glowingly healthy Berlau, could go to Moscow to manage many of Brecht's affairs from there. Reaching the Soviet Union in September, Steffin went first for a brief stay in a sanitorium in the Caucasus. There, she wrote an allegorical play for children, *If I Had an Angel.* The play was written, so she told Walter Benjamin, "in the middle of a club, amidst speaking, storytelling, piano-playing people."[15] She felt the tone of the play was a little too close in its first draft to agitprop style, which she meant to change as soon as possible. This was evidently her earliest effort to write an entire play on her own. Reminiscent both in language and its biblical orientation to works of Brecht-Hauptmann and Goethe's *Faust,* and clearly anticipating key features of the Steffin-Brecht play *The Good Woman* of *Setzuan, Angel* is a morality play where people deal with a heaven that proves unable to help with real problems on earth. By the play's end, one sees clearly that human beings must find their own salvation rather than counting on heavenly intervention. When she returned to the West, Hanns Eisler set the songs to music. It is a very performable work still, though there are places where references are as dated as the kolkhoz scene in *The Caucasian Chalk Circle* and the Control Chorus in *Measures.*

Besides her tuberculosis, Grete was also having serious trouble with her appendix. But the nearest doctor who could operate on her was seven and a half hours' away by train and a further four hours' by bus. Instead, she tried to wait the illness out, still working for Brecht. There is a deeply disturbing, self-denigrating note in her letters to him by this time. She begins to say she has long realized she is "enslaved" to Brecht and that she "belongs entirely" to him. He does not challenge this in his responses.

While she expressed herself as his slave, at the same time, she continued to dream of a world where women would not be enslaved. When still in Georgia, she read the history of the area and was particularly taken with the fact that Georgians agreed the finest ruler they had ever had was a woman, Queen Tamara, who had ruled in the twelfth century. In a warm letter to Walter Benjamin, she said that she wanted to do a book on this queen.[16]

But she had reckoned without Brecht's insistent demands. In mid-January 1935, at Brecht's urging, Steffin left the warmth of the Caucasus and its medical help for Moscow to promote Brecht's interests and what both saw as the revolutionary cause itself. She and Brecht saw Marxism and the Soviet Union as the best hope to achieve peace and equality on earth. Steffin particularly saw Marxism embodied in women's equality in the Soviet Union at that time. She poured every ounce of her energy into making the entire world accept the same principle. Brecht's writings, she was convinced, needed to be published, distributed, and played in order to help this effort. Against smaller questions such as recognition of her contributions and her royalties, "the third thing," the revolution itself, was immeasurably more important, more important even than her health and her life.

She was lonely, freezing, and ill, as she guided his publications through the Soviet bureaucracy. According to David Pike, the world authority on German writers in the Soviet Union during the Stalin era, Steffin's efforts resulted in several works being sold in the Soviet Union. Brecht had begged her in a September letter to sell *The Threepenny Novel*, and by December, she had arranged for it to appear both in German and in Russian. Valentin Stenich, an associate of Meyerhold and translator of Joyce, Faulkner, and Kipling, was the translator. She was also able to get a Soviet contract to bring out *Round Heads, Peak Heads* in the Moscow journal *International Literature*.

In September 1934, Brecht received a long, rather desperate letter from Hauptmann in Saint Louis. She had stayed in Paris, ill most of the time, until February, when she had sailed for the United States on the liner the *Lafayette*. Still unwell upon her arrival, she stayed a few days in New York before continuing her journey to Saint Louis. Limited in job opportunities both by the fact that she was an unknown writer and by her visa, she had been forced to take a room in the home of a mentally unbalanced woman who needed a companion. It was an almost impossible place for her to write. "I do not," she wrote, "have anyone here who interests himself in my things."[17] Hoping for help, she asked him to send her research materials from Europe and offered to provide him with what he might need from America. Her requests went unanswered, but he did ask her to do some German translations of Chinese poems from Arthur Waley's English versions. When he got the poems, he then published them in Moscow with no significant changes under his own name and without paying Hauptmann.[18] Hauptmann believed that Brecht was lost without her and in bad shape. She wrote to Benjamin, "I wrote him a couple of short letters, put some money into the envelope for him that he could use for doing some research for some things that I needed."[19] Hauptmann never received what she had asked for. The money was used for Brecht's own ends. She was finally able to get a room of her own after becoming an instructor in German at a Saint Louis University. The job paid her fifty dollars a month for nine months of the year. She remained generous to a fault to people like Peter Lorre, who was now in Hollywood, and to Brecht in Scandinavia. Both borrowed money from her, as her meticulously kept account book shows.[20]

At the time of Hauptmann's cry of pain from Saint Louis, Brecht was in Copenhagen to talk with the director Per Knutzon, a close friend of Berlau. He hoped to persuade Knutzon to do a Danish production of *Round Heads, Peak Heads.* The original Hauptmann-Brecht script had now been revised by Steffin and Brecht, but the central problem remained. The play argues that eventually "Nazi leaders and the rich Jews would combine against the working class, irrespective of race."[21] Knutzon did not see this as a problem and planned a 1936 production.

Soon after meeting Brecht in August 1933 and stealing a copy of the play, Berlau translated *The Mother.* In the fall of 1934, she directed a production of it, starring Dagmar Andreasen, for the Revolutionary Theater company she had founded. After rehearsals, Andreasen scrubbed floors all night at the Copenhagen train station. Brecht (who had learned little Danish) sometimes attended rehearsals. He said to Berlau on one occasion, "It's comic when workers want to play actors, and tragic when actors don't know how to play workers."[22] Brecht's remarks about worker actors did not stop Red Ruth. Her production of *The Mother* was remarkable not only for its fine worker actors, who are still very much remembered in Denmark, but also as a recruiting tool.[23] "Very few Communists were there when rehearsals began," said Berlau proudly, "but there were lots by the time we were done."[24] The work was important also as the virtual beginning of a new way of recording theater history. Berlau made an extensive photographic record of the production. From now until Brecht's death, she would photograph every production with which he and she were involved.

In early October 1934, before *The Mother* opened, Brecht left for London eager to negotiate with publishers and to see if he could get any work as a film writer, though he knew very little English. He stayed at a small pension at 24 Calthorpe Street, where his Berlin Marxist teacher Karl Korsch was also staying. Despite Brecht's many contacts in London (Hanns Eisler had already established himself in film and music circles), the visit was not a success. His double dealings over the rights to *The Threepenny Novel* made him something of a persona non grata in publishing circles. He and Leo Lania, a screenwriter who had worked on the Pabst version of *Threepenny*, worked on a treatment about the cause of puerperal fever, but it was rejected by emigré film impresario Alexander Korda.[25]

He attended one of the five private performances given that winter of T. S. Eliot's *Sweeney Agonistes* together with W. H. Auden's clearly epic *The Dance of Death*.[26] Though he told Group Theatre director Rupert Doone that he considered this "the best thing he had seen for a long time and by far the best thing in London," that did not say a great deal. He told Weigel the London theater was "antediluvian."[27]

Brecht was often at loose ends in London, and as usual when that happened, he turned to revising some of the erotic sonnets he had produced years before in Augsburg. To Steffin in Moscow, he sent poems with lines such as:

> I love my women who cheat
> And hide their full lap from me
> They see my eyes staring at their lap
> (It turns me on to look at them at times like this).[28]

The reference to women in the plural and the poet's fascination with betrayal were hardly what Steffin wanted to hear, freezing and ill in Moscow. Fortunately, he also seems to have sent some of his other London poems, including the fine fighting song "Keine oder Alle," set to a rousing tune by Eisler. The songs written with Eisler at this time mark the highest point of Brecht's commitment to explicit political verse. However, for reasons not yet adequately explained, a rift now occurred between Brecht and Eisler, and their work together broke off.

Mixed with the fighting songs is a poem for Steffin marked by touching tenderness:

> Write me what you have on! Is it warm?
> Write me how you lie down! Is it soft?
> Write me how you look! Is it the same?
> Write me what you lack! Is it my arm?[29]

He may also have sent her at this time one of his finest and most revealing poems, "Questions from a Worker Who Reads." Here he asks why we only remember the names of kings on monuments, not those of the people who actually did the building. In one stanza, he writes, "Every ten years a great man, / Who paid the bill?" The poem is perhaps a tribute to Steffin's unacknowledged contributions to the work that helped make him a "great man," but if so, it appears an unconscious one.

Brecht's letters urged her to "establish my fame in Mecca"[30] even as she guided the Soviet edition of *The Threepenny Novel* through the bureaucracy. But she was still writing and looked to him for some response. He made her feel guilty about it. A typical letter runs: "Bidi, Bidi, whether or not I have the right, despite everything, to load you down with my plays? Don't you find it extremely ugly of me? Because of these things, I have not done things for you for a long time—that is bad!—it is as if I have committed a crime when things appear in your letters that look like appeals to my conscience."[31]

While Brecht was in London, Weigel left Svendborg for the second time, trying again to pick up the pieces of her own career. She now spoke rudimentary Danish but felt professionally comfortable only in German. She wanted to see what her prospects might be in her hometown of Vienna and in the German-speaking theaters of Prague. Brecht also learned that Mari Hold, with whom he had now lived since she was fourteen, was planning to leave him in order to marry a Svendborg butcher.

The domestic difficulties of the now thirty-six-year-old Brecht were accompanied by professional ones. His first important works published in exile were not proving very successful. The du Carrefour volume, while it had a few new poems ridiculing Hitler, basically repackaged previously published and not very good political verse. Hauptmann wrote to Walter Benjamin that she liked only one poem in it,[32] one on which she had originally worked from a Kipling model.

The Threepenny Novel, Brecht's first and really last attempt at a novel, appeared in German in Amsterdam to mixed reviews and sluggish sales. Set in an improbable, allegorical London that Brecht barely knew, it wholly lacks the verve of the original *Threepenny Opera*. Not familiar with the English milieu, Steffin had confined her work to rewriting its turgid German, and indeed the only thing critics praised was the clarity of its language. In a note to Steffin using the nickname "Muck," Brecht acknowledged her contribution; "It [the novel] gives the impression you have achieved a masterwork, old Muck, in particular, your clear language is being praised."[33]

Leftist writer Bodo Uhse said the novel's language was on a par with three of the greatest names in the history of German literature—Luther, Kleist, and Büchner—but it was widely criticized in the party press as not presenting an accurate picture of the proletariat and of not conforming to socialist realist norms. Brecht complained to Johannes R.

Becher, who had sought asylum in the Soviet Union, that an attack by Becher's "secretary" Alfred Kantorowicz constituted an official attack on Brecht,[34] which it was. Brecht, however, remained useful as a propaganda tool. Stalin, like Brecht, was a past master at simultaneously attacking and praising those useful to him. So while Brecht's work would be criticized, every effort was made to make him an ally of and spokesperson for the Soviet Union in the West.

On December 1, 1934, Sergei Kirov, the head of the Communist party apparatus in Leningrad, the most popular political figure in Russia at the time and the sole remaining person who could have challenged Stalin for leadership, was assassinated. Years later, it was suggested that Kirov's murder was rigged by Stalin and that the whole incident was strikingly similar to Hitler's assassination of Ernst Röhm.[35]

A few months later, without any evidence, Stalin announced that the assassination was inspired by one of Lenin's oldest companions, Grigory Zinoviev. Nearly one hundred thousand people, supposedly part of Zinoviev's "oppositionist group," were arrested by the NKVD in Leningrad alone. Stalin declared: "We were obliged to handle some of these comrades roughly. But that cannot be helped. I must confess that I, too, had a hand in this."[36] People were routinely killed without trial or defense counsel. The following year, Stalin would personally set quotas for NKVD arrests.[37]

With torture and murder ubiquitous in the winter of 1934–35, the Soviet Union was anxious to improve its external image. Erwin Piscator was authorized in the winter of 1934–35 to invite Brecht to Moscow as a guest of the Soviet Union. Brecht accepted his official invitation, though some of his closest friends discouraged him. From Switzerland, Bernard von Brentano wrote to say the Soviets were indistinguishable from the fascists. Brecht replied that the Soviet leadership was fully justified in its actions by the fact that they were so few and their enemies so many. Throughout his life, Brecht felt that use of authoritarian force by a political elite was justified, as long as it was a political elite of which he was a part.

Brecht left in mid-March 1935, hoping to understand the situation better in person, to offset the bad publicity he had received for the publication of "formalist" works, and to see what new deals could be made there. It was also a chance to see Grete again and to resume relations with Carola Neher, who was now living and working in the Soviet Union. Anticipating his arrival, he had sent off a note to Bernhard Reich. He enclosed a poem and note for Carola Neher, hoping to resume their old affair.[38]

With the wave of arrests after the Kirov murder the previous December, "there was," in the words of Georg Lukács, "no sane person in Moscow who had five healthy senses who could have failed to recognize that . . . traps were being set all the time for enemies."[39] Lukács does not say, however, that he was a prime setter of traps, nor that he worked for decades to undercut Brecht. In 1935, as the West still dallied with Hitler, and even Winston Churchill wondered whether Hitler would join the forces of civilization, opposition to Stalin was a dangerous proposition. For anybody committed to Marxism, it was a terrible thing to admit that instead of the state withering away, the Soviet police state was growing at cancerous rates and was directed by a paranoid sadist. With his fundamental lack of interest in democracy and his core belief in the use of violence from above to achieve supposedly benevolent ends, Brecht could accept the Soviet reality. Killing, endorsed by a Moscow Control Chorus, had been and would remain central to his own system of belief.

Despite a growing undercurrent of fear that it was essential to publicly ignore, Brecht was to find Moscow wonderfully exciting in many ways during his stay there from mid-March until mid-May 1935.[40] It was a watershed moment in history. The stages and screens glowed with the last rays of a sunburst of creative activity that had dawned in the first brilliant years of the twentieth century. In the physically grubby Moscow theaters of the twenties and early thirties, Meyerhold, Stanislavsky, and Tairov rubbed shoulders with Mei lan-Fan from China, Piscator, Gordon Craig from England, French writer André Malraux, and a host of Americans including Joseph Losey, Hallie Flanagan, Harold Clurman, Lee Strasberg, and Stella Adler—all visibly dazzled by what they saw and heard.

The Soviet Union, it seemed, was in the vanguard of the arts. It seemed also to be on its way to the triumphant unfolding of the human spirit and a classless, nonracist, and nonsexist society. This was a dream still widely believed in 1935 both inside and outside the Soviet Union. In a book published in London at this time, Ada Chesterton described Sergei Tretiakov as "an ardent feminist." His daughter was a student of aeronautics, whereas "in England Tatiana would probably have been relegated to an office, her talents leashed to other people's correspondence," Chesterton said. "A career as air designer, who could pour life and movement into wood and metal, would have been impossible [elsewhere]."[41]

Brecht was shown everything that would support an impression of a society making great forward strides. There were special tickets for him to see Mei lan-Fan do his superb repertoire of female roles from the classical Chinese repertoire. He also met the avant-garde novelist and theorist Viktor Schklovski. Schklovski used the Russian term "Otchysdenie" to describe work he and Meyerhold had been doing for many years (something remarkably similar to ideas found in the preface to Coleridge's *Lyrical Ballads*), rendering the strange familiar and the familiar strange. Schklovski, who had lived and worked in Berlin in 1923, spoke German with Brecht. Immediately following the Schklovski meeting, we first encounter the term "Verfremdung" in Brecht's vocabulary. The basic concept would gain international currency as the "Verfremdungseffekt," or V-effect.[42] Though it was a term that would be adopted after World War II by those wanting to work in the Brechtian manner, Brecht himself was rarely bound by the concept when working on an actual production.[43]

Brecht went out of his way to keep a distance from his old Berlin and Thurø friends Ernst Ottwalt and Waltraut Nicolas, who were staying at the same hotel as he. Brecht's attempts to resume his old affair with Carola Neher came to naught. Happily married and a new mother, she had no sexual interest in Brecht. There were a few other sour notes. Weigel's former lover Alexander Granach said: "Brecht, who is also here [Moscow], wants to convince the people here of one little thing, that Tolstoy, Dostoevski, Pushkin, Gogol, Gorki are talentless chatterers from whom the Russian people must free themselves, and instead [they should] prescribe for themselves a large dose of Brecht."[44] The influential director Gustav von Wangenheim complained vigorously about Brecht in party circles. And while Brecht was in Moscow, a damning letter (no doubt read by the NKVD on its way there) reached him from Emil Burian, head of Prague's Collective Theater.[45] Burian was incensed that Brecht showed so little interest in helping genuine workers' theaters. But even if some people were less than enchanted with him, Brecht was wooed in the only Soviet circle that mattered—the one reporting to Stalin.

One key event was a special "Brecht Evening" held on April 21, in a clubroom adjacent to the Mayakovsky Theater. Tairov's experimental theater company presented a skit based on the song "Mack the Knife." Hanne Rodenberg sang some of the songs from *The Mother*. The high point of the evening, however, was Carola Neher's sexy rendition of "Johnny, Take That Cigar out of Your Mouth" from *Happy End*. The important thing about such evenings was who attended and who did not. This event drew a number of top CPG officials, including Wilhelm Pieck; his brother, director Arthur Pieck; and the party poet, Johannes R. Becher. Also in attendance were two top officials from the Executive Committee of the Comintern; the former head of the short-lived Hungarian soviet, Béla Kun; and Vladimir Knorin, the man who dealt daily with Stalin's policies toward Nazi Germany.

Knorin, after beginning his party career in prerevolutionary Minsk, helped Stalin oust his key rivals Zinoviev and Trotsky after

Lenin's death. Knorin had hesitated briefly in 1931 before going over to full-scale glorification of Stalin but then joined with a vigor that made up, momentarily, for his previous hesitancy.[46] By 1935, besides handling Comintern matters concerning Hitler's Germany for Stalin, he was involved in rewriting the *Short History of the Party*, changing key details to artificially increase Stalin's stature at the time of the Russian Revolution. Knorin also helped plan Bukharin's demise.

At some point during Brecht's Moscow visit, Knorin invited Brecht for a formal meeting at Knorin's apartment in Government House across from the Kremlin. Others who attended the meeting were Bernhard Reich (who made a detailed account of it), Asja Lazis, and Johannes R. Becher. In this two-hour meeting, Knorin stated that "the most important assignment for an anti-fascist writer at that time was to warn that Fascism posed the danger of starting a new world war. This he should do tirelessly, using every opportunity."[47] This, expressed by Knorin, amounted to an order. As Reich puts it rather delicately, "It is certainly possible that Knorin in this talk won Brecht over to the assignment of repeatedly and damningly warning against a war of conquest."[48] This is Soviet-speak for Knorin's telling Brecht "get off the fence, start really praising us and attacking the Nazis in your writing!"

Brecht was subsequently taken to see Tretiakov's immediate boss, Mikhail Koltsov. Like Knorin, Koltsov was close to Stalin at the time and served as an associate editor of the official paper, *Pravda*. Brecht was also introduced to Kolzov's common-law wife, German-born journalist Maria Osten, and to Koltsov's assistant, Mikhail Apletin.[49] Apletin himself was a man of considerable power in the hierarchy as he authorized rarely given foreign travel visas and payments in hard currency. The three Soviet executives outlined plans to establish a new antifascist journal to be called *Das Wort*. They were eager to recruit Brecht as one of the three editors of the journal, along with Lion Feuchtwanger and veteran Communist Willi Bredel. Though it would be financed and printed in Moscow, Brecht would be permitted to carry out his duties from Svendborg. Payments would be in hard currency. Though Brecht did not accept right away, he later told Maria Osten he was willing to take on the assignment. At the same time, he began an affair with her.

Béla Kun, the other key Comintern person who had attended the "Brecht Evening," also arranged to meet the distinguished German visitor. He decided to throw a big party at his home, an apartment the size of several regular Moscow apartments. Light and attractive, it was filled with fine antiques bought at a fraction of their value in the desperate years immediately following the Russian Revolution. Despite the effort made by the Kuns for their honored guest, the evening was not a complete success. Reich and Piscator, remembering Brecht's electric performances as a singer in the old Berlin days, repeatedly urged him to do a few songs. At first he refused, but when he finally did get up and sang his very early work "The Song of the Dead Soldier," it was clear much of the old electricity was gone. Applause was merely polite.

Perhaps the "Dead Soldier" song itself had not been the best choice that evening. This was a country where, certainly since the death of Kirov in late 1934, arrest and death without any form of real trial was an increasingly likely possibility. Bukharin privately told the visiting Malraux that blood would be spilled as Stalin would assume complete dictatorial powers.[50] It was a world where any incorrect word could cost one's life, but there was never a clear sense as to what the correct word might be. The general party line could and would shift as rapidly as Stalin's moods and his moves on the chessboard of Soviet and world politics.

Brecht was so exhausted by all the attention he had received that he took to his bed for two weeks. Tretiakov also became ill. Brecht wrote a couple of his usual businesslike letters to Weigel, who had just returned to Denmark after her visit to Prague and Vienna. There she had found that with the shadow of Hitler growing longer every day, the opportunities for a not conventionally pretty, no-longer-young actress of Jewish origin were virtually nonexistent. She returned to a deeply unsatisfying existence in isolated Svendborg.

By April 27, Brecht had recovered enough to be taken to the formal opening of the Moscow Metro, that marvel of engineering carried out under a mid-level Soviet manager, Nikita Khrushchev. In Stalin's view, Khrushchev had done superb party work in 1929 in the Ukraine. By 1935, the Ukraine was, as a later commentator put it, "like one vast Belsen,"[51] with one quarter of its inhabitants dead or dying and the rest without the strength to bury the rotting dead. Khrushchev had proved to be a superb choice in driving the Metro project at bone-crushing speed.[52]

For his Soviet hosts, Brecht prepared a small poem to mark the Metro's completion. Brecht wrote that the subway system had been built by "laughing young men and girls" in just one year.[53] Actually, as any inhabitant of Moscow knew, it had taken three years and had not been so much a laughing as a dying matter as safety was deliberately sacrificed to speed. Either Brecht had no idea of the real building process or had decided to flatter his Soviet hosts. It is a poem uncannily similar in tone to the advertisements written for the Steyr firm in exchange for cars in the Weimar days.

On May 1, Brecht was given a rare privilege for foreigners, a permit to view the annual military march from Red Square itself. Later, he was interviewed by the Moscow-based *Deutsche Zentral-Zeitung* (German Central Newspaper). He was asked to sum up his impressions of Moscow. "Here," he said, "the changes are for centuries and millennia." "Yes, I can imagine," he went on, "that there have been difficulties in making changes, but this makes them even more praiseworthy."[54]

At the time, Stalin was wiping out the old Bolshevik cadres, as well as ordering the "repression" of hundreds of thousands of farm owners or kulaks. This was open knowledge at the time, particularly among top writers. Pasternak, for instance, wrote: "In the early 1930s, it became fashionable among writers to visit the collective farms and gather material about the new way of life in the villages. I wanted to be like everyone else and also set out on such a trip with the intention of writing a book. But there are no words to express what I saw. There was such inhuman, unimaginable misery, such frightful poverty, that . . . I fell ill and could write nothing for an entire year."[55] Tretiakov had spent several years examining collectivization and remained a staunch supporter of a policy that depended on mass murder and starvation. Brecht, from the remarks he had made to Tretiakov in Berlin in 1930, was aware of "problems" with Stalin's collectivization. But in Moscow, after his meeting with Knorin, he said it was more praiseworthy because it was difficult.

On May 2, Brecht was negotiating for more Soviet editions of his work.[56] He still had details to settle about royalties for the Soviet edition of *The Threepenny Novel* in German, but there were still no firm offers for production of any of his plays. Though there were promising signs that the experimental director Nikolai Okhlopkov would like to tackle *Round Heads*, this was his only real lead, and even this would come to nothing.

The point of the original invitation to Brecht to visit Moscow in the spring of 1935 was crystal clear by the time he left. He had been ordered to be extremely explicit in opposing the Nazis in his own writings. He'd agreed to help edit *Das Wort*, assisting the Moscow-orchestrated effort to involve other writers in the effort against Hitler. The Soviets were prepared to pay him, often in hard currency, for book versions of his work but would remain cold toward the idea of producing his plays. Under relentless pressure, he was forced to get off the political fence and publicly represent the Comintern point of view. A propaganda campaign commenced at once. He was featured on Moscow radio. Soviet propaganda made him, ex post facto, a great hero of the antifascist movement, out of all proportion to his real efforts.

After Brecht and Steffin left Moscow for Denmark, they stopped for several days in Leningrad where another Brecht evening was arranged. Accompanying herself on her own small accordion, Grete sang a number of Brecht's cradle songs. Brecht read a number of his poems aloud. "Bert Brecht," wrote the official *Red Newspaper* the next day, "an unpretentious person, almost, one might say, shy, read from his works. From his world-famous *Threepenny Opera*, he read the 'Ballad of the Reichstag Fire' and the 'Song of the Housepainter, Hitler.' These poems, full of soul, reveal the great master, perhaps the greatest antifascist writer in all of Europe." Neither of the pieces cited by the Soviet writer as having been in the "world-famous *Threepenny Opera*" actually occur in that work, but the fiction of Brecht as longtime anti-Nazi required their placement there. The Soviet writer had also conveniently forgotten far more active anti-Nazi writers such as Feuchtwanger, Heinrich and Thomas Mann, Gide, and Malraux. With an offer in hand to be paid in hard currency if he would work for Moscow and dubbed "the great master," Brecht returned to Svendborg.

"I Do Not Want to Get Involved in Any of Your Hierarchical Games, No Matter How Fine" (1935–36)

Perhaps it was only a coincidence, but a month after Brecht's Moscow trip, on June 8, 1935, the Nazis finally took away Brecht's German citizenship. He commemorated the occasion with a few brief, rather pedestrian lines of unrhymed poetry.[1] Now, like tens of thousands of others, he was stateless. Fortunately, many governments still recognized passports such as his, as long as they had not expired. His still had some months before it would be invalid.

Brecht went to Paris in late June 1935 to attend a Soviet-backed conference on the theme "The Defense of Culture."[2] The Comintern rescinded the policy of not allowing Communists to cooperate with bourgeois elements.[3] That the Comintern had opposed cooperation for years was left unexplained, but the reason was obvious to those in the inmost circle of the Comintern. Karl Radek had once pointed to Stalin's office in the Kremlin and indiscreetly remarked, "there sit those who bear the guilt for Hitler's victory."[4] Witnesses such as Radek would now be murdered.

The new Comintern position produced some strange bedfellows. E. M. Forster, whom the NKVD suspected of involvement in a British attempt to assassinate Lenin in 1918, attended, as did as Aldous Huxley, whose 1932 novel *Brave New World* was widely seen as a critique of the Soviet Union. The French delegates included André Gide, Romain Rolland, André Malraux, Henri Barbusse (author of a highly laudatory, Soviet-commissioned biography of Stalin), and André Breton. The Soviet Union was represented by a relatively minor poet, Nikolai Tikhonov; an undistinguished novelist, Alexei Tolstoy; Mikhail Koltzov; and Ilya Ehrenburg. When there were complaints in Paris that the Soviet delegation was second-rate, Stalin ordered Pasternak to go there at once. The main German participants, besides Brecht, were Anna Seghers, Johannes R. Becher, Heinrich Mann, and Lion Feuchtwanger; Walter Benjamin was present as an observer.

As the news reached Paris of more arrests, including that of international journalist Victor Serge, anti-Stalin noises were heard. Malraux, an admirer of Trotsky, now defended Stalin as the only remaining way to oppose Hitler.[5] Anna Seghers did the same, claiming efforts to defend Serge "can only have a counterrevolutionary effect!"[6] Tikhonov and Koltsov made the dishonest claim that Serge was involved in Kirov's assassination though he had been in jail at the time.[7] Serge had been Tikhonov's close friend and official translator, but Tikhonov's own life now depended on the public vilification of Serge.

However, international pressure forced the Kremlin to buckle on this one case. Upon his release in April 1936, Serge published a devastating account of a revolution betrayed by Stalin.[8] Serge wrote of the hundreds of thousands arrested in the wake of the Kirov murder. He described in detail what one critic has called "a literary mandarinate," a group paid well for continued docility while the less docile were sent to concentration camps.[9] Serge's account of the Soviet Union concluded with the open question: "We're fighting fascism, but how do we fight fascism with so many concentration camps in our rear?" But in 1935, at the Paris conference, such things were still only rumors.

Brecht spoke on the third day of the bitterly contested Paris conference. "Kameraden," he began, "let us speak on the question of property rights." Few there knew how vigorously he defended his own property rights, but at the conference, he decried them as pernicious. He sent a copy of his speech to Moscow.[10] At the same time, he denounced Heinrich Mann in a number of letters, spreading the rumor that Mann showed his own speech to the French police before delivering it.[11]

Pasternak arrived in the middle of the conference. In his public speech, he urged a return to nature and said not a word about the horrors of collectivization that he had personally witnessed. After five days and 104 wary and weary speakers, the conference was brought to a close by the deft Malraux. It broke up before it could break apart over the issue of whether being against Hitler meant automatically backing the lawlessness and concentration-camp terror that many knew Stalin had unleashed against his own best people.

When Brecht got back to Denmark, he visited Ruth Berlau. He gave Ruth one of his collection of inexpensive rings; gold, he told her, was too conventional. Only the two of them, he said, would know what her iron ring meant. Then, one beautiful starlit night when they had taken a blanket and gone down to a nearby beach together, he gave her two other gifts. He had taken a small, polished beach stone and had scratched in it with his pocket knife the letters "epep" for the Latin motto *et prope et procul* (whether near or far). She was to place it in her lap—a combination chastity belt and dildo—to remind her of him while he was away.[12] He also drew her attention to the night sky, pointing out the W-shaped outline of the five stars making up Cassiopeia. Wherever they might be in the future, he said, however physically distant they might be, if each went outside and looked up at Cassiopeia, they would really be together. "So he had brought," Ruth said later, "heaven down to earth." They kissed under Cassiopeia, "a tentative kiss, a heavenly light kiss, a kiss of the stars, an eternal kiss."

Not realizing how standardized Brecht's gestures were, Berlau thought they signaled real permanency. She hoped they would work together in art and politics. On the personal plane, she hoped her frank enjoyment of his naked body would allow him to be more open. She, at least as sexually experienced as he, saw herself as his teacher. She wanted him to learn to shed all his clothes with ease rather than unbuttoning his fly briefly and hoisting her skirt above her waist for a quick one (as he apparently did at the time of their first intimacies).[13]

Berlau hoped her love would overcome his bourgeois inhibitions, his insistence on secrecy about their relationship. Rather like a child, he acted as though if he closed his eyes, nobody else would see what was really going on. Everyone, of course, saw. Not even the children in their two households could miss the smoldering looks the two exchanged when together. Berlau was prepared to give up a marriage she considered more comfortable than satisfying, and she hoped Brecht would have the courage to do the same. But comfort was his satisfaction and that he would never dare to give up.

Berlau longed for the honesty and parity she had dreamed about ever since encountering the "new world" of the Soviet Union in 1930. She ran her Revolutionary Theater without sexual preferment or hierarchy, thinking, as did Virginia Woolf, that if the world was to change, the changes must begin in one's immediate circle. Sexual openness and equality were central themes of her writing, notably her 1935 novel *Videre* (Forward). Like *The Threepenny Novel*, *Videre* has not worn particularly well. It is too sentimental to be wholly convincing, but it expresses well her enduring concerns about women's rights in a male-dominated society and her hopes that socialism would make genuine equality in love and work the new norm. The central figure of *Videre*, Katja, has similar beliefs but sees that her rather old-fashioned Danish husband, Preben, cannot follow her.

Berlau showed sections of the novel to Brecht, but his suggestions surprised her. In her story, the husband, distraught at the idea of losing his wife after a quarrel has a serious accident and is then saved by her. Brecht recommended that after the argument, Katja should find him later nonchalantly playing cards with his male buddies. This, after all, was what Brecht would have done. Berlau found the suggestion "shattering," as it missed several key points of her work. She changed neither the novel nor her ideas. But though she was intellectually aware of

Brecht's incapacity to share her central beliefs, her love for him did not waver. Her next novel described the great gulf that can open between what one knows intellectually to be true of a person and "that fearsome compulsion," or "deadly longing," the passion that could lead to madness or death for the one so possessed.

In the summer of 1935, a long-buried "leftover" surfaced for Brecht. Bie wrote from Germany to say that she had finally brought Frank, the child she had with Brecht in 1919, to live with her and her husband in Augsburg. She asked Brecht to send money for his education as a dental assistant. Brecht argued that Frank should learn a cheaper and less demanding trade but that he would (with no guarantees) try to send fifty marks per month to help out with Frank's expenses.

That same summer, Brecht got a request from Paul Peters, on behalf of the Communist-led Theater Union in New York, who wanted to put on an English-language production of *Mother*. Brecht replied that they could do the play if he could come to New York at the Theater Union's expense. After some bickering, they agreed.[14]

As he prepared to leave for New York, he was interviewed by a young Danish journalist, Fredrik Martner, known to friends as Crassus. In the very positive article in a local paper, Brecht praised Denmark as a free country and even had kind words to say about its Social Democrat government. Crassus was clearly overwhelmed by Brecht's personality, becoming what one critic calls, "sein treuer Diener" (his faithful servant).[15] When Brecht resumed the Herr Keuner series, Crassus wrote some of them, which were later published in Brecht's collected works.[16] Klaus Völker points out that in Denmark, "It gradually became the custom to address [Brecht] as 'master' when speaking or working with him."[17] Virginia Woolf has said, "The public and the private worlds are inseparably connected: . . . the tyrannies and servilities of one are the tyrannies and servilities of the other."[18] Brecht's everyday life and his politics clearly illustrate this point. A master in the microcosm of his personal circle, he saw nothing odd in Stalin's mastery over those around him. For both, the Marxist theory of equality in human relations went out of the window in everyday practice. Barely concealing contempt for those around them, they expected obedience and generally got it, in the same way that Hitler ruthlessly divided the world into masters and subjects.

In all three cases, it would seem their fear of "the other" and their compulsion to be "in control" was so great that they would systematically sacrifice even those closest to them. All three lives are littered with suicide attempts or actual suicides in the immediate circle. Each insisted on the creation of historical fictions radically at variance with the facts of his history. Each treated women as commodities and seemed incapable of establishing committed relationships. Each justified the sacrifice of others.

On May 25, 1935, Stalin permanently withdrew the civil rights of those he scorned as "kulaks" by his simple marginal notation, "pravil'no" (correct) on an NKVD document. The faithful servant who had drafted the document, NKVD chief Henrikh Yagoda, was both a Jew and a man who knew too much. Having helped Stalin create the terror that would rack the Soviet Union for decades, Yagoda and his successor, Yezhov, would be accused of having gone too far. Stalin would then benevolently eliminate these mass murderers. He replaced them with the even more deadly Lavrenty Beria.

On September 15, 1935, Hitler's rubber-stamp "parliament" passed the Nuremberg Law restricting intermarriage between Jews and Gentiles, and prohibiting any role for Jews in public life. Brecht noted the occasion with a bitter and very fine poem about the public denigration of a Gentile woman who had slept with a Jew.[19] The poem does not deal with what happens to the Jewish lover.

On October 7, 1935, Brecht sailed for New York aboard the *Aquitania*. Before he left, a poem referring to Brecht as a "classic writer" was created and for years has been treated as though it were his. It was, however, one of the many that Steffin wrote capturing his style precisely. (Though the head of the Brecht Archive said for years that the poem is by Steffin, it has again been included in the new Brecht edition of poems.)[20] Steffin gave the work the cumbersome title: "When the Classic [Author] Departed on Monday, October 7, 1935, Denmark Wept." She ironically compared his leaving to Columbus's setting sail for the New World. At one level, however, the poem may well have been serious in intent. Had not the Soviets called him "the great master"? Was not Crassus treating him as such? Did not Steffin say in some letters she was "enslaved" to him? Did not Benjamin, one of the great critical minds of the twentieth century, treat him with awe?

As he left for America, Brecht was worried about the domestic situation he was leaving behind. Mari Hold was planning to marry while he was away, and her fiancé was chronically jealous of Brecht. Brecht wrote a three-page poem to Mari, ostensibly on her marriage.[21] Poetically inconsequential but psychologically revealing, it described Brecht's reliance on servants to heat the stove and pull his bedroom curtains before he was up in the morning, to tend him all day, and finally to clean up after he went to bed at night. Perhaps because it so frankly revealed his pampered existence, Brecht did not publish the Hold poem during his lifetime. That he wrote it at all suggests how deeply he felt the loss of Mari. Decades later, Mari Hold-Ohm said she had not heard of this poem's existence and wondered if he had really written it.[22]

On December 21, Steffin boarded the SS *Ilmatar* to spend yet another winter in the Soviet Union. Once again, she felt harassed by the police in Denmark, and she also knew that the "master" wanted her in the Soviet Union to handle affairs there. Given the warnings that she had received in 1933 of the dangers of damp sea air, it is difficult to imagine a much worse thing than a trip to Russia by ship in late December for an active tuberculosis patient, but it was the cheapest way to go. Steffin and Crassus became close but chaste friends. As Crassus seemed to show no sexual interest in women, Brecht was relaxed about the friendship. When Steffin traveled, she and the Danish writer wrote to one another usually in Danish. Both to improve her Danish and to promote feminist ideals, Steffin translated Berlau's *Videre* into German though she had no hope of publishing a German edition of a work expressing such advanced views on women's rights.

Soon after Steffin's arrival in Moscow, the deadly visits of the NKVD fulfilling Stalin's quotas decimated those closest to her. *The Threepenny Novel*'s translator, Valentin Stenich, was to be one of those taken. Steffin wrote later to Benjamin, "It was an unpleasant winter, that is to say, the most unpleasant of my entire life, may God protect me from ever repeating it."[23] She was frequently on the move: on December 24 in Leningrad; on January 3–4 in Moscow; on January 26 in a sanatorium; on April 1 in Tiflis; on April 7 in Atatumen; on May 4 back in Moscow; on May 16 back in Leningrad.[24]

Steffin got Stenich's translation of the novel and took it to the publishers. As she knew, any association with "formalism" could lead directly to death. She wrote to Brecht: "I really desperately need your love, your love. Perhaps things are too difficult for me . . . my stomach heaves that I am nowhere 'at home.' Nowhere. I always have to beg for a place for me and my suitcase. I can't even buy books, where would I put them."[25] He did not respond to her pain but did send a long list of jobs to be done in "mecca." Thanks to Steffin, the German edition of *The Threepenny Novel* was on sale in the Soviet Union by March 1936. Brecht received three thousand convertible rubles for the Soviet edition. (A Soviet worker would have needed two full years of work to earn three thousand vastly inferior, nonconvertible rubles.) In addition, Steffin managed to get him six hundred rare gold rubles. The scale of Steffin's achievement was all the more staggering since the Soviets did not really want to publish Brecht's allegorical, nonsocialist realism.

Steffin wrote Brecht that she has been told "privately" "that it would not make much sense for Brecht to visit here [the Soviet Union] now."[26] In the middle of the Moscow winter, she wrote to Brecht: "It is cold here. I freeze a lot." She added she only managed to sleep four hours a night and that she longed to get letters from him.[27] Despite being ignored by Brecht except when he needed something, she did complete and sell to Koltsov a short story for 250 regular rubles.

Fortunately for Steffin, others were more considerate. She and Walter Benjamin, both somewhat lost souls overwhelmed by Brecht, had become warmly supportive of one another. Each seemed to instinctively understand the other's difficulties and accomplishments. In one of her frequent letters to Benjamin, she urged him to write something suitable for *Das Wort* as he would be paid in hard currency.[28] He was prone to suicidal depression, and his situation was barely helped by the minuscule monthly stipend from the exiled Frankfurt Institute. But Benjamin could not somehow adjust his writing to Moscow's needs, and Moscow was certainly not willing to adjust to him. A piece he had written on Goethe for the *Great Soviet Encyclopedia* in 1927–28 had been rejected by no less a figure than Anatole Lunacharski. Benjamin had felt even then that the Moscow editorial board had been too conservative and had acted "opportunistically."[29] Encouraged by Steffin, he tried again to write something to Moscow's taste. His perhaps most brilliant, enduring, and influential theoretical essay "The Work of Art in the Age of Mechanical Reproduction" would be rejected by the Moscow staff of *Das Wort* and privately by Brecht, who called its central concerns "fairly dreadful."[30] Nonetheless Benjamin, like so many others, could never make a real break from the charismatic Brecht.[31]

Before Brecht had sailed for the United States, he had written to Elisabeth Hauptmann in Saint Louis asking her to come to New York to meet him and take care of his affairs. She replied on June 29, asking for some financial help as she could ill afford to go to New York. Instead of addressing the money issue, Brecht attacked her, demanding she agree to resume the kind of intimacy they had had in Berlin. Hauptmann wrote back, saying his letter sounded as if he were "writing to a prison inmate." Deliberately using the formal "Sie" and alluding to his relationships with other women, she said, "I do not want to get involved in any of your hierarchical games, no matter how fine," and then said, "Let us completely end this kind of relationship between us, Brecht."[32]

She was fully aware, however, that with his rudimentary English, Brecht was likely to get little accomplished in New York without help. Though her sister was in Saint Louis, Hauptmann longed to be involved more fully in the pro-Communist, antifascist causes in which she so deeply believed. Her writing had not gone well in Saint Louis. She had a crushing teaching schedule and was living in a tiny flat, scraping by on an annual income of $450. As she was receiving no royalties in the

United States for what she had written with Brecht in Berlin, her only luxuries came out of a small inheritance she had from her mother. By the middle of 1935, all she had was $32.44, less than the $38.06 needed for a bus ticket to New York.[33] She decided to go anyway but not just to help Brecht. She hoped to persuade Soviet officials in New York to send her to Moscow in order to try to make a bigger contribution to the fight against Hitler.

At a lunch counter in Havre de Grace, Maryland, where she stopped during the trip, black passengers were supposed to sit at a separate counter. Always the activist for her beliefs, Hauptmann ostentatiously went and sat at that counter herself, and in solidarity rode the whole way in the back of the bus.[34] These experiences in America helped confirm her belief in communism, with its explicit credo of equality for all—black or white, male or female. She thought she detected less racism in New York. She was pleased to see plays like *They Shall Not Die* and *Stevedore*, which she thought sympathetic to blacks.

Brecht arrived at the end of October. Before coming to America, he had expressed some apprehension to Hanns Eisler (who was now touring the United States and would meet Brecht in New York) that America's current anti-Comintern stance could lead to difficulties for both of them. However, he was apparently helped by the fact that he was married to Weigel. "Your Jewish origins," he wrote to her, "really paid off."[35]

Brecht plunged into Theater Union rehearsals, controversy, and a new affair. Hauptmann had rented an apartment at 225 West 69th Street, with separate bedrooms for her and Brecht; and at all hours, he brought back the translator who had been assigned to him at the theater. Perhaps it only sounded as if the woman Brecht brought home really weighed 220 pounds, as Hauptmann later claimed.[36] That was not all that was causing Hauptmann concern. The Russian consulate had told her that no position could be found for her in Moscow. She was to stay on in America working for the party.

At the Theater Union, Brecht was trying to establish what he called in a note to Weigel "a nice little dictatorship."[37] Only the American set designer Mordecai ("Max") Gorelik seemed to understand what Brecht wanted when the playwright bellowed that he wanted a restrained style. Deeply taken with Brecht, Gorelik was not surprised when Brecht announced to him one day that he, Brecht, was "the Einstein of the new stage form." Eric Bentley believes Brecht could not have been serious. In 1969, I had a chance to speak with Max Gorelik. Asked whether Brecht was joking, Gorelik said, "No, certainly not."[38] Unlike Gorelik, most of the Theater Union people were appalled at the new Einstein's behavior. George Sklar remembered Brecht's outbursts as being "Hitlerian," exhibiting, he said, "the same apoplectic indulgence, the same ranting and shrieking associated with the German dictator."[39] Albert Maltz came to loathe him as a person who not only displayed "contentious arrogance" but also whose unbathed stench made working with him extremely difficult.[40]

When Brecht did not get unquestioning obedience from the cast, he went to the cultural head of the American Communist party, V. J. Jerome, to demand that the Theater Union as a whole submit to strict party discipline and begin obeying Brecht. Jerome did. The cast tried to accept Jerome's ukaze but found Brecht incapable of working in any kind of reasonably democratic way with them. Finally, composer and author were ordered to leave the theater. When the play opened on November 19, both Brecht and Eisler pointedly stayed away from the opening and went to a movie instead.

The Mother closed on December 15 after financial losses so great that the company never fully recovered. Brecht was wholly unwilling to acknowledge his role in the collapse. Instead, in a letter to Piscator, Brecht said he was through with the "so-called party theater" in New York and that he was turning his attention to Broadway producers who at least had some technical skills, whatever else they might lack. What Brecht did not say was that his interest in noncommercial political theater, though theoretically strong, was in everyday practice minimal. From his letter to Piscator and memo to Jerome, it seems clear that Brecht's alienation from the official Communist theater in New York was complete, except for personal ties to Gorelik and flattering letters to V. J. Jerome. Jerome seems unaware that in letters to others, Brecht regularly denigrated him.

Hauptmann accompanied Brecht to American publishers, hawking *The Threepenny Novel;* on their visits to producers, they brought with them *Round Heads, Peak Heads.* Neither work found takers. Through Hanns Eisler, who had managed to obtain a position at the progressive New School for Social Research in New York, Brecht was able to meet a number of people who were already prominent or who would become prominent in the American theater, including John Gassner, Archibald MacLeish, Marc Blitzstein and his wife, Eva Goldbeck. Brecht had an immediate effect on Blitzstein, whose 1936 experimental play *The Cradle Will Rock* was dedicated to the German playwright. Brecht also met briefly with Weill and Lenya, who had gotten back together again in Europe and who had emigrated to America in September 1935. Weill was beginning to flourish as brilliantly in America as he had in Berlin. Brecht also saw Georg Grosz, the great chronicler of the horror of Weimar Germany, but Grosz seemed wholly lost in New York.

Through Joseph Losey, Brecht met a young actor, John House-man. Houseman and Losey were deeply involved with the Federal Theater Project, run by Hallie Flanagan, who had studied theater in the Soviet Union. At the time of this meeting, they were just about to open an "epic" spectacle on the history of farm problems in the Midwest in the twenties and thirties, *One Third of a Nation*. The work involved "a rapid succession of short takes—pantomimes, skits, and radio broadcasts."[41] Though they had no prior knowledge of Brecht's work, they were familiar with Brecht's own source, the experimental theater of Tretiakov and Meyerhold.[42]

Brecht also met a young man by the name of Lee Strasberg. Despite the fact that Strasberg later became the high priest of the Stanislavsky school of method acting in America—the exact opposite of Brecht's preferred technique—they rehearsed a few scenes from *The Measures Taken* together. On January 27, Brecht told Strasberg, "The few rehearsals with you and your group have at least shown me that a revolutionary pedagogic theater is possible here too."[43] Brecht knew enough about the "Living Newspaper" by this time to know that federally funded performances of pedagogic theater were being done by Hallie Flanagan throughout the United States using out-of-work actors. So radical was Flanagan's work (and so influential, as radically outspoken plays would open with different casts simultaneously throughout the country) that a conservative Congress soon cut off her government funding.

Brecht had an encounter in New York with philosopher Sidney Hook, whom he had first met in Berlin some years before. Hook told Brecht of his doubts as to the legitimacy of the arrests that were taking place in the Soviet Union.[44] Zinoviev and Kamenev had already been in jail at the time of Brecht's visit to the Soviet Union in 1935. Brecht said, "The more innocent they are, the more they deserve to die." It was a statement as extreme as those Brecht had often made in Sternberg's hearing back in Berlin. Horrified, Hook showed Brecht the door and never saw him agin.

As 1935 came to an end, Brecht, still in New York, badly missed his traditional Christmas. A second Christmas would have to be held in Svendborg he instructed Weigel. He said he missed Christmas Day with her, Christmas night, and the Christmas tree. Meanwhile, she should "keep [him] in [her] memory" and should sign letters "deine" (yours), with the word used here, as the context makes plain, not in the merely polite sense but in the sense of real possession. In a separate note to his then eleven-year-old son Stefan, he told the child that in the absence of his father he was to consider himself the head of the household.[45] A few days later, in a New Year's Eve note to Weigel, Brecht complained that Christmas in New York had been a dull affair "in the bosom of the childless Eislers" as someone sang "Scottish ballads without end." He closed the letter: "I would have liked to have taken you to bed, Helli, the same as every year. I kiss you. b." Then he tacked on a business postscript almost as long as the letter itself. She was to send a copy of the original *Threepenny Opera* contract to Weill who was now back together with Lenya and living at the Hotel Saint Moritz, Central Park South, New York. And she was to send also only the paragraph concerning *The Threepenny Opera* from the other disputed general contract with Wreede.

Before leaving New York, Brecht saw every current gangster movie. He also took in several Broadway shows including *Waiting for Lefty, Porgy and Bess*, and *Green Pastures*. Hauptmann collected for him, just as she had in Berlin, a suitcase full of clippings, including material on the murder of the gangster Dutch Schultz, which happened while Brecht was in New York, and anything else that could be found on "gangland wars and slayings, loan-sharking, robberies, corrupt public officials, murders of respected citizens, and other ills of life in the capitalistic metropolis."[46] She also appears to have translated for him sections of Louis Adamic's novel *Dynamite*. These will show up later, virtually verbatim, in the Brecht poem "How the Ship *Oskawa* Was Taken Apart by Her Crew."[47]

On the eve of leaving, Brecht went to the German consulate in New York and asked to have his passport renewed. Unless Brecht had inside information that he would somehow be protected, this was an extremely risky move. German consular officials were under specific orders to confiscate the passport of anyone appearing on the official list of those whose German citizenship had been taken away. Despite his name being on this list as of the previous June, for some reason an official turned a blind eye. Instead of his old passport being confiscated, Brecht was issued a new German passport, valid until January 27, 1941.[48] With this priceless document in hand, he boarded the *Majestic* to return to Europe. He left having undercut by his behavior his ties with American theater on the left.

Apparently, during the journey back to Europe, he wrote the short but touching poem "Why Should My Name Be Remembered."[49] These moments when he is indubitably alone are of particular importance to anyone trying to establish who wrote what in the Brecht canon. When he is alone, he almost always expresses himself in poetry rather than in drama. Often, the poems are either about himself or devoted to various kinds of violent subjects. Such poems vary enormously in quality. Sometimes, as is the poem about the loss of German citizenship, they are almost completely lifeless and wholly lacking any sign of having been written by one of the very greatest masters of the German language. But then, another poem will come along that has the radical phosphorence that marked the verse that won over Herbert Ihering in 1924 and Elias Canetti in 1928.

Brecht's shipboard poem of January 1936 is somewhere at the midpoint between his best and worst verse. He says he used to think he would be remembered in times to come, but now, just as melted snow is displaced by new snow, so his poems will be replaced in future generations and his name will not be remembered. The thought of being forgotten will haunt him until his death. Back in Denmark, he will beg Berlau to learn all his poems by heart, apparently fearing that they might otherwise not survive. Perhaps he knew that Soviet poets fearing NKVD raids tried to have their poems survive by having close friends and relatives commit them to memory.[50]

"A Quagmire of Infamous Crimes. All of the Scum . . . , All the Parasites . . . Were All Nested Together" (1936–37)

Back in Copenhagen, Brecht wrote at once to Moscow to explain the delay of some long-overdue work. The fault, he said, was Steffin's hospitalization, but "she will be out in the next few days, and you can rely on the fact that everything will be taken care of promptly."[1] In fact, she was so ill at this time that she barely had the strength to write a letter.[2] She told Walter Benjamin that she was suffering desperately from the cold in the Soviet Union and that she was having recurrent problems with an ear that was now tubercular. Nevertheless, she checked herself out of the Alekein Memorial Sanitorium and went back to work for Brecht.

With his new passport, Brecht presented himself to the Danish police on February 20. He had "spent some time abroad," the police report casually notes. A nearly ritual six-month extension was given him, and he soon left for London.

In March, *The Measures Taken* was produced in England as *The Expedient,* featuring the London Labour Choral Union under Alan Bush. Performances were given in London at the Westminster Theatre, the Shoreditch Town Hall, and the Co-operative Hall at Tooting.[3] We do not know whether Brecht felt odd about producing this particular play when, as we know, his doubts about the infallibility of Moscow had existed privately for years. Brecht wrote to Walter Benjamin that he had come to London to write a filmscript.[4] German emigré actor Fritz Kortner had arranged to get him a job working on the film *Bajazzo.* Though he had little knowledge of screenwriting, Brecht was still paid the comparatively large sum of six hundred pounds for a couple of weeks work.[5] He also arranged a deal for an English edition of *The Threepenny Novel.* Desmond I. Vesey, who had bought and translated *The Threepenny Opera* for the firm of Robert Hale, had known Hauptmann in Berlin prior to the Reichstag fire. Vesey led Brecht to W. H. Auden and Christopher Isherwood, both of whom would become useful to him in the years ahead. Another deal was struck with the emigré Berthold Fles to supervise the translation of three Brecht plays, for which Auden was to be paid 150 pounds.[6] Though Hauptmann had played a major role in creating all three, and she was expert in English, she was not informed of the deal.

Having finally completed her Moscow assignments, Steffin got herself to London by May 30. From 134 Abbey Road, she wrote to Benjamin: "Healthwise unchanged, that is to say, not improved, but not worse."[7] She saw little of Brecht though he was just up the street at 148 Abbey Road. He was attending, in a rather desultory way, yet another Moscow-organized writers' conference. Though he failed to attend a conference session devoted to the idea of producing an encyclopedia modeled on Diderot's original French work, he wrote to say he was "extraordinarily interested in the idea" and that he had proposed just such a thing sometime before to Comrade Johannes R. Becher.[8] Then he wrote a poem, not published for many years, in which the idea of doing an encyclopedia is lampooned and the person who had proposed it, André Malraux, is mercilessly satirized.[9] According to Steffin's unpublished diary, in London she and Brecht met a young photographer named Ellen Rosenberg who had just left the Soviet Union. Her experiences with the NKVD reminded them of Dante's *Inferno*. Brecht was visibly frightened by these accounts but said he was determined to keep the information strictly to himself.

Steffin returned alone to Scandinavia in late July. Brecht said he had business in Paris. What he actually had was an assignation there with Koltsov's common-law wife, Maria Osten, whom he now also tried to persuade to join him in Denmark.[10] Steffin was so sick upon her arrival in Copenhagen that she went straight to the Øresunds Hospital. But soon, needing once again to renew her residence permit, she had herself discharged again. Steffin's position was desperate in every way. Her illness advanced unchecked as Brecht's demands or police harassment prevented her from staying in the hospital long enough for serious treatment. As her illness had advanced, Brecht's sexual interest had shifted elsewhere, and she felt ever more abandoned.

In the Soviet Union, now seemingly random arrests were a nightly occurrence. In the West, Steffin's connections with the Soviet Union reduced her chances of getting a residency permit. She decided to resort to a radical expedient. On August 29, 1936, she entered a pro forma marriage with a man she had barely met, a Dane named Svend Jensen Juul. The "husband" came courtesy of the Communist party. Neither Juul nor Steffin was sexually interested in the other, but as the wife of a Danish citizen, she could finally get residence papers and an invaluable Danish passport.

With three thousand convertible and four hundred gold rubles from Moscow, the *Threepenny* and *Measures* proceeds from England, and the house paid for, Brecht was wealthy by rural Danish standards.

By comparison, when Hanns and Hilde Eisler came for a long stay, they paid eleven kroner (a dollar a day per person) for what amounted to a three-room suite at a local tourist hotel.[11] Brecht could keep several Danish neighbors on his payroll. Lazar Rasmussen emptied his toilet every day; Solveig Hansen handled the wood for the stoves and emptied the ashes; and Mie Andersen and her daughter did the household work that Mari Hold had done before she married the local butcher.[12] Visitors for Brecht and Weigel were housed by neighbors such as the Sørensens who needed the money from the rental of rooms. Exile had become gemütlich and even sometimes crowded as a stream of visitors came to this remote, peaceful, cheap, and comfortable area of Denmark, mainly to see Brecht. Weigel's Jewish family and friends could not readily obtain travel documents, but Brecht's "Aryan" father and brother came to visit, as did his daughter Hanne. Several old friends from the Augsburg and Berlin days, including Orge Pfanzelt and Rudolf Hartmann, came there also on holiday.

Developments in Germany and the Soviet Union were worrisome. In one letter so faded in the archive copy that it is not possible to say with absolute certainty who sent it (but almost certainly from Bernard von Brentano), Brecht was clearly warned about the extralegal activities of Stalin, referred to in the letter as a "wretched Georgian." The NKVD was destroying people without any semblance of due legal process, while others such as Maxim Gorki were living in luxury. Brecht, who had defended the activities of Soviet intelligence agencies in an earlier letter, denounced neither the NKVD nor the "wretched Georgian."

In Nazi Germany, Jews were being routinely dismissed from employment. When the Jewish family owning the distinguished publishing firm of S. Fischer Verlag were forced into exile, Brecht's old friend Peter Suhrkamp—who had befriended and apparently tried to help protect the Fischer family—was permitted by Goebbels to take over. When Goebbels later included Austrian cultural enterprises under his Ministry of Propaganda and forced Max Reinhardt and Carl Zuckmayer into exile, Nazi party–member Herbert von Karajan, Caspar Neher's intimate friend composer Rudolf Wagner-Régeny, and Brecht's old supporter Herbert Ihering all advanced.[13]

As the state radio was purged of Jews, the "Aryanized" Arnolt Bronnen was placed in charge of the embryonic television capability of the Third Reich. While his colleague and friend Leni Riefenstahl filmed the 1936 Berlin Olympic Games, Bronnen was there with television cameras. Riefenstahl's film showed the world a clean, orderly, peaceful Berlin with Hitler holding an olive branch and surrounded by cooing doves;[14] however, Bronnen shot Hitler applauding only warlike sports. It was becoming clear to Bronnen that he was working for people wholly bent on war. But he remained intrigued by the possibilities of television, developing programs that gave Hitler and Goebbels, in Bronnen's own words, "nice private pleasure."[15]

In Moscow, hard currency funds, which were derived overwhelmingly from the use of slave labor, were used both for a global intelligence network and for propaganda. When Brecht saw the first issue of *Das Wort*, he told Piscator it made him "want to throw up."[16] But he gave up neither his editorship nor the hard currency income. Brecht was preaching to the converted. Though Piscator had been a deeply committed Communist since at least 1918, he now believed that Lazar Kaganovich, head of Russian railroads who supervised Soviet film production on the side, had "reduced Russian film making to the same abysmal level as the worst crap produced in Hollywood."[17] After Piscator told Kaganovich this to his face and then left the country, word reached him in Paris that the organization that he had headed in the Soviet Union, MORT (Mezhounarodvoe Objedinenie Revoljutsionnykh Teatrov— the International Association of Revolutionary Theaters), was dead and that there was "no need for him to return."[18] Piscator was lucky that only MORT was dead. In ferocity and scale of pursuit of "enemies," Kaganovich earns a place in history comparable to Himmler, Hitler, Beria, and Stalin.[19] "During the years [Piscator] had spent in the Soviet Union," writes Günther Rühle, "the political dreamer had been brought face to face with the hard, brutal reality of Stalinism. Brief notes—a poem written on the murder of Trotsky, for example—indicate that he was planning to write a play of his own which would question the right of a State or Party to kill people."[20]

Piscator now sought to follow Hanns Eisler to New York's New School for Social Research. This unique institution was run by Dr. Alvin S. Johnson, who was extraordinarily understanding of the problems of emigrés. A job was found for Piscator, and he began to coax Dr. Johnson on Brecht's behalf. As Piscator knew, the Soviet Union could no more be a haven for the maverick Brecht than it had been for him. German emigré writers in Moscow raced to denounce their closest friends, relatives, and colleagues, hoping to postpone the day when they themselves would be taken.[21] There were vehement denunciations of Carola Neher, Maria Osten, and Koltsov from the very same people who had been on Koltsov's capacious foreign payroll. Carola Neher was arrested in Moscow on July 25, 1936.[22] The NKVD claimed Gustav von Wangenheim and Neher's husband, Anatol Becker, gave evidence against her.[23] Among those attacking Neher were the future leaders of the German Democratic Republic, Walter Ulbricht and Wilhelm Pieck.

By late 1936, many were aware that the Soviet Union was a regime of lawlessness and terror. André Gide's indictment of Stalin's policies *Back from the USSR* argued that "from month to month the state of the USSR gets worse. It diverges more and more from what we had hoped it was—it would be," and that Trotsky "is far more the enemy of fascism than is Stalin himself, and it is as a revolutionary and anti-fascist that he denounces Stalin's compromises." Gide's attack came just as Nikolai Bukharin, at a meeting of the Central Committee in September 1936, accused Stalin and the secret police of a "terrible plot against the Party and the State."[24] Astonishingly, a majority of the Central Committee at first backed Bukharin, but Stalin was able to bludgeon enough people to change their votes later so that Bukharin again became the accused.

Koltsov and Osten, who had invited Gide to the Soviet Union, were now in mortal danger. To further complicate things, Thomas Mann wrote asking Koltsov if the Soviet Union was no longer an asylum for refugees but a prison cell?[25] Victor Serge was known to be writing his indictment of the Soviet Union. Finally, an article in Switzerland by Ignazio Silone, the well-known Italian writer and former staunch supporter of the Soviet Union, charged that the show trials in Moscow were based on torture. Silone pointedly drew parallels between fascist practices, which were known to him personally in Italy, and what Stalin was doing in the Soviet Union. Silone said he "refused to become a Fascist, not even a red Fascist."[26] He ostentatiously withdrew from any contact with *Das Wort*, whose first issue was now in preparation in Denmark and Moscow. Koltsov needed to find a Western writer willing to offset these well-known voices. To Koltsov's relief, Lion Feuchtwanger agreed.[27] Meanwhile, a transparently anti-Semitic campaign against Gide began in the Soviet Union. (Gide's name was pronounced in Russian like "Yid.")

Brecht was already receiving payment for work (mainly Steffin's) on *Das Wort*. Berlau was working with Brecht on a play called *Die Leiden und Freuden der kleineren Seeleute*, or *The Sorrows and Pleasures of Common Sailors*, apparently never finished. Brecht was making suggestions for Steffin's play *The True Life of Jakob Geherda*. Steffin was also working intensively with Brecht on a cycle of one-act plays about contemporary Germany to be called *Fear and Misery of the Third Reich*. Of great importance to this latter project was the visit of Grete's mother and father from Berlin, whose experiences she used as her factual basis for writing the play.[28]

In November 1936, a commercial production of *Round Heads, Peak Heads* was due to open in Copenhagen. Brecht urged the theater company to break with its usual practice of operating as a nonhierarchical ensemble.[29] He said the company should exploit the name of its most famous member, Lulu Ziegler. Just before opening night, Maria Lazar (who had helped Michaëlis rescue Weigel and Brecht in 1933) was told in Weigel and Brecht's presence that it would be best if she did not attend the premiere.[30] Lazar saw this (as she told Karin Michaëlis) as a direct attempt to avoid having immigrants of Jewish origin antagonize the bourgeoisie of Copenhagen. "With such methods, Karin," said Lazar, "nazism was brought into existence in Germany."[31] The response to the play was in any case lukewarm.

Berlau had managed to get the Weill-Brecht ballet, *The Seven Deadly Sins*, on the program of the Royal Theater for a couple of performances. Brecht wrote Karl Korsch in New York that he had been lucky to get his residence permit extended in Denmark after putting on plays like this. In fact, Danish police ignored the entire issue. The middle- and upper-class population of Denmark was largely committed to key elements of social progress advocated by both the Communist party and the Social Democrats. Brecht's plays were not earthshaking or particularly radical, which is why they could be produced at the state-financed Royal Theater.

As Steffin worked on the plays on which much of Brecht's world fame now rests and on the translations that were often the main source of income for Brecht and his collaborators, her diary records his frequent absences, her sexual frustration, and her horror at his stream of affairs. One poem admonishes:

> *Imagine: all the women you've ever had*
> *Come to your bed now. oh, only a pitiful few*
> *Are still handsome. none, you think, is worth looking at now.*
> *But they all stand stern and silent*
> *They all want their pleasure from you tonight*
> *And after you've done it for one*
> *She stands aside and gestures toward the next.*
> *Lustfully they line up. you*
> *Are lost. those you had once picked out*
> *For your own pleasure now use you as the butt of a bitter joke.*
> *I also join this line*
> *Totally without shame, I wait my turn*
> *You lie there wretched, ill and pale.*[32]

By late 1936, it seemed doubtful that Steffin would survive the year, though getting her into a hospital was difficult.[33] On one occasion, Lund said that Steffin needed treatment at once but Brecht replied, "Now's not the time for her to be lying in the hospital, when I need her."[34] Fortunately, Lund insisted, and Steffin was placed on a ward for the desperately ill, which she saw as "a bastion of death."[35] On November 26, a woman in the adjoining "dying room" expired and was replaced by an old man. Grete watched as the old man died, and nurses washed him, bound up his jaw, and adjusted his limbs so that he lay there "nice and orderly and symmetrically."

But Grete's powers of recuperation and her wish to get back in harness were so strong that two weeks later she had herself discharged from the hospital. On December 10, she wrote to Benjamin: "I got very good news here, my lungs are completely quiet, and my ear is healed . . . I have things good here with a single room and with my typewriter."[36] The hospital record does not agree. The doctors said that though there might be periods of remission, she was on an irreversible course toward an early death.

Stress in the inner circle never subsided. One New Year's, when the Berlau-Lunds were visiting Skovsbostrand, things boiled over. Berlau and Weigel had been peacefully playing chess together when suddenly one of Lund's children saw the two rolling around on the floor of the house in a hair-tugging match.[37] At times, Berlau wondered if Brecht deliberately promoted fights in the entourage. She wrote later, "With astonishment I experienced years ago how Brecht would get into a fight with Helli or Grete in order that he could then leave with me, or that he was then left in peace if he went to his own room, as that was what he wanted."[38] In this same letter, Berlau claimed that during the emigration years, Brecht was "Unmenschlich grausam" (inhumanly horrible) to Weigel, a view that was repeatedly confirmed by various male and female observers, party and nonparty members alike.

The rather plain legal wife and the tubercular lover sometimes tried to set up a united front against their beautiful, healthy rival, but whenever anyone complained, Brecht talked loftily of communism and its goals. They owed it to this "third thing" to get right back to work and not give in to the bourgeois disease of jealousy. But apparently the "third thing" did not prevent him from feeling jealous of other men and of the women together. While Berlau and Weigel were talking one night, they caught him peering through the keyhole to "find out what we might be doing in his absence."[39]

Despite having been repulsed by Carola Neher during his visit in the spring of 1935, Brecht asked Feuchtwanger to try to deliver a poem to her during his visit to Moscow in late 1936. Brecht's short, erotically charged poem begins:

> *I showed you years ago*
> *How you should wash yourself in the early morning*

With little bits of ice in the water
In the small copper washbasin.

At the end of the poem, he says he has heard she is in prison. "How,"
he asks, "are your mornings? Are you still able to do things for yourself?
Full of hope, responsibly, with lovely movements, in an exemplary
way?"[40] Brecht was grotesquely far from reality if this was how he
imagined Moscow penal conditions. The reality is that Neher attempted
suicide when first taken to Moscow's central political prison, the Lu-
bianka.[41] Later, Neher was held in solitary confinement for four years,
where she was often starved and had at least one near-fatal bout with
typhus. Carola Neher was not alone among Brecht's friends then in the
hands of the NKVD. Even as Feuchtwanger was arranging to interview
Stalin, Béla Kun was in an overflowing Moscow prison, the Bytykri.
The bloody, beaten Kun was made to stand for as long as twenty hours
at a stretch before he would collapse.[42] Just weeks before Feuchtwanger's arrival, Ernst Ottwalt and Waltraut Nicolas were arrested.
Nicolas would survive the camps and write two volumes of extraordinary memoirs. Ottwalt would die in the middle of 1943 in the gulag.

As an honored guest of the Soviet Union, Feuchtwanger and a
lovely female traveling companion were put up at the best hotel in
Moscow. Early in his stay, he met the newly assigned American ambassador, Joseph E. Davies, whose views partly shaped his own. In his long
memoir *Mission to Moscow*, the ambassador would write glowingly of
Stalin: "His brown eye is exceedingly kindly and gentle. A child would
like to sit in his lap and a dog would sidle up to him."[43] Of the Radek
trial, Mr. Davies wrote, "To have assumed that this proceeding was
invented and staged as a project of dramatic political fiction would be
to presuppose the creative genius of a Shakespeare and the genius of a
Belasco in stage production."[44] Unfortunately, as we now know, the
trials were dramatic political fiction. After a prisoner was first broken
by NKVD torture, their physical health was then restored as far as
possible while their script was prepared and rehearsals commenced.[45]

Before the Radek trial got under way, Feuchtwanger met with
Stalin. The meeting began with an exchange of politenesses.[46] "Might
he," asked Stalin, "smoke a pipe?" Feuchtwanger said, "I am just recovering from a bad cold," at which the Soviet leader put down the pipe.
When asked about his impressions of Moscow, Feuchtwanger answered at first in general terms, praising the beauty of the city before
going on to ask almost offhandly if "Stalin was not bothered by the fact
that his enormous picture decorated all the streets of the city?" Stalin
answered indirectly, "One must shout very loudly in order to be heard
in Vladivostok." Feuchtwanger said that he knew Radek personally

from Radek's work in Germany and asked if Stalin could not pardon at least some of the accused. Turning to the person who was serving as his interpreter, *Pravda* editor B. M. Tal, Stalin said, "This is the kind of person you bring in to meet me." Stalin's seemingly casual remark to Tal was deliberate, as was most of what Stalin did. Once Feuchtwanger left the Soviet Union, the NKVD seized Tal after they were given a red pencil note from Stalin himself.[47] At the meeting with Feuchtwanger, absentmindedly lighting his pipe, Stalin said that he had already pardoned Radek once but he, like the others on trial, was an incorrigible Trotskyist.

Presumably not knowing that in Stalin's Soviet Union such charges were routinely invented, Feuchtwanger wrote: "When I saw Pjatakov, Radek, and his friends, and heard what they said and how they said it, I was forced to accept the evidence of my senses. . . . If that was lying or prearranged, then I don't know what truth is."[48] When Feuchtwanger left to return to France on February 5, 1937, he presumably guessed nothing of the systematic breaking, then the careful restoration, of the physical health of individuals that preceded appearances in theatrical productions presented as "courts of justice."

Feuchtwanger's view would be adopted by countless other Soviet and Western intellectuals (despite warning signals from people such as Gide, Silone, and Thomas Mann). Brecht, for instance, wrote: "We must try to discern behind the actions of the accused what was to them a conceivable political conception—a conception which led them deep into a quagmire of infamous crimes. All of the scum both domestic and foreign, all the parasites, the professional criminals and spies, were all nested together: with all of this scum, they shared the same goal. I am convinced that this is the truth, and that this truth will sound likely even in Western Europe and even to hostile readers."[49]

Brecht echoes two of the supporting cast at the Grand Guignol spectacle masquerading as a legal trial. Andrei Vyshinsky, Stalin's direct accomplice, spoke of the defendants as "scum," "stinking carrion," and "dung."[50] Koltsov wrote: "When they stand up and start describing their monstrous crimes in detail, sometimes with the crestfallen look of repentant sinners, sometimes with the cynical familiarity of inveterate rogues, you feel like jumping up and shouting, thumping your fist down on the table and seizing these filthy, blood-smeared blackguards by the throats, grabbing hold of them and finishing them off yourself."[51]

27

" 'Is This Signature Yours?' 'I Put It There, after Torture . . . Terrible Torture.' " (1937–38)

It was an unusually harsh winter on the Riviera when Feuchtwanger returned from Moscow. Over the nearby Pyrenees, civil war was raging with Hitler and Mussolini backing Franco as he tried to topple Spain's democratically elected government.[1] While Western governments turned a blind eye, the Soviet Union tried to stop the establishment of another fascist regime in Europe. Against a backdrop of rapidly advancing fascism and anti-Semitism, Feuchtwanger completed *Moscow 1937—A Travel Report for My Friends*. By May, it was in print in England, with editions in other languages following fast.[2] The book gave the Soviet Union and Stalin an almost perfect report card. Trotsky was denounced in ringing terms; the guilt of those who had been tried in Moscow was confirmed; the use of court martial proceedings in the Soviet Union was explained as a precaution in face of the war that everyone saw on the horizon; and, Feuchtwanger said, the rights of Jews were being safeguarded in the Soviet Union in an exemplary manner.[3] Though a large number of those included in the purge trials were Jewish, Feuchtwanger had become convinced that their Jewish origins played no part in their having been brought to trial.

The work was a propaganda bonanza for Stalin. A Russian edition of two hundred thousand copies was brought out at breakneck speed with tens of thousands of rubles going to Feuchtwanger's account.[4] Apparently, when Bukharin was arrested in 1937, the NKVD handed him a copy of the book to convince him his case was hopeless.[5] Bukharin agreed to participate in a farce of a "trial," but Bukharin's wife, Anna Larina Bukharina, had memorized her husband's last testament before the NKVD had taken him away. "I feel my helplessness," Bukharin told her, "before a hellish machine, which, probably by the use of medieval methods, now possesses pulverizing power, which manufactures organized slanders while striding audaciously and confidently ahead. The organs of the NKVD are now made up in the majority by depraved organizations which are themselves made up of demoralized, idealless, well-cared-for bureaucrats who use the authority of the former intelligence agency the Cheka to cater to Stalin's sickly suspiciousness."[6]

Bukharin himself faced the full force of the "hellish machine." He was brutalized until he was willing to say the opposite of the statement he had left with his wife. He hoped to save his young, beautiful wife and his infant son; and he hoped that eventually Russia would have sane leaders who would put the original goals of the revolution back on track.

A call went out from Moscow for another Paris conference of intellectuals—this one in the late summer of 1937. Malraux and Antoine de Saint-Exupéry came prepared to lend aircraft and piloting skills to the imperiled Spanish government. Hemingway and Langston Hughes came from the United States. From the Soviet Union came Koltsov, Osten, and Ehrenburg. Ruth Berlau was there as a reporter. Brecht arrived when the show was really over. All was not harmony. Gide's recent defection still cast a shadow that Feuchtwanger's book could not wholly blot out. Franz Werfel said Feuchtwanger's work was a cover-up for Stalin. Marta Feuchtwanger jumped to her husband's defense, apparently unaware of Stalin's privileged intelligentsia, "When one speaks of the sufferings of the Russian people, one shouldn't forget that everyone shares in that poverty—there are no class differences there." "Shut up," said Werfel, "you don't understand a thing about politics."[7]

Many speeches at the conference were long and fiery, including one Brecht had sent by mail.[8] He arrived late, complaining his invitation had arrived at the last minute.[9] "Culture," he had written in his speech, "for long, much too long, now defended only by intellectual weapons though attacked by material weapons, culture must now be defended with material weapons."[10] These fighting words were exactly what Ruth Berlau wanted to hear from the usually politically timorous Brecht. Koltsov, now a general in the Soviet forces in Spain, was also delighted. He arranged for a private aircraft to take him to his duty station in Madrid, and hoped Brecht and Berlau would join him. Brecht had no such intention. "I can't imagine," he said, "living in a Madrid hotel being hit by thirty whistling shells a day and, as it were, writing a play on the side."[11] Appalled at Brecht's decision and encouraged by Koltsov (as much a womanizer as Brecht was), Berlau decided to fly to Madrid with the general. On the night before her departure, Brecht brought a half-bottle of champagne to the hotel where he and Ruth were staying.[12] Slatan Dudow had been waiting all day long to see him about a Paris production of a Steffin-Brecht version of J. M. Synge's Riders to the Sea, but Brecht said he was too tired to talk. Upstairs with Ruth, after a glass of champagne, he fell asleep at once.

After Berlau left, Brecht spent some time with Maria Osten and with the Feuchtwangers at lovely Sanary-sur-Mer. He returned to Paris at Ernst Josef Aufricht's invitation to attend rehearsals of The Three-

penny Opera due to open at the commercial Théâtre de l'Etoile on September 28. Brecht evinced little interest in a production done in a language he barely understood, which he had not been invited to direct. He engaged a lawyer to try to collect some royalties from it despite the still-unresolved dispute he had with Felix Bloch Erben in Berlin. The play opened to poor notices and did poorly at the box office.

After Maria Osten left to cover the war in Spain, Helene Weigel came from Denmark to play the lead in Dudow's Paris German-language production of the Synge adaptation *Señora Carrar's Rifles*. Based partly on newspaper accounts about the Spanish Civil War, the play was about a mother who wishes to keep her sons from going to war. (Later, after the war had been lost, the play's pacificist orientation would be changed.) Brecht showed his usual desultory enthusiasm for an emigré production that paid him nearly nothing. Before the show opened in late October, he had returned to Denmark. From there he nagged his lawyer about *Threepenny* royalties. Steffin's diary for October 20, 1937, reads, "b COMING." With Berlau in Spain and Weigel in Paris, Steffin hoped to have Brecht to herself. But, by November 1937, with the Spanish situation rapidly deteriorating, Ruth Berlau had decided to return to Scandinavia to help the Spanish war effort in her own way by staging a Copenhagen production of *Señora Carrar's Rifles*.

With Brecht gone, Weigel met with friends, trying to find a way to support herself and finally leave Brecht. She talked extensively with the actress Steffi Spira, whom she had met in *A Man's a Man* in Berlin. Spira had great sympathy for Weigel's difficulties, but she and Weigel could find no way out that Weigel was able to accept.[13] Weigel spent most of the rest of 1937 shuttling between Paris, Zurich, Vienna, and Prague, desperately trying, as she had the year before, to establish a separate existence.

Sensing Weigel's dangerous dissatisfaction, Brecht wrote an unusual number of letters to her while she was away. He reminded her constantly of the children and their need of her. Either not willing or not able to take care of the children himself, Brecht lodged the two of them either at a nearby hotel or with their neighbor, Mie Andersen, who also came over regularly to prepare all Brecht's meals.[14] He sent Weigel a small poem, "The Actress in Exile," praising her way of preparing to perform, "letting her noble shoulders fall forward in the manner that those who work hard do."[15] He sent lists of tasks for her to do, checking his Swiss bank account, buying a copy of Mommsen's *Roman History*, and trying to collect royalty money from Universal Edition in Vienna.

Though Weigel did get a few small offers to perform in Prague and Paris, it became clear that her quest for an independent financial base was nearly hopeless. It did not help that Brecht had not put his full weight behind the Paris *Señora Carrar's Rifles* production nor that in Prague, Brecht had pointedly ignored requests for cooperation from Emil Burian, the main exponent there of the kind of political theater for which Weigel was best suited. Meanwhile, Brecht constantly called her back to domestic duty. Finally, Weigel returned in time to arrange the kind of old-fashioned Christmas on which Brecht doted. Not that she saw a lot of him otherwise. Once he had succeeded in getting her to return to him, he largely ignored her. By December, Berlau was back from Spain, and he was often with her in Copenhagen trying to set up Scandinavian productions that could produce some cash. He made sure Steffin was working as fast as possible, despite her illness and poverty.

While Berlau had been away in Spain, Brecht, all too aware of Koltsov's allure, worried about losing Berlau to a man far bolder in his commitment to revolution than himself. Hemingway, who used Koltsov as his model for Karkov in *For Whom the Bell Tolls*, wrote, "Karkov was the most intelligent man he had ever met. He had more brains and more inner dignity and outer insolence and humor than any man he had ever known."[16] Hemingway gives Karkov a wife (clearly Maria Osten) but notes a mistress in Spain, someone "well constructed" with a "mahogany-colored head," a description that fits Berlau. Unwilling to deal directly with his worries, Brecht sent Berlau a poem as a kind of mantra. She was to say to herself all the time:

> *I must look after myself*
> *Carefully choosing my path*
> *And fearing any drop of rain*
> *That could hit me.*[17]

In besieged Madrid, the danger to Brecht was from Koltsov; and the danger to Berlau was from bombs and shells not rain.

From Madrid, Koltsov spoke regularly on a private line to the Kremlin. "A telephone call reached me direct from Moscow," wrote Koltsov, "I heard a voice on the line, one of the editors of *Pravda*: 'How does the situation look?' 'The Fascists have almost reached the river . . . A real battle is being fought.' 'A real battle is being fought?' 'Yes, a real battle, we hope for reinforcements.' 'You're to receive substantial reinforcements?' All I had really said was 'we hope for reinforcements,' but the voice on the other end of the line asked again with renewed emphasis: 'You're to receive substantial reinforcements?' The voice and the question reminded me all of a sudden that outside beleaguered Madrid, helpless and isolated as we were, there was a world divided into two enemy camps and that both were waiting for news as to how this battle would end . . . I yelled with all my might into the receiver: 'Yes, very strong reinforcements expected any day now and even without them we will be able to hold the city.' "[18] On one occasion Koltsov told Ehrenburg: "Other people write novels. But what will remain of me after I've gone. Newspaper articles are ephemeral stuff. Even [a] historian won't find them useful, because we don't show in our articles what's going on in Spain, only what ought to be happening."

As had been the case in Germany before 1933, Moscow regularly divided and lied to friends and enemies. Those who supported Trotsky, though dying by the thousands in Spain, were nevertheless called by Stalin "agents of fascism." Antonov-Oysenko, hero of the storming of the Winter Palace, tried to build a bridge between the various groups. For his pains, he would be charged with trafficking with the enemy and executed. In Hemingway's account, Karkov says: "Certainly we destroy such veritable fiends and dregs of humanity and the treacherous dogs of generals and the revolting spectacle of admirals unfaithful to their trust. These are destroyed. They are not assassinated." The reality was more bizarre than anything Hemingway's fiction might make of it.

In real life, in order to stop the collaboration that a paranoid Stalin feared among Trotskyists, anarcho-syndicalists, and Communist feminist groups who wanted to fight equally with men, German emigré Walter Ulbricht toured Spain identifying anyone deemed not totally loyal to Stalin. People were killed on the spot or sent to Moscow for examination by a tribunal like the one in Hauptmann's and Brecht's *The Measures Taken*.[19]

From Spain, Ulbricht went to Paris to reshape on Stalinist lines the so-called Popular Front Committee (PFC). By October 1, 1937, a number of committee members, including Heinrich Mann and Jakob Walcher, signed a letter addressed to the Central Committee of the German Communist party in exile protesting Ulbricht's behavior. In a November 13, 1937, in a letter to Ulbricht himself, the PFC charged, "You are weakening the popular front movement at a time when its establishment within and outside Germany is more necessary than ever before."[20] But Ulbricht, with Stalin, held to his position. By 1938, virtually all the writers who had previously been willing to work closely with the Comintern and their publisher Willi Münzenberg would be driven out or murdered by the NKVD.[21]

Before leaving Spain, Berlau apparently told Brecht in a fairly offhand way that she would be arriving in Denmark by ship perhaps on such and such a date. Brecht met the ship, but, though he recognized Gerhart Eisler as he came down the gangplank to report back to his Comintern station in Copenhagen, he did not see Ruth Berlau. With boldness typical of her, she had taken up with a man she had met aboard ship and had decided to sail with him to the next port. The man was

Georg Branting, who happened to be both very charming and a highly influential Swedish parliament member.

Brecht was furious as he made his long way home, but by the end of November they were together in Copenhagen where Berlau's Revolutionary Theater staged *Señora Carrar's Rifles*. The play opened in mid-December with Dagmar Andreasen playing Carrar, and was reviewed in *Das Wort* by Martin Andersen-Nexø, with hardly any mention of Ruth Berlau. From Berlau's photos of the production, it is clear that a scene in which Señora Carrar views the body of her dead son anticipates a similar scene in the 1949 Berlin production of *Mother Courage*. Berlau also arranged a one-time guest appearance by Helene Weigel in a German version of the play the following February. After Weigel's strongly moving performance, Danish actress Bodil Ipsen read a Danish translation of "The Actress in Exile." For one evening, Weigel's worth as a professional would be beautifully recognized.

Though the professional and then the sexual relationship of Berlau and Brecht had quickly resumed after her return from Spain, problems remained. He continued to cling to his bourgeois attitudes and got angry when Ruth dared to point out the discrepancy between his words and his deeds. He saw his own perquisites as appropriate to a "great master," a teacher of morality, so he thought, comparable to Confucius, and "the Einstein of the new stage form." Through all his bravado, Berlau saw his constant jealousy, his fear of being abandoned, his chronic fears that not only had prevented him from going to Madrid with her but even stopped him from going to the dentist alone if he could help it. She saw his need for servants, his inability to prepare his own meals, or light a stove, or finish a piece of writing of any length on his own; but, paradoxically, to Berlau and others, his helplessness, which made her feel really needed, was as appealing as his genius. It was Bertolt, the human being behind the facade of greatness, that Berlau loved and for whom she felt the "fearsome compulsion" or "deadly longing" described in her own writing.

When Brecht went off to join Berlau in Copenhagen in late 1937, Steffin felt abandoned in Svendborg. As usual, however, she kept working on their joint projects, the sole area where she really felt, and correctly so, that she was irreplaceable.

By December, however, again very ill, she left for Moscow where she could both check whether that country could possibly be a haven for Brecht, Weigel, the children, and herself, and get further treatment for her tuberculosis. Her X-ray records show that a section of her ribcage was removed at this time, a procedure apparently no longer practiced at that time in western Europe. Like all the operations done before, this one also failed to provide anything but brief relief.

Though Steffin's daily pain had long been obvious to anyone else

who saw her, Brecht had established ways to maintain his own emotional distance from the pain of others. In one of his most famous
poems of the Danish years, the "Dark Times" poem, he argues:

> Ah we
> Who wished to prepare the ground for friendliness
> Could not ourselves be friendly.

The poem ends with the request:

> Those of you, however, when things are far enough along
> That people help people
> Think of us
> With pity.

The poem transfers the reason for coldness and ruthlessness away from
self to the convenient "other," the "dark times."

It is not an accident, I believe, that the creator of the "Dark
Times" poem returned around this time to one of his most enduring
persona, Keuner, the man who stole money from a helpless child in one
of the early Keuner stories. In a later story, Mr. K. is challenged. He has
said elsewhere that he is usually hungry whereas in reality he obviously
has plenty to eat. K. replies that it is not important whether or not he
is hungry; it is his opposition to hunger that is important. In one
revealing K. story, the argument is advanced that one person alone
cannot create anything but small works. In another vignette, K. is asked
what he does if he loves someone. "I make a sketch of that person," he
says, "and ensure that it is a good likeness." "The sketch?" asks the
questioner. No, replies Mr. K., the person is to adjust to his sketch.

"The Ambassador," one Mr. K story of the 1930s, is an unusually
direct comment on what was happening in Moscow. Mr. K. endorses
the murder of a former ambassador. He says that the person in carrying
out his duties had to eat and drink with and flatter the enemies of his
homeland. Therefore, he must be eliminated on his return. "Of course,
that's the way to do it," says Mr. K. "He had the courage and made the
contribution of taking on a deadly assignment. As a result he died.
Should they now, instead of burying him, let him rot in the air and
[themselves] put up with the stink?"[22] Again, as happens so frequently
in Brecht's writings of his teens or the poems of his twenties about
Hedda being dead or people going up in smoke, living beings are routinely treated as corpses.

Mr. K. permits Brecht to imagine eliminating the line between life
and death. Mr. K. is the incarnation of brutal wisdom about a world

where humans (as one K. story has it, repeating part of the imagery of "Mack the Knife") are worse than sharks.[23] In this brutal world, Keuner declares in the fragment "On the Carrying of Wisdom," "The person who carries wisdom is not permitted to fight; nor to tell the truth; nor to help people; nor [not to] eat; nor [not to] accept honors; nor [to] be recognizable. The only virtue the carrier of wisdom has is one: that he carries wisdom."[24] How to distinguish real wisdom from circular reasoning in defense of cowardice, lies, and self is not explained in the Keuner tales. Wisdom and "morality" in Keuner's world (very like what we know of the universe according to Brecht, Hitler, and Stalin) is a self-defined condition within a closed system.

By the mid-thirties, Brecht also began to slip into the poetic persona of a "Chinese" character he called Kin-jeh, modeled on the fifth century B.C. Confucian philosopher Me-ti.[25] Kin-jeh would comment on the land of Su (the Soviet Union), on Ni-en (Stalin), and speak to and of Lai-tu (Ruth Berlau). But the comments would not be published until years after Brecht was safely dead.

In addition to Mr. K. and Kin-jeh, he had also begun to create (as though it were a recently discovered chronicle from preimperial Rome), the "diary" of Varus, slave and financial counselor to a local politician on the make called Julius Caesar. The work was titled "The Business Deals of Herr Julius Caesar." When Brecht tired of a role for himself or for others, he could drop it without any apparent qualms or apparently any sense of genuine pain or loss. In a universe where people, including himself, were interchangeable with fictions, trying to find a real person with real opinions and real affections within his unending metamorphoses was an impossible task.

Steffin visited the Soviet Union again in late 1937. Once Stalin had wiped out virtually all the old Bolsheviks who had surrounded Lenin, he turned to the top ranks of the Red Army and Soviet intelligence services. Cannibalistic denunciation had become absolutely routine.[26] The frenzy was at its height during Steffin's 1937 visit. Most of the prominent artists and intellectuals she and Brecht had known since their first visit to the Soviet Union in 1932 were being seized. Bernhard Reich and Asja Lazis were taken away in the winter of 1937–38. Reich's arrest order charged him with the crime of "Knowing Knorin." Both Steffin and Brecht, of course, also knew Vladimir Knorin. On July 16, Tretiakov had been taken from the Kremlin hospital directly to prison, accused of "having worked for the Japanese and German Intelligence services."[27] Olga Tretiakova was also arrested, and their daughter, Tatiana, was forced out of the aeronautical engineering school where she had been a star student.

Young and idealistic, Olga Tretiakova was by no means an isolated instance. Where women had had prominent roles in government and were admitted for study of all professions under Lenin's regime, and virtually as many women as men were in the top ranks of the arts community, under Stalin, women disappeared from the best schools and from most prominent positions in the Soviet Union, and women's rights guaranteed since the early, heady days of the Russian Revolution, including the right to divorce and abortion, were undercut. The right to an abortion was done away with altogether in 1936, and premiums were placed on women having more than seven children! From accounts of those who spent time in Stalin's company, which tell of his almost nightly all-male dinners where he routinely humiliated his guests, we see that Stalin seemed to have little use or respect for colleagues and/or women, either in his personal life or in more general political spheres. Many thought his wife's suicide in 1932 was her only way out of an impossible situation. Her suicide note made it clear she felt her husband had betrayed the original goals of the revolution.[28]

Ilya Ehrenburg has left a graphic account of the atmosphere in Moscow in late 1937. Returning from reporting assignments in Madrid and Paris, he was met by his friend Irina. They laughed together on the way to their apartment in the high-rise building in Lavrushensky Lane where writers in Stalin's favor were housed. In the elevator, Ehrenburg was struck by the sign reading "It is prohibited to put books down the toilet. Anyone contravening this order will be traced and punished."[29] "What does this sign mean," he asked Irina. She glanced at the elevator operator and said only, "I'm so glad you've come." Upstairs in the flat, Irina was more explicit. "Don't you know anything?" she asked in a low voice. Much of the rest of the night was spent bringing the returnee up to date on the names of those who had been taken while he had been away. He learned for the first time that Tretiakov had been arrested. The next day, he dropped in at the *Pravda* offices and went to see Koltsov. Ehrenburg started to talk openly of those who sent greetings from abroad—Koltsov's wife, Maria Osten, a certain Lisa, and so on. Koltsov looked appalled and (apparently fearful of speaking in his own office) took him into the large adjoining bathroom. Here he told Ehrenburg a joke involving the Spanish city of Teruel recently overrun by Franco. "Here's the latest anecdote for you." "Two Muscovites meet. One says[:] 'Have you heard the news? They've taken Teruel.' The other asks: 'Oh, and what about his wife?'" Koltsov smiled and asked: "Funny, isn't it?"

One day that same winter, Ehrenburg ran into Boris Pasternak, who waved his arms about amid the snowdrifts on the open street and said, "If only someone would tell Stalin about it." Even Meyerhold, it was rumored, before he was led away by the NKVD had said simply,

"They conceal it from Stalin." The truth was otherwise. As the Soviet historian Roy Medvedev has recently written: "Stalin almost always took a sadistic pleasure in listening to the accounts given by the chief executioners of the last minutes of those people whom he had openly or secretly hated."[30]

At that distant time, not everyone was blind and deaf, or too scared to talk about what was really happening. The poet Anna Akhmatova said of the "trials," "It's time you understand that people are arrested for nothing."[31] Akhmatova knew, just as Georg Lukács knew, that a jealous neighbor who envied a person his slightly larger apartment could denounce him to the NKVD as a "Trotskyist Wrecker" and that he could then be rewarded with the suddenly empty larger apartment, until, that is, another knock would come on that same door.

In Das Wort, the journal that Brecht was supposedly editing from Denmark and where Steffin's translations were published, their friends were attacked, while the associated journal International Literature attacked Brecht. One of the attackers was Georg Lukács. But anyone could attack anyone else. An article in Das Wort in the spring issue of 1938 (written by Herwarth Walden) stated: "Those who involve themselves with literature . . . must be aware of the fact that they do so in the interests of progress and the development of the entire collective. If they are unwilling or unable to do that, then their pen or their typewriter must be taken away from them. By whatever means necessary."[32] In March 1941, Walden went down the gulag path, never to return.

Stalin sometimes came out of the shadows to take things personally in hand. One day in 1938, Stalin asked Koltsov if he had a gun. "Had you ever thought," asked Stalin, "of killing yourself?"[33] Soon after, on December 12, 1938, the NKVD picked up Koltsov. He was tortured by the NKVD until he signed a manufactured "confession." He was "tried" in less than twenty minutes on February 1, 1940. His "judges" were three NKVD accomplices: Vasily Ulrikh, the obscure Kandybin, and Bukanov. Before the "judges" lay Koltsov's signed "confession." He had been a spy, it said, for German, French, and British intelligence agencies, and "a member of the anti-Soviet underground since 1923."[34] He had planned assassinations and "had popularized the leaders of Trotskyism." Ulrikh asked Koltsov, "Do you wish to add anything?" Koltsov replied: "Not add but deny. Everything that is written here is a lie. From start to finish." "Well how is it a lie? Is this signature yours?" "I put it there," Koltsov said, "after torture . . . terrible torture." The reply was ignored. "Execution by shooting" was the verdict.

When in late 1938 the news reached Paris of her husband's arrest, Maria Osten ignored all advice and hurried back. Feuchtwanger told her she could draw five thousand rubles from his Moscow royalty account. She took with her a child that she and Koltsov had adopted in Spain, a boy called José. She went first to her old Moscow apartment, now occupied by another adopted son, Hubert, now adult. He blocked the apartment doorway and declared loudly enough that all the neighbors could hear that he would not listen to the name of the traitor Koltsov. "I don't want my name dragged in the dirt," he added.[35] Putting his arm around his wife, he declared before sending his mother and her child away, "We've started a family, Luisa and I."

Osten managed to find a room in a shabby, small hotel. When she looked for work, the Writers' Union behaved with typical shabbiness. Neither Fritz Erpenbeck nor Brecht's and Feuchtwanger's fellow editor on Das Wort, Willi Bredel, lifted a finger to help.[36] Alexander Fadayev, the head of the Writers' Union, asked whether the German Section under Johannes R. Becher would take Osten in. Becher said that since she had not been a part of his section before, he would not take her on now. At a secret sitting of March 7, 1939, Walter Ulbricht signed a protocol that put Maria Osten in the same category as Carola Neher and Koltsov, and distanced the CPG from her.[37] Fadayev also washed his hands of the matter. Yet somehow, as we shall see later, Osten survived anyway for the next two years. Even the book Osten and Koltsov had commissioned from Feuchtwanger, Moscow 1937, would be confiscated because of its strictures against Stalin, however mild.[38] Every available copy of the two hundred thousand that had been printed were now collected and pulped.

After Steffin's return from the Soviet visit in late 1937 with a firsthand report, Brecht became aware that simply blaming victims for their own demise was not an adequate reaction. But still he could not bring himself to speak out in public, nor did he make a sustained effort to leave Europe. That Christmas, assuming the role of Kin-jeh, Brecht wrote a poem to Steffin.[39] Addressing her from a grand historical distance, he stylized her as his "little soldier." Like the child on the playground at Augsburg years before, he imagined himself commanding entire battlefields.[40] Kin-jeh now directed "little soldiers" fighting for that distant "third thing." Steffin saw through his self-aggrandizement. Several poems of 1937–38 are usually published as Brecht's but are obviously hers. The "The Good Comrade M.S." (dated in Steffin's hand, December 1937), the "Song of the Soldier of the Revolution," and "Standing Orders for the Soldier M.S." capture too well a sense of the muck of the trenches to have been written by a führer who stayed behind the lines in his Gemütliche Hauptquartier. Steffin's voice comes through particularly clearly in the lines:

> *Mostly it's not the place that's bad*
> *But the gang that has the gall to rule over it.*
> *This is the pack that has to be faced down*
> *And only then will life on earth be made bearable.*

Or, in another poem of this same period:

> *Say what you want about things*
> *Life's a real mess.*
> *Let's stop this:*
> *Now the soldier will speak.*
> *Let me give you some advice*
> *Don't start things with me!*
> *I am a soldier.*
> *So stop this stuff.*

A later verse stresses that this particular soldier is a woman, and even her rifle is given a woman's name:

> *What I need I have in hand*
> *My untearable dress*
> *My rifle called Emmi*
> *My understanding as a soldier*
> *Every detail no matter how small.*

Tellingly, it was Steffin who, after her late 1937 visit to the Soviet Union, lit a fire under the group, saying: "I am all for getting to America as quickly as possible. If that can still be done."[41] But Brecht would risk the lives of all of them by not making an all-out effort until late 1940 to get visas to flee Europe altogether. In doing so, he was ignoring Steffin's firsthand account of the murder of the "Formalists" by the NKVD.

Moscow doctors had removed several of her ribs, and X-rays showed a "goose-egg-size hole in her right lung" and a "hen's-egg-size hole" in the left lung.[42] Still weak after her lung operation (and apparently by at least one additional abortion) and psychically drained both by what she had seen in the Soviet Union and by Brecht's demeaning treatment, Steffin seems to have carried most of the Brecht workshop's workload in the late 1930s. In early 1938, she helped the workshop produce what would become classics of world literature. Early in the new year, she finished with Brecht seventeen scenes of *Fear and Misery of the Third Reich*. She continued to handle almost all correspondence as Brecht rarely answered letters.[43]

On top of all this, by March, Martin Andersen-Nexø and Brecht pressured her to work on a German translation of Andersen-Nexø's interminable memoirs, to be published both in Switzerland and Moscow. The job had to be rushed since Brecht told Nexø he did not know how much longer Moscow would continue to publish such things. About authorship credit for the work, Brecht wrote to Nexø: "I have nothing against having my name attached, though then it would need to say 'Margarete Steffin and Bertolt Brecht' because I, as everyone knows, do not understand Danish, and I know that the main work will really be done by Grete."[44] In the same letter, Brecht pressured Nexø for payment for the project, with the money to come either directly from the publisher or from Nexø himself. By this time, Nexø was heavily dependent on money earned from the sale of his books in the Soviet Union. A letter from Nexø to Tretiakov in the middle of 1937 (immediately prior to and possibly one of the causes of Tretiakov's arrest) talks of how, "thanks to Soviet-Russian honoraria," he plans to add central heating and another bedroom to his country house.[45]

Meanwhile, as usual pleading poverty but now sharpening his appeals by stressing his opposition to Hitler and the attendant dangers of that position, Brecht had been working to line up additional sources of income—this time in the United States. By May 28, 1938, his efforts were rewarded; he had in hand the first monthly check for fifty dollars from the American Guild for German Cultural Freedom. In his thank-you letter, he claimed he was receiving income "neither from publishers nor from theaters."[46] The claim was untrue on both counts. Money still came to him at that time for the Soviet work for which Steffin was actually responsible, and Wieland Herzfelde was paying him for a two-volume edition of Brecht's Collected Works that Herzfelde brought out in London in 1938. In addition, two weeks before Brecht's letter to the American guild, he had received 4,300 francs from Aufricht's 1937 Threepenny Opera production in Paris.

"Master, What Grounds Do You Have for Your Antipathy toward Women?" (1938–39)

In May 1938, Weigel again left for Paris, this time to play in a small, emigré production of scenes from the Steffin-Brecht *Fear and Misery of the Third Reich*. Brecht came to Paris briefly but, as he had with the similarly low-budget *Señora Carrar's Rifles*, left before the play opened.[1] Back in Skovsbostrand with the visiting Walter Benjamin, Brecht was now openly bitter about what he called Georg Lukács's priestly "camarilla" in Moscow. Speaking of his conversations with Brecht, Benjamin felt "a power being exercised over me that was equal to fascism itself; that is, I would say, it sprang from the same depths of history as the fascistic."[2] It is rare that someone so clearly articulates, as Benjamin does here, Brecht's ability to seize and transform an audience as Hitler was able to do.

Speaking from the depths of his rage, Brecht said, "Every one of their pieces of criticism contains a threat."[3] Lukács's associate Julius Hay had recently said in print in Moscow that Brecht's (Steffin's) *Round Heads* "was water over the Fascist mill." It was tantamount to signing Brecht's death warrant. Brecht quite correctly guessed that Hay would not have done this unless he had powerful backing. Among Hay's backers were Lukács and Alfred Kurella, who was thought to have fingered his own brother, Heinrich, to the NKVD.[4] Kurella was secretary to Comintern head Dimitrov, and close to Fritz Erpenbeck and Stalin's "woodcutter" Walter Ulbricht. The group was out to get Brecht. On June 8, 1938, Alfred Kurella wrote the following letter to Erpenbeck: "Quickly a new intermezzo: the enclosed letter from Brecht just arrived. Tahu-tata! Now the cat sticks his head out of the bag." Kurella goes on to say he hopes to "stimulate" Brecht to respond and says, using an intimate first-name form of address, "I'll give a copy of the letter to Walter, and will also speak with him and see how we should react."[5] This "Walter," as the context of Kurella's letter makes clear, is Walter Ulbricht. Brecht did not respond to the provocation. Even when he and Hanns Eisler were attacked by Lukács in the July 1938 issue of *International Literature*, Brecht confined his response to scribbling on his copy of the journal, "Lukács's decadents."[6] In early 1937,

Bernard von Brentano had told Brecht that the time had long since come for Brecht to speak out against what was happening in the Soviet Union. In the same letter, Brentano had then pointed out that Brecht's former co-worker Ernst Ottwalt was now charged with "counterrevolutionary activities." Couldn't Brecht help defend his old friend?[7] Brecht refused.

On October 4–5, 1938, in the Parisian Trotskyist journal *Our Word*, Brecht was publicly attacked for failing to help friends arrested in the Soviet Union. German emigré Walter Held wrote in an open letter: "You, Herr Brecht, knew Carola Neher. You know that she is neither a terrorist nor a spy, but rather was a brave human being and a great artist. Why do you remain silent? Is it because Stalin finances your publication *The Word* [*Das Wort*]—this, the least truthful, most depraved publication ever put out by German intellectuals?"[8] Held's questions (never answered by Brecht) and comments on the Soviet Union were to cost the lives of Held, his wife, and child. Fleeing from the Nazis in 1940 and needing by that time to cross the Soviet Union to try to reach America across the Pacific, the entire Held family was pulled off the Transsiberian Express and murdered by the NKVD.

Playing chess with Brecht in the quiet garden at Skovsbostrand in the summer of 1938, Benjamin said of Moscow, "But you have friends there." Brecht replied no, he no longer did, and then added, "And those in Moscow do not have any friends either—like the dead."[9] On July 25, 1938, Benjamin noted: "He follows Russian developments and Trotsky's writings. These prove that there are grounds for suspicion, justified suspicion, that one needs to react sceptically to the way Russian affairs are now being handled. . . . Should these suspicions one day be actually proven, then one would have to fight this regime and fight it openly."[10] Brecht did not openly attack Stalin, however, and showed Benjamin a poem he had just written, which he said was a form of praise to Stalin. In it, a great ox is praised, and fear is expressed that it may die before the sowing season ends.[11]

The workshop was now busy with a volume to be called *The Svendborg Poems*, privately funded by Ruth Berlau but published by Malik Verlag. In London, where the press had moved from Czechoslovakia, Malik had brought out in 1938 a two-volume edition of Brecht plays. The edition went forward even though the head of Malik, Wieland Herzfelde, complained to Steffin about Brecht's lack of interest in the battle against fascism. Herzfelde claimed Brecht only responded to letters about his own works. Questions about other writers who really were battling fascism went unanswered for years.[12]

When not in the hospital or working for Brecht, Steffin worked on two plays of her own (one scene of which was to be accepted and published in Moscow within the year).[13] She had hundreds of pages to complete on the Martin Andersen-Nexø memoirs and had translated one of his short stories for the February 1938 issue of *Das Wort*.[14] Her translation into German from Norwegian of Nordahl Grieg's play *The Defeat* came out in three issues of *Das Wort* in 1938.[15] After her death, Brecht ransacked this play. Adding all the translations that Steffin was primarily responsible for, works that she wrote entirely on her own, and the editorial work she did for *Das Wort*, by 1938, her writing had become the primary financial support of the Skovsbostrand group.

In November 1938, after almost six years of exile, Weigel helped Steffin get a small place of her own. After years of moving from one rented room to another, living with borrowed furniture, Steffin was happy to finally have both a sleeping and a working room, and her own furniture. She wrote to Benjamin that the new place helped her forget "that Skovsbostrand is actually somewhat lonely."[16]

In Saint Louis, Hauptmann was still helping the group's finances by allowing Brecht's illicit use of her creative work. In the July 1938 issue of *Das Wort*, Brecht published six "Chinese Poems" he claimed to have translated. A book on Brecht's Chinese poems accepts his claim and makes no mention whatsoever of Hauptmann's role.[17] However, Paula Hanssen has shown that the translations are Hauptmann's.[18]

Though Steffin's translations and adaptations were still being sold on the Moscow market in late 1938, there was almost no interest there in the kind of plays produced under the Brecht name. The charges of the Lukács clique usually resulted in not only no demand and payment for such work but in a one-way trip to the gulag for their author. In view of the naked threat posed by the Moscow clique, the group's thoughts now necessarily turned toward America as a potential haven, beyond reach supposedly of the NKVD. But, even now, though repeatedly warned of NKVD danger by Steffin, Brecht seemed paralyzed.

To improve her English in the prospect of moving to America, Steffin, like Hauptmann before her, was reading Arthur Waley's English versions of Chinese poems and rendering them into German. She was also reading, at Brecht's insistence, a volume of Confucius in Waley's translation. Steffin was appalled at the reactionary positions the Chinese philosopher held, particularly those regarding women. Noting with horror that Brecht was now identifying with Confucius, she wrote to Crassus, "He understands nothing of women."[19] Her allegorical tale "Confucius Understands Nothing of Women" holds its own with any of Brecht's allegorical writing. When it was published in 1991, one reviewer compared her writing to that of the female troubadours of the Middle Ages who exchanged brilliant poetic texts with male admirers.[20] Another reviewer spoke of Steffin's "greatness" and her "sovereign command of style."[21]

While ostensibly writing about Confucius, Steffin gives us a portrait of Brecht written in a style that is like a samurai sword—graceful, balanced, deadly. Her Confucius says, "One of the most intelligent men I have ever met is the poet Ken-jeh." But Ken-jeh is primarily concerned about his reputation. Wrapped up in his own concerns, Ken-jeh offers no reaction when a student asks of Confucius, "Master, what grounds do you have for your antipathy toward women?" The Master simply replies, "None." Steffin's short piece ends with this observation: "on subjects such as souls, religion, astrology, and the arts of war, Confucius, one of the greatest teachers of all time, said almost nothing or only generalities to his students, funnily, women also belong to this category."[22] Though Steffin told Brecht that Confucius was "enormously reactionary," particularly toward women's rights, Brecht continued to see himself as a Confucian figure, the great sage driven out of his homeland by those who did not comprehend his wisdom.

One day Berlau and Brecht drove down a lonely country road in a heavy rainstorm. They saw an old man who signaled them for a ride. Ruth said they should stop to pick him up, but Brecht insisted they go on. Ruth so raged about this later that Brecht finally sent her a poem admitting, in a typically distanced manner, that this had been a mistake.[23] Yes, he was shocked by his own behavior, but then he was shocked by "this whole world."

For Ruth, Brecht's behavior with the hitchhiker was part of a pattern. He used this sense of shock to justify his own behavior in both his professional and private life. While more or less living with Weigel, he constantly nagged Berlau to leave her husband, deriding her for relying on her marriage as a crutch.[24] Finally worn down by Brecht and hoping to set an example, Berlau moved out of the huge apartment she shared with Lund and took a small attic apartment at a far less fashionable Copenhagen address in 1938. She paid for it entirely on her own. She also bought a small country house where she could spend private weekends with Brecht. To fully establish her independence from Lund, she gave up the use of the Lincoln and bought a large, fast BSA motorcycle. The always dramatic Red Ruth was often now seen and heard on her BSA, roaring along, Brecht clinging behind for dear life. One winter week, with Brecht on the back of the BSA, she drove to her little hideaway in the village of Vallensbaeck, about an hour from Copenhagen. By the time they arrived, they were frozen, and the house was frozen also. Berlau hurried to get a fire made, and since the well pump was frozen, she thawed snow to make hot tea. Brecht sat, angrily chomping on his cigar, while Ruth made the fire and the tea. They stayed eight days at the country house and wrote together a comedy called *Alle wissen Alles*, or *Everyone Knows Everything*.[25] The play deals with a famous thief in Denmark, a wizard at break-ins. He staged a robbery once every seven years, making off with enough to live for the next period. Due to the regular pattern of his thefts, the police were finally able to catch him, but his case so took the fancy of the Danes that the king was moved to pardon him. He was released to the custody of Karin Michaëlis, who allowed him to live in one of the small houses on her estate.

A few days after they had returned from Vallensbaeck, Brecht-Kin-jeh gave Berlau-Lai-tu a poem in which he objected to the time it had taken her to give him his tea. This had improperly delayed the purpose of their visit to the country house, that is, "to write the truth about oppressors." Ruth was furious. But later, passion both for the work and for him overcame prudence, and once again she was lighting fires and making tea while the "Chinese sage" worked on *The Book of Twists and Turns*, where he discussed not only Lai-tu but Ni-en (Stalin), and what he thought was going on in Su (the Soviet Union).

Berlau continued acting full-time in the Danish commercial theater, running her antifascist Revolutionary Theater company in Copenhagen, writing, and serving as Brecht's theatrical and publishing agent for Scandinavia. Though her 1935 feminist and pro-Soviet novel *Videre* was almost completely ignored and brought little income, she was not discouraged. With Brecht providing some good and some hostile suggestions about her theme, the sexual situation of women in a society dominated by sexually insensitive males, she was completing a strongly feminist book, *Ethvert Dyr Kan Det*, or *Every Animal Can Do It*.[26]

Like most of Berlau's work, the new volume drew on her own experience, and that of family and friends. She did not mention the Soviet Union, either positively or negatively. But the new work was revelatory with regard to sex. Indeed, it was so explicit that she delayed publication for over two years and eventually brought the work out under the pseudonym Maria Sten. Lightly disguised, *Every Animal* tells the story of her sister Edith. Apparently, Edith had had her first sexual experience with a man in 1938 when she was already thirty-four years old. Edith had gone for psychological advice to a Dr. Krabbe, and they became sexually involved, despite Krabbe's marriage. When Edith understood that he had no intention of getting a divorce, she was devastated. Krabbe, with the complicity of medical colleagues, had Edith committed to a mental institution where she remained for eighteen years.[27]

Berlau saw her sister's case as a warning. When she visited her sister at the asylum, she was particularly horrified that the toilets had no doors—this detail stayed with her forever. Edith's birthday on December 24 was always traumatic for Ruth, who wondered if she too might go over the edge. Most disturbing for Ruth was the suspicion that her sister was locked up to protect the man who had put her there, rather than for Edith's good. During Ruth's visits, Edith seemed wholly rational. Speaking one day about the world political situation, Edith wondered whether the slow change of social democracy might be better than the violent path of communism in the Soviet Union. "Can it be done with kindness?" asked Edith wistfully.

The case of her sister and Krabbe, as well as her own relationship with Brecht, provided ample evidence for Berlau that loving, committed relationships seemed virtually impossible for the male of the human species. Though any animal (hence the title of her book) engaged in sex, human males could not fully give themselves in love. In story after story, Berlau showed the havoc wrought on women by the inability of men to love fully. Each of a series of stories ends with a woman saying of her inept "lover," "May the devil take him."

Berlau would say, quite correctly, "Men do not like to read the book as it is a critique of men." She was particularly aware that Brecht disapproved of it. Berlau claimed later he had wanted to add a final chapter that would be a "critique of women."[28] Summing up both Brecht's reaction to her book and his attitude toward women, Berlau said later that Brecht "despises us women deeply." But though Berlau knew this, she, like Steffin, still loved him and found nobody else with whom to realize her dream of a full, equal relationship between a woman and a man.

With unrest in the female ranks, Brecht welcomed the distraction of visits by old male friends. Sternberg visited Skovsbostrand at the end of September, and the two discussed turning the life of the early seventeenth-century scientist Galileo into a play. In late October, Brecht met with Ferdinand Reyher, a German-speaking American novelist and screenwriter who had briefly met Brecht and Hauptmann in Berlin in 1928.[29] Reyher was now touring Europe with a male friend. He recommended doing the Galileo theme as a screenplay for Hollywood. After Reyher left, the screenplay idea was dropped, since no one had much screenwriting experience. They turned instead to what they knew best, hoping to create a play suitable for Broadway. By November 17, Steffin reported progress on *Galileo* and "giant steps forward" on the huge Nexø translation.

Galileo was a stalking-horse for the Soviet Union and Bukharin's recantation.[30] The group marked up the German translation of the transcript of Bukharin's "trial" while working on *Galileo*.[31] Brecht said privately: "With the representation of Galileo, the problem of representation at the Soviet trials is also solved . . . In Bukharin's self-analysis, he climbs further above himself in the moment of that analysis than anyone else in the courtroom."[32] Brecht had correctly surmised that Bukharin, like Galileo, had confessed only after being threatened with torture.[33] Obviously, it would have been mortally dangerous for the authors of this play if these connections had now been seen by the NKVD. Therefore, in an evasive cover note, Steffin claimed the play was "a purely historical piece on the life of the great Italian physicist. Its contemporary applicability consists solely of the fact that it considers the problem of freedom of research."[34]

Galileo, Brecht claimed later, was finished in little more than three weeks. This was almost certainly not true. *Galileo* is, together with *Measures* and a handful of his best poems, perhaps the most superbly crafted work with which Brecht was ever associated. It has, as Schumacher has pointed out, and as Brecht himself was aware, the symmetry that is "an essential feature of the classical drama."[35] Each scene in *Galileo* leads inexorably to the next. We see him stealing the original idea of a telescope from one of his students who had seen such a device in Holland. We watch as Galileo not only claims the idea is his, "the fruit of many years of effort," but then turns it toward the heavens and comes up with a new vision of the universe. The earth, he claims, is not flat but round, and but a tiny speck in space. After threats by the Inquisition, Galileo will then publicly renounce what he and the pope know to be proven scientific discoveries. Then under virtual house arrest, Galileo will secretly continue his heretical writings. Galileo is both hero and coward, a thief of other people's ideas and someone capable of enormous originality.

With *Galileo*, Brecht and Steffin have returned to the world of the classic drama with its towering but flawed central hero. The rise and fall of the action, with its deliberate retardation as we are forced to wait to discover whether Galileo will stand up to the Inquisition, is constructed in the prescribed Aristotelian manner. The play is as carefully constructed as a watch, each cog precisely driving the other. In its free use of historical sources, its use of music and dance, and its chronicle structure, it clearly echoes precisely the devices used by Shakespeare in his great history plays. It should not surprise us perhaps that Eric Bentley, arguably *the* keenest eye and ear of drama criticism in the twentieth century, should sum up his view of *Galileo* as "theatre on the grandest scale,"[36] and that he should include the play in his two-volume anthology of the greatest drama the world has so far produced. We might wish to remember also that the great actor Charles Laughton would seriously compare this work with the plays of Shakespeare.[37] I believe the comparison is apt. In my view, *Galileo* is one of the two (*Mother Courage* is the other) greatest Elizabethan-style chronicle plays written in the twentieth century. Both in *Galileo* and *Mother Courage*, the techniques of exposition that served Shakespeare so well enjoy a radical renaissance in these two carefully rounded (in the end is the beginning), archly "modern," yet wholly classical, plays. Brecht was surely right in noting of the play that, in contrast to his earlier writing about "epic" modern subjects, "technically, *Galileo* is a large step backwards."[38] It was a step back to the late sixteenth century. Again, the way to the drama of the future lay in the past (as it had with *Measures Taken* and other *Lehrstücke*, with their explicit medieval antecedents).

For all of the great dramatic strength of *Galileo*, women in the play (as is so often the case in other major classics) are presented mainly as caretakers, beings whose lives are dictated by the whims and wanderings of a "great" man. Galileo is a man alone. He does not appear to express any real concern for the lives of those closest to him. His daughter's life is wholly sacrificed to his own. If, as Steffin claimed of Confucius-Brecht, they "understood nothing of women," the figure of Galileo is cut from the same cloth. In Steffin's intense work on this play, we see how she worked dialectically as she had in the poem archly speaking of how "Denmark wept" when the "great master" Brecht left for America in late 1935. For Steffin, these figures that history might present as great were, no matter how great their talents, deeply, deeply flawed human beings. It is, I think, the central human weakness of Galileo, as Steffin and Brecht present it, that, in dramatic terms, paradoxically constitute one of the play's greatest, and specifically Aristotelian, strengths.

No sooner was the first version of *Galileo* finished than it began to take on a new layer of meaning. From Berlin came the news that Einstein's former colleagues Otto Hahn and Fritz Strassmann had split the atom. Not understanding the implications of the discovery, Hahn wrote of it to the great Jewish physicist Lise Meitner, a former colleague who fled abroad after Hitler had seized her native Austria.[39] Meitner discussed the question with her nephew Otto Robert Frisch, an atomic physicist who was working with Niels Bohr in Copenhagen. From them, the news spread within Bohr's research institute. Frisch and a lab associate, Dr. Møller, participated in a January 27 radio program on the applications of atomic energy. When the host of the program was told that probably there would not be a feasible military use, he expressed thanks, saying he thought the human race "was not ready for responsible use of such awesome power."

Supposedly wanting to know more about the work of Niels Bohr, Brecht asked Berlau to arrange for him to meet Dr. Møller. However, as Møller said later, Brecht asked him nothing about Bohr's work but instead "lectured him on science."[40] Niels Bohr left for America. Within weeks of the original Berlin experiments, they were duplicated in the basement of the physics building at Columbia University. By August 1939, pacifist Albert Einstein would write to President Roosevelt that the danger of the Berlin experiments was so great that America should conduct a crash program to build an atomic bomb.

Though Steffin and Brecht were only vaguely aware of the implications of the Berlin discovery, *Galileo* was revised to suggest that physics itself could become deadly to the human race. Steffin prepared multiple copies of the revised text and sent them, as her diary records, to the following list of people in America: "einstein, korsch, kortner, geis, granach, hauptmann, reyher, gorelik."[41] Another copy went to England for Desmond Vesey to translate. The hope clearly was that *Galileo* might provide a foothold in the English-language theater.

That same year, Hitler had been greeted in Austria by jubilant crowds and had murdered potential opponents there. Chamberlain had sought to placate Hitler in Munich to buy a few more years of peace. It had been the year of the successful scripting, rehearsing, and staging of the Moscow Show Trials. In America, Congress created its own kind of Inquisition, the House of Un-American Activities Committee.

Clearly frightened at the tide of new developments, in a January 1939 diary entry (not published until years after his death), Brecht wrote: "Koltsov also arrested in Moscow. My last Russian connection with over there. Nobody knows anything about Tretiakov, who is supposed to be a 'Japanese spy.' Nobody knows anything about [Carola] Neher, who is supposed to have gotten involved in Prague with her husband in some Trotskyist business. Reich and Asja Lazis don't write anymore [they had also been arrested]. Grete doesn't get any answers from her acquaintances in the Caucasus and in Leningrad. Also Béla Kun has been arrested, the one politician I saw there. Meyerhold has lost his theater. . . . Literature and art have been turned to shit, political theory has gone to the dogs, and what we see is an officiously propagated proletarian humanism that is thin and bloodless."[42]

But, like Galileo, Brecht maintained public silence, hiding his various heresies in his desk drawer. Never, in his own lifetime, would Brecht dare publicly to challenge anything done by the Soviet Union. Brecht did one thing privately while appearing in public to be doing something else. When his brother Walter came to Svendborg on a visit, Brecht told him to return to Germany and join the Nazi party. Brecht recommended Walter work his way up "if possible to the rank of gauleiter within it—because otherwise the anti-Nazi activities of his Bolshevik brother might get him into trouble."[43]

Steffin reported to Crassus as 1939 began: "I've had a lot to do: wrote out all of *Galileo*. Must write the whole thing out again. People on every side are asking for the new book of poems, and the Nexø needs to be sent off, and copies of *Caesar* are also needed—I hardly know where to begin."[44] It was now certain that her operation in the Soviet

Union in late 1937 had been far too late to stop her tuberculosis. The disease was now exerting massive strain both on her heart and her liver. She had constant headaches and fevers.

Though repeatedly urged by Robert Lund, Brecht made no effort to get Steffin consistent treatment. Telling her to think about her health, Brecht would also point out the urgency of this or that writing project and its supposed importance for that vital "third thing." Unless she was literally in a state of collapse, she would devote herself to writing rather than her own health. Danish critic Harald Engberg described all this activity as a "workshop, working at top speed, like the German war industry."[45] Steffin's dream of a better world seemed worth any sacrifice. The plays seem almost to have become the children that she repeatedly aborted during her years with Brecht. She poured whatever energy she had into them, hoping they would help others reach a promised land of friendship, peace, and equality that she was now sure she could never reach.

Whether or not she was aware of it, she and Brecht had entered a creative period where, beset by the horror of Hitler on one hand (as he absorbed Austria into the Third Reich without significant international protest) and of the NKVD on the other, they created works that consistently deal with the human condition at its most naked and vulnerable. *Galileo* is largely free of the doctrinaire assumptions that had dictated much of the work written since *The Measures Taken*. It returns to the oldest dramatic verities. A towering figure, neither wholly good nor wholly bad, faces choices so profound and dramatically compelling that he elicits fear and pity in the audience. Not too specifically about Bukharin's struggle with Stalin, the subject becomes the universal struggle against any kind of repression.

But in early 1939, Hitler's march across Europe could, at any time, overwhelm neighboring Denmark. A London *Times* editorial of September 7, 1938, said Britain should yield to Hitler's demands for the Sudetenland. In its final issue of 1938, the American news magazine *Time* declared Hitler to be the man of the year. The fate of Czechoslovakia was sealed. Plans were now finally made by Weigel and Berlau to help move the Brecht-Weigel family and the seriously ill Steffin further away from the aggressively expansionist Third Reich. The urgency intensified when Brecht, driving his old Ford, ran down and injured a child on a bicycle. Whatever Brecht's responsibility, he had a deserved reputation as a dangerous driver. Georg Grosz had said in 1934 that Brecht was "one the fastest and least careful" drivers of his acquaintance.[46] He had driven his first Steyr into a tree. In October 1938, *Politiken* reported that Brecht had run into a car with five people in it.[47]

Steffin, who was in the car when Brecht ran down the child, had a severe psychosomatic attack including a loss of hearing. She thought of suicide.[48] Berlau took her to Copenhagen where the long-suffering Lund tried to bring her out of a deep depression. She slowly recovered some of the hearing in her one good ear (the other, the tubercular one, remained problematic); but her hearing was now permanently affected, and she felt more and more isolated and unwanted as a person. She knew they had to get out of Denmark and out of Europe altogether. She wrote to Benjamin: "I preach constantly: America!"[49] In another letter, she asked Elisabeth Hauptmann about whether she thought Mexico might be a good alternate haven if America itself could not be reached because of visa problems. Hauptmann replied in the middle of 1939 that Mexican visas were a viable option.[50]

In the spring of 1939, terrified both by Hitler and what the local court might do to him for running down the child, Brecht was desperate to get away.[51] Finally, with the help of Berlau's influential Swedish friend Georg Branting, Brecht was invited to lecture in Sweden, and Weigel was supposed to come to give acting instruction. To go, however, they would need Swedish visas. Using all his pull in the Swedish parliament, Branting soon obtained the necessary papers for Brecht and Weigel to "visit" Sweden. Weigel went to work at once on travel arrangements and on the sale of the Danish house.

All the while, Brecht was busy negotiating more contracts for the sale of present and past work published under the Brecht label. Hauptmann's *Happy End* had interested one of France's most popular directors, René Clair. Nobody in Paris apparently knew it was not Brecht's work to sell, and he was not about to tell them. Through his Paris attorney, Martin Domke, Brecht proposed to collect option monies of three thousand francs a month for three months, with two conditions: first, he did not want his name to be used; and second, he wanted to exclude the songs (the only part he had partially written) from the contract. Domke wrote back on March 17, 1939, "As you certainly know, the film is to be made by René Clair, and it can only be in your interest to have your name mentioned."[52]

But as Brecht had no legal right whatsoever to Hauptmann's *Happy End* (particularly to the play minus the songs), he was on very dangerous ground. A letter to Hauptmann does not mention that the sale of her play is imminent.[53] Only once the deal was set did Steffin, not Brecht, send a note to Hauptmann claiming Brecht had sold *Happy End* for a total of $250. Hauptmann wrote back at once: "On this *Happy End* matter, I can say nothing. I believe that they have taken Brecht for a ride with this price. Even in Paris and today, a film company pays more than $250 for film rights." As to what she should receive from the $250, she replied simply, "I cannot say, those were [. . .] other times. The contract with Felix Bloch Erben was in my name. But, as I have said, today is '39."[54] After World War II, Hauptmann found out from the person who had acquired *Happy End* from Brecht that the cost to him had been 50,000 marks, or about $15,000 at the exchange rate of that time. That amount would have been ten years of income for Hauptmann in the United States in 1939. It would have bought her her independence and the time to write that she so desperately wanted and could never afford.

While stealing Hauptmann's money and lying about what he had earned, Brecht did not mention the transaction to Weill at all. Nor did he mention he had collected 4,300 francs for a *Threepenny Opera* done in Paris. Brecht directly lied to Weill in a March 1939 letter, saying "they do not give us our royalties," as he pocketed Weill's and Hauptmann's share.[55]

By the spring of 1939, with care provided by Dr. Lund, Steffin was again able to hear and to resume work. Even as preparations were made to leave Denmark, she began to rework a story with Brecht either he or Hauptmann had written years before in Berlin, a story whose punning title in German could be translated in English as both "True Love" and "Love for Sale." The revised story, now using American writer Agnes Smedley's work for background material on China, was to be called *The Good Woman of Setzuan*.[56] Like *Galileo*, the play was written for America but unlike *Galileo*, *Setzuan* revolves around a woman. For the first time in a Brecht play, somebody who does good will not be executed.

On Easter Monday, 1939, after Hitler entered Prague, and Franco had taken Madrid, while Mussolini seized Albania, Brecht left Skovsbostrand and the unresolved case of the accident with the child. Brecht also worried that the Germans would cross the Danish border at any moment. Crassus noted of the scene of departure: "He had a cap on his head, and in one hand he held a small bag holding his most essential items, and in his other hand, a volume of Chinese poems in English translation. With a sad smile he looked around the garden where the trees and bushes were starting to turn green. Spring that year arrived on time. As Ruth Berlau started the car to drive him to Copenhagen, he lifted his cap to us, the ones remaining, and said: 'Aufwiedersehen, and many thanks.' "[57]

Writing to Crassus, Steffin described the situation after Brecht left Skovsbostrand with Berlau: "Frau Brecht and I could not do any more in the end. You see, we worked every night until one o'clock and had to get up early."[58] She said Crassus was not to tell Brecht about her night work because "for my health I'm supposed to go to bed early, you understand." After a week of day-and-night packing, and after Weigel was able both to sell the house and collect the money for it, Weigel left to join Brecht. The children were left behind in Steffin's care, and she still had to guide the volume *The Svendborg Poems* through the printer. The last stage required continuous access to a mimeograph machine. Crassus found her one, but despite its weight and her now severe heart problems, she had to carry it home herself. But the home to which she brought it was dissolving. After only months of occupancy, her first apartment in all the years of exile would again be given up. She lost the one and only room of her own.

29

"How Can a Tiny Tree Blossom When So Much Snow Falls on It?" (1939–41)

Once Brecht got to Copenhagen, while waiting for a visa for Sweden, he also put in a visa application to the American embassy. He knew a response would take at least six months. Quite deliberately, on tactical grounds, no attempt was being made as yet to try to get Swedish visas for the children, or to get Steffin out of Denmark.[1] This would be attempted if and when Weigel and Brecht got to Sweden.[2] On April 8, a Saturday, Brecht made a hysterical phone call to Henry Peter Mathis, another friend of Berlau, who was working with Branting to arrange for the visas. In advancing Brecht's case with the immigration authorities in Sweden, Mathis and Branting stressed Brecht's fame as the author of *The Threepenny Opera*, which had played extensively in Sweden from 1929 on. They said the author would be a cultural asset. The ploy was successful. But once the Swedish visa arrived, Brecht said he now planned to delay his coming from April 20 to 23.[3]

When Weigel, Berlau, and Brecht first arrived in Stockholm, they stayed in several rooms at Stockholm's Hotel Pallas, whose rundown, bordello atmosphere would have suited Mack the Knife.[4] On May 4, Brecht gave a formal lecture on his work at the Stockholm Student Club. The Swedish students seem to have been impressed by the fame of the lecturer and the impenetrability of his epic theater text, and were not put off by Brecht's mumbled delivery of the lecture.

While Brecht lectured, women were taking care of his needs. The Swedish actress Naima Wifstrand, a great admirer who had visited Brecht briefly at Skovsbostrand the year before, made arrangements to have a large, comfortable house loaned to them. The house was owned by the sculptress Ninnan Santesson. "The house," as Brecht noted in his diary after moving in, "is ideal. It lies on the island of Lidingö, with pine forests coming up to it on two sides. My workroom, formerly a sculptor's studio, is twenty-four feet long by sixteen feet wide. I have lots of working tables."[5]

After seeing Brecht and Weigel installed in Stockholm, Berlau returned to Copenhagen and helped Steffin with trips to the printers. Berlau carried the heavy duplicating machine back to its owner, and the last set of proofs was read. In their haste, neither Steffin nor Berlau thought to put any reference to themselves in this lovely, revealing, and concealing book.

The Svendborg volume ends with the extraordinary "Dark Times" poem, as fine a work as anything Brecht ever produced. The poem is a deeply moving plea to those "who survive the flood" to think "with indulgence" of those who were not friendly during the years of "the flood." The second-to-last poem in the book "Chased out with Good Reason" is also quite good and is often cited as though it described Brecht's own life. We learn in the poem that the poet was brought up as the son of "well-off people" who taught him "the customs of being served and the art of giving orders."[6] But, "once I grew up," claims the poet, "the people of my class did not please me, nor did the giving of orders, nor being waited on, and I left my own class and went over to people of a lesser class." The poem goes on to say that the poet has become a traitor to his own class, deliberately translating (as did Galileo in the Steffin-Brecht play) the Latin of the ruling class so that the proletariat could understand the discourse of power. The poem ends with the line "You, I hear, they had good reason to chase away."

The poem shows us a towering figure of courage and foresight, friend of all "those without possessions," a man who has himself lost (because of his outspokenness against those in command in his own country) "that which I had earned through my own labor." The poem is not about the person who published almost no anti-Nazi work before the Reichstag fire, the man who stole a colleague's work regularly in the Nazi years and treated her as his employee, the person who was so attached to his own domestic servant that he brought her with him into exile, a man who was treated with consistent respect by the Danish police and whose works were produced even at the elitist Danish Royal Theater.

As an artifact of revolution, without reference to the real life of the poet who wrote it, this poem is a model of what the middle and upper classes could do if they really wished to commit themselves to the cause of the disenfranchised. Problems with the poem arise only when it is read in a biographical context, which reveals how much sheer fantasy is involved. When Brecht's servant Mari Hold cited the "Chased Out" poem, she did so with considerable irony. She, of all people, knew just how little it had to do with Brecht's own life.[7]

Georg Branting was successful in getting Swedish visas for Steffin and the children, and they left for Sweden on May 7. Berlau continued to perform regularly at the Royal Theater in Copenhagen, to write feminist works, and to direct her Revolutionary Theater group in anti-fascist plays. Even with the Germans poised to invade, she felt Denmark was the best place for her to help in the struggle for a new world of peace and equality. Long since separated from Lund, though she remained on friendly terms with him, she began divorce procedures. Once divorced, by progressive Danish law, she would be entitled to a small pension. Wanting to be equally available (and eligible for the Danish pension), Steffin decided to divorce her pro forma husband.

Soon after Steffin reached Stockholm, the news arrived there of the death of Brecht's father on May 20. Whatever effect it may have had on him, no mention of it is found in his son's diary. On Lidingö Island, the large Brecht-Weigel house and attached studio rapidly filled up with all the furniture and books shipped to Brecht and Weigel—dishes, furniture, the portable billiard table, and everything else they had had sent to them from Berlin and Augsburg in 1933. To this had been added in Denmark an antique church pew and a collection of lovely old copper pots. Naima Wifstrand was surely wrong when she said later the Brecht-Weigel goods had filled "several railway cars,"[8] but her general sense was certainly accurate and wholly at variance with Brecht's stylized image of taking only a portable radio and a handful of small objects that could be fitted into a small footlocker.

With the clouds of war darkening daily, Brecht still managed to move his affairs along. The Erich Reiss Verlag that Brecht had first signed with in Berlin was now based in Switzerland, representing German authors stranded by the tide of nazism. Brecht worked out a contract with Reiss in the late summer of 1939, weeks before the outbreak of World War II.[9] At the same time, a telegram dated July 18, 1939, came from Hollywood, saying that "a topflight producer" was interested in producing *Galileo* in New York.[10] The play had been shown to this unnamed producer by the German emigré actor Fritz Kortner, who was now in New York. The telegram was signed "Gerda"; almost certainly this is Gerda Goedhart, a photographer Brecht had met in London. Gerda was now working with Elisabeth Hauptmann, who was temporarily in Hollywood.

As fall turned to winter and winds swept across the Swedish island, Steffin became psychologically and physically desperate. Except on ever-rarer occasions, she had long since been sexually displaced by casual partners and by Berlau, who visited Lidingö as frequently as her work permitted. Again alone and friendless, Steffin's lifeline was her correspondence with Crassus and Walter Benjamin. "My new room," Steffin wrote to Crassus, "is quite nice because it is bigger than my old one, but, unfortunately, it is so badly heated that I can only work in it if I wrap myself tightly in blankets and a shawl. Now I sit from early in the morning till late in the evening in Brecht's huge atelier that warms up immediately even with just half a bucket of coke. It is a miracle to come into this beautiful, warm atelier."[11] After working all day, she returned alone to a cold room. Brecht walked up a few steps to his large bed in his heated studio. In the morning, Weigel lit the fire again to warm the atelier before Brecht was up. Steffin, often insomniac, crying and shouting into her pillow, worked through the night, huddled in blankets, the typewriter on her lap. She was aware of what she called Brecht's "many small swindles" but believed that she was vital to the writing of the plays.

Weigel received unusual attention at the Lidingö house. Ninnan Santesson visited often and began a clay bust of Weigel. Naima Wifstrand—a striking figure with her short haircut, trousers, unisex jacket with watch chain, her string tie, and a cigarette always dangling from her lip—invited Weigel to participate part-time in Wifstrand's school for actors. Brecht assisted also, rewriting scenes from plays such as *Macbeth* and *Romeo and Juliet*, placing the action in the hands and mouths of the servants rather than their masters and mistresses. The idea (one that still works well with actors) was to get actors to see classic texts in a fresh and liberating way.

In the year spent on Lidingö, Steffin worked on the radio play *The Trial of Lucullus, Mother Courage*, translated two more volumes of Nexø's memoirs for the Soviet Union, rendered two novels into German from Danish, and completed two plays, *Geisteranna* and *The True Life of Jakob Geherda*.[12] The language of *Geherda* is often very down-to-earth, reflecting her proletarian background. Central to the story is the sexual harassment and rape of the dishwasher Sylvia by drunken patrons of the club where she works. Her recriminations about what has happened go unanswered except in Geherda's dream where, imagining himself to be the Black Knight, he defends her. In Geherda's imagination, he helps the helpless; in reality, he contributes to an appalling climate where Sylvia is raped as part of her job. The cynicism of the males in the play is best summed up in one waiter's remark: "Is Sylvia still not here? I'll eat my head if she is not a bigger attraction to guests than the cutlets." The play's preface states that the club where Sylvia works could be on a German river, or on the Thames, or on the Hudson.

Berlau completed an adaptation of Flaubert's novel titled *The Case of Madame Bovary*. She wrote the work for broadcast on Swedish radio and insisted on using her own name. In addition, Brecht and Berlau would complete two small political plays, *Dansen* and *What Is the Cost of Iron?* for a workers' theater group, with Berlau directing.[13] Brecht, as usual with worker productions, only occasionally looked in.[14] Berlau arranged for the production, with its "knockabout" or circus-style arrangements that she and Brecht used as a leitmotif, to be photographed throughout.[15] *Dansen* openly criticized Sweden's shipping large quantities of iron ore to the Third Reich. The ironmonger Herr Svendson (Mr. Sweden) eventually has to face his customer (obviously Germany), with the customer holding a gun made of Swedish metal. Thinking it politically expedient to hide his part, Brecht briefly took on the pseudonym John Kent.[16]

In conversations about subjects for new plays, Wifstrand happened to mention a classical Swedish tale by Johan Ludvig Runeberg. A Swedish subject drawn from the early seventeenth century when Sweden was a major European power was a good choice if there was to be any hope of getting a Swedish production. The story was about a woman called Lotta Svörd, who lives by running a canteen for soldiers. Wifstrand wanted a play where she, now fifty years of age, could play the lead. She prepared a translation for Brecht of one section of Runeberg's work.[17] A few days later, Brecht read aloud to her the first section of what would now become the play *Mother Courage*. As the idea was developed in the collective, a second powerful woman's role was created, that of the canteen owner's daughter who loses her speech after a soldier "shoves something into her mouth." This "dumb" role was designed for the non-Swedish-speaking Weigel. The text drew both on the Runeberg text and the early seventeenth-century work by Grimmelshausen *A Narrative Description of the Arch-Rogue and Camp-Follower Courasche*.[18] Another model was Widow Begbick, product of the Weimar years and Hauptmann's work with Brecht.

The earliest extant version of *Mother Courage* reflects joint work; it has innumerable handwritten notes by both Steffin and Brecht.[19] The second extant version, both from the typing style and from its thematic content, appears not to be by Brecht though it takes lots of Brecht from the earlier version.[20] In the text that now emerged, the sheer brutality of Courage's mercantilism is offset by her mute daughter, Kattrin, who deliberately gives her life for others when, under the cocked guns of soldiers down below, she climbs on the roof of a peasant hut and powerfully beats a drum to awaken a city about to be attacked by marauders. As she is shot down, the cannons of the nearby city that she has awakened with her drumming are heard in the distance. The scene in which Kattrin is shot down would be described by Eric Bentley later as "possibly the most powerful scene, emotionally, in twentieth-century drama."[21] Such scenes of personal heroism are not usually found in work that we know for certain was written by Brecht. Structurally, the play is unusually strong for a Brecht play. *Mother Courage*, like *Galileo*, follows a line of dramatic development consciously taken from Shakespeare's chronicle, or history, plays.[22] Organized episodically, each episode sets up the next one, so that the work builds to tremendous dramatic force with the death of Kattrin and the horror of a woman whose children have all died violently.

The opposition of the life-destroying values of Mother Courage and the life-affirming values of Kattrin serves to dramatically supercharge the play. *Mother Courage* is a supreme example of how productive it can be to combine radically different points of view in a work. Courage acts in the over-dead-bodies-to-get-one's-own-way style so characteristic of virtually all Brecht's own writing. In contrast, Kattrin reflects the values of Steffin and Berlau. Kattrin puts her life on the line to help change the world. She is *not* willing to allow brutal mercenaries to get things their own way through rape and murder. She is *not* willing to postpone goodness, waiting for some never-never land of the future. She is *not* willing to cooperate with the forces of evil in order to save her own skin.

Whether aware or not of the full grandeur of what had been created with *Mother Courage,* a play that would help reshape the modern stage, Steffin shipped it off in November to Switzerland and the United States. At the same time, Wifstrand attempted to put together a production for Scandinavia, but none of the Scandinavian countries would risk it. Only tiny Switzerland, surrounded on every side by fascism, would dare to do so. The play's world premiere would be in Zurich on April 19, 1941.

In 1939, Berlau still came up periodically from her home base in Copenhagen to work with the Lidingö collective. Weigel had put her foot down and told Brecht she did not want Berlau under the roof of the Lidingö house. So Berlau set up a large, white tent on the lawn. Bursting with energy, dashing about on her motorcycle, she gathered material for use in the writing factory. Production went on even though it was proving more and more difficult to get anything into print or staged, either in the West or in the Soviet Union.

Money seemed to always be a problem. After Mikhail Koltsov was purged in December 1938, it had looked as though Steffin would not be paid at all for her Nexø work. Brecht had written to Fritz Erpenbeck to complain, but Erpenbeck, who had been scheming with the grim Walter Ulbricht against Brecht, arranged for a payment of only 180 kroner (worth $20 at the time). Later, Mikhail Apletin and Johannes R. Becher were somewhat more help; and in 1939, one thousand of the four thousand rubles owed were sent in hard currency. Despite the risk to himself, Becher still accepted some original work from Brecht and Steffin for *International Literature,* including one section of *Mother Courage* in late 1940.

An agent in Scandinavia wanted to take a ten-year option on Brecht rights. On the brink of the outbreak of World War II, and despite the deal just signed with Erich Reiss Verlag, Brecht signed a contract with Arvid Englind for him to represent Brecht's major plays in Europe. Brecht also asked Englind to take out an agency contract in Englind's name for the American copyright to *Mother Courage* and *Galileo*.[23]

The factory hardly paused when the news crackled over Brecht's portable radio that, on the night of August 23, 1939, Joseph Stalin had drunk the health of Adolf Hitler and that the Soviets had signed a nonaggression pact with Nazi Germany, whose secret protocols allowed the Soviet Union to swallow half of Poland and the Baltic states in their entirety.[24]

Once the pact was signed, all anti-Nazi publications in the Soviet Union came to a stop; and the work of anti-Nazi emigré writers, Steffin and Brecht among them, was no longer welcome. Reacting to these latest Soviet developments, Brecht wrote lines that would not be published until years after his death, "i do not believe that more can be said other than that the union is trying to save itself at the price of leaving the world proletariat without a solution, without hope and without support."[25]

On September 1, 1939, Hitler and the Red Army began to dismember Poland. Both armies drove as far as Lvov, the agreed dividing line. Nikita Khrushchev was in charge of "political education" on the Polish front and in the neighboring Ukraine for Stalin at the time. Under Khrushchev's direct supervision, the huge NKVD cadre accompanying him worked out deals with the Gestapo to hand over hundreds of Jewish emigrés who had sought political asylum in the Soviet Union. In addition, tens of thousands of the Polish intelligentsia and the cream of the Polish officer corps were marked for murder by the NKVD. While the Nazis now murdered Jews in their section of Poland, Soviet newspapers remained silent. As one critic has said, "Stalin thus paved the way for the extermination of 1.5 million unsuspecting Jews in White Russia and the Ukraine."[26]

Listening to the Berlin broadcasts proclaiming a grand victory over Poland, Brecht wrote in his diary that Hitler should not be celebrating. After Britain and France entered the fray on September 3, he wrote that if the West did not sign a peace of capitulation, then Hitler was already lost. "The outcome of his war is decided, either he breaks through or dies of hunger." What Brecht was describing was the scenario of World War I. If Germany was to break the alliance with the Soviet Union, she would again be fighting on two fronts against the world. A one-page fragment of Shakespearean-style Brecht dialogue survives from this period, the beginning of a play about Stalin. In a fragment, Brecht has Voroshilov ask: "If we march, what will become of our friendship [with the Nazis]? Where will we stop?" Stalin replies, "We'll decide that tomorrow and today we'll give the order to march."[27] Completed at about this same time was the Steffin-Brecht antiwar play *The Trial of Lucullus*. Set in ancient Rome, the general is tried for his responsibility for over eighty thousand deaths. A deal was immediately signed to sell the play as a Brecht text to Swedish National Radio. A check for four hundred kroner was issued to Brecht on November 21, 1939.

Later, reflecting again on the war against Poland, Brecht created one of his finest poems arising out of World War II, "The Children's Crusade." This work, which is written in four-line stanzas with rhyming first and third lines of an almost childlike simplicity, tells the story of fifty-five wandering children attempting to survive in the midst of a war that threatens them from every side. The children "seek a land of peace, without thunder, without fire."[28] When two of the children seek love together, it is too cold for love. "How," asks the poem, "can a tiny tree blossom when so much snow falls on it?" Lost in the driving snow that weighs down the young tree, the children send for help. They paint a sign to hang around the neck of a dog they have befriended. They hope the dog can survive long enough to find someone to save them, but the dog dies of hunger. In its sensitivity to the plight of the lost children of Poland, this chronicle of failure is perhaps Brecht's single most compelling contribution to the cause of peace. "Children's Crusade" shows us that a nightmare of innocent, freezing, hungry, lost children (who are so clearly us) must be brought to a permanent end.

During the year at Lidingö, evenings were often spent meeting with disappointed veterans of the Weimar years and of the International brigades who had fought against Franco in Spain. As the veterans talked about divisions in the Communist party ranks in Spain, and how Stalin's agents had weeded out supposed Trotskyists, Steffin took shorthand notes. An occasional visitor at the Lidingö house was a young man named Willy Brandt, who had fled Germany to continue the anti-Hitler struggle abroad. During these discussions, Brecht rarely ventured an opinion, confining himself mainly to asking questions.

One of the most frequent visitors was Herman Greid, who had acted with Weigel in Weimar's commercial theater before dedicating himself to helping working-class theater groups get established.[29] He had read widely in Soviet publications and trained himself also to read between the lines, which made him fear that a new, immoral dictatorship had now replaced that of the czars. After the Reichstag fire, he worked in the Soviet Union for a time and confirmed his worst fears. Nevertheless, Greid fought on the Soviet-backed side against the fascists in Spain. After the fascist victory there, he came to Sweden, married into a wealthy Jewish banking family but kept up his work with anti-fascist workers' theater groups.

Greid had determined that what was lacking in the Soviet position was any real sense of ethics.[30] When Greid showed a manuscript to Brecht that argued this position, Brecht was polite to Greid's face but contemptuous behind his back, labeling the work "extremely dilettantish."[31] Brecht put his own thoughts on this issue into the mouth of Me-ti, under the general heading "The Condemnation of the Ethicists."[32]

All the comings and goings across the bridge leading to the Brecht and Weigel household aroused the concern of the Swedish police.[33] The police questioned a frequent visitor to the island house, a student named Alfred Giehsman. Giehsman only provided the first names of people, and mentioned "Grete" (Steffin) and "Willy" (Brandt), whom the police seemed to think were most dangerous. It is an odd historical note that the Swedes felt Steffin was as dangerous as Willy Brandt, one of this century's most influential politicians after Hitler's defeat.

In December 1939, the Soviet Union overran a portion of Finland, but with the officer corps having been decimated in the purges, the Red Army was inadequate faced with the fierce, effective Finnish resistance. Brecht's diary condones the Soviet action, arguing correctly that the Russian invasion was a preemptive strike to create a buffer zone around Leningrad.

Despite the war and the constant threat of a Nazi occupation of Denmark, Grete Steffin decided to return to Copenhagen for a long-delayed appendectomy. Right after completing her work on *Mother Courage*, she made the sea journey south. From the hospital, she wrote to Crassus: "You mustn't believe that I'm happy when I'm lying this way, very scared, feeling so lonely . . . I can only endure pain. Unfortunately, I cannot get anesthesia, that makes it worse." After her operation on December 18, 1939, Grete found she could remain out of bed for only twenty minutes without collapsing. Lonely and ill, she was deeply touched that Brecht had arranged to have a small Christmas tree delivered to her. His gesture overcame for a moment the pain of neglect and made her think again of returning to him.

Steffin was particularly frustrated because she wanted to finish divorce proceedings from her pro forma husband. But she was too ill to get things done, and the case made little progress before she left in the spring to go back to Lidingö. She was leaving just as Hitler massed to move against Denmark. In Sweden, Brecht ignored her. Sexually frustrated, she wrote to Crassus that anyone would do as "a man's a man."[34]

Brecht was busy with questions of contracts and property rights.

Somehow, his interests in Nazi Germany were still being recognized. Through the Augsburg notary, Otto Linder, assisted by Legal Counselor Deiler, in January 1940 the Utting estate was transferred to Bertolt Brecht's now seventeen-year-old-daughter, Hanne, whose legal guardian was Brecht's former wife, Marianne. In the transfer document—signed by officials in Landsberg am Lech, Oberbayern, Augsburg, Vienna, Munich, and Berlin—Brecht's ownership is recognized, and he is described as the "current location unknown writer Bertold/Bert Brecht of Berlin." The document also states that Frau Marianne Schmitz-Lingen, resident of Berlin-Zehlendorf-West, had declared herself "not a Jewess in the sense of paragraph 5 of the first version of the Law of Citizenship of the Reich of November 14, 1935."[35] Nobody in the Reich in 1940 seems to have questioned a transaction between a man the Soviets declared to be "perhaps the greatest anti-Fascist writer in all of Europe" and his half-Jewish former wife.

On March 5, 1940, in Moscow, Lavrenty Beria and Joseph Stalin signed a document disposing of the lives of some 11,700 Polish officers and 11,000 other prisoners captured in the war they had conducted jointly with Hitler. The document states that all these people are to be executed "without summoning of the arrested people to court and without presenting them with indictments."[36] The document was then acted on at once by the NKVD. It has gone down in history as the Katyn Forest Massacre.

A month after Stalin's mass murder of Poles, on April 9, Hitler invaded Denmark while moving simultaneously to take Norway. Suddenly, in Sweden, Brecht began to see the island of Lidingö as a trap and was frantic to get away. Ruth Berlau, who had been asked to help, called on a friend in Finland, Hella Wuolijoki. Wuolijoki agreed to help. While the move to Helsinki was being arranged, the police came in search of subversive materials. Nothing too damning was found. On April 17, abandoning most books, including *Das Kapital*, Brecht, Weigel, Steffin, and the children left by ship for the fourteen-hour journey through spring ice to Finland.[37]

Just before leaving, Brecht wrote an urgent letter to Berlau, clearly fearful she might be seized by the Nazis. The prospect of losing a lover or needed co-worker always made him redouble his efforts. "I love you," he wrote to Berlau. "From now on I will be waiting for you, wherever I go I will be counting on you. And it is not of your welfare that I think when I think about your coming, but about my own, Ruth." She was, he said, to memorize and then destroy this letter. The letter ended: "Dear Ruth, come soon. Everything is unchanged, is certain and is good. J.e.d. And things will remain unaltered no matter how long our separation may last. Even in ten or twenty years. And for Lai-tu, she is given the assignment to look after herself and to bring herself through all the dangers until our thing can begin, the real thing which one must save oneself for. Dear Ruth e.p.e.p. Bertolt."[38] For Brecht, this was an unusually direct declaration.[39] The "J.e.d.," she knew, stood for "I love you" in Danish. The long-term commitment he mentioned was unprecedented.

With a signal like this from the man she loved, Berlau was tempted to leave. Furthermore, in the early days of the occupation, after performing one night at the Royal Theater, she returned home to find her apartment had been smashed by Nazis. When she checked with Communist party authorities about whether they wanted her to stay on in Denmark, they saw that her antifascist work with her Revolutionary Theater had been so public that she was in immediate danger of arrest or murder. They told her to leave and, under party discipline, continue the struggle against nazism from abroad.

For Berlau, Hitler's attack on Denmark had come at the worst possible moment. Her daringly feminist and very lively novel *Every Animal Can Do It* had been issued under the name Maria Sten. With the arrival of the Nazis, the novel would be almost wholly forgotten for half a century. With a few copies of her new book in her luggage, together with jewelry to pawn or sell later, Berlau prepared to escape. The journey north would be hazardous as heavily armed German vessels crisscrossed the Baltic, the skies were controlled by the Luftwaffe, and the Nazis were watching the railways. Leaving her family and beloved Revolutionary Theater troupe behind, in late April, she left her homeland to try to join Brecht, Steffin, Weigel, and the children in Helsinki.

"I Saw That without Me He Really Didn't Get Anything Done" (1941)

Steffin, Weigel, Brecht, and the two children reached Helsinki from Sweden on April 18, 1940. There was ice in the harbor as they landed, and piles of dirty snow lay head high. Sandbags and taped windows were reminders of the recently ended so-called Winter War where the Soviet Union had seized a large section of Finnish territory and bombed Helsinki. The new arrivals were fortunate that Finnish comrades, alerted by Wuolijoki, "Finland's Number One Lady," quickly provided a comfortable flat and equally comfortable furniture for them.

Though much of the library had been left behind in Sweden, as well as their furniture, they had still managed to bring with them some twenty pieces of luggage. But Brecht would transmute by poetry the facts of their condition in Finland into carefully constructed accounts of an impoverished great master fleeing before the enemy and relying on workers to save him; he would establish legends of his poverty that persist to the present day. Only occasionally has Brecht's view of his conditions of exile been factually examined. In a fine study of the Brecht group in Finland, Hans Peter Neureuter notes matter-of-factly that the group was given an apartment in the typically middle-class area of Tölö.[1] Brecht described the new apartment bleakly as "small and empty," but with Helsinki crowded by 150,000 refugees from the area of Finland recently annexed by the Soviet Union, and 90,000 homeless as a result of Russian bombing, the apartment they got was extraordinary.[2] In Brecht's first poetic account of the arrival in Helsinki, it is friends who provide "a pair of beds in clean rooms,"[3] and by 1942 he says of himself, "Finnish workers gave him beds and a writing table."[4] The friends, as Neureuter points out, were all middle- or upper-middle-class—directors, composers, a major landowner, a member of Parliament, and the spouse of a future minister of state. Neureuter is also unusually sensitive to the psychologically disastrous situations of Weigel, Steffin, and Berlau as they are pushed, pulled, and periodically fucked into providing him with the life-style that Brecht felt was essential if he, the great master, was to publish "his" masterworks on the needs of the poor. On her deathbed, Steffin would say she often thought of stopping work with him, "but, then it pained me as I saw that without me he really didn't get anything done."[5] Neureuter says, and I agree, "Brecht's paralysis after her death is evidence that she saw things correctly."[6]

Steffin, the only member of the group who knew what real proletarian conditions looked like, wrote to Crassus: "We are fine. We have moved into a 4-room apartment with an icebox and all that kind of luxury in the kitchen. The old one [Brecht], could you guess, has of course the best room. He has a big room and also the dining room. The children [Stefan was now fifteen and a half and Barbara almost ten] live together in one room, so the last room will probably be for me."[7] In a note to herself, she said: "I am a piece of shit. No one wants to admit that of themselves [sic]."[8] In the same diary entry, she wrote: "It must look funny to others looking at me when I throw myself down on my bed and, a model of bad taste, cry and scream into my pillow, screaming out what I never dare to say right to someone's face. . . . For two years at such times I neither ate nor slept. The third year I walked around with an angry face. Now I try to not let it get to me, at least not more than once a day, thank you very much. But everything's OK because I am a piece of shit. Every year I bought myself a new calendar. But eventually, for months on end, there were no entries made in it and no notations made there in his own hand. I so liked his handwriting. I must have had a wonderful time back then when I was not yet a piece of shit."[9]

Steffin could sometimes shake off her depression long enough to complete and sell a few of her own works. To Crassus, she wrote of her difficulty around the more famous Brecht: "I'd also very much like to be productive, but I have to admit something to you. Always when I begin something, I get scared that people will say I haven't done it myself. And that's why I stop. Also I think it's not good." But then, a few sentences later, some confidence returns and she adds: "Now I took out two old pieces by me personally and liked them a lot. But also most of it is missing. Why don't I keep order in my own things?"[10] Her question was rhetorical. For years now, only through her contributions to the work that she knew would be published under his name had she been able to get any attention from "the old one."

The project that absorbed most of Steffin's remaining energy was *The Good Woman of Setzuan*. The earliest extant typescript has extensive handwritten notes by both Steffin and Brecht.[11]

In his working diary on June 11, 1940, Brecht wrote, "i go through word for word with Grete for the xth time *Good Person [Woman] of Se[t]zuan*." Only when Grete was present was there any real progress on this or any other of the major projects. As is usual for works where Steffin is involved, which is true also for those Berlau and Hauptmann worked on, the text features a strong woman seeking to do good in a world that demands evil. So marked is this gender division in *Setzuan*, as in so many other plays, that Oscar Mandel (not knowing at the time of writing—1968—who else had a hand in the writing of all the plays), has taken Brecht to task saying: "his women and even his children are often heroic. Now it is is true that Communism gives women a solid masculine [sic] role to play in society . . . Still, Brecht goes a little too far. The revolution is not, after all, an exclusively feminine business, as one might gather from reading his plays."[12] However, in the inner Brecht circle, as in so many of the plays, when heroic roles were played, they were not played by men. It was Hauptmann who stayed behind to deal directly with the Gestapo in Berlin in 1933. And it was Berlau who went to Madrid during the Spanish Civil War to report on conditions there, and she was the one who remained behind in Denmark continuing to work on behalf of the revolution in which she genuinely believed, right up through the Nazi invasion. And it was Steffin who was told to try and recover Brecht's papers seized by the NKVD in 1932, or who repeatedly went to the Soviet Union at the height of the purge years to see if a haven could be found for the group there. In his own life and in his own writing, Brecht will literally recommend embracing the butcher, suggesting compromises with the Nazis in the case of his own brother and with the murderous Stalin regime when his own neck was at stake, and, as we shall see later, making compromises both with witch hunters in America, and the Stalinist regime of the postwar German Democratic Republic. In real life, Herr Bertolt Brecht was always full of excuses as to why it is too dangerous for him to practice kindness in the present.

The *Setzuan* play, with Shen Te's daring dream of goodness in the here and now, is set in a fantastic, semi-industrialized "China." In it, we are introduced to a mixture of ancient, rather down-at-heel gods, prostitutes, small shopkeepers, and airline pilots. Here, the good Shen Te desperately attempts to do good in the face both of those who seek to exploit her goodness and in the face of her evil "cousin" Shui Ta.[13] Late in the play, it is revealed that the bad Shui Ta is really the good Shen Te in disguise. She has survived only by having her good feminine self hidden by an evil male self. Is this, she asks her audience at the play's conclusion, any way to live at all? The bare tale of the woes of Shen Te-Shui Ta perhaps seems pedestrian, but it is a story that in its very simplicity would prove to be stage dynamite.

The play shouts the agony of Steffin, who lived much of her life as an author wearing a male disguise. Shen Te knows her "lover," Sun, is a brutal man who steals her money, a coldly ruthless and manipulative male figure of the type Brecht so often depicted positively in his own poems. But even when she finds this out, she loves him anyway and puts Sun's brutality to work by having him run her factory, providing jobs for the helpless and homeless. He works for her because he believes the boss is not really the female Shen Te, toward whom he is consistently contemptuous, but rather the tough male Shui Ta, to whom he is consistently fawning.

Ruth Berlau got to Helsinki in mid-May.[14] We do not know how she got through areas overrun by German troops. Almost certainly, she, who had helped so many Comintern couriers in Copenhagen, received party help on her dangerous journey. Possibly in order not to jeopardize the escape route for others, she never (to the best of my knowledge) described this journey to anybody.

Predictably, the arrival of the radiantly beautiful, radically emancipated Berlau was a blow to Steffin and Weigel. Both tried at first to ignore the newcomer, but Red Ruth was not a person to be easily ignored. When Finnish friends extended social invitations to Brecht, Weigel, and "the secretary" Steffin, Berlau came, invited or not, dazzlingly beautiful in her Balmain-style dresses, with a red rose for her astonished host or hostess. People called the new arrival "eccentric, difficult, emancipated."[15]

While Brecht, Steffin, and now Berlau made slow progress on *The Good Woman of Setzuan*, Weigel tried to line up American visas for the family members and for Grete but not for Berlau. Generally speaking, Brecht did little to help the process, usually leaving most of this work to others. In anticipation of the American visas, and noticeably leaving out Ruth Berlau, Weigel booked five tickets for a ship due to leave the Finnish port of Petsamo on August 5, sailing for the United States. However, when the visas did not arrive, the group prepared instead to spend the summer in the lovely Finnish countryside. Steffin wrote ironically to Crassus: "Everybody says there'll be nobody in town in two weeks, but perhaps we are nobody? We are, as you know, waiting for visas. If one is going to go out at all, it might as well be to the country when you have nothing in particular to do in town."[16] Soon, the whole group, including Berlau, to Weigel's and Steffin's horror, moved out of town. The millionaire socialist Hella Wuolijoki invited them to her grand estate of Marlebäck, in the province of Tavstvaland.

Brecht, Weigel, Steffin, and the children were given a separate house in a birch forest on the ocean, furnished with an old sofa and velvet drapes from Wuolijoki's attic. But even the unusually emancipated Wuolijoki had difficulty welcoming Brecht with not one but two mistresses. At some time that summer, apparently Helene Weigel complained to Wuolijoki about Berlau. Wuolijoki's daughter also reported to her mother what the workers on the estate said about Berlau's and Brecht's sexual activities when they went off on walks together. Wuolijoki began to make Ruth feel unwelcome in the big manor house. Berlau moved out, setting up her large white tent near Brecht's house. Here they had some privacy and could also get some work done. One project begun in the summer of 1940 was a new version of the Joan of Arc story set in Nazi-occupied territory. When Berlau asked Steffin to type the new text up, her rival did the work with the greatest reluctance.

Most evenings at the manor house, Wuolijoki held court.[17] In any one of the eight languages she knew, the Finnish Madame de Staël held forth, telling tales of her life as a businesswoman and globe-trotting politician, as well as of her birthplace, Estonia, and her adopted country, Finland. With Berlau sitting at Brecht's feet smiling her "Mona Lisa smile," Steffin discreetly taking dictation, Weigel pouring American coffee from a silver Viennese coffee machine, and Wuolijoki stretched out on a sofa cooled by breezes from the nearby river Kymi, the bloody battles of the rest of Europe seemed far away.

One of the stories Wuolijoki told her guests was about a Finnish relative by marriage, another big landowner, whom she called Puntila. Puntila was a man divided against himself. When he was drunk, which was often, he was a real mensch to his chauffeur, Matti, and even proposed to give Matti his beautiful daughter's hand. But sober, Puntila's character changed completely. He was brutal to Matti and promised his daughter to a wellborn, bloodless diplomat. Wuolijoki (an internationally produced playwright) wrote the Puntila story as a play and showed her German translation of it to Brecht. To Wuolijoki's initial dismay, Brecht, Steffin, and Berlau reworked the material according to "epic" principles. Later, Wuolijoki softened somewhat and began to rather like the new version.

That summer on the Wuolijoki estate, Brecht particularly loved the sauna. He went there sometimes even with Grete, taking "private" photos and also recording such occasions with an erotic poem where he noted, "after the custom of our fathers, / She will serve you in the bath."[18] She was to "sit on his cock" in order "to have her cunt sprinkled upward" and then beat him red with birch twigs so that "in the ever hotter / Balsamic steam you let yourself be refreshed / And sweat the fucking out of the bones."

The sauna was very publicly placed at the end of a jetty. Anyone going there could be seen from far around. At one point, Berlau complained about Brecht's behavior. When Brecht responded in a lordly fashion, saying he was "going to send her home," Berlau left in a dudgeon to go back to Helsinki. She could not, of course, return to her real home in a Copenhagen occupied by Nazis likely to arrest her on sight. Worried, Brecht wrote one of his usual letters, saying, "You must not be disquieted. I think of you and will not leave without you." He concluded his note, "Alles ist in ordnung," their code for "I'm sleeping with nobody else."[19] His letter ended with the letter "d" for "belonging to you," heavily underlined. Despite the obvious lies, the relationship resumed in all its creative and erotic intensity. There was nowhere else for Berlau to go in Nazi-occupied Europe. She was now trapped in exile, much as Steffin had been since early 1933.

Serene and intoxicatingly beautiful though the Wuolijoki estate appeared, events beyond the estate had an impact even there. Comintern agents were secretly flown into Finland from the Soviet Union and visited Wuolijoki and her guests at the estate.[20] A couple of years later, Wuolijoki would be tried on a charge of treason because of these and many other contacts with Finland's neighbor and, at that time, deadly enemy. With the Soviet Union actively opposing any meaningful alliance of the Scandinavian countries against Hitler, Finland drifted in 1940–41 toward a formal alliance with Nazi Germany. At the same time, Brecht listened to BBC reports of the German bombing of London. Though Brecht probably did not know it, among those contributing to the all-out Nazi effort was his abandoned son, Frank Banholzer, now serving in the Luftwaffe as a bombardier.

With Finnish oil supplies being saved for war, Wuolijoki had no fuel to run the farm tractors. Many of her farmhands were taken as army conscripts. Wuolijoki found that she was fighting a losing battle to continue to run her estate. By October 3, she had completed arrangements to sell it, and she and all her guests moved back to Helsinki. Steffin moved in with Wuolijoki for the winter of 1940–41. Wuolijoki noted, "The seal of death was in [Grete's] face."[21] Weigel, Brecht, and the children were housed in an apartment in the harbor section of Helsinki. Looking out of the window there, they could see German transports in the few gray daylight hours. Berlau, as usual, fended for herself at a local pension just around the corner from Brecht and Weigel. One Finnish guest who met her, and who had been told that Berlau was "hysterical and difficult," found instead that she was "healthy and happy," but the kind of woman "who acts by rules she herself had set up."[22]

Steffin tried to keep working. Between October 1940 and May 1941, she did most of the translation from English of the Japanese play Okichi under the title Judith of Shimoda. As is usual with Steffin projects, the Shimoda play turns around a strong central character who is a woman. Steffin also contributed to Puntila, The Good Woman of Setzuan, and a play about Hitler called Arturo Ui. With her hostess as co-translator, Steffin completed a German version of Wuolijoki's play about an independent woman The Innkeeper of Niskavuori. Besides all this, she worked with Wuolijoki on a German version of Wuolijoki's adaptation of the Estonian folk poem *Soja Laul,* or *The Poem of War.* It became in Wuolijoki's version strongly pacificist. And whereas the original text centered around a male figure, Wuolijoki insisted on creating a work where women are as important as the male hero. It was a curious project in a very obscure language, but the very country of Estonia had recently all but disappeared in the summer of 1940, together with Lithuania and Latvia. In December, in almost perpetually dark Helsinki, work on the Estonian poem was interrupted. Wuolijoki was terribly worried about Steffin. Wuolijoki insisted on bringing in a doctor who told Grete she was too ill to write anymore. Only now did Brecht get involved in the work on the *Poem of War,* taking down Wuolijoki's German translation of the text. When the poem was published in German in 1984, it was sold as a Wuolijoki-Brecht project, with Steffin's contribution acknowledged neither on the cover nor in the royalty statements. Her name is only found inside, in the footnotes.[23]

Finland was drawing closer to Nazi Germany. Finally, Brecht wrote, on November 5, 1940, "today chose america." But having left the decision so late, Brecht had drastically reduced the chances that any of them could ever now reach America. The only remaining route, even once Soviet and American visas might be obtained, was across the length of the Soviet Union to the Far-Eastern port city of Vladivostok. In light of the arrest or murder of virtually all the closest associates of the Brecht group in Moscow, a trip through Russia was almost as dangerous as waiting for Hitler to arrive, but it might be the margin between life and death. Weigel desperately set out to find a way to America, fully three years after Steffin had first argued the necessity of this.

Steffin almost continuously ran a high fever and rapidly lost weight. But despite her doctor's orders, by late December, she was back at work on *The Good Woman of Setzuan.* She could only work a total of ten minutes in an entire day, writing by hand, since the doctor had explicitly told her not to use a typewriter.[24] With Steffin often almost completely out of commission, Brecht now spent more time with Berlau, with the usual mixture of sex and work as together they tried to complete *Setzuan.* When the play was finally near completion in late January 1941, Brecht noted only, "work on *The Good Woman of Setzuan* was dragged out by Grete's illness."[25]

When Berlau went to the American consul, Lawrence von Hellens, to apply for a visa, he cabled Copenhagen for background information. He learned she had been "a Communist party member since 1930 and had visited the Soviet Union four times." Red in the face, he raged at Berlau: "You'll never get into the United States. And it won't do you any good to file your request at any other consulate as I'm going to circulate what I have learned from Copenhagen." Somewhat daunted, Berlau went to see the Danish consul in Helsinki, an Herr Baek. Baek had been the Danish consul who had met Berlau in Leningrad when she had made her trip there as a journalist in 1930. Baek told von Hellens that Berlau was a harmless "salon Communist." On March 29, Berlau had her American visa and, with her own funds in hand, could now have left at any time. With her usual courage, she would wait until the other five had American visas.

The case for a visa for Steffin was presented by the influential Wuolijoki who said she wanted Steffin to do research for her in the United States. This story, given Steffin's rapidly deteriorating health, was wildly implausible but the best that could be dreamed up under the circumstances. Brecht, Weigel, Mari Barbara, and Stefan were being handled by the American consul as one entity for visa purposes. Luckily, Brecht was not a Communist party member; he even looked respectable, having put on a suit and even a tie for his meetings with von Hellens. Prompted by Piscator, Alvin S. Johnson, the president of the New School in New York, wrote offering Brecht a teaching post. An "affidavit of support" came in also from the wealthy Hollywood emigré director William Dieterle.

Elisabeth Hauptmann, by this time an American citizen, worked tirelessly on the group's behalf, urging the Feuchtwangers, Weill, Lenya, Dieterle, and poet H. R. Hays (whom she had involved in doing Brecht translations) to send Brecht whatever money they could. In asking for help, Hauptmann wrote: "The worst is that he has been very ill. There is a great food shortage there and that combined with the damp climate was enough. I think it now depends entirely on those of us who are financially able either to let him completely collapse there or try to get him over here. The journey across Siberia is expensive. They also need to be properly outfitted."[26] Dorothy Thompson, whom Brecht and Hauptmann had met in Berlin, lobbied her friends President and Eleanor Roosevelt for a visa for the Brecht group. A special letter on Brecht's behalf came from Väinö Tanner, one of Finland's most powerful politicians, a key architect of the then emerging alliance with Nazi Germany.[27]

Von Hellens still looked askance at the ménage à quatre. He said Weigel must cable Berlin for "a certificate of morality." He insisted also that Nazi-occupied Copenhagen be cabled asking authorities there to renew the group's Danish residency papers so the group could be shipped back there if necessary. Finally, he told them they must have money enough to complete the whole journey halfway around the globe yet still arrive in America with one thousand dollars apiece.

By this time, the normally unflappable Weigel was openly hysteri-cal and tried wherever she could to borrow money from Finnish friends. Not expecting any result, she cabled Berlin for a "certificate of morality." Astonishingly, even as the Wannsee "final solution" was being put together, a Nazi official wrote to say that Weigel's morals were in order. And in Nazi-occupied Denmark, an official with a taste for the dialectic noted in pencil in the margin of the Brecht file that it was best to continuously renew Brecht's Danish papers as this was the best way to keep him away.[28]

It was still a dismal forty-third birthday for Brecht in February. Seeking some kind of relaxation, Brecht went to see a gangster movie called *Invisible Chains*. Soon, putting visa, money, and health difficulties to one side, Brecht and Steffin were hard at work on yet another new work, a play called optimistically *The Resistible Rise of Arturo Ui*, which argued the obvious, that if people had acted together in the early days that the rise of the gangster Hitler could have been resisted. The play is radically uneven, at times almost childish, but rises to a virtually Shake-spearean level of brilliance, particularly in depicting savagery (as the German playwright Heiner Müller has approvingly noted). Müller argues (and *Arturo Ui* is only one of several plays and poems he uses to make this point) that in Brecht and Hitler we find "the same kind of malignant malice, there is an extraordinary affinity."[29] Whether or not this aspect of Brecht or the text was visible to most readers at the time with Hitler at the door, *Arturo Ui* was unstageable at that time and place.

For Steffin, money was not the only anguish. "For weeks," she wrote in an autobiographical dream piece, "I have been aboard the ship of fever. It climbs frighteningly high and then sinks so deep that I feel so awful, so awful. I want to reach the shore of health, but the ship never reaches shore. I jump overboard into the dark water, but with fish nets and with fish hooks, they haul me back aboard." Taken below decks on the "fever ship," through fog Steffin sees a large number of men and women sitting on long benches. She asks her guards who these people are, and one guard replies that they are all actors. What do they want from me? asks Steffin. Their roles, replies a guard. "What are your favorites?" demand the clamorous actors through the fog. "All those plays," the dreamer replies, "that through these bad times could not be staged, *Saint Joan*, *Mother Courage*, *Galileo*, *Setzuan*, these are the ones I love best." Despairingly, the dreamer says, "These new plays can only be played if the times change. However, the times will only change if these plays can now be played." The dream ends, "The swaying bottom opens under me and I fall, fall, fall."[30]

The group tried to extract hard currency from the Soviets for work that still had not been paid for after Mikhail Koltsov's arrest in

late 1938. In November, Brecht had written to Koltsov's former assistant, Mikhail Apletin, urging speedy payment for past work done, particularly the Nexø translations.[31] Apletin was warily polite in his
Russian-language reply of March 12 but sent no money.[32] When it was
clear that nothing might come from Moscow, Brecht asked the Soviet
consul in Helsinki for the Nexø money but was again refused. After
Brecht's failures, the Russian-speaking Steffin made a try. Somehow,
she managed to persuade a Soviet official by the name of Terentiev to
issue the funds *if* Wuolijoki would sign a guarantee to reimburse the
funds if Moscow disapproved the payment. Wuolijoki signed, and
Steffin was given the equivalent of about four thousand dollars.[33]

Steffin's success coincided with the group's receiving Mexican
visas. Hauptmann had recommended this strategy in case American
visas did not come through. Brecht was now convinced, however, that
the group would get American immigration visas and that at least a
tourist visa could be obtained for Steffin.[34] In order to meet the American requirement that Steffin not become a drain on the government,
Brecht asked William Dieterle and the Oscar-winning actress Luise
Rainer to underwrite pro forma any American expenses Steffin might
incur. Insisting on America rather than Mexico, Brecht risked all their
lives.

With some of their own funds, plus Steffin's large amount of
money in hand to show they could arrive in America with one thousand
dollars each, a form was filed with the American consul on April 15
stating that the Brecht group planned to "depart from Bassia, Persia,
and enter the United States at San Francisco, to join Mr. William
Dieterle, 3351 North Knoll Drive, Hollywood, California."[35] Brecht
still hoped to find a way to reach the United States without having to
enter the Soviet Union. But, as a glance at a map shows, with the
German invasion of Bulgaria, Yugoslavia, and Greece in March and
April, by April 15, he could not have realistically hoped to reach Persia
without either encountering German troops or crossing over into the
Soviet Union.

On May 3, 1941, the American immigration visas for everyone but
Steffin arrived. Advancing Nazis had blocked access to all European
ports, and it was clear that Soviet transit visas would now be needed.
While the applications began to work their way through a cumbersome
NKVD-dominated bureaucracy, and final details of Steffin's US "Visi-
tors Visa" were ironed out, twelve German warships dropped anchor
in the Finnish port of Turku. Weigel went into a panic. On May 12,
Steffin's American tourist visa arrived, and Russian transit visas were
issued for the entire group. Immediately, tickets were booked to nearby
Leningrad. There, negotiations with Hitler's ally would be needed to get

authorization for the group to proceed to Moscow and then to America. On May 13, Hitler secretly ordered that final preparations be made for Operation Barbarossa, the invasion of the Soviet Union. Within days, heavily loaded trains would begin to roll east to staging grounds all along the Soviet frontier.

On May 15, in Helsinki, plans were finally in place for the small group of emigrés to leave for the Soviet Union the next day. A *Puntila* contract was signed by Brecht and Wuolijoki. It recognized the play as a "collaborative effort" and specified that all income from the work was to be equally divided.[36] Like other Brecht contracts, it would be routinely violated in the years ahead. That evening, Finnish friends gave a farewell dinner for the group at the elegant tower restaurant Torni. As a farewell present to friends, Berlau gave away copies of her feminist book *Every Animal Can Do It*. When the group got up to leave, Steffin asked Erkki Vala, one of the Finnish guests, if she could give him a hug because, she said, "we will not see one another again."[37]

Late that same night, Grete wrote to her family in Berlin: "Here, it is still not spring, not the tiniest bit of green on the trees, I have such longing for the spring . . . May everything go well for all of you. And *auf Wiedersehen!* Yours, Grete."[38] Then, in anticipation of crossing the dangerous Soviet frontier the next day with its NKVD guards, she sewed into the lining of her coat an emergency fund of fifteen British pounds—all that she had kept for herself of the four thousand dollars of earnings put at the disposal of her comrades.

For her, the journey she was now embarking on, four years after she had urgently counseled the group to get beyond the reach of both the Gestapo and the NKVD, would consume her last strength. Had they left for California, and had she got there the medical care she needed, she would have had a fighting chance for life. Her only consolation would be the great plays to which she contributed so much, and the money she earned in Moscow, now used to finance the group's journey to possible freedom.

31

"I and My People . . . Firmly Believe Your Wise Plan: Hitler Is Not Going to Attack Us in 1941" (1941)

As the travelers left Helsinki on May 16, 1941, final preparations advanced in Berlin for Operation Barbarossa, the invasion of the Soviet Union by air and land forces greater than any ever before assembled.[1] Alongside conventional units, 3,000 men had been organized into four task forces or Einsatzgruppen. They were to carry out mass murder under the rubric "special tasks." On March 30, Hitler had harangued 250 high-ranking German officers from all branches of the service. According to Admiral Halder's notes of the meeting, Hitler stated, "The leaders must demand of themselves the sacrifice of overcoming their scruples."[2] On June 6, 1941, Hitler ordered that the commissars of the Red Army, being "the authors of barbarously Asiatic methods of fighting . . . when captured in battle or in resistance are on principle to be disposed of by gunshot immediately."[3] Just as Kaiser Wilhelm had told German troops leaving for China in 1900 to "take no prisoners," Heinrich Himmler gave orders to Einsatzgruppen and regular army units preparing to leave for the Soviet Union that they were to kill not only all Jews but all " 'Asiatic inferiors,' Communist functionaries, and Gypsies."[4]

As the massive, bloody German plans advanced, the Soviet Union was singularly ill equipped to react adequately. Her intelligence networks, like the armed forces and the party cadres, had been ravaged by the NKVD on Stalin's orders. The one reliable intelligence organization still in place was General Jan Bersin's military intelligence division called the Fourth Channel. Bersin himself had been killed by the NKVD after he had dared to complain of the NKVD's murderous and divisive activities during the Spanish Civil War. In 1941, in a scenario worthy of Kafka, the only reason the Soviet Union still had a properly functioning intelligence service at all was because the NKVD had not yet completed the destruction of all agents put in place at foreign stations by Bersin. Bersin's network still reported but to a Moscow that consistently disbelieved any negative data it received no matter how well founded.

On May 15, 1941, one of Bersin's best agents, Dr. Richard Sorge, reported to Moscow from Tokyo by clandestine radio. Sorge said the German military attaché in Tokyo had given him the plan of the proposed German attack. "Scholl gave me," said Sorge, "a detailed account. The attack would begin on June 20; there might be two or three days' delay, but preparations were complete. 170–190 German divisions were massed on the Eastern frontier. There would be no ultimatum or declaration of war. The Red Army would collapse, and the Soviet regime would fall within two months."[5] Moscow Central responded, "Central cannot believe this." Sorge jumped up in anger and disbelief, "Jetzt langt es mir aber" (that's enough for me).[6] But as disciplined agents, they continued to risk their lives, though all Moscow Central wanted were fictions supporting Stalin's erroneous preconceptions, like those Koltsov had sent from Spain.

At just this time, Brecht, Weigel, Steffin, Berlau, and the children reached the Soviet border. With illegal money sewn into her coat and barely able to either stand or talk, the Russian-speaking Steffin had to deal with the hours of perilous questions. The group had twenty-two pieces of luggage, many of them elegant, bearing labels from all over Europe and even America. In the suitcases were literally hundreds of typescripts in various languages. Some of them were works that had been translated in the Soviet Union either by the "traitor and Japanese spy" Sergei Tretiakov or by Valentin Stenich, who had met his death in 1939. There were works endorsed by the "traitors" Koltsov, Béla Kun, and Vladimir Knorin, and works denounced in print by Lukács and Fritz Erpenbeck.

After hours of questioning and the examination of every scrap of paper they had in each piece of luggage, the NKVD decided to allow the wanderers to go on at least to Leningrad. From there, a mid-level foreign office official named Velichkin sent a cable to Apletin in Moscow saying he planned to put the party on the second-class express "The Arrow," departing for Moscow the following day.[7] Velichkin also said, "Brecht has no money."[8] Together in one room at a Leningrad hotel that first night in the Soviet Union, Grete, despite having piled all the available bedclothes on her bed, shivered uncontrollably and coughed the entire night.

When they got to Moscow on Sunday, May 18, the group was not greeted by a bevy of top privileged intelligentsia. Most of those who had greeted Brecht on earlier visits were dead or in the gulag. They were met by the second-level bureaucrat Mikhail Apletin and the German-speaking secretary of the Foreign Commission, Lidia Ivanovna Gerasimova. Apletin reported to Alexander Fadayev, who reported directly to Stalin. As head of the Writers' Union, Fadayev held the rank of general in a borderland between "culture" (as Stalin understood it) and intelligence.[9] Routinely, Fadayev met with Stalin and personally signed lists sanctioning the arrest and death of members of his union. For his complicity, Fadayev himself admitted later, he was showered "with money and honors."[10]

The new arrivals were given one room at the Hotel Metropolitan. Lidia Ivanovna Gerasimova remembered the way Steffin looked at arrival. "She was a small blond woman, thin, sitting there with her hands up her sleeves, wrapping herself in her brown coat like a sick little boy.... Perhaps," recalled Gerasimova, "this has so engraved itself in my memory because I had to work with her right up to the very last day."[11]

On May 22, the group was invited to attend the fiftieth birthday party of Johannes R. Becher. It was a state-funded evening, with ample food and drink, held at a converted mansion that served as a club for the Writers' Union. The mood was superficially gay; nobody dared to voice their fear of being liquidated. Becher constantly thought of suicide. Bernhard Reich called, risking his own life to warn his friends that the German attack was now imminent.[12] Fresh from arrest himself, he reported that Asja Lazis, co-director of the 1924 Edward II, had also been taken away.

With Steffin as guide, Brecht tried to tap a way to the truth through a minefield of deceptions. He arranged to meet with his powerful enemy Georg Lukács, who protested that he was not Brecht's enemy; unspecified "others" had pushed him to the attack. It was bad enough dealing with Lukács's lies, but it was also frightening that even old friends such as Becher, Willi Bredel, and Reich could have been co-opted by the NKVD.

The group had to know that they were moving among corpses on leave from death. Brecht and Steffin spoke with Maria Osten, still searching in vain for information on her husband arrested two and half years before. Osten told them bluntly of how she had been rejected by her adopted son and by her former CPG colleagues—all terrified of any association with the wholly innocent wife of an NKVD victim.[13]

They tried to get news of Carola Neher, but among her few friends who were not in the gulag, nobody dared talk. We now know from accounts of Eugenia Ginzburg and Margarete Buber-Neumann, who sometimes shared a cell with her, what had happened.[14] The erstwhile star of The Threepenny Opera was last seen by friends in the back of an open truck in the city of Yaroslavl in 1937 where "Carola's beauty and unusual dress drew the eyes of the passersby."[15] In 1940, the NKVD tried to force her to "cooperate" as an agent.[16] She refused and would endure two further years of NKVD brutality before she was shot on June 28, 1942. We know this from an NKVD scribble on her last letter to her tiny son, a letter delivered twenty-six years later.[17]

Steffin was particularly aware of the danger as they met with Reich and Osten, and pursued the fate of Neher. With their own history of association with Koltsov, they could be taken at any moment either in Moscow itself or pulled later from the Transsiberian Express. They had no idea of whether someone they talked with had been "turned" by the NKVD. If Reich had been an NKVD plant, then failure to turn them in for their "defeatist" attitude was enough to insure his and Osten's own instant arrest. Their best hope, they determined, was to continually remind the Soviet authorities of Brecht's association with people of influence in the United States, especially Lion Feuchtwanger and Dorothy Thompson, both of whom were known to have direct access to the White House. If reminded of this, the Soviet authorities might be made to worry about the furor that might ensue in the United States if Brecht were now to disappear.

They needed several things from the Soviets almost immediately: formal permission to leave the Soviet Union; money for the hard-to-come-by reservations on the Transsiberian Express to Vladivostok; finally, boat tickets from Vladivostok to the United States. Each item was delicate and would require extensive negotiation, mostly by Steffin, with the complex and xenophobic Soviet bureaucracy. Steffin tried to obtain the money by writing a letter for Brecht to the state publishing house. Barely able to breathe, she was already aware she was attempting to arrange a journey that almost certainly she would never make. The carefully phrased Russian letter read: "Dear Comrade Chagin, Having learned on the road to America that I would be traveling to the Soviet Union, Lion Feuchtwanger informed me that I could withdraw from his royalty account in Soviet Rubles as much as I might need. I need the money for my trip and for my co-worker, Margarete Steffin-Juul, who is seriously ill and evidently will be forced to remain here and then catch up later. I will be very grateful if you could give me from the current account of Feuchtwanger 18,000 Rubles. Bertolt Brecht."[18]

Berlau looked up old contacts that she had made while visiting Moscow in 1933 with her Revolutionary Theater group. She arranged to meet privately with theater director Arthur Pieck, brother of the Comintern functionary and future premier of the German Democratic Republic, Wilhelm Pieck. While they were out for a walk and hence presumably out of NKVD earshot, Arthur Pieck confirmed what they knew anyway from Reich, that war with Nazi Germany was imminent.[19] Pieck told Berlau to leave at once.

According to a claim Brecht made years later, Apletin offered to let him stay in the Soviet Union on the payroll of the Moscow Art Theater.[20] As Brecht may well have known, the same offer had been made to the great experimental director Vsevolod Meyerhold. Meyerhold's theater was subsequently taken away, and he was sent to work with Stalin's favorite director, the sycophantic Stanislavsky.[21] From the Moscow Art Theater, Meyerhold had been taken to the torture chambers of the NKVD while his wife was murdered in their flat. Apletin said later that he made another offer to Brecht. If Brecht went to America, money from Soviet sources could be made available to him there, as "the USSR will need friends in America."[22] Usually willing to grab money from any source, Brecht must have sensed a trap in this money that would have made him directly beholden to the Soviets. He said he had many friends in Hollywood who would help keep the group financially afloat if they could get there, specifically Feuchtwanger and Gerhart Eisler, who was running American operations for the Comintern in 1941.

Brecht declined Apletin's dangerous offer (or offers), politely saying that his current anti-Hitler writing, assigned to him by the Comintern in 1935, was inappropriate for the Soviet Union in light of the "special relationship" between Moscow and Berlin. He said he understood why the Soviet Union found the Nazi-Soviet pact necessary on tactical grounds. However, he asked, if he could not write against the Soviet tactical ally Hitler, what would that leave him to say?[23] Apletin had to wriggle around this, noting only "life goes on and that things can change." "I just wanted to knock at the door a bit," he concluded. "You can, of course, change your mind." With uncharacteristic clarity, Brecht replied that his mind would never change. He wanted to emphasize that despite his declining Apletin's help, he nevertheless would be completely reliable. "Whatever the papers over there may write about me," he emphatically told Apletin, "you must always believe me. I will never publish anything against the USSR. Everything else may be possible," said Brecht, "but that will never happen." Apletin then seemed to accept Brecht's going to America. The two men worked out a code for communicating with one another. From now on, whenever Brecht wanted to contact Apletin, he was to use the code name John Kent.[24]

It was May 29; two weeks had now passed since the group had left Helsinki. The constant difficult negotiations were Steffin's final undoing. She could hardly breathe or stand up on her own. Apletin and Fadayev arranged a luxurious private room for her at High Hills, Moscow's leading tuberculosis treatment center. It is unlikely that veterans of coercion Apletin and Fadayev did not see some virtue in having one close member of the Brecht group left in the Soviet Union.

With an ambulance scheduled to pick up Grete at the hotel, Brecht and Weigel packed her two suitcases. Into one went "a broken comb, unrepairable stockings, scraps of paper, stumps of pencils, worn-out shoes, faded photos of excursions."[25] Her more valuable possessions consisted of: a portrait on silk by Caspar Neher; wooden and ivory elephants she had been given by Brecht; a Chinese dressing gown; various original manuscripts; lots of letters from Walter Benjamin, Stefan Zweig, Crassus, and from her own family. She also had a number of first editions, a photo of Lenin, and a number of dictionaries. There were also Brecht's letters to her, the "private" photos of the two, her diaries, and her own and Brecht's erotic sonnets. Weigel and Brecht took copies of all the plays she had worked on and would control all access to them for decades to come. Missing at the final packing was the cheap ring that Brecht had given her years before as a symbol of their love.

When the ambulance arrived, the attendants took one look at Grete and wondered aloud whether they could get her to the hospital alive. During the brief journey, she was frequently given oxygen. When the oxygen mask was not over her face, she said again and again to Bert, "Write to me."[26] Barely alive when they reached the hospital, she was carried upstairs to room twenty-three. She was in no condition to see that she had been assigned the loveliest room available, with ceilings three and a half meters high, sculpted harps decorating the corners, and two floor-to-ceiling windows looking out on a lovely park. The physician assigned to her case was Dr. Rachel Shatkan. Years later, Shatkan recalled Steffin's arrival at the hospital: "They carried her in on a stretcher from the ambulance since her room was on the second floor and she was in critical condition. Externally, she appeared to be the usual tubercular patient: a blond with sharp features, her cheeks somewhat fallen in, moist cheekbones, she had a fever and a haircut like that of a boy, and her hair was stuck together from sweat. . . . When she brought up blood—this happened frequently—she looked at me with an imploring gaze and then, for a long time, would not let me go away and held my hand as if in a lock, you know, the way children do it."[27]

Brecht left to arrange tickets for America and to try to buy Grete a new ring. At five that day he returned. He had found a replacement ring. Perhaps it was just a coincidence, but Brecht was suddenly given the tickets, the last five places on a Swedish ship that was due to sail for San Pedro, California, from Vladivostok in two weeks. As there were no passenger air connections, they had also been given tickets to leave as soon as possible on the ten-day, six-thousand-mile journey on the Transsiberian Express. When Grete was told about the now miraculously available tickets, she smiled and said in a strong voice, "That's good."[28]

Brecht was also now given the eighteen thousand rubles from Feuchtwanger's bulging royalty account.[29] These had to be spent in the Soviet Union, so Brecht bought Ruth Berlau an expensive black Persian lamb coat and Weigel a similar fur in brown. On May 30, he visited Grete a last time, bringing her gifts of a small pillow and a tiny elephant. According to Brecht, she said, "I'll follow, only two things would be able to prevent me: if my life is in danger or the war." When he said good-bye, Grete said (Brecht claimed later), "Because of the things you told me, I am completely at ease."[30]

Leaving High Hills, Brecht joined the rest of the group waiting to board the Transsiberian Express. The train accommodations Fadayev and Apletin had lined up were first-class. The train itself was a holdover from czarist days with its carriages bearing the names of czarist ministers like the notorious Stolypin. Brecht, Weigel, and the two children had one sleeping compartment to themselves, and Ruth Berlau, another. There were, as Ruth Berlau recalled, "proper small salons, in which one could play chess, or listen to the radio, or drink tea out of the samovar."[31] Berlau would recall the journey as "gemütlich."[32] Without Grete as translator, an official interpreter (almost certainly an NKVD operative) came with them. The interpreter could communicate with Moscow through telegraph stations along the way.

On June 1, on Grete's behalf, a telegram was sent to the train by Maria Osten: "On the 31st, during the night, I felt only moderately well. On the first, during the day, I felt awful. Greetings Grete and Maria." Each day, Maria Osten sat at the hospital as long as Grete was well enough to have her there.[33] On June 3, Osten stayed from 5 to 6:45 P.M. and wrote to Brecht that same day with details of the visit.[34] Grete asked for piles of books in various languages and told Osten about how things had been for the group in Finland, how she had objected when Berlau had served coffee but gave only Brecht cream and sugar. "I was," Grete told Maria, "very often angry at his many small swindles." At times, she said, she had not wanted to work with Brecht anymore. But, then, she was "pained when she saw he hardly worked at all" without her. Finally, so Grete told Maria, Brecht had seen the light. Things were going to be different when they were all together again in America; he had said as much before leaving, telling her "that she meant everything to him."

Steffin slept well that night. A telegram was there from Brecht when she awoke: "Dear Grete, Are you eating enough and sleeping enough? Good morning. Bidi."[35] She drank three glasses of tea, and ate some pieces of cake and an apple. At 7:30 A.M., she ordered a glass of champagne and asked if her hair could not be washed today. But by eight she was rapidly failing, and Dr. Shatkan telephoned Maria Osten to come at once. Osten's own account runs as follows: "At eight-thirty, they called me up at my place. I should come. Take a taxi and go. Arrived two minutes too late. At five to nine, Grete had died. She had hardly had any pulse. The directress held her hand the whole time. Grete said, 'Bad, very bad,' and held onto the hand tightly. The directress said to her, 'In a couple of minutes, things will be better for you.' Grete nodded in agreement. 'Doctor, Doctor, Doctor' were her last words. The face is totally peaceful. The hands lie quiet, the left closed, the right open. I thought so quietly did she lie there that she could wake up at any moment. Stood there a long time."

At ten in the evening on June 4, as the Transsiberian reached the far side of Lake Baikal, the following terse message came in Russian: "At eight this morning Grete got your telegram and read it quietly. At nine she died. We take your hand. Fadayev, Apletin." Brecht went to stand alone in the train corridor. Worried about him, Berlau went in to the "family" compartment and said that Brecht, in his grief, could move into her compartment. Weigel responded: "Why? He'll soon forget."[36]

On June 5, Maria Osten wrote again: "The doctor found at the autopsy that her lungs were almost completely gone, huge craters, and her heart and liver were far too large. The plaster death mask of her face was made for you as you requested." Later, at the end of an even more detailed account mailed to Vladivostok, we see Maria Osten's final notes handwritten on the edges of the piece of paper: "Later, I will write to you anything that I may perhaps have forgotten. I will dress Grete in the black dress that she wore on her last days here. On the sixth at 3 will be the cremation! All the best. *Auf Wiedersehen*. Maria."

But it was not "Auf Wiedersehen." Within weeks, both Osten and her child were suddenly "taken."[37] We do not know whether she made the cattle-car or cattle-truck journey to Vladivostok and then was shipped up to the Arctic camps.[38] Her NKVD file, which may or may not tell the truth, indicates she was "shot for espionage on August 8, 1942."[39]

Whatever Brecht was feeling as the train steamed east, he made no diary entries at this time about Steffin's death. Berlau noticed that he did not smile for four days.[40] When the train stopped at one Far Eastern station, Berlau observed Brecht standing alone. He watched children selling Grete's favorite little blue mayflowers. Watching Brecht seeing the children and their small bouquets, Berlau thought she detected in him a real sense of loss. However, two days later, he was laughing. He had "already recovered, he had recovered from the fearful blow of losing his best co-worker."[41]

As the group had steamed toward Vladivostok on the Transsiberian, the usual preparations were under way for gulag shipments to the death camps of the far north. Outside Vladivostok was a camp in which over one hundred thousand of the "taken" were held at any given time. High season on the conveyor belt of death was from April to

October when the coast was free of ice, and hundreds of thousands of prisoners were loaded for Arctic Magadan. One eyewitness account of conditions on these trips comes to us from Eugenia Ginzburg, who shared a cell in Moscow with Carola Neher. Ginzburg was loaded aboard the *Dzhurma* during the 1939 "season." Like the five other similar ships making the far northern run, some seven to eight thousand prisoners were crammed aboard per voyage. These ordinary-looking ships, making an average roundtrip in eighteen days, transported half a million of the living dead each shipping season.[42] "When it seemed as though there was no room left for even a kitten," wrote Ginzburg of her voyage, "down through the hatchway poured another few hundred human beings. They were the cream of the criminal world: murderers, sadists, adepts at every kind of sexual perversion." Ginzburg and the other women were at the sexual disposal of both women and male prisoners, and of the crew.[43]

The fleet of blue-and-white flagged NKVD ships carried a total estimated at somewhere between three and twelve million prisoners. The worst camps exacted death tolls as high as 90 percent. Ernst Ottwalt died in the gulag in 1943 after seven brutal years in custody after Brecht failed to try to help him. Ottwalt's wife, Waltraut Nicolas, was perhaps luckier. She was turned over by the NKVD to the Gestapo and somehow survived the worst of both camp systems.[44] For prisoners in Soviet and Nazi slave labor camps, similarities were striking. Over the gates of the NKVD camps stood a sign: Labor Is a Matter of Honor, Courage, and Heroism. In the same years, over the gates of the SS-run camps stood another sign: Labor Brings Freedom. Like the Nazi system of camps, the gulag was productive in material terms. Not only did the Soviet camps eliminate those Stalin wanted out of the way, but the mining camps yielded three hundred tons of pure gold a year.

Brecht, Weigel, and Berlau may never have had a clear idea of the transshipment camps there. The group was taken to a hotel reserved for the privileged intelligentsia. Telegrams were exchanged with Fadayev and Apletin. Apletin graciously arranged to give Brecht $940 that had been left with Steffin to get her into America if she survived.[45] In his letter of thanks, Brecht reminded Apletin that if he wrote from Hollywood, he would use the code name "Karl Kinner or only K. K." For some reason the code had been changed from the previously agreed upon John Kent. Of Steffin's death, Brecht wrote: "The loss of Grete hits me very hard, but if I was going to leave her anywhere, there is nowhere that I would have preferred to leave her than in your great land."[46] With Grete's money and with a few days on their hands as they waited for the boat to leave on the thirteenth, Brecht and Weigel went shopping. Egon Breiner, a young man booked on the same ship, saw Brecht buying German editions of Lenin's writings.[47]

On June 13, Tass issued a bulletin reaffirming the Nazi-Soviet pact and stating that rumors of attack were wholly untrue. That day, the party of four German nationals and one Dane were allowed to board the small Swedish freighter the *Annie Johnson*, with their twenty remaining pieces of luggage. The *Annie Johnson*, with its fifty-one passengers, cleared the Vladivostok harbor and turned toward Manila. It would be the last ship to leave that harbor with passengers for America for years to come. To Weigel and Berlau's dismay, the whole group had been assigned to the same cabin. The thought of a month or more under such conditions struck Berlau as "gruesome."[48] Acting quickly, she struck up a friendship with the ship's radio officer who she learned was hardly using his own private cabin. If war broke out, the ship could be attacked by the Axis Japanese, and the radio officer was on emergency duty on the bridge where he could sleep next to the radio. The officer agreed that Berlau could use his cabin, but to his dismay, his kindness went unrewarded. When he came to call, Ruth made it clear that he was unwelcome and that she only had eyes for the married man whose wife and children were also aboard.

Food aboard the *Annie Johnson* was plentiful and well prepared. The passengers were invited in turn to dine at the captain's table. Games were organized daily in the ship's salons and on deck. The ship even had a small swimming pool. Brecht sometimes appeared in a tiny brown swimsuit, even giving some attention to Weigel and the children.

Brecht wanted Berlau to take up Steffin's work, but she found she could not match Grete's standards either as an writer-editor in German or as a typist. Weigel was never a writer, so the work remained unfinished throughout the voyage. Steffin's death did not merely mean the typing was late. Though Brecht did not yet realize it, her death ended the most fertile period of production of Brecht texts. Except for a handful of plays completed in later years with Ruth Berlau, or after the war by Elisabeth Hauptmann, the career of Brecht the world-class dramatist died with Margarete Steffin in Moscow in June 1941.

As the *Annie Johnson* steamed across the Pacific, the situation in Moscow became ever-more bizarre. Reinforcing Sorge's warning, similar news began to come in from Belgium, England, and from the Soviet embassy in Berlin. Stalin wrote in red ink on an intelligence report from one of the Bersin-appointed agents in Berlin: "This information is an English provocation. Find out who is making this provocation and punish him."[49] Major Akhmedov, the Soviet investigating officer hurried to Berlin, only to find the report had been completely accurate. When he told Moscow this on June 21, he was told to forget it and go to a Russian embassy picnic scheduled for the next day.[50] From France, on June 21, the Soviet General Susloparov reported that German attack was imminent. Stalin dismissed this also as a "British provocation."

That same busy June 21 in Moscow, the top person in Soviet "intelligence," Lavrenty Beria, sent two typical NKVD memos. The one to Stalin read: "I again insist on recalling and punishing our ambassador to Berlin, Dekanozov, who keeps on bombarding me with 'reports' on Hitler's alleged preparations to attack the USSR. He has reported that this 'attack' will start tomorrow . . . The same was radioed by Major-General V. I. Tupikov, the military attaché in Berlin. Relying on his Berlin agents, this thick-skulled general claims that three groups of the Wehrmacht army will be attacking Moscow, Leningrad, and Kiev . . . But I and my people, Iosif Vissarionovich [Stalin], firmly believe your wise plan: Hitler is not going to attack us in 1941."[51] Having told Stalin what he wished to hear, another Beria memo went to his underlings that day saying "For systematic disinformation, grind the secret operatives 'Hawk,' 'Diamond,' 'Loyal,' into the labour camp dust as the abettors of international provocateurs wishing to make us argue with Germany." Even as the word went out that its most reliable agents were to be ground to dust, the Soviet Union reeled under the force of the first waves of air and ground attack. Hardly had the passengers on the *Annie Johnson* settled into their shipboard routine than the news reached the radio officer that Operation Barbarossa had begun during the night of June 21–22.

Before the first wave of the German attack, with characteristic attention to detail, plans had been drawn up in Berlin for a Moscow victory parade similar to the one conducted when Paris had been taken a year before. Goebbels planned a full-scale media blitz on the day of the anticipated Moscow takeover. At Berlin Radio headquarters, Bronnen was asked by his superior to prepare himself to go to Moscow to cover the victory parade planned for Monday, July 21.[52] But Bronnen declined, pleading that there were other correspondents who would be better qualified.

Since 1936 and his close observations of Hitler at the Olympic Games, Bronnen had seen more and more clearly that the Nazis were bent on world conquest. Bronnen had begun moving in the circles of Bersin's bold and amazingly reliable Fourth Channel operatives.[53] Where many other Germans might speak of real resistance, Bronnen saw that there were few willing to put their lives on the line. At the cocktail parties of Mildred and Arno Harnack, and of their close friends and fellow conspirators Libertas and Harro Schulze-Boysen, and of the playwright Günther Weisenborn, Bronnen heard discussions of ways to stop a Hitler clearly bent on world conquest.[54]

On the night of June 21–22, 1941, as the Soviet Union reassured by Beria and Stalin slept, with its 2,740 planes on the eastern front,[55] the Luftwaffe wiped out fully half of the Russian fleet of 10,000 planes, with negligible German losses. Six hundred thousand German motorized vehicles, 3,480 tanks, and 7,184 artillery pieces slashed forward in wedge formations to enclose hundreds of thousands of Soviet troops. Behind the armor came the infantry and the Einsatzgruppen, trained in the techniques of mass murder. Even as the Nazis crossed the border, Beria was at work attacking his own people. NKVD arrests of Soviet military and other vital personnel continued unabated in the weeks following Hitler's attack.[56] Mother Russia was being attacked both in the front and the rear.

Within two weeks of crossing the poorly guarded frontier, the Wehrmacht neared Smolensk. Riga was taken on the morning of July 1, and the first Jews encountered by the Nazi invaders were tied to German tanks.[57] By September, Kiev was taken.[58] On September 27–28, the Kiev Einsatzgruppen posted the following notice, printed on coarse, dark blue paper, in both Ukrainian and Russian script: "Kikes of the city of Kiev and surroundings! On Monday, September 29, you are to appear by 7:00 A.M. with your possessions, money, documents, valuables, and warm clothing at Dorogozhitskaya Street, next to the Jewish cemetery."[59]

Wholly unwarned by the Soviets as to what was happening to Jews throughout the occupied territories, at dawn on September 29, tens of thousands made their way toward the Jewish cemetery and then to a stark ravine called Babi Yar. Here, the victims were shot in the back of the head at point-blank range to tumble, dead or dying, into the ravine below. Only four people are known to have crawled out of that maelstrom of blood.[60] As Barbarossa rolled forward, there is no reasonable basis to suppose that no news of these massive actions, of which Babi Yar was but one example, reached the NKVD and/or the Soviet high command.[61] Yet no efforts were made to warn the Jewish population of what was happening. Within months, over half a million Jews in the western regions of Russia were slaughtered, and a similar number of the Red Army were killed in captivity.

As the *Annie Johnson* steamed toward Manila, reports coming over the radio were hotly discussed. A Belgian diplomat, recalling the overrunning of his own country in 1940, declared: "In ten days, it will all be over." There were more local problems. First, the children, Barbara and Stefan, and then Ruth came down with mumps. As a result, when the ship did lay over in the Philippines for several days to load and unload cargo, Ruth was unable to go ashore. Brecht and Weigel found a shop near the harbor that was having a big sale of clothes at prices made possible by rock-bottom wage scales. Brecht bought Ruth a pair of black silk Chinese pajamas. Between shopping trips, he observed the meals of the dockworkers as they ate a tiny portion of rice from the large leaf in which it had been wrapped. When they sailed from Manila a few days later, the memory of this real detail of a tiny portion of rice wrapped in a leaf would be stored away for use in a future play set in a mythical Far East. The course of the *Annie Johnson* was now set for San Pedro, California, over seven thousand miles away.

In Moscow, in a heightened wave of paranoia against German nationals, Maria Osten was taken away on August 8, 1941. KGB (the former NKVD) records, which were first released in the Soviet Union in 1957 and in East Germany in 1989, state she was shot on August 8, 1942, on the usual faked charge of "spying for German and French intelligence agencies."[62]

With the Germans now at the gates of Moscow and Leningrad, Sorge was finally heard. He now told Moscow Central, "The Soviet Far East can be considered as safe from Japanese attack."[63] With this vital intelligence in hand, the crack Siberian divisions trained in winter warfare were hastily shifted west. They would arrive at the threatened Moscow salient with the first snow flurries. The Siberian troops dressed in ghostly white uniforms that enabled them to blend into the snowy background would face Germans whose guns had frozen in their hands and whose tank engines would not start in the extreme cold. Having anticipated victory in six weeks, the Germans had only been outfitted for summer temperatures. As winter advanced, besides ice and snow, their forces began to face two new weapons. Their shells seemed to just bounce off the newly deployed and extremely mobile Russian T-34 tank, while the new M-8 Katyusha rocket batteries (called "Stalin's organ" by the German troops) penetrated the armor of even the heaviest German tanks.

Russia's unexpected resistance, combined with American lend-lease materiel, made the Russian campaign far more costly than had been imagined. Unwilling to accept blame himself, Hitler declared, "My generals know nothing about a war economy."[64] But his generals, many of whom were members of old Prussian military families, knew something of history. They remembered both Napoléon and the stalemate of World War I.

A month after the start of Barbarossa and well before the tide of war had begun to turn slightly in favor of the Soviet Union, the *Annie Johnson* came within sight of the palm trees and oil rigs of San Pedro, California. A fellow passenger, Egon Breiner, noticed that before the ship entered the harbor, Brecht tossed his edition of Lenin overboard. He told Breiner he thought this was prudent before facing the American immigration authorities.[65]

Despite a few questions about their political background, all members of the group easily got through immigration proceedings. They had their affidavit from William Dieterle guaranteeing they would not become wards of the state. With the money from the sale of the Scandinavian house and Grete Steffin's earnings, they were able to show that each member of the group had at least one thousand dollars. With immigration formalities completed, they entered an America that, so far, had managed to avoid entering the war.

"As Long As They Are Fighting, the War Will Stay away Forever from Our Shores" (1941–43)

When the *Annie Johnson* arrived at the San Pedro harbor, Marta Feucht-wanger and Alexander Granach were waiting at dockside. Berlau re-called later, "I did not greet any of them, because I did not want Brecht and Weigel to have to concern themselves about me."[1] Ignored, partly because she allowed herself to be, she went off from San Pedro to Los Angeles with "comrades," as she put it, whom she had met aboard the ship. She arranged to call Brecht the next day.

Marta Feuchtwanger took the rest of the group to a furnished house she and other friends had rented for them at 1954 Argyle Avenue in Santa Monica. Though it had all the basics, it was smaller than Brecht was used to, and he would soon urge Weigel to find a larger place. Steffin's money was enough to provide a substantial down payment if they should choose to buy a house rather than rent one. They could also count on a Film Fund grant of $120 per month for the first year.

The next day, it took Berlau two hours by bus to reach Santa Monica from Los Angeles. It was clear to her that she would have to either buy a car or find a closer place. Finally, she did both, quickly getting a driver's license and a used car, and renting a room in the house of a Dutch painter in Santa Monica. One day Brecht arrived there and made a scene. Having heard the painter was a physical-fitness buff, Brecht was determined to show his own superiority. He did one impres-sive pull-up on a bar, raising his chin over the bar itself but thereafter confined most of his exercise activities to those that could be done horizontally.

By August, Brecht, Weigel, and the children moved from Argyle Avenue to a larger rented house at 817 Twenty-fifth Street in Santa Monica. At Brecht's insistence, Berlau moved from the Dutch painter's house, though her room there was very cheap. She managed to find a small, cheap wooden shack to rent at 844 Twenty-sixth Street. She had only enough money to last about half a year, along with some jewelry as her "iron reserve."

Brecht and Weigel were immediately taken up in the professional and social life of the generally prosperous Hollywood emigré community. They were now part of those hundreds of the greatest names in European culture who fleeing Hitler and the Russian purges, or simply seeking their film fortune, had settled in or near Hollywood. At a drugstore in Santa Monica or Beverly Hills, one could run into Thomas Mann, Jean Renoir, Greta Garbo, Christopher Isherwood, Peter Lorre, Aldous Huxley, Charlie Chaplin, Igor Stravinsky, or Max Reinhardt. Brecht would have dealings with all these, and many other representatives of world culture during the six years he would spend on and off in Hollywood. Nevertheless, he would claim in late 1942: "The spiritual isolation here is enormous. In comparison to H[ollywood], Svendborg was a world center."[2] In Svendborg, Brecht had been the center of that world. In Hollywood, with its film and emigré stars, Brecht was a marginal figure.

By the middle of 1941, the film community was already a trifle weary of absorbing emigrés no matter how distinguished they were or thought themselves to be. In Hollywood terms, even in his own field, Brecht was at best a has-been, known only as the librettist for the *The Threepenny Opera*. In America, Kurt Weill was now the famous one, with a rocketing career on Broadway. To Brecht's dismay, when he attended his first Hollywood cocktail party, he was asked to spell his name. Brecht neither looked like nor smelled like a success in Hollywood. Viewed strictly in profile with his aquiline nose, his hair cut straight across his forehead Roman emperor fashion and with a scar on his left cheek, he was strikingly attractive; but the cheap-looking wire-rim glasses perched on his nose, the three-day growth of beard, the body odor, wet cigar, and decaying teeth, the stooping, round-shouldered, five-foot eight-inch, 130-pound frame in a gray flannel shirt and perpetually uncreased, very baggy trousers effectively disguised whatever physical attractiveness he had.

Weigel's case was similar. Like many performers, her radiance only really came out on stage. American intelligence reports described her as "mannish looking, brown hair combed back and cut short, dresses very oddly at times wearing ankle length skirts and peasant costumes."[3] Her plain looks, dowdy clothes, and limited English reduced Weigel's chances of reestablishing her acting career at age forty-one to nil in Hollywood. Unable to resume her acting career, Weigel's life at home (with Berlau living right around the corner) was more that of mother to Mari Barbara, Stefan, and forty-three-year-old Brecht than of wife. Ten-year-old Mari Barbara had to have lots of bed rest in the first few months in America as she was diagnosed on arrival as having a relatively mild case of tuberculosis. Stefan, nearly seventeen, could be enrolled in high school. Brecht was mainly off, often with Berlau, promoting various kinds of affairs.

Several friends observed that, at home, when he was there at all, he treated Weigel like a kitchen slave.[4] Weigel was long used by now to putting on the best public face she could. Salka Viertel, her old Berlin friend and now a highly successful screenwriter, would take her shopping at the Los Angeles Grand Central Market with its good but cheap foods so that Weigel could feed the family for ten to twelve dollars a week. Raiding junk stores, Weigel found fine old pieces of furniture at knockdown prices. With these, she fixed up their house with furniture of the style with which she and Brecht had grown up. Further enhancing a sense of home, she started a series of Sunday soirees to which she invited other emigrés. She refused to invite Berlau, saying she never wanted her under the family roof. At Sunday gatherings, amidst old-fashioned furniture and the smells of Weigel's Austrian and South German dishes, Brecht could enjoy a mostly European and mostly German island in the alien sea of Hollywood and America.

Invited often to the homes of friends from Munich and Berlin, he could continue to speak German rather than being plunged at once, as Berlau was, into English. Many of Brecht's German friends had re-created the luxurious surroundings they had enjoyed in Germany. Feuchtwanger lived in California as he had in Germany amidst a collection of incunabula, first editions, and priceless antiques. He told Brecht that he was better off in California than he would be in New York. And so, despite the presence in New York of Aufricht, Weill, Piscator, and Elisabeth Hauptmann, Brecht decided to settle in Hollywood. However, he said in his diary, "In almost no other place was life harder for me than in this showplace of [the] easygoing." But he also noted of the lucky that they could "wash out of the muck chunks of gold as big as a fist."

Within weeks of his arrival, Brecht had been actively included in the life of the German-speaking and financially successful portion of the exile community. Brecht would now be found discussing the strong and weak points of the newly released *Citizen Kane* at the Hollywood home of its primary writer, Herman Mankiewicz, or disputing astrological forecasts of the outcome of the war at the home of director Fritz Lang.

One of the less pretentious homes where Brecht was welcomed was the beachside home of Salka and Berthold Viertel and their three children at 165 Maybery Road at the foot of the Santa Monica Canyon. Very early in the morning, from her house just a few steps up the beach, Greta Garbo would stop by to go out for long walks on the beach with Salka Viertel. Garbo spoke freely with Viertel about new scripts for her at MGM (Metro-Goldwyn-Mayer). Salka Viertel shared some of her script-writing knowledge with Brecht to try to help to get him started.

But even as he derived benefits from his various connections in

Hollywood, his diary is full of contempt for the life-style and attitudes of many of the emigrés. His old hatred of Thomas Mann finds fresh expression, and he hints at his living luxuriously while allowing his older brother, Heinrich, to get by on welfare checks. The charge was untrue and furthermore—coming from a person who had constantly claimed poverty as an excuse for not supporting his son Frank or his daughter Hanne, or for not paying his closest co-workers—was shamelessly hypocritical. He was just as bitter, and just as unfair, to the members of the old Frankfurt Institute for Social Research, which had kept Benjamin afloat with a small stipend and was now supporting Karl Korsch. He had, however, quickly resumed his varied sex life, taking a particular interest in the former Berlin stage and screen actress and dancer Valeska Gert, the androgynous woman who had appeared in Pabst's *Threepenny Opera* film and the Baden-Baden "death" film.

Often, he was despondent at his inability to start new writing, either scripts for Hollywood or new plays. He found his thoughts turning to the times when much of the writing had been done by Grete Steffin. On August 1, 1941, he wrote, "It is as though I had lost my leader [Führer] just as I entered the desert."[5] Since late 1924 and his meeting Elisabeth Hauptmann, the Brecht workshop had always had at least one reliable person capable of generating Brecht texts with little input from him. Now, with Steffin dead and Hauptmann in New York, he found little grew in the creative "desert."

Berlau would not and could not completely fill the gap left by Steffin. She had published her own work in Scandinavia, and was less willing than Hauptmann or Steffin to hand things over for him to publish under his name. Furthermore, as her native language was Danish, she could not, even had she wanted to, write German that could be passed off as his. Trying to co-produce texts with Berlau meant more effort than Brecht had expended since meeting Hauptmann in 1924 and Steffin in 1930. Often, Brecht's thoughts drift back and forth from Steffin to problems he was having as a writer or back to the "bloody carnage 15,000 kilometers away, throughout Europe."[6]

Berlau, meanwhile, was being treated everywhere as a fifth wheel. Since Brecht wanted her to be his general factotum, he had no motivation to help her find independent employment worthy of her talents as an actress, stage director, and writer. She often found herself excluded from the gatherings where Hollywood deals were made. Unlike in Finland, she could not simply crash Hollywood parties at the big estates where they were held. With Hollywood's almost exclusive emphasis on young women in film, Berlau was too old at thirty-five to begin a career as a Hollywood actress. Nor would she necessarily have wished to do so unless she could have played roles with a clear feminist and/or progressive political orientation. She wanted to participate in the anti-Nazi struggle but found that all she was offered were demeaning, part-time secretarial jobs at the studios, work she was as unsuited for as Brecht.

When a British offensive was launched against Rommel in Libya, opinion among the emigrés was divided. Feuchtwanger said the British worked slowly but surely, with a studied absence of "showmanship."[7] Brecht was derisive, saying that any weapon would fail when placed "in the hands of a class as old as the British aristocracy."[8] He then unfavorably compared the British effort to that of the Russians. Though the news of the Japanese attack on Pearl Harbor reached California at about 10 A.M. Pacific time on Sunday, December 7, according to Brecht's often stylized diary, he first heard about it on December 8. Dramatizing the moment, he wrote that he was hard at work with the actor Fritz Kortner on a script for the actor Charles Boyer called *Days on Fire* when Kortner's young son came to announce the news of the Japanese attack.[9] When Ruth Berlau heard about the bombing, she said that she was pleased about it as this meant that America would now have no choice but to openly fight fascism. Unfortunately, she said this to a Hollywood acquaintance who promptly transmitted it to the FBI.[10]

As the United States entered the war against the combined forces of Japan, Germany, and Italy, Brecht took out his "first papers," the first stage in becoming an American citizen. He noticed that the United States now proceeded to round up people of Japanese origins and put them in camps.[11] In a poem called "The Fishing Tackle," he speaks movingly of the plight of Japanese fishermen sent to camps as "suspect aliens."[12] For him, things were less dire. An evening curfew was put in place for Caucasian "enemy aliens" like Brecht and Weigel. Only a few of the more obvious Nazi sympathizers were arrested.[13]

The Russian winter helped slow down the Germans, and reports of modest Soviet victories began to arrive. Brecht wrote: "The Russians have smashed Hitler's 'greatest army in the world': Hitler dismisses his generals and takes command himself. Churchill flies to Washington to confer with Roosevelt."[14] Brecht was not alone in his views on the latest Russian developments. In late 1941, the former American ambassador to Moscow was finishing up a book called *Mission to Moscow*. In it, he quoted Bill Batt, President Roosevelt's special Soviet envoy, as saying "as long as they are fighting, the war will stay forever away from our shores."[15] Viewed in this manner, suddenly the Soviet Union became a marketable commodity for publishers and for Hollywood.

Though Hollywood was eagerly producing films such as Ronald Reagan's *Desperate Journey* or *This Is the Army*, or Davies's *Mission to Moscow*, Brecht continued to work on the fluffy Boyer script and another called *Bermuda Troubles*. He and Kortner began an adaptation of Arthur Schnitzler's erotic work *Reigen*.[16] But though *Reigen* exactly paralleled Brecht's own views of interchangeable sex partners and sex unencumbered by "love," he got nowhere with it. With very little English, he was happy to bring in as a collaborator the German-speaking American writer Ferdinand Reyher, whom he had first met in Berlin and who had visited him in Denmark.[17] Besides being virtually bilingual, Reyher was an experienced screenwriter. Throughout the American years, Reyher always remained willing to subjugate himself to Brecht and to work (not without resentment) without acknowledgment.

Trying as always to have several irons in the fire, Brecht began work with Berlau on a piece first called *The Snowman*. After Berlau apparently wrote up the first plan for the work, they began together to rough out another play set in France in 1940, involving a kind of twentieth-century Joan of Arc, which would be called *The Visions of Simone Machard*. Marta Feuchtwanger who was present during much of the work; Lion Feuchtwanger's secretary, Hilda Waldo; and the contract originally drawn up for the work—all confirm the role Ruth Berlau played in its creation. Marta Feuchtwanger told the American writer Bruce Cook in an interview in 1970 that the original idea for the piece was Berlau's, and Berlau told Bunge the same thing.[18] As both the Feuchtwangers had experienced firsthand the German invasion of France and had escaped by the skin of their teeth, they could provide authentic details to be combined with Berlau's experiences during the first stages of the Nazi takeover of Denmark. Feuchtwanger's inclusion in the project also brought potential cash benefits. Neither Brecht nor Berlau had any reputation as a screenwriter, but Feuchtwanger had superb connections with the major studios. A contract was drawn up to split the take, with 50 percent to go to the Feuchtwangers and the other 50 percent to Berlau and Brecht.[19]

As was true of virtually all the work in which Berlau had a hand, the story evolved around a strong, central female character. Simone Machard, like Joan of Arc, dreams of driving the invader from French soil. Simone acts boldly, sabotaging the stocks of fuel that would have driven Nazi tanks and trucks. When she is finally captured, she is placed, like Berlau's sister, in a mental hospital run by nuns. The young woman's straightforward and successful heroism is highly unusual in the Brecht canon, so much so that he would never be comfortable with it.[20] Brecht heroes-heroines either bend to force or, like the character of Kattrin in *Mother Courage* or the Young Comrade in *Measures*, die as a result of openly showing either compassion or courage.

Christmas 1941 in America was celebrated by the Brecht-Weigel family around the Christmas tree that he always insisted on having.

They were joined by a glittering circle of old friends. Elisabeth Bergner (whom Brecht was eyeing) was there with her husband, producer Paul Czinner. The Feuchtwangers and Alexander Granach also came, and Fritz Lang dropped by later. Brecht gave Weigel a small make-up mirror that he had had made for her that morning in Los Angeles. New Year's Eve, always a big occasion in Brecht's life, was spent at the palatial Bergner-Czinner place. Granach and the Feuchtwangers were there again, and Erich Maria Remarque, the author of *All Quiet on the Western Front*, dropped in also. He had the actress Lupe Velez, "the Mexican bombshell," on his arm.

In the distant Third Reich, though the Russians and the British were proving far more stubborn opponents than Hitler had predicted, cultural appearances were maintained. Film, opera, and the stage flourished. Caspar Neher was designing almost thirty superb productions a year. When his *Marriage of Figaro* opened in Vienna on October 27, 1941, a reviewer praised "the graceful delicacy of a curved space in Caspar Neher's magical set. . . . Moving walls, only in white and gold, provide variety in the set, which seems to architectonically match the central movement of Mozart's rhythms."[21]

Under the watchful eye of Dr. Goebbels's organization, much culture was available for off-duty Nazi officials. There were the newest films of Pabst, Riefenstahl, and Ernst von Salomon. Among stage directors, Gustav Gründgens and Heinz Hilpert were thought to be the best. Among the most admired actors were Heinrich George, Lothar Müthel, Theo Lingen, Emil Jannings, and the great musical star Hans Albers. Brecht's daughter by Marianne Zoff completed her training as an actress and began work in both theater and film. Herbert Ihering was made head of one of the crown jewels of the Third Reich, Vienna's prestigious Hofburgtheater.[22] Brecht's publisher Peter Suhrkamp was running Fischer Verlag, the firm he had taken over after the Fischers were forced by the Nazis to "emigrate." Brecht's brother, Walter, was still a professor at the thoroughly Aryanized Darmstadt University. Brecht's son by Bie Banholzer, having helped earlier with Luftwaffe attacks on London, was now in the Wehrmacht.

Arnolt Bronnen was trying to distance himself from the Nazis. As early as 1937, Brecht and Hitler's old friend from the Munich days Hanns Johst tried to get Bronnen thrown out of the Nazi writers' union. In 1940, Bronnen was formally charged with being a Jew and belonging to the opposition. He was in fact part of a circle in Berlin that included two of the most implacable foes of nazism, Harro Schulze-Boysen and Arno Harnack, whose network regularly broadcast intelligence data to Moscow from 1939 until the second half of 1942. Fortunately for Bronnen, in 1940 the Nazis were still unaware that the Schulze-Boysen–

Harnack circle constituted the most effective resistance group in the Third Reich.

Bronnen was dismissed from his jobs in Berlin radio and television, but, amazingly, he was reinstated after a court fight that ended in May 1941 with him being declared an official Aryan. Blood tests confirmed what he had long maintained, he was not the child of his mother's Jewish husband. It was at this time that Bronnen turned down the assignment to cover officially the anticipated Nazi victory parade on Red Square. Instead, he attempted to earn a living writing novels and plays that did not praise the Nazis. But after a novel of his was rejected by Peter Suhrkamp, and Gründgens was not allowed to stage Bronnen's most recent play, he left Berlin altogether and later joined the Communist resistance in Austria.

Meanwhile key Nazi personnel were assembling in Berlin for a conference called by Reichs Sicherheitsdienst head Reinhard Heydrich to be held on Monday, January 20, 1942. The meeting place was a lovely villa on the Wannsee, Berlin's beautiful lake. Here, at a brief and largely cordial meeting, detailed plans were made to make Europe totally "Jew free." Killing factories would now be set up at key points having railroad access for bringing Jews from the major ghettos.

At the time of the Wannsee Conference, news of the earliest, rudimentary efforts at mass extermination had begun to leak out. The Allies learned that at Auschwitz, Dachau, Mauthausen, Bergen-Belsen, Buchenwald, Theresienstadt, and in Poland, preparations were being made to create large-scale killing factories. The victims had no opportunity to organize resistance that could have tied down Nazi forces. Jacob Schulmann, rabbi of Grabow, wrote the following letter to friends in nearby Lodz: "Alas, to our great grief, we now know all. I spoke to an eyewitness who escaped. He told me everything. They're exterminated in Chelmno near Dombie, and they're all buried in Rzuszow forest. The Jews are killed in two ways: by shooting or gas. Do not think this is being written by a madman. Alas, it is the tragic, horrible truth."[23] But the truth proved too horrible to be believed in the ghettos themselves, and when it was leaked abroad, the Allies decided not to make the issue a special priority.[24]

Everywhere under German occupation, similar methods were employed. Populations marked for death were lured with promises of settlement in new lands. But, in fact, as at Treblinka in Poland, trains made up of sixty cattle cars, with the number of occupants—150, 180, or 200—written in chalk on the outside were quickly and brutally killed. Ordered to undress, the train's occupants were then herded directly down a path that the Germans called the "Schlauch" (funnel) or the "Himmelweg" (path to heaven). Prisoners were driven naked, five in a row, with raised hands, down a straight avenue of clean white sand, 140 yards long and thirteen feet wide, lined with flowers, fir trees, guards, and dogs. Beyond all pretense and hope, hurried by blows, screaming in terror and deafened by shouts so loud that they could be heard in the nearby village of Wulka, they stumbled down the "path to heaven." Within half an hour of the prisoners' having left the train alive, the new corpses would be piled up in the gas chambers. Eighteen thousand corpses a day could be produced at Treblinka.[25]

In Russia, the camps went unreported but not Soviet deaths. In the spring of 1942, American newspapers told how disturbed Russian Foreign Minister Molotov had been when he learned of the murder of 7,000 Russian civilians by the German occupying forces in the city of Kerch. In fact, the massacre at Kerch was not against the general population but was directly mounted against Jews, as Molotov surely should have known. But Kerch was one of the smaller massacres. As Molotov had to have known, most of the Jewish population of Kiev (as many as 80,000 people by one estimate), of the town of Berdichev (some 30,000 people), and of the Black Sea ports of Kherson and Nikolayev (35,782 known killed)[26] had been abandoned by Soviet forces. Among the tens of thousands murdered in Kiev was Sarra Maksimovna Evensona, the Russian translator of the works of Lion Feuchtwanger.

At that time, it was widely known in America that the phenomenon we now call the Holocaust had already claimed well over a million Jewish lives.[27] A May 18, 1942, *New York Times* story, for instance, spoke of the obliteration of 400,000 people in portions of Eastern Europe alone. A BBC program of June 2, 1942, estimated Jewish deaths in Poland at 700,000. Both the *Boston Globe* and the *New York Times* picked up the BBC account. Ben Hecht would write a series of brilliant ads in 1943 drawing attention to the horror in Europe. He also joined forces with Kurt Weill to create a Madison Square Garden pageant to call world attention to the desperate plight of European Jewry. The pageant, entitled "We Will Never Die," then toured the United States, including Los Angeles.

Salka Viertel's reaction to Molotov's grief about the citizens of Kerch was shared by many who had escaped. She felt guilty at having been spared when so many others were dying. The next morning, she found a Brecht poem slipped under her door:

I, the Survivor
I know, of course, that it's only through luck
That I have outlived so many of my friends. But in a dream last
  night
I heard these friends say of me: "It's the stronger ones who survive."
And I hated myself.

A few weeks before writing this poem with its rare note of self-hatred, Brecht made a diary note about the death of Grete Steffin. On June 4, 1942, he wrote "Anniversary of Grete's Death." Later that month, he wrote, "I have not done and will not do anything to 'get over' Grete's death." In two other diary entries, he speaks of the constellation of Orion and how it still reminds him of her. In a poem, he said her death was due to "exhaustion from the many journeys forced upon her by Hitler," "the cold and the hunger in wintry Finland," and having to wait for a passport on "another continent." Never would he see that his persistent neglect of Steffin's obvious needs was a central factor in her suffering and early death.[28]

At the same time, Brecht learned of the suicide of Walter Benjamin the previous September and wrote a poem entitled "The List of the Lost." Typically, he begins with a reference to himself, whom he sees as "fleeing from one sinking ship to another." He then notes the loss of Grete. In the next line, he writes, "So also left me . . . Walter Benjamin," thus telescoping the death of Steffin and Benjamin, and presenting himself (though *he* had left *her* in Moscow) as the one who has been left. This poem repeats the stance taken in the poem on the death of his mother; there, he saw her as abandoning him.[29]

In poems from every period of his life, when he is not boasting of being an Einstein, or a Columbus, or a new Confucius, he swings instantly to the other pole where such extremes so obviously meet. He instantly can become a child, helpless victim, the one left. It is one of the great paradoxes that he, of all people, would often claim that his poems deliberately exclude the personal and that the hundreds of poems dealing with this theme have no basis in his psyche. Bébé would always feel himself the vulnerable child who is in such fear that he whistles in the dark, saying he is really the greatest and the most powerful, and that God himself has a benevolent eye on this particular Bébé. Always frightened of loss, and yet unable to form close attachments, he seeks security in numbers. He maintains a mutual fund of the emotions, his investments spread over many, so he can still feel protected even when part of his diversified portfolio fails.

For those involved in Brecht's self-protection, the struggle for his attention often seemed too difficult to be worth it. Orge Pfanzelt and Caspar Neher had left him quite early, as did Bie Banholzer, Marianne Zoff, and eventually even Mari Hold. Hauptmann had finally opted out of his "hierarchical games." Though Weigel had the legal title of wife to sustain her, Berlau had nothing. In Hollywood, nobody appreciated her importance in Danish theater. Nobody knew her fight against fascism even as the Nazis had invaded her country. Nobody recognized that she was a writer or even spoke the language of her tiny country. When she did write, Brecht or others stole it. She said that in early 1942 she gave the screen and radio writer Arch Obeler her radio play on the Norwegian resistance movement, but (so she claimed) he sold it under his name.[30] Brecht did the same whenever he got a chance. Describing his general situation in Hollywood in 1942, he wrote one of his shortest yet most famous poems:

> Every morning, in order to earn my bread
> I drive to the market where lies are bought.
> Hopefully [or "patiently" as the first version has it]
> I join the queue of sellers.[31]

Less patient, less hopeful, and less experienced than Brecht in the selling of lies—and tired of being exploited—Berlau wanted to play a real role in the effort against Hitler. In the spring of 1942, she met a Quaker activist who invited her to give a talk at a Danish-American women's congress in Washington, D.C. that May. Berlau finally had a chance to speak of her own anti-Nazi efforts in Denmark. One of those who reacted most warmly to her speech was Ida Bachmann, a fellow Dane. Bachmann worked for the American Office of War Information (OWI) in New York, where she was responsible for resistance broadcasts to Scandinavia. Appreciating Ruth's deep voice, her real knowledge of the resistance leaders in Denmark, and her ideas about addressing such an audience, Bachmann suggested that Ruth could come and stay with her in New York and explore the possibility of also getting a job with OWI. Before leaving for New York with Bachmann, Berlau visited the Danish consul in Washington and arranged to receive the seventy-five dollars a month due to her under Danish law as a result of her divorce.[32] With this, plus her reserves, she would be able to take care of her own needs for a time.

After a successful tryout at OWI, Berlau was appointed to the regular staff at a salary of $2,600 a year. She rented a home with Ida Bachmann at 124 East Fifty-seventh Street for seventy-five dollars a month.[33] The location was a fashionable one, a couple of blocks from Broadway, Carnegie Hall, and Central Park, and close to OWI's offices in the General Motors Argonaut Building at the corner of Fifty-seventh and Broadway. At OWI, as did all the broadcasters, she had to have her text in English approved before going on the air. As a result, her English rapidly improved.

Predictably, Brecht now felt abandoned. She tried to help him, sending the key to her new apartment so that he could come there at any time, and writing him the poem "My Key":

> His voice is so lovely
> So distant yet near and wonderful

Hello
Hello
I have no peace
If he has to knock
At my door.
My door is open
My heart too
And my lap
For him—for him
Alone.[34]

He wrote almost daily special delivery letters begging her to remain faithful and to return. Occasionally, he would include a small poem of his own, a stylized account of reality that often recycled images used before. In one poem, he speaks again of "dark times," and, using one of their code formulations for fidelity, claims his "forehead is unwrinkled."[35] Much of this verse is lifeless, a stringing together of the hackneyed sentiments that Brecht (ever the literary ecologist) endlessly recycles.

Together with occasional poems of varying merit, Brecht was busy writing lists of projects for Berlau in New York. He would often forget (as he had before with Hauptmann and Steffin) the most elementary of her needs, consistently failing, for instance, to send her money owed to her and to acknowledge her birthday or to remember her at Christmas.[36] When she dared to complain, he immediately attacked, making her complaint the problem. She should remember, he whined in one note, that his days were difficult because he had to work in a foreign language. He said he now planned to stop defending himself altogether.[37] Immediately, the stream of assignments flowed again, often overwhelming Berlau who had little time to spare after getting home after a full day at OWI, where she too worked much of the time in a foreign language.

33

"He's Behaved, in the Worst Word I Can Find, Like a 'Hitlerite' " (1943)

At times when the workload sent to Berlau was too heavy, Berlau would ask Hauptmann to help out a bit. "One doesn't help out a bit with Brecht," said Hauptmann, "you work for him 24 hours a day."[1] Hauptmann was attempting to maintain her independence and write fiction and plays; as it was not known she was the primary author of *The Threepenny Opera*, she was not a marketable name in America. Being half-American through her mother, she had become an American citizen quickly. She could travel without notifying the FBI, and restrictions on employment were largely lifted. Importantly for a Communist, she could safely sign affidavits of support for fellow emigrés, many of whom were also party members.

Hauptmann lived in New York with a man called Dr. Horst Bärensprung at apartment 604, 243 Riverside Drive.[2] Bärensprung's background was similar to Hauptmann's, and though he was born into the Prussian aristocracy, he rarely used "von" or the title "Baron" in the United States. He had served as chief of police of the city of Magdeburg in the Weimar Republic and had been an outspoken anti-Nazi. When the Nazis gained power, Bärensprung was put in a concentration camp; but with the aid of colleagues in the police, he escaped and fled to the Far East. He served as police aide to Chiang Kai-shek on intelligence matters and was rumored to have been recruited by Soviet intelligence. Since coming to the United States, Bärensprung had been on the research faculty of the "university in exile," The New School for Social Research. He also had a regular job with CBS as part of a team of broadcast journalists and (recruited apparently by Dorothy Thompson) did regular stints with OWI.[3] In addition, he was a paid informant for the Office of Strategic Services (OSS), the predecessor of the CIA.[4] His detailed knowledge of espionage in China made him useful to the Far Eastern Division of OSS. His OSS contact, Emmy C. Rado, began to use him to track German emigré activities in New York. "He is," she wrote, "on the inside of all the German refugee organizations and their plans."[5] Living with Hauptmann, he was ideally placed to oversee activities in left-wing circles in New York.

Though both the OSS and OWI hired Hauptmann's roommate, one FBI faction suspected him of being a Nazi double agent, while a different FBI group advanced the idea he was a double agent on behalf of his Communist flat-mate Hauptmann. This latter faction was working on the FBI's mysterious MOCASE,[6] a code designation that probably stands for the *Moscow Case*, the Russian attempts to steal secrets of the atomic bomb. Hauptmann and Bärensprung spent every summer in Larchmont, New York, and had their vacation place maintained by a domestic servant. The servant was an FBI informant who reported every detail about their lives.

On June 9, 1942, a month after Ruth Berlau had left for New York, a young, lanky, bespectacled instructor at UCLA (the University of California at Los Angeles) came to call at the Brecht residence in Santa Monica. Eager to translate German poetry, Eric Bentley began, with Brecht's help, to render his deceptively simple German poems into English.

Around the time that Brecht first met Bentley, there was a much less welcome visitor. Supposedly alerted by neighbors, the FBI came to check on this family of "enemy aliens." One of these "aliens," Stefan Brecht was not at home by now. Having finished high school in Santa Monica, he had left to study philosophy at Harvard. Oddly, it was eleven-year-old Mari Barbara who supposedly had brought the unwelcome FBI attention. She had been seen by her suspicious neighbors eating lunch at a place frequented by workers from the nearby Douglas Aircraft factory. Brecht was not told the real reason for the visit. He notes, "Two FBI people came and looked at my registration booklet, apparently checking up because of the [enemy alien] curfew."

If the diary can be trusted, Brecht seems to have been unaware he was a likely target for FBI suspicion. If so, he was very naive, given his trips to Moscow, his involvement with *Das Wort*, his contact with Hauptmann, and his meetings in America with Hanns Eisler, composer of what was generally referred to as the anthem of the Comintern and brother of Gerhart Eisler. Brecht was also known to have met Grigori Kheifetz of the Soviet consulate in Los Angeles, who was suspected of being head of NKVD operations in California and responsible for efforts to penetrate J. Robert Oppenheimer's old academic base, the radiation laboratory at Berkeley. FBI suspicion of Brecht increased in 1943 when he began to work on filmscripts with Vladimir Pozner, a friend of Oppenheimer in Berkeley. Pozner, a mysterious multinational fluent in Russian, had been part of the Comintern Apparat in Paris before the war.[7]

Despite all the leads the FBI was following, they completely failed to uncover the real spying that was going on around the Manhattan

Project. They never discovered Gerhart Eisler's shortwave radio hookup with Moscow. They failed to find anything wrong with Klaus Fuchs until Fuchs made a statement of guilt to his British superior after the Soviets had already exploded a bomb built partially from his blueprints. The FBI consistently missed the sharks while chasing scores of minnows, such as Berlau and Brecht. Brecht and Berlau's erotic arrangements added piquancy. It was an open secret that the FBI director liked erotic details and leaked them (whether or not they were true) to try to destroy opponents' reputations. He kept a secret bedroom tap on the then young naval officer John Fitzgerald Kennedy and extensive notes on Eleanor Roosevelt's supposed extramarital affair, through which Hoover clearly hoped to get at her husband.[8]

What seems to have begun in May 1942 as a fairly routine FBI inquiry about Brecht turned dangerous a year later when his file was transferred from the general category of "enemy alien control" to "internal security" cases of suspected espionage. Just when the FBI began to interest itself in Brecht, he managed to get his first real break as a screenwriter in Hollywood. Following the assassination of Reinhard Heydrich, the brutal Nazi "protector" of Czechoslovakia, by the Czech underground in late May 1942, Brecht and Fritz Lang began to explore turning the Heydrich assassination and its aftermath into a film about resistance to Nazi tyranny in Europe. Soon, Lang induced another emigré, successful Hollywood producer Arnold Pressburger, to become a partner on the project and to engage Brecht for the script (despite Brecht's inexperience with film writing). Pressburger insisted on yoking Brecht to a more experienced English-language scenarist, John Wexley, to work on *Hangmen Also Die*.

With Brecht working on this script, the FBI found itself deep in literary analysis, comparing Brecht's work on the *Hangmen* script with *The Measures Taken*. As a note in the 1,100-page Brecht FBI file correctly puts it, "When viewed in the light of previous writings of Bert Brecht, 'Hangmen Also Die' takes on something of the complexion of Brecht's education plays in that it emphasizes the conduct required of persons working in an underground movement." Though the FBI heard distinct echoes of *Measures* in the *Hangmen* film, Brecht felt too few of his ideas were included. Although the finished film was above the usual Hollywood standard and indeed won a 1944 Academy Award for its music by Hanns Eisler, Brecht distanced himself from it. He consoled himself, however, with his salary, which was between eight and ten thousand dollars for ten weeks' work.[9] At a time when an American industrial worker's salary was $200 a month and Berlau made $2,600 for a full year and a large villa could be bought outright in California for less than $10,000, Brecht did well on the *Hangmen* film. Characteristically, he told Berlau he had made only $250.

He now moved to a larger house in Santa Monica, 1063 Twenty-sixth Street, which increased his monthly rent from $47.50 to $60. Here, he noted, he was beginning "to feel halfway OK." On August 17, he even admitted: "The house is very lovely. In this garden, one can even read Lucretius again." Berlau told him she was appalled that he would not leave his marriage. She saw this as part of his general timidity and addiction to middle-class comfort. Eric Bentley, who saw Brecht frequently in the coming years, would later not be taken in by Brecht's proletarian affectations, observing "the man was bottomlessly bour-geois."[10] Despairing of Brecht's ever leaving Weigel, Berlau tried hard to break with him. She began an affair with a young co-worker at OWI, Bernard Frizell. He enjoyed her untrammeled sexuality,[11] but she could not shake Brecht. He wrote to her virtually every day, signing with his usual multiply underlined "d," and demanded she remain faithful to him. Thinking once again there was hope with him, she would some-times refer to herself as "a backstreet wife" of Bertolt Brecht. Despite all her attempts at independence, she still loved him and wanted to work with him on plays that would help reshape the future.

Around the tree on Christmas Eve, Brecht, Weigel, and Mari Barbara were joined at their spacious new house by the Feuchtwangers; Hanns Eisler with his wife, Lou; Oskar Homolka; and Ferdinand Reyher. New Year's Eve was spent at the home of the Kortners, who were also joined by the Eislers, actor Ludwig Donath (who could be relied upon to enliven emigré parties with chillingly accurate renderings of Hitler's speeches), Berthold Viertel (now separated from his wife, Salka Viertel), and emigré producer Robert Thören.

After Christmas, Brecht told Berlau to expect him in New York. Piscator had invited him for a lecture at the New School, and this got him the travel permission that as an enemy alien he needed. Elisabeth Bergner and her husband, Paul Czinner, wanted Brecht to do an adapta-tion of Webster's *The Duchess of Malfi* for New York, with Bergner to play the lead. In a note to Berlau, Brecht spoke of mentally "already walking down Broadway with you." On February 8, a few days after getting the encouraging news that the play *The Good Woman of Setzuan* had had its world premiere in neutral Switzerland, he boarded the train for New York. The address and telephone number he left with Weigel was that of Berlau. He told the FBI, however, that Piscator's address was the place to reach him.

The FBI was now following Brecht closely. When he boarded the Southern Pacific train "The Californian" on February 8, at 5:30 P.M., the FBI was there as he checked two bags and took one with him to upper berth 15 in Car, California.[12] Almost certainly his luggage was searched in the baggage car as this was routine for the FBI. Every aspect of his life was now being examined. A report prepared in Los Angeles for J. Edgar Hoover stated: 1) "On February 26, 1943, Source A advised that she knew Mr. and Mrs. BRECHT in Germany, where they were Communists." 2) "On March 5, 1943, Source B advised that he knew BRECHT by reputation in Germany, where he was considered a radical and an associate of people with Communistic inclinations. Source B stated that he became acquainted with BRECHT personally in the United States and found him still a radical and an enemy of Capitalism." Another informant told the FBI: "Brecht is looked upon by German Communists as their poet laureate." As words very close to these were used in published statements in 1944 by Ruth Fischer, sister of Hanns and Gerhart Eisler, it is quite possible that she was the unnamed informant. In this same "poet laureate" paragraph, much weightier cases now are tied in. After heavy FBI censorship in this important section, the Brecht file reads, "Due to the fact that the [blank] investigation had been developed along extremely confidential lines, it is not desired that BRECHT'S present significance be presented to an enemy alien hearing board if this can be avoided, for fear of disclosing valuable sources of information thereby."

A strategy had emerged in the handling of the case: Brecht was to be allowed to continue to run free in the hope that he might provide leads to others. From scattered references left in the heavily censored files of the Brecht circle, we can reconstruct the outlines of three important cases where the FBI assumed Brecht's involvement. As of the end of the summer of 1943, he was part of an investigation of a group of emigrés who were concerned about what shape a postwar German government would take. Another investigation was the so-called MO-CASE. The third case was COMRAP, perhaps to be read as "Communist Radiation Penetration" as the file deals with Communist penetration of the Lawrence Radiation Lab at Berkeley, Oppenheimer's academic home before he left for Los Alamos. The central espionage figure for the FBI was Grigori Kheifetz, who was in turn linked to Gerhart Eisler. Both figures were directly tied to Brecht. What is not clear from the released FBI files is whether the FBI knew of Brecht's Comintern meeting with Knorin in Moscow in 1935 or the pact that he had made with Apletin in Moscow in 1941.

Whatever the FBI did or did not know about Brecht's past, they felt they had ample material to go on in the present. One FBI report read: "On February 8, 1943 Subject left by the Southern Pacific train, the Californian for New York, after having duely [sic] applied for permission to travel, and having received a permit from the United States Attorney at Los Angeles. BRECHT stated in his application for this permit that he was going to New York for a period of eight weeks to attend to business of a theatrical nature. He said he could be reached in

New York through ERWIN PISCATOR, 66 West 12th Street, New York City. The New York Field Division was informed of BRECHT's travel to New York."[13]

Brecht's ostensible host in New York was already expressing disgust with Brecht's behavior. On January 21, 1943, Piscator wrote to his and Brecht's acquaintance Max Gorelik: "He is quick to write[,] even phone or send telegrams to me when he needs me. At other times he's behaved, in the worst word I can find, like a 'Hitlerite.' "[14]

Arriving in New York on February 12, Brecht wrote nothing in his journal about Ruth or the apartment at Fifty-seventh Street. On the way to New York, he had written one poem to Ruth of their having "made love between the battles," and, anticipating his arrival, he wrote, "My lips caked with the dust of the journey, I kissed her."[15] Ruth had asked Ida Bachmann to live elsewhere during Brecht's visit and had taken Ida's room for herself. This gave Brecht a working room with a large balcony and view of the skyline, but he complained that his room was smaller than Ruth's and insisted on switching.

Soon after arrival, Brecht met with the sinologist Karl August Wittfogel, whom he had known in Berlin. Wittfogel told Brecht that Stalin had deliberately encouraged Hitler's rise to power. Wittfogel claimed, according to a Brecht diary entry, that Karl Radek had told him in 1932, "This is a burden that the German workers will have to bear for two years."[16] Wittfogel's position, though it may have seemed exaggerated in early 1943, is one that grows ever-more plausible as we look at recently opened Soviet archives.

At Berlau's instigation, John Houseman, who had met Brecht in 1935, asked him to prepare some demonstration antifascist broadcasts for OWI. Houseman thought that though the work had some excellent artistic points, "as propaganda it didn't work. . . . There seemed to be absolutely no communication between Brecht and the Germans of the Nazi Third Reich."[17]

Brecht's failure with propaganda was as nothing compared with his failure to produce new plays. Without a replacement for Steffin, he had finished no new plays for well over two years. He made a renewed effort in New York to get Hauptmann to come back, but she flatly refused. He became desperate at least to sell some old work and signed up with agent Ann Elmo. Brecht met with Paul Czinner for an adaptation of *The Duchess of Malfi*. As Brecht's English was still very shaky and his knowledge of New York commercial theater nil, he was given a partner, little-known poet H. R. Hays. Without telling his collaborator, Brecht also tried to involve Auden. In the poet's Fifty-seventh Street apartment, his shirt slipping out of his trousers, sliding about in huge felt slippers, Auden received his guest in fractured but fluent

German. Auden smoked around the clock. His curtains were never drawn and his windows never opened.[18] The talk turned to *Malfi*. Before the year was out, Auden was working on the adaptation, and eventually Brecht let H. R. Hays know he was no longer needed.

Almost at the same time, Hays completed a fine English translation of the Steffin-Brecht *The Trial of Lucullus*, which appeared in the prestigious New Directions Poets of the Year series that included work by Dylan Thomas and e.e. cummings. The dust jacket of the *Lucullus* volume described Brecht as: "a German exile now living in California. He is not well known in America, having published only a brilliant satirical novel, *A Penny for the Poor*, and plays and poems in advance guard magazines and anthologies." Steffin was not mentioned, and with her death, the process of making her a nonperson began. Her name was not noted when *Fear and Misery of the Third Reich* was staged and published in New York in 1945. It was a pattern Brecht had used for decades. On *Schweik*, he first had his friend Alfred Kreymborg do one version and then involved Ferdinand Reyher, but told neither party about the other. When Reyher finally noticed this pattern, he was very angry, though he could never bring himself to make an explicit break with Brecht.[19]

Perhaps unaware that many of the people he met were under FBI, OSS, and NKVD surveillance, Brecht met his old "Marxist teacher" from the Berlin days Karl Korsch, who was visiting New York briefly from Boston. There, with an academic grant of one hundred dollars a month from the Frankfurt Institute's New York office, he pursued his interest in geopolitics. Brecht also saw Jakob Walcher, the former student and friend of Rosa Luxemburg; Walcher's wife, former Soviet courier Herta Gordon; and, of course, Gerhart Eisler.[20] Karin Michaëlis, now living in New York with her sister, Baroness Dahlerup, also welcomed him. Michaëlis was deeply involved in the effort to help Jews escape the Nazi death machine, which does not seem to have interested Brecht. When Piscator tried to involve him in 1943 with a "musical play for a pro-Jewish cause,"[21] he again refused, as he had in Paris in 1933 with the *Threepenny* production.

Brecht resumed contact with the left-wing editor Wieland Herzfelde, whose Malik Verlag had published a two-volume edition of Brecht in 1938. Herzfelde now arranged a showcase "Brecht Evening" for March 6 at Piscator's Studio Theater at the New School for Social Research. By all accounts (including that of the FBI), the evening was a success, with performers that included Elisabeth Bergner and Peter Lorre. The applause at the show's conclusion went on and on as Brecht joined Bergner and Lorre to take bows. Brecht liked the evening enough that, at the party at Piscator's Chelsea apartment afterward, he agreed to a repeat performance of the show. When he left the lovely apartment, purchased with money brought into the marriage by Piscator's wife, widow of an electronics tycoon, he told Berlau, "There one sees that with electric light bulbs one can even buy . . . the greatest living stage director."

In 1943, with the tide seeming now to be turning against Germany, the subject of many of the discussions held with other emigrés in New York and with various Americans concerned what were the resistance movements in various parts of Europe doing to hasten the demise of the Hitler regime, and what should happen to Germany once she was defeated. These themes would now show up regularly in several of the plays on which he and Berlau worked.

Turning again to Hasek's novel *The Good Soldier Schweik* and the adaptation that he had worked on with other writers for Piscator in 1927–28, Brecht and Berlau began to consider transposing the play from its original World War I setting in Prague to a Prague occupied by the Nazis. What could a "little man" such as the dogcatcher Schweik do to resist something as brutal as the Gestapo? Echoing the theme of the *Hangmen Also Die* film and the *Simone* material, the new *Schweik* play tries to show little people resisting the Nazis in small but important ways.

Looking for a commercial hit, Brecht hoped that *Schweik* could be done on Broadway with the old *Threepenny* team of Brecht, Weill, Aufricht, and Lenya. Aufricht tried to line up the rights to the Czech novel from the Czech government-in-exile. This was done secretly as Piscator, who was planning to stage the work again, had introduced Brecht to the actor Zero Mostel as a potential lead, and thought he and Brecht would do the play together. But Brecht wanted to work not with Piscator's experimental and political theater but to try for a commercial hit with the famous and successful Weill.

Alternating with the work on *Schweik,* and hoping to have two shots at Broadway, Brecht and Berlau returned to *The Good Woman of Setzuan,* a play he had first begun in Berlin with Hauptmann and had completed with Steffin in Scandinavia. The lead role of the good woman, the prostitute Shen Te, who in the course of the play disguises herself as her tough, male, businesslike cousin, Shui Ta, was a role that Brecht hoped would appeal to Lenya. If so, then Weill could probably be induced to do the music.

In May 1943, Weill and Lenya invited him to spend a week as a houseguest in the suburban community of New City on the Hudson. It was a difficult time for Weill. He had recently been deeply stung when the American composer Virgil Thomson, in a *Herald Tribune* review, accused him of not only having "avoided working with serious poets" but also avoiding themes with "social significance." Brecht might present an opportunity for Weill to redeem himself. As for Brecht, Weill was his best bet to establish a commercial foothold on Broadway.

But the old collaborators, behind a facade of politeness, approached one another warily. Not only was there the old problem of the division of the royalties for *Threepenny* but there had been a more recent problem. Right after arriving in America in 1941, Brecht had tried to act unilaterally in getting an all-black production of *The Threepenny Opera* staged in California. Weill, who had not been shown the patchwork English translation and so had no idea if it would fit with his score, said he must see the text before approving the project. In an April 8, 1942, letter written from Hollywood to Lenya in New York, Weill had spoken about Brecht's plans for *Threepenny*. Weill saw what he called "the good old swinish Brecht method." Receiving this particular letter, Lenya had replied in her marvelously fractured English: "The whole Brecht schit [sic] is just too funny for words. . . . You know what they will do, if you would give in. Cut the music to pieces and make the whole thing cheap and ridiculous. And this stupid Brecht, this chinese-augsburg Hinterwäldler [hick] philosopher. It's too much already, that letters from him, soil our mailbox."[22] Lenya cautioned her husband about renewing any relationship with Brecht. She wrote: "I never believe, that he can ever change his character, which is a selfish one and always will be. . . . I always believed in diccency [sic] and a certain fairness. And Brecht hasn't got much of it."

By 1943, the old Brecht–Weill and Lenya power balance of the Weimar days was reversed. With *Johnny Johnston, Knickerbocker Holiday*, and his most recent and greatest success of all, *Lady in the Dark*, completed with the celebrated Moss Hart and sold to Paramount for $283,000, Weill was far more successful than the virtually forgotten Brecht. With Weill's six-figure earnings from Broadway and Hollywood, he had bought a large, eighteenth-century farmhouse near New City, on fourteen wooded acres including a trout stream. It was a place not unlike Brecht's old estate in Bavaria, and precisely the kind of place he could no longer afford.

Lenya and Weill gave a party to introduce Brecht to some of the neighbors, people prominent in the American theater who might prove helpful. But Brecht seemed determined to show his least charming side. He did not hit it off with either the playwright Elmer Rice or with Maxwell Anderson. The party was not a success. Brecht clearly felt that Anderson was hopelessly reactionary, and Anderson was convinced that Brecht was a Communist. And though Weill and Lenya were Brecht's hosts, they were very wary of any proposal coming from him as they were sure he was a crook.

On the train back to California, Brecht wrote a letter to Berlau instructing her to remain faithful.[23] He recalled Ruth in the white Mother Hubbard nightgowns she had worn at his insistence during his visit. These were ones like those he himself still wore, though his had a tiny red hem. The pure white version was the kind his mother and all the maids had worn—all the women who had cared for him. In his letter to Berlau, he worried that if Ida Bachmann saw the nightgowns she would suspect that he and Berlau were having an affair. The fear is a very odd one as it was very clear to Bachmann why she had been asked to move out of her apartment during his visit. In what was for him an unusually effusive letter, he told Berlau of his hopes for times to come, and he even used the Danish formula "J.e.d." for "I love you."

Brecht stopped briefly in Chicago to visit his son, Stefan, who was now in the American army being trained as a translator of Japanese. Brecht told his son about the *Schweik* project, but Stefan declared that Hasek's *Schweik* would "hardly have bothered himself with Baloun's difficulties."[24] Brecht was not willing to change his and Berlau's conception, however. Brecht wanted to believe that the "common man" in Prague and other parts of occupied Europe was capable of more than self-interest, and was trying to bring about Hitler's downfall.

Years before, Brecht had created a tiny Herr Keuner story called "Measures to Be Taken against the Powerful."[25] In this fairy-tale-like piece, anticipating key elements of *Schweik*'s strategy for dealing with powerful enemies, a fat "agent of the government" comes to the apartment of a citizen and asks, "Will you serve me?" Taking his host's silence as assent, the fat man moves in and is served for seven long years by his secretly seething "host." After seven years, the fat man dies. After his death, his host now "answers" the question that was put to him seven long years before. His answer is now a clear "No!" but his actions for those seven years said something quite different. In non-fairy-tale terms, the real question was, what would need to be done in a postwar world with all those people who had taken care of the fat men and had committed unspeakable atrocities as part of such "service." Brecht's position on these matters was totally inconsistent with German realities. It was, after all, Brecht who had advised his own brother to join the Nazi party and work his way up to the level of gauleiter. And it was Brecht who had left his son Frank behind in Germany, a son who then helped bomb Britain and later helped invade the Soviet Union. This was not German resistance. Nevertheless, on the train to Los Angeles, Brecht's diary presents a dream of millions of Schweiks busily undermining Hitler.[26]

The position Brecht was articulating was close to one being formulated at this time in Moscow. The Free Germany National Committee, a Moscow group, including German prisoners of war, exiled party and labor leaders, and intellectuals, had been given official endorsement to publish a full-page manifesto in German and in Russian in *Pravda* on July 21, 1943. The statement called on German soldiers to mutiny and for German factory workers to sabotage the war effort. The hope clearly was that millions of "little people" could be mobilized to undermine the Hitler regime. Like almost all other assessments of Hitler by the Stalin regime, this too proved to be complete fantasy.

When Brecht got back to Hollywood, he was anxious to finish up *Schweik*. As insurance, in case Weill would not join the project, he got Hanns Eisler to begin composing music for the show. For help on the text, he now involved Salka Viertel and J. Robert Oppenheimer's old friend Vladimir Pozner. As they worked together, Brecht would sometimes play the part of one of the characters. Playing a Nazi, he declared: "The Jews don't have the slightest idea of humor. Look." Then, as though he were brutally kicking a body, Brecht went on: "He doesn't laugh at all, this Jew. He doesn't find this at all comical."[27]

Sometimes the group would switch from *Schweik* and work on a screenplay that they hoped would earn them lots of money. But when Salka Viertel would ask about the context of a dramatic figure, Brecht would reply that one should only provide information in the text that was essential to forwarding the action. Brecht refused to explain further what he meant. Stubbing out his cigar, he declared: "Because I say so. That's all!"[28] This did not endear him to Salka Viertel, one of the most successful screenplay writers among the German emigrés.

In between other work, Brecht was finishing up the *Simone Machard* play that he had begun with Ruth Berlau and Lion Feuchtwanger. It was hoped that Feuchtwanger would be able to sell it to MGM. Brecht also took on some well-paid, hack script work with Peter Lorre. While working with Lorre, he asked him to consider playing the role of *Schweik* in a potential Broadway production. But Lorre did not think his American career would be enhanced by playing a man who butchers a dog and gives it in a bloody package to his starved friend Baloun. He was not the only one turned off by the work. When Weill came out to Hollywood on a brief visit during the summer, he took one look at it and knew that it would never do for Broadway. This news was bad for Aufricht who had raised $85,000 to float a Broadway production of the work.

With or without the support of Weill, Brecht would persist in trying to conquer Broadway. He sent Berlau an occasional poem and a constant stream of instructions. He told her to go around to the offices of the Czech government-in-exile to see if they would give him exclusive rights to *Schweik* and forget the prior claims of Piscator, Aufricht, and

Weill to the material. But then, to Berlau's joy, he would add something about his own feelings, telling her in a June 23, 1943, letter: "A silver haze filled the evening sky, and no stars were visible. But I knew you were looking up, and I stood, so to speak, next to you."[29] In September, he sent her the tiny but lovely poem "Ruth," in which he used their code term to claim he was remaining faithful. Boosted by sentiments such as this, she would work ever harder to promote his affairs and dream her old dream that he might finally have courage enough to leave Weigel and join her.

Meanwhile, he sometimes gave the frequently disaffected Weigel a small poem, even, very occasionally, an erotic one. In one he praised her peasant-style skirts. He liked such skirts, he said, because they would ride up when she was sprawled on a sofa so that he glimpsed her flesh and could dream of lovemaking that night.[30]

"For a Moment I Crossed My Fingers for Hitler" (1943–45)

Immediately after the publication of the Moscow Free Germany National Committee statement, the New York and Los Angeles German emigré communities began to formulate a position on the same issues. Salka and Berthold Viertel made their house at 165 Mabery Road available for a meeting on August 1, 1943. Tactically putting aside his usual rabid hostility toward Thomas Mann, Brecht urged him to attend this meeting. Mann agreed to join the Viertels; Brecht; physicist Hans Reichenbach; Thomas Mann's older brother, Heinrich; Lion Feuchtwanger; Bruno Frank; and historian Ludwig Marcuse. Leaving the women downstairs to furnish refreshments, the men retired upstairs to work on a document.[1]

According to Brecht, whose observations on Thomas Mann must be taken with a block of salt, Mann leaned back in his chair and declared: "Yes, a half million will have to be killed in Germany."[2] After four hours' discussion, the group had their joint communiqué. This largely innocuous statement ended with the sentence "We are convinced that there can be no enduring world peace without a strong and democratic Germany." The men signed it. No women were invited to sign. The next day, Thomas Mann called Feuchtwanger to say that his name had to be removed. The declaration, Mann felt, could be seen as a stab in the back of the Allies. After Mann withdrew, Brecht said in his diary that Mann was spreading rumors about Brecht being a Soviet agent and that Mann's main concern was selling his own books. In fact (as we shall see later in the case of the House Committee on Un-American Activities [HUAC] hearings), Mann was better informed politically, both in the Weimar years and in America, and often more courageous than Brecht.

With the Mabery Road effort stymied, a New York group, which was ostensibly led by Paul Tillich but organized by Elisabeth Hauptmann, tried to work out a statement expressing the views of the German exile community. At once, an interoffice OSS memo went from Emmy C. Rado to Mr. DeWitt Poole, noting that the original Mabery Road memo had failed to "take" as "it was felt that it was leaning too much on the Moscow announcement." Rado then refers to another draft statement by the same people in Hollywood. These two memos, Rado goes on to say, were "sent to Dorothy Thompson for advice, and she advised against them." However, continues Rado, Miss Thompson had then come up with another draft herself, which, according to Rado, was "Dorothy Thompson's idea. It has been drawn up by Dorothy Thompson, [her researcher] Dudislawsky [sic] and Carl Zuckmayer." "This last resolution," continues Rado, "was airmailed to the Hollywood signers. . . . They hope to force the Government through this act into action obliging them to select an equivalent 'Free Germany' Committee."[3]

At this watershed point in the war, when worries about the depth of the Soviet threat to postwar Europe increased, interagency memos made their way from the FBI to the OSS to OWI deeming this person or that a Soviet sympathizer and hence a security risk. High on the list were Berlau and the "Proletarian bordering on an Anarchist," as Brecht was called in one FBI report. As Berlau prepared her broadcasts to occupied Denmark, she was monitored by the FBI.[4] When she called the National Maritime Union of America headquarters in New York on July 9, 1943, the FBI recorded the wholly innocent conversation. Her follow-up calls on July 12 and 13 were recorded, and on July 23, a note was sent to J. Edgar Hoover. Within days of the July 23 memo and a warning note from Hoover to OWI, Berlau was summoned to talk with her superior, the Dane Hans Bendix.[5] He accused her of having been in Spain "on the wrong side," that is, according to Bendix, she should have been on the fascist side. On August 17, she was fired at OWI but allowed to say she had resigned in order "to write a book." Berlau, an extraordinarily effective broadcaster, had become a casualty of the war that had begun within the war. It was no longer enough to be anti-Hitler; one also had now to be anti-Soviet. When on August 27, 1943, Kurt Weill had his American citizenship hearing, he was asked, "If we were fighting Russia, would you take up arms against her?"[6] It is now very clear that long, long before the hot war had ended, the first rounds in the cold war had long since been fired.

On November 13, 1943, the town cinema of Porchow in northwest Russia received a direct hit by Russian artillery. The cinema was full of off-duty German troops. Two years before, Brecht had written a poem "To the German Soldiers in the East":

> So, I must die, I know that . . .
> And I will never see again
> The land from which I come,
> The forests of Bavaria.

Among the dead on November 13 was Brecht's son, twenty-four-year-old Private Frank Banholzer. Frank had first been drafted on October 6, 1939. He flew Luftwaffe missions against England before being wounded in 1943. Just before his death, he had spent a home leave visiting his father's old friend in Berlin, Dr. Müllereisert and to see his godfather, Caspar Neher. While Frank Banholzer was on leave, his godfather had one show running in Vienna and two in production in Berlin. The theater of which he was now one of the leading lights was now almost completely "Judenfrei." Paul Morgan and Fritz Grünbaum both died in Buchenwald in 1941. Kurt Gerron (who had worked in various Brecht and Neher productions) and Otto Walburg were gassed at Auschwitz. Neher went on to do *Don Giovanni* in Hamburg. By the time the show opened, his godson was dead. Neher continued to provide high-level cultural relaxation for Nazi officials tired after their day at this and that office running the death machines.

In the fall of 1943, amidst the palms and orange trees of southern California, Brecht was trying to complete the *Schweik* play. Berlau praised what he had already done with *Schweik* and helped him with problems of character or scenes. He would sometimes thank her in a letter, but when the play was published, he gave her no acknowledgment. In daily special delivery letters and telegrams, with notes on Schweik entwined with notes about her pure white nightgowns, he spoke of possibly returning to New York. In October, Brecht earned a substantial sum from the filmscript with Lorre (not named in his diary and in all likelihood never produced), with which he intended to finance the trip.

Since Ruth had lost her OWI job, he urged her to devote herself to his business interests. He would try—but couldn't yet promise—to pay her two hundred dollars a month for all the work done for him. He instructed her to stay healthy, sober, and faithful; to send him any extra ration coupons she might have; to improve her typing; to go out on her balcony and look up at "their star" at night; to remember him always; and to line up Zero Mostel for the role of Schweik. "The more practical and realistic a production with Mostel seems," he wrote, "the easier it will be for me to sell it to Lorre or to get him to make a counteroffer."[7] His letters often close with the admonition that she was to remain his creature and to write to him at least once a day to report on her efforts on his behalf.

Brecht was preparing to avoid paying Berlau's legal share of income from *The Visions of Simone Machard*. The original deal had given half to the Feuchtwangers and half to Berlau and Brecht; but in February 1943, Berlau agreed to a modification that would give Brecht 35 percent, Lion Feuchtwanger 30 percent, Berlau 20 percent, and Marta Feuchtwanger 15 percent. However, in the fall of 1943, unbeknownst to Berlau, the two men agreed to allow Brecht to collect both his own and

Berlau's legal share.[8] He was still contractually obligated to give her the 20 percent of income due her, of course.

Berlau was increasingly unhappy with Brecht's thoughts and actions. She had long been aware that his interest in party matters, the "third thing" central to her life, often seemed minimal. She repeatedly reminded him of the need for political action, but he spent most of his time plotting ways to make money and reestablishing his world fame. In all the years of exile in America, the only explicitly Communist work she persuaded him to do was to begin a verse version of *The Communist Manifesto*. She was not reassured about Brecht's claim of faithfulness to her when she had called him at 2 A.M. California time and he was not home yet. He assured her in letters of his love, "but you choose to accuse me of simply wanting to preserve a bourgeois idyll here."[9] He was equally ambiguous about leaving Weigel and about Ruth's own creative work. Sometimes he said that she should get up early and devote at least two hours a day to writing, but he would then ask why yesterday's assignment for him was not yet completed? She feared that she had not yet completed any large piece of her own work by which she would be remembered. He responded in a "fictional" fragment, speaking as Kin-jeh. He told Lai-tu not to worry. Yes, her ideas were taken over in his work, but "an apple," said Kin-jeh to Lai-Tu, "achieves fame by being eaten."[10] The metaphor is wholly consistent with the "bull consumes grass" images of his twenties. Thousands of his letters, poems, short stories, or plays chronicle his endorsement of any means to obtain control over the "other."

By 1943 at the latest, Berlau's life as a proud, practical, imaginative, independent writer, manager, director, announcer, and actress had disappeared. Brecht had reduced her to discrete functions and psychological fragments, each answering to his needs and each with a different name. When he writes to her as "Ruth," this person is usually the one designated to carry out urgent, complex business and creative tasks for him. She is an adult, though an adult totally under his control. When sex is the issue, he usually uses Berlau's childhood nickname of "Ute." "Ute" is to be kept at a constantly infantile level. She is enjoined, while Brecht is away, to guard her chastity with the stone that Brecht had given her in Svendborg, to wear her white nightgown while thinking of him, and to go out on her balcony at night to look up at the heavenly link with Brecht. "Lai-tu" is used when he wishes to chastise her or to demand submission. Occasionally, simultaneously drawing her closer and pushing her away sexually, he assigns her the role of his mother or sister. Most chilling of all the names used, however, is "Kreatur," where she is both his "creature" and his "creation," (or, as the word is used in Danish, one of his herd of cattle).

After Ruth was fired from OWI, this formerly independent and highly successful actress-novelist-broadcaster, who was at the same time a childhood victim of abuse, took over the same kind of psychically fragmented, self-denigrating vocabulary Brecht was using toward her. The person she loves is Bertolt or Bert, and the vulnerable, human, funny, frequently childlike Bébé. However, the man she carries out hundreds of assignments for is "the master." She says "Ruth" has carried out this and that assignment, that "Ute" misses him in her bed, and often signs some letters with the deeply denigrating "deine Kreatur."

Berlau's domination by a "master" who is also a "baby" was becoming total. The independence she had enjoyed at the time of meeting Brecht was now radically reduced both by her joblessness and by Brecht's applied psychology of bait and switch. Longing for him, Berlau would rejoice in a telegram that read, "I love you, ute, bertolt,"[11] or one that said: "Mailing you 200 dollars. Dear Ute, don't worry only try to save our autumn in Newyork love, Bertolt."[12] Then she would be hurt when the two hundred dollars, like almost all the checks Brecht ever claimed to have put in the mail, failed to arrive. Then she would rejoice when she received on August 23 the message "Tell UTE I need her so she must take care of herself. BERTOLT." But the next day, he had not only ignored her birthday but admitted he did not even know when her birthday was. But in October he would write, "Stay firm and cheerful, and remain my good creature, yes?"[13]

Constantly seesawing between dreams of his loving presence and his frequent physical and psychological absence and brutality, she would reach for the smooth Danish stone he had given her at Skovsbostrand. "Sometimes," she said later, "my lap would burn with longing for him and I would place his wonderful cool present there."[14] So often did she use the stone that by 1943 the message etched on it was worn away.[15] No longer could she make out the letters *epep* standing for his Latin message to her of his closeness to her "whether near or far." More and more often now, the stone was not enough to assuage her sexual longing or grief. She occasionally sought solace in alcohol or with another lover.

On September 20, 1943, there was a less than gemütlich evening at the Brecht-Weigel house in Santa Monica when Christopher Isherwood came to dinner. Brecht had arranged to get a copy of the latest update of The Good Woman of Setzuan into Isherwood's hands so that he could read it at his Indian-ashram home in the suburbs of Los Angeles. It did not seem to cross Brecht's mind that a play that revolves around three Oriental gods who are mocked for their inability to change social conditions might be offensive to a man who lived his life according to Hindu practices. At dinner, when Brecht brought up the play, Isherwood expressed discomfiture at the way in which religion was handled. At this, another dinner guest, Berthold Viertel, accused Isherwood of having been "conquered by India." Brecht attacked Isherwood's motives, saying he had been bought. At this, Isherwood glanced at his watch and left. Brecht said he felt like a surgeon whose patient leaves before an operation is completed.[16]

The FBI suspected both might be working to turn the Indian subcontinent over to the Soviet Union. The FBI file notes, "While there is no known connection between the Hindu contacts of BRECHT and those of HEINRICH MANN, and the above mentioned Soviet officials, it is believed that the same may have some significance of interest to this investigation." And sure enough, one thing did lead to another as Brecht's FBI file reveals, "This source [unnamed in the file] reflects surveillance information to the effect that on October 25, 1943, GREGORI KHEIFETS [sic], described above, visited the residence of BERT BRECHT from approximately 1:45 P.M. to 3:05 P.M." Then, the plot thickened further for the FBI when, on October 28, Karin Michaëlis, known for her efforts on behalf of the oppressed on all continents, arrived to settle in for an eight-month stay at the Brecht-Weigel home in Santa Monica! The FBI noted, "The exact nature of MICHAELIS's activities in the BRECHT residence or the purpose of her living there is unknown."

The exact nature of Michaëlis's visit to California was human. She was trying to raise money to ransom Jews from Hitler. In a letter to an Austrian friend in New York, she wrote: "I speak on the radio and at banquets, and should give lectures and write. I do what I can. It is, for me, the most important question of all. We can save more than a million people, a million innocent men, women, and children."[17] Brecht, like so much of the rest of the world, made no known effort to help.

Weigel, with Jewish relatives left behind in the Reich, deeply appreciated Michaëlis's efforts. She also valued the opportunity to repay the hospitality Michaëlis had extended in Denmark. In her invitation, Weigel had written: "Look, Karinoli, see if you can't come here for a bit. We have a garden here, and I would like to show it to you and sit with you there and shoot the breeze together."[18] Later, Weigel would say to her: "My modest purpose in life shrinks further and further. I can hardly find any way to see myself as important."[19] Often abandoned or ignored by Brecht, she was desperately lonely and unhappy. She had to ask him for every cent needed for household expenses, to which he would usually claim that he had no money or, when he was away, that money was in the mail.

In Moscow, his old Munich friend Johannes R. Becher had just published an essay attempting to rescue some remnants of pride in the achievements of German culture. "Hitler had the wrong nationalism and now Becher has the right kind," wrote Brecht derisively. Brecht had grounds for concern about the Soviet situation. By the middle of 1943, Brecht had read Boris Souvarine's detailed and devastating 1939 book on Stalin. From Souvarine, who was there as the events had unfolded, Brecht learned the gruesome details of Stalin's destruction of the old revolutionary cadres and other imagined enemies. Brecht, in a diary entry of October 16, 1943, made a damning assessment not of Stalin's politics of mass murder but of the arts under Stalin: "In point of fact, not only is there no novel of any significance, but the kitsch novels of Alexei Tolstoy are held to be good. And there is not a single drama, not one dramatic figure, neither comic nor tragic, nothing achieved in the language, and no philosophical qualities in a single play and that in a theater with excellent prospects."[20] But the diary entry was a private one. Even in the narrow area of the arts, Brecht would not speak publicly against Stalin. He had made a pledge to Apletin in Moscow in 1941 as the price of his exit visa, and he would keep that pledge no matter what he learned about the systematic criminality of the Soviet Union under Stalin.

In November, Brecht rejoined Ruth Berlau at her Fifty-seventh Street apartment. Typically, Weigel was not told when he expected to return and was given only a pittance to run the household despite his recent windfall from the Lorre script work. In a letter to Brecht in New York of November 29, she writes only: "I ask that you give information about your coming or not coming Christmas. I am a bad writer. There isn't anything new otherwise. Good-bye. Helli."[21] The articulate Berlau was still not willing—if it would destroy him—to insist on tugging him out of the family circle. She attempted to make up for her inferior legal status by trying harder. Always generous, she gave him what he wanted in the way of creature comforts, newspapers (German and English), stacks of English-language murder mysteries, the select and expensive cigars that he now favored, beer, and an "orgy of cheeses." She had little interest in cooking, and instead tended to send across the street to a Danish delicatessen for the things he had particularly liked in Denmark. His appetite seemed to grow with feeding. Never was what she sent or gave enough.

Unlike the rather homely Weigel, now forty-three, the thirty-seven-year-old Berlau was still fairly secure in her beauty and sexuality. She loved to caress his slender calves when she sat at his feet before they went to bed and to cup his shoulder blades in her two hands as they made love. She teased him about his shyness about being seen naked. She loved him naked and aroused, and told him how much she liked the sight of his "cock" or, in the German slang he had taught her, his "Schwanz" (tail).

From the Fifty-seventh Street base, he sallied forth, tripping FBI and OSS wires everywhere. With Hauptmann, he wanted to help put together what would eventually be called a Council for a Democratic Germany, a kind of German government-in-exile. Pursuing this end, Brecht reluctantly turned again to the man he privately called a "reptile," the recognized "dean" of the German exile community, Thomas Mann. Brecht had tried, as best he could, to make his letter a model of carefully constructed politeness and historical conciliation. He finally admitted, as he had never been able to in Weimar and in his support of Stalin's decisions later, that "it was the division between the two largest workers' parties in the Republic that was mainly to blame for Hitler's seizure of power."[22] But Thomas Mann, who had argued publicly in the twenties that the left must unite—while Brecht did nothing to bring that about—had no reason to trust Brecht's so obviously wrong political judgment then or now. Mann thought it sheer fantasy when Brecht wrote to him of massive resistance within Germany, which was tying down "50 divisions of Hitler's elite troops, the SS." In Mann's estimation, resistance on this scale was wholly imaginary. Mann correctly believed that Hitler could not have achieved what he had without near-total cooperation from every segment of German society.

Brecht got a telegram from Paul Robeson asking him to address a rally at Carnegie Hall on December 22, 1943. Robeson described Brecht "as [the] foremost representative [of] free German culture." This endorsement (highly reminiscent of the one given to him in Moscow in 1935) proved irresistible. Three days before Christmas, Brecht looked out over a crowd of three thousand people in Carnegie Hall to speak on the subject "The Other Germany." Though he cut the number of SS divisions tied down by the "resistance" from the fifty he had claimed to Thomas Mann to thirty (or "half a million able-bodied men" as Eric Bentley's English-language version of the speech had it), he more than made up for this by increasing the numbers of people he claimed to represent the "other Germany" of his lecture's title. This group of "resisters," Brecht said, included 99 percent of the population. The German people themselves, Brecht said, once Hitler was defeated, must be allowed to take destiny into their own hands rather than have some form of government imposed from without by what he called in his speech "the great democracies." These "great democracies" (plural in Brecht's formulation and so supposedly including both the Soviet Union on one side and the United States on the other) would not be able, said Brecht, either to effectively occupy Germany or to "forcibly educate a whole people."

After his Carnegie Hall speech (largely ignored by the press),

Brecht sought to advance his point of view through the Council for a Democratic Germany. Through Hauptmann, Brecht met Tillich, the nominal head of the operation. Immediately thereafter, a soberly dressed and even shaved Brecht emerged as a key figure in a group that had some serious prospects of becoming the Germans in charge of postwar Germany. An interoffice memo by Sergeant Friediger of the OSS, which, together with the FBI, was monitoring the council, accurately stated that the council platform "seems to include the following main points": "a. to struggle for independent German foreign policies towards East and West, b. to protest against dismemberment of the Reich, c. to establish a constitution in Germany following the Weimar lines with the addition of socialization of industries and the liquidation of large estates." The council wanted a united Germany governed by people like themselves. Although it was argued that the council must represent the whole spectrum of the old Weimar parties (exclusive of the far right), at Brecht's insistence, two Communists were invited to join as formal members. Tillich was reported to have said: "We have two and one-half Communist representatives on the council. The half is Bert Brecht."

During the maneuverings to broaden the council, the FBI noted that on January 17, at the Fifty-seventh Street apartment, Gerhart Eisler, "an alleged Comintern agent," had come to call. He had remained "for approximately one hour and a quarter." Two days after Eisler's visit, Brecht was formally placed on the National Censorship Watch list. Ruth Fischer, head of the German Communist party until she had been displaced by Stalin, began to talk openly about exposing Brecht as a Soviet sympathizer. Fischer's threats alarmed Aufricht.[23] Somehow he managed to persuade the two combatants to get together to try to iron out their differences. Brecht, anxious to maintain the viability of the council, agreed to have Fischer and Aufricht over for supper at Berlau's.

Fischer had difficulties getting up the four flights of stairs as she had a heart condition compounded by obesity. Upstairs, things seemed to go well at first, but then Fischer declared, "Brecht, you with the brainpan of a freshman in high school, began to interest yourself in the Party at the time that it had already been ripped apart by Stalin."[24] After she had left, Brecht declared: "That sow will be shot. One does not take ideological disagreements between comrades to the police." He then added, "That rat will be drowned." Internal working paper 187 of the OSS summed up the spirit of such encounters: "Both in the Social Democratic refusal of cooperation with the Communists, and in the anti-Stalinist line of former Communists may be seen the perpetuation in German exile politics of the issues which unhappily divided republican Germany during the period of its struggle for and failure in democracy." But though splits existed in the emigré community, American intelligence, terrified of a united Germany, deliberately widened the fissures.

At the same time as the work of the Council for a Democratic Germany was being deliberately undermined, its views were being given powerful poetic form in the plays Brecht was working on with Berlau and various others. In early 1944, Brecht managed to get Luise Rainer interested in a project that would provide her with a starring role for Broadway. The new project was a play he had begun with Steffin and Wuolijoki in Scandinavia,[25] and he was now working on it again with Berlau. The play's new title was *The Caucasian Chalk Circle*.

The central idea of the play, the Solomon-like judgment made with the child placed in a circle of chalk, was taken from Brecht's friend Klabund's 1925 play, *Der Kreidekreis*, or *The Circle of Chalk*. Poetic passages about Georgia were lifted without acknowledgment from the expatriate Georgian poet Grigol Robakidse's work *Das Schlangenhemd*, or *The Snake's Skin*, published in German in 1924.

Set in an imaginary "Caucasus," the work has dominating male and female leads. One is Grusha, a maid in the royal palace. When the governor of Grusinia is killed by revolutionaries, and the royal son and heir, Michel, is abandoned by his luxury-loving mother, Grusha gathers the royal child in her arms and flees with it as her own. As the flames of revolution still glow on the horizon, the other dominant figure in the play appears. He is an anarchist, a poacher by the name of Azdak. He happens upon a scene where a judge has just been hung by the revolutionaries. Suddenly he is clad in judicial robes that cover his rags and told he is now to serve as the circuit judge of Grusinia. While Grusha flees to the Northern Mountains with "her" precious baby, Azdak serves the new rulers. But he does so in a sycophantic yet subversive, Schweikian way. He openly takes bribes from the rich but tries, wherever possible without risking his own none-too-clean skin, to render judgment on behalf of the poor. At the end of the play, with the revolution finally crushed and the wife of the former ruler needing the child Michel in order to claim the royal inheritance, the paths of Azdak, the Governor's Wife, and the adoptive mother cross as the women vie for the child.

Azdak, after sexually harrassing a woman who had brought a charge of sexual harassment before him, acts more responsibly in the case of Michel. He sets up a test in which the child is placed in a small circle of chalk and both "mothers" are urged to tug on one arm to determine which one is the true mother. The biological mother, with no emotional attachment to the child but anxious to get the inheritance, yanks brutally. Grusha, unwilling to hurt the child she loves, lets go. At this, the paradoxical Azdak awards her the child and then gathers up his robes to flee.

The fairy-tale-like story of Grusha and Azdak would later be framed in the published and staged text by a prologue and an epilogue set in a supposedly realistic, contemporary collective farm in Soviet Georgia shortly after the Germans have been driven out. Here, the "child" in the test of the circle of chalk is explicitly identified as a metaphor for the problems of now making the best possible postwar division of land. In 1944, particularly as the child was called Michel, the German nickname for a German, the child in the circle could clearly be seen as Germany with America tugging on one of its arms and the Soviet Union tugging on the other. The great virtue of the metaphorical circle would always be that it could reflect new historical meanings for new historical situations in times to come.

Though the plot of the play turns upon a number of improbabilities, it has proven very effective in production. Though Brecht had dismissed Shakespeare years before as creating a drama "for cannibals," it is Shakespeare's characters who serve as obvious models for those in *The Caucasian Chalk Circle*. Brecht, who attended readings of *Measure for Measure* and *The Tempest* in California in early 1944, saw Azdak as a "Shakespearean wise fool."[26]

For Berlau, this new play was intimately tied up with her own life. She learned in early 1944 she was pregnant. For her, the child, Michel, of the play was not only Bébé himself, torn between her and Weigel (as well as a Germany being ripped apart by the competing forces of capitalism and socialism) but also the real child in her womb. Despite Berlau's pregnancy, it was clear to everyone that Brecht was "not immune to the strange charms" of the star of the *Malfi* production, the slender, boyish Elizabeth Bergner. At about this time, another woman entered the picture, a young American poet named Naomi Replansky.

At this same time, Brecht was receiving a series of business letters from Lion Feuchtwanger concerning *Simone Machard*.[27] Feuchtwanger had recast the material as a novel. Knowing that a deal with Sam Goldwyn of Metro-Goldwyn-Mayer could be struck immediately if Goldwyn was convinced he would get clear title to the rights, Brecht signed and had notarized on February 21 the following document. "In consideration of ten Dollars in hand to me paid and for other valuable considerations, receipt whereof is hereby acknowledged, I, Bertolt Brecht, hereby shall assign, transfer and release to Lion Feuchtwanger and his heirs and assignees forever any and all right, title and interest of every kind and description whatsoever which I heretofore have had, now have or hereafter may have in or to the novel SIMONE by Lion

Feuchtwanger and Bertolt Brecht, together with all my right, title or interest in or to any play, drama, scenario, film producion [sic] or other derivative work heretofore now or hereafter based on either said novel or play in any way connected therewith."[28] His signature on this de jure assignment of the work was witnessed by a notary public, James M. Angus. However, Feuchtwanger would have to kick back half the proceeds once MGM bought it.

Without the agreement of Berlau, the co-copyright holder (whose earnings were to be collected by Brecht anyway), Feuchtwanger's agent sold the film rights to the novel to Sam Goldwyn at MGM for $50,000. In his February 25 letter to Brecht informing him of details of the sale, Feuchtwanger mentioned he had already given $2,000 of the proceeds to Helene Weigel as she was obviously in need of money. Brecht neither told Berlau of the sale nor gave her any of the money.[29] By keeping her money, Brecht was keeping control over Berlau. And by concealing the $22,000, he could continue to maintain for her and others the legend of "poor Bert Brecht." Brecht "made Hollywood acquaintances think," as one critic puts it, "he and his family subsisted on the brink of poverty."[30]

Berlau should have received about $10,000 after deducting the agent's fees. This was four times her annual salary and more than the Feuchtwangers paid for their palatial villa in Pacific Palisades overlooking the Pacific Ocean.[31] After boasting to Feuchtwanger's secretary "we are rich now,"[32] Brecht used some of the money for the large house where he and Weigel lived (already partly paid for in 1944 by the money received for *Hangmen*). He kept for his own use a balance of almost $20,000. He nevertheless encouraged Berlau and Weigel to think he was broke. Weigel was fortunate to have landed a small, silent but well-paid role in a Spencer Tracy film, *The Seventh Cross*.[33] Weigel used this money to help pay off the house.

In late February, Brecht headed back to the West Coast, with an assignment from the New York council to get support in Hollywood. He told Berlau to hide the fact of her pregnancy. He was clearly worried about what could happen if she spoke with a mutual friend such as Karin Michaëlis, and the news of the pregnancy got back to Weigel. As Berlau told a later interviewer about the pregnancy: "I was very happy, and Brecht was too, even though he made extreme efforts to keep my condition secret."[34] At the same time, he told her to keep a personal eye on the latest *Malfi* translation as paid for by Bergner and Czinner. She was to maintain pressure on Kurt Weill, despite his obvious reluctance, to participate in both a *Schweik* and a *Good Woman of Setzuan* production on Broadway. And, despite Piscator's smoldering anger at the dubious way he had been squeezed out of the proposed *Schweik* production, Berlau was to persuade him to direct a production of Eric Bentley's new translation of *The Private Life of the Master Race*, the new title of *Fear and Misery of the Third Reich. The Caucasian Chalk Circle* needed to be nursed along, and, finally, she was to encourage producer Jed Harris (who had successfully mounted Thornton Wilder's *Our Town*) to look at *Galileo*.

In California, Brecht convinced a number of key film, stage, and publishing figures—Lion Feuchtwanger, Peter Lorre, Paul Czinner, Oskar Homolka, Heinrich Mann, Alexander Granach, Elisabeth Bergner, Berthold Viertel, and Leopold Jessner—to sign the manifesto of the Council for a Democratic Germany. While lining up these signatures, he was introduced at one of Salka Viertel's parties to Charles Laughton,[35] star of *Mutiny on the Bounty* and *The Hunchback of Notre Dame.* Laughton was smitten with Brecht, and Brecht saw how useful a major Hollywood star could be in promoting plays produced in the Brecht factory. Like so many others who were swept off their feet by Brecht, Laughton was prone to questioning his own self-worth both as actor and as human being. He lived a double life, married to the actress Elsa Lanchester but bringing home a stream of young male lovers.[36] Feeling guilty about not fighting for his native Britain, Laughton had become a superpatriot, who, between films, traveled the United States selling war bonds.

Just then, Ruth Fischer published her attack on Brecht, provocatively using the former name of the NKVD: "Bert Brecht, Minstrel of the GPU." The FBI duly noted all goings-on at the Brecht household: "This source reflects surveillance information to the effect that on April 27, 1944, GREGORI KHEIFETS [*sic*], described above, visited the home of BERT BRECHT from 3 to 5 P.M." Kheifetz's visit, Fischer's attack, and FBI and OSS suspicions about the Council for a Democratic Germany being a Soviet tool could not have come at a worse time. On May 2, the official formation of the Council for a Democratic Germany was announced in New York with Brecht's name prominent among the co-signers under the leadership of Paul Tillich and with Elisabeth Hauptmann as council secretary.

Though the council had widespread support in the emigré community, it could gain no official support in the United States. FBI and OSS documents persisted in describing it as a "Communist front organization." On June 16, 1944, ten days after D day, Kheifetz again visited Brecht's home and "stayed from 2–3:50." When news came through in the American press about the July 20 plot to assassinate Hitler by the bold and dedicated Colonel Claus Schenk von Stauffenburg, and that Hitler had survived and had begun to wipe out the plotters, Brecht wrote in his diary on July 21: "As some news came through about the bloody events between Hitler and his Junker generals, for a moment I crossed my fingers for Hitler; otherwise, if not he, who else is going to destroy this band of criminals?" After having written for years that Germans should rise up and get rid of Hitler, when a member of the general staff (the only group with regular access to Hitler during these years) makes the attempt, paying with their lives to do so, Brecht endorses Hitler's doing away with his opposition.

In June, getting no money from Brecht, Berlau borrowed enough from Peter Lorre to fly to California to wait for the birth of her baby. She lived for a time at the drug-addicted Peter Lorre's luxurious home in Pacific Palisades. Unhappy there, six weeks later, she moved to a room at the Chalet Motor Hotel at 3212 Wilshire Boulevard in Santa Monica. Her arrival on July 26, 1944, was duly reported to the FBI, who now wrote in her file: "Advised that BERLAU came to the Chalet Motor Hotel alone but that shortly thereafter a man brought her belongings to her new living quarters. They described this individual as a little fellow with dark hair, who could hardly speak English, and who drove a 'wreck of an automobile'. This is undoubtedly BERT BRECHT." Through the summer months, growing rounder day by day, and needing to be kept out of sight of anyone who could report on her condition to Weigel but never out of the sight or the hearing of the FBI, Berlau and Brecht worked daily on *The Caucasian Chalk Circle.*

The play was completed, as Brecht's diary notes, on September 1, 1944, but reality suddenly intruded. Without time to even check out of the Chalet Motor Hotel, Ruth was rushed to the Cedars of Lebanon Hospital where a stomach tumor was discovered and removed two days later. Her child, now in its seventh or eighth month, was delivered by cesarean section. The child, a little boy who Berlau named Michel, was born with a serious heart defect. As the doctors fought for Berlau's and Michel's life, the FBI was everywhere. When Brecht left a note to be delivered to Ruth in her room number 314, it was copied at once by the agents: "Love, I am so glad that you are fighting so courageously. Don't think that I do not want to see you when you are ill. You are beautiful then too. I am coming tomorrow before noon. Yours, Bertolt." As Berlau's condition began to improve, Michel lost his struggle. When the head surgeon, his face down almost to his tie, began to say, "there is something I must tell you," Ruth knew at once the news he was bringing and said, "I know already, Michel is dead." Adding to her pain at the hospital, she was also told that one of the consequences of her operation was that she could never have another child. Brecht told her not to worry about the loss, saying "Why so sad? When we get to Berlin, we'll immediately adopt a child. So many children without fathers, without mothers."[37]

All too conscious of the cost of her private room at Cedars of Lebanon, and unaware of the $22,000 Brecht had recently collected, Ruth got herself discharged before she was at all recovered. The hospital and doctor's bills would remain unpaid as Brecht maintained the fiction of being poor. Salka Viertel generously gave her a room over the garage. Having hidden her pregnancy at Brecht's behest, she did not now permit herself to grieve openly for her loss. Desperate for some release, she talked about it in letters in Danish to Karin Michaëlis in New York. This put Michaëlis on the spot. Was she not to tell Helene Weigel, her friend since 1918?

At this time, Ruth happened to see an entry Brecht had made in his diary, saying simply "ruth operated on." This was then followed by a notation for an expenditure of $40, the combined amount he had spent for the cremation of Michel and an urn for the boy's ashes.[38] Ruth got extremely angry. She saw the entries as typical of his evasiveness and cold-bloodedness concerning anything that constituted a danger to him and his way of life with Weigel. He could not openly acknowledge what had happened, even in his own diary. Despite the chronic strain between them, a few weeks after Michel's cremation, Brecht asked if they could sleep together again. And she again said yes.

"The Jews Have Now Had Their Six Million Deaths, Now They Should Give [Us] Some Peace" (1945)

With one child dead and unable to have another, Berlau consoled herself with the idea that the plays that she had written with Brecht were their children. As her physical health gradually improved, she began to study photography in order to make microfilm copies of all the Brecht texts and to improve her photographic records of the productions of the plays. Predictably, the FBI suspected a link between Berlau's studies of photography and Soviet espionage. They wondered why she went for "photographic instruction" to Professor Reichenbach of UCLA, a physicist with knowledge of atomic research and a friend of Albert Einstein. What about her connections to Grigori Kheifetz and to Vladimir Pozner, who dropped by Mabery Road supposedly to work on filmscripts?

The tangle of threads seemed to run in every direction. Why, the FBI asked in the Brecht file, was his car parked outside the Soviet vice-consulate in Los Angeles on the night of October 14, 1944, as their source had advised? On March 15, 1945, the FBI noted: "The New York Office . . . called the Bureau's attention to the fact that Horst Baerensprung [sic], who is of interest in connection with Brecht, was given a 'special introduction' to Professor L. Simpson and Dr. Haakon M. Chevalier, University of California, by a Miss or Mrs. Page, initials unknown, while Baerensprung [sic] was in Los Angeles." This meant the target of all these suspected spies might well be Chevalier's personal friend J. Robert Oppenheimer, head of the American atomic bomb effort at Los Alamos.

Though Paul Tillich may have described Brecht half-jokingly as only half a Communist, the FBI continued to find evidence of Brecht's Communist leanings. Their point of view was given a boost in early 1945 as he began to circulate for comment his attempts to put the *Communist Manifesto* into verse form. Though Feuchtwanger, as usual, criticized Brecht's hexameters, Karl Korsch found the content of the versified section of the *Manifesto* absolutely superb. The FBI made no comment on the merit of the hexameters but saw it as confirming their most extreme suspicions. On March 27, 1945, J. Edgar Hoover wrote:

"MEMORANDUM FOR THE ATTORNEY GENERAL. In connection with this Bureau's investigation of the Comintern apparatus, which includes espionage agents, it has been determined that Bertolt Eugen Friedrich Brecht, 1063 26th Street, Santa Monica, California, telephone Santa Monica 5-4943, has been contacted by an individual known to have engaged in espionage activities. Brecht has been closely associated with German Communist leaders in the Los Angeles area and is allegedly a Soviet agent.

"I recommend authorization of a technical surveillance on Bertolt Eugen Friedrich Brecht for the purpose of developing additional information relative to Soviet and Communist espionage activities.

"Respectfully, John Edgar Hoover, Director"

Berlau prepared to return to New York. "On March 31, 1945," now read the FBI report, "BERT BRECHT'S car was again observed at the SALKA VIERTEL residence at 10:15 A.M. BRECHT, however was not there on this occasion . . . At 4 P.M. BRECHT and BERLAU left the VIERTEL residence in the same Packard and drove to the Eastman Kodak Store at 202 Santa Monica Boulevard, Santa Monica, California . . . After stopping at the Eastman Kodak Store, BRECHT and BERLAU continued to the Union Station at Los Angeles where BERLAU was observed to board the Union Pacific Challenger for New York City. She carried with her a suitcase and two briefcases which BRECHT carried aboard the train for her."

Before Brecht left the train, he handed Berlau a letter that she was to open during the journey. Berlau's four remaining suitcases were put in the baggage car. From the FBI files, we see that pursuing agents boarded the train and went to the baggage car to search (without a warrant) Berlau's suitcases. The agents found developed and undeveloped microfilm scattered haphazardly throughout the various bags. They took particular note of a typescript entitled *They Owe Us Love*, an English version of her erotically explicit feminist novel *Every Animal Can Do It*. She also had packed various unpaid medical bills.

In her train compartment, Ruth opened the letter that Brecht had handed her. She immediately replied: "Bertolt. I have opened your letter. O you. I became so quiet. I am happy. I thank you. Think of you. I will become just as you wish. I will be worried again now and then, it is mostly fear that you might become unfaithful. But that is only a tiny backslide. Now I am happy. You can understand how it was, I thought that you would be thinking 'glad that she's finally left, that's good riddance,' then you told me 'come back as soon as you can. I love you.' You can understand that was a good thing for you to let me travel this way with a sleeper and with meals. Thanks for all the new clothes you bought me. It is snowing. I'm so glad to have my fur coat. Jed elsker dig

[Danish for "I love you"]. I'll get this off to you when we stop in Salt Lake City. Everything is all right."[1] Despite her momentary delight, none of her basic problems had been addressed. He was still with Weigel. He had failed to give her money owed her from the sale of *Simone Machard*. Occasional presents from him failed to take care of her most basic necessities. The physicians who had taken care of her and Michel were never paid. Berlau apparently knew nothing of Brecht's various sources of income nor of the numerous invasions of her privacy by the FBI, not even that the janitor in her building examined her belongings and her correspondence when she was out and passed whatever he found to the FBI.

The Ruth Berlau who had left New York pregnant and full of hope the previous June seemed odd and listless, at a lower energy level than before, to Ida Bachmann. Hauptmann was disturbed at how generally rundown she looked and at her manner of speech. Berlau asked Hauptmann: "Wouldn't you want to work for Brecht again, I and Brecht are quits."[2] But Hauptmann, despite her sympathy for Ruth, was reluctant to work again with Brecht. Clearly Ruth was weakened physically and psychologically. Though she wanted a future with Brecht, she knew that she should break with him. He, meanwhile, urged her not to see her Danish friend Karin Michaëlis and talk over difficulties she was having as "[Michaëlis] would never keep her mouth shut."[3]

Dunned by bill collectors, and without any regular source of income, Berlau worried constantly about money. She had no savings and no regular income other than her $75 Danish alimony check. Blocked by the FBI from meaningful employment, and only occasionally getting a small check from Brecht, she was forced to take jobs like housecleaning and bartending. She could no longer be a paid employee of OWI, but her commitment to the Danish resistance remained so strong that she returned to OWI in the closing weeks of the European war as an unpaid volunteer broadcaster. She stayed up much of the night trying to carry out the assignments that poured in from Brecht. By the summer of 1945, she had Brecht's formal power of attorney to act on his behalf with publishers and actors' agents. She set up a darkroom in the flat to develop her microfilms of the play manuscripts.

Letters between Berlau and Brecht spoke of love and also of Ruth's next visit to the Chalet Motor Hotel. The Los Angeles FBI office telexed J. Edgar Hoover: "At the present time it is desired to request of the Bureau blanket authorization for the installation of a microphone surveillance in whichever unit of the Chalet Motor Hotel BERLAU might reside upon her return." With the cooperation of the hotel, a bug was installed, and the trap was set to be sprung as soon as she returned to California. Surveillance was also maintained on the Council for a

Democratic Germany. The American government took the position that these people were dangerous, a policy clearly set before Roosevelt's sudden death on April 12 and continued by his successor, Harry S Truman.

In late April, before the shooting had stopped in Berlin, a hand-picked group of German exiles who had spent the Hitler years in Moscow landed on the outskirts of the miles of rubble that was all that was left of prewar Berlin. The Ulbricht Group, named for its leader, was charged by Stalin to take over, under Russian supervision, whatever was left of a governmental apparatus in the ruins of Berlin. On May 8, in Los Angeles, Bert Brecht, member of the now fragmented and helpless council, noted: "Nazi Germany capitulates unconditionally."

At the time of the German surrender, Brecht was concerned about a production of *Fear and Misery of the Third Reich* in rehearsal in New York, now under the title *The Private Life of the Master Race*. About May 11, Brecht talked with Berlau in New York. The FBI log of the call reads: "BERLAU requested a little part for herself, undoubtedly in BRECHT'S play 'The Private Life of the Master Race.' At that time BRECHT stated that he would think it over." Brecht made no effort to have Berlau cast in *Master Race*, nor did he mention the coauthor of the play, Margarete Steffin. Giving Berlau a part in the play would invite Weigel's ire, and mentioning Steffin would involve recognizing the claims of any surviving relatives now that the war in Europe was almost over. As an enemy alien, Brecht still needed clearance to travel. Weigel called on Charles Laughton, who successfully intervened. "At 4:10 P.M. on May 19, 1945," notes the FBI report, "BERT BRECHT was called for at his residence by Mr. and Mrs. HANNS EISLER and was driven by Mrs. EISLER to the Union Station in Los Angeles, where EISLER and BRECHT boarded the Union Pacific Challenger for New York City."

As the war came to a close in Europe, Berlau's OWI broadcast script read: "First I direct thanks to all those at home who have risked their lives in the battle against the Nazis. It is good to know that now you can continue the battle in the open, for I will tell you something. This time we will not have fought in vain. We must clean out all the Nazis and the Fascists, every one of them. Bring all the guilty ones out into the open, so they can be judged."[4] To gather material, Berlau made a number of visits to a Danish seaman's home at 25 South Street, next to the wharves of the Fulton Market. The home was run by a Dane called Meta Juul, and the two women became friends. On May 17, Berlau's broadcast began with a quote from an Icelandic saga: "Oh Lord, give peace to the dead and healing to the living." But where the saga spoke of healing, a sailor called Verner Hansen from Mrs. Juul's home, spoke of revenge: "Find the guilty ones, but do it thoroughly, so that we can keep the peace we have fought so hard for." Berlau replied on the air, "Thanks for those words, Verner Hansen." After only a handful of broadcasts, again Berlau's work at OWI was terminated. One FBI report approvingly notes, "As a result of an investigation and inquiry by the Civil Service Commission in connection with her services at OWI, the subject's services were discontinued and since then she has done no work, voluntary or otherwise, for the OWI." Once again, Berlau was without work that could bear her own name and give her an independent sense of purpose.

In New York, Brecht was appalled at what was being done to *Master Race* by an ad hoc off-Broadway theater company called the Theater of All Nations, pulled together by a young producer named Ernest Roberts and directed by Erwin Piscator. Always jealous of Piscator's legitimate prior claim to having created "epic theater" in Germany, Brecht insisted on a new director, Berthold Viertel. Eric Bentley stopped by Berlau's place to say hello to Brecht, whom he found on the phone yelling, "Verbrecher" (crooks). Replying to something said on the other end of the telephone, Brecht next yelled, "No, no, no, *little* crooks—we can't even sue them to any good effect!"[5]

By the summer of 1945, Bentley had few illusions about dealing with Brecht. "His paranoia," writes Bentley, "was as outrageous as that of anyone I've ever met with the single exception, perhaps, of the critic F. R. Leavis."[6] The paranoia, was accompanied by frequent apodictic shifts from one extreme statement to another. Sometimes Brecht would declare that one should trust the German people. But, then, just as emphatically, Bentley noted, "he would angrily give up on the German people as hopeless." In a 1945 letter, Bentley said of Brecht: "He has neither good manners nor elementary decency. He lives out his own theory that it is impossible to behave well in this society. . . . He is like Dubedat in [Shaw's] *The Doctor's Dilemma*—a scoundrel but an artist."[7] In a despairing letter to James Laughlin at the New Directions press, which had published *The Private Life of the Master Race*, Bentley wrote: "He suggests me as his general editor but upon impossible terms. I'm to do all the dirty work and Brecht is to boss everything. Unless he withdraws his demand to supervise the whole show I must be counted out. I've had enough of Brecht and his female followers. He even asks that my introduction contain no criticism of his work!"[8] But despite his threats to quit, Bentley was persuaded to return to promoting Brecht's affairs in America.

Brecht learned with *Master Race* that on Broadway a contract actually is a contract and cannot be altered at will. Brecht was terrified that a failure with *Master Race* could make New York backers less interested in *Galileo*. Therefore, as with *Mother* in 1935, he tried to stop the show before it could open. James Laughlin, who attended some rehearsals and saw Brecht violently arguing with actors, claimed that Brecht "destroyed his own work."[9] Bentley, who had worked so hard to prepare the English version of the play, thought Brecht's tirades wild and unconscionable. Brecht wanted "to destroy the actress and defy the producer." Berthold Viertel pointed out that since the war with Hitler was now over, the play had lost much of its immediacy. He proposed an American army intelligence officer, a German-Jewish emigré, interrogate the characters, whose recollections of the Hitler years would be flashbacks.[10] Brecht rejected this vivifying idea, and slashed scenes and lines till the play made no sense. He then said: "If I can't stop the show, I'll exclude all critics! Viertel, arrange with Bentley to keep all critics out." On opening night, Elisabeth Bergner was seen openly weeping at this deliberately contrived disaster of a production. Predictably, critics panned the inchoate show.

Brecht's behavior comes from radically different views of what was permitted to a director in the United States and Germany. His rantings were no worse than those of at least two other German directors working in New York. According to John Houseman, Berthold Viertel in everyday life was mild and cultivated, but as a director he was "violent, tyrannical, and obsessively concerned with personal prestige."[11] When Fritz Kortner directed Dorothy Thompson's *Another Sun* in 1939, he shouted at her, as she put it, "like a crazed gorilla, his face purple, his eyes bulging."[12] Brecht, Viertel, and Kortner, opposed as they were in theory to Adolf Hitler, repeatedly used an apoplectic style of directing in the American theater. Bentley later saw Brecht in a Munich theater behaving in a way that reminded Bentley of Hitler's tirades. But, as Bentley observed, neither the German stage staff nor the actors complained.

Having done his best to sabotage one production in New York in 1945, Brecht turned with Berlau to the *Duchess of Malfi* adaptation. The play's sponsors, Czinner and Bergner, were at their summer place in Vermont. As Dorothy Thompson and her private secretary, Hermann Budzislawski, lived near Czinner and Bergner, Brecht and Berlau decided to join the Vermont colony for a few days. The FBI went too. The work on *Malfi* was particularly difficult for Brecht since he did not have final say on the project, but Czinner and Bergner insisted on extensive revisions before they would pay him.

On his way back to Los Angeles in mid-July, Brecht again stopped in Chicago to visit Stefan. By this time, Stefan was an American citizen and had completed his military training as an interpreter of Japanese. When his father came to visit him, he was in a military hospital suffering from "mental exhaustion." The twenty-year-old was having headaches that seemed to have no physiological cause, but which blocked sending him to the war zone.

At dawn on July 16, 1945, at a site in New Mexico named Trinity, the world's first atomic bomb imploded. In its spectral light, J. Robert Oppenheimer quoted the Indian epic the Bhagavad Gita, saying "I am become death, destroyer of worlds." Over Hiroshima at 8:15 A.M., August 6, the bomb bay of the Enola Gay was opened by Thomas Ferebee. At 8:16:02 A.M. shock waves crushed the central strike zone, the Shima Hospital. On August 9, a nuclear device was detonated over Nagasaki. On August 15, Emperor Hirohito spoke over the radio announcing the surrender of imperial Japan.

Various FBI agents and informers report that Brecht was horrified to hear, after the deliberations of the victorious Allies at Potsdam, that Germany was to be divided.[13] In a moment of unusual candor, Brecht expressed dismay that in the splitting of Germany, "the greatest part was going to the soviet." The FBI also reports him saying "that it would be possible to destroy whole continents now and that this would make the need for Socialism imperative."

While trying to grasp the implications of a new world order that included atomic weapons, Brecht was almost constantly haunted by fears that perhaps he was losing his hold on Berlau. He demanded that she write to him more often and that she provide details of any moment not spent on his affairs. He reiterated in letters that she is vital to plans he might later make to return to Europe. He began to call her at 2 A.M. New York time to see if she was home. On one occasion when he talked with her, he imagined someone else was with her. In one desperate missive from around this time, he writes, "Love, why don't you write my name anymore? Please, write to tell me if everything is in order." The note ends, "Do you still know how much we need truth?"[14] The more aloof she was, the closer he wanted to be. The closer she came, however, the more distant he then became.

In August, a cautious letter to Berlau recalls a visit by Soviet agents in Finland in 1941: "Do you remember the people that we met at Hella's? They asked me whether I intended to see Berlin again. I answered that that would be a while, but then I would like to. They agreed with me. They would be helpful to me."[15] As the Soviets now controlled a large portion of Germany and much of Berlin itself, this feeler was significant. Brecht had carried out the pledge given to Vladimir Knorin in 1935 and to Mikhail Apletin in 1941. He had proven reliable and would be rewarded.

In the same letter, Brecht went on to say, "You know that under no circumstances will I make plans without you." He signs his letter with his large "d" for "deine" (yours) and adds the initial letters of the formula "Whether near or far." But, in his next letter, he told her to expect the arrival of a young woman who had been with him in California, a young and wealthy woman also named Ruth. He wanted Berlau to train the new person in photography. The FBI described her as "a girl about 20 years old, of Slavic type, and who spoke English very brokenly."

At the time of the Japanese surrender, Brecht was working on the *Malfi* revisions, which he hated doing, and on yet another English version of *Galileo* with Charles Laughton. Brecht was disappointed when Lion Feuchtwanger turned down an opportunity to cover the Nuremberg war crime trials. Feuchtwanger said, "You know it is not cowardice." Brecht replied, "I know something worse, it is comfortableness."

Secure in his own comfort, Brecht was still trying to conquer Broadway and to take advantage of the coming peace to market Brecht work in Europe. He made no immediate plans to go back to Germany, though he recommended that Feuchtwanger do so. In a poem called "Germany 1945," Brecht wrote:

> In the house is black death
> Outdoors is death from freezing.
> Where shall we go then?
> The sow shits in its feed
> This sow is my mother
> O mother mine, o mother mine
> What are you doing against me.[16]

This small poem hearkens back to many of his poems of World War I and the years immediately after: the world is female and filthy; his mother's acts are seen as directed specifically against him; the "human" animal is inhuman.

Another 1945 poem about Germany reveals an almost Swiftian sense of humor. "Der Krieg ist geschändet worden," or "War's Reputation Ruined!" says archly, "In the best circles it is being said that, from a moral point of view, the Second World War, did not maintain the same standards as the first." The poem closes with those in "the best circles" observing sadly "Though of and for themselves wars are necessary, through this method [of Hitler] which went beyond the bounds and was even inhuman, for some time to come war is likely to be discredited."[17] The brilliant use of language that deliberately undercuts the speaker is Brecht at his best as poet engagé. More of the poems from this period are simply not very good; and worse, the images (the "sow in the feed" is a good example) show little development since his teenage years. Describing the search for Hitler's body at the chancery in Berlin, for instance, he speaks of the "narrow foreheads" of several of the bodies found there.[18] This recalls the writing of Cesare Lombroso and Hitler's own bizarre physiognomic theories, suggesting that people be judged by the height of their foreheads. Later, in his bitter and often clever reworking of Shelley's "The Masque of Anarchy," Brecht refers to the judges appointed in the western zones of Germany as "lice."[19] Hitler used the same expression, for similar purposes, to describe those sections of the population he planned to annihilate.

At his deepest levels, Brecht was profoundly undemocratic, seeing himself as immeasurably superior to those around him. Berlau was an apple to be consumed. Friends were bridges over which he could drive his "1,000-ton goods train." When he denounced Ruth Fischer, he used metaphors typical of the Nazis and of the Stalin camp. Fischer was a "sow," the expression used to describe Walter Rathenau, who was murdered in Weimar, and she was a "rat" who "will be drowned," the expression used by Brecht and others at the time of the Moscow Show Trials to describe defendants whom we now know were innocent, as Brecht himself surmised at the time.

In Europe, as elsewhere, "Brecht's idea was to obtain several offers, in order to get the best terms he could."[20] Nineteen forty-five found Brecht dealing with Erich Reiss Verlag in Basle, Englind in Stockholm,[21] de Lange in Amsterdam, Malik Press of Wieland Herzfelde, and taking up the cudgel against Felix Bloch Erben in Berlin. His first postwar sale was to Mundus Verlag in Switzerland of Steffin's translation of Martin Anderson-Nexø's Childhood (without, now or later, either notifying Steffin's heirs or Nexø himself, who was still very much alive). Allert de Lange wrote him, describing the Nazi occupation and the violent death of the firm's head, Walter Landauer, during his attempt to escape to Switzerland in 1944.[22] By the time the Germans fled, all that was left were the prewar copyrights. Brecht ignored de Lange's inquiry about reprinting The Threepenny Novel and looked for better offers.

As firms in Europe sought German-language works as free as possible of Nazi taint, the work of Brecht and many of the other emigrés in California could now command large sums. Producers in Europe were eager to mount the surefire Threepenny Opera. Brecht said that the firm of Felix Bloch Erben should not be allowed to represent the play as they had failed to pay him his royalties and instead had given the money to the Nazis. This was not entirely true, as Edward Hogan, whom Brecht had met in California and who was now in charge of denazifying the American zone, wrote to Brecht on November 1, 1945: "Your suspicions of this old and utterly reliable firm are groundless.

Everything was grabbed by the Nazis, particularly royalties with foreign exchange value. The firm itself was swallowed by the Reichskulturkammer and had to call itself Die Drehbuhne—the Turntable Stage [now the name Felix Bloch Erben is back on the letterhead]. Frau Wreede (Fritz killed himself you know due to the whole situation) is in charge and the offices are at Schlueterstrasse 41 in the British zone. The staff has voluntarily submitted to investigation by us."[23]

In the same letter, Hogan cleared a production of *Threepenny* then running in Berlin. Hogan said (apparently in response to a note from Brecht): "That *Die Dreigroschenoper* ever led to Unstimmigkeiten [disagreements] is a bare untruth. The production now current under Karl Heinz Martin is successful in every way." Hogan gave Martin's theater a clean bill of health against charges of nazism, saying "Martin's theatre is the cleanest in Berlin in this respect." None of this was what Brecht really wanted to hear. He had hoped to regain control of the rights to *Threepenny* by his charge of nazism.

Peter Suhrkamp wrote, representing S. Fischer Verlag, the old Jewish firm that he had taken over in 1936 after the Fischer family had made a forced sale under terms set by Joseph Goebbels. Late in the war, Suhrkamp was briefly held as an enemy of the Reich, but afterward he resumed running Fischer Verlag. When the original owners returned from exile, Suhrkamp refused to return the firm to them.[24] After a bitter battle, the assets of the company were divided. With his portion, Suhrkamp established Suhrkamp Verlag, which would feature Brecht for many years as its principal author. The Fischers were left with, in their words, "a mountain of debt."[25] Brecht's attitude toward Peter Suhrkamp was typical of his method of determining who were "old Nazis." Eric Bentley later gave Brecht a copy of Herbert Ihering's Nazi-oriented book on Emil Jannings.[26] Pressed for an opinion on Ihering's nazism, Brecht said, "I'm sure that what he [Ihering] said in favor of the Nazis was an absolute minimum."[27]

Brecht's one-man tribunal on denazification permitted him the luxury of interpreting old contracts as he wished, breaking some and keeping others. As long as he was paid and repaid for the same text, he signed multiple agreements giving supposedly "exclusive" power of attorney to: Eric Bentley, Ruth Berlau, Ferdinand Reyher in America, Suhrkamp and Desch Verlag in Germany, Reiss and Mundus in Switzerland, Englind in Scandinavia, and Einaudi in Italy. And while appointing all these agents, he often ignored them, issuing other "rights" and collecting additional option monies. In the midst of this, Bentley wrote to James Laughlin: "Our friend Brecht has created a god-awful mess. Just after I had given Roberts an option, he wired another to somebody else in New York, I am now hectically trying to straighten things out. What a man!"[28]

An article now appeared in the Los Angeles *Daily News* about the production of *The Threepenny Opera* in Berlin, describing Brecht "as one of the most famous Jews in Germany." To which Brecht (according to the FBI) is reported to have replied: "A 'Jew,' did you say? They have murdered so many Jews over there that they need a new crop and so they enlist me among them." The actor Leopold Lindtberg claims that Brecht said to him in 1945, "The Jews have now had their six million deaths, now they should give [us] some peace."[29]

On December 11, 1945, Charles Laughton read aloud the new version of *Galileo*. His audience included: Brecht, Weigel, Stefan Brecht (now recovered and discharged from the American army), Hanns Eisler, the atomic physicist Reichenbach, and Salka Viertel and her son Hans. The reading was a great success. Brecht's star was rising in the West: Laughton made *Galileo* a strong theater and film property, *Simone Machard* was sold to MGM, and Bentley was publishing Brecht plays in English translation and praising Brecht in critical essays. Brecht wanted to return to Europe in a position of power after having had a New York production of *Galileo* with Laughton, a film and stage star of the first magnitude.

Hauptmann had finally consented to work semi-independently with Bentley on an English-language version of the Steffin-Brecht *Private Life of the Master Race*. She confidently and fully on her own authority changed and again changed Brecht texts. Usually, when Bentley would ask about Hauptmann's changes, Brecht would reply, "Yes, yes, let that stand."[30] Bentley, who knew little of her work in the old Berlin days, saw her as a commissar whose changes did not help the literary merits of the texts. Hauptmann, sympathetic to the abuse Berlau was taking from Brecht, read some of Berlau's work and thought her writing very good. One piece that struck her particularly was a story called "Helli." Ruth was also working at this time on a novel and a stage play. These were both, Ida Bachmann told Hauptmann, very good indeed.

Suddenly Brecht's otherwise upbeat affairs were clouded by a phone conversation with Berlau. His journal for December 2, 1945, reads, "Called r[uth] at night and heard unpleasant things." In the course of her visits to Meta Juul's Danish seaman's home, Berlau had become close friends with two Danish sailors. One was described by the FBI as: "38 to 40 years of age, 5' 9" to 5' 10", 175 lbs., Hair, Iron grey, cut short, Eyes Blue, Complexion Dark and swarthy, Build Stocky, Appearance German or Jewish; no glasses." After a brief affair, this man, a writer who warmly encouraged her work as a writer, had left to return to Denmark. Ruth brought home a second man, described by the FBI as: "30 years of age, 5' 10" tall, 190 lbs, blond hair, light complexion, Nordic appearance, with tattoos on both arms." On December 15, Brecht railed darkly, "It is hard and it is dangerous to try to learn from deceptions."[31] Then he sent Ruth Berlau the poem "The Writer Feels Himself Betrayed by a Friend." The poem, a fine example of "Kunst als Waffe"—"art as weapon"—shows typically Brechtian telescoping of inanimate and animate objects:

> What the child feels, when its mother goes away with a strange man. . . .
> What the airplane feels, if it felt at all, when its pilot steers it drunkenly.[32]

After years of attacks on Ruth's own self-esteem, this poem was an emotional hand grenade with the pin already pulled. On Christmas Eve, her sister Edith's birthday, Ruth identified anew with the anguish of Edith's relationship with a married man that had put her in an insane asylum. She had lost Michel, again been fired from OWI, and the sailors she had befriended were returning to Denmark. Both Karin Michaëlis and Ida Bachmann would soon be leaving also. She was not only losing her friends, but also the financial help that had made the New York apartment affordable. As he had done with Hauptmann, Zoff, and Weigel when they had moved toward independence, Brecht exerted more and more pressure to bring Berlau back to heel. After Ruth told Brecht about her lovers, her condition seemed to improve. "She seemed happy for a while," Bachmann wrote to Brecht later, "with a certain feeling of freedom at having told you the truth."[33]

Brecht's accusatory poem had arrived as the first of Berlau's sailor lovers left. "From then on," Bachmann wrote in a long report that she sent later to Brecht, "her desire to be free, her admiration for you, and her anxiety for the Dane out at sea formed a growing conflict in her mind. One afternoon, around the 19th or 20th of December, I came home and found her in what can only be described as ecstasy. She declared, when she saw me, that she 'saw the whole truth.' 'Now when I have told the Master the truth, I have found the truth and I am free,' she said. She talked with the gestures and the voice of a prophet, and I found it wisest to not contradict her, although much of what she said was incorrect. 'I know that this is going to cost me my life,' she said. 'I am going to die.' She talked about her sister, Edith, [still in a Danish asylum] and she asked me to drive out and see her when I get to Denmark. 'Take her a pair of shoes, last time I saw her she needed shoes. And there you will see a Communist gone mad. Shortly before she went mad she asked me' (Ruth said about her sister) 'Can it be done with friendliness? Maybe social democracy is the right way after all.' "[34]

When Bachmann returned home from work on Christmas Eve, "a stormy conversation" had been going on between the younger, apprentice photographer Ruth (sent to Berlau by Brecht) and the older Ruth. Ruth Berlau now announced to Bachmann: "I have handed everything over to her. She can take over now, she is young and intelligent and beautiful. I put Brecht's leika [sic] over her shoulder and said to her it is yours." The next day, the two Ruths had a violent quarrel, and the younger one fled never to be seen by Bachmann again.

Berlau proposed to Bachmann that they write a play together "for Broadway," as Ruth said, "in order to make fast money, for that is the only way you and I can make fast money since we are not whores." Ruth's play was to be about an actress who always acted her current role offstage. Its title was to be *Who Are You?* This question, Bachmann writes, "took possession of Ruth," as Ruth began to ask: "Who am I? Who are you? Who is everybody?" As Bachmann put it in her letter to Brecht, "At the time it was impossible for me to see whether it was her vivid imagination (which I always admired) and her sometimes brilliant intelligence that was at work, or whether she had lost control over these faculties." As Christmas Day neared, things got worse. "She began," Bachmann writes, "reading the [B]ible in order to find everyone portrayed in it. You were Jesus Christ, later on King Solomon. She herself was first Jeanne d'Arc, then the [V]irgin Mary, Mary Magdalena—and finally Revolution. I was the 'goddess of Liberty.' A young sailor who was in her room day and night—the proletariat being treated to a home—was 'Satan' (the tempter) and 'an angel whom god had touched.' Another sailor who had mentioned that he wanted to study social science was 'Denmark's Lenin.' "

"For Christmas Eve," remembered Bachmann, "Ruth had promised Meta Juul to come down and help prepare the dinner party at the sailors' home . . . I was not with her that evening, but from Meta Juul I hear that Ruth got into violent arguments with several people during the half hour she spent at the sailors' home, and everybody thought she had been drinking too much." "On Christmas day," Bachmann wrote, "she told me that it had been the most wonderful Christmas [E]ve she had ever had, and she was absolutely normal and quiet that morning, lay on her bed and read . . . and she declared that now she had got over it (realizing that something had been wrong)."

Two days later, it was clear to Ida that this had been the calm before the storm. "But from then on," wrote Bachmann, "she got steadily worse, and I don't believe she slept one night. Her eagerness to start the revolution was present in her mind, and it gave her no rest. She quoted you all the time and she wrote down much of what she thought and said and what other people said. The sailor, Bernhard, stayed in her room. He would not leave and she would not let him leave until Thursday evening when he had to make for his ship. It was Thursday (Dec.

27th) that it became clear to me that she was ill. It may seem strange to you—now that I had not realized it before. But during these years I had grown accustomed to her behavior which had often been what many people would call unusual and theatrical, and I said before much of what she said, in fact most of it, was logical and right."

The situation worsened: "But on Thursday evening she became violent, and I asked her if she wanted to see Meta Juul (for whom she had great admiration). 'No,' she declared, 'from now on I shall see Meta very seldom. She told me to step down from the table" (on Christmas [E]ve). Then I telephoned for [D]r. Sternberg, who was not at home, and Elisabeth Hauptmann came in shortly after with a doctor, having been notified by Mrs. Sternberg." Ruth physically attacked the doctor, and he had wanted to call the police, but the women dissuaded him. Fritz Sternberg, Brecht's old misogynist friend from the Berlin days, got on the telephone and talked guardedly with Brecht in California. Brecht called Ferdinand Reyher at the Chelsea Hotel and asked him to go by the next day with a doctor to see what could be done to help. However, when the sympathetic Reyher arrived with Dr. Grünthal, he concluded the police should be called if only to prevent Ruth from doing violence to others or herself. The police took Ruth to the huge, public Bellevue Hospital. Two days later, with Paul Czinner and Elisabeth Bergner as signatories for the bill, Ruth was transferred from Bellevue to South Oaks Hospital in the small town of Amityville on Long Island.

There, Brecht was allowed to speak with her by telephone. "I can imagine that Ruth will come to her senses," Brecht wrote to Reyher, "at least for a time (when I telephoned her she was very rational throughout). If so, she should be able to read the enclosed letter. It would help her."[35] He explained he could not come himself. "Unfortunately, I have a bad case of flu with a rather high fever. The fact that she is so far away and in strange hands naturally upsets me very much." "The nervous breakdown," he explained to Reyher, "did not come out of a clear blue sky. She did some dumb things and thought I would send her away. In any case, the doctors ought to be made aware that [a] certain amount of mental agitation preceded it." In a postscript, he asked, "What shall I send in the way of money??" There is no evidence he actually sent any money. Paul Czinner paid most of Ruth's bills at Amityville. Brecht argued later that Czinner's expenses for Ruth should be considered as partial payment for work done on *Malfi*.

After a telephone conversation with Brecht on January 8, Hauptmann wrote down her own sense of the situation. Hauptmann told Brecht it was a five-hour roundtrip to Amityville by public transportation. Ruth, reported Hauptmann, was very bitter about "deceptions and losses" with Brecht and had declared "my poor head is chopped up into pieces." Hauptmann stated firmly in her January 9 report to Brecht that if Ruth was to recover she would need more independence, would need to do far less mechanical work, would need to be free to do her own creative writing, and in the early stages of her release at least, "she urgently needs someone who will watch out for her as she cannot be alone." The next day, she sent Brecht another letter urging that he provide a modest amount of money to transfer Ruth from distant Amityville, to the closer and better facilities of the New York Medical Center. As far as can be determined, Brecht never responded to this idea, and Ruth was left at a place where it was difficult for someone without a private car to visit her.

In early January, while trying to wind down affairs to return to Denmark, Ida Bachmann and Meta Juul made the five-hour roundtrip by public transportation to Amityville. Bachmann wrote on January 11: "She was much quieter, and it was evident that she was very happy to see Mrs. Juul and me. She had forgotten much of what had gone before her going to the place where she is now. . . . Her only thought was that she wanted to get away from that place, she implored us to take her back home with us." Bachmann also had a talk with Ruth's doctor, a Dr. Rollo, whom Ida thought to be "quite unpleasant." The doctor held out hope of Ruth's recovery if a course of electric shock treatments was undertaken. The treatments themselves, as the doctors told Bachmann, "are apt to make the patient more confused in the beginning, and to eliminate the memory." The treatments may well have been performed, as they were on Sylvia Plath a few years later, with no friends or relatives of the patient present.[36] As Bachmann observed after her Amityville visit: "I do not know much about that sort of institutions [sic], but it seems to me that any normal person would go insane in such a place."

Bachmann now recommended what she felt Ruth would need if she was to have a real chance to recover. "I am, of course, not a doctor," she wrote, "but it would seem to me that after a few more treatments, [her own] work would be the only thing that would bring her back, together with proper care and rest. . . . she was longing for peace to work on her novel." Bachmann's letter pointed out also that her own sailing date was set for January 20, and that she felt that the New York apartment should be kept for Ruth to come back to after her discharge.

Brecht's diary mentions neither the letters from Hauptmann and Bachmann, nor Ruth herself. There is a long diary entry for January 5 in which he says the Russians were doing in their sections of occupied Europe what the Europeans should have done themselves. He means by this what he calls "agricultural reform." He seems to have forgotten what havoc Soviet "reform" of agriculture had wrought throughout the Soviet Union in the mid-thirties.

On January 7, he was finally able to sign a formal contract for a fall 1946 production of *Galileo* in New York with Laughton. He wrote a detailed business letter to Peter Suhrkamp giving him "power of attorney" for a number of plays, including *Galileo* and *Mother Courage*.[37] He made no mention of Steffin or provision for her heirs to collect royalties. On January 18, he wrote to Erich Reiss Verlag in Switzerland challenging modest expenses that the firm had charged against his royalty account.[38] Weeks later, Brecht declared himself well enough to go to New York. Laughton was now preparing to give press conferences there on the upcoming *Galileo* production, and Brecht wanted to be involved in the preproduction publicity they hoped to generate.

"I Am Jealous, So Jealous That the Devil's Fire Is Burning All over in My Body" (1946–47)

Brecht reached New York about February 9 to join Charles Laughton for press conferences and work on *Galileo*.[1] It was a crucial and lucrative time for Brecht affairs both European and American. Relatively large sums of money show up in his accounts. From the FBI file, we know, for instance, that on February 1 $2,743.33 was deposited from a source that the FBI did not identify, along with $10,000 of other earnings from this same period, which was hidden from Berlau and Weigel.[2]

Brecht may have made one trip out to Amityville to see Berlau during his first few weeks in New York. In a February 16 letter mainly about revisions of *Malfi* that he wanted Hauptmann to do on his behalf (but which he did not want to pay her for), he said he had seen Berlau.[3] Disputing this later—and her recollection may understandably be faulty in this period—Berlau claimed he first saw her on February 27. Whenever it was, he went with Paul Czinner and Elizabeth Bergner in their limousine. Berlau recalled years later that during the visit to Amityville, Brecht had muttered to Bergner that "no one was as crazy as a crazy Communist." When he first spoke with Berlau about her being able to leave the asylum, she pointed to the other thirty-two patients on her barred ward and shouted he would have to find cars for all of them.

In March, still disoriented from the electric shock treatments, she was released in Brecht's custody. It was a particularly busy time for him. *Galileo* negotiations were at a make-or-break point. February and March were the period of what James K. Lyon has called Brecht's "most intensive collaborative efforts" with W. H. Auden on another reworking of *Malfi*.[4] At the same time, Brecht was pushing Auden to finish up a translation of *The Caucasian Chalk Circle*. The atmosphere was tense. Ferdinand Reyher, jealous of his own contribution to *Galileo* and anxious to spend time with Brecht, worried about Brecht's work with Laughton. Laughton, ever in need of reassurance, hated Brecht's absences with Reyher. Czinner, anxious to get *Malfi* finally staged, was furious at the constant delays and could not ignore Brecht's obvious sexual interest in Bergner; nor could he get Brecht to reimburse him for Ruth's long stay at Amityville. Auden was also at the end of his tether.

The British publisher Charles Monteith claims, "Auden said to me
. . . that of the literary men he had known only three struck him as
positively evil: Robert Frost, Yeats and Brecht!"⁵ Auden finally got
Brecht out of his hair by delivering the Malfi adaptation to him on
April 4.

The plays painfully echoed Ruth's own situation. In Galileo,
women are expected to forget their own concerns in order to serve the
daily needs of "the great man." In Malfi, the Duchess suffers from
economic exploitation and from the insane jealousy and incestuous
lusts of her brother. She is forced to hide her pregnancies, and her
newborn babies are killed and their bodies hidden in a wardrobe. The
same people who have done this plan to lock her away in an insane
asylum.

Ruth Berlau made two notes on her own situation. "How and
what happened," she wrote in Danish, "I don't know—the last thing I
really remember is that I said to Brecht on the telephone: 'everything is
not in order,' that was in December 1945—I don't remember the date.
I was picked up, so they told me, by some 'watchmen' from a mental
hospital and put into a straitjacket on December 28—and the next day
I was brought to another mental hospital in the country. Brecht came
from California February 27th and took me out of the hospital. From
about December 24 to about February 24 I don't remember anything or
just fragments. Nearly one year of my memory has slipped away because of the electric shock treatments so they told me. The diagnosis:
schizophrenia—possibly psychosis."⁶ In her second note, dated March
25, 1946, she wrote: "What I was about to write down was about
uncertainty, jealousy, suspiciousness, the fear of loneliness from the
one you love carries great weight on the one scale and even the luck, the
joy of the lust still has the upper hand. I love. I am in love. I am jealous,
so jealous that the devil's fire is burning all over in my body and the
damned devils are tearing at me."⁷

Brecht came to realize that he was not going to get Czinner to pay
Ruth's hospital bill and (as we know from the FBI file) had to pay it
himself. He now called Weigel to tell her that accommodations would
have to be made for Berlau on the West Coast. James Lyon reports:
"Rhoda Riker, a friend of the family, remembers receiving a phone call
from Weigel in the spring of 1946, saying her husband had just phoned
from New York. If she did not take in Berlau, he had said, he would not
come home."⁸

Brecht's latest demand was part of a pattern going all the way back
to 1924 and Bie Banholzer. When Weigel had first met Rhoda Riker,
whom Stefan Brecht had met at UCLA and then introduced to his
father, Weigel had bluntly asked, "Are you one of the sisterhood?"

When Riker asked what this meant, Weigel asked more explicitly, "Are you one of Brecht's women?" Riker answered no, and said that she had only realized later "what a large society she was asking me whether I was a member of."[9] But if Riker was not "of the sisterhood," her enthusiasm for Brecht would always suggest she could easily become part of that company. When she was handed a copy of *Galileo* and told she was the first English-speaking person to see it—a claim she knew to be untrue—she was nevertheless "immensely flattered."[10] James Lyon describes Riker as "an eager follower who was overwhelmed by the dramatist's creative gifts."[11] After Weigel was convinced Riker was not "of the company," she said (Riker recalled), "Brecht was a genius and needed all kinds of inspiration and care to keep his thoughts flowing and she said she thought she could tolerate all this as long as he was able to work."[12]

Still on the East Coast with Berlau, Brecht made a quick run up to Boston to see Orson Welles's production of Cole Porter's *Around the World in Eighty Days*. Brecht told Welles, "This is the greatest thing I have seen in American theater," but he was one of the few people to like it. Brecht told Welles he was definitely the man to direct *Galileo*. But Welles, in a note to Laughton, wrote, "Brecht was very, very tiresome today until (I'm sorry to say) I was stern and a trifle shitty. Then he behaved. I hate working like that."[13]

By early May, *Malfi* plans were set for the fall. He was now rewriting *Galileo* with Berlau and Reyher. Many lines and whole scenes from the version Laughton considered final were discarded. Reyher noted: "Really did a job of work on the play, and repaired it greatly." In the same diary entry, dated May 7, 1946, Reyher expressed outrage at Brecht's cavalier treatment of him, saying: "Broke out he's leaving for California at 5 a.m. tomorrow—and 'thought I knew.' He uses the papal legate shift not infrequently."[14] Despite hurt feelings, Reyher had lunch with Brecht on May 7 at Costello's and went shopping with him at Macy's, Brooks Brothers, and an Army-Navy surplus store. Observing Brecht's strategies in clothes buying, Reyher told friends that "Brecht was the most expensively worst-dressed person" he ever knew.

Just before Brecht and Berlau left for California—in Charles Laughton's chauffeur-driven limousine while Laughton went back by plane—Reyher advised Brecht on how to register at motels: "[I] told him to bunk with [the] other man and keep her [Berlau] separate." The day after they had left, Reyher wrote: "Sticking in my craw, Brecht's departure without a word. Something demoralizing in this. Not the grace or imagination of a word. A cheap view of one; a subconscious wish to make my work on *Galileo* unimportant, even unnecessary." A little later in the same entry, Reyher adds: "Never or rarely credits a line, idea, suggestion, correction, etc. Taken, and credit with it. Too bad; I can be had so cheaply, too, if not cheapened; ask so little, if not denied in advance . . . bad."[15] Brecht sensed Reyher's disaffection and later sent him a note saying "Many thanks for your enormous effort."

When the limousine reached California, Berlau was installed at a apartment house called The Uplifters. She went to work at once with Brecht and Laughton on *Galileo*, taking apart again what had been put together with Reyher. They considered who should produce and direct the play. Orson Welles had been assured that he was the chosen one, but when Mike Todd offered more money, Laughton and Brecht made an agreement with him. "That's protection," Laughton said. When Welles learned of Todd's involvement, he backed out. Now more protection was sought from, among others, Elia Kazan, Alfred Lunt, and Joseph Losey.

Brecht was still tinkering with the text and had now brought in three younger people to work with him: Morton Wurtele, a physics student at UCLA, who was now living at the Brecht-Weigel home in Santa Monica; Naomi Replansky, a young, aspiring woman poet whom Brecht had met in New York and who had followed him to Santa Monica; and Rhoda Riker. These young and obviously adoring women deeply threatened Berlau, now nearing forty. She invited Eugen Tumantsev, the Soviet consul in Los Angeles, for dinner (as the FBI noted), but Brecht did not join them.

In the fall, Berlau and Brecht rode back to New York, again by chauffeur-driven limousine. When they reached New York, Reyher noted: "Remeeting [with Brecht]. Helly [Helene Weigel] not with him— Ruth Berlau. Sudden painful insight into Helly's feelings: trapped in Santa Monica, bored, not out of L.A. since she arrived eight [*sic*] years ago, passed, by, and around."[16] Reyher's insight about Weigel was correct. To Michaëlis, Weigel wrote: "With me it's the same old thing, I could, with a little reflection, make a few tragedies out of my life, but I absolutely don't want to, probably my lack of *Weiberei* [woman's reactions] is the stupidest thing I could do. Otherwise I am depressed that I cannot come to New York. It is boring here."[17]

Things were not better for Ruth Berlau who, in her fragile state, was now torn constantly by jealousy. Though she did not know it at the time, often when she left the Fifty-seventh Street flat, Brecht used her place for assignations with the spouses of various emigrés and any young woman he could persuade to come over. Hanns Eisler told Berlau of this years later and also claimed that Brecht's sexual approaches had been pared down to two words: "Say yes."[18] Edith Schloss agreed.[19] Daughter of one of the emigrés, she met Brecht by accident in 1945 at a party at Berlau's apartment. "Brecht's unwashed appearance, the smell of cigar smoke and drinks that always hung around the studio, the smart cracks and tired cynicism of his friends, and everyone's outdated bourgeois mannerisms confused me," she said. "I could not believe," wrote Schloss, "that old and tired revolutionaries behaved like that." She saw Brecht as exactly like his businessman father who, he told her, had run a paper factory in Augsburg.

Later, Brecht invited Schloss to come by the Fifty-seventh Street flat again. He was alone. Looking at her quizzically he said: "Draw yourself." When she asked what he meant by that, he was more explicit: "Yes, draw yourself. Nude." As Schloss recalled later, he sucked on his cigar, smiled, and said: "You know, in one of those unzüchtig [unseemly or immodest] attitudes you sat in the other night when you were here." Schloss was horrified. She had sat cross-legged but did think that unseemly as she had worn trousers to the party. Now Schloss was all too conscious of the "cigar smell" and the "unshaven cheek" as Brecht chased her around Berlau's apartment. This "peculiar minuet," as she put it, was interrupted by a ring of the doorbell as a bespectacled gentleman arrived. Schloss thought it might have been Kurt Weill. Whoever it was, it gave Schloss the chance to get away.

In earlier years, his charm and vivacity had usually helped him carry the day. But there was something tired and hackneyed about his sexual approaches now. The sedentary years had taken their toll. Thicker around the middle and in the face, most of his teeth now rotten and foul smelling, his movements were more shuffling than graceful. He was often seen now walking with a cane that Berlau had given him. But the physical signs did not mean that all his charm was gone. His words could still dazzle. And he was a past master at the skilled use of time-honored aphrodisiacal supplements: the promise of fame or marriage, the use of the casting couch, and an occasional gift.

In December 1946, Brecht returned to Hollywood for still more work on *Galileo*, leaving Berlau behind to spend the first anniversary of her breakdown alone. Elisabeth Hauptmann, somewhat at loose ends with the war now over, decided in September 1946 to move out to Hollywood where she would try to resume her writing career and take over some of the work Ruth Berlau's deteriorating health no longer permitted her to do. Her relationship with Baron von Bärensprung had ended, and she took up with a great Brecht admirer, the moderately talented composer Paul Dessau, whom she soon married.

Clearly, Hauptmann again hoped—all the betrayals of the past notwithstanding—to work as a real writing partner with Brecht in California. She did editorial chores for an edition of Brecht in Bentley's translations, and she also began work with Brecht in late 1946 on a film adaptation of Gogol's famous novella *The Overcoat*. They designed the script as a vehicle for Peter Lorre. She made sure her name appeared on the title page in letters just as large as those of Brecht's name. But, with Lorre by this time known as a drug addict, the script found no buyers.

Otherwise, Brecht's affairs were booming as 1946 drew to an end. He had been prominently and positively featured in Bentley's 1946 book *The Playwright as Thinker* and in Berlin, Ihering was finishing a book in which Brecht was treated as the German theater's greatest hope. Charles Laughton praised him more and more openly now as the greatest playwright since Shakespeare. Hauptmann and Bentley's English edition of his plays was about to appear. *Galileo* was penciled in for a production in 1947, with a West Coast tryout and then a good prospect of moving it to New York. Laughton had needed to delay the premiere somewhat in order to complete film roles but insisted that Brecht be given a job rewriting a script, as well as paying Brecht $5,000 from his own earnings on *The Paradine Case.*

Still, Brecht was finally beginning to think of returning at least for a visit to Europe. In early 1947, Brecht and Weigel filed for American exit and reentry permits for themselves and teenage Mari Barbara. Stefan, now twenty-two years old, an American citizen and a graduate student at Harvard on the G.I. Bill, seemed likely to want to stay in the United States. In February, half-wary of a rival and half-encouraging a kindred theatrical spirit, Brecht asked Piscator whether he planned to return. Brecht told Piscator that the Soviets had approached him to return to the Soviet sector of Berlin to take over the old Schiffbauerdamm Theater.

It was becoming clear that getting out of the United States might soon become an urgent necessity. In October 1946, the former editor of the *American Daily Worker*, the radically disaffected Louis Budenz, had made a series of public allegations about a vast Soviet intelligence network in the United States run by a man known as "Edwards," "Brown," and "Berger." The man with the many names was Gerhart Eisler. To investigate Budenz's story, the FBI recruited Eisler's former wife, Hede Massing,[20] and the House Committee on Un-American Activities began a public inquiry.

HUAC, as the congressional committee was now called in the press, traced its origins back to the 1938 attack that had been launched on supposed Communist infiltration of President Roosevelt's New Deal, but which had petered out when America became allied with the Soviet Union. But even after Stalin was an official ally, the FBI continued to monitor those having any contact with the Soviet Union. Hoover saw Communists everywhere, even believing that "the Communists had engineered Roosevelt's New Deal."[21]

Hoover was convinced that HUAC was not doing enough to root

out Communists. In the margin of Ronald Reagan's FBI file, Hoover says in a handwritten note, "It is outrageous that House Un-American Activities Committee got cold feet and dropped Hollywood Investigation."[22] Hoover sent a team to work over Reagan, who had been an FBI informant since 1943.[23] According to Reagan, the three FBI agents who were sent to see him in 1946 were very blunt. When told he had been called "that sonofabitching bastard Reagan" at an FBI-infiltrated meeting the night before, he named names, under his FBI code number, T-10.

The strong-arm tactics used against Reagan was part of a carefully coordinated strategy. Hoover, aware long before most people of the influence exerted by Hollywood films, was to push HUAC into aiding him to bring the motion picture industry into line with his own views. And Reagan, president of the Screen Actors' Guild, cooperated fully to have the studios brought under political scrutiny. Pressured by Hoover, HUAC now sent a memo to studio heads that "if necessary, Mr. MAYER would be subpoenaed."[24] In 1945, HUAC's John Rankin had railed about "alien-minded Communistic enemies of Christianity" and spoke of Albert Einstein as a "foreign-born agitator." Mayer, who had fled the pogroms in Minsk, now tried to preempt HUAC by setting up his own committee to fight "Un-Americanism." Mayer hoped self-censorship might keep HUAC out of Hollywood. What might be said, for instance, if HUAC was to ask Mayer why his company had paid Lion Feuchtwanger (and Bert Brecht) some $50,000 just the year before for the rights to *Simone Machard?*

Not impressed by Mayer's committee, HUAC now led the attack on Hollywood and the real enemy behind all its charges—the kind of social activism that had been introduced in America under Franklin and Eleanor Roosevelt. At 10 A.M., on February 6, 1947, under the presiding chair, J. Parnell Thomas, the hearing of Gerhart Eisler began in Washington.[25] In response to Counsel Robert Stripling's summons, "Mr. Gerhart Eisler, take the stand," the witness's first words were: "I am not going to take the stand."[26] HUAC member Mundt moved "that the witness be cited for contempt." The motion carried, and Gerhart Eisler was led from the room.

Ruth Fischer was then sworn in. She stated of her brother Gerhart: "I regard him as a most dangerous terrorist, both to the people of America and to the people of Germany, where he wants to go and whom he pretends to love so much."[27] She then alleged: "He is particularly responsible for the death of the German Communist Hugo Eberlein, the leader of Eisler's own caucuses, and of Nikolai Bukharin, the great Russian theorist, his one-time friend and protector." She also implicated her other brother, Hanns Eisler.

At this time of sensational allegations, Hanns Eisler was hard at work with Brecht in Hollywood on the stage production of *Galileo*. When Laughton was asked whether Hanns Eisler was a Communist, he replied: "Eisler, a communist? Nonsense: his music is just like Mozart!"[28] Each scene in the play was now to be introduced musically. Rehearsals would begin with the cast sharing the Hollywood spotlight with HUAC when the committee opened a Hollywood office in May 1947. The cooperation between the FBI and HUAC was very close. HUAC was provided with lists of "unfriendly" witnesses, including Brecht, and the "friendly" ones, such as Reagan.[29] The FBI deliberately leaked raw file data to HUAC, an explicitly illegal action.

When the *Galileo* rehearsals began in Hollywood, it was clear to the cast that though Joseph Losey was the director of record, the real directors were Laughton and Brecht. The producers were trying to work within a budget of $50,000, half of it from Laughton, and the other half from a young and idealistic producer named T. Edward Hambleton, known as T to his friends. Brecht ignored budgetary restrictions and as John Houseman, one of the show's producers, wrote later: "The horror stories I had heard of his theatrical behavior in Europe and America were confirmed and surpassed."[30]

After one encounter, Losey stormed out vowing never to return unless Brecht apologized. Laughton was asked to tell Losey: "Brecht says please come back, and he also says you should know Brecht never apologizes." Somehow Losey was persuaded to return anyway. But Brecht's blowups were not the only problem. Charles Laughton had insisted that his current lover be given the role of Andrea, a part well beyond his real ability. When Eric Bentley asked Ruth Berlau about this, she agreed that the casting was wrong but said of Laughton's male lovers and the subject of homosexuality in general, "Brecht doesn't want to hear about such things."[31] Similarly, Brecht had put his own entourage on the payroll. Rhoda Riker and Naomi Replansky were on it; as were Ruth, who made a detailed photographic record of the production; Elisabeth Hauptmann, who kept tabs on the script; and Weigel, who did much of the costume work. The executive director of the production, Kate Drane Lawson, wrote a detailed memo in which she noted that Brecht was changing everything at will with no attention whatsoever to budget restraints.

After late rehearsals at the Coronet Theater, "die Herrschaften" (the gentlemen) (as Berlau ironically and rather bitterly dubbed them)— Laughton, his current lover, Brecht, and Eisler—went off in Laughton's limousine for champagne and oysters. Berlau went back to Pacific Palisades. She had been given a room in a house owned by Ann Hunter, a wealthy friend of hers from OWI. Eric Bentley, who had come west for the production, stayed at the same house.[32] At Hunter's place, Berlau had set up a lab where she developed three thousand still pictures and a sixteen-millimeter movie version that she shot of Laughton in *Galileo*.[33] She worked most nights to do this so Brecht could see the photos early the next morning.[34]

On July 30, 1947, an unusual number of Beverly Hills limousines headed for the 260-seat Coronet Theater in Hollywood for the premiere of *Galileo*. Brecht and Berlau's friend and supporter Charles Chaplin arrived with Oona, Eugene O'Neill's daughter, the latest of his young brides. Also there were Charles Boyer, Ingrid Bergman, Anthony Quinn, Van Heflin (whose wife, Frances, was in the cast), John Garfield, Gene Kelly, Sydney Greenstreet, Richard Conte, Howard da Silva, Sam Wanamaker, David Loew, Lewis Milestone, and Frank Lloyd Wright. Eric Bentley had a rather good spot. He was seated beside Peter Lorre, behind Ingrid Bergman, and just in front of Charlie and Oona Chaplin. Bentley saw Brecht was nervous just before curtain time. Brecht dashed out to the nearest drugstore muttering "Ich muss ein Seven Up haben."[35]

Galileo had been written in Scandinavia against a backdrop of the Moscow Show Trials, and revised in 1945–46 under the shadow of the atomic bombs dropped on Japan. In 1947, in Hollywood, Galileo's confrontation with the Inquisition became a mirror held up to HUAC, though Laughton seemed oblivious of all such political dimensions of the text. In its mixed review of the production, *The Hollywood Reporter* seemed to confirm Laughton's view when it wrote: "both in staging and in the dialogue the play approaches the old English Shakespearean style of presentation, wherein scenery is but illusionary and the actors move the props around themselves." In the *New York Times*, Gladwin Hill correctly noted that the episodic structure of the play and its use of a relatively bare stage were similar to techniques widely used in America in the 1930s for WPA "living newspaper" productions. Laughton also got mixed reviews.[36] Gladwin Hill felt he had made of the scientist "an appealing human figure." *Variety*, while expressing doubts about the script and the production as a whole, deemed Laughton's performance a "personal triumph." However, Patterson Greene of the *Los Angeles Examiner* dismissed Laughton as "a porcine boor."

Hardly a week after *Galileo* had opened in Hollywood, a letter from the Los Angeles FBI bureau to J. Edgar Hoover in Washington noted, "It is pointed out that during 1943 and 1944 BRECHT was contacted by KHEIFETS [sic], alleged espionage assistant to the chief of the N.K.V.D. in the United States, at least twice at his residence"; and later in same letter, "It is requested that Philadelphia and Washington Field expidite [sic] the leads set forth inasmuch as the Bureau may desire that BRECHT be interviewed before his departure for Europe in case he does not apply for a re-entrance permit." But while the Los Angeles office was concerned about whether Brecht should be given a reentry permit, on August 18, the Philadelphia office sent off a Teletype marked "URGENT" saying "BERTOLT EUGEN FRIEDRICH BRECHT, WAS., ISR. RELET FROM LOS ANGELES TO DIRECTOR EIGHT EIGHT FORTYSEVEN. SUBJECT ISSUED RE-ENTRY PERMIT ONE FOUR THREE SEVEN NINE ONE ON THREE ELEVEN FOR-TYSEVEN TO VISIT SWITZERLAND, SWEDEN, DENMARK, FRANCE, AND ITALY FOR EIGHTEEN MONTHS FOR PUR-POSE OF NEGOTIATIONS WITH THEATERS AND PUBLISHERS HOUSES. INTENDS DEPARTING FROM NEW YORK DATE, UNKNOWN, BECAUSE QUOTE DEPENDS ON SWISS VISA QUOTE. ADDRESS ABROAD WILL BE CARE PRAESENS FILMS, WEINBERGATR FIFTEEN ZURICH, SWITZERLAND." Reacting to this urgent cable, Los Angeles responded on August 25, "In view of subject's plans for an 18 month trip to Europe departing in September of this year from the United States, it is requested that permission be granted to interview BRECHT concerning his contacts with GREGORI KHEIFETS [sic], former Soviet vice-consul in San Francisco and alleged N.K.V.D. agent."

While the FBI considered bringing Brecht in immediately for questioning about MOCASE and COMRAP, or waiting for a better moment, the Brecht team was preparing for departure. Weigel put their large house on the market. Brecht remained busy trying to sell *Galileo* to the movies and, with Laughton's active encouragement, still hoping for Broadway productions of not only *Galileo* but also *Setzuan* and *Chalk Circle*. He hoped all this, together with the sale of the house, would yield plenty of cash for him to buy an American car to take to Europe. He rather liked the thought of the then popular Nash, but he wrote to Reyher asking him whether he would recommend a Chevrolet over a Nash.[37]

On September 19, a United States marshal turned up on the doorstep of the Brecht-Weigel house. He had come to serve a subpoena for Brecht to appear before HUAC, which had now returned to Washington. Weigel invited the man in and gave him coffee. He was inclined to chat and offered advice on how to get more money out of the American government. The thing to do, he said, was to take a train from the West to the East Coast but to bill the American government at the higher rate paid for driving a car. As the government paid a roundtrip fare in advance and provided a per diem for the trip, this all added up.

After a report from Weigel, Brecht spoke by phone with set designer Max Gorelik, who asked him if he had in fact done anything "un-American." Brecht is supposed to have replied: "No, I'm not an American. If they had accused me of doing nothing for Communism, they would have been correct."[38]

On September 24, Hanns Eisler, described as "the Karl Marx of Communism in the musical field," made a feisty appearance in Washington. He did not cooperate with HUAC. He repeatedly risked his own neck to protect Brecht. When asked about *The Measures Taken*, he suggested that both words and music were entirely his. When asked about an appearance with his brother Gerhart at Communist party headquarters in New York in 1935, however, he replied in tones worthy of Watergate or Irangate, "My best recollection is I do not remember."[39] Stripling sought to link Hanns to Gerhart by quoting a letter in which Ruth Fischer had stated that both brothers were "agents of the GPU." Rankin said the Eisler brothers had been admitted to the United States only after Eleanor Roosevelt had written a letter on January 11, 1939. In her letter, she had urged the State Department to at least give Hanns Eisler a fair hearing before turning him down.[40]

Rankin now launched into a diatribe against the widow of the author of the New Deal, and referred to a recent article by Mrs. Roosevelt in the *Ladies' Home Journal*. Of this article, Rankin said: "It is the most insulting, Communistic piece of propaganda that was ever thrown in the faces of the women in America. I am just wondering if she was familiar with all this Communist infiltration when she was trying to get Hanns Eisler into the United States." In light of such attacks, I believe a strong case can be made for Eric Bentley's contention that "arguably [Eleanor Roosevelt] was the principal target of HUAC in its early years."[41]

37

"No, No, No, No, No, Never" (1947)

To oppose HUAC was to risk both clandestine attacks by the FBI seeking any kind of dirt on opponents and to be tarred by the committee with the "Commie" brush. Among those who directly opposed HUAC at this dangerous time was Thomas Mann. In a radio talk, Mann said: "I have the honor to expose myself as a hostile witness. I testify that I am very much interested in the moving picture industry and that, since my arrival in the United States nine years ago, I've seen a great many Hollywood films. If Communist propaganda had been smuggled into any of them, it must have been most thoroughly hidden." Mann concluded, "I am painfully familiar with certain political trends. Spiritual intolerance, political inquisitions, and declining legal security, and all this in the name of an alleged 'state of emergency' . . . that is how it started in Germany. What followed was fascism and what followed fascism was war."[1] Albert Einstein attacked HUAC in a letter that he allowed to be made public. I. F. Stone said of Einstein's position: "I propose an association of American intellectuals to take the 'Einstein Pledge' and throw down a fundamental challenge to the establishment of an inquisition in America."[2] Einstein, Mann, and I. F. Stone saw that failure to oppose HUAC was an invitation to the American right to strangle legitimate ideas of social progress. HUAC, backed by the FBI, wanted the public to throw out the baby of Eleanor and Franklin D. Roosevelt's social agenda with the bathwater of real Soviet agents.

Another who dared take on HUAC directly was Joseph Losey. Losey organized a rally to help pay the huge legal bills of those subpoenaed by HUAC as "unfriendly witnesses." Attended by five thousand people, the rally was held at the Los Angeles Shrine Auditorium on October 15. Risking his career, Gene Kelly served as master of ceremonies. Shortly after a discreet appearance at the Shrine rally, Brecht left Los Angeles by train for Washington and the reopening of the HUAC hearings in Washington on October 20.[3] He would not be late. HUAC had arranged the schedule to get "friendly witnesses" on the record first. Brecht, as a presumed "Unfriendly" witness, would not be called until late October.

The "friendly witnesses" were coached by HUAC counsel illegally supplied with raw FBI data. FBI records show that Robert Stripling, who would be questioning Reagan, visited him the night before to rehearse his testimony.[4] The early exchanges with Reagan on October 23 were friendly and deliberately humorous. When asked how long he had been an actor, he replied, "Since June 1937, with a brief interlude of three and a half years—that at the time didn't seem very brief." The remark was placed there to introduce Mr. Reagan's "service" record. No mention was made of the fact that he never left the world of Hollywood during those three and a half years, and never stopped acting. When asked by Stripling for details on the Screen Actors' Guild of which he was at that time the acting president, Reagan simply referred to the earlier friendly testimony of George Murphy and Robert Montgomery. Reagan was not asked to name publicly supposed Communist members of the Screen Actors' Guild. Toward the end of his HUAC performance, Mr. Reagan fervently quoted Thomas Jefferson. The quote, in his recollection, went like this: "If all the American people know all of the facts they will never make a mistake." This then gave the HUAC chairman his cue: "There is one thing that you said that interested me very much. That was the quotation from Jefferson. That is just why this Committee was created by the House of Representatives: to acquaint the American people with the facts. Once the American people are acquainted with the facts there is no question but what the American people will do the kind of a job they want done: that is, to make America just as pure as we can possibly make it. We want to thank you very much for coming here today."[5]

Despite having now been dismissed, Ronald Reagan, in his distinctive throaty, actor's voice, seized the last word and declared: "Sir, I detest, I abhor their philosophy, but I detest more than that their tactics, which are those of the fifth column, and are dishonest, but at the same time I never as a citizen want to see our country become urged, by either fear or resentment of this group, that we ever compromise with any of our democratic principles through that fear or resentment. I still think that democracy can do it."[6] With its tone of embattled yet confident fervor, its attack on an undefined "their philosophy," combined with an endorsement of a mysterious "it," this speech gave a foretaste of just how formidable Ronald Reagan could be later as a candidate for ever-larger political office.

Often, the FBI acted without one hand knowing what the other was doing. On October 14, 1947, Hoover gave "Bureau permission" to "interview" Brecht with a view to deportation. However, a note from Los Angeles, dated October 11, discreetly reminded Hoover that an FBI "interview" of Brecht now could interfere with the FBI-guided HUAC proceedings. Hoover reversed himself, saying now "postpone interview in light of pending HUAC appearance of BRECHT."

Piecing together clues left in heavily censored FBI files, it is clear that no full-time watch was apparently in place on Brecht himself by October 1947. However, Gerhart Eisler (now out on bail), the adventuresome Manhattan socialite Martha Dodd Stern, who had worked earlier with the NKVD, and Hermann Budzislawski (Dorothy Thompson's secretary) were all staked out. Each time, Brecht or Berlau was in contact with any of these figures, FBI alarms rang. On one occasion, while Brecht was consulting with the Eisler brothers, an unexpected visitor arrived. It was Charles Laughton, in New York for the upcoming New York production of *Galileo*. In the recollection of Elisabeth Freundlich, who was there, the conversation suddenly took a decidedly nonpolitical turn until Laughton left.[7]

One tactical question presumably discussed with top-ranking party figures such as Gerhart Eisler and Hermann Budzislawski was how to deal with the routine question the committee asked of any suspected Communist: "Are you now or have you ever been a member of the Communist party?" The party required members to plead the First Amendment. I have seen no evidence that Brecht was instructed not to act in accord with this general Moscow policy.

They thought about how to dress, how to comport themselves, and how to gain time to think through an answer. The Eisler brothers had appeared without interpreters. Budzislawski felt, however, that Brecht should have one though he now spoke English about as well. The translation would give Brecht extra time to think about his reply. Care was also given to the question of dress. Brecht could not appear in his stylized "proletarian" clothes but would be the picture of middle-class propriety in a conservative suit and tie. There remained the question of props. Eyeglasses were good; they could be polished at times if needed. And what about a cigar? After determining that the chair of HUAC was a cigar smoker, it was decided Brecht should also be presented as a cigar smoker. With the mise en scene set, Brecht was ready for rehearsals. Budzi, as Budzislawski was affectionately called in party circles, began to interrogate him on *Mother* and *The Measures Taken*, the plays about which HUAC had quizzed Hanns Eisler. Brecht followed proceedings on the radio and in the *New York Times*, which now openly asked if HUAC was worse than the "disease" it was supposed to cure. With *The Caucasian Chalk Circle* about to appear in the Eric Bentley and Maja Apelman translation, Brecht told Bentley to remove the play's preface set in a Soviet kolkhoz in the Caucasus.[8]

On October 26, accompanied by the *Galileo* backers, T. Edward Hambleton and Joseph Losey, Brecht went to Washington. He stayed at the Shoreham Hotel, with eighteen of the so-called Unfriendly Nineteen. Speaking in the hotel's Rose Garden—as it was felt that the rooms in the hotel were probably bugged—consultations took place with the two key attorneys representing the nineteen, Bartley Crum and Robert W. Kenny. Kenny told Brecht that "in spite of being an alien, he enjoyed the same protection and rights under American law that citizens did,"[9] something he had already been told by his attorney in Los Angeles, Ben Margolis. Later, Brecht repeatedly lied and said that since he was not an American citizen, he was not protected by the First Amendment.[10]

The first of the "unfriendly witnesses" was called to testify on October 27. Brecht listened to the radio as John Howard Lawson declared that "this Committee is on trial here before the American people." When he was asked the "are you now or have you ever been" question, Lawson responded, "It is unfortunate and tragic that I have to teach this Committee the basic principles of American—"[11] After several such exchanges, Lawson was removed and cited for contempt of Congress. Subsequent witnesses carefully evaded the key question without ever directly refusing to reply to it.

Martha Dodd Stern telephoned Berlau on October 28 to invite her and Brecht to a social occasion. On October 30, amidst a drumbeat of HUAC press releases announcing surprise testimony, Brecht made his way to the old House Office Building. He appeared with Ring Lardner, Jr., and Chester Cole. At ten-thirty, lured by the promise of surprise testimony, the press was there in force. Flashbulbs popped, and the glare of special lighting for movie cameramen lit and heated up the room.

In response to the formulaic "are you now" question, Lardner replied, "I could answer, but if I did, I would hate myself in the morning." The choleric J. Parnell Thomas spluttered, "Any real American would be proud to answer the question," and ordered, "Sergeant, take the witness away."[12] The case of Cole was dealt with similarly in under seven minutes. There seemed little doubt that Brecht, with his somewhat faulty English, could be dealt with at least as easily, and linked to Gerhart Eisler and the NKVD.

Film footage of Brecht on the stand shows him through a haze of cigar smoke. In his glasses, formal suit, and tie, he does not look like a revolutionary. He has an air of benign cooperation about him that is in signal contrast to the embattled truculence that the Eislers and the members of the "Unfriendly Nineteen" showed. In a thick accent, Brecht started to provide his date and place of birth.[13] At this, HUAC's counsel, Stripling, volunteered to provide Brecht with an interpreter, and a Mr. Baumgardt from the nearby Library of Congress was sworn in. Hearing Baumgardt's accent, Thomas muttered into an open mike, "I cannot understand the interpreter any more than I can the witness."

Though Brecht had given his date of birth correctly as 1898, Stripling now gave it as 1888. One of the attorneys representing the Unfriendly Nineteen broke in, "I think, Mr. Stripling, it was 1898." It was a small slip by Stripling, but it showed he was not in full command of the material. Very slightly, the prosecutor had been placed on the defensive. When Stripling went on to the "are you now or have you ever been" question, Brecht responded, making reference to a typed statement he had brought along with him: "May I read my statement? I will answer this question but may I read my statement?" The statement itself argued that Brecht had seen the need to oppose Hitler at an early date (a lie) and that this explained his actions in the Weimar years. As to his present behavior, Brecht said he saw the greatest danger posed to the planet was nuclear weapons. As a result of these weapons, he argued, "We may be the last generation of the human species on earth." After the committee had read it, Rankin declared, "It is a very interesting story of German life but it is not at all pertinent to this inquiry."

Stripling now again asked, "Are you now or have you ever been a member of the Communist Party of any country?" To Stripling's apparent surprise, Brecht responded: "Mr. Chairman, I have heard my colleagues when they considered this question not as proper, but I am a guest in this country and do not want to enter into any legal arguments, so I will answer your question fully as well as I can. I was not a member or am not a member of the Communist Party."[14] When now asked other questions, Brecht often seemed the very model of the absentminded professor. When asked about articles that had recently appeared in a Soviet publication, very mildly Brecht responded: "No; I do not remember to have written such articles. I have not seen any of them printed. I have not written any such articles just now. I write very few articles, if any." Undeterred, Stripling pressed on, handing what he claimed was an article to Mr. Baumgardt to be identified. But Brecht asked to see the piece in question. He dismissed it: "Oh, yes. That is not an article, that is a scene out of a play I wrote in, I think, 1937 or 1938 in Denmark." The "article" he was shown was a scene from the play *Fear and Misery of the Third Reich*.

With this "article" turning out not to be an article, Stripling turned to *The Measures Taken*. Stripling barked, "Now, Mr. Brecht, will you tell the committee whether or not one of the characters in this play was murdered by his comrade because it was in the best interest of the party, of the Communist Party; is that true?" Brecht replied, "No, it is not quite according to the story." Switching (knowingly or unknowingly), to a quite different play of the same period, *He Who Says Yes*,

Brecht continued, "No; it is not really in it. . . . He jumps into an abyss and they lead him tenderly to that abyss, and that is the story." It was Stripling who was being led to an abyss. When Stripling read from a translation of the play *The Mother*, "You must be ready to take over," Mr. Baumgardt jumped in with the far less inflammatory wording: "The correct translation would be, 'You must take the lead.' "

At another point, in response to whether many of Brecht's writings were "based upon the philosophy of Lenin and Marx?" Brecht blandly replied: "No; I don't think that is quite correct but, of course, I studied, had to study as a playwright who wrote historical plays. I, of course, had to study Marx's ideas about history. I do not think intelligent plays today can be written without such study. Also, history . . . written now is vitally influenced by the studies of Marx about history." The witness was turning the hearing into a lecture room and casually suggesting the absolute necessity of the study of Marx. Stripling sought safer ground, barking "Have you ever made application to join the Communist Party?" Brecht replied, "No, no, no, no, no, never." This was certainly emphatic, but the chairman still asked, "Mr. Brecht, did Gerhart Eisler ever ask you to join the Communist Party?" Brecht replied simply, "No, no." Rankin closed the session at 12:15 P.M., saying "Thank you very much, Mr. Brecht. You are a good example to the witnesses of Mr. Kenny and Mr. Crum." As Rankin saw, Brecht had deserted the position of his colleagues. By answering HUAC's "are you now" question, he had supported the disputed right of HUAC to ask such questions at all.

Like Galileo before the Inquisition, Brecht helped strengthen the hand of his inquisitors. He left with their gratitude. He weakened the case of his colleagues in the Hollywood script-writing community and anybody else who was under attack by this unscrupulous body. As at other key moments in history where he could have stood up and been counted, Brecht chose public cooperation: he did not directly confront the Nazis; he did not support the Jewish cause; he did not defend people like Bukharin and Tretiakov though he privately believed they were innocent; and he advised his brother to join the Nazi party. He acted exactly like the man in the Keuner stories who supports his fat lodger until the lodger dies and is no longer a threat to him, and only then says No! Not that Brecht's word alone could have turned the tide of political events (except perhaps later in the GDR), but he was among the millions whose tacit complicity helped turn the tide toward Hitler, Stalin, and McCarthy.

After being thanked by HUAC, Brecht rode back to his hotel in a cab with Lester Cole. According to Cole, Brecht was in tears as he tried to explain that he had wanted to take the same position as the other witnesses but had "betrayed us by taking a different position."[15] According to Dalton Trumbo, when Brecht got back to the Shoreham after his testimony, he apologized to the other eighteen witnesses "for the position he had taken." For the two members of the eighteen who knew him best, John Howard Lawson and Albert Maltz, Brecht's break with them could not have come as a surprise. For Lawson, Brecht's work represented "discredited and thoroughly un-Marxist theories";[16] and Maltz, who knew him from the 1935 production of *Mother* at the Marxist Theater Union, had always considered Brecht an example of "contentious arrogance."[17]

Many party members in America later told Berlau of their disapproval of Brecht's behavior.[18] Brecht later wrote a letter to Hanns Eisler in which he mentioned the bad press he was getting on this matter.[19] Brecht said his strategy had been the result of advice he had received from the attorneys who had advised the Unfriendly Nineteen. In lying to Hanns Eisler, Brecht would have assumed he was addressing Gerhart Eisler indirectly, who could transmit Brecht's view to Moscow Central.[20] Any hope Brecht might have of working in the Soviet Zone of Germany depended on Moscow's satisfaction with his behavior in America. It was essential that he promote his own version of his behavior in Washington and that it become the accepted one. In the main, in this case as in most others, he was generally successful.

Brecht had more to worry about than disapproval from the New York left and possibly Moscow Central. Of more immediate danger were outraged reactions on the other flank. In Philadelphia, an anti-Communist German emigré (whose name is expunged in the FBI documents as released), a former head reader for Dreimasken Verlag in the Weimar days, had listened to the testimony on the radio. This man called the FBI office in Philadelphia and told them he could prove Brecht had lied about his Communist party affiliation.

On the same day that Brecht appeared before the committee, HUAC heard their promised mystery witness, Louis J. Russell, an ex-FBI agent now in HUAC's employ as an investigator. Russell spoke about the Eisler brothers and their links to Haakon Chevalier and Grigori Kheifetz. Next, he talked of an American scientist by the name of George Charles Eltenton who had once worked in the Soviet Union and who had approached Haakon Chevalier. Stripling asked, "Can you tell the Committee whether or not J. Robert Oppenheimer subsequently worked on the atomic project at Los Alamos, New Mexico, in the development of the atomic bomb?" Russell replied, "He was in charge of it." Using the Eislers and Hollywood witnesses as stalking-horses, HUAC fired at the far larger "commie" targets: Eleanor Roosevelt (and by extension, the Democratic party), Albert Einstein, and

J. Robert Oppenheimer. With this, the so-called Hollywood Hearings ended. The process of purging Hollywood of writers committed to social progress was well under way.

On the evening of October 30, Brecht, Weigel, and Budzislawski listened to a broadcast of portions of Brecht's HUAC testimony. In his diary, inventing a self-exculpating version, Brecht wrote: "The 18 are very satisfied with my testimony, and also the lawyers."[21] The next morning, Brecht noted, "Met with Laughton this morning, who is already wearing the Galileo beard and is pleased that it will not take any special courage to play Galileo, as he says: no headlines about me."[22] By cooperating with HUAC, Brecht had protected his best shot at mounting a major play with a topflight cast in New York.

Later that day, Brecht left for La Guardia Airport to catch an Air France flight to Paris. According to Ruth Berlau, who accompanied him, flights were delayed due to weather. At 3:20 that foggy afternoon, a bulletin came over the "urgent" wire to J. Edgar Hoover from Philadelphia, stating that Brecht's HUAC testimony could be shown to be false. Standing in the departure lounge at La Guardia, Brecht waited nervously for the fog to lift. Two uniformed New York police officers entered the lounge, bought candy bars, and left. Finally the departure of Brecht's flight was announced, and he walked off into the still-lingering light fog to board his flight for Europe.

Soon after he had left, an anonymous postcard came to the FBI from California saying "You let yourselves be told by BRECHT that he was never in a Communist Party! If anyone was ever a Communist, and if anyone gave a false oath, it was he. I am an old lady and know all the people from Berlin. BRECHT was always a Communist and no less a one than EISLER, who at least half told the truth." The card ended, "Don't let them all out!"

On November 3, wholly unaware that Brecht had long since left, the FBI office in Los Angeles asked Hoover whether moving against Brecht could put the MOCASE involving Martha Dodd Stern in jeopardy. Ignorant of Brecht's departure, Hoover replied on November 12: "Your letter of November 3 was considered but it is not believed that subject's association with Martha Dodd Stern is sufficient reason to hold up the interview. HOOVER." This message, labeled "Routine," was sent six days after it was written.

It was not until November 20, 1947, that the New York office finally sent a memo to Los Angeles and to FBI Director Hoover that read, "BRECHT left country October 31, 1947." Hoover finally realized that Brecht had left three full weeks before, with whatever secrets he may or may not have possessed concerning Kheifetz, Eisler, Stern, Chevalier, Pozner, Oppenheimer, and Soviet networks. A week after learning of Brecht's departure, Hoover wrote a memo to the CIA.[23] His memo said nothing of the FBI's failure to notice Brecht's departure. Hoover also failed to mention that FBI files had repeatedly directly linked Brecht both to the NKVD operative in California and to Haakon Chevalier, who in turn was directly linked to J. Robert Oppenheimer, head of the Los Alamos laboratory. In failing to promptly provide such information to the CIA, Hoover placed his own self-interest ahead of central national security concerns. His bland memo to the CIA notes of Bert Brecht: "A confidential source, believed reliable, advised the Bureau on November 5, 1947 that Brecht planned to travel to Europe; would visit Switzerland, and might try to move into the Eastern Zone of Germany in order to work for his Communistic ideas. Please furnish any information you receive or develop on the subject's activities in Europe of a Soviet intelligence nature, and any indications of his return to the United States."

"We No Longer Stand before a Choice between Peace and War, but between Peace and Annihilation" (1947–48)

In Paris, Brecht met two wealthy American friends, Ella Winter and her husband, screenwriter Donald Ogden Stewart. Brecht had first been introduced to them in New York.[1] When they saw him in Paris, Brecht wore what looked like a battered overcoat and cheap cloth cap. Thinking him broke, they paid for his hotel room and took him out for what Brecht said were "fabulous meals." Brecht noted of the city: "Paris shabby, poor, one single black market."[2] He saw in Paris another New Yorker, Joe Forster, editor of *New Masses*. Forster promised to speak to Picasso about him, though there is no record that he did.

On November 4, he saw an acquaintance from prewar days, Anna Seghers. Now forty-seven years old and with a shock of white hair, Seghers had spent many of the Hitler years in Mexico, where she had worked closely with the Comintern activist Otto Katz. After she returned to Berlin, Seghers derived much of her ample income from the Soviets, but in order to preserve some independence, she lived in the Western Sector at the home of the hastily denazified Herbert Ihering.

"Berlin," Seghers told Brecht, was "a witches' Sabbath." Glad to be out for a time, she was visiting her children, who were studying in Paris. "It is clear," Seghers said to Brecht, "that one must have a residence outside Germany itself." Without privileges for such basics as food, coal, footwear, clothing, and paper, it was almost impossible for a writer to live in Berlin. To work there, she advised, one had to be "part of a strong group." Brecht wrote at once to Berlau: "You are going to be unbelievably needed in Berlin, after everything that Seghers has related to me."[3] In another letter, he stressed, "Alone, or almost alone, one cannot have an existence there." "I'll kind of need to use you," he added and closed with the familiar "dein" (yours) with the "d" underlined four times.

In New York, Berlau supervised the opening of *Galileo* with Laughton, a delicate balance between stopping him from making any changes in the original staging and from withdrawing from the production altogether. Brecht wrote to tell her that Stewart and Winter might be able to get her a job in Europe as a correspondent for the *Manchester*

Guardian. He also wanted Berlau to try to find cash for him in Holly-wood or New York. In fact, he was doing well financially. He had several new contracts with European publishers, and his plays were being produced again, including (though he hid this from Berlau) a *Simone Machard* production in socialist Prague. In Switzerland, he still had prewar gold mark money from Felix Bloch Erben.

On November 5, Brecht left Paris for Zurich to meet Caspar Neher. The American Military Authority's chief of the Theater Control Section for Bavaria stated that Neher had been "thoroughly cleared politically."[4] Brecht never questioned this conclusion. Neher took Brecht home to a supper cooked by Neher's wife, Erika. Later, the man who had exchanged so many loving letters with Brecht thirty years earlier wrote: "It was good to see one another after such a long time. He had become stouter, more masculine, more withdrawn and with his gentleness turned outward more than it had been before. His facade of hardness has fallen away from him completely. His natural goodness could now be seen."[5] Neher's rosy view of Brecht's "new" character would soon begin to vanish as Brecht treated Neher, as he had decades before, as someone there to do Brecht's bidding.

Their discussion was about where and how creative work could best be done by a German. Between the Soviet and the Western camps, nowhere looked safe anymore. George F. Kennan had warned the Tru-man government about radical Soviet expansionism that was gaining ground every day. Marxism, Kennan warned, "is the fig leaf of their moral and intellectual respectability. Without it they would stand before history, at best, as only the last of that long succession of cruel and wasteful Russian rulers who have relentlessly forced their country on to ever new heights of military power in order to guarantee external security for their internally weak regimes."[6] Simultaneously, moderate socialism rapidly advanced to power in the Scandinavian countries and in Britain via the ballot box. The Dutch and British empires were unraveling, with the Soviet Union poised to pick up the pieces.

A CIA report to Harry Truman of December 17, 1947, warned that the Soviets planned to "cause the collapse of the French and Italian centrist Governments," using "a hard core of militants, possibly oper-ating underground."[7] The West responded with fair means and foul. The CIA set out in the winter of 1947 to fix the upcoming Italian election, the first in a series that would eventually lead to attempted government takeovers. The Marshall Plan was intended to fight the rising Communist tide with massive aid. All of Germany, all of Europe, the entire planet was now the child in the chalk circle. An all-out war, where the United States might use nuclear weapons before the Soviet Union could develop its own, seemed possible at any moment. A

number of artists gathered on November 9 in Zurich to draft a memorandum of opposition, essentially to both parties in the conflict. Brecht
was invited, as well as German playwright Carl Zuckmayer, newly returned from exile in the United States, and Swiss architect and playwright Max Frisch. The document drafted by the group, partly written
by him, echoed the concerns of Brecht's written statement to HUAC:
"We may be the last generation of the human species on this earth."

Whatever duplicities Brecht practiced in other areas, in the face of
a nuclear holocaust, he was completely sincere in his opposition, all too
aware of his own utter vulnerability. In some distant place, someone
could push a button and end everything. The Swiss manifesto read in
part: "The expectation of a new war is paralyzing the effort to rebuild
the world. We no longer stand today before a choice between peace and
war, but between peace and annihilation. To those politicians who do
not yet recognize this we say decisively, that the people of various
nations want peace. . . . The undersigned writers, who have met in
Zurich, have established that the very existence of two different economic systems is being used to create propaganda for war."[8] This peace
declaration was largely ignored by the press but not by intelligence
agencies. "Peace" had been successfully made a dirty word. Within two
weeks of his reaching Switzerland, Brecht was under CIA observation.[9]

Within days of Brecht's arrival in Zurich, his poverty-stricken
appearance and his reputation of being the reshaper of the modern
stage, ornamented by his explicit commitment to the peace effort, had
an extraordinary effect. He was loaned a studio apartment by Utz Oet-
tinger, a Schauspielhaus dramaturge, and offered another by Reni and
Hans-Walter Mertens. Caspar Neher noted laconically of what was
happening, "It is a revelation how he is handed what he needs from
every side."

Having staged the world premieres of both *Mother Courage* and of
Galileo during the war, the Zurich Schauspielhaus was well disposed
toward Brecht's plays but less convinced that they wanted Brecht as a
director. He had a well-deserved reputation as an expensive tyrant. The
Schauspielhaus could take refuge in Swiss law, which would not permit
a foreigner without working papers to direct a commercial production.
Weigel, who had returned to Europe soon after Brecht, was similarly
blocked from anything but experimental theater. After stopping briefly
in her old home city of Vienna, she and Mari Barbara, now seventeen,
were installed with the Mertenses, which left Brecht free to meet people
in town without having to account to Weigel.

Berlau, meanwhile, was very angry at being left virtually penniless
in New York, managing Brecht's tangled affairs in the face of anger on
both the right and the left at his HUAC behavior. All she got was his

usual letter claiming there had been a mix-up at his Swiss bank. Berlau
added huge exclamation points in the margin of this letter next to "I
now have an apartment for Helli and Barbara 20 minutes from Zurich.
I myself have an atelier in Zurich, so everything is in order. And Helli
will have something to do in the theater in January and will perform for
a while in Chur." The news that Weigel would again be performing,
even in the small Swiss town of Chur, upset Berlau. But his letter ended
with the old and still-beguiling triply underlined "d" and the parentheti-
cal notation about the much underlined "d," "you must believe this,
bertolt." Ruth added her own notation to his and wrote, with a line
drawn to that triple-underlined "d," "but living with Helli so that will
make him inaccessible."[10]

Despite clear premonitions of how things would be for her if she
rejoined him, that was what she planned to do. *Galileo* closed after a
four-week run as Laughton had not been able to raise enough money to
finance it longer. Instead of thanking Laughton for his years of effort,
Brecht wrote a poem in his best "versified invective" form,[11] saying of
Laughton:

> *Speak of the weather and*
> *Bury him deep, for*
> *Before he spoke,*
> *He recanted.*[12]

After finishing up her assigned chores in New York—finding a
disc recording of Brecht's HUAC testimony and buying a large supply
of Brecht's favorite cigars—Berlau flew to Zurich. Arriving on January
22, 1948, she found she would have to largely fend for herself to
reestablish herself in Europe. Her main income in the first year came
from journalism, primarily for the Scandinavian liberal press.

When the Schauspielhaus rebuffed Brecht as a director, he turned
to Hans Curjel, an old friend from the prewar Berlin days, who now ran
a small experimental theater in Chur. They discussed various plays,
including *Phaedra, Macbeth, Mother Courage, Saint Joan of the Stockyards*,
and the one that was finally chosen, Hölderlin's version of Sophocles'
Antigone. In the relative obscurity of Chur, outside the glare of big-city
publicity, Weigel saw what she could still achieve. She was now forty-
seven years old and had hardly appeared on the professional stage for
the last fourteen years.

For Caspar Neher, this Chur production was small potatoes. He
was used to coming into Europe's main theaters for a brief period,
supervising the work on his sets and costumes, and then hastening to
another well-paid job. But Brecht wanted "his" people there for the

entire rehearsal period to change sets and costumes at need. Neher insisted on commuting between the theater in Chur and Milan's La Scala.

Part-time as it was, Neher's work in Chur would help reshape the modern stage. Fortunately, we have a very complete record of what he did there from Berlau's detailed series of photographs of every stage of the work. She used high-speed film that gives her photos a gritty, moody, documentary look. Taking photographically striking shots of her rival Weigel was a process difficult for both the women.

The result of the troubled photographic sessions was a model book, which Berlau would edit later. The book combines the text of the play, Berlau's detailed photo series, and notes on the creation of the props. Her book created a high, now widely imitated standard of production documentation. Looking at Berlau's work on *Antigone*, we see the essential features of the Brechtian postwar style. Neher said, "Brecht is trying to get rid of all mythological and religious bric-a-brac."[13] Where Brecht's ideas end and Neher's begin is difficult to determine. Often, the Neher drawings are taken verbatim as a matrix into which the actors were placed. Directing credit was shared in the program.

As backdrop, Neher had a semicircle of screens covered in red rush matting. In front of the screens stood long pewlike benches on which the cast sat waiting to come forward to play their roles, a device now widely used even in mainstream theater.[14] There was no curtain. The acting area was marked by four posts on which hung the boiled skulls of freshly slaughtered horses. Props and masks were hung on a rack and taken down by the actors in the full view of the audience, another practice that would henceforth become widespread in contemporary theater. The production was starkly modern, but, paradoxically, this very starkness echoed the bareness of the Elizabethan and classical Greek stage. The future of the modern stage drew on classical stage history.

Rehearsals of the play often erupted into arguments between Brecht, Neher, and Curjel. Brecht viewed the production as a kind of preview for Berlin. He did not want to be rushed into a premiere, particularly because he felt Weigel needed time to raise her performance to the highest possible level. But Neher had other engagements, and Curjel needed the income. When Brecht did allow *Antigone* to open on February 15, 1948, it was largely ignored. Despite a solid performance by Weigel and Neher's fine set and costumes, Brecht was invited to bring the show to Zurich only for a single Sunday matinee.

Though audiences were sparse, two influential figures from nearby Salzburg, Gottfried von Einem and Oscar Fritz Schuh, were impressed.

Schuh had worked closely with Neher during the Third Reich, much as Neher had worked with Brecht during Weimar. Schuh and von Einem made an attractive proposition: both Neher and Brecht should be permanently attached to the new Salzburg Festival they were organizing. Austria had just gained a large measure of independence from both the East and the West. It had a long and distinguished history of German-language theater, albeit less than Berlin's. Most interesting, Brecht and Neher were both married to Austrians, and with a little help, they might be able to get Austrian passports. Brecht, who had been stateless since 1935, found the prospect of citizenship in an independent country tremendously attractive at this time.

Schuh and von Einem returned to Austria unaware that Brecht was using their offer as a bargaining chip. He approached Benno Frank, then the American officer for cultural affairs in Bavaria, to ask whether he might be able to settle in Munich. The request was denied after a check with the FBI and CIA. Brecht turned to the Soviet Zone, specifically Berlin, and investigated living in northern Italy, where Rod Geiger hoped to film Galileo. Brecht also wrote Otto Katz.

Meanwhile, he sent Berlau to help his Weimar agent, Jacob Geis, negotiate with Desch Verlag for The Threepenny Novel. They succeeded in providing him with a new advance and the Mercedes he asked for, despite de Lange's prior right. He persuaded Kurt Hirschfield, the Schauspielhaus manager, to mount a main stage production of Puntila in Zurich. Brecht ignored the rights of both Steffin's heirs and Wuolijoki, the latter of whom had an agreement that "both authors will share all income in equal amounts."[15] Brecht was annoyed that Neher was too busy to work on Puntila. Brecht's second choice was Teo Otto, who had designed the wartime world premiere of Mother Courage. Nor could he get his first choice for the lead: Hans Albers, one of the most popular film stars of the Third Reich. By default, the role went to Swiss actor Leonard Steckel.

His daughter by Marianne Zoff, Hanne, visited him in Zurich. Now twenty-five, Hanne had spent the war years with her mother and her stepfather, Theo Lingen. She studied acting and had played a few roles under the name Hanne Hiob. At least one was in a Nazi film. There was some talk of her taking a small part in the upcoming Puntila, but finally neither Hanne nor Weigel appeared in the production.

Less welcome was Wuolijoki's daughter, Vappu Tuomioja, who discovered that her mother was being ignored in the production. Wuolijoki told a Swiss reporter that Brecht was not correctly describing the play's creation. A small note on the differences between the original and the Brecht play was published in the Neue Zurcher Zeitung on July 15. No matter how different the two plays were, Brecht was

49. On June 4, 1930, as reported in the leading Danish paper, Politiken, Berlau leaves for Moscow on special assignment to the paper. However, she was fired after she refused to send back negative reports. Berlau was impressed by the fact that women seemed to have equal rights in the USSR.

50. Berlau's workers' theater company on its way to attend a Revolutionary Theater festival organized in Moscow in the spring of 1933. By this time, Stalin had consolidated his hold on total power in Moscow and was personally directing the NKVD; he would systematically roll back the liberal gains women had made in the first period of the revolution.

51. Ruth Berlau with Robert Lund (seated at center) at his fiftieth birthday party in Copenhagen

52. *Berlau meets Brecht at the home of Weigel's friend the then world-famous Danish novelist Karin Michaëlis on the island of Thurø, August 1933. Berlau wrote later: "He was very funny, and I was too. I didn't know then I already loved him."*

53. *Brecht/Weigel house in Denmark, bought with a combination of Weigel's money and income from the pedestrian and distinctly non-anti-Nazi book the Brecht/Steffin Three-penny Novel*

54. Steffin, 1934

55. Helene Weigel, Ruth Berlau, and the worker actress from Berlau's Revolutionary Theater, Dagmar Andreasen. At night, Andreasen scrubbed floors for a living in the main Copenhagen railway station.

57. The Mother, directed by Viktor Wolfson with Helen Cook playing the title role, New York, 1935. Brecht's dictatorial interference contributed to the virtual destruction of the financial base of the leading left-wing company, the Theater Union, and alienated him from much of the theater left.

56. Elisabeth Hauptmann in Saint Louis, where (totally unknown as a writer) her financial situation was such that she was forced to live for a time as the paid companion of a mentally disturbed woman. Later, as a university instructor in German, she earned $450 a year.

58 and 59. *Cropped and uncropped versions of a photo of Feuchtwanger with Stalin and the Pravda editor Tal in 1937. His usefulness to Stalin over, Tal went down the memory hole after Feuchtwanger returned to the West.*

60. *Mikhail Koltsov, model for Hemingway's brilliant and cynical Soviet representative in* For Whom the Bell Tolls. *Upon his return to Moscow, taunted by Stalin to commit suicide and not doing so, he was, after "terrible torture" and the extraction of a fake confession, murdered by the NKVD.*

61. *Maria Osten, who also appears in* For Whom the Bell Tolls. *After nursing Steffin through her final days in Moscow in 1941, Osten was picked up by the NKVD and murdered the following year, August 8, 1942.*

62. Berlau's production of Señora Carrar's Rifles, Copenhagen, 1937. Note this scene of
a woman viewing her dead son, a clear anticipation of the use of the same image in Mother
Courage and Her Children in 1949.

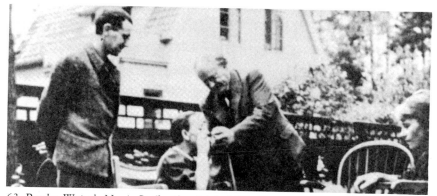

63. Brecht, Weigel, Nexø, Steffin (far right), 1939. Nexø and Brecht insisted that Steffin
translate Nexø's memoirs, though by this time she was so ill and emotionally neglected that
she saw herself as "a tiny piece of shit." Nexø used money from Soviet publications such as
the Steffin translations to build on to his country house.

64. Fear and Misery, Paris, 1938, directed by Slatan Dudow with music by Paul Dessau.
Brecht did not stay in Paris to see Weigel's performance.

66. *Ninnan Santesson creates a portrait head of Weigel, Sweden, 1940*

65. *Ruth Berlau on the motorcycle she bought to give her more independence from Robert Lund and the family Lincoln*

67. *Hella Wuolijoki, politician and playwright. She was sentenced to death during WWII for collaboration with Soviet agents, but her sentence was commuted. After her release in 1945 she would unsuccessfully attempt to collect earnings legally due her from work written jointly with Brecht.*

ГРЕТЕ СМЕРТЬ НЕ ОЖИДАЛА ДУМАЛА ТОЛЬКО
О ЖИЗНИ ПРОСИЛА КНИГИ ВСПОМИНАЛА ВАС
ЕДИНСТВЕННОЕ ЖЕЛАНИЕ СКОРЕЕ ВЫЗДОРОВЕТЬ
ПОЕХАТЬ ВАМ ТЧК ПОСЛЕДНЯЯ НОЧЬ СПОКОЙНА
ЗАВТРАКАЛА ХОРОШО ЧИТАЛА ВАШУ ТЕЛЕГРАММУ
ПРОСИЛА ШАМПАНСКОЕ СКОРМ ПОЧУВСТВОВАЛА
ПЛОХО ОНА ДУМАЛА ОБЫЧНЫЙ ПРИСТУП

68. *A Russian telegram sent by Fadayev announcing the death of Steffin on June 4, 1941. Fadayev, Stalin's right-hand person in the murder of members of the Russian intelligentsia, would commit suicide in 1956 after Khrushchev began to reveal the extent of Stalin's crimes and of those who helped Stalin.*

69. *Weigel and Brecht's first California house, rented and furnished for them by the Feuchtwangers and Elisabeth Hauptmann*

70. *Legal document specifying how all Machard income was to be divided*

Romans oder einer solchen Novelle aber werden unter alle Autoren
des Stückes nach dem in Paragraph (6) angegebenen Schlüssel geteilt.

6)   Alle wie immer gearteten Einnahmen aus dem Stück, aus Auf-
führungen, aus dem Verkauf von Filmrechten, Radiorechten, usw.,
werden so geteilt, dass

BERTOLT BRECHT	fünfundreissig Prozent
LION FEUCHTWANGER	dreissig Prozent
RUTH BERLAU	zwanzig Prozent
MARTA FEUCHTWANGER	fünfzehn Prozent

aus diesen Einnahmen erhalten.

71. Marta and Lion Feuchtwanger in the library of their beautiful Pacific Palisades home

72. Eric Bentley at about the time of his first meeting Brecht

73. The house bought with Machard money. Brecht told Feuchtwanger's secretary, Hilda Waldo, "we are rich now." Rich or not, Brecht failed to pay Berlau $10,000, her legal share of the Machard money. This amount was four times what Berlau earned per year as a federal employee in New York before the FBI got her fired and slightly more than the Feuchtwangers paid for their Pacific Palisades mansion.

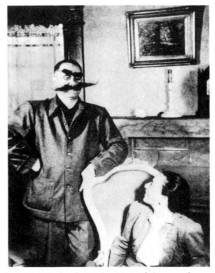

74. Brecht, safe in the United States, does a Stalin imitation for Weigel. This same act in the USSR would have cost Brecht and Weigel their lives. The poet Mandelstam was shipped to the gulag, where he died, for one unflattering mention of Stalin's mustache in a privately circulated poem.

75. *Frank Banholzer in Wehrmacht uniform before his death by Russian artillery fire on November 13, 1943*

76. *Berlau covers her head with a scarf in the first months after disfiguring electroshock treatments at a hospital in Amityville on Long Island in 1946.*

77. *Hauptmann in California in 1947. She had married by this time the composer Paul Dessau. The marriage would not last long as Dessau would take up with a younger woman immediately upon his return to Germany in 1948.*

78. Charles Laughton plays the lead in Galileo, New York, 1947

79. Brecht blows clouds of smoke before the House Un-American Activities Committee. He betrayed his colleagues by answering the committee's question about his party affiliation. His later claim that he had no protection under the United States Constitution was a self-serving lie.

80. FBI memo: Brecht has fled USA. What Hoover did not admit to the CIA was that the FBI had let him get away without knowing for some three weeks that they had done so.

81. *Caspar Neher design,* Antigone, *1948*

82. *Bentley visits Brecht in Zurich*

83. *October 22, 1948. The creation of an iconography of "normalcy" for a Soviet zone that was prudish and deeply conservative, not least in the matter of sexual mores. Brecht and Weigel are here portrayed (with Berlau conveniently absent) as a married couple. In a publicity coup for Stalin, they return to the zone at the height of the Soviet blockade of West Berlin.*

84. Opening scene of Mother Courage, Berlin, January 1949. George Steiner would say of Weigel's performance as she fails to recognize the body of her son: "It was the same wild cry with which the tragic imagination [of classical Greece] first marked our sense of life."

85. Closing scene of Mother Courage. The Soviet critic Boris Sachawa notes that "the heart of the viewer is unwillingly seized" and that the final scene "is a terrifying symbol of the fate of an entire people."

86. Mother Courage: the death of Kattrin. Kattrin gives up her own life in order to awaken the nearby city by her drumming. Eric Bentley has called this (I believe correctly): "possibly the most powerful scene, emotionally, in twentieth-century drama."

87. Hans Albers, one of the greatest and wealthiest stars of films and theater of the Third Reich, was cast as Mackie Messer in the 1949 Munich production of The Threepenny Opera. Brecht made a personal plea to the great star at Albers's Bavarian estate to tour in a production Brecht hoped to direct.

88. Following standard Soviet practice, people deemed useful were given privileges totally inaccessible to the population at large. Besides huge salaries, cars, and chauffeurs, Brecht and Weigel are given a fourteen-room villa with the staff to run it and the coal to heat it at a time when East Berliners were huddled in ruins with little food, heat, or clothing.

89. Brecht and Wuolijoki with Puntila poster. Though the ubiquitous NKVD-trained secret police, the Stasi, could not be unaware of the fact that Brecht regularly appropriated Wuolijoki's money, the conventional public view that everything was all right between the two authors was allowed to prevail. Wuolijoki died in 1954 with her money still unpaid.

90. *Käthe Reichel in Urfaustus. Directed by the young Egon Monk with some assistance from Brecht, the work was explicit in its sexuality. Its failure to treat Goethe and the play as iconic classics attracted Ulbricht's personal ire. Ulbricht tried to withdraw Brecht's personal privileges, but the death of Stalin temporarily undercut Ulbricht's position in Moscow.*

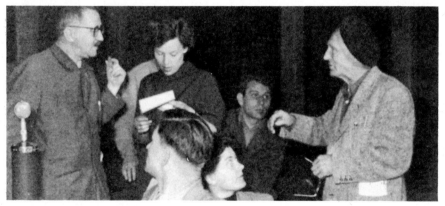

91. *Back row: Brecht, Isot Kilian, Manfred Wekwerth, Ernst Busch. Front row: Hans Bunge and Käthe Rülicke. Weigel, however reluctantly, helped to give Brecht what amounted to a kind of droit du seigneur, first sexual "rights" to Ensemble members.*

92. *The restored Theater am Schiffbauerdamm. Brecht was very much a public figure now. As long as Brecht remained a drawing card for Western intellectuals, Ulbricht tolerated him. Only one sixth of the Ensemble's (and Brecht's and Weigel's) income came from the box office; the rest was from Ulbricht.*

93. *Brecht's and Weigel's house, where each had their own apartment. As with his childhood home in Augsburg, Brecht had a place where he could do his thing without interference (but with servants) while also having the comfort, when he chose, of a comfortably appointed bourgeois home downstairs.*

94. *The Caucasian Chalk Circle. The child in the circle is, like Berlau's child who died after only a few days, called Michel. Michel is also the German equivalent of John Bull for Britain or Uncle Sam for the United States. No attempt was made in Berlin to adopt the child Brecht had told Berlau they would adopt when they got to Berlin.*

95. *On May 25, 1955, in the Kremlin, Brecht receives the Stalin Prize from the hands of Nikolai Tikhonov, longtime tool of Stalin's practice of destroying anyone progressive who threatened Stalin's deeply old-fashioned views on artistic expression. The Stalin Prize, worth roughly a quarter of a million dollars, would mainly be deposited in one of Brecht's Swiss bank accounts.*

96. *Brecht's death mask. This copy, owned by Berlau and frequently carried around by her in a hatbox, would sometimes become the object of her ire. On one occasion she threw it down so violently the nose was broken, giving it even more of a classically severe Greek or Roman cast.*

97. *Elisabeth Hauptmann in the early 1970s. During her last years she had a bout with cancer and, after her recovery, would occasionally talk discreetly about her contribution to plays published under Brecht's name ("eighty percent of Jasager" for instance). She left her papers to the East German Academy, which failed to catalog them promptly and, toward the end of the regime (and against her wishes) planned to subsume them in the Brecht Archive.*

98. *Ruth Berlau in East Berlin, 1973, shortly before her death by fire in the Charité Hospital, where she had gone for a periodic check-up. To this day Berlau's legal rights have not been recognized by the primary publisher of the "Brecht" works.*

legally obligated to pay Wuolijoki. But in the end, nothing was done either for her or for Steffin's heirs. This story of a grasping tyrant when sober who becomes the spirit of generosity when drunk proved consistently profitable for Brecht and his heirs in productions from Calcutta to Cincinnati. Brecht sold *Puntila* both to Desch and to Munich Radio, but in neither case did he make provision to pay Wuolijoki her share.[16] The staff at Munich Radio had seen reports of Wuolijoki's involvement and asked for an explanation. Brecht was unhelpful, and as long as Wuolijoki did *not* explain publicly what the real history was (something she was reluctant to do to a fellow socialist), Brecht was able to keep stealing her money.

Brecht had still not decided where to live. In an April 1948 letter to Karl Korsch, he said, "I do not want just now to decide to settle down in G[ermany]."[17] He still hoped Austria might provide a passport, giving him freedom to work throughout the German-speaking world.

In any case, Ruth Berlau was essential to many of his business and personal affairs. Her Danish passport and press pass allowed her to travel to places that were off-limits to Brecht and Weigel. He wrote Berlau saying "believe that all i want is to find a car ready for me, what I want is only you." This letter ends with a large "D" with a circle drawn around it.[18] Like hundreds of other letters Brecht wrote to Berlau, this one is not included in the posthumous collection.

During the summer of 1948, Brecht had a pleasant and amusing meeting with Eric Bentley.[19] Though he had earlier described Brecht as a scoundrel, Bentley thought him a charming one. They went to films together, including *The Gold Rush.* After Chaplin sweeps the villain away in an avalanche, Brecht poked Bentley in the ribs and whispered, "Our playwrights would have taken twenty minutes to get rid of the man!" Bentley notes, "I rather think there is more theatre wisdom in this off-the-cuff comment than in any hundred pages of his abstract theorizing and programmizing."[20] Brecht played his HUAC recording, claiming to Bentley that he had not been entitled to plead the First or Fifth amendments. Though it was a lie, Brecht seemed to believe it.

The next day, Bentley saw Brecht with Paul Dessau, who had now left Hauptmann for Brecht. His hair was cut in the Brecht style, and he wore the jacket with a high collar that would soon be associated with Brecht and Mao. Dessau had brought along some music for *The Good Woman of Setzuan.* Brecht rejected it and croaked out a rhythmic pattern. The next day, Dessau's tune was exactly what Brecht wanted. In Dessau, Brecht had found a composer who was not specially talented but more than willing to subjugate himself to Brecht's needs.

Brecht was beginning to assemble the team he wanted for what would now become his main work, directing. Steffin's loss had proved irreparable. With the help of Berlau—and contributions from Laughton, Reyher, and Auden—some good work had been done in the American years, but his career as a playwright had moved forward only fitfully. With his return to Europe in 1947, his main effort was to find the right stage form for the many brilliant works that Brecht & Co. had completed during the years of exile: *Puntila, Mother Courage, The Trial of Lucullus, The Caucasian Chalk Circle*, and *Galileo*.

During production delays in Zurich when Neher was at La Scala, Brecht worked on his single most important piece of theoretical writing on theater, a long essay published later as *A Short Organum for the Theatre*. The piece was a direct response to Eric Bentley's *The Playwright as Thinker*.[21] Bentley had pointed out that Brecht's earlier theoretical statements were riddled with inconsistencies. Unlike others who accepted this as evidence of Brecht's genius, Bentley noted that the underlying thinking was confused and many issues were not addressed at all. Bentley observed: "I felt that you brushed aside all modern art except your own kind. You brushed it aside; you did not really cope with it."[22] "Like Shaw," Bentley wrote to Brecht, "you are more eager to explain your politics and your morality than your art."

Under Bentley's prodding, *A Short Organum* became Brecht's most consistent and accurate description of his own work as a post–World War II theater director. The reader should, however, be warned that Brecht throws away, or retreats from, many of his more radical ideas from the twenties and the thirties. He now recognized that most of his old ideas obscured at least as much as they illuminated. From now on, constantly shifting terms such as "epic theater," "Verfremdung," "distance," and "playing one segment against another" will hardly ever be used.[23]

However, Brecht's abandonment of much of what he had written earlier has had almost no impact on critics and contemporary theater and film artists. To this day, Brecht's prewar, more radical ideas of staging are what continue to intrigue theorists and practitioners. Perhaps because, as John Willett has long since pointed out, the earlier formulations are almost impossible to pin down to a consistent meaning, they remain extraordinarily useful in theatrical, cinematic, and feminist discourse. Like grains of sand in an oyster, these terms continue to serve as magnificent irritants. Though they sometimes confuse, they also often help practitioners and critics around the world create fine work not bound by the parameters of nineteenth-century realism. Among those who have used early Brecht theory effectively are theorists and artists as distinguished as Roland Barthes, Jean-Luc Godard, Kenneth Tynan, Peter Brook, Judith Malina, Dario Fo, France Rame, Fredric Jameson, Armand Gatti, Utpal Dutt, Badal Sircar, Edward

Bond, Augusto Boal, Peter Handke, and Robert Wilson, to name just a few among literally hundreds of others.

The pearls formed by others surely continue to justify the original irritant. If Brecht's early theories and his fast-moving 1954 production of *The Caucasian Chalk Circle* inspired The Royal Shakespeare Company to create something as dazzling as *The Life and Adventures of Nicholas Nickleby* in 1980, then that is what is important. Whether audiences maintain "distance," as characters are moved in *Nickleby* with a rapidity that Mollie Panter-Downes in *The New Yorker* correctly calls "a sort of Brechtian sleight of hand,"[24] is an issue best left for the high priests guarding the flame of Brecht orthodoxy to argue over. Panter-Downes matter-of-factly notes that audiences were "pulled into" the *Nickleby* production from the first moment of their entering the theater, and that the actors then proceeded to "break our hearts on the way."

In order to see what Brecht himself was backing away from in 1948 as he jettisoned the main elements of his earlier theories with their call for audiences to remain "distanced," it is helpful to recall that Brecht had often dismissed Aristotle and classical theater constructs as having provided "a theater for cannibals." With *A Short Organum*, Bentley noted a 180-degree shift. "You started out," Bentley told Brecht, "as an anti-Aristotelian critic. But the ORGANON [*Organum*] champions 2 great Aristotelian notions: first, that pleasure is the end of art as of life and, second, that the heart of drama is plot."[25] Bentley's remarks were apt. Significantly, when Brecht was writing *A Short Organum*, he was working in Chur on a classical Aristotelian drama and staging it with fundamental elements of the classic Greek and Elizabethan stage: verse, music, choral or narrative passages commenting on action, the use of dance, and a complete lack of both a stage curtain and any kind of detailed, realistic, or naturalistic set.

Bentley was one of the few critics who noted just how far-reaching the changes were in Brecht, and he also began to risk Brecht's ire by pointing out to Brecht where reality did not seem to square with his various—as usual, extreme—political announcements. Did he "really believe," Bentley asked Brecht the next year, "that the communists in the East zone stand for rule of the Germans by the Germans in the fullest and sincerest way?"[26] Brecht would have Ruth Berlau complain to Bentley about comments like this. Brecht was incensed when Bentley had said outright in one of his publications that Brecht "would be a better writer if he gave up Marxism."[27] Was Bentley, demanded Ruth, ever going to get enlightened politically? Bentley, however, felt he was the one who was not wearing political blinders. Bentley would usually be a lone voice in telling Brecht to his face when he was wrong. Bentley warned Brecht, for instance, that ex-Nazi sympathizers were at work in

East Berlin.[28] He also warned Brecht that he would be attacked in Berlin as a "formalist."

Brecht spent some time in Zurich with Max Frisch. After the architect-author had taken Brecht around a housing block for workers that he had designed, Frisch noted: "Brecht has an astonishing eye, with intelligence as a magnet which attracts the problems in such a way that they emerge even from behind the solutions. You explain to him how a tower came about, how the architectural form developed from the static formulae, and not only how it developed but how the form should not only fulfill its purpose but also explain this purpose to the eye—such explanations become a real pleasure, a shared pleasure."[29] Brecht's diary describes the day differently: "Frisch takes me through a municipal housing project with three- and four-room flats in large housing blocks. The fronts of the houses turned to the sun, between the houses a bit of green space, inside 'comfort' (bathtubs, electrical stoves), but everything small, these are cells for prisoners, tiny spaces for the recuperation of an object for sale, strength to go back to work, improved slums."[30] Brecht's frustration may have come from what was the real issue, the very existence of such houses for workers. If Swiss workers were happy with their working and living conditions, Brecht asked Berlau, "when would they ever rebel?"[31] The question was not limited to Switzerland. If capitalism could provide this for workers anywhere, this was a problem for world communism, Soviet style. But, like Marx, who did the same thing in the nineteenth century, Brecht usually ignored all evidence of improvements in working conditions in capitalist countries. Such improvements were a serious ideological problem for Moscow, especially because they were usually achieved in spite of Moscow through the efforts of labor unions and moderate socialist parties.

Brecht seemed determined to denigrate efforts such as Frisch's and to emphasize widespread corruption in the world not directly controlled by Moscow. Frequently, he notes the latest revelation in the Nuremburg Trials. In a diary note of April 13, he writes: "The camps where people were gassed built by [the firm of] IG-Farben were monuments to bourgeois culture in this decade";[32] but, as Bentley pointed out to him, he failed to ask himself similarly tough and obvious questions about things going on in the Soviet Union and in countries directly dependent on Moscow.

For all his reservations about western Europe, he remained there for over a year. He was worried about going back to Berlin and trying to work with the Soviet authorities. As Brecht sat hesitating in Zurich, Berlin had been trying for over a year to sound out Piscator in New York.[33] Dramatist Friedrich Wolf asked Piscator if he would like to return to the Soviet Zone. The offer was a threat to Brecht if he himself wished to live in that zone, because Piscator was the originator in Germany of "epic theater" and thus his rival as an innovator of modern theater. Fortunately for Brecht, the Soviets were perhaps bluffing. Friedrich Wolf attacked Piscator in a later letter.[34] It is likely that Wolf, checking back with Soviet authorities, found that Piscator was persona non grata because of his previous attacks on the Soviet apparat. Whatever the case, negotiations with Piscator slowed in 1948, and an offer was extended to Brecht. The chief Russian cultural officer in the Soviet Zone, Alexander Dymschitz, gave Frisch a sealed letter to deliver to Brecht in Zurich. Weigel immediately said they should take the offer, but Brecht, though obviously pleased to be invited,[35] remained wary and negotiated only slowly.

The Russians had made a sensible choice in inviting Brecht rather than Piscator. Piscator demanded "the most modern lighting-systems, with lifts and revolves in vertical and horizontal planes."[36] All this would have been daunting in a Berlin that had a perpetual power shortage. Furthermore, Piscator did not control the rights to any new plays. Finally, the theater and film people he trained in America—Harry Belafonte, Marlon Brando, Rod Steiger, Walter Matthau, Ben Gazzara, Tony Curtis, and Shelley Winters—would be less than perfect for German theater in Soviet Berlin.

In contrast, Brecht offered a history of accommodation to Soviet manipulation, a sheaf of new plays, and Helene Weigel to play in them. The fact that Weigel was a party member who could be readily disciplined, insured that this was a controllable package. The Soviets were also pleased that *A Short Organum* clearly abandoned "formalist" ideas. This new postwar Brecht sounded close to the classical theater of the Soviet Union and the satellite states under Stalin.

Brecht continued to hesitate. It was one thing to support Marxism in all its teleological grandeur in the abstract but quite another to back its practical and often unsavory applications in everyday life. The year before, after reading an article on the French Revolution by his old enemy Georg Lukács, Brecht wrote, "Without having our own [revolution], we will now have to rework the Russian one, I think to myself with a shudder." Cultural power in Moscow and in the Soviet Zone of Germany often seemed to be wholly in the hands of Georg Lukács, Alfred Kurella, and Walter Ulbricht—all of whom Brecht had denounced in 1938 as "enemies of production" or the "camarilla." Fortunately for Brecht, he was now sure that the Russian cultural officers in Berlin were more amenable to him than the camarilla could ever be. Soviet overtures in Los Angeles as early as the middle of 1945 had suggested that the Schiffbauerdamm Theater, scene of the original

Threepenny Opera, would be given to him. In two articles published in the Soviet Zone in 1947, Alexander Dymschitz had praised Brecht and suggested flattering comparisons with the Soviet cultural icon Mayakovsky.[37]

But one Russian ally, even as important as Dymschitz, was not enough. Brecht felt (quite correctly, I think) that he also needed some external leverage. Only if he had options outside Soviet authority, such as in Austria or Italy, would he be able to make demands for a position of power and authority in the Soviet Zone. Berlin suggested a nonbinding exploration: Brecht and Weigel would be given Soviet financing for one guest production of *Mother Courage*. The production would be at the Deutsches Theater, run by an old friend from the Weimar days, Wolfgang Langhoff.

Though the chance to direct the antiwar play in Berlin with Weigel in the title role was tempting, several things complicated the idea at this particular moment: first, Stalin had tried to cut off debate within the socialist camp as to different possible roads to socialism by putting Marshal Tito of Yugoslavia on the enemies list; second, at Stalin's prompting many Jews would be arrested and tried in 1949–50; third, Stalin had put a land blockade of West Berlin into place on June 23, 1948, trying to force the Western Allies out. It was a bad time to go. But Brecht was barred from the American Zone, and his application to Austria had not yet been acted on. He decided at least to try Berlin.

In August 1948, Swiss authorities allowed him to make a one-day visit across the frontier to a theater in the small German town of Konstanz. With Max Frisch and actor Wilfried Seyferth, Brecht stepped on German soil for the first time since 1933. He hated the production, seeing it as a continuation of the Goebbels style of inflated "heroic" theater, and he extrapolated what he saw there to the rest of Germany. He was more anxious now than ever to get to Berlin to show how, in his view, things really ought to be done.

Practical details demanded his attention. On October 7, writing from Munich, Brecht's agent Geis reported, "All of the affairs you wished to be handled, and that I do not want to report on here in writing, have been carried out and positively so."[38] Geis added, "I therefore expect you to give me the authorization to hand over the *Threepenny Novel* contract to Desch as you have already received the order form for the car. A Mercedes cabriolet is not being built at present, and the shipping of a limousine would take twelve months and would further be made impossible [now] that Mercedes demands an iron coupon for 1,500 kilos that Desch has not been able to obtain. What an iron coupon is, that would be too boring to explain." This was disappointing, but Geis closed on a bright note. "From Munich

Radio," he reported, "in a lightning strike, I've seized 3,000 marks." The money "seized" was for *Puntila*, with, as usual, nothing for Wuolijoki. But rumors kept popping up about Brecht's stealing from Wuolijoki. In response to a terse inquiry on the subject by Peter Suhrkamp, Brecht said Munich Radio was spreading rumors of plagiarism. Brecht told Suhrkamp he was merely collecting money to pass a portion of it on to his coauthor.[39] He never paid her what was due her.

On September 20, Brecht wrote to Caspar Neher in Austria, "Finally I have my Swiss papers and can begin to make plans." Brecht told Otto Katz, a middleman in Prague for the Soviets, that he had "a Soviet permit for Berlin."[40] Brecht asked Katz about obtaining money from Czech royalties for a *Simone Machard* production there, implying that he needed the Czech money to get to Berlin. While conning Katz, he also had to reassure the Salzburg authorities that his heart still really belonged to Austria, and he only planned a brief visit to Berlin.

On October 18, Mari Barbara's eighteenth birthday, Brecht and Weigel left for Salzburg and Prague, retracing the path followed in leaving Germany in 1933. He found Salzburg, with its thriving black market, "exhausted." Here the poor had very little, and the rich could have anything whatsoever. The next stop was socialist Prague. Brecht would later say generally of the West and the East, "they are both whores but the eastern whore is pregnant." "Justice," he noted approvingly in Prague, "is undemocratic: the rich, when caught, are punished more than the poor." In an unusual comment for Brecht, he noted in his diary that of the 37,000 Jews who had lived in Prague at the time of the beginning of the German occupation, only eight hundred were there now. One of the few Jews left alive in Prague was Otto Katz. Katz did not as yet know it, but a new officially sanctioned pogrom was in the works. Stalin would soon kill Katz and most of his Jewish colleagues in the Czech party apparatus.

On Friday, October 22, 1948, the day arrived for which Weigel and Brecht had waited for fifteen and a half years. With tickets Katz had paid for, they boarded the train for the German frontier.

39

"Possibly the Most Powerful Scene, Emotionally, in Twentieth-Century Drama" (1948–49)

Brecht's and Weigel's arrival in the Soviet Zone, while the Russians were attempting to starve and freeze out West Berlin, was a propaganda coup. The press photograph of the returnees taken at the border is dominated by a shiny, large, Soviet-made car.[1] Everyone is well dressed but not too well dressed. Brecht wears the middle-class suit he had put on for HUAC but, with a proletarian touch, wears no tie. Weigel has a large, new leather bag on one shoulder and another large bag in her hands. That day, she wore a wool coat, rather than one of her several furs. They were carrying enough luggage to require a second car. Berlau was making her way separately to Berlin. Her absence gives the appearance of marital propriety. Brecht's diary gives his view of events: "We leave early from Prague and are at the border by noon. Shrecker picks us up with a car. He has the car we are in overtake the other car, the one carrying our suitcases: 'do you have something along with you, I am hungry.' Chewing on bread with sausage, he speaks further on the subject, that one has the power but that there are still great difficulties. A meal, with speeches, in a suburb of Berlin. Those who are present, [Ludwig] Renn, theater people, and party people, very nice and very hungry. . . . The head of the party states that the situation now is: 'first comes morality, then one gets to eat.' "[2] The dig about morality does not pass unnoticed. Clearly, there were doubts in German party circles about Brecht's morality, but it is equally clear that the Russians desperately needed him there at this time.

Arriving late in Berlin, they were taken to the surviving section of the Adlon, the best hotel left operating. Berlau arrived soon after Brecht and Weigel, and as "Brecht's assistant," she was given a room at the Adlon just down the hall from them. The entire visit was conducted amid the privileged intelligentsia. Ludwig Renn was born Arnold Friedrich Vieth von Golssenau. The wellborn Georg Lukács, the dean of socialist realist critics, was also there. Johannes R. Becher, now a top cultural official in the zone, grew up with a father who was a superior court judge. Becher would be rewarded with a chauffeur-driven Mercedes limousine with West Berlin plates, hard currency accounts, and hunting rights on the former feudal estates. Lavish benefits at the top and a steeply descending scheme of benefits through the pyramidal hierarchy were essential parts of both Stalin's and Brecht's systems of control. When theater director Walter Felsenstein tried to distribute food and privileges on an equal basis to his company members, the Russians insisted he stick to a strictly hierarchical scheme.[3]

Brecht woke before dawn his first morning at the Adlon and took an early walk. With land access to West Berlin cut by the Russians, the air shuddered with the roar of the planes of the Western powers bringing desperately needed supplies to the Western Zones around the clock. Because of the blockade and the need to conserve fuel, the darkness was unrelieved by any city lights. At dawn, as the silhouette of ruins around the Brandenburg Gate became visible, Brecht walked the few yards to the ruins of Hitler's chancery, as he said, "to smoke my cigar there." This stylized gesture in the best Brecht stage manner was a "quotation" of Churchill, who had performed the same symbolic, Freudian act on his first postwar visit to Berlin.

The rest of Brecht's day was packed with carefully scheduled events, many involving contract negotiations. In the morning, there was Weiss Verlag; in the afternoon, a reception at the Soviet-funded House of Cultural Relations. The key speakers were Herbert Ihering; the head of the Deutsches Theater, Wolfgang Langhoff; and the chief Soviet Cultural officer of the zone, Alexander Dymschitz. Brecht declined to speak publicly, saying he needed to orient himself first. That evening he was taken to see the Hungarian Julius Hay's German-language play *Haben*. Hay had been one of the group that had tried to trap Brecht in Moscow in the mid-thirties. Animosity between them had not subsided, however polite they might be forced to be in public. In his diary, Brecht wrote of Hay's play, "Miserable performance, hysterically cramped, totally unrealistic."[4] Amid Stalinist politicized aesthetics, Brecht would almost always publicly pretend enjoyment or maintain silence, and privately revile it.

Brecht had seen one bright spot in Hay's play, a stocky young actress named Angelika Hurwicz. He invited her to the Adlon to discuss a part in his upcoming *Mother Courage*.[5] She was, it turned out, just right for the large, silent role of Courage's daughter, Kattrin.

Sunday, October 24, Brecht, Weigel, and Hanns Eisler (who was also visiting Berlin with a view to perhaps settling there) attended a peace rally at the Soviet-funded Cultural Relations Club, which paid Brecht's bills in Berlin. Again, Brecht elected not to speak. Later that day, Brecht got together with Jakob Walcher and Herta Gordon. Brecht noted, "[Walcher] spoke about the difficult situation, sober and positive as usual."[6]

The situation that Walcher saw was, in many ways, a repetition of the 1920s and 1930s. Events in the zone were determined by events in Moscow. If Moscow had decided that a system of collective farming in agriculture was right for the Soviet Union and had adopted the bizarre genetic theories of Trofim Lysenko, that is what the zone would have to do also, no matter how inefficient it was. If a one-party system had been adopted in the Soviet Union, a similar system had to be established in the zone. Torture, murder, and blackmail to force compliance with the one-party system would be routine, with the Russians serving as enforcers until they could train East Germans to do most of this work themselves. Orders from the Kremlin were transmitted through Ulbricht, and all orders came from a central command system, itself often hysterically cramped and frequently out of all touch with reality. In one instance that reflects thousands of others, an opponent of unifying the old parties under Ulbricht's control was told by a Russian major that either he would speak enthusiastically for unification, or he would be tried as a "leader of a Fascist group opposing the state."[7]

If Brecht and Walcher had any chance to help change the course of political life in the zone, it was obvious they would need allies. Brecht hoped to recruit Berthold Viertel, who was directing *Mother Courage* in Vienna. "Our own standard of living, as it depends on 100 privileges," Brecht wrote to Viertel, "is very good. We are living comfortably at the Adlon." Brecht's comforts were further enhanced by his access to Western goods at the American army exchange, the PX, a result of his continued contact with Edward Hogan. With her Danish passport and the few precious dollars she had, Berlau crossed to the PX, returning loaded down with cigars, grapefruit juice, eggs, white bread, beer, cheese, canned milk, and real coffee.

Though cocooned at the Adlon, Brecht could not avoid seeing how deeply the Russian occupation and the blockade of West Berlin was resented. The memory of bloodshed and widespread rape when the Russians took Berlin was still a pervasive nightmare. One night, he, Weigel, and Walcher were accosted by a drunken Russian army lieutenant waving a pistol in each hand. The drunk was finally persuaded to let them leave in Walcher's car. "On the question of the Berlin blockade," Brecht noted, "here one is clearly on the defensive."[8] Only a small part of the population believed that "imposed socialism [by the Russians] was better than no socialism at all."[9] Brecht thought the mixed Soviet-German government must address basic everyday needs. Why not, he asked, bring in the work of artists of the caliber of Picasso to help design simple consumer goods, which could then be mass produced? But such ideas were anathema. Picasso's public affiliation with the Communist party in France was useful as propaganda, but Stalin had no intention of accepting Picasso's art.

By early November, in borrowed rehearsal space at the Deutsches Theater, using a pickup cast of actors (except for Weigel), Brecht began to shape his vision of Mother Courage's world of war. The schedule was unusually fast, for him, for an opening in the first half of January. Partly to save time and partly because Neher was not available, he used much of Teo Otto's Zurich designs. This included what was to become perhaps the single most famous prop of the twentieth-century stage, the wagon of Mother Courage. Brecht's host, Wolfgang Langhoff, had played a lead role in the Zurich production. Music for the Berlin version was by Paul Dessau, who though still married to Hauptmann, had not waited for her to join him in East Berlin and had quickly taken up with a younger woman.

The choice of Helene Weigel to play the demanding role of Courage was a gamble given her long absence from the stage. Just as bold was the choice of Angelika Hurwicz as Courage's daughter, Kattrin. Brecht also included two actors that one critic labeled "among Hitler's most spoiled children,"[10] Werner Hinz as the chaplain and Paul Bildt as the cook. He also brought in, though in a minor role, a Brecht/Bronnen lover from prewar days, Gerda Müller. As he often had earlier, Brecht elected to work with a co-director on this production, Erich Engel. Though half-Jewish, Engel had worked in the German theater throughout the Third Reich.[11] Ruth Berlau, though only officially acknowledged as "production photographer," was one of the directors, rehearsing segments of the play just as she had in Scandinavia in the 1930s.

By mid-December, Brecht had settled into a working rhythm. Getting up at 5:30 at the Adlon, he would read for an hour or so, usually some Goethe or, in order to orient himself toward the dominant socialist realist position, Lukács. By the time it was light, his assistant, Heinz Kuckhahn, would arrive to order breakfast and get things ready for the day's rehearsals. At nine, they would head for the theater, where Brecht's secretary, Ilse Kasprowiak, would wait to take dictation. Rehearsals began at ten.

While working hard every day at *Mother Courage* rehearsals, Brecht also tried to put together some poems and songs that halfway met the lamentable taste of most of his Soviet-German cultural bosses. However, when he had completed a couple of small pieces, they had not liked his line "No führer can lead us out of this mess." Trying to find other leadership models, Brecht harked back to Lenin and Luxemburg, speaking often with the socialist mavericks Walcher and Gordon, who had known both leaders personally. But Luxemburg, who had predicted that Moscow leadership of world Communist affairs would be a disaster, was not of interest to his hosts. Unhappy as he was with the antediluvian Stalinist aesthetics of the zone but not daring to say so publicly, Brecht was delighted when Hanns Eisler showed him some poems by Mao Tse-tung. He wrote in his diary on December 29, 1948, "My calculations on a renaissance of the arts, spurred on by an uprising in the Far East, seems to have paid off sooner than one might have thought."[12]

On January 6, 1949, a week before *Mother Courage* was to open, he met with German officials to talk about the possibility of having his own company in Berlin. The mayor of Berlin at this time was Friedrich Ebert, son of the Social Democrat Friedrich Ebert, first president of the Weimar Republic, who had put down Luxemburg's and Liebknecht's Spartacist rebellion in 1918. This new Ebert arrived, said neither hello nor good-bye, and never addressed Brecht directly. He spoke only one sentence, something about "unclear projects that could endanger that which already existed." Brecht was furious. "For the first time," he wrote in his diary, "I feel the stinking breath of the provinces here."[13] It had been a whiff of a discredited past, a past where Germany had missed a chance to have her own revolution. Again, it appeared to Brecht that Germany was failing to establish her own revolution, one not wholly dependent on Soviet models.

Living now in a nominally socialist state, Brecht could daily see the difference between his original dream of 1927, in which Marx was the perfect spectator for his plays, and the government who thought his work "formalist" and drenched with decadent Western ideas. Every move he made in Berlin for the rest of his life would be a delicate balancing between what he understood Russian wishes to be and lip service to "the Ulbricht group." Ulbricht barely tolerated him. Even those who would prove sympathetic to Brecht were disturbed that he was not particularly well-read in Marxism, had read the wrong people— dissidents such as Korsch, Sternberg, and Trotsky—and had never joined the party. He saw the future in other forms of communism, ones that harked back to Liebknecht and Luxemburg. One senses this as Brecht's diary reads, "The victory of the Chinese Communists has fully changed the face of the world."

The news of the Chinese victory helped somewhat to offset other deeply disturbing news. Just at the time that Mao had risen to power in China, and Yugoslavia's Tito was beginning, against great odds, to establish his independence from Stalin, the Soviet defector Victor Kravchenko, in his book *I Chose Freedom*, described a vast system of death camps that he said existed in the Soviet Union. When the magazine *Les lettres françaises* tried to discredit the book by suggesting it was a CIA plant, the resulting lawsuit amply confirmed the existence of the Soviet death camp system.[14] It was a grim reminder of the disappearance of Carola Neher, Tretiakov, Koltsov, Osten, Mandelstam, Meyerhold, and hundreds of others Brecht had personally known. But disappearances were not just a thing of the past. Since 1945, the Soviet secret police had set up eleven concentration camps on German soil, killing or allowing to die by neglect tens of thousands of Germans.[15] Among those declared "enemies of the people" would be anyone who opposed efforts by the Stalinist Socialist Unity party, the boa constrictor–like SED, to absorb and control the old Social Democratic party.

As the signature half-height curtain, familiar to Berlin audiences from the one used by Neher for the 1928 *Threepenny Opera* opening, was whisked back at the January 11, 1949, premiere of *Mother Courage*,[16] the audience heard Dessau's rousing music together with Weigel's voice singing:

> *Cannon on an empty stomach,*
> *Captains that's not healthy.*
> *But once they've fed, then with my blessing*
> *Lead them into the maw of hell.*

The audience saw *Mother Courage* sitting on her wagon, she and her children against a stark, gray semicircular backdrop. Next to Courage, playing a mouth organ, is Kattrin. Courage's other children, the teenage boys Eilif and Swiss Cheese, pull the wagon, walking briskly against the movement of the turntable stage, staying in a constant position center stage.

At the play's end, when she has lost all her children to the war that she has helped supply, the gaunt Courage staggers against the relentless drive of the turntable stage to follow a war that seems to have had no beginning and that will be without end. Those who were there that first night remember that when the curtain finally closed, the audience sat in a mesmerized silence, broken only by sobbing. Deeply, deeply moved by what they had just seen, the audience stood and wept and clapped to exhaustion as Weigel, Hurwicz, Brecht, and Engel came forward for countless curtain calls.

What Brecht, Engel, and Berlau had achieved with a pickup cast, in borrowed space, in a matter of a few weeks, with the lead played by an actress who had hardly performed at all since 1933, was a near miracle. Eric Bentley had flown into Berlin on an American army plane and saw the audience in tears during the climactic scene where Kattrin is shot and Courage makes her final exit. After the show, he asked Weigel about this emotion, "Is this all right in a play by Bertolt Brecht?"[17] Her satisfied smile said, thought Bentley, "Certainly, and I love it." Bentley would describe the climactic final scene, directed by Brecht, as "possibly the most powerful scene, emotionally, in twentieth-century drama."[18] What Bentley saw was that Brecht's "epic drama" and its downplaying of emotion was gone.

When the Soviet critic Boris Sachawa came, he saw the play's final scene as "a terrifying symbol of the tragic fate of an entire people."[19] In *The Death of Tragedy*, George Steiner says of Weigel's "silent scream" after she is forced to view the body of her just-executed son, "It was the same wild cry with which the tragic imagination first marked our sense of life."[20] "The curve of tragedy," said Steiner after seeing *Mother Courage*, "is, perhaps, unbroken." Brecht's way forward to modern theatrical performance had led backward, through Marlowe and Shakespeare, through Elisabeth Hauptmann's rediscovery of the Japanese and Chinese theater, to the kind of theater performances seen in Shakespeare's Globe and in the arenas of classical Greece.

Alexander Dymschitz and the Soviet commander of the zone, Vladimir Semyonov, shared the enthusiasm. After seeing the show twice, Semyonov took Brecht aside and said: "Comrade Brecht, you must ask for anything you want. Obviously, you are very short of money."[21] When Brecht asked him what made him think so, he replied: "But it all looks so poor. No rich decorations, and that's what the people want to see." Semyonov did not yet know that the "poor look" achieved by Brecht, whether in his personal dress or in stage productions, was expensive.

For the longtime theorist of "epic theater," it was clear that audiences identified both with Courage herself and her heroic daughter, Kattrin. Of the death of Kattrin, critic Albrecht Schöne writes, "If anywhere, it is here that Brecht's theory of alienation is itself alienated; here the critical distance of the (calmly) smoking audience is destroyed."[22] Bowing to the reality of audience reaction, Brecht now rather grudgingly said, "Spectators are permitted to identify with Kattrin in this scene."[23] But he also, in one of his radical reversals, began to wonder if his method of working did not elicit more emotion than traditional methods. "It is advantageous (in performance)," he now writes, "to avoid the direct or 'immediate impression' of the apparently singular (nonrecurrent) event in order to reach a different stratum of fear, where frequently recurring misfortune has forced mankind into ceremonialization of its defense mechanisms, which of course can never save man from fear itself. We must break, in performance, through this ceremonialization of defense."[24] And break through they did. As Brecht saw for himself, on the streets people pointed to Weigel and said, "Mutter Courage."[25] When director Sam Wanamaker saw Weigel play Courage, he said her acting was "indistinguishable from that of a superb Stanislavsky trained actress."[26]

These examples take us to the heart of something essential to

Brecht the postwar director. What he realized in 1949 was that his longtime assumption—cool acting leads to cool audiences—was wrong. In a rapid about-face, he now acknowledged that an audience may become more emotionally involved by cool acting.[27] As the production of *Mother Courage* repeatedly showed, silence proved to be more eloquent and more deeply moving than words. Kattrin who utters not a single word in the play reduced audiences to tears. It had been wrong to assume, as Brecht had in the twenties, thirties, and the first half of the forties (and as many critics still do), that the understatement of a scene or the stylization of a scene through masks, wooden figures, or revealing the lights or scene changes, cools scenes down for audiences. Fleisser had said this emphatically when Brecht had used stylized whiteface to represent fear in the *Edward II* production in Munich in 1924. And in 1929 at Baden-Baden, Hanns Eisler had told Brecht that sawing off the head of the obviously wooden clown elicited tremendously strong emotions.

In 1949, Brecht realized that his kind of staging could help audiences reach deeper levels of the Aristotelian elements of pity and of fear than were reached by other directors. To miss this crucial reorientation of Brecht from the late forties on, both in theory (*A Short Organum*) and in stage practice (*Mother Courage, Galileo, Chalk Circle,* and so on) is to fail to see that he achieved his breakthrough as a postwar director by going back to Aristotelian roots, where audiences are deeply moved.

Semyonov approved ever-larger budgets, and the approval of key Soviet functionaries in Berlin was far more important to Brecht than Ebert and his ilk in Berlin, who viewed him as "a position-seeking artist who over-rated himself."[28] With the Soviets on his side, he could succeed even though Fritz Erpenbeck now attacked him with great savagery. Using the same vocabulary that had been used at the height of the Moscow Show Trials, Erpenbeck asked of the *Mother Courage* production, "Where does it lose itself, despite the wish to be progressive and the highest formal skill, on the path into decadence that is alien to the people?"[29]

Denunciatory language of precisely this sort had been tantamount to a death sentence in the Soviet Union during the thirties; but in an act of courage that Brecht would not forget, a young philosopher, Wolfgang Harich, denounced Erpenbeck.[30] Nor would Erpenbeck and Ulbricht forget. Despite the views of the "camarilla," Brecht and Harich seemed to prevail. The play had forced critics in the East and the West to recognize Brecht as a world-class playwright-director and establish Weigel as a world-class actress.

Ever more self-confident now, Brecht signed an agreement with his friend Peter Suhrkamp that specified that Suhrkamp was entrusted with "the licensing of public performances of Brecht's stage plays in all theaters in all zones of Germany." Though Brecht was not free to dispose of *The Threepenny Opera*, he included it in the list. The contract also specified: "Bertolt Brecht can entrust Mrs. Elisabeth Hauptmann-Dessau with the final drafting of the texts. Moreover, Mrs. Hauptmann-Dessau represents Bertolt Brecht in all transactions with the theaters." It was stated in the contract that Hauptmann would get small fees from Suhrkamp for her work.

"A Small Hole of a Room" (1949)

By the time Brecht signed the Suhrkamp contract, Hauptmann was back in Europe. Her marriage with Paul Dessau was in disarray. Like Brecht, Dessau was attracted to younger women. Not wanting to rejoin either her husband or her former lover, Hauptmann was of two minds about going to East Berlin. She tried first to establish herself as a writer in West Germany. But, with much of her best work published under Brecht's name, she had no reputation on which to build. Also, the fact that she was openly a Communist party member was a strike against her in the West.

Under these discouraging circumstances, she agreed to come to Berlin to edit Brecht's work for a small salary. This almost exactly repeated her situation in the twenties and early thirties. In early 1949, the *Versuche* series was resumed. Each volume appeared in plain paper covers, with Brecht's name in large letters outside and her name in minuscule print inside. Though the task was distasteful, she believed the works to which she contributed so much would help establish real socialism and genuine equality between men and women.

By February, Weigel had been given a suite of offices at The Seagull, the Soviet-German cultural club in the Luisenstrasse. Here, Weigel was to begin planning the establishment of a repertory company under her direction, with Brecht serving as head artistic advisor. Distributing perks largely as she saw fit, Weigel took the largest offices for herself and Brecht and assigned a broom-closet-size "office" to Elisabeth Hauptmann, and no office at all to Ruth Berlau. Brecht held court at the restaurant in The Seagull, just as he had at Schlichter's in the Weimar years. Often Brecht was seen there with the key Soviet cultural officer in the zone, Alexander Dymschitz,[1] who spoke excellent German and was most interested in the maverick "formalists" Tretiakov and Mayakovsky.[2]

Brecht decided to fly to Zurich with Berlau to recruit for the budding enterprise. Weigel stayed behind due to both her role of Courage and her administrative work. Berlau was happy to get away and to have the chance to be with him. She had hurt desperately as she listened to the chorus of praise for Weigel. At the party following the *Mother Courage* premiere, Berlau had gotten drunk and caused a scene. Besides, she saw Brecht using his personal charm and his powerful position in East Berlin to start affairs with young staff members. Berlau shared her frustration with Bentley. "It was at that time that I learned in a kind of touching way," said Bentley later, "of how this triangle system didn't really work, at least for the women. It was supposed to work because we were all Marxists and didn't believe in jealousy and that sort of thing. But actually there was plenty of jealousy all around and Ruth didn't mind admitting to it."[3] When Bentley left, Berlau felt very much alone. Of the baby Brecht had spoken of adopting at the time of the loss of Michel in Los Angeles, he now said nothing. As their plane lifted for Zurich via Prague (their tickets paid from royalties in Czechoslovakia released by Otto Katz), Berlau fell asleep. While she slept, Brecht read *Defeat*, Grete Steffin's German version of Nordahl Grieg's play on the Paris Commune of 1871. On the cover was the notation: "Autorisierte Übertragung aus dem Norwegischen von Margarete Steffin."[4] When Berlau woke up, Brecht said he planned to take over the play. Berlau pointed out this would violate Grieg's and Steffin's copyright.[5] But Brecht was adamant.

Berlau and Brecht checked into two rooms at the pension Au Bien Etre in central Zurich. She would often stay up very late in her own room reading and marking up books for Brecht who had gone to bed early in his room. The next morning, in front of his door, he would find the books and Berlau's ideas for scenes for the Grieg-Steffin play. Berlau was happy when he would take over a couple of sentences verbatim or an entire scene that she had written.[6] Though working with him to revamp the original play, Berlau remained uncomfortable about the use of the Grieg-Steffin material. Brecht now invented a fictitious "original author," claiming the work was "an adaptation from the French of Jacques Duchesne." Neither Berlau nor Brecht had enough expertise in French to work from that language. The "new work" was called *The Days of the Commune*, a play by Brecht (written large) and by R. Berlau (written small). The names of Grieg and Steffin were dropped altogether.

A draft was sent to Eric Bentley, who wrote back: "I do not think that *Tage der Commune* is a good play. Considered stylistically it is made up of imitations of yr earlier work. It seems to be lacking in all freshness and spontaneity. A big disappointment."[7] Whether because of Bentley's reaction or Brecht's dubious copyright, the play was dropped. It would be one of Brecht's last serious efforts to produce a "new" play.

Expecting formal authorization soon to hire people for Berlin, Brecht began drafting contracts. He reported to Weigel on actors and directors who might be willing to come to Berlin, and provided details of what he assumed the newcomers' financial and other needs would be.[8] But he had no intention of putting all his own eggs in the blockaded, Soviet-controlled Berlin basket. On March 5, when Gottfried von Einem came to Zurich, Brecht encouraged him to think Berlin was not going to take precedence over Salzburg. At the same time, Weigel wrote that she had gotten them assigned a large villa overlooking a lake in the Berlin district of Weissensee. Brecht seemed delighted and urged her to buy the fourteen-room house outright with her own large earnings from the sold-out *Mother Courage*.[9]

In Zurich, Brecht saw Mari Barbara, now eighteen, and reported to Weigel that there were no signs of recurrence of the mild case of tuberculosis that she had had ten years before. Brecht and Berlau began obtaining travel documents from the Swiss so that Mari Barbara could go back to Berlin with them. Mari Barbara's return to Berlin caused enormous frustration as she was not at home either in German or English. She felt neglected by both Brecht and Weigel. They would provide her with a job and a car, perhaps to make up for the fact that she was radically insecure, felt less intelligent and talented than other members of the family. In a typical letter with her mixture of badly spelled English and grammatically insecure German, her family was one of "high ambitionts [sic] and realizations."[10] This letter is signed "Mari Barbara Brecht," the first name reminding us of her "second mother," Brecht's old servant Mari Hold, who had stayed behind in Scandinavia in the 1930s.

In April, a letter signed by Walter Ulbricht indicated that the politburo of the ruling Socialist Unity party, the SED, had approved the creation of a theatrical ensemble in Berlin. Hedging its bets against the nonparty member Brecht, the politburo placed formal authority in Weigel's disciplined hands. Berlau knew this was not good news for her. The letter said: "A special Ensemble will be put together under the management of Helene Weigel. This Ensemble will begin its playing season on September 1, 1949, and will present in the 1949–50 season three progressive works. These productions will be mounted either in the Deutsches Theater or in the Kammerspiel, and will be included in the repertoire of these theaters over a six-month period. For five further months the Ensemble will go on tour in the Zone."[11] The first year budget was 1,465,500 marks, $10,000 of which was in hard currency. This was a huge amount for a country in ruins and making huge indemnity payments to the Soviet Union.

Stalin lifted the blockade of West Berlin, which had succeeded only in alienating those who saw it as Soviet expansionism. Removal of the blockade made it easier for Brecht to recruit staff, but it was accom-

panied by the recall of Dymschitz to Moscow. His place was taken by
Ilya Fradkin. To Brecht's relief, Fradkin told him he had read and liked
Brecht's work in Tretiakov's translations.

As soon as Weigel had received official approval, she set to work
scheduling at the Kammerspiel and the Deutsches Theater, and acquiring the necessary perquisites for the entire company. Her achievement
was formidable for, at exactly the same time, the Russians were reorga-
nizing to set up a nominally "independent state," the German Democratic Republic, in response to the establishment of the German Federal
Republic in the Western zone.

Following precedent, contracts at the Ensemble reflected Weigel's
and Brecht's sense of the relative importance of the members. She and
Brecht were at the top of the pyramid.[12] In addition to the fourteen-
room villa, Weigel assigned them a scarce official car and gas to run it
(although public transportation was convenient). Weigel furnished the
villa with antiques available at laughable prices to those with Western
money. More furniture arrived from Stockholm where it had been in
storage since 1940, along with most of their books. Most important of
all, the trunk in which Steffin had kept her copies of the manuscripts she
had written with Brecht arrived from Moscow.[13] None of Steffin's
belongings were returned to her heirs. Brecht commemorated moving
into the villa with a poem, "Driving through the Rubble":

> I am reminded daily of the privileges
> This house gives me. I hope
> It will not make me patient with the holes
> In which so many thousand sit.

Berlau and Hauptmann were among those assigned holes in which
to both live and work. As a foreigner, Berlau's life was more difficult.
She was not given an apartment and was told she could no longer stay
at the Adlon now that Brecht and Weigel had moved to their villa. She
took the only room available in a rundown place called the Schmidt
Hotel, whose only other occupants at the time were Russian soldiers,
usually drunk. Berlau lived in constant fear of rape.

Hauptmann was somewhat better off, with some hard-currency
income from Suhrkamp. She found herself living in what she called "a
small hole of a room," where she would later become so depressed that
she would again attempt suicide as she had done in 1929.[14] As in the
twenties, Hauptmann took on a string of translations to make ends
meet. By this time, Berlau realized that "Brecht had money like I don't
know what,"[15] and she was furious at the way Hauptmann was treated.
Berlau pounded on Brecht's desk, demanding that Hauptmann "at least

be given money." Brecht gave Hauptmann nothing but was angry at Berlau's pointing out how miserly he was. Soon, rumors began to circulate in the Ensemble about how "difficult" Berlau was. This would be used to "justify" keeping her salary low. Instead of paying her the earnings from the model books she produced in a constant stream, Brecht gave her an occasional handout. When she asked that her directing be credited and paid for, Brecht refused.

Though Hauptmann seethed privately about the inequities at the Ensemble, she maintained a loyal public demeanor. Her commitment, like that of Berlau and Steffin, was not to Brecht but to the success of communism and to a world of equality and peace. Unless we accept these women's commitment to these ideals, it is hard to understand the level of personal pain and self-effacement they tolerated. Danish psychologist Peter Elsass has argued that "to place oneself in a closed system without self-criticism and without interaction with one's opponents is to risk self-dissolution."[16] One can see this happening very clearly in the lives of Berlau, Weigel, and Hauptmann. Socialism was the closed system into which they had voluntarily entered. They believed that equal rights were given greater importance in socialism than in any other political system on the planet. This was their light at the end of the tunnel, and they tended not to look for another. They would always try to explain away any problems they saw within the system as temporary. Their expectations for their personal needs remained extremely low.

I witnessed this with Russian dissident Lev Kopelev. In 1972, as editor at that time of the *Yearbook of the International Brecht Society*, I had secretly commissioned an article on Brecht by him. In November, I visited Kopelev at his Moscow flat to deliver a Western typewriter as payment for his essay and to discuss his article. He, however, wanted to discuss an article I had published in which I argued that when Georg Lukács denounced this or that writer as a "formalist" or a "decadent" in Moscow in the thirties, it was tantamount to signing a death warrant. Kopelev, a former student of Lukács, told me I was using the wrong standard of measurement. He said that Lukács only agreed about 96 percent of the time with Stalin's aesthetic judgments. Kopelev wanted me to understand that what was important to those who lived in Moscow in the mid-thirties was that vital residual 4 percent of disagreement. That 4 percent was the one hope that desperate people had to begin to break out of the stranglehold Stalin had on the country.

Most who live outside self-referential systems of terror will see a success rate of 4 percent as unacceptable. But as Kopelev went to some pains to impress upon me, it was his view that if Lukács had only slightly increased the percentage of artistic experimentation he tried to protect in the deadly 1930s, he might well have been the next to go. "Lukács," Kopelev told me, "belonged to the opposition." Astoundingly, perhaps 4 percent was enough to place one in "opposition" to the deadly system in which Lukács operated.

From 1949–53, amid Stalin's paranoia, party members like Hauptmann, Berlau, and Weigel were in a position analogous to Lukács's in Moscow in the mid-thirties. They only expected change in small increments. The differences Brecht introduced were therefore praised out of proportion because of their "opposition" to the practices of Stalin and the Ulbricht regime. It was more important to Weigel, Berlau, and Hauptmann to help maintain that 4 percent edge of opposition, the edge that would improve socialism, than to allow their own personal situations to become so public that they could jeopardize the goal itself.

The profoundly conservative Ulbricht was not enthusiastic about the Ensemble, as everyone in the inner circle knew. Heiner Müller bluntly states in his post 1989 memoirs: "[Brecht] only got the theater because the Russians ordered it. He [Brecht] was under deep suspicion."[17] For the Russians, Brecht's theater had the same function in the zone as those shop windows filled with generally forbidden goods. These windows were for Westerners to see in the center of Berlin; but exhibiting such "goods" at all in the GDR had an immediate side effect. I was told literally thousands of times in the GDR that the Berlin Ensemble's quirky, semi-secret opposition to the worst excesses of socialist realism was a margin of hope. Those who were part of the dazzling company in its early years genuinely felt the work they were doing was helping to bring a new dawn closer.

With that dawn still distant, Brecht's old pattern of stealing from co-workers continued as it had for years. When *The Caucasian Chalk Circle* was published in 1949 in a Soviet Zone journal, *Sinn und Form*, no mention was made of Steffin or Berlau. Similarly, when a number of what he called his "Chinese Poems" were brought out in the tenth volume of the *Versuche*, Hauptmann's name was given inside in tiny letters with nothing indicating she was the sole author of most of them. Brecht seems to have really believed that he was building for a future of greater justice and of peace. The beam of inequality in his own eye seems to have been invisible to him. But what he failed to see was obvious to those who paid that he might live in luxury. The surviving heirs of Steffin—mother, sister, brother-in-law, and nephew—lived in converted garden sheds, with only bare necessities, on the remote outskirts of Berlin. When I visited the family in 1989, washing water was still carried from outside. Their horizon set extremely low, they diffidently asked if I could not help them get enough money from Margarete's estate to buy a down comforter. They had had no legal advice in the "workers's state" on what might be done to help them in the face of Brecht's extremely rich heirs.

Apparently, right after the war, Helene Weigel did try to send a care package to the Steffin family, but later, she and Brecht were too busy to find the Steffin family. It was only at a reception at the Metropolitan Hotel in Berlin in 1949, that Herta Hanisch, the younger sister of Grete Steffin, happened to see Brecht and Weigel crossing the lobby. She went up to reintroduce herself. She had not seen them since visits to Grete in Denmark in the 1930s. In 1949, Herta apparently finally got news of her sister's death in Moscow in 1941.[18] When she asked what had happened to Grete's belongings, Weigel claimed they had disappeared. Brecht had, in fact, kept most of Grete's effects from Moscow, though they were of considerable historical and monetary value.[19]

Sometimes, in the early fifties, Weigel would invite Herta Hanisch to visit her at the otherwise off-limits Seagull for coffee and cake. Sometimes, Höppchen (as her friends called her), her husband, and their son Bernd were invited to the fourteen-room Weissensee villa furnished with seventeenth-and eighteenth-century antiques, where they always felt thoroughly uncomfortable. Though *Mother Courage* alone was an enormous success, Steffin's heirs had no idea of their rightful share of the income. Lied to about Grete's possessions, they could not demand the return of that valuable collection. They were helpless as Brecht dictated terms. Instead of paying them himself, he had his Berlin publishers make a one-time payment of five thousand marks to be divided between Joanna Steffin and her daughter. They were given this sum much later, at a time when a loaf of good bread cost eighty marks,[20] and when annual earnings from Steffin-Brecht works were in six figures, much of that untaxed and in hard currency.

Brecht was not unique in his treatment of Steffin's heirs. When a new edition of Steffin's translation of the Martin Andersen-Nexø work was published in the zone, nothing was paid to Steffin's heirs. Only after numerous delays and arguments were they given 360 marks. At one point, when Höppchen and her mother complained about how little they had been given, Weigel gave them another two hundred East German marks. Steffin had saved the lives of the whole group in 1941, and helped create the works Brecht and Weigel were living on: *Mother Courage, The Good Woman of Setzuan, Galileo, The Trial of Lucullus, Puntila, Arturo Ui, The Private Life of the Master Race,* and early drafts of *The Caucasian Chalk Circle.* Weigel, hardly ignorant of how the plays were created, did not help Hauptmann, Steffin's heirs, or Berlau receive even a small portion of their royalties or recognition as writers of "Brecht" texts.[21]

Though a few crooked deals for small sums were made soon after

Brecht's return to Europe, the biggest stake, involving millions in the years to come, would be for the rights to *The Threepenny Opera*. For years, Brecht had been anxious to find a way to take it from Felix Bloch Erben. His earlier ploy of accusing the firm of being a nest of old Nazis had failed. Brecht then asked his agent Jacob Geis and Wolf Schwarz, an attorney in Zurich, to try to find a legal way to get back the *Threepenny Opera* rights; but both said the chances of legally taking it from Felix Bloch Erben were slight.[22] It was complicated by the fact that Brecht had not revealed to Weill and Hauptmann the details on his general contract with the publishing house.

Brecht decided against the expensive, personally damaging, and probably hopeless legal route. Getting Berlau to go along, the two made a kind of guerrilla-theater appearance at the Felix Bloch Erben offices on July 11, 1949. Upon entering the office, they began loudly shouting the lie that the Felix Bloch Erben people were all "a bunch of old Nazis."[23] Frau Wreede, fed up with this shameless spectacle, told her staff to bring her Brecht's general contract (on which he still owed 42,000 gold marks) and the *Threepenny Opera* contract. Frau Wreede threw the two documents at him and announced, "There is the door young man." Later, she dictated a letter dissolving the legal arrangement between the firm and Brecht. Brecht was delighted. By his clever and wholly unscrupulous antic, he had gained control of one of the most remunerative contracts in twentieth-century theatrical history.

Though Peter Suhrkamp was glad to hear that Felix Bloch Erben had given up its claim to *Threepenny*, soon he was having his own trouble with Brecht. No sooner was an agreement signed than Brecht argued Suhrkamp should retroactively pay Hauptmann for work previously done.[24] Suhrkamp refused but continued her small salary. That meant Brecht did not have to cover any costs of preparing his publications. Weigel's two salaries, as head of the Berliner Ensemble and as the lead actress of the company, as well as her control of the repertoire, guaranteed a steady income. Ruth Berlau's minimal salary from the Ensemble for handling directorial chores, photography, and some business matters meant that the various divisions of "Brecht Enterprises" now ran either at Suhrkamp's or at the state's expense, without any drain whatsoever on Brecht's numerous foreign and domestic accounts.

By this time, he also received a special income of fifteen hundred marks a month for his services to the Academy of Arts. There was the income, often in the form of advances, from the multiple sale to publishers in various countries of works that were only marginally his to sell. There was box-office income at theaters in both western and eastern Europe: *Mother Courage*, for instance, was scheduled in Vienna and in Wuppertal, and *Threepenny* would soon open in Munich. As a free-lance director, he could charge whatever the market would bear. He was now getting offers for film rights in the mid-five-figure range in hard currency that could be hidden, untaxed, in his Western bank accounts. On the tiny portion of their income that they did declare, he and Weigel paid taxes of only 14 percent and had state-subsidized rent. They also had the use of a company car, special allowances for anything that was in short supply, and Western currency to use when they wanted to buy luxuries in West Berlin. They were living at a level hundreds of times higher than the rest of the population of the GDR.

Brecht remained, technically at least, a kind of consultant to the Ensemble, receiving honoraria rather than a salary. Thus (though his income from the GDR was as regular as Weigel's), he could demand a salary and a contract in Salzburg. Therefore, he further argued that, with an Austrian-born wife, he should be given an Austrian passport. In making his claim for a passport, Brecht maintained to the Austrian authorities that he was a "stateless person." But, by the fall of 1949, technical governance of the zone was due to pass in a few weeks from the Russians to the German Socialist Unity party. This new state could then begin issuing passports, for which Brecht would be immediately eligible.

Though Brecht maintained by de jure technicalities his condition as a stateless person and as a "consultant" at the Ensemble in his negotiations with Salzburg, in Berlin itself he acted on a totally different basis. Weigel was in charge of things like the subsidized canteen, housing permits, furniture allowances, and so on. Unless Brecht needed favors given to a new or old mistress, or to this or that employee for personal services rendered, he was too busy to bother himself with the day-to-day details of running the Ensemble. As long as Weigel was willing to run the Berliner Ensemble as a branch office of the international conglomerate that was Brecht & Co., he had no reason to interfere.

He now collected royalties from a repertoire consisting almost exclusively of plays he both in fact and claimed to own. The Ensemble was financially supported by a generally impoverished state that paid most of its workers near-starvation wages at that time. Only one mark in six of its funding came from box-office sales. Brecht placed his friends and relatives on the payroll, sometimes regardless of talent or lack thereof. He set salaries at levels that enabled him to maintain his own personal system of control over all those contributing to Brecht enterprises. Such acts, in the Western democracies, would have constituted blatant conflicts of interest. However, as the Soviet system throughout the satellite states was a top-down model, the Ensemble management situation of feathering the manager's nest was not an exception.

41

"He Despises Us Women Deeply" (1949–50)

On August 28, 1949, using Russian documents that allowed "inter-zonal" travel, Brecht left Berlin in his Ensemble car, bound for the Czech-Austrian border, where he was met by Erica von Einem and taken to Salzburg. He completed the paperwork for his Austrian pass-port, and discussed the Salzburg Festival and possible sites for its out-door stages. Drawing on his hard-currency funds, he bought a new car. It was a large, open Steyr, much like the one he had driven during the Weimar era.[1] The newly established West German government, more cooperative than the American military authorities, allowed him to visit Munich.

He went to visit Hans Albers, one of the best-known stage and film actors of the Nazi era, at his estate on Lake Starnberg, near Brecht's old estate.[2] Brecht wanted Albers (then playing in a Munich production of *Threepenny*) to play Mack the Knife in a Brecht-organized touring pro-duction of *Threepenny*, though he had just taken the play from Felix Bloch Erben on the ostensible grounds that the company had cooper-ated with the Nazis. Albers's stardom and his personal charisma were irresistible. Angelika Hurwicz said later, "Brecht loved stars."[3] Though Brecht failed to recruit the greatest star of the Third Reich, it was not for want of trying. Now joined by Berlau, he signed a contract to direct *Mother Courage* in Munich in 1950. On September 3, Berlau and Brecht drove to Augsburg where they met with his boyhood lover Orge Pfan-zelt. Brecht noted that Orge had not changed but that the city "[is] somewhat bombed, strange, leaves me fairly cold."[4] That day, he and Ruth began the drive back to Berlin.

On September 4, the United States learned that the Soviet Union, years ahead of American intelligence estimates, had exploded its first atomic bomb. Immediately, questions were asked about how the Sovi-ets had obtained the information that enabled them to build the bomb? Had Gerhart Eisler and those associated with him been involved? The Western intelligence effort around the Brecht circle was now intensi-fied, long after the horse of atomic secrets had bolted.

Ironically, at this same time, Stalin ordered a closer watch on anyone who had spent time outside the Soviet Union during the Hitler years, and Walter Ulbricht, more Catholic than the pope, met with General Serov of Soviet intelligence. Serov was a veteran of Stalin's deliberate starvation of the Ukraine, and he would later smash the remnants of the 1956 rebellion in Hungary. Ulbricht got the latest instructions. He was to identify and mercilessly root out presumed Western agents in the GDR. Within months of the 1949 Serov and Ulbricht meeting, the GDR established a Ministerium für Staatssicherheit (called the Stasi for short), whose agents were trained by the NKVD, whose name would soon be changed to the KGB. With Ulbricht and Wilhelm Pieck at the controls, the newly established secret police exhibited cancerous levels of growth. Nobody was beyond their purview. No one knew whether the person next to them at table or at work or in bed was reporting to the Stasi. The odds were with someone if one guessed one was being spied on, one's telephone tapped, and one's letters read. Nor was one necessarily safe if one fled abroad. The Stasi would boast in the GDR press: "No agent of warmongering imperialism can sit in safety, regardless of whether he is in West Berlin, Bonn, Paris, or even in Washington."[5] The Stasi threat was: depart from the party line and wherever you run, you will be caught, brought back, and handed over to the Soviets or shot in the back of the neck or guillotined in a Stasi prison.[6]

Under Ulbricht, only those who, like himself, had spent years in Stalin's Soviet Union were eligible for the inner circle of governance. When new government agencies were created to regulate cultural life in the GDR, Brecht was not offered a position of importance, despite his supposed closeness to Wilhelm Pieck. In a letter to Arnold Zweig, Brecht complained that he was not included in meetings.[7] The new government's position was clear. They would pay him well, give him the necessary privileges, and showcase him to the West; but they would slap him down the moment he attempted to spread "formalist" heresies within the GDR.

In the late fall of 1949, the Berliner Ensemble prepared to make its formal debut before both the old Soviet and the new German governments of the GDR with *Puntila*. Its debut on November 12 formally marked the creation of the Ensemble as a state-supported theater company. The furor over the play's authorship created by Wuolijoki's daughter in Zurich and Munich had not been forgotten, and her name was in the Ensemble program. But she was only credited with having told Brecht stories about Puntila, not as the author of the original play.

Though she had been rich at the time she had sheltered the Brecht group in 1940–41, Wuolijoki had been badly battered by the war. Jailed as a Russian spy in Finland in the middle of the war, she had at one time been sentenced to death. Though later reprieved, at war's end she left prison with her health and her fortune gone. She tried to get Brecht to pay her directly for her share of *Puntila*, but he evaded her, saying that the Munich publisher was responsible for her royalties. The Munich publisher rejected her claim, stating correctly that Brecht was legally responsible. Hoping that a personal discussion with Brecht might help, Wuolijoki came down to Berlin for the *Puntila* production, and Brecht had a photo taken of her in front of the poster for *Puntila*. The picture would be used to "prove" that Wuolijoki agreed with what he was doing. In fact, though *Puntila* appeared in a *Versuche* volume published in both East and West Germany, she got nothing. Nor would she get anything when the film rights were sold to a Viennese company. Toward the end of her life (she died in February 1954), she wrote to Weigel that she had been seriously ill, was broke, and desperately needed the *Puntila* money to pay her large hospital bills.[8] Her request brought no response that I have ever seen.

The same *Versuche* volume that included *Puntila* also contained a number of items by Elisabeth Hauptmann: a group of Chinese poems that she had first worked on in the thirties and had now resumed work on since her return to Berlin; and a play, *The Exception and the Rule*, heavily based on Hauptmann's 1929–30 translation of the French version of a Chinese play.[9] One long poem that Brecht really did apparently write and that was published at this time is called "The Raising of Millet." It consists of fifty-two stanzas in praise of the charlatan geneticist Trofim Lysenko, who virtually destroyed the genuinely scientific study of genetics in the Soviet Union and directly caused the death of countless rivals. Brecht's poem speaks of Lysenko's sponsor, Stalin, as "our great harvest leader." As John Willett observes of this bizarre poem, it "is hard to stomach for all its technical skill."[10]

By 1947, except for an occasional short poem still exhibiting technical skill, Brecht's writing was no longer of great interest. Except for the *Antigone* adaptation with Neher in Chur and the adaptation of *Defeat*, he completed no significant new plays and very few poems during the rest of his life. What was published in his last years was usually mainly Hauptmann's or work completed during the exile years with Berlau or Steffin, or an occasional good short poem. His time was spent managing copyrights and the lives of those closest to him, or poured into his work as a world-class stage director.

When the audience filed into the Deutsches Theater for the *Puntila* that Brecht directed on November 8, 1949, the first thing they saw was Picasso's famous drawing of the dove of peace sewn on the main curtain. It was a belligerent gesture, since Picasso was artistically persona non grata in the socialist states.[11] Käthe Reichel, playing the part of one of Puntila's many "lovers" in the play, slipped Brecht a note just before the curtain rose. "Bert, my dear Bert!" she wrote, "When we first begin to play your plays we will reap fame such as that of no other theater in the world, because you are the greatest of all playwrights. That I believe and know firmly. And that is why I am so full of joy."[12] Both the German and the Russian officials applauded the performance. *Puntila* was a hit and a money-maker.

By late 1949, Brecht's position seemed secure, even gemütlich. At the villa, assisted by suitable help and amidst her antiques, Weigel provided the Viennese cooking that he loved. He again had his own car. His affair with Reichel was going well, and Weigel eased things along in the madamelike way she had since meeting Brecht. At year's end, Brecht wrote, "Dear Helli, Thanks for a good year, in which you were the greatest. b."[13] When his old friend Wilhelm Pieck took formal office as president of the newly established GDR, Brecht sent him a note using the intimate "Du" form: "Dear Comrade Wilhelm Pieck, May I send you, in order to express my joy at your taking office, a small poem, that you could read better than the poet? With very hearty greetings, also from Helli, Yours, Bertolt Brecht."[14] It reiterated Brecht's concerns about a new and perhaps more terrible war:

> *Do not march off to war you poor ones*
> *As though the old wars had not been enough:*
> *I ask you, have mercy on yourself!*

But though Brecht was on a "Du" basis with the nominal head of the new East German government, this was a government that showed little real interest in what he represented.

Several "Brecht" works were on the assembly line. Therese Giehse was doing an adaptation of Gorky's play *Wassa Schelesnowa;* and a new version of Jakob Lenz's *The Private Tutor* was being prepared by Brecht and Berlau. Beginners Benno Besson and Egon Monk worked with veterans such as Elisabeth Hauptmann and Ruth Berlau, with Brecht's occasional involvement. There was a Besson-Brecht version of Anna Segher's Joan of Arc material and a Hauptmann-Wekwerth adaptation of a Chinese folk play. New and brilliantly stageable versions of plays such as Molière's *Don Juan* and Farquhar's *The Recruiting Officer* (by Hauptmann and Besson), Shakespeare's *Coriolanus* and Ben Jonson's *Volpone* (by Hauptmann) were prepared by staff members and then, despite private objections from Hauptmann and Besson, stamped for sale with the Brecht label.[15] Benno Besson told me that Brecht served as an "assistant" to him on *Don Juan* and the evidence in the archives supports Besson's assessment. Brecht neither had the skills in French

(French is Besson's native language, and Hauptmann was fluent in it), nor did Brecht spare time to work on it. Further, according to available records, Brecht contributed even less to *Trumpets and Drums*, the adaptation of Farquhar's *Recruiting Officer*. Nevertheless, to this day, the Hauptmann-Besson *Don Juan* and the Farquhar adaptation are published as Brecht works.[16] The production process at the Ensemble was similar to what Marieluise Fleisser described in 1929–30 in her play *The Deepseafish*, in which Bébé hired young people to write and then signed their work as his own.

One of the few people besides Hauptmann and Besson who knew how Brecht plays were created at the Berliner Ensemble was Ruth Berlau. She told Brecht that his actions were arbitrary and that he was not being a very good teacher. To the horror of the old and committed party member Berlau, he declared, "I don't have students, I have employees."[17] Life in East Berlin remained a dangerous struggle for Berlau. Still technically a foreigner, she was under the kind of constant surveillance that had haunted her years in the United States. She was caught between constant attention from the Stasi and frequent neglect by Brecht, and was further saddened by the obvious inconsistency of Brecht's socialism. But Berlau still thought she could work in socialist Berlin for that all-important "third thing." After her first year, she managed to escape the Schmidt Hotel with its dangerous Russian guests. Despite Weigel, Berlau got East German residence papers and found a rather pleasant apartment at 3 Charitéstrasse, near the Charité Hospital.

Berlau furnished her new place with Brecht's preferences in mind. Chronically short of money, particularly hard currency, she found simple and elegant Danish furniture of the sort he had liked when she had first met him in 1933. She also bought one large Biedermeier chair like those he knew from Augsburg. It all proved attractive for a while. When they were finished with rehearsals, he would come over and she would serve him lunch. He had his afternoon nap and conducted meetings with co-workers. But he came and went on his own schedule, never mentioning the adoption of a child once they got to Berlin. Often, he seemed to want her far away. At his request, she spent the last part of 1949 in Leipzig doing a production of *Mother* for Brecht to take over later in Berlin. Her absence helped get Weigel, who obviously could not stand Berlau, off his back for a bit, while he also made headway with his affair with Käthe Reichel.

Others at the Ensemble were envious, but the young, lovely, and talented Reichel was getting ever-better roles. Born Käthe Levi in 1926, she was in her early teens when her Jewish father was taken to the Sachsenhausen concentration camp.[18] Soon after, she began to correspond with soldiers at the front using her mother's "Aryan" maiden name of Reichel. A postmistress watched the blond, blue-eyed teenager pick up hundreds of German soldiers' letters addressed to Reichel, and helped her get a lifesaving identity card. Despite her new name, she lived every day in fear of a Gestapo knock at the door. Her brother had broken under the strain and committed suicide.

From quite early on, Reichel had decided that if she survived, she would become a professional actress. She had auditioned for Brecht and Weigel very soon after they reached Berlin. Brecht had liked what she did, on- and offstage, and she thought him a genius who could help her achieve her full potential. Small and very aware of how young and inexperienced she was, she thought it natural to address Brecht as the "master," while she became "Käthe the Tiny." Though begun in jest and in recognition of his fame and her own small stature, in the phrases lay the seed of the essential repetitive Brecht pattern of dominance and submission.

On her return from Leipzig, Berlau could neither ignore nor accept what was going on between the twenty-four-year-old Reichel and Brecht, now about to turn fifty-two. As Berlau came to realize that Brecht was hardly ever available to see her, she began to lose hope and control. She accused Hannah Budzislawski in Leipzig of having had an affair with Brecht since the New York days and both Budzislawskis of spying on her at Brecht's behest.[19] In one letter, she cited (in English) the "Sonnet from the Portuguese": " 'Guess who holds thee?' 'Death,' I said. But there the silver answer rang: 'Not death but love.' "[20] Sometimes visitors to her flat were shown a rope that she kept in a drawer and the hook that she said she planned to tie it to one day.

Berlau's insecurity was now often more than she could bear. In one frantic, often incoherent letter to Weigel, Berlau claims that Brecht "liebt mich" (loves me). Weigel, all too aware of Brecht's appetite for other and younger women, found absurd the now forty-two-year-old Ruth's claim of his love. Other claims were less absurd. "Don't tell people," Berlau wrote, "that you don't have money, someone who can buy a fourth fur coat for 1,030 marks could return my clock to me."[21] Weigel feared that Berlau might make such accusations public. Having several fur coats in a country where for most one warm cloth coat was unattainable was a problem. After one public incident where Berlau blew up at Brecht at the Ensemble, Weigel seized the opportunity to take her rival off the payroll, hoping Berlau would go back to Denmark where she might be less dangerous.

But Berlau was not going to allow herself to be driven out, even if it meant her own destruction. Her work as a director, photographer, and driving force behind the creation of the model books detailing

Ensemble productions was still essential to the operation, though Weigel could hire other photographers for the new productions. Despite this treatment by the nominal head of the Berliner Ensemble and by Brecht, Berlau could not really push herself to leave Berlin permanently. As with Berlau's many predecessors, when she tried to leave, he sent her a stream of letters signed with that old, multiply underlined, still-magnetic "d."

Often depressed, she now combined drinking with prescription tranquilizers. In the first week of March 1950, Berlau "played Ophelia a bit," as she wrote later. One evening, unable to get Brecht to sleep with her, she drank some of the highest proof vodka available and swallowed sleeping pills, some obtained by prescription and some, she claimed later, left in her bed by Brecht. Luckily, some visitors happened to drop by and called Brecht. He arranged with his childhood friend Dr. Hans Otto Münsterer to have her admitted to a locked ward at the state-run Charité Hospital.

Berlau returned to consciousness at the hospital, alone in a barred and padded cell that reminded her of her sister's confinement. She was under the supervision of a Professor Thile and a Dr. Hegemann, who both seemed genuinely interested in her welfare, rather than in catering to the wishes of the famous and powerful man who had had her committed. A March 4 letter to Brecht in her expressive but largely untutored German begs: "Comrade and friend help me now. I need your help now, until now I am the one who has helped you. I love you. Always your creature. Ruth. Now I need it that you be great and mighty-magical Bertolt. I know best how to get healthy. Here there are too many memories of Edith, the toilet without a door etc. etc."[22] On March 8, she had identified her main problems: "I have spoken with Dr. Hegemann about how things should go from now on. Even if Professor Thile thinks I am well enough to leave here, we must work something out so that everything will not then repeat itself. I have proposed to Dr. Hegemann that a 'basic problem' that must be removed is that I get a contract from you that is deposited directly in my account every two weeks, so that you will need to have nothing to do with my money matters, similar to a Berliner Ensemble contract."[23] Another practical problem was the need to get proper credit for her directing and contributions to numerous plays. She had created the basic Brecht archive of manuscripts and done almost all the work leading to the creation of the model books, which were so useful for spreading Brecht's fame abroad.

Aware that he might not want her to continue working with him, she indicated she would be happy to rebuild her career in Scandinavia, working as a journalist. She felt that she could be fully independent within four months but would need payments for past work to sustain her during the transition period. Finally, she asked for clarification of their personal and sexual relationship. As she put it: "FOR ME THE FIRST THING IS THAT YOU FINALLY AND HONESTLY TELL ME WHETHER YOU ARE GOING TO LOOK SERIOUSLY FOR AN ATTIC APARTMENT FOR YOURSELF, RATHER THAN AL-WAYS MOVING BACK AND FORTH BETWEEN ONE PLACE AND ANOTHER WHICH HINDERS YOUR WORK. WHERE YOUR TYPEWRITER IS THAT IS WHERE YOU WILL LIVE. DON'T MISUNDERSTAND ME: I AM ONLY ASKING WHETHER YOU ARE GOING TO KEEP YOUR WORD OR WHETHER YOU ARE NOT THINKING OF THAT ANYMORE. I AM NOT ASKING WHEN BUT RATHER WHETHER OR EVER???? IN THAT WAY WE CAN FINALLY REACH SOME CLARITY ON THAT QUESTION AS I AM NOT IN AGREEMENT WITH YOUR LAST PROPOSAL, 'I WILL COME TO YOU ONCE A WEEK.' "[24] Again, she got no answer.

In her locked and barred room, she dreamed of a playwright coming to visit her. On March 11, she described a visit the night before of Lenz, the eighteenth-century author of *The Private Tutor*, then being rehearsed by Brecht with Reichel.[25] Berlau was overjoyed when she turned out the light and found Lenz in bed with her. "My brother," said Berlau, "I love you." Lenz said, breaking down in tears, "I visited him, the one who calls himself a master . . ." Ruth replied, "He's doing your play, Lenz, and he has no time for you?" "But this master," Lenz replied, "did he himself not say that he who had outrun the tiger was now nourishing bedbugs and being eaten by mediocrity?" "THAT'S THE WAY IT REALLY IS!" she replied.

In the 1950 May Day parade celebrating international Workers' Day, the exultant "master" Bertolt Brecht, with Helene Weigel and Mari Barbara Brecht together as "a family" for the photo, waved from their chauffeur-driven open car. On the sidewalk, mothers held up their children so that they could see "Mother Courage" and the author who was being shaped into an icon of socialist culture. When Eric Bentley came to visit in 1950, he told Brecht he was amazed at how rapidly the new company had been raised to the level of a world-class theater. Brecht replied that he had definitely "inherited the crown." When Bentley asked, "What crown was that?" he remembers that Brecht answered, "The German theater always had a king. In his [Brecht's] youth, it was Gerhart Hauptmann, in his early maturity it was Georg Kaiser, now it was himself."[26]

But if he was the king, rivals saw him as mere pretender. A Ger-man critic told Ilya Ehrenburg that Brecht was an "impenitent formal-ist."[27] Ehrenburg had little patience with such attacks. Many of his and

Brecht's closest friends had been murdered for being "formalists." Now, as Ehrenburg knew, Stalin's chosen enemies were often Jews. By 1950, in the Soviet Union, arrests and individual murders of Jews were routine.[28] Sometimes, these acts were carried out with the cooperation of Alexander Fadayev.[29] In the three years that Stalin had left to live, his anti-Semitism would violently spill over to client states.

Despite the clouds rolling in from the Kremlin, life in the GDR looked normal enough in the middle of 1950. When summer came, the GDR privileged intelligentsia went off to the Baltic beaches that had seen generations of top-level German functionaries vacation there. A favorite resort (before the privileged intelligentsia developed the system of taking over their own private islands including "nature preserves") was the picturesque town of Ahrenshoop. In August 1950, first Brecht and Berlau, and then Brecht and Weigel, were there rubbing shoulders with the elite.

On September 2, 1949, Brecht left with Berlau to drive to Munich to direct a production of Mother Courage with Therese Giehse in the lead. Eric Bentley went there also, and Brecht took him on as an unpaid assistant.[30] That was the only place where money was spared. Bentley notes: "For their Mother Courage, the Bavarians went out and chopped down forests, they 'spoiled' this superb new wood with a blowtorch to make it look old and worn. Ruined postwar Munich could afford what Broadway never in this world would have considered."[31]

One thing that surprised Bentley was that Brecht would not consult with Giehse as to how a certain scene might be arranged.[32] Bentley asked her if she always allowed directors to push her around. "Only if he's a genius,"[33] she replied. Perhaps because Brecht had been known in the Munich theater for almost thirty years for his dictatorial behavior, the stage personnel did not seem surprised and offended when Brecht shouted at them in what Bentley calls Brecht's "Hitler imitation."[34] (This description of Brecht's voice and tone is echoed by East German playwright Heiner Müller in his writings on Brecht.)[35] Ironically, Brecht's standard imprecation was that everyone was an old Nazi. But, as Bentley points out, there really were unreconstructed Nazis in Munich. At the Oktoberfest, as Berlau, Bentley, and Brecht were sitting at one table, students at a table nearby were singing a song about the "Saujud," (the Jewish swine). Brecht almost turned purple. After Brecht had jumped up and kicked over the bench on which they had been sitting, he turned to Bentley and said: "And they say these people have changed! Good liberals now, are they? I know this sort! They will never change! And in the East, they know this. Over there these hoodlums would be behind barbed wire! And never, never would they be let out."[36] Brecht's recommended treatment of extremists was extreme.

His "solution" was the mirror image of the "problem." Brecht never dealt with the less dramatic but far tougher problem, that of designing a legal system that protects the rights of individuals and of the body politic as a whole.

While in Munich, Brecht was visited by his former lover and collaborator Marieluise Fleisser. Having barely survived the Third Reich, suicide attempts, and a breakdown that put her in an asylum, she had begun to write again. She brought along her newest play, written in Bavarian dialect, called *The Strong Breed*. With the help of Brecht and Werner Bergold of the Kammerspiel, she was able to get it performed for at least a short run. But there was little general interest in it, and she returned to Ingolstadt.

Also in September, Brecht told Gottfried von Einem that his Austrian papers had now finally come through.[37] What Brecht probably did not know was that various branches of American intelligence continued to track him, and they knew at once about his Austrian citizenship.[38] But the knowledge was kept in the files until it was deemed the most damaging moment to leak it.[39]

Brecht's personal ties from the American years were growing looser. When Ferdinand Reyher came to visit in September 1950, Brecht had little time for him.[40] Reyher saw the Brecht-Weigel villa filled with "the antique furniture which Weigel had been acquiring all over Berlin."[41] The cars, food, and clothes were all conspicuously above the general standard of the GDR, "in a State that was allegedly striving to erase class differences." Most disturbingly, perhaps, Reyher saw that Brecht's circle consisted of intellectuals and theater people, with little or no contact with workers. Leaving Berlin much sooner than he had planned, he told his daughter, "I'm tired of broken promises."[42]

As the traumatic Christmas season and anniversary of her 1945 breakdown came around, Berlau left to direct her own "Brecht-authorized" production of *Mother Courage* in Rotterdam. Her letters were routinely signed "Ruth," "Ute," and "your creature."[43] His "letters" to her often were just that, a single letter, a "d" (with or without underlinings) or a "b."

On January 12, Brecht had a business meeting to discuss joint publication terms between his West German publisher, Suhrkamp, and Kurt Wendt of the East Berlin Aufbau Verlag. He was preparing a version of *Mother*, which Berlau had directed in Leipzig, for a mid-January premiere. The servant "girl" in the play, the role that Margarete Steffin had played in Berlin in 1932, was now played by Reichel. The affair with Reichel echoed in many ways that with Steffin. Where he had been for Steffin "der alte" (the old one) or the "master," for Reichel, he was usually "the master."[44] As the year ended, she gave him a gift of fall leaves, and he had written to her, "The year is almost over, love is just beginning."[45] He had not said whose love was just beginning; but as love began, so did it wane.

On January 16, 1951, after Berlau returned to Berlin from her assignment in Holland, Brecht bitterly called her to task. After receiving the gift of the yellow leaves from Käthe, he had decided that he looked older than his years. "I want to tell you something very bad, Ruth," he said to Berlau, "but it's something you must know: if I fall down tomorrow in the street, you will be to blame. You have cost me five years of my life. I am now 53 years old and I look five years older than that and you're to blame."[46] The attack was fundamentally unfair. He had psychologically abused her for so many years that it was a near miracle she could even still function effectively.

Berlau was devastated by Brecht's charge, as well as his unwillingness to hear her side of things. In another effort to reestablish her own independence, on January 16, 1951, she queried Peter Suhrkamp on a German edition of *Every Animal Can Do It*,[47] describing the work: "The book is modern and new and Brechtian. It is also a fact that men do not like to read the book as it is a critique of men." She told Suhrkamp that she and Brecht had once almost completed a kind of alternate final chapter (a chapter that had never been published) that was a "critique of women." When it comes to critiquing women, said Berlau, "believe me, Brecht is great. In fact, he despises us women deeply; only on the subject of Rosa Luxemburg and Krupskaya, Lenin's wife, can one force him to say anything good. Yes, and naturally about Weigel!!! Me, he has handled like the last piece of shit—unfortunately, I love him."[48] The letter continues: "Here, all I am for people is Brecht's girlfriend, someone who was once lovely. Now, however, Brecht looks for young flesh. That's what people say. And my work is for me finally—now that I am forty-four years old—that which is most important. I don't want to make photographs anymore. I wanted to do it before only to help Brecht, in order to make a record of his plays. Here, in Berlin, there are enough good photographers, and now he can pay them. In America, I was cheap labor and I wore myself down to a wreck. I want to write and to be a director. That is my specialty, my profession. That's what I can do." As far as I can determine, Suhrkamp never seriously considered bringing out Berlau's book and only in recent years has it been published in Germany by the feminist press Persona Verlag.

Around the time of her desperate letter to Suhrkamp, Berlau wrote in her diary: "Whether I am now declared to be sick or healthy, since I left Denmark, I am mostly alone, all the long evenings, every Sunday, at Christmas, on New Year's Day, on my own and on his birthday. During my three years in Berlin, I have never been invited over. Yes, sometimes I was allowed to go along when it was convenient and when it was assumed I would not make a scene and when perhaps there happened to be a place in one of their various cars. Does one deal with a guest like a piece of shit?"[49]

Her despair again reached a crisis, and she was again committed to a locked ward at the Charité. In a letter dated simply February 1951, she begs him to let her have the money that is due to her for her work on the various model books. She begs that her money be deposited directly in her own checking account so that she does not have to come to him all the time to ask for it. She says that Herr Walbrecht, Brecht's accountant at this time, had told her Brecht did not have his own checking account.[50] (Brecht, in fact, wrote his own checks.) Knowing that Walbrecht was lying on his master's behalf, she wrote directly to Brecht: "Hardly any capitalist would behave like such a swine: NOW YOU ARE SUPERFLUOUS: GET OUT!!! Posterity will certainly wonder about this."[51]

But no matter how bitter Berlau's attacks, Brecht did not arrange to make regular payments for her past or present work. Only when it looked as if he would have to pay her out of his own pocket unless she was put back on the Ensemble payroll did he finally intervene and insist to Weigel that her job be restored. He remained unprepared to let her live her own life. He had no time for her when she was in Berlin but felt abandoned the moment she left the city, usually on a special assignment for him. He sent streams of letters saying how important she was to him. But, as with Bie, Marianne, Hedda Kuhn, Caspar Neher, Arnolt Bronnen, Steffin, Hauptmann, and Reyher, as soon as Berlau responded, he would instantly become distant. Always, he seemed incapable of articulating his own pain at his entire series of dysfunctional relationships. It is difficult to believe he was himself without pain and terror as he clung privately to others while publicly posing as tough and self-sufficient.

42

"I Regard Myself As a Criminal. I Am a Jew." (1951–53)

Though the Ensemble drew a stream of foreign visitors and thus was useful to the GDR in foreign propaganda, Brecht's relationship with the authorities was cool at best. As Bentley had predicted, not only had Brecht been accused of formalism with *Mother Courage* in 1949, but, in 1951, Fred Oelssner, a member of the party's Central Committee, called Brecht's Berlin production of *Mother* (taken over largely from Berlau's production in Leipzig) "a kind of mixture between Meyerhold and Proletkult."[1] Meyerhold had, of course, died for "formalist" sins. One of Brecht's Weimar friends, Hans Rodenberg, tried to defend him, acknowledging Brecht was making mistakes but saying this was because he had not learned his lessons in the Soviet Union in 1936. "We must," said Rodenberg, "give Brecht some time."[2]

Even as Rodenberg wrote, Brecht took another "formalist" piece out of the baggage he had brought from his years in the West. This was an antiwar opera he had created with Steffin on the brink of World War II. It was called *The Trial of Lucullus*. With no mention of Steffin and no payment to her heirs, Brecht sought to revive it now as a warning against the rearmament that seemed imminent in both East and West Germany. In the play (with music by Paul Dessau), the Roman general Lucullus is tried before a tribunal of the dead who note his responsibility for at least eighty thousand deaths.

When the work was attacked during rehearsals both for its "decadent" music and the "excessive pacifism" of the libretto, Dessau wanted to back off at once. Brecht counseled the composer sternly, "One must never fear criticism, one either meets it or turns it to account, that is all."[3] When it opened on March 17, it was taken off after one performance. On March 24, Dessau and Brecht were brought in for a half day meeting with Walter Ulbricht, Otto Grotewohl, and Wilhelm Pieck. To Dessau's horror, Brecht, who had told him never to fear criticism, said nothing at the meeting. Instead, Brecht had sent Ulbricht two conciliatory letters. Werner Mittenzwei notes, "The letters had not the slightest impact on Walter Ulbricht."[4] When the meeting at which he failed to defend Dessau or himself ended, Brecht asked archly, "Where else in the world can you find a government that shows such interest in and pays such attention to artists?" The answer was in the Soviet Union, where this kind of "attention" from Stalin often meant death. The incident was profoundly damaging to Dessau, but Brecht, with behind-the-scenes maneuverings, had managed to avoid an open confrontation with his patron Ulbricht.

Still under suspicion after the *Lucullus* incident, Brecht tried to create something to please the government. He chose as his subject a recent clash between some Communist youths who had been held up at the east-west border of the two Germanies by the West German border guards. This work, titled *The Herrenberger Report*, was no better or worse than much of the work he had done for cash during the Weimar period or while in Hollywood. It deals with freedom to export and import political beliefs between two Germanies without undue governmental interference, certainly an important topic at that time. In the middle of 1951, when the GDR still hoped for the possibility of a reunited Germany, the *Report* was well received. By late 1951, he had sufficiently quieted GDR government fears, and he was given the National Prize for Literature, accompanied by 50,000 marks in cash.

On October 18, when the United States thought the news would be most damaging, the information about Brecht's Austrian passport was leaked. Gottfried von Einem lost his job in Salzburg after a press campaign attacked him for cooperating with the "Commie" Brecht. But Brecht seemed to come out unharmed. The GDR authorities chose to overlook their National Prize winner's explanation that the whole business of getting a foreign passport and proposing to go to work in a capitalist state was harmless and that his real home was the GDR.

In November, Käthe Reichel was being treated at the Schloss Wispersdorf Clinic for an undisclosed ailment. From there, on November 13, 1951, she wrote: "Dear Brecht! How are you? Are you sleeping in the afternoons? Look after yourself, rest a little. I love you, don't catch cold, look after yourself."[5] After these few introductory sentences, the letter continues: "I read to the end of *Education sentimentale*, don't get angry about my stupidity. Forgive me. I will read it once again once you have spoken about it with me. Be nice and do not laugh at me. Good night, Bert, I am not clever, but I will become cleverer, help me! Everything is difficult and I am fearful." As the letter progresses, the previously adult writer suddenly becomes fearful, turning to an older, more powerful, better-read, sometimes sternly critical person.

In this letter, Reichel worries about not understanding Flaubert's *L'Education sentimentale*, which Brecht has assigned. The book probably reminded Brecht of his own whorehouse experiences, but Reichel is not sure how it applies to herself. For all Brecht's theoretical arguments for the value of the "new," his teaching assignments gravitated not to *Madame Bovary, Lady Chatterly's Lover,* or the writings of Alexandra Kollontai or Virginia Woolf but rather back toward the nineteenth century or even to an ancient China of repressive patriarchy and flagrant misogyny.

Generally, he seemed more comfortable with the past than the present. His interest in modern art was minimal, as Eric Bentley has pointed out.[6] If he dealt at all with a Picasso, it was with Picasso's most conventional work, a representational dove of peace. Over Brecht's bed hung not a modern work but a print by Brueghel the Elder. He showed no interest in music, modern or classical, as an independent art form. His reading showed scant interest in innovative modern fiction in general but remained a daily diet of crime novels. His basic interests in drama similarly drift to the violent and classical. Whether as a fourteen-year-old with a puppet theater in Augsburg or a fifty-year-old in the GDR, the dramatic events, figures, and emotions he puts upon the stage—Schiller, Büchner, Lenz, Marlowe, Webster, Goethe's *Faust*—are incest, jealousy, castration, infidelity, murdered and abandoned children, violations of women, "attractive" murderers, brutal soldiery, rape, burnings, and suicides. These plays are filled with males beyond the law, men who deny their feelings and preach a philosophy of hierarchy, control, and dominance. Heiner Müller is, I think, correct when he says of virtually all of the plays Brecht worked on either as writer or director: "Terrorism is the real power [in Brecht]."[7]

Nowhere in this landscape is there a loving or genuinely present father, or indeed a biological mother who does not by default or design allow her children to be slaughtered. Even the loving and protective "mothers" or semi-independent women who begin to enter Brecht's work with Hauptmann, Steffin, and Berlau, are usually either whores like Shen Te in *Setzuan* or servants like Grusha in *Chalk Circle.* Real biological mothers—the mother in *The Mother,* the Governor's Wife in *Chalk Circle,* or Mother Courage in the play of that name—sacrifice their children to war, a cause, or commerce. Nowhere is there a strong, caring, and committed adult male in an enduring relationship with either a female or a child. The poetry and the plays reflect the Brecht circle in its most intimate life, a Grimm fairy tale of submission and dominance, of unstable, deliberately divided personalities. In Brecht's last years (reiterating his early years), he spent hours daily trying to break up alliances of former lovers or friends to insure that his control over another person remained unchallenged. All his known letters show that it was virtually impossible for him to be close to another human being.

With frankness and insight typical of her, in early 1952, Reichel writes, "Afternoon—regrettably alone—lying in the sun (instead of a letter)." She continues:

> *You say, come here, give me your cunt.*
> *I can't keep my legs together*
> *A slit is made to be opened*
> *Says logic.*[8]

Reichel adds to the several similarly erotic stanzas: "Above and below to be read in bed. One cannot write a love letter to you, all that mad silliness that one thinks about but never says, but, at best, could write— but not to you—that's bad. I'm sure you don't even understand what I mean. I mean the urge to stroke someone, to kiss their eyes—your eyes are both humorous and cunning—such human responses for classic authors like you, I believe, are absolutely inaccessible. You 'contemplate' everything with a view to using it—that is to say, there are just a few tiny moments, very rare seconds, where you give up 'contemplation.' These few tiny moments are the ones I love."[9] Life "with Brecht" for Reichel was often lived not physically "with him" but with her projecting herself onto his erotic fantasy.

As Hauptmann saw him amidst the real and fantasized affairs he had with young "lovers" (of which the ones I mention here include only the longer lasting ones), she tried to go on with her work. Often, that was impossibly hard. In her presence, Brecht had complained in the spring of 1951 that in the old days of Weimar, "We did not have to work so hard, only until one in the afternoon at the latest."[10] He had not worked many hours perhaps, but she had worked around the clock, even as she was doing now. In a note published years after Brecht's death, Hauptmann wrote of the Weimer years: "Up until thirty-three I either wrote or wrote down most of the poems. There was hardly anyone else there who wrote. Hardly anyone to provide material, no one else from January '25 on."[11]

When Hauptmann complained to Brecht in a November 5, 1951, letter that the royalty arrangements he had made for *The Threepenny Opera* in France ignored her rights,[12] he ignored her objection. Soon after, using the third person, Hauptmann jotted down some notes on her second known suicide attempt. "Now here was another damned Sunday morning. Something that really began on Saturday evening when it began to grow dark. She had lived in this city for almost three years now—that would be one hundred and fifty Sundays. On one hundred and twenty-five of those Sundays she had been alone, the whole day, and often she thought she would not be able to stand it anymore. Once she had not been able to stand it anymore it had piled up even more, but it was not in this apartment here, but rather in a little hole of a room, and there she had had bad luck: it had to be that particular night that somebody had decided to stay on and work in the building and apparently had heard her moaning. Then the doctor had come and in three days she was together again."[13]

With Brecht and Weigel's foreign and domestic bank balances mounting, and now that he had received the National Prize from the Ulbricht government, they began to think of buying a country estate in the GDR. On February 14, 1952, Brecht noted: "With Helli in Buckow in Marckian Switzerland, looked at country houses. Find on a nice piece of land on the water on the shores of Lake Scharmützel, under large old trees an old, not ignobly built small house with another, roomier, but also simple house nearby, about fifty steps away. Something of this sort would be manageable, also in terms of upkeep. One could invite people to stay at the larger house."

The estate that Brecht describes here in what he and the Berliners call "Marckian Switzerland" (Buckow is a village about an hour by car from central Berlin) still dominates the finest view in the area and includes a hundred meters of lakefront. Several life-size sculpted figures in stone grace the grounds. Its large, paved patio looks out over one of the most serenely beautiful views left in an East Germany that even then was becoming a nightmare of untrammeled industrial pollution. The estate was and is surrounded on the landward side by a high fence and is prominently marked Private—No Entry. The local inhabitants call the holders of such pieces of property "the Buckow millionaires."

As was so often the case in Brecht's life, an action in the present is a clear "quotation" of something in the past, the reestablishment of something that was or that he imagined to have existed. The houses on the lake at Buckow echoed the house bought at Skovsbostrand in Denmark in 1933 and the very similar property bought in Bavaria in 1932. His new estate recapitulated his life in the dying days of Weimar when in 1932 he had retreated to the serenity of the Bavarian landscape even as Germany was on the brink of a maelstrom of blood and fire. Now, in 1952–53, if he had been able to listen, he would have heard within the GDR a rising cry of radical disaffection from hundreds of thousands of workers against their nominally "socialist" masters.

By late 1952, the blanket of paranoia eating up a slowly dying Stalin spread inexorably over Eastern Europe. If Stalin opposed "cosmopolitanism" or advocated the crushing of all forms of experimentation, the satellite states hastened to do the same.[14] Bizarre charges of "Titoism," "Zionism," and "working for British or American Imperialists" were made. A wave of NKVD-manipulated "trials" of "oppositionists" rolled through Bulgaria, Poland, Romania, Hungary, and Czechoslovakia. The GDR quickly conformed.

Following Ulbricht's 1949 consultation with NKVD General Serov, a new prison with the most up-to-date torture facilities had been set up in Berlin's Schumannstrasse. Techniques learned from the NKVD were used to prepare prisoners for East Berlin's own first show trial. Under the guise of attacking "enemies of the state," personal scores were brutally settled by Ulbricht. Paul Bertz, who had worked throughout the Nazi period to rescue comrades in Nazi territories and whose work had brought him necessarily into contact with similarly minded American relief organizations, committed suicide before he could be taken away.[15] Among those who were caught was the party functionary Hans Bergmann. Terrified after his first arrest and a preliminary hearing, Bergmann fled to the West.

People who, like Jakob Walcher and the Eisler brothers, had spent the Hitler years in the West rather than in the Soviet Union were under particularly close watch. Walcher, who had openly opposed Ulbricht's deadly activities in France in the mid-thirties,[16] was removed from his post, as was Gerhart Eisler from his post as propaganda chief. Paul Wandel, who had come out on Brecht and Dessau's side in the *Lucullus* controversy, was demoted. Those who had not only been in the West but also were of Jewish origin had two strikes against them. Stalin was proposing a "final solution" to the Jewish problem in the Soviet Union.[17] Jewish artists and intellectuals were forced to sign a "petition" saying that they agreed with a plan to deport all Soviet Jews to the Soviet Far East. And, in the GDR, the special protections that Jews who had suffered under Hitler were receiving were suddenly removed.

Partly out of conviction, partly out of a growing sense of the need for self-defense, Brecht and Weigel (who was usually far bolder in such matters than he) would sometimes show up when behind-the-scenes discussions of alternate roads to Marxist goals took place. When they visited Warsaw briefly in February 1952 to discuss bringing *Mother Courage* there, they met both with regular party officials and members of the Polish dissident intelligentsia such as Andrzej Wirth, editor of *Kultura*. Brecht, with his history of association with "spies," "traitors," and "cosmopolitans" like Koltzov, Tretiakov, Knorin, Kun, and Otto Katz (now about to subjected to a show trial in Prague), and Weigel, with her Jewishness and comparative outspokenness, were ideal surveillance subjects.

Financed and controlled by a state directed by Stalinist values, Brecht and Weigel produced works described by Heiner Müller as "[plays with] the Stalinist brakes on."[18] The Ensemble's position would always be dictated by the belief that if it did more to oppose Ulbricht, everything could be lost with one blow. However, without an alternative to turgid socialist realism, Ensemble members might defect to the West, where they could work without overt government interference.

Trying not only to limit losses but to extend the circle of allies in Berlin, Brecht persuaded the Academy of Arts to finance some "master students" to work with him and whom he hoped to train in his own kind of non–socialist realist art. In 1952, one of these "master students" was a young homosexual poet named Martin Pohl.

A delicate boy, Pohl had grown up during the Nazi years in a household where his father rejected him as not manly enough. In the last weeks of the war, the then fifteen-year-old Martin tried to flee the Russian advance with his mother and younger brother, who were trapped in a building and set on fire by the SS. Unable to save them as they burned before his eyes, Pohl went on alone. He reached Berlin after the shooting stopped and tried to establish himself as a writer. The chance to work with the Brecht group seemed like bliss to him at first. "Years ago you led me," he addressed Brecht (then deceased) in a poem, "out onto the ice . . . and I dug for your darkness."[19]

Much of Pohl's time was spent at Berlau's apartment, which Brecht still visited daily at lunchtime. Like Brecht and Berlau themselves, Pohl was deeply needy, and he soon began to see the curious couple almost as his surrogate parents. They were, he thought, seeking "Geborgenheit" (a place of safety). But Pohl saw that Ruth had no security with Brecht who, wandering between mistresses's homes, seemed himself homeless. Pohl saw Berlau submit to a stream of indignities by Brecht and Weigel. In 1990, in answer to a question whether Berlau was ever insane, Pohl replied, "No! No! I would say with Polonius in *Hamlet*, 'Madness has its methods.' "[20] Her behavior, he suggested, was a sane response to an often insane situation, in which she was caught between the push and pull of Brecht's contradictory desires.

In January 1952, Brecht asked Marieluise Fleisser to turn some materials that he had sent her into a play. Fleisser was still locked in a marriage with Josef "Bepp" Haindl, a man who wanted her to run his tobacco shop in West Germany rather than write. Brecht wanted her to write but on his terms. Finding herself getting nowhere with his material, she wrote, "I am returning the material which you sent me, perhaps you can use it some other time."[21]

Rebuffed here, Brecht had other irons in the fire. A photographer he had met in Western Europe before the war, Gerda Goedhart, decided to settle in Berlin. She took over some of Berlau's photographic work. Each such appointment by Weigel and Brecht tended to lower Berlau's self-esteem, even when it involved jobs she had only done with reluctance. Each job lost, even the bad jobs, meant less time with him and made her own position with the Ensemble ever more tenuous. Berlau watched a stream of newcomers arrive, all desirous of working closely with "the master." Meanwhile, she was usually the lowest paid member of the staff, though she was one of the most experienced directors there. Age and experience, as she said to Brecht in one letter, were not what he seemed interested in promoting at all. She wondered whether he would not prefer her dead. "What," she asked, "is one woman now, now that there is such a selection?"[22] Despite increasing despair, she still worked with him when any opportunity presented itself.

In 1952, Brecht, Berlau, and Pohl were involved in a production of the rarely staged early version of Goethe's *Faust*, the so-called *Urfaustus*, guided by the brilliant young Egon Monk. Monk, in consultation with Brecht, decided to stress Faust's own period, the late middle ages and the beginning of the "scientific era." At the same time, costuming, gesture, and the delivery of lines were to accentuate all the sexual references in the text. In the extremely prudish GDR, this was very bold indeed. When the show opened in Potsdam on April 23, 1952, the audience loved it. Goethe, who had been tamed by centuries of dull staging, suddenly had a sexy and savage bite. The *Märkische Volksstimme* stated: "If we, with all our heart, can recommend an evening in the theater for our readers, then it is this production of the 'Urfaustus.' Anyone who has not been to see it has missed something of significance."[23]

But the rulers of the GDR now began to imagine they detected a whiff of dissidence in this production. "The conception which Monk used," declared an anonymous party critic, "shows that he allows the negative, the decadent to be brought forward by every major figure in his production." This is "extremely dangerous both for theater people themselves and for the general public."[24] "The productions of our classics," concluded this essay, "must help us to awaken the national strength of our Volk."

The return to patently Hitlerian language was obviously now well advanced. Writing from the comparative safety of West Germany, Caspar Neher said the kind of art being pushed by the government in East Berlin was just like "in Goebbels's day."[25] Similarly virulent attacks came from the West, where Brecht was seen as a slavish adherent of Stalin and an apologist for Soviet practices. Stung by one such attack, on March 14, 1952, he wrote to "Dear Comrade Semyonov" saying that he had again been attacked in the West on the question of the disappearance of Carola Neher. "It would be useful," wrote Brecht, "if I could learn something of her fate in order to be able to give out information."[26] He got no answer.

On the same day, he sent a letter to the party paper, *Neues Deutschland*, which had asked him to respond to the question of *Puntila* and Wuolijoki's rights. The paper had been approached by Wuolijoki's

German translator, Friedrich Ege, who had offered to do a candid piece on the case. Instead, the paper asked Brecht for his view. Brecht claimed, "I am on the best of terms with Hella Wuolijoki."[27] He stressed that the new play differed from the original Finnish one. He also said she had been happy with the 1949 Berlin production of *Puntila*. This of course was only part of the truth. The paper accepted Brecht's version of the facts, possibly because the government wished to hold any damaging information until such time as Brecht was to be jerked back into line.

While fending off old attacks for stealing the work of others, Brecht was ready for new appropriations. Martin Pohl had proved himself capable of writing verse so close to Brecht in style that experts to this day cannot tell the difference. At least two dazzling sonnets that Martin Pohl wrote in 1952 on the Faust theme have since been repeatedly published as Brecht's work.[28] "Brecht," said Pohl later with a wry smile, "was a great exploiter."[29]

Living in a state where the disappearance of friends without any semblance of a real trial was an everyday reality, Brecht was constantly trying to figure out where the sinuous party line was going to go next. Before the war, Steffin could provide him with firsthand knowledge of events in the Soviet Union. Now, he found a replacement in the Russian-speaking Käthe Rülicke, whom he had invited to join his personal staff in 1950.[30] To Reichel's and Berlau's dismay, Brecht had begun to spend more and more time with Rülicke. The two out-of-favor rivals began to exchange letters sneering at Käthe Rülicke as "overweight" and "that Hitler youth girl."[31] Rülicke was unusually candid about her Nazi upbringing. Unlike most other people of her generation, she was willing to talk openly about her past and the wish to find under real socialism a wholly different existence.[32] In Brecht, she saw someone to love and someone who shared her sense of urgency in the cause of peace. She was not pleased, however, by his various other women, particularly Käthe Reichel. Brecht objected to her objections to Reichel and banned Rülicke from rehearsals until she agreed to remain silent about her rival.

At Buckow, Brecht had the tranquility that he needed to read classical poetry, usually Horace, and to refresh himself generally with one or another of his mistresses and other visitors. His son, Stefan (now twenty-eight), and Stefan's wife, Alma, had come to visit in 1952, and father and son could discuss family business and Stefan's ongoing Harvard dissertation on Hegel. Gradually, in the postwar years, Stefan became more active in Brecht enterprises, involving himself in negotiations over Western productions and new editions. Stefan was glad to take over business responsibilities and the income that came with them from "that asshole Bentley,"[33] as he referred to him in one letter to his father. On the same day, Stefan signed a letter to Bentley, "Most sincerely and in all friendliness."[34] To complete one tiny circle of vituperation, Brecht, speaking to Eric Bentley about sending money to his son, asked aloud, "Why do I send it? He'll probably spend it on whores."[35] In a later letter to Bentley, he avers that Stefan should not get involved in negotiations about Brecht plays in America "as he understands nothing of this."[36]

In the fall, Brecht returned from Buckow to Weissensee, where Weigel, apparently with increasing distaste, played hostess to a stream of guests and Brecht's lovers. One of the visitors was Angelika Hurwicz, the actress who had played the "dumb" Kattrin in the famous 1949 production of *Mother Courage*. Hurwicz came out to Weissensee to stay overnight and brought along her special friend, Gerda Goedhart. Near the entranceway of the house were two same-sex dolls. Impulsively, Hurwicz held the dolls together in an embrace. Weigel was incensed and snatched them apart. According to Hurwicz, neither Brecht nor Weigel was able to deal openly with homosexuality.[37] Though several of the Ensemble's most prominent members, including Hurwicz, were quite open about their sexual orientation, Weigel and Brecht acted as though only heterosexual behavior existed, reflecting the attitude of the government of the GDR. The prudery shown even with dolls was matched by the painfully shy way in which Brecht behaved with regard to his own body. According to Hurwicz, if Brecht was to take a bath, Weigel had to first clear the halls of the villa so Brecht would not be seen going down the hall in a bathrobe.

Brecht had become a special category in the GDR, allowed all kinds of things otherwise forbidden in the Ulbricht state. On his trips to Buckow, he carried a pass stating: "Bertolt Brecht is working at this time in Buckow, Märk. Bergland, Seestrasse 29, to which he must take the above list of newspapers and magazines." On this list were: *Die Welt, Neue Zurcher Zeitung, Spiegel, Revue, Quick, Münchener Illus., Newsweek, Time,* and *Life.* He also carried a required "Sondergenehmigung" (special permission pass), dated March 9, 1952, that read: "The holder of this pass, Herr Bertold [sic] Brecht, has permission, on his journeys from Berlin to Buckow and back to carry a Portable Typewriter Royal A. Nr. 1099815, as well as a case containing theater manuscripts when he passes the Border Check Point Hoppegarten."[38]

With his mobility and special privileges in a Soviet bloc state where reading was strictly controlled and the transport of a typewriter the subject of special negotiations, sometimes he was reminded of how unusual and precarious his position was. In Prague, in late 1952, a massively publicized trial reminiscent of the Moscow Show Trials took place. Before anything as "bourgeois" as guilt or innocence could be established, Moscow denounced the Prague defendants as traitors who "hoped to transform Czechoslovakia into a foreign branch of Wall Street ruled by American monopolists, bourgeois nationalists, Zionists and all manner of riff-raff [sic] steeped in crime."[39] Otto Katz, who had financed Brecht's return to Berlin in late 1948 and whose phone number Brecht had kept on his bedside list for years, was forced to describe himself at the "trial" as a "Trotskyist Titoist traitor and enemy of the Czech people in the service of American Imperialism."[40] Katz was also forced to say in open court: "I regard myself as a criminal. I am a Jew. I stand before the court a traitor and a spy." On December 3, 1952, Otto Katz and ten others were hanged in a Prague prison yard. Brecht made no note of the death of his friend and failed to protest in any way.

By January 1953, Brecht's deceptions were overcoming Hauptmann's party loyalty. First in a telegram and then in an angry letter to Weigel, she protested that her work at the Ensemble was being used but she was not being paid. The Ensemble press releases, which never mention her, were "a pile of waste." "Apparently, you don't know," she said, "that in the last one and a half years, on top of everything else, I have done four play adaptations, two of them entirely on my own, and one of these two that I did alone was an extremely large and splendid one if I may say so myself."[41] Weigel ignored the complaint.

Throughout the first months of 1953, as Stalinist paranoia mixed inextricably with anti-Semitism swept Eastern Europe, Brecht and Egon Monk worked on another production of the *Urfaustus*. Brecht summed up the "plot" of the play to Berlau: "Here is a man who feels old and wants to become young again. He summons up the devil, and he becomes young again. Then he crosses the street, falls in love with a girl, and gets her pregnant. She kills her baby and ends up in prison."[42] Brecht, a man who feared the advance of age, cast the young, lovely Käthe Reichel as Gretchen.

On February 22, as the *Urfaustus* opening neared, the Stasi picked up Martin Pohl. In a jail the Stasi had taken over from the SS, Pohl was subjected to interrogation similar to that used for decades in the Soviet Union to break the will of prisoners. Decades later, his pain was still evident. He said the Stasi agents who interrogated him had the same brutal faces of the SS who had burned his mother and brother in 1945. Terrified, Pohl signed a wholly made-up "confession" that he was a "US intelligence agent." Brecht does not mention the arrest of Pohl in his diary, and I have not discovered any action taken by him at the time to oppose the arrest. Not until July (when such inquiries seemed less dangerous after Stalin's death in March), and only in a private letter to "Herrn Justizminister Max Fechner," did Brecht ask what Pohl was charged with, saying that there was "great uneasiness" in the Ensemble as a result of the arrest.[43] Behind the scenes, Brecht arranged for Pohl to be allowed to write poetry in jail. I am not aware of any effort Weigel may have made to help in any way. Her general attitude toward such arrests was, as she expressed it to one of her former actors, "When you plane wood, shavings fall."[44]

On March 4, three weeks after Pohl's arrest (before his diary then falls silent until early August of the same year), Brecht wrote, "Our productions in Berlin hardly elicit an echo anymore."[45] At this time, around the night of March 5, 1953, Joseph Stalin finally died, till the last moment planing wood and letting the shavings fall, arranging the arrest and death of Jews and of his closest comrades. With Stalin dead, to the very great relief of those in his inner circle, the public apparatus of praising Stalin briefly continued. Writers throughout the socialist world were directed to write eulogies. Many, like Johannes R. Becher, wrote at length of how disastrous Stalin's death was for the Communist world. Brecht's brief and ambiguous statement read: "The oppressed of all five continents, those who have already freed themselves, and all those who fight for world peace must have felt their heartbeats stop when they heard that Stalin was dead. He was the embodiment of their hopes. But the intellectual and material weapons he brought into being exist, as does the doctrine that new weapons be made."[46]

Despite the large investment that had been made in the production, *Urfaustus* was forced to close after six performances. One official wrote of the show, "By furthering cosmopolitanism this constitutes a direct support of the politics of war of the American imperialists."[47] As Martin Pohl had worked on the production and had "confessed" to working with American intelligence, the charge could hardly have been more serious. And, since "cosmopolitanism" was code for "Jewish," this meant Weigel was in danger also. Walter Ulbricht personally entered the debate. "We will not allow," he wrote on May 27, "that one of the most important works by our greatest German writer, Goethe, is formalistically raped, that the great ideas of Goethe's *Faust* are turned into a caricature, as that has occurred in certain productions even in the German Democratic Republic, for instance, in the so-called Faust of Eisler[48] and in the production of the 'Urfaust [*Urfaustus*].' "[49]

Brecht received a letter from the Academy of Arts cutting off his monthly stipend of fifteen hundred marks (roughly three-to-four times the income of a skilled worker in the GDR in 1953). Brecht wrote on April 10 to say: "I require you to fulfill the terms of the contract of March 13, 1952, that is to say, that you continue to pay me my monthly stipend of 1,500 marks from 1.1.53 up to a point in time when we can reach written agreement as per the terms of Paragraph 11, and which, according to Paragraph 2, cannot occur in any case before 28.2.1954."⁵⁰ Brecht pointed out in his letter that he had been officially recognized in the GDR as "Verfolgte der Nazis" (persecuted by the Nazis). As a member of this group, Brecht enjoyed, as he pointed out, special consideration under the laws of the GDR.

Brecht might seem to have been overmatched in his fight with the bureaucracy of the GDR, but, fortuitously, it was Brecht rather than Ulbricht who was now in tune with a new note being struck in the Soviet Union. After Stalin's burial, the unthinkable happened. Despite objections by Malenkov and Beria, the first handful of prisoners were released from the gulag. Among them was the Jewish wife of Molotov, who had been sentenced on a trumped-up charge. Then, in early April, Moscow radio suddenly announced that the so-called Doctors' Plot that had electrified Moscow in the last months of Stalin's life had been made up by him and the NKVD, renamed in 1956 the KGB. It was also publicly admitted that the charges against the mainly Jewish doctors were the result of "illegal methods of investigation."⁵¹

But though Moscow began to admit massive errors under Stalin, the party apparat in the more distant socialist states was not yet ready to change. In early June, GDR building workers learned that the politburo intended to retroactively cut their wages. Such actions had been accepted before, but with stirrings of reform in Moscow, the workers in the GDR were emboldened to protest.

June 16, 1953, began like any ordinary day. Brecht, who had been out at Buckow with Käthe Rülicke, came back to participate in a Berliner Ensemble meeting. Weigel was off on a business trip to Budapest. Brecht's main concern was to send off a letter he had drafted the day before reminding Comrade Grotewohl that he was still waiting for his own theater building. Typically, part-carrot, part-stick, his missive pointed out that the West German press was playing up the differences that had become public between Brecht and the GDR government. By giving him the Schiffbauerdamm Theater, "my ties to our Republic would be documented most clearly."⁵²

That morning, party activist Robert Havemann, *Pro-Rektor* for student affairs at Humboldt University, was eating breakfast in his apartment (granted to him as a member of the privileged intelligentsia) on the seventh floor of a high-rise building at 39 Strausberger Platz in central Berlin. Hearing unusual noises,⁵³ Havemann went to his window and saw below a crowd of workers with a sign saying Down with the 10% Work Schedule Increase. Shocked, he drove at once to see the local district party head, Heinz Brandt, and the two men went to central party headquarters in the Leipziger Strasse, the old headquarters building of Goering's Luftwaffe. Standing on a table set up in front of the building, a construction worker led the crowd in a chant: "We want to speak with the government. Pieck and Grotewohl. Pieck and Grotewohl!"[54] Brandt tried to make his way forward. An old construction worker jumped on the table and said, "This is comrade Heinz Brandt, we want to hear him." The crowd quieting, Brandt shouted, "I have been given the assignment to communicate to you an important decision of the Politburo, the ten percent raise in the work production norms has been discontinued!" The response of the crowd was a mixture of triumph and anger, but anger soon dominated. The crowd yelled, "Where is the government?" and "Get rid of this government," and "We want free elections, we want freedom." Then, in a steady roar, they shouted over and over again, "We are workers, not slaves."[55]

That evening, at a hastily called meeting of the party leadership, Havemann was appalled that they had no idea what to do. Elisabeth Hauptmann was attending the meeting in an official capacity, and she and Havemann listened as the various party "leaders" of the "workers' state" declared that "no mob on the streets" would tell them what to do.[56]

News of events brought the head of Russian intelligence, Lavrenty Beria, to Berlin.[57] The night of June 16 was a night of extreme crisis, but GDR radio remained silent about the "strike" and broadcast mindless operettas. The next morning, the West Berlin radio station RIAS reported strikes throughout the GDR. Brecht was up early, listening to the radio and telephoning friends for news and advice. He immediately proposed to the government that the Ensemble take over GDR Radio for the entire day. Instead, the operettas continued.

At 8:00 A.M. Brecht tried to communicate directly with key officials in the GDR government and the commander of the Russian garrison. He dictated three letters. "Valued Comrade Semyonov," one read, "Please know that I stand with the forces of socialist progress at this historic moment."[58] A letter to Grotewohl read: "Dear Comrade Grotewohl, What can we in the Academy of Arts and from the Berliner Ensemble do? Will you speak on the radio? That would be good. We would be glad, as an introduction and epilogue, to do some songs and some recitations with Ernst Busch and other artists. In enduring solidarity with the Socialist Unity Party of Germany, Yours."[59] The third letter read: "Valued Comrade Ulbricht, History will pay its respects to the revolutionary impatience of the Socialist Unity Party of Germany. Large-scale discussions with the masses on the subject of the tempo at which socialism is being built would lead to a recognition . . . and consolidation of socialist achievements. I need to express to you at this moment my allegiance with the Socialist Unity Party of Germany. Yours."[60]

Brecht was scheduled to join Benno Besson in a rehearsal of *Don Juan*, but he decided to try to see firsthand what was happening on the streets of East Berlin. Among the workers with genuine grievances, he also thought he detected well-clad people from the West, the kind of agents provocateurs that he remembered from the closing days of Weimar.

While Beria ordered Russian tanks to prepare to move on June 17, a CIA cable from Berlin to Washington requested authority to distribute rifles to rioters. Washington replied that they should encourage expressions of sympathy, offer asylum as needed, but not distribute weapons. Meanwhile, the tanks and armored troop carriers of the Soviet Union, Britain, France, and the United States stood warming up in their different sectors of the divided city. In East Berlin, regular public transportation ground to a halt, preventing demonstrators from gathering in the central city to take part. Hundreds of thousands gathered anyway, and Russian tanks began to roll. Brecht watched the Russian advance from the Brandenburg Gate, near the dividing line between East and West Berlin. The Soviet tanks were preceded by a jeep, from which a high-ranking Soviet officer waved at the crowd. According to Manfred Wekwerth, Brecht's assistant and later a politburo member, Brecht waved back.

Also watching the Russian tanks was Heiner Müller. "It was simply interesting, a stage play,"[61] he said later with that flatness of affect that one almost universally finds among those who have lived for years within closed systems. Müller was later interrogated by the Stasi simply because he had been there that June day, but this did not seem to have affected him either; that was the way things were. Later, Heiner Müller (as he himself admitted in 1993) would find himself, like countless others, routinely cooperating with the Stasi.

When Brecht and Wekwerth returned to the Berliner Ensemble from the Stalinallee on June 17, Brecht called a staff meeting. In a highly unusual action, he addressed the Ensemble workers at length. According to Wekwerth, Brecht had little to say other than the obvious, the need for the government to have discussions with workers.[62] There was not, apparently, any hint of a larger view, of doing away with or fundamentally changing the government. The system and the world view still held. Nothing broke through the rituals of defense. The overwhelming evidence provided by the hundreds of thousands of workers themselves was replaced by marginal and schematic postulations about those far fewer people who might or might not have been agents provocateurs from the West. According to Brecht, June 17, 1953, was not so much an internal problem of an incompetent centralized economy and a paranoid Central Committee that treated workers terribly but the work of "doubtful elements," proto-Nazis from the West, supposedly encouraged by the CIA. The CIA was certainly capable of encouraging people and may have marginally done so in this case despite orders directly from Washington not to provide arms; but this did not address the central problem: the GDR government, like Brecht, was out of touch with the realities of workers.

After only sporadic street fighting and some spontaneous arson, the rebellion was quelled. The GDR intelligentsia had uniformly pledged allegiance to Ulbricht; the West had provided no support; and in the face of tanks and guns, the disgruntled workers walked back to their crowded homes. As Brecht drove back to his villa that evening in his private car, the streets of East Berlin were more eerily deserted than usual. On East German radio, the operettas continued even as West Berlin broadcast a constant stream of bulletins on massive uprisings that had occurred that day in even the furthest corners of the GDR.

43

"They Have Taken My Name out with Chemicals. Out of a Handwritten Letter of Lenin!" (1953–54)

After the uprising was put down by Russian tanks, at a meeting held at the Berliner Ensemble on June 24 at 9 A.M. and attended by Brecht, Weigel, and fifty-eight other members of the Ensemble, one worker complained about a salary of only 428 marks a month that was reduced to just 350 marks after taxes. He said he was out of money and coupons for food by the middle of each month.[1] Neither Brecht nor Weigel responded to this, but the actor Günter Naumann supported the previous speaker's point of view. Naumann pointed out that workers can only be provoked if they have something about which to be provoked. "I have very little money," said Naumann, "and have a sick wife and child, and can't get by on the money I make. In contrast, one sees people [here] who make 2 to 3,000 marks, and who then earn other money from film and radio jobs. They cannot understand what it is like for us and they don't even try. . . . The government has no understanding. These gentlemen are brought back and forth in their cars, and do not come into contact with workers. Therefore, when the workers demand that this government should be got rid of, they are right. Then we would not have any need for provocateurs to pump us up." At this, the Ensemble workers broke into spontaneous applause. But neither Brecht nor Weigel replied, though what had just been said was a direct comment on them as they were the ones who took home Ensemble salaries of 3,000 marks, and had other incomes from film and radio. And they, like the representatives of the Ulbricht government, went back and forth in cars, and had little contact with, or understanding of, the problems faced everyday by GDR workers. The meeting broke up at 11:15 with none of the key issues resolved. Brecht's salary remained at its previous level, roughly ten times that of most Ensemble workers. But his salary was only about 5 percent of his GDR income, which amounted altogether to hundreds of times that of a normal worker in that country and was supplemented by countless perks such as his car, his coal allowance, and his subsidized housing.

Four days after the East German uprising, Ulbricht published in *Neues Deutschland* only one sentence of the letter Brecht had sent him on June 17. This sentence was placed in the following carefully constructed context: "National Prize Laureate Bertolt Brecht has sent the General Secretary of the Central Committee of the Socialist Unity Party, Walter Ulbricht, a letter, in which he declared: 'I need to express to you at this moment my allegiance with the Socialist Unity Party of Germany.' " Almost pathetically, in the days and weeks that followed, Brecht would pull out of his pocket the complete text of his original letter and urge people to read what he had actually written. But, in fact, he had not written a great deal besides this one sentence.

Swiss newspaper correspondent Gody Suter recalled, "That was the only time I have seen him helpless, almost small, as he pulled out of his pocket the original—obviously well thumbed and produced many times—of that letter".[2] The red pencil of the party line had destroyed his cunning design and mercilessly exposed the poet, turning him, in the eyes of the West, into a loyal henchman of the executioners. His independent position, the platform of "inner opposition," was suddenly revealed as a grotesque illusion; a well-aimed blow by the party's paw had smashed the reputation Brecht had built up for himself in long, patient efforts.[3]

Feeling Ulbricht's publication of that one sentence made it seem as if he had betrayed GDR workers, Brecht wrote:

> *Last night I dreamed I saw fingers pointing at me*
> *As at a leper. They were gnarled and*
> *The nails were broken.*
> *"You don't know!" I yelled*
> *Guiltily.*[4]

Brecht kept his guilt to himself and a few friends. The "leper" poem was not published until after his death.

He did publish at the time a modest statement in *Neues Deutschland* two days after Ulbricht had published the edited version of Brecht's letter. This statement reads in part, "As it became clear to me on the morning of June 17 that the demonstration of workers was being misused for purposes of war, I expressed my allegiance to the Socialist Unity party." In fact, the available evidence suggests Brecht sent off his letter to Ulbricht before he had seen anything on the streets of Berlin that day. "I hope," continues the new letter, "now that the provocateurs have been isolated and their communication network destroyed, that workers who demonstrated in legitimate dissatisfaction are not placed on the same level, in order that the necessary, widespread discussions over mistakes made on every side will not be destroyed before they have begun."[5] If Brecht had evidence that the demonstration was "for purposes of war," or that any "communication network" between the supposed provocateurs existed, he did not reveal it then or later. In contrast to Brecht, when, at close range, Havemann saw crowds of angry construction workers on June 16 and 17, he believed their grievances were wholly legitimate, provoked by inept government policies, not by the CIA.

Immediately after the crisis, power radically shifted in the Soviet Union. Using Beria's absence in Berlin, Khrushchev lined up enough votes in the presidium to strip Beria of all offices. Upon his return, Beria was charged, among hundreds of thousands of crimes, with more than a hundred sexual offenses against female children. He was then summarily executed. By September, Khrushchev held the party first secretaryship. Under Khrushchev, Marshal Tito was no longer a pariah, and Mao was now treated with respect. Though Brecht told visitors that his whole existence "had been soured by the events of June 17," he gained leverage in the GDR in the aftermath of the uprising. Brecht campaigned a little less secretly now for more open kinds of socialism.

In the West, Brecht's support of Ulbricht on June 17 caused a continuing uproar, and a boycott began to cut into Suhrkamp's sales. Peter Suhrkamp wrote to ask Brecht to explain his position toward the workers' uprising. Brecht replied, "In the fight against war and against fascism, I stood and I stand at its [the government's] side."[6] Despite Brecht's declaration to Suhrkamp about the GDR's fight against fascism, privately he had doubts about the anti-Nazi nature of the GDR. Several poems published after his death refer to fascism in the GDR. Of the Soviet Zone in 1945, he wrote, "Under new commanders, the old Nazi apparat got under way again."[7] Brecht had claimed in the United States in 1943 that 99 percent of the German population opposed Hitler, but, after June 17, he seemed increasingly to see Nazis everywhere, both in West Germany and in the GDR. A 1954 diary entry records his suspicion that, if it were ten years earlier, his assistants would have gone straight to the Gestapo to turn him in.[8] But if he feared for his life in the GDR, he was so tarred by Ulbricht's clever release of his letter that the West would offer no haven for him. In one of the uneven poems gathered under the rubric of "Buckow Elegies," he says:

> I sit at the roadside.
> The chauffeur changes the tire.
> I am not happy about where I come from.
> I am not happy about where I am going.
> Why do I look at the changing of the tire
> With impatience?[9]

He also wrote an ironic poem noting failures by GDR bureaucrats, published in *Berliner Zeitung*:

> *What mistakes? Somehow they couldn't remember*
> *Any particular mistakes, hard as they might try. The things*
> *Brought forward, had,*
> *Not in fact been mistakes, for the Art Commission*
> *Had, after all, suppressed only worthless things, and even here*
> *Not precisely repressed them, just not fostered them.*[10]

Another poem directly responded to a poem that KuBa (Kurt Bartels), Ulbricht's right-hand man in ideological questions and secretary of the Writers' Union, had published right after the uprising. KuBa had written the GDR masses needed to win back the confidence of their government. Brecht's counterpoem ran:

> *After the uprising of June 17*
> *The secretary of the Writers' Union*
> *Had leaflets distributed in the Stalinallee*
> *In which it was said that the people*
> *Had lost the government's confidence*
> *Which it would only be able to regain*
> *By redoubling its efforts. In that case, would it*
> *Not be simpler if the government dissolved the people*
> *And elected another?*[11]

But this brilliantly ironic poem was not published in his lifetime. He gave it to friends, enhancing his status as a liberal. But by not publishing it (as he could easily have done in the West), he again failed to back the population of the GDR.

Though he was a member, Brecht did not attend a special meeting of the presidium of the Kulturbund held on July 3, 1953.[12] The meeting universally condemned the illegitimacy of many of the acts of the GDR government and the Russian masters during the uprising. Theodor Brugsch said that East Berlin's Humboldt University was not a German institution but a Russian one. Ernst Niekisch said the government repeatedly broke the laws of the GDR by repressing strikes that were allowed in the constitution. The government arrested elected deputies though they were protected by law and provided no right of habeas corpus. Protestant minister Karl Kleinschmidt observed that even when trials were held, the defense provided was a farce. Brecht neither attended this meeting nor seconded its sentiments in writing. With at least two Stasi operatives infiltrated into the most intimate Brecht circle (according to Martin Pohl), he only very rarely took any kind of public issue with Ulbricht.

Though he claimed privately to be unhappy with Ulbricht and his camarilla, Brecht seemed to be looking back at the good old days of socialism before Rosa Luxemburg's murder in 1919 and Lenin's death in 1924. He had a series of conversations at Buckow with the old comrades Herta Gordon and Jakob Walcher, whom Ulbricht had later kicked out of the party.[13] Walcher told Brecht of going to Moscow in 1920 as a delegate of the Communist party of Germany: "We had a conflict with the Russians at the time, and the German delegation wanted to leave. Soon after I arrived, there was a meeting with the Russian comrades chaired by Lenin." The "conflict with the Russians" was over the fact Luxemburg did not approve of creating the Comintern. For her, the Soviet Union was not "a dictatorship of the proletariat but a dictatorship of a handful of politicians."[14] Luxemburg feared that central command by a Moscow power elite would be globally spread by the Comintern. The conversation with Walcher and Gordon then turned to Lenin's leadership style. Brecht asked, "Did he answer things very quickly or did he not have ready answers?" "There was no talk then of infallibility and dogma," replied Walcher, "that a person does not make mistakes and already knows everything exactly and correctly." Herta Gordon recalled that at the end of World War I, "Klara [Zetkin] gave me a letter to deliver to Lenin and so I went there. I was there as he did everything. Then he put his stamp on it, with the hammer and sickle stamp, he'd just gotten it—it was exhibited in Paris at the World Exposition—and he wrote next to the stamp, that is the new stamp. But here at the Rosa Luxemburg Exposition they have taken my name out with chemicals. Out of a handwritten letter of Lenin!"[15]

Gordon's account confirmed what had been said for decades in Communist dissident circles, that historical documents were routinely falsified by Stalin to correspond to whatever current view of historical "reality" the party found suitable. Apparently inspired by Gordon and Walcher, Brecht thought briefly of doing a play on Rosa Luxemburg. But he soon dropped the idea, realizing it would be seen as an attack on the current rulers of the socialist states. A note on Lenin's leadership style survives in a poem titled "The Truth Unites."[16] In it, Lenin is honest and decisive, and admits problems and provides immediate concrete solutions. Unpublished in Brecht's lifetime, the poem was sent privately to Paul Wandel, a former government minister in the GDR who was fired by Ulbricht in 1952.

Whether or not Brecht was capable of writing first-rate poetry and new plays at this point in his life (and I think it clear his best writing days were long since over), the decision not to pursue the play on Luxemburg was overly cautious. By the fall of 1953, even the long-suppressed work of the "formalist" Meyerhold was being revived in Moscow. Khrushchev allowed the publication of the novel that named this era, Ilya Ehrenburg's *The Thaw*. At this time, in the GDR, nominal control of the arts was placed in the hands of a man Brecht had known since the Munich days, Johannes R. Becher. For Brecht, the shift was a move in the right ideological direction but only by a small increment. Becher, who had spent the Hitler years in purge-ridden Moscow, backed away from any initiatives that Ulbricht did not support.[17] The party apparatus remained self-protective, and the party continued to determine which books got published in what size editions.

While on the surface there was some improvement in the GDR, Brecht was now forced to deal with upheaval in his private life. Incensed once again by the unrelenting stream of his affairs, his frequent emotional neglect of her, and the contemptuous tone he often used with her on professional matters, Weigel moved out of their Weissensee villa. She rented her own apartment in the Reinhardtstrasse, taking much of her furniture with her. It was now her intention to divorce him.[18]

Predictably, Brecht began to search for ways to get Weigel back. He decided to find an apartment that he could persuade Weigel to share. With friends' help, he found a villa in Pankow, near where top party officials had their villas, of elegant proportions, set in its own park, and surrounded by lovely, old trees. However, it housed a kindergarten, and, despite his pull, he could not get it reassigned. Finally, he was forced to look at something less elegant but in downtown Berlin. It was big enough to be turned into two adjacent apartments. He wrote a carrot-and-stick note to Weigel, who was on vacation at Ahrenshoop: "Hill has found an apartment for me—a painter moved out and he seized it—it had already been promised and promised to a private firm (things like that are handled like raw eggs nowadays)." Describing the new place, Brecht continued: "Chausseestrasse, 2d block from the square that one crosses on the way to the Academy. Back part of the building (like the front part very old, two stories, from the 30s, that is to say, very lovely, somewhat impoverished, built for small people), one giant room with very large windows, a middle-size room, and a smaller room (not very small). . . . It will be free as of August 1." He continued with a list of plays for the Ensemble, presented as final rather than as suggestions for her, the head of the company, to consider. Finally, he mentioned that his servant, Frau Mutter, "does not cook badly." This was a hint that Weigel might be becoming unnecessary and turned the tables on her. Though she was the one who had threatened divorce, what if Brecht now did what she knew he had done before with

Marianne Zoff, filing for divorce as complainant before she could do so? What if he now gave one of several other contenders the legal status that Weigel had had since 1929? Weigel, an expert businesswoman, knew the works published under his name were worth millions. As his wife, she could legally expect a share in earnings from them. Any hint of divorce coming from him was a serious threat. He, a master of dosage in such matters, signed the letter in the way reserved for when Weigel was most disaffected: "dein" (yours).[19] Using the most conventional of gestures, when Weigel returned to Berlin, he presented her with a bouquet.

In September, Brecht got word that the Berliner Ensemble had been granted the old Schiffbauerdamm Theater. Writing to Berlau, Brecht mentioned both the new apartment he now expected to get and noted that the "Schiff," as the old theater was called, was supposed to be available as of January 1, 1954. His letter closed with a triply underlined "d." Berlau had spent the summer and fall of 1953 working on a production of Mother Courage at the Royal Theater in Copenhagen, where she had received her own training. His almost daily letters are not only signed with his underlined "d" but sometimes also with the abbreviation "e.p.e.p.," for "I am yours whether near or far." He also told her that because of the growing West German boycott of his work, Scandinavia was becoming very important.

By this time Brecht had begun to have his mail and his phone calls screened by whatever mistress or companion was currently in the highest favor. Knowing that another mistress would probably read her letters, Berlau hoped Hans Bunge would help. A gracious and seemingly tireless young man, a former Wehrmacht officer and Russian prisoner of war, Bunge had helped her on a production of The Mother in the GDR. She in turn had recommended Bunge be engaged in Berlin. Soon he was taken into Brecht's confidence while continuing his friendship with Berlau.

After a thirteen-year absence, Berlau was gradually reestablishing herself in Copenhagen. She had visited her sister, Edith, who was finally released after being locked up in an asylum since 1938. Edith successfully adjusted to life outside, married, and emigrated with her husband to Australia where she led a completely normal life. Berlau's former colleagues at Copenhagen's Royal Theater were now stars with the leading Scandinavian film company, Nordisk. Her former husband, Robert Lund, though now remarried, was kind and understanding. Noticing Ruth was not hearing well, he fitted her for the best hearing aid that money could buy. She wrote in her diary, "What a quiet, strange world were the last years for me—and I did not know that until yesterday."[20]

Only gradually was Berlau coming to realize that the promise she thought she had from Brecht, a promise of that longed-for time when they would really be together and would adopt a child, was never going to come. It was one thing to know this rationally but another not to dream when letters with "dein" and "e.p.e.p." arrived constantly. She dwelt on times she spent with him while he spent more and more of his time with younger women. Typical of Berlau's thoughts is the following:

> I stand and walk about with my burning, throbbing, wet cunt.
> And his lovely cock gets big and he puts it in elsewhere.
> He puts it in elsewhere.
>
> My eyes seek his, brown, burning and my eyes get wet
> Like my cunt, because his cock is not looking for mine
> But looks elsewhere.
> He puts it in elsewhere.
>
> Stiff in the air stands his cock, my mouth snaps it up
> And then my cunt.
> And it is only my heart that asks
> Where were you so long.
>
> As intelligent lovers, we both fuck not only with cunt and cock
> But with our brains.
> Don't be so small-minded, give me something too,
> Even an old dog is given a crust
> And, certainly, a mercy shot.[21]

Brecht was now living, in his way, with Rülicke while hustling Weigel to reestablish the facade that substituted for marriage. Between one-night stands, he was keeping constant pressure on Käthe Reichel and beginning a sexual relationship with Ensemble member Isot Kilian, the disaffected wife of his friend and defender, Marxist philosopher Wolfgang Harich.

Kilian's mother had been a Communist party official and her father had worked for a party publisher during the Weimar years.[22] The Gestapo arrested and beat her father in 1933, and he never fully recovered. Isot began acting lessons in Hamburg in 1940 and, while working on the side as a secretary during the Third Reich, completed her acting training in 1942. In 1948, she came to Berlin as part of a small, left-wing troupe with Egon Monk and auditioned for Brecht and Weigel. Kilian sang Carola Neher's and Lotte Lenya's lascivious songs from The Threepenny Opera. Weigel put Kilian on the payroll.

Kilian and her husband, together with their two small children, were given a four-room apartment in Luisenstrasse. Weigel arranged for special food coupons, furniture, and advances on salary. In the years to come, Weigel would try to insure that Brecht's interest in Kilian not be disturbed by other lovers. One day, when Kilian was seen arm-in-arm with the visiting Polish director Konrad Swinarski, Weigel had Swinarski brought to her office. There, "she discreetly explained the situation. It distracted the playwright when other men behaved intimately with the women he loved."[23]

Even as Brecht's affair with Reichel reached one of its jagged series of heights, he had started to single Kilian out. She was given the task of delivering Brecht's daily directorial notes to various actors in the company. Once, when such a note had not been delivered to Therese Giehse just before a premiere in 1951 (Egon Monk had pocketed the note as he did not want to have Giehse made too nervous by criticism just before the play's opening), Brecht had bellowed at Kilian so loudly in public that she had broken into tears.[24] At the rehearsal following this incident, Kilian deliberately sat a distance away. Veteran of "shooting birds who flew away," Brecht said: "Your daughter probably likes cigar boxes, I've brought some along, quite a few of them. I'll give them to the porter at the Rehearsal Building." Soon Kilian was sitting close to him again.

Theoretically, Wolfgang Harich, like Brecht, wanted to believe that monogamy and jealousy were holdovers from the presocialist past. And yet, theory or no, Harich was deeply hurt that this older man was alienating his wife's affections. Harich told others that he had remonstrated with Brecht, who replied, "Divorce her now and then marry her again in two years." According to Kilian, her husband had made up this story in order to try to embarrass Brecht and bring Isot to her senses,[25] but Brecht's pattern of replacing "lovers" every two years or so made the story plausible. Though Killian was aware of Brecht's pattern in relationships, she could not succeed in maintaining distance. If there were any signs of her drifting away, a small gift or a plum assignment at the Ensemble usually brought her back. Hans Bunge noticed that one of Brecht's controlling devices was to put a current sexual favorite in charge of a small fund to buy Brecht small items on a day-to-day basis.[26] Giving and withdrawing control of this fund allowed Brecht to play one lover against another.

In the fall of 1953, even if Brecht was beginning to put June 17 behind him, others remained disaffected. The promising sounds of preparing the Schiff for spring occupancy were offset by other, more discordant sounds. Martin Pohl was still in jail, having been sentenced in November 1953 to a four-year term on the invented charge of spying for American imperialists. In jail, he wrote to Brecht about the translations he was doing of medieval German poets. It would be over a year before Pohl was released. He immediately defected to the West. Therese Giehse was so disheartened by events in the GDR that she spoke of giving up acting altogether. Eisler had not recovered from the attacks on his *Faustus* opera and was threatening to move to Vienna. Caspar Neher, tired of Brecht's demands and Ulbricht's Goebbels-like artistic "standards," found working in the GDR difficult at best and impossible at worst.

After Brecht's delivery of the bouquet, he had managed to work out a rapprochement with Weigel. She agreed to separate apartments in the same building in the Chausseestrasse. The rebuilding necessary to make this possible moved forward in the fall of 1953. As the flats were being remodeled, Brecht and Weigel were both able to get away for a time. The strongly left-wing La Scala theater in Weigel's native Vienna (a theater now being managed by the person who had introduced Brecht and Weigel to one another, Arnolt Bronnen) had invited them to produce the Brecht group's *Mother*. In addition, Brecht had just worked out a deal with Wien Film for the rights to *Puntila*. The contract of September 3, 1953, made no mention of Wuolijoki's 50 percent interest.[27]

In Vienna, he was joined by Hauptmann. Brecht talked with Hanns Eisler about the possibility of expanding a play on a GDR subject. He wanted, he told Eisler, to have some scenes with music, modeling the new play on the experimental style of *Mother* or *The Measures Taken*. Brecht hoped to persuade the disaffected Eisler to return to work with him in Berlin. He spoke about including a full act in this new play on the events of June 17, another of the dreams he would not be able to realize.

The project had a long prior history, and Eisler had shown little enthusiasm for it before. It was to be a kind of exhortatory *Lehrstück* musical play about a GDR worker called Hans Garbe. Brecht had read about Garbe in 1949 when he was being publicized as the GDR equivalent of the Soviet Union's Stakhanovites, those workers who were supposed to have overproduced norms by several hundred percent. Quite possibly Brecht was unaware that however capable Garbe himself might have been as a worker, many of these widely publicized "achievements" were faked by party management.[28] All that was needed was a capable worker willing to be touted as a hero and paid accordingly. That person's production was overreported at the expense of co-workers. These usually faked "heroic results" were then reported in the party-controlled press. Having shown through the heroic worker that more was possible, this was then used to demand higher productivity from workers at large. It was, of course (though I doubt Brecht spotted the similarity), a system not unlike the one he had used for decades now to inflate his own writing "norms" and enhance his own income. Brecht interviewed the superworker, Hans Garbe. But he then generally left the project in Käthe Rülicke's hands, hoping she might be able to turn it into something usable. But Rülicke did not have the necessary creative skills, and what he got was a pedestrian book of Rülicke's notes rather than a usable play.

Brecht had hoped in one play to be able to tie the June 17 uprising to the story of Garbe. To give some excitement to the enterprise, Garbe, he thought, should rape someone and then try to bribe the state's attorney to get him off. Then, putting a violent fictional event in a factual frame, on June 17, Garbe's jealous co-workers would kill him. It would end almost in the style of Chinese Communist drama. A student of Garbe's would turn up after his death to carry the battle further as a triumphant Red Army liberated Garbe's old factory. According to surviving notes, Hanns Eisler was to write music in the style of *The Measures Taken*. In triple fortissimo, under the guns of the Red Army, choruses were to exhort workers on lessons to be learned from June 17 and the direction they should now take. Like the prewar *Fatzer* and *Joe Fleischhacker*, *Garbe* was inchoate and mercifully remained so. I believe it would have been a serious embarrassment had it ever been finished in the form and with the content Brecht envisaged. For Heiner Müller, the *Garbe* project was an example of Brecht's compulsion to organize plays around a central, usually terroristic protagonist. The old dream of a general representation of contemporary history in a play eluded Brecht as much as it ever had.

With neither of his two historical projects about Rosa Luxemburg or Garbe having come together, Brecht tinkered most of the year with an allegorical work to be called *Turandot, or the Congress of Whitewashers*. Set in a mythical China where cotton prices are manipulated by the emperor, the play's central concern is with "the Tuis," or intellectuals, who sell their ideas to the corrupt court. As the work was never finished, it is difficult to tell what the final point of all this was supposed to be. A number of hints in the play suggest it was supposed to be a commentary on GDR history, particularly the June 17 uprising. When, years after Brecht's death, it was staged in Zurich, Max Frisch thought it already "antiquated."[29]

By the time Brecht returned from Vienna to Berlin in November to begin rehearsals of his and Berlau's *Caucasian Chalk Circle*, he seemed to have lifted Hanns Eisler's spirits a bit. Eisler's disposition was helped further when the newly revamped Academy of Arts of the GDR voted to bring out his collected works. Now, despite all the attacks that had been mounted on him the previous spring, Eisler became convinced he would again be able to work in the GDR and now would not have to sacrifice the highly experimental side of his work that owed much to his teacher Arnold Schönberg.

Brecht and Weigel moved to their separate Chausseestrasse apartments. Measured by the standard of people very high in the GDR government, Wilhelm Pieck, for instance, who literally had a castle (satirized by Brecht in a private poem),[30] the Chausseestrasse complex might seem modest. But, by general standards of the population, the two apartments were large. It would eventually recapitulate his childhood home in Augsburg. Weigel's several rooms on the ground floor looked out on a small garden for her private use. His had high ceilings and large windows. He was free upstairs but had instant access below to Weigel's apartment, a museum piece of overstuffed or carved oak furniture, recalling the faraway and long ago of Augsburg's Bleichstrasse and Weigel's rich, comfortable bourgeois upbringing in imperial Vienna. At Weigel's, the language spoken was upper bourgeois with a Viennese lilt. The smell of rich food and the clutter of Biedermeier furniture spoke more of past than future.

The two of them would travel in their separate cars, often driven by chauffeurs, either to the country estate at Buckow or the rich plush of the turn-of-the-century Schiffbauerdamm Theater. The apartment took a great deal of coal to heat, but Brecht and Weigel were among those for whom such things were possible. On September 18, Herr Eichler, administrative director of the Academy wrote to the "Very Honored Herr Brecht" to say that "the Government of the German Democratic Republic, the Ministry of Trade and Allowances, has arranged to provide supplementary coal allowances for the intelligentsia and an assignment has been made. Of this amount we are holding coupons in readiness for you that will entitle you to receive 120 hundredweight."[31] In mid-winter, Eichler would write to say another one hundred hundredweight of coal were now available for Brecht. Eichler's February 1, 1954, letter ended with a cautionary note, "In order to reduce the chance of difficulties, we would be grateful to you if you would treat our giving you these coupons as a confidential matter."[32] Brecht was a veteran of maintaining such appearances and complied with Eichler's request. The general public was not to know of these perks, prizes, medals distributed in an endless, self-congratulatory round. Grateful for Brecht's support on June 17, the government not only authorized the new theater building and turned a blind eye to Brecht's using it as his private milk cow, but also gave Helene Weigel a prize with a cash sum of fifty thousand marks.

When the literature professor and longtime Brecht supporter Professor Hans Mayer came from Leipzig to visit Brecht at the new apartment, he remembers looking out of the window at the cemetery next door. Mayer, a man of encyclopedic memory, mentioned to Brecht that the cemetery below was full and that nobody else would ever be buried there. Brecht grinned and replied that "through pull," he expected to be able to get in anyway.

On November 15, when Brecht and Weigel had moved into their separate but adjacent apartments, Ruth Berlau was in Scandinavia. On a boat between Helsinki and Stockholm, she typed a long piece of writing, part diary entry and part letter, addressed to a figure that combines Ovid and Brecht: "I was outside, dear Bertolt, looking at Cassiopeia. How lovely it is at sea. Do you remember our long sea journeys? Your thin blue trousers. The Chinese pyjamas that you bought me in Manila and that you said I was only to wear when I was with you. How I would get angry if you took a bath without telling me: I always wanted to see more of your body as your cock is so lovely. Just now, when I was in Finland, I remembered so clearly our big white tent and the woods where we made love. Such a long time, so many years, Bertolt, since you held me lovingly in your arms. I went back out on deck again to shake my fist at Cassiopeia that so relentlessly follows me.

"I curse at Ovid too, although I have talked with him a lot during this night at sea—but I must say that I think that he is wrong. 'If he cheats on you, so what, what have you actually lost? You get everything back again. Even if he has sheathed it with thousands, you still have lost nothing. The steel goes in and out, and the sharpening stone is itself worn away. Men keep their potency, it is not lessened by use. Believe me!' Oh, Ovid, you old fool! And you want me to learn your poems by heart so you will not be forgotten? You'd be pleased with yourself, Ovid, if we women were to sing: Ovid was our teacher. Everything that you say, however, I already know since long, long ago. But why didn't you write that we should be able to cheat with thousands of lovers. Why did you not teach us women to cheat also? Why are we supposed to experience what you call 'this great pleasure' only when we are in love? Of course, I would have liked to have slept with you, Ovid. I am sure you would have been wonderful in bed, but I find myself screaming aloud: why are there so few sensitive men? You say that we should speak to one another even at the peak of pleasure, but what are we to do when the members of your sex tell us the stupidest things, where is my pleasure then? And I believe that the self-confident way in which you claim to have been so good in bed, that kind of talk disturbs me.

"And yet perhaps Ovid is right. I took it so seriously when he slept with others. First, he doesn't have enough potency, and I won't get him at all if he sleeps with thousands of others. Second, Bertolt changes so much, him, the one who said to me that I was not allowed to sleep with anyone else (yes, when I reached forty he said to me one day that he didn't give a shit anymore if I slept with others) because he was worried that if I slept with other men my feelings toward him would change. But he is the one who has changed. He now even lets the other one get him his cigars, and he goes shopping with her. Yes, he has taken away even my smallest pleasures. I am a shattered human being that's for sure, and it is his lies that have contributed to my destruction. Too many lies, horrible ones. And we were friends, FRIENDS! only Cassiopeia has survived all this untouched—unreachable, no dirt, no lies, no scorn can reach her. The cold calls to my burning lap. Ute has become superfluous."[33]

She swung between thoughts of suicide and of returning to Berlin, writing as three separate people. Her letter ends: "Write to me at once please in the enclosed envelope a few words, dear, dear Bertolt and have Bunge send it off immediately. Write to tell me where you would most like to meet me? Certainly you will want to see me in the Charité-strasse—at the airport you can certainly not pick me up? Certainly my arrival will be in the middle of a rehearsal or some meeting, and I want to have you for a whole hour so that I can report to you (Ute smiles, be quiet, Ute, Ruth will quietly report and you will stay quiet though it is permitted that you get wet, no one can forbid anyone that. So goodnight—great, distant master—beloved Brecht. Your creature, Ute, Ruth."[34]

While Berlau, her deteriorating mental and physical health permitting, staged Brecht abroad, Hauptmann published old plays and created new ones for Brecht in Berlin. Working with the French-Swiss director Benno Besson, she completed the translation-adaptation of Molière's *Don Juan*. As an indication of Brecht's noninvolvement in its creation, she presented him with a copy of the play on the day of the premiere.[35] To this day, despite evidence in print for twenty years, Suhrkamp still publishes it as a Brecht play.[36]

Hauptmann tried to explain to Brecht in late 1953 how financially and psychologically difficult her situation was while trying to exist in his shadow as honors were showered on him for their work and she was ignored and poorly paid. Mixing German, French, and English, she wrote:

Lieber Brecht:

Too bad. Anarchy is no good. *Jours fixes, après midi fixes, soirs fixes.* Everything *fixe*—Letter: I am neither a lady of leisure nor a call girl. [The letter here switches to German.] As a matter of fact I must work. Not always doing what I want but nevertheless working. Perhaps I can again achieve a situation where I work on what I want.

That brings me to the point where I will show you in figures what my working conditions look like purely in financial terms. I am leaving your greatness and fame out of the game here. 1953, 1 - 3rd quarter, Essays, under which are included two new works (*Carrar* and *Good Person*) [*Señora Carrar's Rifles* and *The Good Woman of Setzuan*)]

October	445.90
Berliner Ensemble	<u>250.00</u>
	695.90

Taxes minus 14%

In addition, *Volpone* Brecht-Besson: 4 days in Vienna (I would very much have liked to have stayed longer), a warm winter overcoat (finally). I paid for the journey to and from Vienna myself. That the income from Suhrkamp has disappeared is due to Adenauer. 1953 was a year in which I was quite ill for half the year with a hospital stay and an operation; that is to say, for half the year I could hardly work at all. Unfortunately, I was supported by nobody, got no special treatment, was not given prizes, not singled out in any way, altogether never praised, something which is hard to take over the long run, as I am only a human being.

To create plays as though I were bringing in groceries and [as though] working on them is a pleasure; that I could not, due to other work, come to the *Caucasian Chalk Circle* and the *Millet for the Outlaws* rehearsals was no fun; also, many of the translations I am forced to do are no fun either.

But it is through [here the text switches from German to English] translations, articles, etc., I have managed to earn this year about 12,000 marks; it was not enough. And I have to change this. I am not against the good things of life, and I love to make small presents. So I have to change my way of working and probably that of living.

What I want to say is this: in spite of the fact that you are now living around the corner, we are drifting more and more apart because of anarchy and *Lebensunterhalt* [roughly, your style of living].

I thought I [would] put this in writing. Although I am afraid it may make interesting reading for others besides yourself.

No oral or written answer or commentary requested. B[ess].[37]

Hauptmann's letter was as futile as the others she had written to both Brecht and Weigel. But, as a party member, she knew she had few options. Publicly stating that Brecht regularly stole her work would provide grist for the Western anti-Communist mill. So, she kept her thoughts as private as her mental state would permit.

For Hauptmann, there was irony in her knowledge of the system of privilege behind the socialist facade. She was herself a cog in the wheel of the machine that permitted this to happen. By 1953, she was a member of the Parteiaktiv of Berlin, the group that acted in lieu of the old, bourgeois institution of a parliament. But although it was a parliament of sorts, surely she was aware it was controlled by Ulbricht's Central Committee. The relationship of the Parteiaktiv to the Central Committee resembled that of the Comrades and the Moscow Control Chorus in *The Measures Taken.* Dominating courts, newspapers, radio, banks, agriculture, industry, and unions as fully *gleichgeschaltet* now as they had been in Germany under Hitler and in the Soviet Union under Stalin, the Central Committee did no wrong. How could Hauptmann complain about her subservient status without drawing Western attention to an apparatus that supported the obviously exploitative behavior of the socialist icon Bertolt Brecht?

44

"Should I Wander around like a Wreck, Muttering His Poems to the Survivors?" (1954–55)

By late 1953 and early 1954, Brecht's official position within the GDR seemed to have switched 180 degrees. The year before, he had been under attack by Walter Ulbricht, but after the uprising, he was made a member of the Artistic Council of the Ministry of Culture and then vice-president of the German Academy of Arts. The newly refurbished Schiffbauerdamm Theater was given to him with a massive annual subsidy. Though Weigel took care of the daily administration, Brecht received letters from the business manager asking whether to push Frau Reppel's salary up to the 1,000 marks she wanted or to stop the bidding at 900, whether Herr Schwabe should be raised from 1,200 to 1,300, or whether to negotiate with Herr Waldmann or fire him.[1]

The Ensemble had a budget of three million marks. It took in only one-sixth of its income at the box office; the rest came from the state. The money was used to support a staff of 212 people, including fifty-five actors. The actress Angelika Hurwicz speaks of the luxuriousness that the company enjoyed: rehearsals lasting up to a full year, for instance, or props in historical plays that looked like museum pieces.

The building the company took over in March 1954 provided few hints that the twentieth-century theater was being remade here. Flanking the traditional proscenium arch, newly regilded, bare-chested titans stared at a restored theater that was the standard of theater design during the reign of Kaiser Wilhelm. Arranged hierarchically under the imperial eagle, like the society that the theater mirrored, were tier after tier of balconies. With its virtually unlimited rehearsal time, Ensemble performances could be polished to a dazzling gleam. Brecht began to think of conquering a wider world. He wanted to take the Ensemble abroad, to enter into competition with the best world theater. The venue he chose for this was the 1954 Paris summer International Festival of Dramatic Art. By the time the company would leave for Paris, *Don Juan*, directed by Benno Besson, and a reworked *Mother Courage*, mainly directed by Brecht, would run with clockwork precision.

For Helene Weigel, the late spring of 1954 was hectic. Not only was she the administrative head of the company but she was the lead actress as well. To her fell the responsibility for sorting out bureaucratic tangles so the Ensemble could take two major productions to the world competition in Paris, with a stopover in Brussels. In addition, rehearsals for *The Caucasian Chalk Circle*, with its huge cast, needed to be scheduled for an opening the following fall. Weigel arranged passports and visas not only for all the actors and lovers chosen to go abroad but, at Brecht's insistence, for the company's stage technicians and costumers as well. It was then discovered that the Paris festival theater did not have a turntable stage, and Brecht demanded that a seventy-five-ton "portable" turntable stage would have to be installed at the Théâtre Sarah-Bernhardt for the four-day run.

Just weeks before the Berliner Ensemble left for Paris, a historical event occurred that prepared the way for the French opening. After years of trying to hold Vietnam, France was finally forced to leave Vietnam when she was defeated at the battle of Dien Bien Phu. The play that had dazzled George Steiner and Eric Bentley in Berlin was just as effective in a Paris that watched the return from Vietnam of the dead, the wounded, and the survivors. *L'Information* said Brecht was "the theater for which we have so long waited, that we all have sought." *Le Monde* compared the beauty of the staging to the work of Callot, the Le Nains brothers, and Georges de la Tour. The Ensemble received the first prize at the Paris festival for best play. Brecht, as both playwright and director, would now be spoken of as perhaps the greatest practitioner of theater art in the modern world. From now on, the Schiff would become the place of pilgrimage that the Moscow Art Theater or Meyerhold's Moscow theater once had been. Brecht, ostensibly on the side of peace and the angels, became the master to whom anyone in theater circles with a claim to being artistically or politically progressive would bow.

At Paris press conferences, Brecht not only took all the credit for *Mother Courage*, where he was in fact the main director, but also for Besson's *Don Juan*. Besson was furious that neither his direction nor his and Hauptmann's writing was recognized. When they got back to Berlin, Besson demanded that Brecht write to at least one Paris critic about Besson's role. Berlau, of course, had helped in the early development of *Mother Courage* (as had the forgotten Steffin), as well as in the first postwar stagings of the play, and had provided the model books used for the new production. But she was not on Weigel's list of invitees. Berlau went anyway, traveling with her Danish passport and paying her own way.

Less lucky was Käthe Reichel. She did not have a foreign passport and foreign currency to get herself there. Since Brecht had insisted that his latest special favorite, Isot Kilian, make the trip on the Ensemble tab, as a kind of consolation prize, Reichel was allowed to stay at the Buckow lakeside estate while Brecht was away. Ruth Berlau sent her a report from Paris. Afterward, Reichel wrote:

Dear Ruth,

Many thanks for your lovely letter from Paris, I was very pleased. I am happy to hear everything and get everything told to me. Brecht unfortunately never talks about it when he has been off somewhere. In Berlin, quite by chance, I spent a very happy evening with Eisler and with Mr. and Mrs. Kantorowitsch (or something like that). How pleasant it is to sit with friendly people a little bit and to talk about things, with everything unforced, natural and friendly, I get so happy and am pleased to be alive, because they have remained human beings. Also, I must tell you, that the enthusiasm with which Eisler spoke of my role as the Governor's Wife [in *The Caucasian Chalk Circle*] did me a lot of good, and I need that so much because the enmities within the Ensemble, which are blessed by our Lord, cause me deep pain. I look forward to seeing you in Buckow and wanted to let you know quickly that there are no potatoes to be had here (neither new ones nor old), so get yourself a few, and there are no lemons either. On the 6th I am going to Berlin to pick up my paycheck, and I could also bring you yours? Until we see one another again, greetings, Your small Kattrin."[2]

By this time, Berlau and Reichel were helping one another in much the way that Fleisser and Hauptmann had tried to do in the Weimar years. Even now, Hauptmann had tried to help those she saw suffering in the way she had herself for so many years. On Ruth's birthday, Hauptmann wrote: "Dear Ruth, From a small plum tree that only wants to do a little bit for us, here are four (4) BIRTHDAY PLUMS with many hearty wishes, Elisabeth."[3]

Often, Reichel and Berlau compared the pain of the circumstances in which they found themselves. They could not ignore the stream of casual bedfellows, star fuckers, and the growing number of sex partners available to the quintessential casting-couch director. His power and prestige, particularly with the success in Paris, grew daily. His stage methods were now recognized as a model for the world to follow. The fact that they could not be followed, as his "simple" effects were achieved at a staggering cost that was totally beyond the resources of theaters in nontotalitarian countries, did not prevent people coming to study with him.

The situation was startlingly similar to the political entities or religions led by charismatic, often sexually alluring personalities that we encounter with extraordinary frequency, and usually with catastrophic results, throughout the twentieth century. The Berliner Ensemble under Brecht was a box within a box. It existed within the closed system of the GDR itself, which, in turn, was part of a larger closed system of socialist bloc states directed in all major particulars by Moscow. The system as a whole preached a teleology of peaceful world conquest. To leave the socialist system was to risk psychic annihilation, a risk that most people prior to glasnost simply could not bring themselves to take.

Similarly, to be allowed to stay within Brecht's orbit was to feel one was contributing to the creation of plays and theatrical productions acknowledged to be world class. As he privately opposed some of the worst aspects of Stalinism and could be devastatingly charming, he appeared vastly more attractive than the Ulbricht camarilla. The temptation to remain part of this world was very great indeed. If one did manage to get up the resolve to leave, Brecht, in old age as in youth, "shot at birds that tried to get away."[4] The Danish psychologist Peter Elsass, in his study of strategies for survival, warns, "To place oneself in a closed system without self-criticism and without interaction with one's opponents is to risk self-dissolution." Such systems are designed to reduce the sense of self-worth of everyone other than the master. Persons within such systems, often as individuals or as class victims of deprivation and/or sexual violation, seem almost wholly unable to summon the will to attempt escape.

Drama offstage at the Ensemble was often as intense as on. One day, Brecht came into his workroom to find Käthe Reichel on his casting couch with a young man lying next to her. Brecht was furious and accused her of "besmearing the workplace with affairs with second-best men."[5] Then, echoing what he had written of Marianne Zoff in his twenties, he noted of Reichel in his diary: "I find I have lost all respect for her; she seems cheap to me. Not without some feeling of relief, I confirm that I have lost all feeling of being in love with her." As she now, in Brecht's view, tried to get back into his graces, he remained professionally polite but privately inaccessible. He used Reichel's transgression to openly advance his affair with Kilian.

To the inner circle with its patterns of dominance and submission was now added another jealous observer who would try to get between Brecht and any other visitor, sitting for hours at his feet gazing at him lovingly. Nobody seems to know for sure when this latest admirer, a German shepherd dog called Rolf, first arrived; but he and Brecht were quickly inseparable. Berlau wondered as she saw them together whether Rolf was the only living creature Brecht trusted and with whom he really wanted to be.

Though Kilian played minor parts on stage, for a time she had the lead role in Brecht's rigidly scheduled personal life. With Brecht's help, in 1954 she moved away from the still-jealous Harich and got her own apartment. On the day of the move, Brecht sent her a small trunk. It contained a vase, some Russian wine, curtains, nails, and a hammer.[6] She was to hang curtains immediately. He also brought her vitamin C tablets, bought in West Berlin. From her new place, Kilian could walk up the street with her two children to call on Brecht. After a few minutes of visiting, she would leave again with the children, taking Rolf for a walk. When Brecht went to Buckow with Rülicke in the late summer, leaving Kilian in Berlin, he called and wrote almost daily in his routine manner. He sent her an occasional poem and urged her to do the impossible, conceal their relationship.

On September 17, Brecht met with the Russian composer Dimitri Shostakovich and Vladimir Pozner to discuss work on a Joris Iven's film *Song of the Rivers*. The very fact that Shostakovich was allowed to go abroad to work on a joint project was cause for rejoicing in dissident intellectual circles. His magnificent (pre–socialist realist) opera of 1934, *Lady Macbeth of Mtsensk,* had been attacked by Stalin for not being "optimistic in spirit and popular in tone." As a result, Shostakovich had had no commissions for years, no productions of his work, and he expected at any time to be "taken." He was one of the few survivors.

With the Paris triumph confirming his monarchy of the modern stage, Brecht had even less time for Berlau, Steffin's relatives, Hauptmann, or even for Weigel or Reichel. He now held court for visitors from every part of the globe. With his increased fame came those who wanted to share his bed, despite the fact that he had now grown flaccid and frequently suffered from urinary tract ailments. What he still had was the allure of an international star, and power to make or break careers.

Every word of the master was now being written down for posterity. When Brecht resumed rehearsals of *The Caucasian Chalk Circle*, Hans Bunge recorded everything and transcribed it for Brecht to edit later. Bunge's recordings and his own observations provide a very complete record of what happened throughout the full year that it took to prepare this production with Brecht as the main director but with Berlau, Monk, and Wekwerth taking on directorial responsibilities with the sprawling cast.

In the fall of 1954, Bunge saw Brecht's personal life spill over into the production. Brecht was trying to work as a director while what was going on between Brecht and Reichel, Rülicke, Kilian, and the one-night stands was all too obvious. Kilian was forced to share an office with her rival, Rülicke. Reichel, playing the Governor's Wife in *Chalk Circle*, was becoming more and more desperate as Brecht paid attention to Rülicke and Kilian. Reichel demanded he pay more attention to her, or, as she said, have cause for regret. When he continued to ignore her, she attempted suicide. She was rushed, like Berlau before her, to the Charité. There she was placed on the psychiatric ward under Brecht's friend and admirer Professor Brugsch.

Reichel's hospitalization seemed to threaten the opening of the play, but Weigel took over Reichel's role in a matter of days, reshaping it in her own playing style. Reichel had grown up in a poor household without servants of any kind; while Weigel had had servants virtually her whole life and had managed the Ensemble for half a decade. The older actress immediately grasped the role, rapping out orders in a cold, peremptory manner that was thoroughly convincing.

Michel's adoptive mother was played by Angelika Hurwicz, the famous Kattrin. Hurwicz's role in *The Caucasian Chalk Circle* was as carefully built in months of rehearsals as that of anyone who worked with Stanislavsky, although from a different approach. From the rehearsal transcripts, we learn that at one point Brecht noticed that Hurwicz, on her own initiative, had reduced the size of the bundle she carried as she fled with baby Michel. Brecht asked her why the bundle was smaller. Hurwicz replied: "That's only logical. Originally, I took a whole bunch of things from the place. But in the meantime I have had to use things for the baby out of my bundle. Besides that, because it is now cold, I am wearing a shawl around my shoulders, and that shawl was in my bundle before. Besides that, I have had to exchange pieces of clothing [to get things] for the baby. Therefore the bundle must have gotten smaller and I am trying to show that realistically."[7] To this Brecht responded: "You are starting from a position that logical reflection must always be right. But that is by no means the case. Here, for instance, this is based on the presupposition that Grusha hasn't stolen anything during her flight. Probably this would be argued on the basis of Grusha's 'character,' that for her stealing would be out of the question. And that is dangerous. One should never start out on the basis of a figure's character because a person has no character. For Grusha, given the circumstances under which she lives, the times even demand that she steal, at least when it's essential, and this reinforces her 'positive character.' It is consistent with the main thrust of the play to show what it costs Grusha to take care of the child. So, in future, we will make the bundle bigger again, perhaps even making it bigger than it is at the beginning. There is, of course, the question of whether our spectators will recognize the background of this measure, but that is not so important. If you think about it, and you could do that anyway if the bundle were smaller, perhaps you will come to a similar conclusion. What is good about what we are doing is that we are creating the basis for a many-layered person, which Grusha is. And what is of interest, at least for the directing staff and all those who think this through with us, is the conscious use of contradiction."

This "conscious use of contradiction" is, I believe, central to Brecht's work as a director at every stage of his career. If one has built up in one rehearsal "good qualities" in Grusha, then one must be sure to go back to add layers of what some might see as less positive qualities. Likewise, if one has stressed slowness and "breaks" in one rehearsal, then one must be sure to build up speed and continuity in other rehearsals. And as one does this, one must not in any way resolve the contradictions inherent in the method. Complex individuals and complex stage action within the Brechtian stage universe is a composite of multiple, contradictory layers. It is this quality, I believe, that Andrzej Wirth was trying to describe when he writes of the "stereoscopic nature" of Brecht's work. The physics of stereoscopy is that each eye sees different a thing, not the same thing, and it is the mental superimposition of one image over another that produces depth. As in the case of Grusha and her bundle, it is the simultaneous difference of unresolved contradictions that gives the characters much of their depth and three-dimensionality.

The highly contradictory role of the crook-judge Azdak was given to the German singer and actor Ernst Busch, who had appeared in the Pabst film *The Threepenny Opera*. Just how dedicated Brecht was to the idea of conscious use of contradiction is revealed in a remark Brecht later made to Eric Bentley about Busch's playing of Azdak. Even after a year of rehearsals in the part, Brecht still felt "the whole tragic side of the role" was missing.[8] For Brecht, apparently, the role of Azdak should be played so that the comic and the tragic is simultaneously present. The 284 pages of transcript of *Chalk Circle* rehearsals make plain why the rehearsals needed almost a full year. It was essential to Brecht's working method as a director that he have time to develop all possible contradictions of persons and plot, and then have time to speed and polish continuity between the contradictory parts so that the contradictions become virtually invisible at the conscious level to the spectator who sees the play only once. As Brecht insisted to Bunge (describing himself as aptly as the stage characters he was directing), "People don't act on the basis of only one motive but always out of various motives that are in part contradictory."[9]

The conscious guiding model for the production as a whole was the nativity scene that had been brought out every Christmas in Brecht's childhood home in Augsburg. Scenes were to combine and contrast a kind of mangerlike simplicity with the rich gaudiness of the three kings who visit the child. Central to the production concept of *Chalk Circle* (and this can be said also of the Ensemble *Mother Courage* and *Galileo*) is that there is no "fourth wall," no attempt to pretend that the performance is real life caught in the act. It is clearly a theatrical representation of life, one that invites audiences to piece together its "imperfections with their own thoughts" (to paraphrase the prologue to Shakespeare's *Henry V*). Brecht and the designer Karl von Appen discussed the fact that this approach had more in common with the Shakespearean stage and Chinese stage practices than it did with the highly technological stage Brecht had frequently called for (though never used) in the 1920s.

Dessau was brought in to do the music. Brecht asked for music that tied the play together, rapidly driving the action forward from one scene to the next. Instead of stressing divisions between scenes as the early Brecht theories had called for, the demand now was for continuity. To further the continuity, Brecht worked with von Appen so that set segments could be taken on and off without stopping the turntable stage between scenes. Each scene had a painted backdrop that was deliberately unweighted at the bottom so that when it was dropped from the flies it would billow down with a pleasing aesthetic effect. Against a backdrop of the Northern Mountains, as Grusha flees with the child, she is made to appear to be moving very rapidly by having the scenery move toward her on the turntable stage. The curtain that Neher had invented in the Weimar years was dispensed with altogether. Brecht chose to use a regular curtain, which was lowered nine times during the performance.

Generally absent from the production was the technical vocabulary that many people today think essential to understanding and staging Brecht. As the photographer Gerda Goedhart and the actress Angelika Hurwicz remember the rehearsals, "That long-awaited word 'Verfremdung' was used only once during the *Chalk Circle* rehearsals."[10] The actors were asked at one point to speak their lines in the third person, but this was used only to aid them in understanding their lines. As soon as they had grasped the meaning, they went back to rapid, first-person delivery.

When *Chalk Circle* opened on October 7, 1954, it had reached a dazzling level of polish and seamless continuity. At the technical rehearsals, Brecht literally stood with a stopwatch, insisting that the scene changes be made at breakneck speed. In contradiction to his "epic" theory of coolness and distance, every trick of heightening audience suspense was used. Would Grusha and her baby manage to cross a breaking bridge before the pursuing soldiers caught her? Would Azdak lose his judgeship before he could help Grusha? Would the obviously corrupt judge who had taken a bribe from the grasping Governor's Wife dare now to give the child to Grusha? The spectator was drawn deeply into the action and the drama of the play's conclusion, the test of the "real" mother in the circle of chalk. Not by accident did the poses of Angelika Hurwicz holding her tiny baby to her breast suggest the timeless beauty and drama of the Madonna and Child, a peasant Mary fleeing from a brutal Herod.

Weigel, claiming that Berlau was a drunk who might disturb Brecht at rehearsals, kept her away from the theater whenever possible. Her contribution to the text was of course ignored. But Brecht had her privately rehearse actors in a number of the smaller parts for *Chalk Circle* and plied her daily with notes and phone calls. Berlau began to take extensive notes on what he said in these phone calls.

A few weeks after *Chalk Circle* had opened and she, Brecht, and a number of other staff members had gone to Buckow for a bit of a vacation, Berlau wrote:

I am in the Tower at Buckow which Brecht has made available to me. He himself is living in his Garden House. We don't have any direct telephone connection. But my neighbor has a telephone, so I can reach Brecht that way. All day long I have waited for him, thinking over his usual habits. He could have come at nine in the morning, if he was bored—he did not come. He could have come at eleven, after he had done some work—he did not come. Then he could have come at four in the afternoon after his siesta—he did not come. Now perhaps he will come by quickly just before he has his supper? No. Now I call him up.
Him: You're here? I didn't know if you'd already left . . .
Me: No . . . what are you up to?
Him: I'm digging around in old manuscripts . . . it has to be done sometime . . .
Me: Yes . . . when are you driving back to Berlin?
Him: Tomorrow . . . tomorrow early . . . how's the stove?
Me: Wonderful. A great stove. Starts right away and lasts a long time . . .
Him: Is the bath working?
Me: Yes. It's all working.
Him: I tried to call, but nobody was there.
Me: My neighbors were away on Saturday and Sunday. They just came back.
Him: I thought maybe you'd gone out for a walk, but . . . I could have you driven to Strausberg tomorrow. Would that help you?
Me: A lot. The journey here was horrible.

Him: Yes I know . . . I know . . .
Me: There's probably no room in the back of your car?
Him: Ha, my car? My car isn't even here, and the other one is full of people.
Me: OK, good, when can the chauffeur pick me up?
Him: Eight o'clock.
Me: I'm very glad of that. Then I'll see you tomorrow at the office.
Him: Yes, I'll go directly to the office and spend the whole morning there.
Me: There was something I wanted to show you. Good night . . .
Him: Good night, Ruth.
It is ten minutes on foot and two minutes by car—that is the distance between our two houses. But oceans separate us. As I went back to my tower after this conversation, the moon was illuminating two slender poplar trees, and the strophe came to mind: "our never-ending conversation, like a conversation between two poplars, our conversation of many years is silenced . . ." "You should be happy when I have fun," he said to me. Am I frigid? Only a frigid woman could carry out this instruction—pleased and rejoicing when he kisses others. He also wrote to me: "those who love one another are great people . . ." Why does he then kick something that is great on account of three or four female kids?[11]

On November 7, 1954, the conversation was lengthy and turned partly around thirty pages of autobiographical jottings she had given Brecht to read. As usual, with no preamble, the conversation began as follows:

Him: I read it . . . the thirty pages.
Me: OK, does it have any value to continue?
Him: Absolutely . . . but I would avoid the tragic.
Me: I can cut that out.
Him: As long as you describe things, it is very lovely. But the tragic becomes novelistic-conventional.
Me: Already cut.
Him: And that business of the silk shirt in Denmark, the one you almost stole . . . there what you must do is describe how I'm dressed otherwise. Otherwise, it sounds so elegant . . . with his silk shirts . . .
Me: But that is the only thing I'm stealing. That isn't tragic, I mean it to be funny.

Him: Yes, but why is it a silk shirt that is lying there . . .

Me: Tell me, why do you wear silk shirts. Do they feel comfortable next to your skin?

Him: Murmurings.

Me: Now you've had some silk shirts tailored for you again.

Him: I don't know, but it strikes me as being too elegant. Write a page about how I'm dressed. And it's a shame that you don't describe my workroom at Skovsbostrand.

Me: At that place where I now am in the manuscript, I'd not yet been in your workroom.

Him: That point where Helli goes off with the architect . . .

Me: But I wasn't part of that. Couldn't you write out for me on half a page what your workroom looked like?

Him: I'll try to do it . . . You must also write why I am great . . .[12]

"The conversation," concludes Berlau, "ended in the usual way: 'I'll call later . . . ,' 'many thanks . . . ' and so on. I sat back. What went through my head had not gone over the telephone wires. I should describe why he is great? But if somebody is reading this, they would already know why Bertolt Brecht was great. My god, is he still frightened that he could be forgotten . . . ? Once, in Denmark, he asked me to learn his poems by heart. Was he already thinking about the atomic bomb? Should I wander around like a wreck, muttering his poems to the survivors?"

As is clear from these notes, Berlau, when sober, recognized that for all his brilliant public successes now, his basic insecurity remained. He needed to be told by as many people as possible of his greatness, and he constantly needed to reshape the past to the image he wished to promote of himself. Paradoxically, it often seems that the appearance of the insecure child in him brings Berlau back. They shared "that desperate longing."[13] Like many others who have been abused in childhood, she recognized and responded to the bottomless depths of his neediness. He expressed his needs and fears only in private; in public, he seemed a tower of strength. Berlau, who saw no need to hide her fears and desires in private or in public, would be seen after one of her public outbursts as weak, hysterical, and dependent. Since their first meeting, she had been vital to his work. The model books on productions give us our primary sense of Brecht theater from the mid-thirties to the mid-fifties, and they are still in daily use. She never had the confidence to insist he not mix cruelty with what he still sometimes called love.

The case of Käthe Reichel shows similarities to that of Ruth Berlau. She too risked showing in public what she felt privately. She too sometimes dared challenge the master and was made to pay dearly for doing so. *Chalk Circle* was rehearsed without her while she was held at the Charité. Apparently not aware as yet that Weigel had taken over her big role, she wrote a biting letter to Brecht's admirer, the man ostensibly treating her, Professor Brugsch:

> Very Honored Professor Brugsch,
> You will hear today my views on what the available possibilities are for my immediate future, about that which is planned for me. Now, as I am neither rich nor powerful, I am absolutely not in a position to permit myself to have my own opinion. And I cannot permit myself any kind of contradiction, because for that the prices are much, much higher, one would have to be a monopolist—but I am proletarian and therefore unable to pay. Not only that, but I am also bankrupt. For that reason, I have to look about as quickly as possible for ways to bring in money, at least enough so that I can exist on it, and, here now in the middle of the playing season, no other way remains open to me but to take up my work again in the Brecht Ensemble, because that's what I live on. . . .
> You tell Herr Brecht that I'm going to Frankfurt as soon as he can make the arrangements. And that I do not want to play the role of Grusche [Grusha] in Görlitz and, if possible, not the role of the Governor's Wife in Berlin. Perhaps he can play the role.
> Yours,
> Little Katherine the Tiny.[14]

On November 23, 1954, Brugsch wrote to Brecht:

> Very Honored Herr Brecht,
> As promised, I have spoken with Käte [*sic*] Reichel. I give you her written answer.
> Personally, I have one request: don't let her leave your Ensemble as she has grown attached to it whether to flourish or decline. I believe I have straightened her out a good deal, and, I assume, as she is talented, that she will be a usable force for yc Ensemble.
> With very, very friendly greetings from one who admires you, Th. Brugsch.[15]

Reichel returned to the Ensemble where she reported to Helene Weigel, who was playing the stage role that was hers before she had challenged Brecht. Her only hope of escape was the Frankfurt *Chalk Circle* production in the spring, directed by the prominent West German Harry Buckwitz.

45

"He Sat on a Chair Placed at a Great Distance from Human Beings" (1954–56)

By 1954, people released from the gulag as a result of Khrushchev's efforts began to arrive back in Germany. Zenzl Mühsam, who had known Brecht and Steffin in the Weimar days, was brought to see him by a socialist comrade.[1] Her husband, anarchist Erich Mühsam, had been arrested and murdered by the Gestapo in 1934. She had fled to the Soviet Union, where she was arrested with Carola Neher. Thomas Mann and André Gide successfully lobbied for her release in 1936, but she was not allowed to leave the Soviet Union. After the Hitler-Stalin pact, she was again "taken," to be handed over to the Gestapo.[2] For some reason, however, Mühsam was sent to the gulag.[3]

Brecht could no longer dismiss persistent reports of wholly arbitrary arrests going back to the 1930s and the disappearance into the gulag system of so many friends. Mühsam's experience was supported by books by gulag survivors such as Erich Wollenberg (also a friend of Carola Neher), Elinor Lipper, and Alexander Weissberg-Cybulski—all published in the West as early as 1951. Brecht had read Boris Souvarine's and Arthur Koestler's accounts, though he did not speak out about Stalin's crimes. Though he was occasionally speaking out a little more boldly (even, on one occasion, telling Ulbricht's close associate Alfred Kurella to kiss his ass), Brecht continued to carry out publicity tasks for the government. At just this time, Brecht learned that an international committee in Moscow had awarded him the Stalin International Peace Award, with its prize of 160,000 convertible rubles.[4]

Brecht did not go at once to Moscow. January was taken up with directing Becher's turgid Stalingrad play *The Winter Battle*. Becher, in turn, helped Brecht obtain a new car, since the Steyr had collapsed. It was replaced by a two-seat BMW. In February 13, 1955, he went to Dresden as a featured participant in a peace congress sponsored by the GDR. When he returned to Berlin, he looked in on rehearsals of Besson's and Hauptmann's adaptation of Farquhar's *The Recruiting Officer*. Its theme was if one recruited soldiers for war, eventually they would be used for war. This was not what the GDR government wanted to hear at the moment they were reintroducing (to Brecht's dismay) the draft. Brecht thought that if Suhrkamp published the play in the West, the GDR could then be pressured to allow it to be printed and staged as Bertolt Brecht's *Trumpets and Drums.* Brecht would get 5 percent in royalties while Hauptmann and Besson each got only half that amount.[5]

Brecht was simultaneously juggling the six-figure sale of rights to other works. The film rights to *Puntila* were acquired by the Anglo-Brazilian director Alberto Cavalcanti, while the co-owner of these rights, Hella Wuolijoki, lay penniless and dying in Helsinki. The project nearly collapsed later, despite hard currency payments by the GDR. Brecht didn't like the script written by Vladimir Pozner and Cavalcanti, whom he called "that fag Brazilian."[6] Pozner was removed from the project altogether, causing a bitter, temporary rift between him and Brecht. At the same time, Brecht asked his agent Jacob Geis whether the film rights to *The Threepenny Opera* and *Mother Courage* might now be worth a quarter of a million marks in West Germany. Although his West German income had sunk in the period immediately after June 1953, sales had bounced right back after the big Paris successes of 1954. Brecht plays were now being produced all over Europe, and from South America to New York, Tel Aviv to Tokyo. The song "Mack the Knife" even became a popular hit in the United States, opening yet another tributary of hard currency that mainly flowed to Brecht.

Brecht still maintained his common-man image in the GDR. If the porter rushed to open the door of his BMW, Brecht ostentatiously slid across his seat to get out on the other side. He wore a deliberately shabby overcoat, a Mao jacket buttoned to the collar to hide his silk shirt, a cap that looked as if it came from the Depression years, and a three-day growth of beard. Though overcoat, jacket, cap, and shirt were all handmade for him, he managed to look more like a candidate for a Salvation Army hostel than a man whose earnings from around the globe were in the mid-six-figure range and rapidly growing.

In the spring of 1955, Harry Buckwitz of Frankfurt's Stadt theater produced the *Caucasian Chalk Circle* that Käthe Reichel had hoped would give her some independence from Brecht. Predictably, Brecht wrote, urging her to read some acting lessons he sent her. On the eve of the opening, he came for a visit and worked enough of his old charms that Reichel agreed to return to Berlin.

While in West Germany, Brecht looked up the disaffected Caspar Neher, who, though willing to work on Brecht's next project, a *Setzuan* production in Munich, was never again to be won back to East Berlin. Brecht also saw Hanne Hiob (his daughter by Marianne Zoff). He was impressed with Hanne's acting ability, and, after a few scenes with her as Shen Te-Shui Ta, he told her he hoped she would be able to understudy the lead in the Munich *Setzuan*.[7] Brecht returned to Berlin at the end of April to prepare to collect the Stalin prize. He did some fence-mending with Paul Dessau, who was upset that Brecht had unilaterally changed the music for *Chalk Circle*.

By this time, the problems between Berlau and Brecht were almost continuous and harder to hide. Berlau reminded him how several of "his" plays and productions had come into being. He and Weigel tried to fob off her claims that he robbed his co-workers as the ramblings of a drunk, but they knew better. Berlau pointed out in 1951 that she had already received over a thousand letters from him, letters that detailed work she had done.[8] As she could leak these at any time, Berlau constituted a danger to the image that Brecht and his sponsors in the GDR and the Soviet Union wished to present of him.

By now, with inadequate medical care within an establishment that cared more for Brecht as icon than it did for the mental health of his co-workers, Berlau's life was a roller coaster. Sometimes, as during the Buckow telephone conversation incident she was thoroughly lucid, but, at other times, she would become pitifully incoherent from a mixture of alcohol, tranquilizers, and electric shock treatments. Sometimes, as Steffin had done before her, Berlau would write down her terrible visions. "The roof collapses and I feel that I am on fire," she wrote of one such dream. "Strange, the hair around my crotch was the first to be attacked by the flames. That I can extinguish. I reach there with both hands and try to smother the flames with the wetness of my crotch. I lift my right hand high. It burns like a torch, my right hand. I am pointing to him—for now he has arrived. He is standing a few yards away and is talking to many people. He is looking diagonally towards me while continuing to talk. I snap up some of the sentences: for you it is a matter of life and death for your works. But I, once more, show the torch, my burning right hand, and I cry softly through the night, 'Bertolt.' Once more, he looks around and begins to quote his own poem: 'Lovely is that which burns in fire without turning to cold ash. Sister, see, you are dear to me, burning, but not turning to ash.' Menacingly, he then says to me, 'I don't get anything from cold ashes!' I am trying to send him a signal: there is a star missing in Cassiopeia; that is what started the fire, this missing star has hit me. He is shaking his head and won't even look up at the sky. He believes that I have gone mad again. Then W[eigel]. grabs his arm and says: 'Get the fire squad. Only the fire squad can do something about this. When there is a fire, one must get the fire squad! You cannot help!' Quickly, I see how he gives the order to call the fire squad. At that moment, a second star falls out of Cassiopeia. But the fire squad has already arrived and carries me away and covers me up."[9]

Ruth was taken away more and more frequently to the Charité or St. Joseph's Hospital. Without friends present, without muscle relaxants, and without the general anesthesia that would later become virtually mandatory, she was repeatedly jolted with powerful shots of electricity. In one letter to Kilian, who was screening Brecht's mail at the time, she described what she regularly went through at St. Joseph's: "The small trolleys with electrical shock equipment disappear into the five cells called 'The Bunkers,' " she wrote. "As you can understand, I am very frightened. I am given electrical shock treatments in 'The Bunker' without anyone to talk with. I feel myself falling down a pit. Please tell me if it would be better for me to return to Denmark where my former husband still lives. He's a doctor. . . . Don't show this letter to Brecht, or his hate will grow faster than the grass outside the bars of my window."[10]

In and out of the revolving door of East Berlin institutions, often radically disoriented and with inadequate follow-up care, Berlau made periodic efforts to reestablish herself in Denmark. As soon as she did, Brecht would insist on reestablishing the connection. On May Day, 1955, he wrote to her in Denmark urging her to work on more model books, something that could only be done in Berlin, saying the books would serve as an antidote to much work in the GDR that was usually, as he put it, "formal, superficial, mechanical."[11]

It was an unusually hectic time. Preparations were being made to take *Chalk Circle* to Paris in June as an entrant in the 1955 world theater festival. Journalist Erwin Leiser told Brecht the Stockholm rumor mill had him as a leading candidate for the Nobel Prize in literature. Leiser wanted to translate some of Brecht's best work quickly so that the Nobel Prize committee could read the work in Swedish before making their choice.

Despite Brecht's now ever-growing fame in both East and West, he was still harassed periodically by the Stasi. Just before he was due to leave for Moscow to collect the Stalin prize, he went by car to West Berlin. He was unceremoniously stopped, searched, and interrogated by the Stasi. Reminded perhaps by this that no matter how famous he now was, he was still vulnerable to the secret police both in the GDR and the Soviet Union. Before his upcoming trip to Moscow, he quickly tried to arrange his affairs in case he should die. He produced two documents: one for the GDR Academy; and the other a last testament. The testament read:

Bertolt Brecht *Testament*

It is my wish that after my death the following occur:

1. What belongs to me and the future income from my work I leave to Helene Weigel Brecht and my children Hanne, Stefan, and Barbara with the following exceptions:
2. Ruth Berlau is to receive the Tower House and the garden at

Buckow. To her also are to go half the income from the play *The Good [Woman] of Setzuan*, as well as half the income from the play *Days of the Commune* and half of all the income from the small book *Tales of the Calendar*.

3. Half of all income from the play *Mr. Puntila and His Servant Matti [Puntila]* is to go to Jakob Walcher.

4. The land at Buckow and the small house being built on it are to go to Käthe Reichel.

5. One third of all the income from the play *Threepenny Opera* and half of all the income from *The Threepenny Novel* are to go to Elisabeth Hauptmann.

6. One third of all the income from my poems is to go to Isot Kilian and her children.

7. My manuscripts and model books are to be given to the Academy of Arts.

8. One third of all the income from the play *The Mother* is to go to Käthe Rülicke.

9. The right to use my literary work shall go to Helene Weigel Brecht and Elisabeth Hauptmann; after their deaths, this shall then go to someone they will name. The use and application of the model books shall go to Ruth Berlau.

Berlin the 15th of May 1955. Signature of Brecht witnessed and signed by Isot Kilian.

Brecht's instructions to the Academy read: "In the case of my death, I do not wish to have my bier be publicly displayed. No speeches should be made at my grave. I wish to be buried at the cemetery next to the place where I live in the Chausseestrasse."[12]

He invited Russian-speaking Käthe Rülicke along with him and Weigel to Moscow. According to Rülicke, Brecht seemed very frightened ten minutes before the plane was due to land in Moscow.[13] But once they landed, he was the first off the plane. He was relieved to recognize three familiar faces from his visit in 1941: Mikhail Apletin, poet Konstantin Fedin, and director Nikolai Okhlopkov, who had staged *The Threepenny Opera* in Moscow in the thirties.

The visitors were taken to the Hotel Sovyetskaya. Brecht and Weigel were given a luxury suite with a double bed. All three were chauffeured about in Moscow in the kind of SIM that usually carried heads of state. When they were not using the limousine, it sat ostentatiously in front of the main entrance of their hotel.[14] They were also given an aide-de-camp, ostensibly there to make any special arrangements that might be desired. As they surely knew, such "assistants" reported directly to the KGB.

Soon after arrival, Brecht sent a note to Bernhard Reich, who was in Latvia with Asja Lazis. After more than a decade of prison and exile, they had been allowed to return to a provincial city, where Lazis ran a small theater. When Lazis and Reich had first learned that Brecht was to receive the Stalin prize, they had sent him their congratulations and their address. Replying to them now, Brecht asked if the two of them could come to Berlin to do some directing at the Ensemble? "Let me know what steps I should take," he went on as, "people are very friendly to us [here] and would help us, I think, fulfill such wishes in whatever way possible."[15] Now, instead of merely replying to Brecht by a letter that could be interdicted, Reich and Lazis hastened to get permission to go to Moscow to meet with Brecht and Weigel.

Brecht had now written out his Stalin prize acceptance speech and asked Boris Pasternak to translate it. Pasternak had been largely silenced under Stalin but allowed to publish again under Khrushchev. On the morning of May 25, Brecht, Rülicke, and Weigel were driven across Red Square to the Spasski Tower entrance of the Kremlin complex. The event was held at the newly built Sverdlov Hall holding about 350 spectators. Like everything else done by the Kremlin, the list of attendees was controlled, and only those currently in favor in the arts received invitations.

Brecht was introduced by the poet Nikolai Tikhonov, who had first achieved prominence as a poet by his membership in the Serapion Brotherhood, a group of experimental poets of the 1920s.[16] In those distant days soon after Lenin's death and long before Stalin had managed to ease out all his rivals for Lenin's mantle, Tikhonov was one of those who had dared sign a strong protest against incipient socialist realism. Many of the signers of the 1924 petition had either committed suicide or died in the gulag, but Tikhonov had survived by becoming an accomplice in Stalin's attacks. He lied on command at international conferences and hosted occasions such as this one.[17]

With his round, ruddy, and smiling countenance giving no hint of the blood he had helped to spill, Tikhonov stuck to the safest channel he could find. He was not about to be caught in the deadly battle still being fought over realism and formalism. He stressed Brecht's anti-Nazi works, saying: "In the active fight against fascism, you developed your towering talent. It became a weapon in the service of peace, for the happiness of mankind." After this wary opening, excitement increased in the hall as Nikolai Okhlopkov came to the rostrum.[18] Okhlopkov had been removed in the middle of staging a Brecht production twenty years before, and his appearance was seen by the audience as a retreat from Stalin's socialist realism. As Okhlopkov spoke, Rülicke looked around and saw the smiles of the artists there who drew hope from the reappearance of this old and feisty "formalist" who had miraculously survived.

When he got up to speak, Brecht relied more on what he had to say than how he said it. He fancifully reconstructed his behavior in Augsburg and Munich in 1918–19. He told his Kremlin audience: "I was 19 years old when I heard about your great revolution, 20 when I glimpsed the reflection of the great fire in my hometown. I was a medical orderly in an Augsburg army clinic. The barracks and even the clinics emptied out, and the old city became filled with new people coming in great clumps from the suburbs, with a liveliness not known before in the streets of the rich, of officials, and of business people. For some days, working women spoke at the speedily improvised councils and washed the hair of young workers wearing military smocks, and the factories listened to the orders of the workers. For just a few days, but what days! Everywhere fighters, but, at the same time, these were peaceful people, people building up things. The fights did not lead, as you know, to victory and you know why."[19] It was quite a different story than the one he had told HUAC. He left to his Russian audience the problem of answering the question of why the revolution had failed in Germany. Nor did he tell his Moscow audience that he himself had gone out of his way in 1919–20 to write plays and sing songs ridiculing the very idea of revolution. But this, as those gathered at Sverdlov Hall surely understood, was a time for quotable quotes and photo opportunities. With photographers' bulbs flashing, the cherub-faced Tikhonov shook Brecht's hand, and handed him a plaque and a certificate for the Stalin prize worth roughly a quarter of a million dollars. Within minutes, the ceremony was over, and he was in his limousine on the way back to his hotel.

After various delays, Asja Lazis had been able to get a ticket to come to Moscow. Bernard Reich, fresh from prison, followed later. They stayed with Asja's friend Estonian critic Lidia Toom, just around the corner from the Pushkin Theater. When the Brecht entourage arrived, Mrs. Toom served real coffee, a great rarity at that time. As they drank the coffee, conversation turned to who was perhaps still alive and who had died in the camps. Lazis, who had been deported for ten years to Kazakhstan on a trumped-up charge, wanted news of her former lover Walter Benjamin.[20] Brecht, hiding details of Benjamin's suicide, told her only he had died fleeing from Hitler.

When Reich came by the hotel, Brecht described work being done by the Ensemble. He told Reich the reason they were doing *Trumpets and Drums* was because it was a play satirizing military recruiting. Fully aware that the GDR, like West Germany and the Soviet Union, was building up its military might, he boasted of the play, "We are almost certain to run into difficulties with it." He arranged to have Rülicke take Reich to the GDR embassy to fill out forms for a Berlin visit. As part of this process, Reich wrote a short vita. In it, he said he had been "repressed" in the thirties for "having known Knorin."[21] He was released in January 1951. For Brecht, who had known Knorin as well as Reich had known him (it was Knorin who had personally recruited Brecht for a Comintern "assignment" in 1935), this note was a reminder of how much danger he must have been in Moscow in June 1941.

Speaking alone on one occasion with Asja Lazis, Brecht admitted that he was disappointed that the Soviet Union, though it had given him the Stalin prize, was not yet staging his plays. As he may now have begun to understand, he might be a useful figure for the Soviet Union in external propaganda, but this did not mean they approved of his art. But, as a useful tool, he had luxurious appointments. From the handful of very particular Moscow shop windows that Brecht's limousine passed, he concluded, quite wrongly, that the Soviet Union's consumer economy was booming. When he saw one full bread shop, Käthe Rülicke recalls, he extrapolated to full bread shops everywhere in that country, which his Soviet friends and even Rülicke knew was wrong. When he saw the faces of people of different races, he concluded that racism did not exist in the Soviet Union. Seeing a SIM limousine parked in a small garden in a Moscow suburb, in Rülicke's recollection, he spoke of "the countless cars" on the streets of Moscow.

Perhaps he no longer knew the difference between the facade of a socialism that kept him in luxury, and the poverty, fear, and unrest that lay behind it. As had Feuchtwanger, Malraux, Shaw, and countless other Western cultural icons, he was moving about Moscow within the well-appointed world of the privileged intelligentsia. Perhaps, Brecht really could not see that most of the people he met now lived on islands of privilege in a sea of want. The Jutkevitches (whose case may serve as a particularly glaring example of life among the Soviet privileged intelligentsia) had a large apartment, a live-in servant, two chauffeur-driven cars, walls decorated with original Léger plates, and shopping privileges at the Kremlin commissary.[22] By 1955, it had long since become the general practice that privileges were now inherited. Those at the top pulled strings to get their children admitted to the key foreign service and party academies. Graduates of these academies got the most remunerative party jobs and placed their children in the elite academies.

Returning from Moscow, Brecht felt vaguely ill. Käthe Rülicke was instructed to send Skobelsyn in Moscow the following note, drafted by Brecht: "Please transfer [the Stalin prize money] in francs to the bank account of Lars Schmidt, Union Bank of Switzerland, Bahnhofstrasse, Zurich, Switzerland. Thank you. Brecht." "This is," said

Brecht, "an English bank that can send money anywhere in the world."[23]

While preparing for the Ensemble's return visit to Paris in mid-June, there was a brief reunion with Lotte Lenya who was visiting Germany with her new husband, George Davis. Davis described Brecht and Weigel as "two shady con artists, or a couple that might be running a pawnshop as a blind."[24] Brecht asked Lenya to go with the Ensemble to Paris to do a song program there.[25] Lenya's memories of Brecht's dealings with Weill, as well as Brecht's rising status as Communist icon, discouraged her. "It's awfully sweet of you," she said, "but I really value my American passport too much for that." She did, however, rehearse a song program with him and recorded it in Hamburg, emphasizing Weill's name in the program and playing down the librettist.

Berlau was again excluded from the list of those going to Paris for the theater festival, even though she was a coauthor and a member of the Chalk Circle directing team. Käthe Reichel was also not invited. Kilian, last year's favorite, was now off the list. Käthe Rülicke accompanied him to Paris.

Vladimir Pozner, despite how he had been treated on the Puntila film, served as Brecht's translator and general factotum at the Théâtre Sarah-Bernhardt. After rehearsals, Pozner would take Brecht and a few key comrades to a small bar-restaurant on the quay across from Notre Dame and the Petit Pont. Nearby, at the famous Shakespeare and Company bookshop Brecht found a number of the English-language detective stories he loved.[26] One evening, he brought back to the restaurant some thirty books. On one side of the table stood the pile of mysteries and on the other an enormous plate with some thirty different cheeses that the gourmet Pozner had ordered. Each cheese had a little tag attached to it giving its name. Pointing to the collection, Brecht said, "I would like to display this cheese tray in the foyer of my theater in order to teach the Germans what culture is."[27]

At the same time, Brecht was showing Paris what German culture could achieve with The Caucasian Chalk Circle. Reviews praised the verve and style of the Paris production, which was positively reviewed but did not take the first prize. Quite possibly, the jurors did not feel they could reward the same company two years in a row. I believe this was not fair to the Chalk Circle production, which presented greater challenges in staging than Mother Courage with its smaller cast and less complex plot.

When the Ensemble returned to Berlin at the end of June, a number of major writers active in the world peace movement—among them Sartre, Lukács, and Ilya Ehrenburg—convened in Helsinki for a peace conference. Brecht had other commitments. He was involved in an expensive international co-production in the GDR of a film version of *Mother Courage* with Simone Signoret as the prostitute Yvette and Weigel as Courage. He wanted something rather old-fashioned, essentially a film document of the staged play; and when he saw the film makers would not do what he wanted, he lobbied to kill the project.

By the end of August, he was involved with Ruth Berlau and Peter Palitzsch in producing a model book of the adaptation of Sophocles' *Antigone* that he had originally produced in Switzerland. The book was to be brought out that fall with the GDR state publisher Henschel. Brecht and Berlau were also pushing the GDR authorities to bring out his book of war photographs and short poems called *Kriegsfibel*, or *A Primer of War*, written in America.[28] When the GDR refused to publish this explicitly pacifist work, he threatened to give it to the World Peace Council in western Europe. Bowing to the threat, a small GDR edition was finally authorized in late 1955.

On September 19, a text daring to satirize Ulbricht was put into rehearsal, the same day *Trumpets and Drums* opened. Adapted and directed by two young Ensemble directors, Carl Weber and Peter Palitzsch, it was a version of an old and anonymous Chinese farce called *The Day of the Great Intellectual Wu*. It did not require a great deal of acumen to read "Wu" as "Walter Ulbricht."

Importantly for the future of the Ensemble and general intellectual honesty, *Wu* was not credited to Brecht. Brecht increasingly attempted to transfer his theater responsibilities to others. The younger directors were now gaining full maturity in the Weigel-Brecht Ensemble. They were, in the main, a largely unisex cadre, with a relatively large number of women as directors. Hurwicz, Giehse, and Berlau did not always get credit for their work, but they did get to direct at a time when women directors were few and far between. This kind of opportunity made the Ensemble attractive to women despite the various other drawbacks of working in East Berlin.

Brecht spent much of the day filling out forms and writing letters asking for special exceptions for himself and those he chose to support. A note to the minister of the interior requested a government pass so that he would not always be stopped by the Stasi when he crossed the east-west border.[29] On November 21, he nagged Herr Thomas in Leipzig to supply another fur coat for Helene Weigel. A gray or black Persian lamb, he said, would be best.[30] He explained to the Ministry for Inter-German Affairs why he needed seventy meters of silk for his daughter Hanne Hiob.[31] To the Ministry of Culture, he explained why his other daughter, Mari Barbara (married to the actor Ekkehard Schall), should, despite the rarity of such things in the GDR, have her own new car.[32]

His globe-circling tangle of contracts also required attention, and not all of these matters could be handed over to Hauptmann. There were upcoming productions of *The Private Tutor* in Japan, of *Chalk Circle* in Tel Aviv, and of *The Threepenny Opera* in Buenos Aires and Edinburgh. Then, there were contracts for Italian, Swedish, Russian, and British editions, and Eric Bentley's complaints about Brecht, Suhrkamp, and Stefan Brecht unilaterally tampering with long-standing agreements. There was the saga of Allert de Lange's *Threepenny Novel* contract. Joining a chorus of complaint, Pozner said his name had been left off the screen credits for the Viennese film production of *Puntila*. There were continued complaints from Berlau and Hauptmann, and the possibility of an uproar from Steffin's heirs if they ever got adequate legal advice and realized the enormity of what he had done to them. But no matter how his earnings and fame grew, it never seemed enough. His appetite for deals increased, and he did not correct even the most glaring inequities with regard to his coauthors.

Increasingly, people wanted to see him after years of absence to ask for help. There had been Zenzl Mühsam, a wreck after her years in the gulag. Now much in need of help, Arnolt Bronnen was invited to Berlin by Becher. His meeting with Brecht, however, as Rülicke remembers it was terse.[33] Brecht had no time for Bronnen, no matter how much Bronnen had helped him in the Weimar years. A recurrent voice was Marieluise Fleisser.[34] Unable to get her career restarted in West Germany, in late 1955, she wrote asking "for help in great need."[35] He replied briefly, asking her whether she would be prepared to move to the GDR, and she came to Berlin for a few days to see if this could work. Fleisser was struck by how much Brecht had changed since 1950. "He sat on a chair placed at a great distance from human beings," she wrote later. "I saw a tragic face."[36] To Lion Feuchtwanger, she wrote: "In no way do I wish to put myself in the hands of the cultural officials there, which I would have to do if I [were] living in Berlin, the thought of this has a crippling effect on me."[37]

Amidst the everyday demands, and still not feeling well after his Moscow trip, Brecht was nevertheless eager to begin staging *Galileo*. Not wanting to interrupt his schedule to get treatment for a persistent "Grippe," he tried to get himself a mail-order treatment. He asked an old Munich friend, Dr. Johann Ludwig Schmitt, to prescribe something and send it to Berlin. When the "Grippe" nevertheless persisted, he visited Dr. Martens's clinic at the Westsanatorium on September 21 and was given Cordalin for his heart. He believed that he had suffered a heart attack as a ten-year-old and had had a heart seizure in 1922. Whether or not the condition went back to childhood, the Charité reported at the end of May that "the heart appears to be somewhat enlarged," and "though pulsation on the left is recognizable, hardly any pulsation is registered on the right."[38]

The "Grippe" persisted, and he went to the internist Dr. Hude-pohl. Hostylakin was prescribed for the infection; but, when the pain and the slightly raised temperature persisted into October, Brecht sub-mitted to a urinary tract operation at Dr. Hudepohl's clinic. Even this produced no improvement. Kilian, back in favor but more nanny than sexual partner, worried that he was overdoing things with *Galileo*. When Kilian and Brecht went to the cinema to see an old Valentin film on December 26, Brecht had to leave when he felt unable to breathe.

In a December 14 letter to Berlau, Brecht complained as usual that she had not written to him enough. He described the *Galileo* rehearsals and said that the photos she had made of the New York and California versions of *Galileo* were proving to be most helpful, as was her sixteen-millimeter film of the play. Toward the end of the letter, he wrote: "I want to write something to you sometime what I think about the future, and what I think you must do. I will need leisure to do this and reflection. Perhaps at Christmas. Immediately, you should so arrange things that you feel well and establish yourself a bit. That is important for things here also."[39] Brecht decided to arrange to buy Berlau a small house in Copenhagen, which was to go to Weigel at Berlau's death. He did not imagine that Weigel's death might come first.

Brecht asked Benno Besson to try to find a house for him to buy in Switzerland. He was increasingly dissatisfied with the estate at Buc-kow. Too many visitors bothered him there. Furthermore, the fifty thousand marks' worth of changes he was having done were not satisfac-tory to him, and he was suing the contractor.

On December 31, he again wrote to Berlau and again complained she was not writing to him enough. He added: "Things are going better now with the heart, I'm getting digitalis."[40] Casually he mentions that he will be off in a couple of weeks to Rostock with Käthe Reichel and Benno Besson to work on *The Good Woman of Setzuan*, but he ends with "J.e.d.," for the Danish "Jed elsker dig" (I love you).

Whatever his ongoing problems with leftover relationships and failing health, the tapes of his rehearsals in late 1955 and early 1956 show how immensely he was enjoying the work. When he rehearsed the scene where Galileo, a virtual prisoner of the Inquisition and of his own daughter, slips a copy of the *Discorsi* to Andrea, he instructed the actors to convey a sense that the contents of the book were like the technical secrets that would lead to nuclear fission. He said to the two actors in this scene, "It must work on a colossal scale, like the H-Bomb." He also told Käthe Rülicke, as he had said to Steffin in the 1930s, that the play actually was a commentary on the behavior of Bukharin at the Moscow Show Trials.[41] At times, he wandered off the subject of Galileo and talked about his own appearance before HUAC. Galileo's caving in before the Inquisition and Brecht's appearance before HUAC seemed deeply entwined with Brecht's view of himself and of the doomed figure of Bukharin at the rigged Moscow Show Trials. He returned often to the play's haunting declaration: "In time you may discover everything that there is to discover and that the advances you will make will only carry you further away from humanity. The chasm between you and humanity can become so great one day that your cries of joy about some new achievement may be answered by a universal cry of horror."[42]

The "chasm between you and humanity" speech described Brecht at this time. Surrounded by those he kept dependent on him, he was lonely, trusted nobody, and his health was failing. He was very rich, but his chin and neck now hung loosely like a turkey. Tobacco juice dribbled down his chin from both sides of his mouth. His fingernails were filthy, and he smelled.[43] He would shuffle across the Schiff courtyard using a walking cane and with one or another of the actresses of the company.

Sporadically, Brecht considered who should inherit his enormous property. As legal wife, Weigel knew, and was part of, the international business complex that was Bertolt Brecht. The GDR did not permit separate tax returns by married couples, so Weigel's name was copied on much of the GDR correspondence. Frau Tinzmann, Brecht's and Weigel's accountant and tax advisor, reported his financial holdings in the GDR at the beginning of 1955 to be 65,700.57 marks in a Berlin checking account. In addition, he cleared 142,640.37 marks in 1955, for a total of 208,340.94 marks. However, Tinzmann recommended transferring 181,154.24 marks to scattered savings accounts so that Brecht could then, taking advantage of a nuance in GDR law, pay less taxes. After the necessary shifts, he wrote the Berlin tax office that his "bank account has gone down by more than one third" and that his taxes should now drop. He enclosed a check for 285 marks.[44] As he had done in the Weimar years, he found stratagems that enabled him to pay only a pittance in taxes. An even larger flood of money earned abroad was not showing up on the GDR books at all and was not revealed to Weigel. These earnings he kept either in his own Swiss account, in the Lars Schmidt account he had used for the massive Stalin prize deposit, or in an account managed for him in Munich by the ever-compliant Jacob Geis, or in various Scandinavian and American accounts run through a network of agents. Only Brecht knew the total.

He made one will that left virtually everything to Weigel, but had then dictated another one to Isot Kilian.[45] Having done so, Brecht never found time to have it notarized, and it was therefore useless. The multiple wills that Brecht would leave continued a lifelong pattern of undergirding his personal, professional, and sexual arrangements with mutually conflicting agreements. Where he had made a legal agreement to marry Zoff in 1922, he had also prepared a "legal" agreement to marry Bie Banholzer. When he sold a work to Allert de Lange, he also sold it to Desch. Where he made Bentley or Berlau his agent, he gave Stefan Brecht authority also, thus guaranteeing a legal tangle that enriches lawyers to this day.

The web of conflicting agreements insured that all questions of moment would need to be referred back to him as long as he was alive. As faithless and mendacious in business and in bed, he projected such behavior onto others. He said that women were unreliable as they were "in a perpetual state of arousal." Comparing a late "love" to his earliest one, he had written in 1954, "And of both, I don't know if they love me."[46]

By 1956, as in his teen years, his most trusted companion was a dog. Sometimes he now had an overnight nurse. Downstairs was the person who played all the mother roles in the plays. Piled up on a bedside table were the detective stories he had used for decades to help him get to sleep. But ever since the Stalin prize trip, sleep had proved elusive. He constantly took his temperature and weighed himself. His weight was up to around 74.5 kilos (165 pounds), but it looked flabby and bloated on his increasingly stooped frame. Kilian, often over Brecht's objections, would ask a doctor to come round to the Schiff. Sometimes he would go to a doctor when a specific ailment became too painful to bear, but, for all his worries about his health, he seemed to have about as much notion of preventive medicine as a child might have. He was frightened of doctors and dentists, and would not go near one unless someone went with him. He had cut back on alcohol at Hudepohl's suggestion, but he got virtually no exercise and continued to eat rich cheeses and to smoke and chew constantly on cigars.

Next to his bed, he kept a list of numbers he thought most important. There were two numbers (so he could call at any time of the day or night if he needed help) for Isot Kilian, two for Hauptmann, and two for Dr. Otto Müllereisert. There were also two numbers for the Charité Hospital and for Dr. Martens in the Western section of Berlin. There were three Frankfurt numbers, as well as a Berlin number for his main publisher, Peter Suhrkamp. Among various other medical numbers were those of the kidney specialist Dr. Hudepohl; the emergency number of the best equipped hospital in the GDR, the Government Hospital at Pankow; and Dr. Schmitt's number in Munich. There were numbers for Weigel, Reichel, Rülicke, his brother, Walter, in West Germany, and a much-changed number for Berlau.

While directing as many *Galileo* rehearsals as his health would allow, Brecht tried to use his position as Stalin prize winner to meet personally with Ulbricht. But Ulbricht broke an appointment they had made and, instead of suggesting another time to meet, wrote patronizingly:

> Dear Comrade Brecht,
>   I had the intention of discussing some questions concerning literature with you, and I ask for your forgiveness that that will no longer be possible before the Writers' Conference as, before everything else, I must busy myself with questions concerning the peoples' economic plan.
>   With friendly greetings! Walter Ulbricht.

At the Writers' Conference in Berlin on January 11–12, 1956, Brecht did not confront Ulbricht directly but spoke in tortured bureaucratic language of change in the GDR.[47] When he did speak clearly, he claimed West Germany was sinking in the swamp of bourgeois barbarism. Ulbricht spoke guardedly at a March conference, hinting only vaguely at possible change. The old political campaigner had picked up a nuance less observant people had missed. Mao's China might be swinging to a conservative position away from Khrushchev. Ulbricht sent Otto Grotewohl to China to investigate this promising development.

Brecht worked on *Galileo* and prepared to go to Milan, where Giorgio Strehler was doing a new *Threepenny Opera*. Brecht agreed to attend the premiere and spend his fifty-eighth birthday there on February 10. Elisabeth Hauptmann would accompany him. As usual, he did not want to use his own funds so he asked Suhrkamp for money for their journey. On February 4, he visited Peter Suhrkamp in a clinic in West Berlin, and the two friends discussed going to "Wasser" Schmitt's Munich clinic for part of the summer for a water cure.

In Milan, Hauptmann and Brecht were installed in separate rooms at the Hotel Manin from February 6–13. Their days were spent at the final rehearsals of *Threepenny* and with Erwin Leiser, who was working on the Swedish edition of the plays. Strehler had transposed the text from the nineteenth-century world of the 1928 *Threepenny* to an early twentieth-century world of garages. It evoked more the Chicago of the St. Valentine's Day Massacre than Victorian London. Leiser attended the premiere and the party that followed. He noted Brecht's fatigue and the fact that somehow, despite all his fame and wealth, none of the younger women seemed attracted to Brecht. Brecht himself was vaguely aware that something was wrong. He had again been troubled by "Grippe," and an Italian doctor he consulted suggested that it seemed connected with his heart. Brecht wrote to Berlau that the production was "brilliant in detail, very aggressive, lasted until two in the morning." His letter ended with the formulaic "e.p.e.p."[48]

When he returned to Berlin on February 13, there were so many business details to be taken care of that, with his "Grippe," he had no time to resume *Galileo* rehearsals. He did take time to pursue a legal case against the contractor working on the Buckow estate. In a three-page, single-spaced, typewritten letter dated February 21, 1956, Brecht told his attorney, Dr. F. K. Kaul, why he should not make a final payment of 3,972.86 marks to the contractor.

On February 25, the historic bombshell of Khrushchev's address to the Twentieth Party Congress, entitled "On the Cult of Personality and Its Consequences," shook the socialist world. Security for the fifteen hundred congress delegates on the day of the speech was particularly tight. Astonishingly, at Khrushchev's insistence, one hundred former gulag inmates who had now been rehabilitated were present. Khrushchev began with a brief description of the leadership style of Marx and Engels and of their efforts to avoid all adulation of themselves, and then showed how Lenin had continued this style. Khrushchev then turned to "Lenin's Testament," whose existence had been long suspected, but which had disappeared into party archives and had never been openly discussed. In this "Testament," Lenin anticipated problems with Stalin and recommended that he be removed from his post of general secretary of the party. There was commotion in the huge hall.

Khrushchev spoke of how Stalin had originated the concept of "enemy of the people," which allowed "the usage of the most cruel repression, violating all norms of revolutionary legality, against anyone who in any way disagreed with Stalin. . . . This led to glaring violations of revolutionary legality, and to the fact that many entirely innocent persons, who in the past had defended the Party line, became victims." Among such victims were 98 of the 139 members of the party's Central Committee at the 1934 Party Congress. Khrushchev read aloud a telegram dated September 25, 1936, in which Stalin complained that the NKVD had not been doing enough and that it had fallen four years behind in its arrest quota! "This directive," said Khrushchev, "directly pushed the NKVD workers on the path of mass arrests and executions." Filling Stalin's quotas, the NKVD "made lying, slanderous and absurd accusations concerning 'two-facedness,' 'espionage,' 'sabotage,' preparation of fictitious 'plots,' etc."

During the war years, Stalin had declared himself to be a universal military genius. "And what was the result of this?" asked Khrushchev: "The Germans surrounded our army concentrations and consequently we lost hundreds of thousands of our soldiers. This is Stalin's military 'genius'; this is what it cost us." Khrushchev concluded that he hoped loyalists would put the Stalin era behind them and join a party-led program of reform. "We are absolutely certain that our Party," he said, "armed with the historical resolutions of the 20th Party Congress, will lead the Soviet people along the Leninist path to new successes, to new victories . . . (Tumultuous, prolonged applause ending in ovation. All rise)."

Among the foreign leaders in Moscow on February 25 was Walter Ulbricht, who had risen to power in the darkest years of Stalin's reign. In early March and in the March 4 issue of *Neues Deutschland*, Ulbricht declared that Stalin could no longer be considered one of the "classics" in the Marxist-Leninist tradition. He also spoke of the damage Stalin had done to "Leninist norms of Party life."

While the Twentieth Party Congress was still in progress in Moscow, Brecht discussed its implications with Jakob Walcher and up-and-coming playwright Erwin Strittmatter, and later with activist Protestant pastor Karl Kleinschmidt. But Brecht made no public statement that could be construed as supporting Khrushchev's, or even Ulbricht's, position on Stalin.

Reluctance to back Khrushchev was in fact general at the March party conference in Berlin. Otto Grotewohl, back from his exploratory trip to China, made vague remarks about the need to "stabilize democratic legality." This was party code for a legal system that protected rights of defendants. Only one speaker at the March conference spoke openly about ridding the GDR of Stalinism. Brecht's old friend and coeditor in the thirties of *Das Wort*, Willi Bredel, asked if elders like Ulbricht should not now exercise self-criticism? Bredel's speech was greeted with stormy applause by the liberal minority wing of SED delegates, but no other delegate spoke out against Ulbricht in public. In fact, the old party chiefs managed to push through a motion at the congress congratulating Ulbricht for his "extraordinary contributions."

After Khrushchev's address, major changes seemed to be happening everywhere in eastern Europe except in East Berlin. On March 15, Bernhard Reich sent Brecht a telegram: "Rehabilitation positively completed. Greetings. Reich."[49] Olga Tretiakova wrote on March 17 to "Dear Helli and Comrade Brecht," saying, without further elaboration, that she was sorry that she had "not been in any condition"[50] to see them during their visit to Moscow the previous May. But now she could reemerge, as her husband had been posthumously "rehabilitated" on February 29. Without going into details in a letter, she asked Brecht if he wanted his works in Russian to include translations made by Sergei Tretiakov, adding "I would be very grateful to you if you could confirm this for me." Instead, on March 28, Brecht wrote a cautious letter to the Writers' Union functionary Mura Pawlowa[51] asking her advice about bringing out his work in Russian. Later, he did authorize publication of some of the works translated by Sergei Tretiakov, but he also began to distribute other commissions. On April 25, he sent a batch of poems to Pasternak. "I can imagine," Brecht wrote, "that these [poems] published now could be very useful."[52]

Wishing to get a better understanding of what was really going on in the wake of Khrushchev's speech, Brecht tried to meet Paul Wandel, Brecht's closest contact in the government and someone who had discretely opposed Ulbricht. In March, Brecht had pointed out that suggestions he and Hanns Eisler had made for discussion at the 1952 Party Congress had not been taken up then. He now asked: "Can I talk over these things with you? Perhaps you could give me a time some evening next week when you could come by to see me."[53] (I have not been able to determine if Wandel did come over to see Brecht as requested.)

More and more frequently now, Brecht said he did not feel well enough to attend public political meetings, though his schedule was otherwise full during the period between his return from Milan on February 13 and up to the end of March. Instead of going to an Academy of Arts meeting where the distribution of National Prizes was discussed, he suggested Willi Bredel for the prize,[54] a bold idea in light of Bredel's opposition to Ulbricht and a clever one if Ulbricht was now to be displaced.

Brecht met privately with Walter Janka, head of the prominent East German press Aufbau Verlag, and with Kilian's husband, dissident Marxist Wolfgang Harich, and seemed to encourage both. Thinking that a change from Stalinism was about to really begin, Janka in turn met with Becher, who proposed giving far more independence to the newspaper *Sonntag*, and handing the chief editorship of the paper to someone Ulbricht had previously removed as an "agent of western imperialism," Gerhart Eisler.[55]

The next year, after brutal Stasi interrogation, Harich would claim that Brecht "had exercised an unhealthy influence"[56] on him in 1956; but generally Weigel rather than Brecht ran the risks of public opposition. She ostentatiously withdrew her party membership after the Khrushchev address, an action that was extraordinarily bold for the time.[57] When Harich spoke openly of introducing substantive change in the GDR, and organized clandestine meetings with Soviet and West German politicians, it was Weigel who sometimes attended, not Brecht.

Concerned about the strain of the *Galileo* rehearsals, Kilian arranged to have Dr. Martens come to the Schiff from West Berlin to examine Brecht on March 28. "Don't you think the rehearsals are a heavy strain on him?"[58] asked Kilian. Martens said: "No, no. I'm satisfied with his condition." Later that day, his temperature was 39.5 degrees Celsius. Brecht was convinced his normal temperature was 36.05 degrees Celsius. Kilian again called Martens, who repeated that rehearsals were no problem. But by March 31, Brecht turned *Galileo* over to Erich Engel, whom he had managed to coax back to East Berlin from West Germany.

Brecht was worried about how he was going to be cared for over the long Easter weekend. Helene Weigel asked that a doctor used by several members of the staff at the Berliner Ensemble, a Georgian expatriate, come by. Since the well-known woman doctor Dr. Tsoulukidse was not available, she sent over her son, Georgi, who was then completing his residency in Berlin. When the young doctor arrived on his bicycle at Brecht's door on Easter Friday, the door was opened by Mari Barbara. When Weigel saw how young he was, she got up at once on her high horse, as Georgi Tsoulukidse remembered it. He cut her off immediately, demanding to know if she would have spoken in this arrogant way to a doctor while she was an immigrant in the United States. Somewhat chastened, Weigel told Tsoulukidse that the important thing was that he not talk overly long with Brecht, who lay in a nearby bed with his omnipresent cigar. Tsoulukidse said that if he was to act as a doctor here, he would have to get Brecht's medical history from him and would have to have an opportunity to carefully examine him. After getting this history and examining the patient, the doctor asked about Brecht's drinking and smoking. Brecht replied, "Ich drinke Bier." When the doctor said he should give this up and his foul cigars, Brecht simply replied, "Das kann ich nicht" (That, I can't do). Then, said Tsoulukidse, Brecht should have himself admitted to the Charité right after the holiday. Meanwhile, the doctor would look in every day and would remain on call if Brecht needed him.

On another visit, young Dr. Tsoulukidse asked Brecht about the play *The Caucasian Chalk Circle*, which is set in Georgia, the homeland of Tsoulukidse's parents. The doctor noted that the play used lines from the work of the expatriate Georgian poet Grigol Robakidse's *Schlangenhemd*, or *The Snake's Skin*. Brecht admitted to the borrowing. Brecht seemed unaware that, in the Nazi years, Robakidse had written book-length encomiums to Hitler and Mussolini. But Nazi encomiums or no, the lines would stay in the play. And the beer drinking and smoking would continue until finally Brecht would consent to enter the Charité Hospital for a general checkup by Tsoulukidse's superior, the famous Dr. Theodor Brugsch.

Brugsch, in 1956, was renowned but already, in Tsoulukidse's view, arteriosclerotic, with memory lapses that seemed glaring to his younger colleague, but which were apparently ignored at the hospital itself. Brugsch, in Tsoulukidse's recollection, was a tyrant to those placed under him and totally submissive to those above, telling Tsoulukidse one day, "Whoever pays for the song, that person's song I sing." Brugsch was a little like the hospital where he now practiced. It was a place that in its 250-year history had sung a number of songs. It had been home both to the famous surgeon Sauerbruch and had participated in the ghastly "medical" experiments of the Third Reich. Once it had been perhaps the finest hospital in Germany. After 1945, the Soviets let Charité standards slide and built the Regierungskrankenhaus, a hospital for top officials of the Soviet Zone near their villas in the suburb of Pankow. Though Brecht was high enough in the ranks of the privileged intelligentsia that he had a Pankow Regierungskrankenhaus card, he chose not to go there.[59] In choosing the Charité, where he had been admitted for "malnutrition" in 1922, Brecht returned to his own and Germany's past.

Brugsch himself had continued his upper-class prewar Berlin practice during the Hitler years, with Rommel among his list of patients. Brugsch openly supported neither Hitler nor the resistance. Somehow, he was tolerated by the Nazis though it was widely known that both his mother and his wife were Jewish. After the war, the Soviets allowed him to continue his practice. Brecht was given a large private room at the Charité, which overlooked an inner courtyard where every few days a man with a scythe swiftly and silently cut the grass under Brecht's window. Lying in his bed, he wrote some poetry about death while continuing to negotiate royalty terms by mail.

One fierce letter went to the East German Reclam Verlag, insisting they increase his royalties. Another letter went to Lion Feuchtwanger, who had written to say there was interest in the United States in doing a stage production of *The Visions of Simone Machard*. Brecht wrote to recommend that the play be done both in the United States and in Europe, without telling Berlau. The matter was rather delicate. If she got any wind of these developments, she could legally claim her right to 20 percent of the play's income. He had never told her about the MGM contract in 1944 or a production in Prague, nor that Leningrad wanted the play for 1955. After Brecht's death, the practice of stealing Berlau's share continued, despite Weigel's and Suhrkamp Verlag's certain knowledge of her share in the original contract.[60]

The seventy-seven-year-old Brugsch put Brecht on his own personally developed regimen of mysterious injections. Brugsch was soon sure he saw marked improvement in his patient, but Brecht noted that even a five-minute conversation still left him completely exhausted.[61]

With every encounter a major effort, there were few whom Brecht wanted to see at all. He trusted none of his young lovers, nor his assistants, and was at almost continuous odds with older lovers. He had a family, of sorts, but it was long since more business combine than family.

On May 3, Elisabeth Hauptmann wrote to Peter Suhrkamp about rights to various plays, along with a description of Brecht's health: "The good thing is that his heart is of and for itself a whole lot better than was first supposed. The bad thing is that one of his valves has been overcome by this bad infection that is hard to do away with. Medically, he is in very good hands."[62] On May 10, she reported to Suhrkamp: "Things are going wholly and decidedly better with Brecht, and he is going to get out of the hospital and go home the day after tomorrow, with the full agreement of the professor."[63] In fact, Brecht had realized he had made no progress whatsoever. He had himself discharged and driven to Buckow. Here, he spent most of June and July and the first week in August with only brief trips to Berlin for Brugsch's injections and to attend to some of his most pressing affairs.

In the first week of June 1956, the full text of Khrushchev's Twentieth Party Congress speech was published in the West. In the Soviet bloc, however, it remained a document officially accessible only to highly placed party officials. Brecht, with his access to Western papers, got his own copy at once. In May, the now openly oppositionist Wolfgang Harich had toured Poland for ten days and met there with anti-Stalinists. When Harich returned to Berlin, he said, "Our Polish friends are way ahead of us, and they are disappointed that we have done nothing about Ulbricht."[64] Ulbricht was seen by Harich as "among the most orthodox supporters of Stalin in the entire East bloc."[65] In Berlin, there was a round of urgent meetings of the Harich group, sometimes including Helene Weigel but usually not Brecht.[66] It seems unlikely that only questions of health kept Brecht away. He still participated in many meetings but only the ones he chose. Generally, as he had in the Weimar years, he stayed away from those that were thought most dangerous.

"Organized Schizophrenia" (1956)

In the summer of 1956, the tide of change seemed to rise throughout eastern Europe. In Hungary, Czechoslovakia, and Poland, students protested compulsory classes in Russian and Marxism-Leninism. On May 13, the head of the Soviet Writers' Union, Alexander Fadayev, shattered by the return of writers he had helped ship to the gulag and aware that "very many honest people" had died after he had sanctioned their arrest, committed suicide.[1]

In the GDR, Walter Ulbricht sensed the need to at least appear to change. Robert Havemann remembers Ulbricht attending a special meeting of the party organization of the Humboldt University called to discuss Khrushchev's address. "Our Soviet colleagues," said Havemann, "have broken out of the devil's trap. And we in Germany, of course, have certainly had our fill of the cult of personality."[2] No sooner had Havemann ended his speech than a young woman shouted: "This is something unheard of. This is an insult to the Party. I certainly did not expect from you, Comrade Havemann, in the presence of Comrade Walter Ulbricht, that you would speak so intemperately and shamelessly." But, astoundingly, Ulbricht responded, "One thing I must tell you, the only person here who has shown that he grasps what it is all really about is Comrade Havemann."

For students of the dialectic, Ulbricht had just offered an advanced practicum in this abstruse science. Just as his model Stalin had done so frequently in the twenties when he had seized the program of his opponents as his own, Ulbricht seemed suddenly to go further than his critics. The hard-liners saw Ulbricht as admitting too much about Stalin, while liberals raged that Ulbricht did not admit mistakes he himself had made. But consummate politician that he was, by placing himself in the middle, Ulbricht would ride out both currents of rage.

Thinking Ulbricht could now be ousted, Harich and Hans Mayer, a Leipzig Germanist and music historian, said publicly that GDR cultural policy as articulated by Ulbricht "had not stood on the best of terms with truth."[3] Prochange forces led by Harich were convinced they had the support of Walter Janka, Weigel, and Brecht. But Brecht would not add a public stone to a balance that now seemed virtually certain to tip against Ulbricht and Stalinism. Instead, at Buckow, he told Käthe Rülicke he wanted her to go to Yugoslavia and the Soviet Union to pick up any useful information on the political situation.[4] He needed her to go away anyway; their relationship was near breaking apart over his various other tangled sexual, political, and business affairs.

Eric Bentley was shocked at Brecht's appearance when he visited in June: "Shrunken in the body, swollen somewhat in the face, flaccid."[5] While Bentley tried to mask his dismay at Brecht's obvious ill health, Brecht admitted only he was "etwas reduziert" (somewhat reduced); and they spoke about Berliner Ensemble productions. Bentley told him the presumably pirated production of Synge's copyrighted *The Playboy of the Western World* was "all wrong." Brecht shrugged, "Oh, well, what else could we make of the play in this benighted land." "Then why do it at all?" Bentley asked. The discussion turned to *Trumpets and Drums*, the adaptation of *The Recruiting Officer*, which Bentley felt was in "excellent taste." Of *The Caucasian Chalk Circle*, Bentley told Brecht, "It was the greatest modern theatre in my life since *Mother Courage* in 1949."[6]

During Bentley's visit, he heard that Brecht had been writing poems critical of Stalin. Bentley saw an open volume of the renegade Communist Arthur Koestler in the room, a book on the GDR's version of the Inquisition's index. But, as Bentley later noted, "If Brecht had daring thoughts, he didn't usually dare to make them known."[7] Bentley noticed Hauptmann kept drifting in and out of the room, almost as though she was monitoring the conversation. The situation reminded Bentley of Galileo's situation where the scientist is a prisoner of the Inquisition but is secretly writing the subversive *Discorsi* to be smuggled out by a former student. But Brecht did not ask Bentley to smuggle anything out. Though Bentley felt they were parting for the last time, both of them uttered conventional lines. "Thank you so much for coming," said Brecht. "Write me from New York." Bentley replied, "Definitely, I trust you'll be fully recovered very soon."[8]

Brecht told Peter Hacks that Khrushchev's address should not be published in the socialist countries.[9] He said to Hacks that socialism was like a lame horse: as long as one did not have a better one, it was best not to look at the faults. While opposing publication and hence open discussion of the Khrushchev speech, Brecht began to comment on it in poetry. In a small prefatory note, he wrote: "The historical evaluation of S[talin]. has, at the moment, no interest and, because of insufficient facts, cannot yet be undertaken." But, he concluded, the "damage done by his example must be liquidated."

In one poetic fragment, a figure who is never named but from the context is obviously Stalin is compared with the czar of Russia and declared to be "the honored murderer of the people."

This figure:

The most intelligent student of Lenin
Smashed his master in the mouth.

Typically, the lines both attack Stalin and praise him: he is both murderer and Lenin's most intelligent student. One poem, with the simple title "Der Führer," asks:

Does the Führer drag those he leads
To a mountain peak, which only he knows?

A third poem sums up:

He who gave the orders
Did not carry them out himself.

Brecht put them into his desk drawer, and their very existence would be disputed for forty years. "Brecht exercised—in contrast to Ernst Bloch—reticence," writes German critic Michael Rohrwasser; "he . . . put his 'political statements' into his desk drawer, or did not finish them, or only sent them to conversational partners as test exercises."[10] Rohrwasser calls this "Brecht's organized schizophrenia."[11]

The phrase is apt not only for Brecht's political statements but all other areas of Brecht's life, his "conscious use of contradiction." His personal and business life for decades had rested on innumerable contradictions—all of which he apparently needed to survive: master and child; a wealthy man who compulsively presents himself as poor; a Communist who mercilessly exploits those around him; a man who denigrates women and then proudly presents their work under his own name. In 1920, he said: "I don't think I could ever have as grown-up a philosophy as Goethe or Hebbel, who, as far as ideas are concerned, must have had the memories of tram conductors. I keep forgetting my own opinions and can't make up my mind to learn them by heart. Even cities, adventures, faces disappear in the wrinkles of my brain faster than the life of grass."[12] He had also said, "A man with only one theory is lost. He must have several, four, many! He must stuff his pockets with them like newspapers, always the latest, one can live well between the theories, one can be comfortably housed between theories."[13] The man of fifty-eight, like the man of twenty-two, housed himself between irreconcilable theories and irreconcilable facts.

There is virtually no issue on which one cannot find arguments by him for both sides: *He Who Says Yes* and *He Who Says No*. He told Hurwicz, "One should never start out on the basis of a figure's character, because a person has no character," and there is every indication that he believed this. He saw himself as a genius in a self-created universe of the dominant and the dominated, a world where he could advocate liberty and practice tyranny, where he held others to promises and contracts while breaking them himself at will. In almost all matters, Brecht remained from first to last, inflexibly inconsistent, as divided as any of the characters in the plays to which he attached his name. The one area in which he does seem willing consistently to stand up and be counted is the issue of peace. *Mother Courage* is a play that warns against war. The same can be said of *Trumpets and Drums*, Hauptmann's and Besson's adaptation of *The Recruiting Officer*, which Brecht insisted be included in the repertoire though he knew it would be seen as pacifist. He argued with GDR authorities in 1955 about publishing his antiwar photographs and brief poems in *A Primer of War*. When he saw both West and East Germany introduce legislation to reintroduce the draft, he published an open letter to the West German Bundestag in which he said: "Do you really want to make this first step towards war? Then the last step, that into nothingness, we will all do together. . . . None of our parliaments, no matter how they have been elected, has from the general public either the assignment or permission to introduce a general draft. As I am opposed to war, I am opposed to the introduction of the draft in both parts of Germany, and, because it is a question of life and death, I propose a public referendum on the question in both parts of Germany."[14] Though the letter seemed to have little effect in either part of Germany, Brecht felt it was essential. Whatever portion of trust he might enjoy anywhere, this was a just cause in which to expend that trust.

Otherwise, Brecht remained locked in a pattern of presenting irreconcilable points of view in public and private. Others took a public stand against what Stalin had represented and Ulbricht continued to represent. On June 14, the head of the Department of German at Humboldt University, Alfred Kantorowicz, published an article opposing Walter Ulbricht and his policies in the *Berliner Zeitung*. On June 17, the anniversary of the uprising of 1953, there were reports in the GDR press on the meetings at which Hans Mayer and others attacked Ulbricht as a liar, and poems by Polish dissident Adam Wazyk. Though not publishing his own anti-Stalin poems, Brecht was now working on a translation of Wazyk's anti-Stalinist "Poem for Adults."[15] In December 1955, he had translated a section of a Wazyk poem that ended with the following line: "They live in their dreams of the future, and lies are their daily bread." But the translation went into the desk drawer.

At this same time, Brecht urged the prominent editor Comrade Just, "Could you publish more and more in *Sonntag* on the political and cultural life of our fraternal states?"[16] But Just, like Brecht, was walking a knife edge, unsure if Ulbricht would manage to hang on or would be deposed. The KGB and the Stasi were waiting for an opportunity to strike back at any hint of dissidence. Khrushchev's revelations, like those of innocent people back from the gulag, threatened them, for they were those who made up cases and murdered innocent people.

Brecht's main GDR publisher, Walter Janka, was under constant surveillance. Brecht could hardly have the illusion that he was not being watched. With his foreign bank accounts, Austrian passport, and his following in the East and the West, he could be far more dangerous to Ulbricht and the Stasi than Janka, Harich, or any other GDR artist, intellectual, or politician. Brecht's poems were no safer in his desk drawer than his house or Berlau's flat had been to the FBI. Ulbricht had to know that Brecht's anti-Stalin and anti-GDR work would be a deadly danger to the Ulbricht regime at this particular historical moment. Brecht was a loose political cannon both within and outside the GDR.

Preparing for a planned August visit of the Ensemble to England, British translator and editor John Willett came to Buckow, where he saw Brecht, Hauptmann, and Weigel. Hauptmann said that the encouraging changes in Russia seemed to make a visit by the Berliner Ensemble to the Soviet Union a real possibility for 1957.[17] When Willett asked why Brecht did no contemporary political plays in the GDR, Brecht replied: "If I put in Ulbricht's policy, then that must be criticized. I don't write for Ulbricht as an actor, I write for him to be in the audience and learn something." The answer was evasive. A case could rather easily be made for saying that Brecht was more Ulbricht's audience than the reverse. Brecht did speak vaguely to Willett of "this ghastly Stalinism," that "had cost twenty years of development,"[18] but the talk remained private.

By June 25, Elisabeth Hauptmann was back in Berlin trying as always to unscramble Brecht's contracts. In exasperation about just one of hundreds of such disputes, *The Threepenny Novel*, she wrote: "Dear Brecht, Desch has sent here the letter to Allert de Lange, to which he has made alterations, that is to say, the first paragraph is entirely by Desch, the second is from our letter. As it would be very nice to get this whole story out of the way, I am sending it to you despite convalescence and holidays. Please don't just chuck it away but rather bring it with you when you come on Thursday. Greetings. Elisabeth Hauptmann."[19]

On June 28, fifty protesters were shot by hard-line Polish governmental forces. The next day, Brecht learned there was some hope for change in the GDR. An official communiqué stated: "It is necessary that all of our work in the past be self-critically examined, with determination to reveal and cast aside all hesitancies and mistakes, and to seek new solutions for various questions."[20]

On July 18, the twentieth anniversary of the outbreak of the Spanish Civil War was commemorated in Berlin. Ulbricht's outspoken opponent Kantorowicz had written in the 1930s about Ulbricht's (and Stasi chief Mielke's) unsavory actions in Spain purging non-Stalinists. Kantorowicz's book circulated in Berlin in a bizarre version that was like an edition of Romeo and Juliet in which Juliet is missing.[21] Ulbricht's NKVD involvement had also been pointed out in 1948 in a book by Ruth Fischer. Many of those who had served in Spain knew of Ulbricht's deadly role there. At the July 18 Spanish Civil War ceremony in Berlin, stormy applause had greeted those who received awards for fighting in Spain, but there was a "deadly silence" when Ulbricht went up to get his award.[22]

Käthe Rülicke, who attended a dance held as part of the ceremonies, wrote to Brecht later about sharing a dance floor with the GDR leaders: "grotewohl with clever eyes and the sour face of a person with a sick stomach; ulbricht, impenetrable, cold, stand-offish—both dancing waltzes (with their wives) as though they were carrying out a five-year plan, both stared at from all sides (and bashed by me with my elbows three times, in the crush, so to speak): denigrating, questioning. It was very remarkable. They left at midnight without a smile."[23] But, perhaps, there was not much for them to smile about. The anti-Stalinist Yugoslavians flourished, and news came in that the Stalinist Rakosi had been booted out in Hungary.

At the end of her letter, Rülicke speaks openly of introducing Yugoslav practices in the GDR: "what a good position that would be to be in, to have to hide nothing." "I only just notice now," she writes, "how the last years have burdened me, how I have swindled myself defending things that were not worth defending. It was all duty and more duty, too little laughter and too little pride in a thing of wonder." Brecht's reply was unresponsive to her political hopes. He wrote about problems "in our personal relationship" and asked her to not let the "thin ties be broken."[24] The words have a tired air. They are well-worn ones, precisely those he had used with Zoff, Weigel, and Berlau over four decades.

For all the surface appearance of change, plans were being made in secret police offices in Moscow and the satellite states to mercilessly roll back such changes. Where in most official offices portraits of Stalin had come down after Khrushchev's February speech, Spanish politburo member Jorge Semprun noticed when he visited Berlin and the Soviet Union that "the yellow stare of Josef Stalin," was still on the wall in offices of the "organs."[25]

In late July, Brecht suggested to Peter Suhrkamp that they get together for a few weeks rest and recuperation at "Wasser" Schmitt's clinic in Munich. By the beginning of the second week in August, Brecht felt strong enough to resume a regular work schedule. However, he told Wekwerth, he planned to reduce both his writing and his directing.[26] "You all can do that," he told Wekwerth, "why else do I have students?" In fact, as he and the Stasi knew, his contract with the Ensemble was due to expire on August 31, and he had not signed a new one. He had asked Besson to help him buy a house in Switzerland, where he could go on his Austrian passport whenever he wanted, and where he could easily live on the huge amounts of hard currency he had already deposited there. Beyond the immediate reach of Ulbricht, he could, if he so chose, say whatever he wanted about Ulbricht and the hated old Moscow camarilla.

On the morning of August 8, there was a productive session revising the *Days of the Commune* text. Afterward, with what Wekwerth described as Brecht's "typical global exaggeration," Brecht described "a glowing future for the new class of freed workers."[27] Wekwerth asked, "Brecht, name the play you think best represents the form the theatre of the future will take." Like a shot, back came the answer: *"The Measures Taken."*[28] Unless we wholly separate the murderous content of this work from its form, this implied endorsement of murder of those who step out of line is extremely chilling.

Early on the morning of Friday, August 10, Brecht and Wekwerth left Buckow for Berlin. Brecht insisted on driving. He drove the two-seater fast, hurtling past the high, cement block walls of the huge Soviet army camp on the main road out of Buckow. By noon, Brecht and Wekwerth were at the Schiff attending a rehearsal of *The Caucasian Chalk Circle*, then being polished for the upcoming London performances. Brecht left Wekwerth to carry on alone. Leaving the Schiff with Kilian, he had her call Dr. Hennemann, Brugsch's associate at the Charité, and ask him to make a house call to the Chausseestrasse. Hennemann, who was substituting for the vacationing Brugsch, "was not eager to interfere in [Brugsch's] treatment." But he agreed to come. Brecht told him he was going to be examined by Brugsch on August 15, and would leave later for Munich and Dr. Schmitt's clinic. Hennemann prescribed medicinal tea. As the doctor was leaving, however, Kilian told him that the trip to Munich was planned for August 14, before Brugsch's return. Hennemann said he saw no reason for Brecht not to leave for Munich as planned.

On August 11, Franz Spelman, the Munich correspondent of *Newsweek*, wrote asking to interview Brecht on the upheavals shaking eastern Europe. In her reply on August 13, Kilian said "regrettably,

Brecht is not yet healthy, and he will soon be in Munich where he will undergo a cure. I cannot tell you today when it will be possible for him to have a conversation with you and must let that be left to the decision of the doctors. Should I see an opportunity to make an appointment, you will hear from me at once."[29] It would have to have been a totally inept intelligence organization that could ignore the potential explosiveness of one of Ulbricht's oldest enemies giving an interview in West Germany to *Newsweek*.

On August 11, Hauptmann wrote Suhrkamp, not mentioning Brecht's health.[30] She asked Suhrkamp whether or not they should sue Electrola, who had, no doubt at Lotte Lenya's instigation, deliberately brought out a recording without Brecht's name on the cover. Lenya was, of course, simply trying to give Brecht a little of his own medicine. Suhrkamp decided there was little wisdom challenging Lenya on what he knew to be heavily mined terrain.

On August 13, Dr. Hennemann made another house call to the famous patient. Apparently, he was pleased with what he saw and heard. He noticed nothing different in the sound of Brecht's heart. He noted there was "some amelioration of the pain associated with the cystitis."[31] After seeing Hennemann, Brecht wrote to Brugsch: "From what was gained by the treatment, nothing has been lost, but no recovery has taken place. We turned to your deputy, Prof. Hennemann, and even he, if only with reluctance, had nothing against the hurrying up of our stay at Schmitt's sanatorium. Schmitt will report to you, and I hope to be back with you again soon."[32]

Apparently, later that day, Mari Barbara was sent on a medical errand, to try to get the amiable and gifted young Dr. Georgi Tsoulukidse to come and see her father. But, when Mari Barbara arrived at the doctor's flat near the Schiffbauerdamm Theater, the doctor was not home. Instead, another doctor who lived in the same house, Dr. Kroker, was persuaded to come instead. Dr. Kroker told Dr. Tsoulukidse that he had examined Brecht, and that Brecht had told him that he had wanted to see a doctor because "mich ergriff eine grosse Müdigkeit" (I was overcome by a great tiredness). But, apparently, the general practitioner Kroker spotted nothing that would warrant having the famous patient taken to a hospital.

Apparently, according to Kilian's recollection, she then decided to ask Dr. Beyer of the famous Virchow Hospital in West Berlin to come to see Brecht. It was only after this, Kilian said later, that she called the East Berlin Regierungskrankenhaus in Pankow and asked them to send an electrocardiogram unit to the Chausseestrasse. Why Brecht did not go to a West Berlin hospital or to Pankow where emergency aid could be administered if the electrocardiogram turned up anything untoward, rather than having an electrocardiogram unit brought to him where no follow-up care was available, has never been explained. Whether they feared what could happen at Pankow is not known. The trip to and from Pankow might have seemed too far with his departure for Munich imminent. However, among the assassination techniques employed by the secret police under Stalin was the inducement of "heart attacks."[33] Martin Pohl believed, based on remarks Kilian had made to him in 1954 about his release from Stasi custody being imminent, that Kilian herself was one of the at least two Stasi agents recruited to report on everything Brecht did or said. Since the practice of recruiting the most intimate partner to spy on a mate was a regular feature of KGB and Stasi practice, Pohl's suspicions warrant further investigation as the Stasi files have now become accessible.

Even as the Regierungskrankenhaus staff brought their equipment to the Chausseestrasse, Brecht's car was being loaded as though he was about to leave on the Munich train. All the key people at the Ensemble on the morning of the fourteenth acted on the assumption that Brecht's Munich trip would take place that day. A clean copy of Brecht's August 13 letter to Brugsch was typed and dated August 14. Several other notes and letters of the same date are also in the files. One is signed by Karl von Appen, Hauptmann, Kilian, and six other members of the Berliner Ensemble staff.[34] The stagehands sent a letter saying "We will stand at Helli's side as long as you are not in Berlin."[35] Weigel also wrote a letter dated August 14:

> Dear Doctor Schmitt,
> I am concerned in the deepest way about Brecht's condition. He is entirely lacking in strength and, besides this, has the feeling that he is very ill. I must ask you to make yourself available for his needs at all times, even when you have your vacation, so that every day, yes, every hour, he can speak with you, because he trusts you and needs you now.
> The bad thing is that I do not see any way to break off the planned tour in order that I could stay with him in Munich. There will, of course, always be a person there who will concern himself for him; our son will stay, as long as you think it is right for him to do so. Mrs. Kilian will help wherever it is possible for her to help.
> I ask you to absolutely be there for Brecht and do whatever or consult with whomever it may be that you think is right. The cost of this plays no role and must not be allowed to play a role.
> I thank you very much."[36]

Weigel's letter to Schmitt, as was usually the case when she wrote of Brecht's health, was part truth and part evasion. Even had she not been on her way to London with the Ensemble, it would have been the current favorite, Isot Kilian, who would have been at Brecht's bedside. The reference to Stefan is also important. If Weigel had any inkling of the fact that Brecht had dictated a new will to Kilian that assigned many of the most remunerative rights to others, having a Brecht family member at the Munich bedside made (as did most of Weigel's actions) excellent business sense.

That same busy August 14, Hennemann also prepared a letter: "Esteemed Colleague Herr Schmidt! [*sic*]" he wrote:

Herr Brecht has asked me to give you a short report on the status of his illness in the last eight days, and I am glad to provide this herewith.

I visited him at his apartment on August 9, 1956, and there examined him for the first time. Based upon the picture I was able to form then of his complaints, I postulated a reoccurrence of the inflammation of his bladder. This was confirmed by a microscopic examination of a urine sample where the sediment showed a massive number of leucocytes. Other evidence, except for a certain number of uric acid crystals, was not found. I prescribed certain dietary measures, as well as warm local compresses and medicinal tea (Ba-Rentraubenblättertee), as I did not want to prescribe any chemical therapeutic treatment in view of the fact that the patient planned to have himself examined by Professor Brugsch upon his return from his vacation on August 15, 1956.

From my general examination of the patient, I had the impression of general arteriosclerosis with particular coronary and aorta-valve sclerosis, which would partially account for his lack of energy and general sense of weakness. On my own initiative, I suggested climatic treatment, and Herr Brecht enthusiastically told me of his own plan to put himself in your care in Munich.

When I visited him for the second time yesterday, I had the impression that there was some amelioration of the pain connected with the cystitis. One would need to check further to determine how much his old prostate condition might be responsible for his cystitis. We therefore advised him that upon his return from your clinic in Munich that he should again present himself to us where we could do a Rest-N-Kontrolle examination of the prostate and a thorough examination of his urinary tract.

With the very best collegial greetings, I remain very humbly yours,

H. H. Hennemann[37]

With so many letters written on August 14—all presupposing Brecht's leaving for Munich that day—the key question is: what then happened to force a change? Thirty years later, Isot Kilian still had great difficulty in bringing herself to talk of specific details. What we do know is that as of about noon, a number of doctors, including staff from the official Regierungskrankenhaus, gathered at the Chausseestrasse apartment. Supposedly, tests on the portable electrocardiogram unit showed that Brecht had suffered a serious stroke three days before. Yet, as we know, Dr. Hennemann had examined Brecht just the day before, and had seen and heard only positive changes in Brecht's condition from the earlier examination on the ninth.

At some point on this tumultuous day, Helene Weigel moved to try to insure control of his financial affairs. Like the famous scene in *War and Peace* where the contenders for the vast fortune of Count Bezuhov maneuver to get the dying man to sign their version of a will, a similar scene now played itself out around Brecht. Though Weigel already had in hand one signed and notarized will, she had Brecht sign in the presence of the doctors the following note in English: "Berlin, August 14, 1956. To whom it may concern. My wife, Mrs. Helene Weigel-Brecht, is authorized by me to collect any royalties due to me and to negotiate on my behalf. Bertolt Brecht."[38] Weigel then asserted her rights as legal wife, and ordered that Hauptmann, Reichel, and Kilian (who might have had Brecht sign something different at a crucial last moment) no longer be admitted to his sickroom. The only people allowed to remain were a medical team that included Brecht's childhood friend Dr. Müllereisert, who had apparently learned that something was wrong.

Not content to leave things as he had in the short note to Weigel, Brecht asked Müllereisert to take down his real last will and testament. Müllereisert's notes, as they would be formally submitted to the GDR authorities the next day, read: "Physically Brecht was in a weak condition that did not permit him to write himself, but he was mentally fully alert and able to understand what he was doing. On Tuesday, the 14th of August, my friend Bertolt Eugen Brecht made his last will and testament: My sole heir is my wife, Helene Weigel. She is not only my sole heir but also has power of attorney in carrying out my wishes." But, as Brecht then went on to specify, there were to be a number of exceptions to the "sole heir":

1) My daughter Barbara is to get the Tower House in Buckow.
2) My son Stefan is to get all the income from my plays produced in America. 3) Miss Käthe Reichel is to get the house in Buckow under the condition that she, as promised, plays her

part at the Berlin[er] Ensemble in *The Good Person* [*Woman*] *of Setzuan.* 4) Mrs. Isot Kilian and her children are to get the income from my songs. 5) Mrs. Ruth Berlau, divorced from Lund, is to receive 50,000 Danish kroner under condition that she uses the money to buy a house which, after her death, is to go to Helene Weigel.

I ask that my wife, Helene Weigel, continue to run the Berlin[er] Ensemble as long as she feels that the present style of the theater can be maintained.[39]

As far as is known, these were Brecht's last words. For whatever reason, he forgot Elisabeth Hauptmann entirely.

Manfred Wekwerth, Benno Besson, and Peter Palitzsch were told at six on the evening of August 14 that Brecht had had a stroke. Shaken but trying to concentrate on something practical, they talked for hours about their own work at the Ensemble. At nine, the three men parted and went home.

Upstairs, Brecht had lapsed into a coma. For five hours, his breath was barely perceptible. Just before midnight, the doctors told Weigel that they believed him to be dead. There remained a gruesome task to carry out. Fearing burial alive, and following the ancient practice of Roman emperors, Brecht had apparently given instructions to Weigel that if he should ever be medically determined dead, a stiletto was to be put through his heart. This was done by one of the attending doctors.

As it was a long-standing tradition in Germany that a death mask be made of famous figures, arrangements were made to have the sculptor Fritz Cremer come at once. As Cremer apparently told journalist Rudy Hassing, when he entered the apartment he saw Brecht in a seated position with blood dribbling from his mouth. It also appeared to the horrified Cremer that Brecht's lips were moving as though he were attempting to say something. But the doctors, putting Brecht down flat, told Cremer to begin to make the death mask. Overwhelmed by what he had seen and not feeling that he was up to doing this gruesome job alone, Cremer left the apartment without making the death mask.

In the early hours of the fifteenth, several key people were told Brecht had died, and the news went out on the major wire services and would be heard all day on the radio. When Piscator heard the news in West Berlin, his main feeling was anger as he felt he had been robbed by Brecht. In a note to himself about Brecht and the whole idea of "epic theater," he said bitterly and surely correctly, "He stole my legacy."[40] Later, as Hanns Eisler told Vladimir Pozner, Eisler was reminded of his dead friend when visiting a whorehouse rather like the one Jenny and Mackie sing about in *The Threepenny Opera* and the piano player struck up the tune of "Mack the Knife."[41] When Manfred Wekwerth was called with the news of Brecht's death, he passed the news to Besson and Palitzsch; and the three hurried back to the Chausseestrasse and watched as the Regierungskrankenhaus equipment was packed up for the drive back to Pankow. At 8:30 A.M., Cremer returned, bringing with him his assistant, Gerhart Thieme. The corpse was now lying flat. There was, Thieme told me, no sign of "a death struggle."[42] Running a piece of string down the nose and slightly oiling the corpse's hair so the plaster would not stick to it, Thieme took an impression of the face and ears. While the body still lay in the apartment, Weigel had Berlau brought from St. Joseph's Hospital where, during the whole last period of Brecht's final illness, she had been taken after another relapse. Berlau was allowed briefly to see the body and then returned to hospital.

Supposedly, Brecht's detailed instructions to Weigel had specified that "the coffin be made of steel or iron." It would have to be con- structed virtually overnight. Simultaneously, as Brecht had left instruc- tions that he was to be buried next door in a cemetery that had long since been filled up, the authorities had to move other bodies to accom- modate his.

Kilian, who was cooperating closely with Hauptmann and who thought she had the final version of Brecht's will, wrote to the firm of Suhrkamp asking for an up-to-date accounting of the earnings due there. Hauptmann, acting before she might be stopped by Weigel, sent a telegram to Denmark confirming the final payment on a house that was being bought there for Berlau.

On August 16, with the funeral to be held the next day, Helene Weigel got off the following telegram to a few very close friends and relatives: "The best friends will meet together at nine tomorrow morn- ing. If you can, come." Among those receiving this message were Brecht's childhood friend Orge Pfanzelt and Brecht's brother, Walter. Johannes R. Becher wired Eric Bentley inviting him to come, but the distance was too far and the time too short for Bentley to get away. Peter Suhrkamp tried to attend, but he was held up by the GDR border guards and missed the procession of men who escorted the coffin to the grave: Paul Wandel, Jakob Walcher, Hanns and Gerhart Eisler, Jo- hannes R. Becher, Fritz Cremer, Paul Dessau, and Erich Engel. There were, as Brecht had specified, no graveyard speeches. Amidst banks of huge wreathes around his grave stood many "widows": Hauptmann, Weigel, Reichel, and Kilian.

Though Brecht had said no speeches were to be given at his grave, he had not blocked other possibilities for making his death a state occasion. On August 18, a formal ceremony was held at the Schiffbauer- damm Theater, with the main speech by Walter Ulbricht. This speech,

according to Hans Mayer's eyewitness account, was delivered in Ulbricht's usual dry and official cadences.[43] From a political perspective
and in terms of iconic "photo opportunities," the speech was a vital one
for Ulbricht at this moment in GDR history. Ulbricht claimed, as he
had done at the 1953 uprising, that Brecht was deeply committed to the
GDR. Nobody rose to challenge Ulbricht.

Johannes R. Becher delivered a speech full of what Hans Mayer
called "the prose of official condolences." The reigning dean of Marxist
critics, the key exegete of socialist realism, Georg Lukács spoke next.
After all Lukács's attacks on Brecht through the decades, he had now,
at Weigel's request, returned from the spa where he usually spent the
summer. Weigel's request reflected political reality. Lukács, believing
his new stance was backed by Khrushchev's Kremlin, defended the kind
of work for which Brecht had been known. Lukács, like Ulbricht, was
using the occasion to claim Brecht, but the reformers hoped to use
Lukács to advance their own goals of measured liberalization.

After the carefully calibrated speeches, erstwhile "formalist" and
"decadent" Hanns Eisler strode to the piano. He was joined by Ernst
Busch, who had until just days before been rehearsing the role of
Galileo. Busch sang "The Song of Praise" and "The Canon of Farewell." The latter, in a nominally socialist state, was a particularly odd
choice. A character named Jimmy Appletree from the Hauptmann-
Brecht adaptation of Farquhar's *The Recruiting Officer* sings as he leaves
to fight a war for the American colonies:

> I would leave you,
> Because the great ship of the Queen
> Lies, for men and soldiers, at the quay.
> Take another, Minnie,
> For this ship is going to Virginia
> And love, and this love is over.

To this the girl replies:

> And we stand here two, three thousand
> As with man and mouse and brew
> The great ship of the Queen sets to sea.
> But one thing, Jimmy, you must know
> I will always miss you
> Even as on with others I will go.[44]

After the ceremony, Peter Suhrkamp complained in a letter to Caspar
Neher (who had not attended), " 'The Song of Praise' and 'The Canon

of Farewell' (Abschiedslied) can only be sung as part of a real community. That meant for Brecht only a few men."[45] Suhrkamp got no argument from Neher on Brecht's inability to deal with women as an equal part of "a real community."

47

"The Progress of the Consciousness of Freedom"

After finishing Brecht's death mask, Gerhart Thieme made copies for the people who wanted this final memorial of him. Getting word of this, Weigel ordered Thieme to bring all the heads except the original death mask to Brecht's old apartment. There, under Weigel's supervision, Thieme took a hammer and smashed ten plaster copies of Brecht to tiny pieces. Unbeknownst to Weigel, one intact copy of the mask remained in Ruth Berlau's possession. From this, other copies would later be made.

As summer turned to fall in 1956, leaves in Berlin's lovely Dorotheen Friedhof cemetery drifted onto Brecht's grave and the adjacent grave of Hegel, who had dreamed his dream of history as "the progress of the consciousness of freedom." A seismic shift was occurring in the socialist world. In Poland, Wladislaw Gomulka spoke openly of moving rapidly away from Stalin's murderous heritage. Radio Liberty and Radio Free Europe praised the Polish position and urged support for Gomulka but said any attempts to carry the revolution further at that time would be counterproductive, if not suicidal. In Hungary, Imre Nagy urged following the Poles and withdrawing his country from the alliance of Soviet-dominated states.

Many in the GDR also longed to break with the past. But Ulbricht, with his years of close work with Soviet intelligence, sensed that the tide was about to turn against dissidents such as Nagy and Gomulka. He made a quick trip to the Kremlin in the fall of 1956. The men he met in the Kremlin (the time had long since passed when women formed part of the Kremlin inner circle) were clearly frightened at Khrushchev's demands for liberalization. Khrushchev's speech in February 1956, which outlined in detail Stalin's hundreds of thousands of violations of justice, was seen as endangering the entire Soviet bloc. Conservative members of the politburo thought Hungary and Poland foreshadowed the collapse of communism itself unless liberalization there was immediately repressed. Authorization was given to use whatever force was needed to crush dissidents everywhere in the client states. Ulbricht had a green light to wipe out all opposition to him and to Stalinist rule in the GDR. During the night of October 16, 1956, Wolfgang Harich was taken to a Stasi jail. There, this leader of the opposition was broken in the time-honored way and for the usual purpose, to appear in a show trial that would condemn him.

Other top-level officials of the GDR were still trying to eliminate Stalinism. A top West German official, Fritz Schäffer, and the deputy defense minister of the GDR, Vincenz Müller, met on October 20 to discuss reunification of the two Germanies. The Soviet ambassador to the GDR attended, and a GDR politburo member, Otto Grotewohl, was told of the meeting. On November 1, 1956, Imre Nagy's government announced Hungary's neutrality and independence from the Soviet Union. The Hungarians obviously hoped that the United States and its NATO allies would back their revolt against the Soviet Union. But Hungary had chosen the precisely wrong moment to act. On October 29, Israeli forces had invaded the Sinai, and Israel, Britain, and France tried to wrest the Suez Canal from Egyptian control. On November 4, while the eyes of the West were on Suez, Russian tanks rolled in Hungary. Nagy was tried and would later be executed. Georg Lukács was put under house arrest. Still hoping for change in the socialist states, Johannes R. Becher and Anna Seghers quickly provided Walter Janka with Western money, a car, and documents to rescue Lukács.[1] Ulbricht ordered the operation canceled. He did not want any potential supporter of the arrested Harich brought to Berlin.

According to Janka, soon after the news got out of Harich's arrest, Helene Weigel asked him to come to see her. He was admitted to Weigel's Chausseestrasse apartment by one of her servants. Though not ill, and though it was afternoon, she lay in her large bed. Janka thought the bed and everything else in the room had the air of a stage prop. After a servant brought them tea and left, Weigel said: "This mess with Harich is a regression to the worst times. One cannot accept this without resistance."[2] Weigel did not propose to become the front line of resistance, but she urged Janka to do so. "Have the press come out on strike," Weigel said. "Your people stand behind you. We now need an example." Janka told her that for a strike to be effective, it could not be led by the couple of hundred employees of Aufbau Verlag. He suggested Weigel approach instead the director of one of the biggest factories in the GDR, the Leuna-Werke. As Janka left, Weigel said to him, "We must now defend ourselves. Precisely, we artists must do something." But, as Janka observes, instead of bringing the Berliner Ensemble out on strike, "Three hours later she [Weigel] stood on the stage. The Berliner Ensemble was playing *Mother Courage.*" Night after night in this play, Weigel as Courage stares in horrified silence as her dead son is brought before her and she must disown him. Night after night, she picked up the harness of her supply wagon to rejoin the forces that had destroyed her progeny and for whom she is a key supplier of war materiel. Reality imitated art as Weigel's silent complicity onstage mirrored her real-life behavior. While her friend Harich was being made ready for his show trial, Janka was also taken, and still Weigel did not protest.

Until his own arrest, Janka himself had maintained, as had Weigel and virtually the entire GDR intelligentsia, a public silence. One charge now made against him was that he had wanted to bring Lukács to the GDR to help overthrow Ulbricht's government. Yet Anna Seghers and Johannes R. Becher, who had urged Janka to bring back Lukács, were deliberately not arrested. Nor was Helene Weigel, though she had participated in the plans of both Harich and Janka. Ulbricht knew, just as his teacher Stalin knew, that the threat of arrest was often as effective as arrest itself. The tactic worked in the GDR just as well as it had in the Soviet Union. Neither Becher nor Seghers challenged the state, or came to Janka's or Harich's defense. Weigel did not admit she had urged Janka to strike, nor that she had explicitly supported Harich's political agenda. Only years later, at the collapse of the GDR, would the state recognize that "show trials" such as that of Janka had fundamentally violated the constitution of the GDR.[3]

Within months of Brecht's death, Ulbricht had skillfully smashed the opposition with the silent, if coerced, cooperation of the GDR intelligentsia including Weigel. Harich argued that "till his death, Bertolt Brecht strongly sympathized with our group and saw in us the healthy powers of the party,"[4] but without published Brecht documents or the public support of prominent people such as Weigel, Seghers, and Becher, Harich's case was hopeless. By failing to publish his more outspoken texts in his own lifetime, Brecht left his friends, Hans Mayer told me later, "without protection." A prominent GDR intellectual at the time of Harich's and Janka's arrests who later fled to the West, Mayer wondered aloud as we spoke about Brecht, "Was his silence necessary?"[5] But quite apart from the question of Brecht's failing health in the last months of his life, it is doubtful that Brecht could have ever been anything but the person who said both yes and no, and only when it was reasonably safe to do either. Like his fictional Herr Keuner, Brecht served Ulbricht for seven years, from late 1948 until the middle of 1956, but he never did what Herr Keuner did in fiction. Brecht died before Ulbricht and never had the satisfaction of saying no!

Carefully selected members of the "Harich group" were made ready to stand trial on charges of "high treason." Anna Seghers, Willi Bredel, and Helene Weigel were "invited" to attend these trials as "observers." If Weigel screamed inside, it was a scream unheard in the courtroom. In a system of justice like that in *The Measures Taken*, where the outcome was predetermined, Harich was sentenced to ten years, and Janka followed him to a Stasi jail. Having, like Johannes R. Becher and Anna Seghers, played her role to Ulbricht's satisfaction, Helene Weigel was permitted to return to her handsomely paid job as head of a compliant Ensemble.

Another and less prominent case moved swiftly through the state apparatus, one that would determine which of Brecht's various wills would be recognized. Millions in hard currency and the control of unpublished Brecht documents were at stake. Weigel had in hand a will that gave her everything, the note that Brecht had apparently signed on August 14, and, furthermore, she was the legal widow. But there was also the one that Brecht had dictated to Isot Kilian. It gave fully one-third of the biggest money-maker of all, *The Threepenny Opera*, to its principle author, Elisabeth Hauptmann; *The Caucasian Chalk Circle* to its coauthor, Ruth Berlau; the money-making *Puntila* to the dissident party politician Jakob Walcher; and other valuable rights to the dissident Paul Wandel. But this will had never been notarized. Then there was the will Brecht had dictated on his deathbed to Otto Müllereisert, one of the lovers from his teenage years. That will gave royalties directly to several mistresses.

In the party-controlled courts of the GDR, the cooperative Weigel was declared Brecht's sole heir and guardian of the posthumous papers until her death. Those named in the Kilian and Müllereisert documents received only modest lump sums from Weigel. Not only did the legatees lose millions, but they also lost control of the right to release the materials as they saw fit. Only in the case of Elisabeth Hauptmann was some minor modification of these terms effected. Peter Suhrkamp, who apparently had some idea of what Hauptmann had contributed down the years to the works published under the richly ambiguous title *The Collected Works of Brecht*, persuaded Weigel that Hauptmann must be given a modest share of the rights.

For the rest of her life, Weigel received medals and titles from the grateful government of the GDR. Weigel alone determined who saw what and whether it could be published. Holding unpublished and explosive Brecht materials gave her leverage with the government when it came time to renew or expand the yearly budget of the Brecht Archive and the Ensemble. But, even with all the money and honors, discreet sparks of dissidence did occasionally flash. A CIA file entry dated December 1960 claims: "In Aug 1960 Helene Weigel widow of Berthold [*sic*] Brecht announced in East German cultural circles her intention to allow publication of Brecht works on 17 June 1953 revolt which are unpublished and damaging to SED regime. Weigel was finally dissuaded by senior East German culture officials in exchange for promise of extensive financial support for Brecht archives in East Berlin. Unpublished works allegedly still remain in Weigel's possession in spite of repeated efforts East German culture functionaries to obtain full control [of] Brecht estate."[6] The CIA message requested authorization to try to surreptitiously obtain from Weigel the material in question. The file does not explain how the CIA intended to achieve this. As far as I have determined, CIA efforts to subvert Weigel remained unsuccessful. Though she had formally left the party following Khrushchev's speech of 1956, her loyalties usually remained with the party.[7] In 1961, for instance, the year the wall was built, she personally advised Heiner Müller to make peace with the SED.[8] Her opposition was generally calibrated close to the levels Lukács set in the 1930s in Stalin's Moscow, but she remained in discreet opposition.

Not long before Weigel's death, she gave me direct access to the then off-limits materials on Tretiakov and the Soviet Union in the years of the Moscow Show Trials. These materials were a lit fuse leading not only to the formalism debate itself but to other explosive materials on Stalin. Weigel said she was giving me access because I had shown her that my proletarian credentials were impeccable, after I had deliberately taunted her with the fact this was in contrast to her own bourgeois origins. But had she really wanted me not to see the Soviet items, she could have found an excuse not to do so. I believe the truth was she wanted at least some of the real story to be known.

Weigel died in 1971, after which the flood of royalty payments then started to flow directly to Brecht's children. Control of the Brecht Archive passed to an agency of the GDR, the Academy of Arts, insuring that only officially endorsed lines of inquiry could be followed. Publications that told a different story, those of Hans Bunge for instance, were extralegally blocked by the government and by Mari Barbara Brecht-Schall. In West Germany, Suhrkamp Verlag, as long as it did not rock the GDR boat by insisting on full and timely revelation of the Brecht legacy of deliberately stealing the creation of others, could reap rewards from Brecht sales that helped the company build a dominant hold over a large segment of West German publishing.

Until its final collapse, the GDR government promoted Brecht's posthumous iconic status. A large statue of him was put up on the renamed Bertolt-Brecht-Platz in front of the Schiffbauerdamm Theater. The state porcelain works created a Bertolt Brecht memorial plate. When Ruth Berlau and Martin Pohl came forward to point out their work had been taken without recompense, they were ignored by everyone except Elisabeth Hauptmann. Hauptmann tried to support claims that she knew were legitimate, but she had no effect either.

In 1994, Suhrkamp Verlag continues to publish a multivolume edition of Brecht's works, in which the writing of Steffin, Hauptmann, Berlau, Ottwalt, Pohl, and several others is reprinted without a systematic effort to identify and frankly acknowledge their contribution to the works of Brecht. In 1986, Jan Knopf, one of Suhrkamp's editors, said that this could not be done as "that train has already left the station."[9] When I met him in Berlin at the time of the fall of the Berlin Wall and showed him explicit instances of the illicit use of the work of others, he was again unwilling to deal directly with the issue of who wrote what in Brecht's works. This arrangement continues to be massively remunerative to the holders of the "Brecht" copyrights.

Hanne Hiob, Brecht's daughter by Marianne Zoff, lives in Munich, the city where she was born and where she still works as an actress, and takes passionate part in peace and social justice activities.

After a brief stint as an actress, Mari Barbara Brecht-Schall managed the foreign appearances of her actor husband, Ekkehard Schall. She has her main residence in Berlin and the inherited lakeside estate at "millionaire's Buckow." Under President Erich Honecker of the GDR, she received a five-figure cash prize from the state for her services. She has complained about what I write about her father, but when I ask her for other facts to disprove what I have written, she provides none. In a letter addressed to Hans Bunge dated February 23, 1979, she wrote of Berlau: "Diese Frau war eben ein Parasit und in keine Weise fähig, mit irgend einer Leistung sich das Leben zu verdienen" (This woman was a parasite and in no way capable with any kind of contribution of earning a living).[10] Mari Barbara Brecht-Schall has lived off her husband's earnings or "Brecht" royalties for most of her adult life and recently negotiated an eight-figure deal with the Berlin senate for "Brecht" manuscripts.

The surviving Brecht son, Stefan, completed a Ph.D. at Harvard after writing his thesis on Hegel. One of his residences is in New York, where he writes poetry and works in experimental New York theater circles. When I have asked him to help me get access to unpublished materials, he has, like his mother, quietly and quickly provided the necessary authorization without attempting to restrict what I would say about any member of the Brecht family.

Herta Hanisch, the sister and heir of Margarete Steffin, continued until her death in 1989 to live in poverty in a small house on the edge of Berlin where washing water would need to be carried by hand. First, Helene Weigel and then Mari Barbara Brecht-Schall attempted to get Hanisch to sign over rights to her sister's surviving papers. Occasionally, in her poverty, Herta Hanisch would agree to sell Weigel some things, which were added to the Brecht collection. When some of

Margarete Steffin's papers were brought to Berlin from Moscow in 1961, they were given not to their legal owner, Hanisch, but to the Brecht Archive.

After Hanisch's death in 1990, I was able to begin to set up with Kurt Groenewold the Steffin Stiftung to help unjustly forgotten writers. Finally, the work of Steffin has begun to be published in its own right. Her volume of miscellaneous writings, *Confucius Understands Nothing of Women*, appeared in 1991 to strong reviews.

Only very gradually has Elisabeth Hauptmann begun to emerge from the shadows in which she spent so much of her creative life. She died on April 20, 1973, largely ignored as a writer. The writings that guardedly reveal her real attitude toward Brecht were not published until 1977. My own notes on Hauptmann's contributions to the Berliner Ensemble plays did not begin to appear until 1974. James Lyon's observations on Brecht's use of Hauptmann's Kipling translations were published in 1975. John Willett's observations that strongly suggest one could not tell who really wrote what from the time of Hauptmann's meeting of Brecht in late 1924 on did not appear until 1985.

In the overwhelmingly theoretical world of Brecht scholarship, facts such as what Hauptmann and others really wrote, and who collected what money from the work, are routinely ignored. The material world had almost no place in this nominally Marxist scholarship. Nor has the real reaction of audiences to Brecht plays, rather than Brecht's intentions for audiences to remain distanced and cool, received much attention. Brecht's mythic retellings of his own history, his "poetic" accounts of why he answered HUAC as he did, his view of himself as "surgeon" and "revolutionary," his claims to poverty, his own view of his devotion to the "class struggle," and his own view of what constitutes "political wisdom" have substituted for scholarly investigation. Even when attempts have been made to substitute historical fact for Brechtian fictions, the efforts are then often ignored by Brecht scholars and those earning money from the sale of Brecht artifacts. In 1977, Hauptmann's old friend Manfred Wekwerth did a television version of the fine but neglected play *Happy End*, a production that won the coveted Prix Italia. For years, Wekwerth has made plain to anyone who would listen that *Happy End* was written by Elisabeth Hauptmann. Still, however, translations of *Happy End* suggest the primary author is Brecht. John Willett, while publishing notes that recognize that at least seven of the eleven so-called Berlin stories are probably by Hauptmann, still allows the stories to circulate as Brecht's Berlin stories.

A few scholars have worked to identify texts previously mislabeled as Brecht. In Europe and America, Shull and Luchessi have shown that the original text of *The Threepenny Opera* is overwhelmingly

Hauptmann's work, as has the German scholar, Klaus Völker. Hauptmann's key role in the creation of *Saint Joan of the Stockyards* is now acknowledged at least in the footnotes of the new Brecht edition. Hauptmann's role in the creation of the *Lehrstücke* has been acknowledged by Willett. Dr. Paula Hanssen has reexamined the manuscripts of Brecht's Chinese poems and attributes them overwhelmingly to Hauptmann. My own essay on Hauptmann's role is in the *Cambridge Companion to Bertolt Brecht*.[11] Gradually, Hauptmann is beginning to be examined in her own right, not as Brecht appendage, apologist, or victim. We were not, I am unhappy to say, alert enough while she was still alive. Most scholars, myself included, hardly knew what questions to ask her. We did not realize that, going all the way back to the Weimar years, she had often held her newspaper upside down to get our attention.

Before her death in 1973, Hauptmann would sometimes speak openly but very quietly of what she had really done. She told me on November 9, 1970, that she hoped to have her own archive so that her work could be studied in its own right. With considerable dignity, she continued to edit the work to which she contributed so much. In the same November 1970 interview, she told me she often had done almost entire poems that were then published under Brecht's name and that she had done much of the work on the *Lehrstücke* but sometimes had forgotten (the case she mentioned was *The Measures Taken*) to put her name on the work even in tiny letters. She hoped posterity would take a closer look at her legacy and reach a fair judgment about it. In her last years, she was able to maintain some measure of independence from Weigel, though Weigel did, Haputmann said, attempt to interfere in her editorial decisions about Brecht texts.[12]

Where Hauptmann had her editing work to sustain her in her last years, Ruth Berlau had the greatest difficulty continuing to work after Brecht's death. She was chronically unhappy in Copenhagen despite her new house. After her sister Edith had married and immigrated to Australia, there was little to keep Ruth in Denmark. Her health problems made a return to the Royal Danish Theater impossible. She also found that her career as a writer in a language as obscure as Danish could not be restarted. When she offered Suhrkamp Verlag *Every Animal Can Do It*, her fine feminist book that had originally appeared in 1940, it was turned down.

In her last years, Ruth Berlau returned to Berlin and gradually sold off her Brecht letters and manuscripts of their joint work together to Helene Weigel or the East Berlin academy, where they were then placed under lock and key. In her last years, she had very few friends. Her behavior was often erratic by that time, and any association with her was frowned upon by Helene Weigel. Despite this, the first head of the Bertolt Brecht Archive, her friend Dr. Hans Bunge, did a series of highly revealing interviews with Berlau. When he attempted to publish them, he was blocked for years by Mari Barbara Brecht-Schall working with officials at the top level of the GDR. In her very last years, Ruth Berlau was almost forgotten. Her hauntingly lovely face was rarely seen at theaters where the work to which she had contributed much was being produced. There was a small moment of triumph when Helene Weigel died before her. Berlau herself died in a fire in a room at the Charité Hospital on the night of January 15, 1974.

Long after her death, Berlau began to get some recognition. Though long-delayed and heavily censcored in the GDR, Hans Bunge's touching memorial to Berlau, *Lai tu*, appeared in several languages, including Japanese and English. Finally, though one of the more revealing autobiographical chapters was left out, *Every Animal Can Do It* came out with a leading feminist press. In 1992, a group of scholar–film makers (myself among them) made a film on Ruth Berlau's life called *Red Ruth: That Deadly Longing*.

Käthe Reichel's position at the Berliner Ensemble under Helene Weigel was very difficult after Brecht died. She took on guest assignments at theaters in both East and West Germany. She began to show other people some of her own writing, including some poems that have since been published. She still lives in the apartment she and Brecht picked out in Berlin. When the GDR fell apart in 1989, she tried to protect some of the hard-won women's rights legislation that had been passed in East Germany. As a woman and Jew, she ran considerable risks from right-wing thugs. To her horror, many women's rights were thrown away by West Germany's ruling coalition led by Helmut Kohl. When the GDR ended, the dream of gender equality Reichel had fought for also remained unfulfilled.

Isot Kilian, with her ex-husband Wolfgang Harich in jail, remained in East Berlin. Now and again, she would publish decorous reminiscences about Brecht. When I interviewed her just before her death in 1986, she provided me with many details on the last months of Brecht's life.

Somewhat better off was Käthe Rülicke, who went on to earn a doctorate and a prominent professorial position in the GDR. She was still working on her memoirs at the time of her death in 1992.

After decades of obscurity, Marieluise Fleisser lived long enough to see a three-volume edition of her collected works brought out by Suhrkamp in 1972. She died on February 2, 1974. At her death, she was working on a final version of her *Deepseafish*, the work that had been suppressed in 1930 because of her accurate, revealing descriptions of the regularly exploitative practices of Brecht & Company.

Gradually, as the years have passed and standards of scholarship have changed from Brecht hagiography to beginning investigations of how the work really was created, Berlau, Steffin, and Hauptmann have begun to emerge from the shadows in which they lived and died. With the fall of the Berlin Wall, and the purchase by the Berlin senate of the original Brecht papers, a new era of scholarship is now beginning and new questions are being asked of the "Brecht" texts. One hopes the era of hagiography is now over, and a period of full, frank, serious scholarship has commenced.

When Brecht and Tretiakov visited a cemetery together in Bavaria in 1931, they noted how in that repressive and unequal society, the class divisions of life were perpetuated in death. Tretiakov wrote scathingly at the time: "The first-class dead were buried along the main path. . . . Third-class was in a far corner."[13] Ironically, looking down on the Dorotheen Friedhof cemetery from the Brecht House at 125 Chaussee-strasse today, one sees exactly the same arrangements in this once "socialist" cemetery as they saw in Bavaria. There is a series of large burial plots alongside Brecht in the main row of this lovely old Hugue-not cemetery: Arnolt Bronnen, Johannes R. Becher, Hanns Eisler, Erich Engel, John Heartfield, and Heinrich Mann. Helene Weigel is the only woman in the front row, next to Brecht. Berlau's and Hauptmann's tiny plots, where their ashes are buried, lie close together. Their graves are placed just about as far away from Brecht and Weigel as the confines of one cemetery permit. They lie in the visually "third-class" area, so far off the beaten track that I had to ask the grave digger who buried them to guide me to them.

Beyond the marked graves of the first-, second-, and third-class dead in Berlin—in places as far-flung as Moscow, New York, Pacific Palisades, Port Bou, Helsinki, Copenhagen, Paris, and London—are the last remains of those many erstwhile members of the circle who were abandoned, or who met violent death at their own or at other hands. The ashes of some are part of the dust of Nazi death camps, and several met their end in what one Soviet poet has called "the Auschwitzes of the North."[14] The whereabouts of the remains of Mikhail Koltsov, Maria Osten, Sergei Tretiakov, Ernst Ottwalt, Vsevolod Meyerhold, Carola Neher, and Margarete Steffin are unknown. Their ashes are scattered somewhere in the Soviet Union, or their bodies tossed into unmarked prison graves or frozen in shallow trenches dug in the perma-frost of the Arctic Circle, identified, if at all, only by an NKVD wooden tag bearing the victim's case number, attached to the left leg.

Perhaps, it is only now in the postglasnost era, that we can even begin to grasp how and why it was that so many intelligent and sensitive people could have tolerated so many lies and so much horror, brutality, and institutionalized inequality. Seeking a socialist millennium of universal peace and justice for all regardless of gender, class, or race, they tried not to see horrors that were clearly there, but which they hoped were only temporary.

But the horrors outlived most of those whom I call Brecht & Company. In much of the world, the dream of the millennium that many of them sought has been rudely thrown away. But the record of the hopes, dreams, and fears of our violent century remains in the plays and poems bearing Brecht's name. In the best of the texts, many with brilliant accompanying scores—*Happy End, The Threepenny Opera, He Who Says Yes, The Measures Taken, Mother Courage, Galileo, Puntila, The Caucasian Chalk Circle*, and *The Good Woman of Setzuan*—are the same dramatic roots that nourished Greek, Japanese, Renaissance European, and modern Norwegian, Russian, French, and Irish drama. In the best work of Brecht & Company, as in other great classics of world dramatic literature, there is a clash of violent, primitive drives, Eros locked in its ancient struggle with Thanatos, good against evil, honor against corruption.

Perhaps, if Hegel's dream of a circular ramp, with its slight upward incline from generation to generation, has some validity, we stand on slightly higher ground as the century ends than when it began. Perhaps, from where we now stand, we can better hear what is said in the work of Brecht & Company. Their work sings of a time when Jenny of *The Threepenny Opera* will have power to control her own destiny; when "Confucius" will genuinely understand women's needs or indeed could as easily be a woman; when a generous Shen Te will not have to hide behind her brutal male cousin. The texts, now recognized as classics of the world's dramatic heritage, point in all their complexity toward a time where neither Courage nor Kattrin will be brutalized. These vivid, dramatic characters may serve to point us toward a wider idea of freedom, a time when the forced silence and namelessness their creators endured in this troubled century will be but a distant memory and a warning to those who come later.

But, of course, in a media-dominated age, we can recognize that progress in the consciousness of freedom depends on promoting consciousness. To bury a Steffin, or a Berlau, or a Hauptmann in a footnote, when they wrote more of the work than Brecht himself, is to deliberately *not* promote consciousness. Those publishing or staging or filming the great works to which Hauptmann, Steffin, Berlau, and Pohl contributed (sometimes in massive ways) can help consciousness by beginning to put these names on the covers of books and in the titles of articles. The names need to be in anthologies and card catalogues as authors of importance.

If "Shakespeare's sisters," to use Virginia Woolf's formulation, wrote much of the works, why should not women everywhere be able to draw strength from the free and open acknowledgment of that fact? It is, in my view, unconscionable (though it happens all the time) to stage *The Threepenny Opera* or *Happy End*, to name but two works for which Elisabeth Hauptmann is mainly responsible. If private property is an outmoded concept, as Brecht argued when accused of stealing in the 1920s, then why do we keep "Brecht" as his and his heirs' private allotment garden?

Should people in future years still be asking the question, Where were the women dramatists of world rank in the first half of the twentieth century, point them under the mask of the brutal male "lover" Shui Ta, at the hidden face of the woman who loves him despite his brutality, Shen Te in *The Good Woman of Setzuan*. Or, having heard the boasting of murderer, rapist, racist Mack the Knife, we can urge people to listen to words sung "in a different voice," the voices of Hauptmann's Polly and Jenny as they dream of a tomorrow when women are recognized in their own right, no longer brutalized and silenced by Mackie and his kind.

Having taken off the stage masks that Steffin and Hauptmann and Berlau and Pohl all donned for reasons they knew best, we can look with new wonder at what they achieved despite living in one of the most brutal periods of human history. If they, in a deeply prejudiced world, could achieve so much, what might now be done?

Acknowledgments

Those who shared with me personal knowledge of events as they observed them are: Elisabeth Hauptmann, Eric Bentley, Marieluise Fleisser, Jorge Semprun, Angelika Hurwicz, Hans Bunge, Erwin Leiser, Carl Weber, Martin Esslin, Heiner Müller, Herbert Marshall, Margo Aufricht, Georg Tsoulukidse, Vera and Joachim Tenschert, Lev Kopelev, Dagmar Andreasen, Marta Feuchtwanger, Hilda Waldo, Mogens Voltelen, Tatiana Tretiakova, Ernst Schumacher, Klaus Völker, John Willett, Manfred Wekwerth, James Schevill, Bernard Frizell, Andrzej Wirth, Käthe Reichel, Mordecai Gorelick, Martin Pohl, Helene Weigel, Herta Hanisch, Irmgild Weber, Jürgen Kuczynski, Annemarie Rost, Ekkehard Schall, Steffi Spira, Johannes Hoffmann, Hans Mayer, Käthe Rülicke-Weiler, Benno Besson, and Isot Kilian.

Those whose research and/or writings have helped me to ask new questions or gain insights on various members of the Brecht circle and modern history are: Gisela Bahr, Inge Gellert, David Pike, Reinhold Grimm, Fritz Sternberg, Dieter Schmidt, Birgit S. Nielsen, Gordon A. Craig, Ekhard Haack, Paula Banholzer, Klaus Völker, Anna Bucharina, Walter Janka, Margarete Buber-Neumann, Robert Havemann, Elinor Lipper, Dirk Krüger, David Drew, Gerda Goedhart, Roy Medvedev, Max Högel, Hans Otto Münsterer, Günther Rühle, Max Frisch, Peter Weiss, Carl Zuckmayer, Elias Canetti, Arnolt Bronnen, Harold von Hofe, Dimitri Shostakovich, Hans Christian Nørregaard, Renate Voris, Isaac Deutscher, Nadezhda Mandelstam, Boris Souvarine, Stephan Bock, Eugenia Ginzburg, Sander Gilman, Wolf Wucherpfennig, André Müller, Werner Frisch, K. W. Obermeier, Morten Nielsen, Hans Peter Neureuter, Jan E. Olsen, Ronald Shull, G. Ronald Murphy, Paula Hanssen, Astrid Horst, Hans Dieter Zimmermann, Joachim Fest, Hans Sahl, Klaus Theweleit, Peter Szondi, Sissi Tax, Fritz Sternberg, Joachim Lucchesi, Bernd Mahl, Andreas W. Mytze, Rudy Hassing, Werner Mittenzwei, James K. Lyon, Dagmar Lorenz, Emma Lew Thomas, Bruce Cook, Erwin Piscator, T. K. Brown, and Eric Bentley.

Background materials, writings, diaries, family photographs, and permission to use all these materials were provided by Margarete Steffin's sister, Herta Hanisch. Steffin's hospital records were obtained for me by Dr. Morten Nielsen. Steffin's extensive correspondence with major figures in modern German history was provided by Moscow's Central State Archive for Literature and Art.

Hans Bunge's unexpurgated interviews with Berlau and Berlau's own diary notes from the Charité, Scandinavia, Leipzig and elsewhere, together with her photos, letters, etc., as provided to me by her heir, Johannes Hoffmann, have provided literally hundreds of day-to-day details that have held up under a rigorous system of cross-referencing to other sources.

Many details on Elisabeth Hauptmann were provided to me directly by her. Others, including a great deal of background information on the Hauptmann family, came from a niece, Irmgild Weber of St. Louis, Missouri. Ms. Weber has kindly allowed me to make unrestricted use of materials on and by her aunt.

Materials on Mordecai (Max) Gorelick's relationship with Brecht came directly from interviews that I conducted with him.

Of particular value in establishing contractual details have been the archival holdings of Felix Bloch Erben in Berlin. Marta Feuchtwanger and Lion Feuchtwanger's secretary, Hilda Waldo, have spoken with me a number of times and provided many details on the Brecht circle in California. Materials on Lenya and Weill's relations with Brecht in the Weimar and the exile years were kindly provided by Lys Symonette and Kim Kowalke of the Kurt Weill Foundation, who gave me direct access to all the relevant archival materials.

More generally, I have benefited from a special seminar taken with Carol Gilligan, who helped me to listen for materials presented "in a different voice."

My understanding of Soviet history has been very much helped by consultations with the Soviet authorities: Klara Hallik, Tatiana Tretiakova, Jack Smith of the CBS Bureau in Moscow, Samuel Rachlin, David Pike, Masha Maretskaya, Sergei Kapitsa, Maria Goldovskaya, Abel Aganbegyan, N. C. Shukov, Arkady Vaksberg, Robert Conquest, Ivan N. Kitaev, Vladimir Rapoport, Lev Kopelev, Georg Zaitsev, Edward Manukian, Juri Oklyanski, Valery Makarov, Vladimir Naumov, Vasily Selunin, and Stanislav Shatalin.

Khruschev's epochal Twentieth Party Congress speech has long been available in most major languages. On the effect of the speech on the Politburo of various parties outside the USSR, I have been helped by numerous discussions with Soviet and German colleagues and by Jorge Semprun, who was a member of the Politburo of the Spanish Party at the time and a direct participant in many of the post–Twentieth Party Congress events that I describe.

Of importance have been the FBI, OSS, and CIA files that I have been able to obtain on various members of the Brecht circle, including Hauptmann and Berlau. My analysis of the raw material in these files has been helped by Athan Theoharis, an expert on the FBI and its often dubious methods.

Other essential source materials have been provided for me by the helpful staff of: Akademie der Künste (then of West Berlin), the Houghton Library at Harvard (access to the source materials of which were kindly provided to me by Stefan Brecht), the Central State Archive for Culture and Art in Moscow, the Central Institute of Mathematics and Economics of the Soviet Academy of Sciences, which kindly provided me with support in Moscow, the Augsburg City Library, internal working documents of the Berlin Ensemble as provided by Manfred Wekwerth, and internal documents of the Schauspielhaus, Zurich.

Financial support has come from a wide variety of sources including NDEA grants in Comparative Literature and Russian Studies, the Fulbright Commission, the Germanistic Society of America, the Humanities Center (Wesleyan), the Center for Twentieth Century Studies (Milwaukee), a brief but important Akademie der Künste Residency (West Berlin), the American Council of Learned Societies (Grant for East European Studies), a National Endowment for the Humanities Brecht Research Conference Award, Visiting Professorships at Harvard, the Freie Universität Berlin, and Wesleyan Universities, a Guggenheim Foundation award, two awards from the Kurt Weill Foundation for Music, a Rockefeller Foundation award, grants from the College of Arts and Humanities and the Graduate School of the University of Maryland, and from the advance paid on this book by Grove/Atlantic.

Various drafts of the book were shown to a number of readers. I am deeply grateful to the following for their reactions to the text and any suggestions they made for improvements: Jo Francis, Jorge Semprun, Robyn Archer, Silvia and Gabriel Cwilich, Len Straub, Sander Gilman, Leon Levin, Rudy Hassing, Glenn Young, Walter Hinderer, Leon Levin, Kristine and Richard Brecht, Catherine Schuler, Leroy and Rosemarie Shaw, Dorothy Wartenberg, Peter Beicken, Yves Lifton, Peter Cook, Kourosh Betsarkis, Paula Palmisano, Karin Reisser, Andreas Ryschka, Anke Wienand, Sven Boedicker, Gerd Breuer, Marianne Brodkorb, Anne Vorhoeve, Carl Weber, Elizabeth Hecker, Mark Forrester, Eric Bentley, and Ileene Smith. Alan Williams (former chief editor of Viking and then head of Grove-Weidenfeld) helped me seek greater clarity in every line of the book. Those who guided the book through at Grove/Atlantic were Allison Draper, Walt Bode, Rachel Berchten, Juliet Nicolson, Kenn Russell, and Morgan Entrekin. I am deeply grateful for the faith shown in the book by the staff of Grove/Atlantic.

Jo Francis provided a positive answer and a human scale model in answer to the basic question, "Can it be done with kindness?" I am deeply grateful to her for years of engaged caring about the things that went into this complex creation.

Though counting heavily on a wide variety of sources for factual information, and having sought counsel from many as to how the mass of new data might be interpreted, I must stress that the conclusions I have drawn are my responsibility.

Notes

Chapter 1

1. Walter Brecht's detailed and unusually accurate account of growing up is given in his *Unser Leben in Augsburg, Damals* (Frankfurt am Main: Insel Verlag, 1984). Hereafter: WB.
2. Cited in Christian Herrmann, *Der Mann, der Old Shatterhand war* (Berlin: Verlag der Nation, 1988), 294.
3. WB, 65. I rely on WB for details throughout this chapter.
4. For a systematic review of the various meanings now attached to the word *mother*, see Sue Ellen Case, "Brecht and Women: Homosexuality and the Mother," in *Brecht, Women, and Politics*, ed. John Fuegi, Gisela Bahr, and John Willett (Detroit: Wayne State University Press, 1985), 65–74. Hereafter: BWP.
5. Directly autobiographical notes are rare in Brecht's work. This observation, surrounded by a number of accurate and verifiable descriptions (though this particular incident has no exterior source to confirm it), is found in *Gesammelte Werke* (Frankfurt am Main: Suhrkamp Verlag, 1967), 14:1414. Hereafter: GW. The best source usually for cross-reference is: Werner Frisch and K. W. Obermeier, eds., *Brecht in Augsburg* (Frankfurt am Main: Suhrkamp Verlag, 1976). Hereafter: F/O. The book is a series of overlapping interviews with those who knew Brecht during his Augsburg childhood and early years in Munich.
6. See Peter Gay, *The Victorian Experience: Victoria to Freud* (New York: Oxford University Press, 1984), vol. 1; (1986), vol. 2; Peter Gay, *Freud: A Life for Our Time* (New York and London: W. W. Norton, 1988); and Gordon A. Craig, *Germany 1866–1945* (New York: Oxford University Press, 1978). Hereafter: Craig, *Germany*.
7. WB, 31. The accuracy of Walter Brecht's observations can frequently be cross-referenced as he kept many of the family artifacts that he describes in his book.
8. Details for this and following paragraphs given in WB, 59–60.
9. WB, 139.
10. See "The Ballad of June 30," in GW 9:520–24.
11. F/O, 33. Franz Kroher.
12. Similarly, as a young man, Wilhelm II was allowed to maneuver with actual companies of soldiers. If he inexplicably lost, he would change the order of battle to his own advantage, prompting the chief of staff to observe, "Originelle idée!" Cited in Craig, *Germany*, 228.

13. F/O, 31.
14. F/O, 175–76.
15. For a discussion of Brecht's possible heart ailment, with a predominantly psychological approach to the subject, see Carl Pietzcker, *"Ich kommandiere mein Herz." Brechts Herzneurose-ein Schlüssel zu seinem Leben und Schreiben* (Würzburg: Müller, 1988).
16. WB, 103, 105.
17. F/O, 44.
18. GW (Frankfurt am Main: Suhrkamp Verlag, 1982), supplemental vol. 3, *Gedichte aus dem Nachlass I*, 149.
19. The notes come from *Bertolt Brecht Tagebuch No. 10, 1913* (Frankfurt am Main: Suhrkamp Verlag, 1989). Hereafter: *BB 10*. 20. GW 11:3.
21. Letter was found in and published with *BB 10*.
22. Given in F/O, 57–58.
23. See Craig, *Germany*, 335ff.
24. F/O, 258.
25. WB, 218–19.

Chapter 2

1. F/O, 225–26.
2. F/O, 239.
3. Craig, *Germany*, 359.
4. F/O, 246.
5. GW 8:6–7.
6. WB, 157.
7. GW 14:1414.
8. F/O, 107.
9. See WB, 268–69.
10. F/O, 277. The poem was published in the local Augsburg paper on 19 February 1916.
11. F/O, 88–90. Eyewitness account of Brecht's fellow student Walter Groos.
12. F/O, 90.
13. F/O, 92. Firsthand account of Marie Aman.
14. Details provided by Paula Banholzer in her memoir, *Meine Zeit mit Bert Brecht*, ed. Axel Poldner and Willibald Eser (Munich: Wilhelm Goldmann Verlag, 1981). Hereafter: *MZBB*.
15. The Augsburg City Library owns the letter to Ostheimer. The diary was published with commentary by Gerhard Seidel in *Sinn und Form* (December 1988). Hereafter: *SuF*.
16. Fritz J. Raddatz, "Ent-weiblichte Eschatologie," in *Text und Kritik, Brecht II*, ed. Heinz Ludwig Arnold (Munich: Richard Boorberg Verlag, 1973), 156. Hereafter: Raddatz, "Eschatologie."
17. *SuF*, 1133ff.
18. F/O, 82–83.
19. F/O, 100.
20. MZBB, 19–20.
21. See John Willett, *Caspar Neher: Brecht's Designer* (London: Methuen, 1986). Hereafter: JW, CN.

Chapter 3

1. In Augsburg, the various festivals were lengthened during World War I.
2. MZBB, 36.
3. MZBB, 39.
4. F/O, 160–61. Hedda Kuhn's recollections are confirmed by Hans Otto Münsterer, who not only notes that Brecht did not study medicine but points out
   the basic ignorance of medicine and the natural sciences exhibited in Brecht's
   published work; Hans Otto Münsterer, Bert Brecht, Erinnerungen aus den
   Jahren 1917–22 (Zurich: Verlag der Arche, 1963), 32. Hereafter: Münsterer.
5. Frank Wedekind, Prosa, Dramen, Verse, 2d ed. (Munich: Georg Müller, 1960),
   43.
6. See Artur Kutscher, ed., Frank Wedekind Lautenlieder (Munich: Georg Müller,
   1920).
7. GW 15:3–4.
8. Compare, for instance, Wedekind's poem "Der Tantenmörder" with Brecht's
   "Apfelbock," or look at "In usum Delphini," "Liebesantrag," "Ilse," "Die
   Keuschheit," or "Der Anarchist"—all Wedekind poems but drenched
   throughout with the style we now tend to call, as Eric Bentley has pointed out
   to me, "typically Brechtian."
9. GW 8:28.
10. Bertolt Brecht, Gedichte über die Liebe, ed. Werner Hecht (Frankfurt am Main:
    Suhrkamp Verlag, 1982), 21. Hereafter: Brecht, Gül. This text was published
    in 1982 in East Germany.
11. Brecht, Gül, 36. The connection between this poem and Herrick's was pointed
    out to me by Alan Williams.
12. F/O, 162. Hedda Kuhn.
13. Münsterer, 12.
14. From Richard Lattimore, trans., The Iliad of Homer (Chicago: University of
    Chicago Press, 1962), xxi, 12ff.
15. GW 8:76.
16. Klaus Völker, Brecht: A Biography, trans. John Nowell (New York: The Seabury
    Press, 1978), 34. Hereafter: Völker, Brecht.
17. GW 8:37–38.
18. Bertolt Brecht, Briefe, 2 vols., ed. Günter Glaeser (Frankfurt am Main: Suhr-
    kamp Verlag, 1981), 20–22. Hereafter: BL. This is perhaps the single most
    shamelessly manipulated volume put out by Suhrkamp on Brecht. The
    volumes contain less than one-third of the known letters by Brecht. The
    letters selected and the ones left out radically diminish the importance of
    Brecht's key collaborators—Elisabeth Hauptmann, Margarete Steffin, and
    Ruth Berlau—and gloss over Brecht's unscrupulous behavior toward them
    and various publishers. In future notes, I will note where, in hundreds of
    instances, I draw on the Brecht letters deliberately not included in this source.
    Unfortunately, the John Willett and Ralph Manheim edition of Bertolt Brecht
    Letters 1913–1956 (London: Methuen, 1990) is, except for the often excellent
    footnote apparatus, as fundamentally flawed as the work of the East German
    state employee Glaeser, on which it is based.
19. F/O, 100–101.

20. BL, 30.
21. BL, 26–27.
22. See Fritz Hennenberg's fine article, "Bruinier und Brecht: Nachrichten über den ersten Brecht-Komponisten," in *The Brecht Yearbook*, ed. John Fuegi et al. (Madison: University of Wisconsin Press, 1990), vol. 15; and Bertolt Brecht Archive East Berlin 800/01–16 (hereafter: BBA).
23. GW 15:3–4.
24. F/O, 119. Hedda Kuhn.
25. A personal letter to me from the Hitler biographer Joachim Fest.
26. The best account of how *Baal* was created is Dieter Schmidt, *"Baal" und der junge Brecht* (Stuttgart: J. B. Metzlersche Verlagsbuchhandlung, 1966).
27. Besides the obvious biblical source for *Baal*, Kurt Wolff of Leipzig published in 1917 the then famous author Paul Zech's *Der schwarze Baal*, in which Baal is treated as a very down-to-earth figure in much the same way as he appears in Brecht.
28. F/O, 87–88.
29. John Willett, ed., *Brecht Poems 1913–56* (New York: Methuen, 1979), ix. Hereafter: JW, *Brecht Poems*.
30. BL, 53.
31. F/O, 133. Georg Geyer.
32. GW 8:224–28.
33. GW 8:77–78.
34. The best accounts of Neher and his relationship with Brecht are given in Max Högel, *Caspar Neher (1897–1962)* (Weisenhorn: Anton H. Konrad Verlag, 1973), 401 (hereafter: Högel, CN); and Max Högel, *Bertolt Brecht, Ein Porträt* (Augsburg: Der schwäbischen Forschungsgemeinschaft, 1962), (hereafter: Högel, BB).
35. Bertolt Brecht, *Tagebücher 1920–1922, autobiographische Aufzeichnungen 1920–1954*, ed. Herta Ramthun (Frankfurt am Main: Suhrkamp Verlag, 1975), 20. Hereafter: Diary 1920–54.
36. F/O, 137. Friedrich Mayer.
37. F/O, 139.

Chapter 4

1. Bertolt Brecht, *Schriften zur Politik und Gesellschaft* (Berlin and Weimar: Aufbau Verlag, 1968), 1:43ff. Hereafter: Brecht, SPG. The first half of this quotation is cited in Werner Mittenzwei's two-volume biography of Brecht, but the telling second half is missing from that work.
2. F/O, 143.
3. See Arnold Brecht (no relation to Bertolt Brecht), *The Political Education of Arnold Brecht* (Princeton: Princeton University Press, 1970), 108ff.
4. Craig, *Germany*, 212.
5. F/O, 166.
6. F/O, 146–49.
7. Högel, CN 411.
8. Cited in Elzbieta Ettinger, *Rosa Luxemburg* (Boston: Beacon Press, 1986), 243.
9. See Stephen Eric Bonner, *Rosa Luxemburg: A Revolutionary for Our Times* (New York: Columbia University Press, 1987), 68ff.

10. See Klaus Theweleit, *Männerphantasien*, (Basel/Frankfurt am Main: Roter Stern Verlag, 1977), 1:84.
11. The written text of Walcher and Gordon is given in BBA 676/49–53. Käthe Rülicke-Weiler separately recalled this detail in an interview with me in Berlin shortly before her death in 1992.
12. The officers involved received sentences ranging from four months to a 500-mark fine.
13. Periodically suppressed in Brecht editions, it is found in *GW* 8:41–42.
14. Caspar Neher diary, Augsburg Library.
15. F/O, 152.
16. F/O, 154.
17. Högel, *CN*, 413.
18. F/O, 156–57.
19. Marta Feuchtwanger, *Nur eine Frau* (Munich/Vienna: Georg Müller, 1983), 130–31.
20. This was told to me by Frau Feuchtwanger, who then confirmed it in a letter.

Chapter 5

1. F/O, 165–66.
2. Caspar Neher diary.
3. F/O, 172.
4. This poem was not published in Brecht's lifetime. It is found in Brecht, *Gül*, 44.
5. See Emile Zola, *Nana*, originally published in book form in 1880.
6. Louise DeSalvo, *Virginia Woolf, the Impact of Childhood Sexual Abuse on Her Life and Work* (New York: Ballantine Books, 1989), 53ff; and Coral Lansbury, "Gynaecology, Pornography, and the Antivivisection Movement," *Victorian Studies* 28 (3): 413–37.
7. Lansbury, "Gynaecology," 421.
8. *GW*, sup. 3:32.
9. See Joan Smith, *Misogynies* (London: Faber & Faber, 1989), 99–105.
10. *GW* 8:52.
11. See Sanford Goldstone, "The Treatment of Antisocial Behavior," in *The Therapist's Handbook*, ed. Benjamin B. Wolman (New York: Van Nostrand, 1976), 419.
12. *GW* 8:108.
13. WB, 319–29.
14. Joachim C. Fest, *Hitler*, trans. Richard and Clara Winston (New York: Vintage Books, 1975), 111.
15. Fest, *Hitler*, 112.
16. Münsterer, 111.
17. *GW*, sup. 3:81.
18. Fest, *Hitler*, 101.
19. Edward Timms, *Karl Kraus, Apocalyptic Satirist* (New Haven: Yale University Press, 1989), 135.
20. *GW* 17:952.
21. Drafted by Lenin and Klara Zetkin, the long-term campaigner for women's rights and German Communist leader, this dubious document, which Lenin

persuaded a reluctant Zetkin was necessary to quiet male fears and thus hasten the revolution, was issued in 1920, by the Comintern under the title *Richtlinien für die kommunistische Frauenbewegung* (Guidelines for the Communist women's movement).

22. Details of the relationship used in these paragraphs are provided by Zoff in her portion of the book *Meine Zeit mit Bertolt Brecht*, ed. Axel Poldner and Willibald Eser (Munich: Goldmann, 1981), hereafter *Meine Zeit* 155–93; and in the volume *Bertolt Brecht Briefe an Marianne Zoff und Hanne Hiob* (Frankfurt am Main: Suhrkamp Verlag, 1990), which, despite its poorly chosen title, contains some of Zoff's own writings (hereafter: Zoff, BB).
23. Zoff, BB, 15.
24. GW 15:6–7.
25. GW 11:20–36.
26. GW 11:37–40.
27. Diary 1920–54, 9 July 1920.
28. MF, 123.

Chapter 6

1. GW 8:232.
2. Bertolt Brecht, *Arbeitsjournal*, 3 vols., ed. Werner Hecht (Frankfurt am Main: Suhrkamp Verlag, 1973), 24 August 1940. Hereafter: AJ.
3. JW, *Brecht Poems*, 526.
4. GW 8:46.
5. GW 8:218–19.
6. See A. O. Lovejoy, *The Great Chain of Being* (Cambridge: Harvard University Press, 1936).
7. GW 8:75–76.
8. GW 8:18–20.
9. Diary 1920–54, 96.
10. BL, 60.
11. See Fest, *Hitler*, 130–32, for details on how the Kapp putsch helped pave Hitler's path.
12. See Völker, *Brecht*, 39ff., for excellent details.
13. BL, 61–62. Note also pages 65–66, for the playful use of violent imagery apparently directed by Brecht against Mannheim.
14. See Craig, *Germany*, 430–33.
15. Diary 1920–54, 88.
16. GW 15:9–11.
17. The best analysis is Gisela E. Bahr, *Im Dickicht, Erstfassung und Materialien* (Frankfurt am Main: Suhrkamp Verlag, 1968), 134–37.
18. GW 18:23.
19. WB, 350.
20. Högel, CN, 420.
21. GW 8:79.
22. Diary 1920–54, 196.
23. Renate Voris, "Inszenierte Ehrlichkeit," in BWP, 79–95.
24. Theweleit, *Männerphantasien* 1:170ff.

25. Diary 1920–54, 111.
26. Diary 1920–54, 28.
27. See particularly Theweleit, *Männerphantasien* 1:172ff.
28. Virginia Woolf, *Three Guineas* (New York: Harcourt, Brace & World, 1938), 53.
29. Diary 1920–54, 162.
30. Diary 1920–54, 147.
31. Diary 1920–54, 32.
32. Diary 1920–54, 87.
33. Diary 1920–54, 41–42.
34. Diary 1920–54, 136.
35. Diary 1920–54, 134.
36. Diary 1920–54, 56.
37. Diary 1920–54, 34.
38. Diary 1920–54, 161.
39. Diary 1920–54, 196.
40. GW 8:78.
41. Diary 1920–54, 27.
42. Diary 1920–54, 41.
43. Diary 1920–54, 79.
44. Diary 1920–54, 78.
45. Diary 1920–54, 78.
46. GW 8:80–81.
47. Diary 1920–54, 24.
48. Diary 1920–54, 71.
49. See John Willett's notes to: Bertolt Brecht's *Diaries 1920–1922*, trans. John Willett (London: Methuen, 1979), 167. Hereafter: JWBD.
50. Diary 1920–54, 62.
51. GW 8:219–22.
52. Diary 1920–54, 48.
53. Diary 1920–54, 57.
54. Diary 1920–54, 98.
55. The existence of these photos was revealed in an interview of Mari Hold with Danish television director Hans Christian Nørregaard, who kindly shared his interview material with me.
56. Diary 1920–54, 52–53.
57. Diary 1920–54, 57–58.
58. Diary 1920–54, 60–61.
59. Diary 1920–54, 55.

Chapter 7

1. Högel, CN, 424.
2. Högel, CN, 415.
3. F/O, 212–13. This account in the *Neue Augsburger Zeitung*, 14 January 1921.
4. F/O, 211–20. This is the full account of the trial stemming from Brecht's published remarks.
5. Brecht counted on being able to get his father to pay, even as he simultaneously claimed his father always abandoned him in times of need.

6. Diary 1920–54, 160.
7. Cited in Högel, CN, 415.
8. Cited in Högel, CN, 421–22.
9. Diary 1920–54, 35.
10. GW 8:235–36.
11. Münsterer, 183.
12. Diary 1920–54, 69.
13. Völker, *Brecht*, 41.
14. Diary 1920–54, 117–18.
15. Diary 1920–54, 117–18.
16. Diary 1920–54, 138.
17. MZBB, 43.
18. Diary 1920–54, 139.
19. Diary 1920–54, 143.
20. Diary 1920–54, 120.
21. It is doubtful that Brecht had enough colloquial English at this time to under-stand the English meaning of the name he had given this bisexual character, pronounced "gal-guy" in German.
22. Diary 1920–54, 160.
23. Diary 1920–54, 161.
24. Diary 1920–54, 160.
25. Diary 1920–54, 161.
26. Guy Stern, *War, Weimar, and Literature: The Story of the "Neue Merkur" 1914–1925* (University Park and London: The Pennsylvania University Press, 1971), 31–32.
27. Klaus Völker, *Brecht-Chronik* (Munich: Hanser Verlag, 1971), 25. An extraor-dinarily useful and mainly reliable collection of facts on the life of Brecht. Hereafter: Völker, *Chronik*.
28. Diary 1920–54, 163.
29. Diary 1920–54, 167.
30. Cited in Gudrun Schulz, *Die Schillerbearbeitungen Bertolt Brechts* (Tübingen: Max Niemeyer Verlag, 1972), 61–64. Hereafter: Schulz, *DSBB*.
31. Diary 1920–54, 170.
32. Diary 1920–54, 171.
33. Diary 1920–54, 172.
34. Diary 1920–54, 173.
35. Werner Mittenzwei, *Das Leben des Bertolt Brecht*, 2 vols. (Berlin: Aufbau Verlag, 1986), 1:167. Hereafter: Mittenzwei, *Leben*.
36. BL, 72.
37. Zoff, BB, 39.
38. Diary 1920–54, 175.
39. Zoff, BB, 44.
40. Diary 1920–54, 178.
41. Diary 1920–54, 166.
42. Diary 1920–54, 82.
43. Given in Trude Hesterberg, *Was ich noch sagen wollte* (Berlin: Henschelverlag, 1971), 95–96. A delicious, equally valid version of this ever-changing skit is in Laurence Senelick, "The Good Gay Comic of Weimar Cabaret," *Theater* (Summer/Fall 1992): 70–75.
44. Hesterberg, *Was ich noch sagen wollte*, 107.

45. Carl Zuckmayer, *Als wär's ein Stück von mir* (Frankfurt am Main: Fischer Verlag, 1966), 368. Hereafter: Zuckmayer, *Ein Stück*.

46. Zoff, *BB*, 44.

47. Wyneken made no attempt to conceal his love of young boys, publishing a highly explicit treatise on the subject, Gustav Wyneken, *Eros* (Lauenburg: A. Saal Verlag, 1922).

48. Bronnen's own account of attending this party is given in two of his books: *Tage mit Bertolt Brecht* (Munich/Vienna/Basel: Desch, 1960), 8–15 (hereafter: Bronnen, *Tage*); and *Arnolt Bronnen gibt zu Protokoll* (Hamburg: Rowohlt, 1954), 97–98 (hereafter: Bronnen, *P*). An extraordinarily frank work, wholly candid about his own sexual proclivities, *Protokoll* was published while Brecht was alive and was never challenged as to its accuracy. *Tage* is equally frank and heavily documented in that it includes facsimiles of many Brecht letters to Bronnen.

49. Bronnen, *Tage*, 8.

50. Bronnen, *P*, 15.

51. Bronnen, *P*, 76.

52. Diary 1920–54, 181.

53. Bronnen, *Tage*, 18.

54. Völker, *Brecht*, 379.

55. Bronnen, *Tage*, 44.

56. Diary 1920–54, 185.

57. BBA 575/24–9.

58. Bronnen, *Tage*, 31–32.

59. Michael Morley, *Brecht, a Study* (London: Heinemann, 1977), 6.

60. Bronnen, *Tage*, 28.

61. Arnolt Bronnen, *Vatermord*, 18. Hectographed Felix Bloch copy (nd., np).

62. Bronnen, *Tage*, 42–43.

63. Bronnen, *Tage*, 50.

64. GW 1:187.

65. GW 1:187.

66. Eric Bentley points out in his notes on this play in his *Seven Plays by Bertolt Brecht* (New York: Grove Press, 1961), 61 (hereafter: Bentley, *Seven Plays*), the similarity of this thought to Jensen's character Evanston, who says: "The only thing that is real in this world is the pleasure of the senses. . . . The only proof that I exist is that I am ecstatic with lust."

67. See Schulz, *DSBB*, 61–62. The theft was made from the translation by K. L. Ammer, who Brecht later ransacked for *The Threepenny Opera*.

68. Mentioned in Diary 1920–54, 66.

69. See Schulz, *DSBB*, 59.

70. Bronnen, *Tage*, 131.

71. Zoff, *BB*, 55.

72. Bronnen, *Tage*, 52.

Chapter 8

1. Bronnen, *Tage*, 145.

2. Fest, *Hitler*, 118.

3. Fest, *Hitler*, 157.

4. Fest, *Hitler*, 152.

5. Bronnen, *P*, 101.

6. Bronnen, *P*, 101.

7. Bronnen, *P*, 103–4.

8. Grossmann published in 1919 an attack on the obviously strongly right-wing German "judicial system" of that time, *Umsturz und Aufbau* (Berlin: Ernst Rowohlt Verlag, 1919).

9. Bronnen, *P*, 106.

10. Bronnen, *Tage*, 59.

11. Bronnen, *Tage*, 62.

12. Bronnen, *Tage*, 63.

13. Bronnen, *Tage*, 71.

14. Bronnen, *Tage*, 71–72.

15. BBA 911/112.

16. Bronnen, *Tage*, 79.

17. Bronnen, *Tage*, 77.

18. Bronnen, *Tage*, 96.

19. Bronnen, *Tage*, 82.

20. Bronnen, *Tage*, 88–89.

21. Cited in Bronnen, *Tage*, 95.

22. *Tage*, 86.

23. MZBB, 82ff.

24. An English version of Ihering's article is found in Hubert Witt, ed., *Brecht As They Knew Him* (New York: International Publishers, 1974), 35–38. I have done my own translation here, however.

25. Reprinted in *GW* (Frankfurt am Main: Suhrkamp Verlag, 1969), vol. 2, *Texts for Film*, 307–12.

Chapter 9

1. MF, 151.

2. BL, 89.

3. Bronnen, *Tage*, 114.

4. Bronnen, *Tage*, 124.

5. Bronnen, *Tage*, 125.

6. Cited in Ronald Hayman, *Brecht* (New York: Oxford University Press, 1983), 95. Hereafter: Hayman.

7. Marianne's letter is in Zoff, *BB*, 86.

8. This sensational work was brought out by Ernst Rowohlt Verlag.

9. Bronnen, *Tage*, 130.

10. See Klaus Völker's excellent *Brecht, Kommentar zum dramatischen Werk* (Munich, Winkler, 1983), 94.

11. MZBB, 88.

12. MZBB, 93.

13. MZBB, 94.

14. BL, 93–94.

15. Bronnen, *P*, 118.

16. Fest, *Hitler*, 157.

17. Fest, *Hitler*, 101.

18. Fest, *Hitler*, 154.
19. Bronnen, *Tage*, 141.
20. Bronnen, *Tage*, 144.
21. Bronnen, *Tage*, 150.
22. Bronnen, *P*, 112.
23. Cited in Bronnen, *Tage*, 154.
24. Bronnen, *Tage*, 161–62.
25. Bronnen, *Tage*, 163.
26. Werner Hecht, "Die Geburt des Dramatischen Genies," *Notate* (April 1990), 2.
27. Hecht.
28. Hecht.
29. Hecht.
30. Hecht, 4.
31. Zoff, *BB*, 88–91.
32. Zoff, *BB*, 92.
33. Zoff, *BB*, 94.

Chapter 10

1. Rudolf Frank, *Spielzeit meines Lebens* (Heidelberg: Verlag Lambert Schneider, 1960), 256.
2. BL, 98–99.
3. BL, 100.
4. See Hecht, 4.
5. Cited in Raddatz, "Eschatalogie," 155ff.
6. Reinhold Grimm has reissued the Heymel text with the Brecht-Feuchtwanger versions in *Bertolt Brecht Leben Eduards des Zweiten von England: Vorlage, Texte und Materialien* (Frankfurt am Main Edition Suhrkamp, 1968). The use Brecht made of Heymel is sensitively discussed by Eduard Kopetzki in his dissertation, "Das Dramatische Werk Bertolt Brechts nacht Seiner Theorie vom Epischen Theater" (University of Vienna, 1949).
7. See John W. Wheeler-Bennett, *The Nemesis of Power: The German Army in Politics 1918–45* (London: Macmillan & Co., 1953), 133–38.
8. Fest, *Hitler*, 112.
9. See Richard Taylor, *The Politics of the Soviet Cinema* (Cambridge: Cambridge University Press, 1979), 144.
10. Bernhard Reich's superb memoirs have been published, though in slightly different form, both in German and in Russian. I cite here from the German text, *Im Wettlauf mit der Zeit* (Berlin: Henschelverlag, 1970), 294. Hereafter: Reich, *W*.
11. See Sissi Tax, *Marieluise Fleisser, Schreiben, Überleben* (Basel/Frankfurt am Main: Stroemfeld/Roter Stern, 1984), 50. Hereafter: Tax, *Fleisser*.
12. Frank, *Spielzeit*, 256.
13. Diary 1920 54, 57.
14. Reich, *W*, 251–52.
15. Fest, *Hitler*, 190.
16. Frank, *Spielzeit*, 271–72.
17. Zuckmayer, *Ein Stück*, 368.

18. *Neue Leipziger Zeitung*, 10 December 1923.
19. GW 8:207–8.
20. MZBB, 98.
21. Reich, *W*, 262.
22. GW 2:313. Marieluise Fleisser.
23. The incident is described in MF, 152.
24. MF, 153.
25. BL, 104–05.
26. Fest, *Hitler*, 193.
27. Fest, *Hitler*, 204.
28. Details of the arrangements with Kiepenheuer (based on direct access to the Kiepenheuer files) that I use here are provided in a letter to me from Friedemann Berger.
29. Early versions of the play and the use of this portmanteau word in John Willett, ed., *Man Equals Man* (London: Eyre Methuen, 1979), 113.
30. BL, 105.

Chapter 11

1. These intimate domestic details are given in a midthirties poem Brecht wrote for Mari Hold. GW 9:527–29.
2. Völker, *Brecht*, 88.
3. Völker, *Brecht*, 88.
4. Zuckmayer's hilarious reminiscences are given in *Ein Stück*, 367–73.
5. Cited in Mittenzwei, *Leben* 1:224.
6. MF, 161–62.
7. For a discussion of this incident and a number of other Brecht thefts, see Schmidt, *"Baal" und der junge Brecht*, 50ff. I consider Schmidt's book to be one of the three or four finest works on Brecht in any language.
8. Hauptmann's comment is found in an anthology named after one of her short stories, Rosemarie Eggert and Rosemarie Hill, eds., *Julia ohne Romeo* (Berlin: Aufbau Verlag, 1977), 204. Hereafter: JoR.
9. Author's personal interviews with Bentley and Schevill, Miami, April 1992.
10. Hauptmann's diaries were neither properly catalogued in the archives of the GDR during the existence of that state, nor were they ever published in their revealing entirety. There is a pressing need to begin a full reexamination and publication of the collected works of this remarkable writer. At the time of the disintegration of the GDR, the Brecht Archiv was attempting to gain physical possession and scholarly jurisdiction over all her unpublished work, though she told me she wanted her own archive. My source is the Brecht Collection at Harvard. Hereafter: HC.
11. John Willett, *Brecht in Britain* (London: TQ Publications, 1977), 14. Hereafter: JW, *BinB*. See also Thomas K. Brown, "Brecht's Thievery," in *Perspectives and Personalities*, ed. Ralph Ley (Heidelberg: Carl Winter, 1978), 70–88. Hereafter: Brown.
12. Cited in John Willett, "Bacon ohne Shakespeare?—The Problem of Mitarbeit," in *BWP*, 123. Hereafter: JW, "Bacon?"
13. JW, "Bacon?" 128.

14. JW, "Bacon?" 128.

15. JoR, 230.

16. Author's interview with Elisabeth Hauptmann, East Berlin, 9 November 1970.

17. Cited in James K. Lyon, *Bertolt Brecht and Rudyard Kipling: A Marxist's Imperial Mentor* (The Hague: Mouton, 1975), 5. Hereafter: Lyon, *BB/RK*. Lyon does not think Brecht went directly to English sources for his Kipling. He writes, "The overwhelming evidence speaks for translations."

18. Details on Elisabeth Hauptmann's mother kindly provided by Hauptmann's niece, Irmie Weber of Saint Louis.

19. See A. G. Gardiner, *Prophets, Priests & Kings* (London: J. M. Dent, 1914), 329.

20. Lyon, *BB/RK*, 55.

21. Lyon, *BB/RK*, 56.

22. Lyon, *BB/RK*, 58.

23. For details on Zelda's writing, see James R. Mellow, *Invented Lives* (Boston: Houghton Mifflin Co., 1984), 340ff. The best book on Rose Wilder Lane's contributions is William Holtz, *The Ghost in the Little House: A Life of Rose Wilder Lane* (Columbia: University of Missouri Press, 1993).

24. See Mathew J. Brucolli, *Some Sort of Epic Grandeur* (New York: Harcourt Brace Jovanovich, 1981), 286.

25. Cited in Mellow, *Invented Lives*, 357.

26. See Sara Mayfield, *Exiles from Paradise, Zelda and F. Scott Fitzgerald* (New York: Delacorte Press, 1971), 146, for details. Zelda's story "Our Movie Queen" was sold under his name to the *Chicago Tribune*. Mayfield also notes of F. Scott and Zelda, "He had published nothing commercially before he met her and very little after he left her" (147).

27. The fact that precisely the same sort of thing happened in the nominally socialist world is attested to by the fact that, through the 1930s, Brecht would sell the work of Hauptmann and of his later lovers and collaborators Margarete Steffin and Ruth Berlau to Moscow journals as though it were his own, and did precisely the same thing after 1949 in the GDR and Czechoslovakia.

28. Cited in Högel, *CN*, 433.

29. Cited in Fritz Sternberg, *Der Dichter und die Ratio*, ed. Reinhold Grimm (Göttingen: Sachse und Pohl Verlag, 1963), 20. Hereafter: Sternberg, *Der Dichter*.

30. Völker, *Brecht*, 89.

31. Here, Brecht expresses sentiments similar to the "natural" misogyny found in Luther's massively influential *Table Talk*. Hauptmann's role is to stay home and use her wide rear on Brecht's behalf.

32. On another level of meaning, Hauptmann with her superb English would see the connection of "Ham" with the flesh of a pig. Incidentally, "Ham" is from the Egyptian *khem*, which means *black*. Multiple prejudices seem piled up in Brecht's story.

33. Zoff, *BB*, 103.

34. Zoff, *BB*, 160–61.

35. Zoff, *BB*, 106.

36. BL, 107.

37. BL, 108.

38. Zoff, *BB*, 114.

39. Zoff, *BB*, 121.
40. *GW* 20:22–24.

Chapter 12

1. JW, *Man Equals Man*, x.
2. JW, "Bacon?" 125. Willett points out that, after Hauptmann's arrival, the work published as Brecht begins for the first time to clearly voice "a woman's point of view." Curiously, to this day, the implications of this observation have remained almost wholly unexplored in the vast, jargon-drenched, and sadly repetitive realm of international Brecht studies.
3. JW, "Bacon?" 123.
4. Cited in JW, *Man Equals Man*, xi.
5. See the published section of Hauptmann's diary in Witt, *Brecht As They Knew Him*, 50–53.
6. When Feuchtwanger presented the same material as a play, he called it *Thomas Brecht*.
7. Jahnn's recollections are given in *SuF*, 2d special Brecht iss., 424–29. Hereafter: *SuF*, 2d.
8. Bronnen, *Tage*, 139.
9. John Willett, *The Theatre of Bertolt Brecht, a Study from Eight Aspects* (New York: New Directions, 1968), 186. Hereafter: JW, *Eight Aspects*.
10. Peter Brook, *The Empty Space* (New York: Avon Books, 1968), 80.
11. *SuF*, 2d, 243.
12. Bronnen, *P*, 144.
13. See John Fuegi, "Russian 'Epic Theatre' Experiments and the American Stage," *The Minnesota Review* (Fall 1973): 102–12. Hereafter: Fuegi, "RET."
14. Edward Braun, trans. and ed., *Meyerhold on Theatre* (New York: Hill and Wang, 1969, 54. Hereafter: *MoT*.
15. *GW*. 7:77.
16. Bronnen, *P*, 148.
17. See Hansjürgen Rosenbauer, *Brecht und der Behaviorismus* (Bad Homburg: Verlag Dr. Max Gehlen, 1970).
18. Hugo von Hoffmannsthal, *Das Theater des Neuen* (Vienna, 1947), 39.
19. Mittenzwei, *Leben* 1:216.
20. Cited in Mittenzwei, *Leben* 1:216.
21. Mittenzwei, *Leben* 1:219.
22. *GW* 15:81–84.
23. Zoff, *BB*, 135.
24. Zoff, *BB*, 143–44.
25. Zoff, *BB*, 147.
26. *GW* 15:89.
27. *GW* 15:89.
28. Tax, *Fleisser*, 69.
29. Cited in Tax, *Fleisser*, 70.
30. *GW* 2:304. Marieluise Fleisser.
31. BL, 115.
32. MZBB, 188. It is quite possible that Brecht actually said "XY" and defined the

person no further. Marianne recollected that this person died somewhat later. The most likely candidate for "XY" would be, I think, the great beauty Carola Neher. As we shall see later, Brecht was infatuated with her for years.

33. BBA 2179/12–13 contains the record of the Berlin-Charlottenburg court.
34. BL, 117.
35. Private papers of the Hauptmann family were kindly made available to me in Saint Louis by Irmie Weber, Hauptmann's niece.
36. JW, "Bacon?" 128.
37. *Not* in BL. BBA 720/14.
38. BBA 720/15.
39. BBA 720/18. Letter is dated June 1926.
40. Fleisser's account, first written in 1962 after Brecht had been dead for six years, was first given the title "The Trauma." It was later published under the title "Avantgarde" in lightly fictionalized form. See *GW* 3:117–68. Fleisser.
41. *GW* 3:135. Fleisser.
42. The story, with Hauptmann's authorship belatedly acknowledged directly, was republished in the volume *JoR*.
43. *GW* 8:294.
44. JW, *Man Equals Man*, xi.
45. A sense of the range of Neher's creations with directors other than Geis and Brecht can be found in editors Gottfried von Einem's and Siegfried Melchinger's large picture book, *Caspar Neher: Bühne und bildende Kunst im xx. Jahrhundert* (Berlin: Friedrich Verlag, 1966).

Chapter 13

1. *GW* 18:137.
2. Völker points out this passage in his biography, Völker, *Brecht*, 93. The text to which Völker refers is found in *GW* 18:60.
3. As we shall see, Goebbels would use this term in the Nazi era to dismissively describe the theater of Gustav Gründgens. The term is still in pejorative use today.
4. *GW* 18:54–59.
5. Hauptmann claims this in the carefully edited section of her 1926 diary notes that she provided for the *Sinn und Form* second special Brecht issue published after Brecht's death. I have never seen the actual letter to which she refers. If a properly independent Hauptmann archive is ever set up and made accessible, this will be an important item to track down.
6. *GW* 15:129.
7. Cited in Paul Johnson, *Intellectuals* (New York: Harper and Row, 1989), 62.
8. Sternberg, *Der Dichter*, 7ff.
9. Sternberg, *Der Dichter*, 8.
10. The description is by Margarete Steffin. See Margarete Steffin, *Konfutse versteht nichts von Frauen* (Berlin: Rowohlt, 1991), 115. Steffin, *Konfutse*. "Masculinism" as a term originates with Virginia Woolf. See *The Diaries of Virginia Woolf* (New York: Harcourt Brace Jovanovich, 1979), ed. Anne Olivier Bell.
11. Sternberg, *Der Dichter*, 12.
12. Brecht, *Gül*, 187.

13. For a list of these and other similar Lenin quotations, see Vasily Selyunin, "Sources," *Novi Mir* (1988).

14. GW 8:267–68. For notes on variant versions of this work, see JW, *Brecht Poems*, 541–42.

15. GW 8:269–70.

16. See Edmund Wilson, *To the Finland Station* (New York: Farrar, Straus and Giroux, 1972), 323ff., for a lucid exposition of the unbroken line of revolutionary terror that stretches from Bakunin and Nechaev to Lenin and Stalin.

17. An early solid account of these multiple mirrorings is given in Boris Souvarine, *Stalin*, trans. C. L. R. James (New York: Longmans, Green & Co., 1939), 673ff.

18. Cited in Fest, *Hitler*, 126.

19. Hans Sahl, *Das Exil im Exil: Memoiren eines Moralisten* (Frankfurt am Main, Luchterhand, 1991), 2:147.

20. GW 8:75–76.

21. Diary, 1920–54, 172.

22. BL, 120.

23. Cited by Raddatz, "Eschatalogie," 155.

24. This is the title given to the work in Eric Bentley's fine English version published by Grove Press.

25. The book was first published in Munich in 1921 by the Kurt Wolff Verlag and is at least as radical in its attack on the "values" of the bourgeoisie as *Hauspostille*.

26. See John Willett's notes to his English-language version of *The Rise and Fall of the City of Mahagonny* (London: Methuen, 1979), viii. Hereafter: JW, Notes, *Mahagonny*.

27. Author's conversation with James K. Lyon, Delaware Brecht Conference, 1 March 1992.

28. See JW, "Bacon?" 123.

29. GW 18:56.

30. Völker, 94.

31. Eric Bentley, *The Brecht Memoir* (New York: PAJ Publications, 1985), 14. Hereafter: Bentley, *Memoir*.

32. Bronnen, *P*, 189.

33. Bronnen, *P*, 191.

34. Günther Rühle, ed., *Materialien zum Leben und Schreiben der Marieluise Fleisser* (Frankfurt am Main: Suhrkamp, 1973), 416. Hereafter: Rühle, *FMat*.

35. In *A Room of One's Own* (New York: Harcourt Brace Jovanovich, 1929), note the understanding with which Virginia Woolf deals with the problem of women being pushed to write novels. Woolf was fully aware that without the circumstance of her own inheritance, her own five-hundred a year, she would not have had the necessary time and "room" to be able to complete longer pieces of work. She, like "Shakespeare's sister," would have been beaten down and forgotten.

36. Rühle, *FMat*, 155.

37. Rühle, *FMat*, 153.

38. The expression is used in Fleisser's slightly fictionalized novella *Avantgarde*. GW 3:127. Marieluise Fleisser. In this story, told entirely in the third person,

and first published in 1963 (seven years after Brecht's death), Fleisser used both characteristics from her own life and Elisabeth Hauptmann's to form the composite character of Cilly Ostermeier. The character of Polly in the same piece is based on that of Helene Weigel, with some traces of Carola Neher. See also Fleisser's first-person essays, "Erinnerungen and Brecht: Frühe Begegnungen," *GW* 2:297–308; and "Aus der Augustenstrasse," *GW* 2:309–14.

39. *GW* 3:129. Marieluise Fleisser.
40. Rühle, *FMat*, 154.
41. See BBA 720/36.
42. See Hennenberg, "Bruinier und Brecht."
43. Cited in Ronald Sanders, *The Days Grow Short* (New York: Holt, Rinehart and Winston, 1980), 78.
44. Statements made by Lenya in an interview published in the *Philadelphia Inquirer*, 28 April 1976.
45. See, for instance, the *Münchner Illustrierte Presse*, 14 April 1929.
46. JW, *Eight Aspects*, 130.
47. The song and its history are discussed by Andreas Hauff in the *Kurt Weill Newsletter*, vol. 9, no. 1.
48. Lenya's jacket notes to her 1956 Columbia recording of what she refers to provocatively in a deliberate inversion of Brecht's usual practice as "KURT WEILL'S [in letters two inches high] in collaboration with Bertolt Brecht [in letters a quarter of an inch high] *The Rise and Fall of the City of Mahagonny*."
49. JW, Notes, *Mahagonny*, 111.
50. Kim H. Kowalke, *Kurt Weill in Europe* (Ann Arbor: UMI Research Press, 1979), 59. Hereafter: Kowalke, *KWE*.
51. Given Hauptmann's (in the original) and Brecht's (in translation) familiarity with French literature, the obvious source for this inn is Rabelais's bawdy 1534 text: *La vie très horrifique du grand Gargantua*. In the Abbey of Thélème, the inhabitants live by the dictum "Do as thou wilt."
52. Sanders, *Days Grow Short*, 92.

Chapter 14

1. See Jürgen Schebera, "Später Epitaph für Carola Neher," *Notate* (January 1990).
2. Cited in JW, *Brecht Poems*, x.
3. JW, *Brecht Poems*, x.
4. BL, 128.
5. See C. D. Innes, *Erwin Piscator's Political Theatre* (Cambridge: Cambridge University Press, 1972), 80.
6. BL, 129.
7. Many years after Brecht's death, a number of these poems were published by the East German scholar Werner Hecht. See Brecht, *Gül*.
8. An excellent discussion of the turn made by Weill at this time is provided in Christopher Hailey, "Creating a Public, Addressing a Market: Kurt Weill and Universal Edition," in *A New Orpheus: Essays on Kurt Weill*, ed. Kim H. Kowalke (New Haven: Yale University Press, 1986).
9. See Mittenzwei, *Leben* 1:277–78.

10. Even after the meeting with Aufricht and sale of the work to Felix Bloch Erben, in a letter dated 9 May 1928 (BL, 136), Brecht still refers to the text as something that Erich Engel plans to do under the original title *The Beggar's Opera*. In FBE's house organ, *Charivari*, of 18 July 1928, they also announce the work as *Des Bettler's Oper*, "translated by Elisabeth Hauptmann." And in the issue dated 8 September 1928, the journal again credits the translation to Hauptmann.

11. Ernst Josef Aufricht, *Erzähle damit du dein Recht erweist* (Berlin, Propyläen Verlag, 1966), 64. Hereafter: Aufricht.

12. For a good discussion of the various layers of the text and the importance of Hauptmann's work in the process, see Joachim Lucchesi and Ronald K. Shull, *Musik bei Brecht* (Berlin: Henschelverlag, 1988), 388–407. Hereafter: Lucchesi and Shull, *MbB*.

13. The date stamps on the contract are fuzzy, but the time frame can be fully reconstructed from internal evidence and from Kurt Weill's records.

14. It is catalogued BBA 1782/1–66. With German reunification, it is to be sincerely hoped that a fundamental reassessment of former GDR archives will be undertaken to strip away the scholarly chaos that has resulted from almost half a century of politically determined labeling of and access to basic research materials such as these. I hope, however, that we do not encounter an opposite kind of tendentious scholarship, where everything is seen from the perspective of what I believe is a far from blameless West.

15. Lucchesi and Shull, *MbB*, 390.

16. Statement made by Völker at his apartment in Berlin on 28 September 1990. See also Klaus Völker, "Induktive Liebe, extensive Mitarbeit," in *Nach Brecht: Ein Almanach 1992*, ed. Inge Gellert (Berlin: Argon, 1992).

17. See my analysis of these and other Brecht financial arrangements with Weill and Hauptmann, "Most Unpleasant Things with the *Threepenny Opera*: Weill, Brecht and Money," in *A New Orpheus*; and, in slightly different form and under the title, "The Business Deals of Herr Bertolt Brecht," in *The Play and Its Critic: Essays for Eric Bentley*, ed. Michael Bertin (Lanham/New York/London: University Press of America, 1986). The essay was also published in German as "Die Geschäfte des Herrn Bertolt Brecht," in *Bertolt Brecht-Die Widersprüche sind die Hoffnungen*, ed. Wolf Wucherpfennig and Klaus Schulte (Copenhagen/Munich: Wilhelm Fink, 1988). The figures I use are based on the original records of Felix Bloch Erben, who kindly made them available to me. The figures were cross-checked against Weill and Lenya's private papers, kindly made available to me by the Kurt Weill Foundation. These essays have now been in print for many years, and no fact given in them has been challenged by anybody, though I know from her personally that Brecht's daughter and heir, Mari Barbara Brecht-Schall, has been incensed by my work since the outset. As I have told her on several occasions, I welcome any correction she might be able to provide from her family files. So far, she has provided none. My offer remains open.

18. Upon Brecht's death in 1956, with Brecht leaving Hauptmann nothing in his will, giving everything to Weigel, we know that Peter Suhrkamp insisted on Hauptmann's contribution being recognized, if only with a tiny share in the millions that were at stake by that time.

19. JoR, 25.
20. BL, 135–36.
21. BL, 139.
22. Here, Lucchesi and Shull, MbB ignores Hauptmann's presence. This may, of course, be due to the sheer cumbersomeness of always mentioning more than one individual as author. This will now become a serious general problem as we learn more about how much we thought was by Brecht is by others.
23. Aufricht, 66.
24. See Lucchesi and Shull, MbB, 390.
25. Canetti's biography, The Torch in My Ear, part 4, trans. Joachim Neugroschel (New York: Farrar Straus Giroux, 1982), provides a detailed account of events in Berlin in 1928. Hereafter: Canetti, Torch.
26. "Brecht . . . As Seen by Lenya," from her husband George Davis's notes. Weill/Lenya Research Foundation.
27. Aufricht, 70.
28. See Lyon, BB/RK, 93.
29. Eric Bentley informs me that Brecht always pronounced "song" as "zonk."
30. Kowalke, KWE, 134.

Chapter 15

1. Harry Graf Kessler, Tagebücher 1918–1937 (Frankfurt am Main: Insel, 1961), 349.
2. Kessler, Tagebücher, 567.
3. See Max Brod, "Die Frau und die neue Sachlichkeit," in Die Frauen von Morgen, ed. F. M. Huebner (Leipzig: E. A. Seemann, 1929).
4. Ernst Bloch, Literarische Aufsätze (Frankfurt am Main: Suhrkamp Verlag, 1965), vol. 9 of the Gesamtausgabe, 393.
5. For salaries paid for translation at this time in Germany, please note the translator who did the English version of The Threepenny Opera was paid a total of 120 marks.
6. One such typical letter (not in BL) is that of 16 December 1927. Here, he argued to the tax authorities that the money he gets from publishers is a loan and hence not taxable. However, when publishers tried to recover any of this money (as Felix Bloch Erben did in the early thirties), Brecht declared that this was money he had earned and was not repayable. But, again, he later told the tax authorities (see his letter of 10 February 1933) that he has no "income," only "loans," and fought an epistolary war over a tax assessment of a total of 128 marks for a period of three years.
7. Records of the Berlin court in Charlottenburg as cited in Mittenzwei, Leben 1:211.
8. JW, "Bacon?" 128.
9. BL, 146.
10. For a transcript of the meeting, see Bertolt Brecht, Schriften zum Theater (Berlin and Weimar: Aufbau, 1964), 292–317.
11. See John Fuegi, "The Form and the Pressure: Shakespeare's Haunting of Bertolt Brecht," Modern Drama 3 (December 1972).
12. It would now seem that the work was done jointly with Bronnen's old friend at Berlin radio Alfred Braun. See GW 15:4.

13. GW 15:115–20.
14. GW 15:149.
15. GW 15:181–82.
16. GW 16:938.
17. Sternberg, *Der Dichter*, 36.
18. Benn cited in André Gisselbrecht, "Autour de Brecht mais sans lui," *Obliques* 20–21:59.
19. GW 3:149. Marieluise Fleisser.
20. GW 3:152. Marieluise Fleisser.
21. GW 3:157. Marieluise Fleisser.
22. GW 3:157. Marieluise Fleisser.
23. Marieluise Fleisser, a lifelong friend and supporter of Hauptmann, told me (author's interview, Berlin, 2 November 1973) that Hauptmann definitely expected to marry Brecht. Fleisser's statement, of course, is sadly ironic as she too had that expectation.
24. Author's interview with Fleisser, Berlin, 1973.
25. BL, 146–48. The letter is undated, and the last section is missing. In the Willett and Manheim edition, Willett dates it as "mid-year 1929" (*Brecht Letters*, 582). The letter appears to be Brecht's attempt to claim the idea of *Happy End* as his.
26. Massary was married to Max Pallenberg, the star of Piscator's *Schweik* (on which Brecht intermittently worked).
27. Rendered in rhyme but with minimal sexual explicitness by Willett and Mannheim as "You can't undress Mimosa Bess."
28. JW and Mannheim, *Brecht Letters*, 582.
29. I first published these private papers of Hauptmann in 1985 (they have never been challenged) as an addendum to John Willett's article on Elisabeth Hauptmann's many contributions to Brecht, "Bacon ohne Shakespeare?," 136–37.
30. I spoke with Margot Aufricht about this in 1983. When Frau Aufricht saw the Felix Bloch Erben evidence of Haupmann's authorship, she agreed at once that she and her husband had been deceived by Brecht and had pursued the wrong author in 1929.
31. Cited in JW, *Eight Aspects*, 94.
32. "Im Theater . . . Von wem ist dieses Stück? Dieses Stück ist von Brecht. Von wem *ist* also dieses Stück?" Kurt Tucholsky, *Lerne lachen ohne zu weinen* (Berlin: Rowohlt, 1931), 346.
33. Not in GW. See instead, Völker, *Brecht*, 133.
34. Erwin Piscator, *Das Politische Theater* (Berlin: Schutz Verlag, 1929), 141.
35. See Gershom Scholem, *Walter Benjamin, The Story of a Friendship*, trans. Harry Zohn (New York: Schocken Books, 1981), 164.

Chapter 16

1. See notes on O. Schirmer's 1966 interview, Reiner Steinweg, *Das Lehrstück* (Stuttgart: Metzler, 1972), 65–66. Hereafter: Steinweg, *DL*.
2. The interview is found in *JoR*, 175–77.

3. This was seen as early as 1959 by Willett in *Eight Aspects*, 96–97, in 1961 by Reinhold Grimm in *Brecht und die Weltliteratur*, 19, and by my Berlin mentor, Peter Szondi, in *Bertolt Brecht, Der Jasager und Der Neinsager, Vorlagen, Fassungen, Materialien*, ed. Peter Szondi (Frankfurt am Main: Suhrkamp, 1966). Not long after publishing this, Szondi took his own life and hence never pursued the topic further. Hauptmann published her own text in 1930 in the relatively obscure magazine *Scheinwerfer* (Searchlight). See also Brown, who confirms Hauptmann's authorship.

4. Heiner Müller, *Krieg ohne Schlacht: Leben in zwei Diktaturen* (Cologne: Kiepenheuer & Witsch, 1992), 226. Hereafter: Müller, *KoS*. Franz Wille in *Theater Heute* (November 1993) argues *Fatzer* is an early example of "Stalinist party doctrine that climbs over dead bodies."

5. Incident cited in Hayman, 140.

6. Mittenzwei, *Leben* 1:305–6.

7. JW, *Eight Aspects*, 186.

8. JW, *Eight Aspects*, 33–34.

9. Reiner Steinweg (*DL*, 219) notes: "Fabelschemata, Notizen und Entwürfe, ausgehend von einem chinesischen Stück 'Die zwei Mantelhälften', das Elisabeth Hauptmann nach einer französischen Vorlage ins Deutsche übertragen hatte."

10. Communication of Karl-Heinz Schoeps, Brecht Symposium, Delaware, 1 March 1992. Additional information came to me directly from Paula Hanssen in letters and in two written versions of talks she has given at scholarly conferences. See Paula Hanssen, "Elisabeth Hauptmann: 'Brechts Federführung ohne Feder'—Hauptmann's Silent Collaboration with Brecht in the Example of the 'Chinesische Gedichte.' " (Paper delivered at the Kentucky Literature Conference, 1991). Hereafter: Hanssen, "Elisabeth Hauptmann." I am very grateful to Ms. Hanssen for sharing her findings with me. There is also evidence that when the workshop again tackled questions of "Chinese" translations (again mainly from Waley's English versions) in the late 1930s, that Margarete Steffin, Hauptmann's successor as of the early 1930s, would do most of the work, but the poems were published as Brecht's work.

11. JW, "Bacon?" 125.

12. See Steinweg, *DL*, notes on original typescripts in Hauptmann's possession (215–26).

13. Author's interview with Hauptmann, which she gave in Berlin 1966, ten years after Brecht's death.

14. The piece was called "Ein lehrreicher Auto-Unfall" (A richly didactic automobile accident), *Uhu*, February 1929, 65.

15. This letter was given to me by Dr. Gerhard Seidel just before the collapse of the GDR.

16. For details see Völker, Brecht, 133, and Schmidt, *'Baal' und der junge Brecht*, 16.

17. For Hindemith's use of *Lehrstück*, see Lucchesi and Shull, *MbB*, 430–34.

18. See Steinweg, *DL*, 217, where he notes an original "Clown Number" typescript, "mit handschriftlichen Verbesserungen von Elisabeth Hauptmann."

19. See Dorothea Friedrich's essay, "Kratz mich, beiss mich, sag Iltis zu mir!"

Frankfurter Allgemeine Magazin, 13 March 1992; and Valeska Gert's autobiography, *Ich bin eine Hexe: Kaleidoskop meines Lebens* (Munich: Franz Schneekluth Verlag, 1968).

20. Gert, *Ich bin eine Hexe,* 461.
21. Eisler in *SuF,* 2d, 97.
22. Lingen's letter to Elisabeth Hauptmann. See also Theo Lingen's memoirs, *Ich Über Mich* (Velber bei Hannover: Friedrich Verlag, 1963), 43–45.
23. E. H. Gombrich, "Meditations on a Hobby Horse and the Roots of Artistic Form," in *Meditations on a Hobby Horse and Other Essays on the Theory of Art* (London and New York: Phaidon, 1971). Hereafter: Gombrich, "Meditations."
24. John Willett was, to the best of my knowledge, the first to ask about Hauptmann's "hand in the writing of the songs." See JW, "Bacon?" 127.
25. Aufricht, 99.
26. Aufricht, 99–100.
27. The Kipling-based and show-stopping "Surabaya Johnny" and the "Bilbao Song" are almost certainly the work of Hauptmann, as well as possibly the "Cannon Song," which so clearly derives from Kipling. See John Willett's version of the song in a deliberately Kiplingesque English in *Poetry Review* vol. 62, no. 1 (Spring 1971): 48.

Chapter 17

1. The text of the song "Surabaya Johnny," for instance, is picked up virtually verbatim from work Brecht and Hauptmann had done with Feuchtwanger in 1925.
2. Weill's comment was made in August 1929 to Felix Jackson. Cited by Guy Stern in an untitled piece in the *Kurt Weill Newsletter,* 10, no. 1 (Spring 1992): 7.
3. Bernard Holland, review of *Street Scene, New York Times,* 7 September 1990.
4. Völker, *Brecht,* 129/30.
5. *GW* 8:291–92.
6. Woolf, *Room,* 48.
7. Woolf, *Room,* 49.
8. Cited in Tax, *Fleisser,* 91.
9. *GW* 1:459. Marieluise Fleisser.
10. Apparently, wholly without irony, the 1976 *Oxford Companion to German Literature* (Oxford: Oxford University Press, 1976), 732, states of the six plays that Roswitha von Gandersheim wrote in the tenth century: "They appear to have received little attention in spite of their lively dialogue and skilful dramatic organization." No doubt it was this almost complete ignoring of a fine woman dramatist that prompted Fleisser to read her autobiographical piece at the Roswitha von Gandersheim celebration entitled "Eine Tagung schaffender Frauen."
11. Woolf, *Room,* 36.
12. Woolf, *Three Guineas,* 53.
13. The firm of Opel was held by General Motors; 25 percent of AEG was held by the General Electric Company; the various divisions of what has now become the Metallgesellschaft, or MG, Services had interlocking relationships with

Standard Oil; Western Electric had a commercial agreement with Tobis; and Nero Film was partially owned by Warner Brothers. The biggest studio of all, UFA, had been taken over by the megaindustrialist and ardent nationalist Alfred Hugenberg in 1927.

14. See Craig, *Germany*, 530.
15. Fest, *Hitler*, 261.
16. The BBA copy of *Unter dem Banner des Marxismus*, 5, no. 3 (October 1929).
17. Diary 1920–1954, 98.
18. Manfred Wekwerth, close associate of Brecht in his last years, said in my presence in East Berlin in 1985: "Brecht did not read the second volume of *Das Kapital*. With him [Brecht], dialectics was a matter of feelings."
19. Cited in John Willett, *Art and Politics in the Weimar Period* (New York: Pantheon, 1978), 175. Hereafter: JW, *APWP*.
20. Cited in Wheeler-Bennett, *Nemesis*, 148.
21. Bronnen, *P*, 224.
22. See John Willett, *Brecht in Context* (London and New York: Methuen, 1983), 160. Hereafter: JW, *BinC*.
23. See Lenya's notes, Columbia recording of *Mahagonny*.
24. On 23 January 1930, Wilhelm Frick was elected on the Nazi ticket to the important post of education minister of Thuringia.
25. Sternberg, *Der Dichter*, 26–27.
26. See Isaac Deutscher, *Stalin, A Political Biography* (Oxford: Oxford University Press, 1949), 407, where Stalin's position is cited: "Social Democracy is the moderate wing of fascism. . . . These organizations do not contradict but supplement one another. They are not antipodeds but twins." In fact, as we are now increasingly aware, the true fraternal twins, and who were sometimes recognized as such even at that time, were Stalin and Hitler, whose tastes and methods were so compellingly similar in such a huge variety of areas.
27. Deutscher, *Stalin*, 399–400.
28. It is possible to cross-reference what happened, as we have an account of the meeting in Piscator's unpublished papers (Piscator Papers, Akademie der Künste, West Berlin), and Bronnen's published account in *P*, 248.
29. Notes, Piscator Papers.
30. Many details on the *Versuche* deal and the general contractual relationship Brecht had at different times with Kiepenheuer were kindly provided to me by two former Kiepenheuer employees, Dr. Friedemann Berger and Dr. Fritz Landshoff.

Chapter 18

1. This point has been made in Sanders, *Days Grow Short*, 161; and in JW, *Eight Aspects*, 37.
2. JW, *BinC*, 160.
3. The printed version of the broadcast is given in *JoR*, 139–65.
4. See Jan Knopf, *Brecht, Theater Handbuch* (Stuttgart: Metzler, 1980), 92. Hereafter: Knopf, *BTH*.
5. Only decades later were reasonably reliable accounts published on methods used by the Comintern and other Soviet-directed intelligence agencies to insert

agents into the Far East. The best accounts are Julius Mader, Gerhard Stuch-lik, and Horst Pehnert, eds., *Dr. Sorge funkt aus Tokyo* (Berlin: Militärverlag der Deutschen Demokratischen Republik, 1976) (hereafter: Mader, Stuchlik, Pehnert, *Sorge Funkt*); and a firsthand account, Otto Braun, *A Comintern Agent in China, 1932–9* (Stanford: Stanford University Press, 1982). Gerhart Eisler himself contributed to the *Sorge* volume, which gives a clear account of the complete absence of anything like the disguises and chinoiserie that are such a dramatically necessary feature of *Measures*.

6. This term was used regularly in Soviet and GDR "scholarship" up to 1989.
7. Hanns Eisler, *Gesammelte Werke: Musik und Politik, Schriften 1924–4* (Leipzig: Deutscher Verlag für Musik, 1982). Hereafter: Eisler, *MuP*.
8. See Eisler, *MuP*.
9. See the three-volume *MuP*, where the only two references to Elisabeth Hauptmann have been added by Eisler's editor. Also see extensive interviews with Eisler, in Hans Bunge, *Fragen Sie mehr über Brecht* (Munich: Rogner & Bernhard, 1970). Hereafter: Bunge, *FSB*. There is no index entry at all for Elisabeth Hauptmann.
10. Hauptmann's contribution to *Measures* is noted in Mittenzwei, *Leben* 1:345.
11. This fragment from the original audiotapes was dropped in the 1970 Munich edition of Hans Bunge, *FSB*; but does turn up in Reiner Steinweg, *Die Massnahme, Kritische Ausgabe* (Frankfurt am Main: Suhrkamp, 1972), 269 (hereafter: Steinweg, *MKA*), a volume that almost wholly ignores Hauptmann's creative contributions to a new genre for which, I believe, she was mainly responsible. When Steinweg speaks with Hauptmann, he typically marginalizes her by only asking her about Brecht rather than her own work.
12. I cite from Bertolt Brecht, *Versuche*, 1st ed., Elisabeth Hauptmann, ed. (Berlin: Kiepenheuer, 1931), 4:139.
13. In fact, the history of Comintern activities in China is an almost uninterrupted chain of error. Stalin repeatedly misread the course of the Chinese Revolution, and was consistently contemptuous of Mao and Mao's working methods. He never seemed to understand that Mao worked from a rural base in a country that had virtually no proletariat.
14. See Völker's (to my mind) rather one-sided discussion of this theme, *Brecht*, 166ff.
15. See Sanders, *Days Grow Short*, 171, for this and other excellent details on the tangled threads of the *Threepenny* film case.
16. Mittenzwei, *Leben* 1:345.
17. Mittenzwei, *Leben* 1:345.
18. Sanders, *Days Grow Short*, 164.
19. Frank Warschauer, *Die Weltbühne*, 26, no. 28 (1930): 70–71. Also in Peter Szondi ed., *Jasager/Neinsager Materialien* (Frankfurt am Main: Suhrkamp, 1966), 71–73. Hereafter: *Materialien*.
20. Heinrich Strobel wrote, "*Massnahme* is a new version of *Jasager*." See *Materialien*, 326.
21. See Jürgen Schebera, *Kurt Weill* (Leipzig: Deutscher Verlag für Musik, 1989), 139. Schebera's discussion of score and libretto in this book is the best I know.
22. See Steinweg, *DL*, 219, for excellent notes on Hauptmann's original typescript.

23. See Lucchesi and Shull, *MbB*, 507.
24. *GW* 9:527–29. In a poem specifically written for Mari Hold, Brecht punningly writes, "Als die Barbarische erschien, hatte sie Ihre Augen und Bald / Hatte sie zwei Mütter" (When barbaric Barbara appeared, she had your eyes, and, soon, she had two mothers).
25. Brecht, however, in his notes, makes reference to a four-hundred-man choir.
26. *Materialien*, 336
27. *Materialien*, 335. Review was signed "A. E." and appeared in the *Berliner Tagblatt*.
28. Cited in Mittenzwei, *Leben* 1:362.

Chapter 19

1. Well after Brecht's death, the story was reprinted in *JoR*, 45–53. Its meaning, however, was once again wholly ignored as the East German state continued, until it collapsed, to tirelessly promote Brecht abroad as an iconic figure.
2. See Carolyn G. Heilbrun's analysis of changes at key points in women's lives in *Writing a Woman's Life* (New York: Ballantine Books, 1988).
3. A solid account of German-Soviet relations in these years is given in JW, *APWP*.
4. Cited in JW, *Eight Aspects*, 148.
5. See Anatoly Smeliansky, "The Last Decade: Stanislavsky and Stalinism," in the Yale magazine *Theater*, vol. 22 (January 1991), 7–13.
6. This version of the interview, with all its glaring factual errors (but with no guide to the errors), has been repeatedly reprinted in Peter Demetz ed., *Brecht: Twentieth Century Views* (Englewood Cliffs, Prentice-Hall, 1962), 16–29.
7. The best published account of these policies and their impact is Robert Conquest, *The Harvest of Sorrow* (New York: Oxford University Press, 1986). After years of denigration, *Harvest* was serialized in the Soviet Union in 1989 in *Novi Mir*.
8. Sternberg, *Der Dichter*, 23–24.
9. Leon Trotsky, *Germany, the Key to the International Situation* (London: 1931), 44.
10. See Scholem, *Walter Benjamin*, 164.
11. See Bronnen's own account of these events in *P*, 264–65.
12. The gossip here was more likely to be about Brecht and Lenya than about Brecht and Hauptmann. Often desperately unhappy with Weill's inattention, Lenya would take various lovers of both sexes; the couple obtained a divorce as Weimar lurched to an end. They would remarry later in exile.
13. Fest, *Hitler*, 190.
14. Fest, *Hitler*, 204.
15. Josephine Hauptmann (née Diestelhorst) died on 29 March 1930. A portion of her small estate went to each of her two daughters and one son.
16. This extraordinary item was *not* included in the published *Brecht Letters*. My copy, from a private source, has no BBA number on it. It is headed simply "Bertolt Brecht, z.Zt. Augsburg" and dated on the reverse side 28 June 1931.
17. See Schulz, *DSBB*, 98–99.
18. For a detailed examination of the play as text and performance, see John Fuegi, *The Essential Brecht* (Los Angeles: Hennessey and Ingalls, 1972), chap. 3.
19. As Bukharin was later murdered and made a nonperson by Stalin, references

to this major figure in the spread of international communism are usually not included in discussions of the Brecht version of *Mother*.

20. See Reinhard Müller, ed., *Die Säuberung, Moskau 1936, Stenogramm einer geschlossenen Parteiversammlung* (Reinbeck bei Hamburg: Rowohlt, 1991), 68–70, 309–10, 552–56. Hereafter: Müller, *Säuberung*.

21. Steffin, *Konfutse*, 176ff.

22. Knopf, *BTH*, 107.

23. Knopf, *BTH*, 105.

24. A few examples may suffice here. Work of Elisabeth Hauptmann, Margarete Steffin, Ruth Berlau, and Martin Pohl has been routinely taken over in so-called Brecht editions without any prior authorization and despite protests made about unauthorized, unrecognized, and unpaid-for use. When Martin Pohl and Ruth Berlau protested to the publisher, their claims were dismissed out of hand. In the case of Steffin, the fact that she was dead and her family was too poor and ill-informed helped make decades of deception possible.

25. Helfried W. Seliger, *Das Amerikabild Bertolt Brechts* (Bonn: Bouvier, 1974), 183.

26. In the Fat Ham story, it is Hauptmann who saves the Ark. In her own stories and *Happy End*, she had dealt in detail with the Salvation Army.

27. The connection to an 1892 text of Engels is noted in Karl-Heinz Schoeps, *Bertolt Brecht und Bernard Shaw* (Bonn: Bouvier, 1974), 47. In addition to the Engels reference, Schoeps provides excellent materials on the myriad other sources used by the collective.

28. BBA 117/13. "Johanna D'ark dreiundzwanzig Jahre alt, gestorben an Lungenentzündung."

Chapter 20

1. Bronnen, *P*, 271.

2. Aufricht, 126.

3. See Weigel interview in Werner Hecht, ed., *Materialien zu Bertolt Brechts 'Die Mutter'* (Frankfurt am Main: Suhrkamp, 1969), 28–34. Hereafter: M/M.

4. For details on her recollections, see Steffin, *Konfutse*, 166ff.

5. Interview with Herta Hanisch conducted by Rudy Hassing and Hans and Gudrun Bunge, Berlin, 17 November 1986, and kindly made available to me. In December 1987, I spoke directly with Frau Hanisch in the village of Fredersdorf to the east of Berlin.

6. Steffin, *Konfutse*, 204.

7. Steffin described the abortion in a poem that she wrote in November 1932, at a time when she had had another abortion, this time of a child by Brecht.

8. GW 2:878.

9. Fest, *Hitler*, 244.

10. Lenya's notes, Columbia recording of *Mahagonny*.

11. Aufricht, 128.

12. M/M, 27.

13. M/M, 32.

14. Steffin, *Konfutse*, 202–3. The original typescript of the poem was one that Steffin showed to Brecht. He penciled in a few changes. He wanted the poem to read throughout as follows: Not, "When he asked me the first time . . . ," but

rather, "When you asked me the first time . . ." The poem as finally printed in *Konfutse* in 1991 is, quite properly I feel, given in its original version.

15. Carol Gilligan, *In a Different Voice* (Cambridge: Harvard University Press, 1982). Using "Jake" to represent a typical boy's reaction and "Amy" as the "different voice" of a girl, Gilligan writes: "Jake sets himself apart from the world by his abilities, his beliefs, and his height. Although Amy also enumerates her likes, her wants, and her beliefs, she locates herself in relation to the world, describing herself through actions that bring her into connection with others, elaborating ties through her ability to provide help" (35). I see "Jake" as a reflection of the core values of Brecht, and "Amy" as reflecting the core values of Hauptmann and Steffin.

Chapter 21

1. Conquest, *Harvest*, 230.
2. This very useful term (modeled obviously on the analogous Russian word *intelligentsia*) is from Conquest, *Harvest*.
3. See Conquest, *Harvest*, chap. 16.
4. My conclusion that Steffin had many abortions is derived from a study of Danish hospital records as obtained by Dr. Morten Nielsen, who kindly provided them to me. Some doubt as to the number still exists as sometimes, even in progressive Denmark, the fact of an abortion was sometimes concealed under another rubric. Helene Weigel, for example, supposedly had her "appendix" removed three times. The abortions we are sure of in Steffin's case were done in 1928, 1930, and 1932. Other highly probable dates are 1934, 1936, and 1937 when Steffin was often in the Soviet Union where abortions were, until circa 1936, available on demand.
5. Apparently, neither was George Bernard Shaw, who had seen the production the year before in Moscow. He saw the play as "an amazing, and at points disgusting perversion of the *Beggar's Opera*, with modern German music." Quoted in George Bernard Shaw, *Collected Letters 1926–1950*, ed. Dan H. Laurence (forthcoming).
6. Though entire books have been published on Brecht and film, this letter and the point of view it represents have been consistently ignored. Dated 11 July 1932, it is in the Brecht Archive as 656/02–3.
7. Georg Lukács, *Gelebtes Denken* (Frankfurt am Main: Suhrkamp, 1981), 149. Hereafter: Lukács, *GD*.
8. The subject has now been treated in the West. See Antonia Fraser, *The Warrior Queens* (New York: Knopf, 1989).
9. MF, 215ff.
10. MF, 225ff.
11. Fest, *Hitler*, 338.
12. Müller, *KoS*, 187.
13. GW 8:418–19.
14. BL, 157. This letter, written from Utting, ends with a handwritten greeting to Eisler from Steffin. Other details in this paragraph come from the unpublished letters in the Central State Archive for Literature and Art (CSALA), File 631/14/388.

15. Fest, *Hitler*, 329.
16. Fest, *Hitler*, 328.
17. Cited in Robert Tucker, *Stalin in Power* (New York: W. W. Norton & Company, 1990), 230.
18. JW, *Eight Aspects*, 194.
19. BL, 157.
20. The letter describing her work of the previous year is dated Paris, 10 December 1933. BBA 480/124–32.
21. "Mr. Nobody" is almost certainly borrowed from *The Odyssey*. When Polyphemus asks who has hurt him, Odysseus replies, "Nobody." Then, when other cyclops ask Polyphemus, "Who has hurt you?" he answers, "Nobody." They then fail to come to help him while Odysseus, "Mr. Nobody," escapes. Before the Keuner stories became a separate series, the character of Keuner had showed up in the violent, never-to-be-completed play *Fatzer*.
22. *Versuche*, 13:456.
23. This account of their visits is given by Natalya Rosenel. *Neues Deutschland*, 10 February 1958.
24. The exchange is reproduced in Mittenzwei, *Leben* 365 1:7.
25. JW, *BinC*, 184.
26. JW, *BinC*, 184.
27. Sternberg, *Der Dichter*, 37. In December 1986, I asked the longtime Brecht scholar Reinhold Grimm, the editor of the Sternberg memoirs, whether he felt this description of the Sylvester 1932 party was reliable. He said he was sure it was. Bronnen's and von Salamon's own memoirs confirm that talk of such a putsch was general in their circle from 1928 on. See Bronnen, *P*, 209ff.
28. Bronnen, *P*, 276.
29. Fest, *Hitler*, 366.
30. Fest, *Hitler*, 367.
31. Fest, *Hitler*, 369.
32. See BBA 722/02. Letter *not* included in BL.
33. Fest, *Hitler*, 392.
34. Mittenzwei indicates that Brecht was visited at the clinic that day by Hanns Eisler just before Eisler left for Vienna to supervise a performance of *The Measures Taken*.
35. Mittenzwei, *Leben* 1:463.
36. Bronnen, *P*, 290.

Chapter 22

1. Carola Stern, *Ulbricht. Eine politische Biographie* (Cologne and Berlin: Kiepenheuer & Witsch, 1963), 116ff.
2. See the eyewitness Evgeni Gnedin's account cited in Tucker, *Stalin in Power*, 236.
3. See the Nazi propaganda volume, *Die nationale Erhebung 1933*, ed. Willi Peschel (Oldenburg: Gerhard Stalling, 1933), 5–6.
4. Cited in Herbert Tutas, *NS-Propaganda und deutsches Exil 1933–39* (Worms: G. Heintz, 1973), 23.
5. Erika and Klaus Mann, *Escape to Life* (Boston: Houghton Mifflin Company, 1939), 60; and Sternberg, *Der Dichter*, 37–38.

6. See Elaine S. Hochman, *Architects of Fortune, Mies van der Rohe and the Third Reich* (New York: Weidenfeld & Nicholson, 1989).

7. Author's personal conversation with Herbert Marshal at Southern Illinois University, July 10, 1980.

8. Details are given in chapter 24 below.

9. See Sanders, *Days Grow Short*, 189.

10. For a discussion of Pabst and the Nazis, see Paul Rotha, *The Film Till Now* (London: Spring Books, 1949), 582ff.

11. Weigel's mother died in 1933, and her father in 1938.

12. Through the help of colleagues in the Academy of Science of the USSR and the special efforts of Georg Zaitsev, I obtained copies of all this correspondence from the CSALA.

13. CSALA File 631/14/388. *Not* in BL.

14 Moscow CSALA File 631/14/394. *Not* in BL.

15. See Schebera, *Weill*, 169–70.

16. James was thought by some to be the illegitimate son of Edward VII.

17. See Donald Spoto, *Lenya, A Life* (Boston: Little, Brown & Co., 1989), 112–13.

18. See BBA 911/47.

19. Felix Bloch Erben Files (hereafter: FBE); and BBA 783/41. *Not* in BL.

20. FBE Files; and BBA 783/42. *Not* in BL.

21. BBA 722/19. The letter is dated 21 May 1933, almost three months after the Reichstag fire.

22. See Tucker, *Stalin*, 235–37.

23. BL, 164–65. A copy of the note survives among Brecht's papers. Tretiakov's papers, however, did not survive. They, like Tretiakov himself, were seized by the NKVD on 16 July 1937 and never returned.

24. Ilya Ehrenburg, *Memoirs 1921–41*, trans. Tatiania Shebunina and Yvonne Kapp (New York: Grosset & Dunlap, 1966), 242.

25. Franz Leschnitzer's Moscow letter to Brecht confirming the arrangement will be placed in the Steffin Archive.

26. See BBA 533/44–45. One version of this sketch is to be found in Steffin, *Konfutse*, 167–68.

27. BL, 166.

28. BBA 722/41.

29. Materials provided to me by Margarete Steffin's sister, Herta Hanisch, and from Berlin, Moscow, and Copenhagen sources. All these materials will be listed hereafter as SA (Steffin Archive). I plan to deposit all these papers, photographs, family documents, and other materials in a public library so they will be accessible for further study.

30. Steffin wrote to Brecht: "I am not going to call friend Eisler anymore. He doesn't have time for me." In another letter, she wrote: "I haven't seen Eisler for a long time. He was supposed to give me the name of a doctor but never has time, and nothing is heard from him" (SA).

31. SA.

32. SA.

33. None of the letters to Steffin are in the volume of Brecht letters published by Suhrkamp Verlag (BL). The same press, however, has often published Steffin's work without obtaining authorization of her heirs or paying for its use.

34. BBA 152/03. "Der liebesakt muss sie von grund verändern bis zur entstellung."
35. This poem was published by Suhrkamp Verlag in 1982 in Brecht, Gül, 195.
36. Typewritten "10th Sonnet" (SA); and BBA 152/13. The German lines are: "Was ich nicht gern gesteh: gerade ich verachte solche, die im Unglück sind."
37. SA. See also BBA 654/32.
38. SA.
39. SA.
40. Statement made to the photographer Gerda Goedhart, who repeated it to Hans Bunge.

Chapter 23

1. Nicolas's account of the horrors inflicted on her and her husband under Hitler and Stalin are given in her book, Viele tausend Tage (Stuttgart: Steingruben Verlag, 1960). Hereafter: Nicolas, Viele Tausend.
2. Cited in Birgit S. Nielsen, "Freundschaft zwischen Bert Brecht, Helene Weigel, und Karin Michaëlis," in Exil 1933–45, ed. Edith Böhne and W. Motzkau-Valeton. Text seen in prepublication form, courtesy of Dr. Nielsen. Hereafter: Nielsen, "Freundschaft."
3. Cited in Nielsen, "Freundschaft."
4. The account I rely on here and in following chapters for the way Brecht and Steffin were treated by the Danish authorities is that of Hans Christian Nørregaard as given in his essay, "Brecht and the Danish Authorities 1933–41," as kindly shared with me in manuscript form. Hereafter: Nørregaard, "Brecht."
5. On Berlau's relationship with Brecht, see Hans Bunge, Brechts Lai-tu (Darmstadt and Neuwied: Luchterhand, 1985). Hereafter: Bunge, Lai-tu. The Lai-tu book is a bowdlerized, heavily censored version of Hans Bunge's recorded interviews with Berlau. He has kindly made the original interviews directly available to me so that I can restore the things the GDR government press and Mari Barbara Schall forced him to delete. It is important to note that when Berlau speaks of things of which she had direct knowledge she is, despite years of battling with alcoholism in her later years, amazingly reliable. This is not true, however, when she speculates about things such as Carola Neher's treatment by the Soviet authorities. For further details on Berlau, see the 1992 documentary film Red Ruth: That Deadly Longing, with Berlau's statements spoken by Liv Ullmann.
6. Voltelen spoke with me in Copenhagen in 1986 about his relationship with Berlau and the Comintern. Both Berlau and Voltelen were working members of the Danish Communist party and its affiliated organization the Moscow-run Comintern.
7. Bunge, Lai-tu, 46.
8. Bunge, Lai-tu, 53.
9. Bunge, Lai-tu, 53.
10. SA.
11. SA.
12. CSALA. Letter dated 30 August 1933.

13. SA.
14. CSALA File 631/14/394.
15. CSALA File 631/14/394.
16. CSALA File 631/14/394. Letter dated 18 August 1933.
17. See BBA 654/37/40.
18. 20 August letter to Paris from Denmark found in CSALA 631/14/394. Not in BL.
19. Letter dated 13 July 1933. BBA 654/45.
20. SA.
21. SA.
22. BBA 2142/34.
23. BL, 178.
24. BL, 179–80.
25. From FBI records, it seems likely that Weigel had yet another "appendix" removed during the American years. If so, this would make three in all.
26. The Comintern worker Katz crossed Brecht's path several times before his death on the scaffold in 1952 on a trumped-up and anti-Semitic Communist party charge of being a "Zionist spy."
27. From other letters Brecht wrote to her, it seems that when Weigel lost weight, she lost it first from her breasts. Brecht seems disturbed at the prospect of such loss.
28. The exchange rate at the time was 100 Danish kroner to 60 German marks, or 360 French francs.
29. Dr. Morten Nielsen of Copenhagen obtained Steffin's medical records and wrote an account titled "Margarete Steffin-en utrættrelig kvindes sygehistorie." This unpublished account was kindly made available to me directly by Dr. Nielsen.
30. Though Kesten's view of this incident was written up years later, its main points are confirmed in Brecht's reply as found in BL, 185–86.
31. See Kesten in Klaus Mann, Briefe und Antworten ed. Martin Gregor-Dellin (Reinbek bei Hamburg: Rowohlt, 1991), 1:364. Letter dated 15 December 1933.
32. BL, 188.
33. See BBA 722/42 for the text of the Gestapo reply to a 17 June 1933 letter of Brecht's father. See also BBA 911/43 for the text of a 1 September 1933 Berlin Tax Office letter to Brecht's father demanding payment of his son's taxes to that date and billing for the payment that would fall due on 10 September 1933.
34. GW 7:229–34.
35. See BBA 480/124–32. See also Astrid Horst's Prima Inter Pares: Elisabeth Hauptmann, Die Mitarbeiterin Bertolt Brechts (Würzburg: Konigshausen, 1992).
36. BBA 124–32. We know this from the letter Hauptmann sent to Brecht's father. See also Astrid Horst.
37. Hauptmann's file obtained by me under the Freedom of Information Act (hereafter: FOIA). The FBI thought Hauptmann got to the United States "about December 1934." From family records that I obtained in Saint Louis, it is obvious the FBI was late by a full year.

38. Berlau's own description given in audio interview recorded by Hans Bunge.
39. Details on these arrangements are given in Hans and Renate Schumacher, *Leben Brechts* (Berlin: Henschel Verlag, 1978), 116. Hereafter: Schumacher, *LB*.
40. See particularly the seventh stanza of the poem "1940" (GW 9:818–19). At the time he wrote this poem, Brecht was actually surrounded by possessions so numerous that, in the view of one observer at that time, they were enough to fill entire boxcars.
41. The legend of Brecht's dire need in the exile years, as promoted in his poems, dies hard. The first director of the Brecht Archive, Hans Bunge, pointed out as early as 1964 that this did not square with reality. For his pains, Bunge was harassed for decades by the secret police of the GDR, the Stasi.

Chapter 24

1. Cited in Ludwig Hoffmann, *Exil in Skandinavien, England, der Tsechoslovakei, Palästina* (Leipzig: Reclam, 1978), 486–87. Hereafter: Hoffmann, *Exil*.
2. The earliest book-length study of the Brecht group in Denmark is Harald Engberg, *Brecht auf Fünen*, trans. Heinz Kulas (Wuppertal: Peter Hammer Verlag, 1974). Hereafter: Engberg, *BaF*. Though this book (originally published in Danish in 1966) contains lots of useful information, it needs to be carefully checked against the more recent work of Berlau herself, Hans Bunge, and the Danish scholars Hans Christian Nørregaard, Birgit S. Nielsen, and Morten Nielsen.
3. Cited in *Kurt Weill Newsletter* 9, no. 2 (Fall 1991): 5.
4. *Weill Newsletter* 9, no. 2 (Fall 1991): 5.
5. See discussion of Steffin's case number 40762 in the Danish police files in Nørregaard, *Brecht*.
6. One side of this exchange is in BL 217ff.
7. Bentley, *Seven Plays*, xxxii. See also John Fuegi, "Feuchtwanger, Brecht and the 'Epic' Media," in *Lion Feuchtwanger: The Man, His Ideas, and His Work*, ed. John Spalek (Los Angeles: Hennessey and Ingalls, 1972), 307–22. Like Bentley, I consider Brecht to have failed as a novelist.
8. See BBA 584/01 for details of contract with Fedin in Leningrad. Material is dated 2 May 1935. *Not* in BL.
9. Margaret Mynatt was the old, close friend of Elisabeth Hauptmann who had provided her with English materials such as Gay, Shaw, and Waley. Mynatt's home at 16 Doughty Street, London, WCI, served as the operating address for Herzfelde's nomadic Malik Verlag. Mynatt's complaint about Brecht's unethical behavior is dated 13 February 1935.
10. For a detailed discussion of the issue, see John Fuegi, "The Soviet Union and Brecht: The Exile's Choice," in *Brecht Heute/Brecht Today*, ed. John Fuegi et al. (Frankfurt am Main: Athenäum, 1972), 209–21.
11. See BBA 477/134–40. My access to this Tretiakov material was provided by Helene Weigel directly. My first article based on this material appeared in 1972 and was never challenged by Weigel.
12. Souvarine, *Stalin*, 580.
13. Souvarine, *Stalin*, 581.
14. Roy A. Medvedev, *Let History Judge*, trans. Colleen Taylor (New York: Alfred A. Knopf, 1972), 148. Hereafter: Medvedev, *Let History*.

15. Steffin, *Konfutse*, 323–25.
16. The text of the letter to Benjamin is given in Steffin, *Konfutse*, 323–25.
17. BBA 480/61. Letter dated 28 September 1934.
18. The stealing of the Chinese poems was discovered by Dr. Paula Hanssen and conveyed to me in letters and in a personal conversation.
19. Walter Benjamin Archive, Berlin, 23/92. Hereafter: WBA.
20. Account book was given to me by Hauptmann's relatives in Saint Louis.
21. JW, *Eight Aspects*, 194.
22. Cited in JW, *Brecht Poems*, 557.
23. See the 1990 Danish film *Dagmar*.
24. Cited in Völker, *Chronik*, 64.
25. Leslie Halliwell, *The Filmgoer's Companion* (New York: Hill & Wang, 1967), 430–31.
26. JW, *BinC*, 61.
27. BL, 223.
28. Brecht, *Gül*, 94.
29. GW 9:541. He wrote on 29 September 1934 saying Steffin should get medical treatment but sent no money to pay for special care (CSALA).
30. CSALA 631/14/415
31. Letter given in Jurij Okljanskij's small but useful book on Steffin, *Povest o malenkom soldate* (Moscow: Izdatelstvo "Sovetskaja Rossija," 1978), 197. Hereafter: Okljanskij, *POMS*. The appearance of this important book in Germany was blocked by Brecht-Schall.
32. WBA (file number indecipherable).
33. Cited in Hoffmann, *Exil*, 488. *Not* in BL. The word *muck* has, as Steffin might well have known, a meaning rather like *shit* in English. In German, it means "little fly."
34. See David Pike, "Brecht and Stalin's Russia: The Victim as Apologist (1931–1945)," in *Beyond Brecht*, vol. 11, ed. John Fuegi et al. (Detroit: Wayne University Press, 1983), 143–93.
35. The most complete statement of the Kirov case is Robert Conquest, *Stalin and the Kirov Murder* (New York: Oxford University Press, 1989).
36. Deutscher, *Stalin*, 358.
37. In the Twentieth Party Congress speech given by Khrushchev in February 1956, he claimed that it was a 25 September 1936 Stalin directive to the then NKVD head, Yezhov, that "directly pushed the NKVD workers on the path of mass arrests and executions."
38. BL, 229.
39. Lukács, *GD*, 181.
40. Details are given in Schumacher, *LB*, 128ff.; and in Reich, *W*, 369–76.
41. Mrs. Cecil Chesterton (Ada Elizabeth [Jones] Chesterton), *Sickle or Swastika* (London: Stanley Paul & Co., 1935), 212.
42. See Fuegi, "RET," 102–12.
43. For supporting details on what may strike many as a surprising point, see my book on Brecht the stage director, *Bertolt Brecht: Chaos, According to Plan* (Cambridge: Cambridge University Press, 1986). Hereafter: Fuegi, *CAP*.
44. Cited in Schumacher, *LB*, 129.
45. BBA 783/80. Letter is dated 5 April 1935.

46. The best currently available source on Knorin is the latest edition of Branko Lazich and Milorad M. Drachkovitch, *Biographical Dictionary of the Comintern* (Stanford: The Hoover Institution Press, 1986). Knorin was born in 1890 in Latvia. He was expelled from the party in June 1937 and died in an NKVD prison, probably in 1939. He was posthumously rehabilitated during the Khrushchev "thaw."

47. Reich, *W*, 372.

48. Reich, *W*, 372.

49. Maria Osten was born Maria Emilie Alwine Gresshöner on 20 March 1908 in West Prussia and grew up under conditions similar to Elisabeth Hauptmann. Osten would be destroyed by the NKVD.

50. See Jean Lacouture, *André Malraux* (New York: Pantheon Books, 1975).

51. Conquest, *Harvest*, 3.

52. There is some suggestion in Medvedev's book on Khrushchev that convict labor, if it was not used in part to build the Moscow subway system, was used on the massive Moscow-Volga canal project where Khrushchev had a supervisory role.

53. *GW* 9:673–75.

54. Cited in Schumacher, *LB*, 130.

55. Cited in Roy Medvedev, *On Stalin and Stalinism*, trans. Ellen de Kadt (New York: Oxford University Press, 1979), 76, from an unpublished Pasternak manuscript. Hereafter: Medvedev, *On Stalin*.

56. See BBA 584/01 for further details. *Not in BL.*

Chapter 25

1. *GW* 9:554.

2. The text of the conference speeches are found in Wolfgang Klein, ed., *Paris 1935* (Berlin: Akademie Verlag, 1982).

3. Knorin argued until late 1934 that "fascism had temporarily gained the day in Germany." See David Pike, *German Writers in Soviet Exile 1933–1945* (Chapel Hill: University of North Carolina Press, 1982), 74. Hereafter: Pike, *German Writers*.

4. Isaac Deutscher, *The Prophet Outcast*, 3 vols. (New York: Vintage Books, 1963), 2; 166. Hereafter: Deutscher, *Prophet*.

5. Lacouture, *Malraux*, 216ff.

6. Pike, *German Writers*, 113.

7. Lacouture, *Malraux*, 189; and Pike, *German Writers*, 112.

8. Victor Serge, *Destin d'une revolution. URSS 1917–36* (Paris: 1937).

9. Tucker, *Stalin*, 360.

10. BL, 259–60.

11. BL, 254 (to Korsch), 258–59 (to Grosz).

12. Berlau's account of the stone is given in Bunge, *Lai-tu*, 257; her account of Cassiopeia, 250. The ring appears in her picture on page 228.

13. One of Berlau's graphic descriptions of Brecht's sexual habits as she knew them is given in an August 1951 poem of hers: "Now he lifts up her skirt. This one, two, three, and already he buttons up his trousers again. . . . He has unlearned that which I taught him." Unpublished Berlau materials kindly supplied by Berlau's literary executor, Johannes Hoffmann.

14. For the full record of the correspondence, see James K. Lyon, "Der Briefwechsel Zwischen Brecht und der New Yorker Theater Union von 1935," *Brecht Jahrbuch 1975*, ed. John Fuegi et al. (Frankfurt am Main: Suhrkamp, 1975), 136–55.

15. Engberg, *BaF*, 95.

16. Völker, *Brecht*, 200.

17. Engberg, *BaF*, 94.

18. Woolf, *Three Guineas*, 142.

19. GW 9:641–42.

20. Gerhard Seidel, longtime head of the Brecht Archive, has lectured on this subject for several years but has not published his findings. For the original version of the poem, see BBA 534/09 bearing the telltale notation "Thurø," where Steffin was living at the time, August 1936.

21. GW 9:527–29.

22. The question was put to Mari Ohm in October 1986 by Hans Christian Nørregaard, who kindly shared his original interview materials with me.

23. Her letter (file number twenty-three 23) is among the Benjamin papers, WBA.

24. SA.

25. CSALA 631/14/415. Dated 5 March 1936. She explicitly mentions formalism.

26. Cited in Okljanskij, *POMS*, 153.

27. Hoffmann, *Exil*, 490.

28. See extensive correspondence with Benjamin, WBA folder twenty-three.

29. Walter Benjamin, *Briefe*, ed. Gershom Sholem and Theodor W. Adorno (Frankfurt am Main: Suhrkamp, 1993).

30. Bertolt Brecht, Arbeitsjournal, ed. Werner Hecht (Frankfurt am Main: Suhrkamp, 1973), 3 vols. Hereafter: *AJ*.

31. Richard Wolin, in his *Walter Benjamin, an Aesthetic of Redemption* (New York: Columbia University Press, 1982), states: "Benjamin's devotion to Brecht would seem to signify in no uncertain terms a death wish vis-à-vis his earlier esoteric criticism and love of literature as an autonomous medium of spiritual expression" (140–41). Did Benjamin, I wonder, enjoy the denigration, the playing out the drama of lies and submission that was part of the continuously playing Brechtian drama of dominance and submission. See the discussion of the Brecht-Benjamin relationship in Hannah Arendt, *Men in Dark Times* (New York: Harcourt, Brace & World, 1968), 167–68. Hereafter: Arendt, *Dark Times*.

32. This enormously important interchange is *not* in BL. Of a relationship that extended for thirty-two years, the BL editor has included in the entire two-volume set only seven Brecht letters to Hauptmann. My sources are the Hauptmann-Warmber-Weber family and the Harvard copies of BBA 480/133/4. These materials are desperately in need of updating by rephotographing the originals. The copies held in Berlin and at Harvard have faded so badly that they are now often virtually illegible.

33. Hauptmann-Warmber-Weber family.

34. Information in a short story by Hauptmann called "Under Way on a Greyhound Bus," in *JoR*, 205–18.

35. BL, 273.

36. Cited in Bunge, *Lai-tu*, 205.

37. BL, 273.
38. Author's interview with Max Gorelick, Milwaukee, Wisconsin, 1969.
39. James K. Lyon, *Brecht in America* (Princeton: Princeton University Press, 1980), 11–12. Hereafter: Lyon, *BinA*.
40. Lyon, *BinA*, 11–12.
41. Jane de Hart Mathews, *The Federal Theatre 1935–9* (Princeton: Princeton University Press, 1967), 71.
42. Fuegi, "RET," 102–12.
43. Private source.
44. Sidney Hook, "A Recollection of Berthold Brecht," *The New Leader*, 10 October 1960, 22–23.
45. BL, 280–81.
46. Lyon, *BinA*, 20.
47. GW 9:670.
48. Supporting documentation kindly provided by the German Foreign Office.
49. GW 9:561–62.
50. See the accounts of Nadezhda Mandelstam of the poems of Osip Mandelstam who died in the gulag, and of Nikolai Bukharin's widow who committed to memory her husband's testament in which he denounced the NKVD.

Chapter 26

1. CSALA 631/14/415. *Not* in BL.
2. WBA (file number 23).
3. JW, *BinB*, 26.
4. BL, 286–87. In this letter, Brecht claims to Benjamin he is at work "smoothing out film dialogue" in England.
5. A small personal note on the value of money in England in 1936. I was born in London that year as the fifth member of a working class (that is to say, more accurately, an often unemployed) family. Speaking of Brecht's money earned in a few weeks, I asked my mother how long it would have taken her and my father to earn six hundred pounds at that time. Her answer, based on their income at that time of twenty-seven shillings a week, was "almost seven years." In *Three Guineas* in 1937, Virginia Woolf quotes an authority who stated of middle-class, educated women: "To earn £250 a year is quite an achievement even for a highly qualified woman with years of experience" (58).
6. The letter, with the amount Brecht is to receive for "his" plays unspecified here, is dated 25 July 1936 and is countersigned by Fles. *Not* in BL. Private source.
7. WBA, 20 July 1936.
8. BL, 289–90.
9. See GW 9:565.
10. CSALA 631/12/143/432. Letter of Osten confirming this is dated 24 July 1936.
11. WBA, details in Steffin letter to Benjamin, 11 February 1937.
12. Details of those working for Brecht and Weigel in Skovsbostrand were gathered by Rudy Hassing.
13. JW, CN, 124; and Högel, CN, 439–48. Högel is frank about the closeness of Neher's relationship with Wagner-Régeny. As homosexuality was officially

punishable with a one-way trip to a concentration camp, homosexual relations were usually hidden, often by marriage.

14. For people attending the Berlin Olympics, things were carefully controlled. Foreign visitors were steered away from the "Red" or working class sections of Berlin.

15. Bronnen, *P*, 347.

16. BL, 295.

17. I am grateful to the Akademie der Künste, West Berlin, for making available to me their holdings of Piscator's unpublished papers.

18. Among the Akademie der Künste, West Berlin, materials is a note wherein Piscator states he believes the mistress he had in Moscow was an NKVD plant, a typical practice of the time.

19. See in Medvedev, *Let History*, observations on Kaganovich's massive role in the millionfold murders of the Stalin era, calculated by reliable analysts as somewhere between twenty and thirty million deaths exclusive of war.

20. Walter Huder, ed., *Erwin Piscator 1893–1966* (Berlin: Akademie der Künste, 1979), 17.

21. See Müller, *Säuberung*.

22. Müller, *Säuberung*, 557–59.

23. For the protocol of the hearing of Wangenheim in the NKVD records, see Müller, *Säuberung*, 560–62.

24. For further details, see interview with Roy Medvedev, *Der Spiegel*, no. 52, 1987. The *Spiegel* piece gives far more details than Medvedev was able to include in his preglasnost account, *Nikolai Bukharin: The Last Years*, trans. A. D. P. Briggs (New York: W. W. Norton & Company, 1980). My own ability to get firsthand accounts of this dark era was materially helped in Moscow by the efforts of Professor Naumov, who personally took me to the Moscow Central Party Archives. I was also helped in Moscow in my archival work by Georg Zaitsev and Tatiana Glovotskaya.

25. See Pike, *German Writers*, 2.

26. Cited in Pike, *German Writers*, 213.

27. Koltsov's own richly ironic account of this meeting is contained in his Spanish memoirs, *Die rote Schlacht* (Berlin: Aufbau, 1960), 518–19. Hereafter: Koltsov, *Schlacht*. For notes on Feuchtwanger and Stalin, see Medvedev, *On Stalin*.

28. An account of this visit and the reactions of her parents to this play in SA.

29. See BL, 295–96.

30. The documentation for this disturbing incident is given by Birgit S. Nielsen in her excellent piece of detective work, "Maria Lazar, eine Schriftstellerin aus Wien," in *Text und Kontext*, ed. Heinz Ludwig Arnold (Munich: Wilhelm Fink Verlag, 1983), 146–47.

31. The letter is dated 6 November 1936. Original in Michaëlis Collection, Royal Library, Copenhagen.

32. Steffin, *Konfutse*, 199.

33. Dr. Morten Nielsen obtained and analyzed the hospital records for me.

34. See Bunge, *Lai-tu*, 111.

35. SA.

36. Document found in WBA, 23.

37. Rudy Hassing interview with Lund's daughter, Ceci Gunlogsson, Copenhagen, 1987.

38. Bunge, *Lai-tu*, 111.

39. Bunge, *Lai-tu*, 62.

40. *GW* 9:606. In the house where Brecht was born in Augsburg (now a Brecht museum), there stands a washstand or dry sink once owned by the Brecht family. The bowls in the stand are made of copper.

41. For a detailed account, see Margarete Buber-Neumann, *Als gefangene bei Stalin und Hitler: eine Welt im Dunkel* (Stuttgart: Deutsche Verlags-Ansttalt, 1958), 164. Hereafter: Buber-Neumann, *Gefangene*.

42. See W. G. Krivitsky, *Agent de Staline* (Paris: Cooperation, 1940) 253ff. This book is one of the earliest accounts of what really went on in Soviet prisons. Krivitsky claims that the torturers of Kamenev and Zinoviev reported to Stalin's private secretary directly every two hours. Anton Antonov-Ovseyenko, in *The Time of Stalin: Portrait of a Tyranny*, trans. George Saunders (New York: Harper & Row, 1981), 127, claims that Kun was finally broken before his death on 30 November 1939. Hereafter: Antonov-Ovseyenko, *Portrait*.

43. The events of this period can be cross-referenced from three sources: Joseph E. Davies, *Mission to Moscow* (Garden City, New York: Garden City Publishing, 1941), *Moscow 1937—A Travel Report for My Friends*; and MF.

44. Davies, *Mission*, 217.

45. See Anna Larina Bukharina, *Nun bin ich schon weit über zwanzig*, trans. Eva Rönnau (Göttingen: Steidl, 1989), 387ff., for an account of such rehearsals. Hereafter: Bukharina, *Nun*.

46. Feuchtwanger, *Moscow 1937*, 135.

47. Tucker, *Stalin*, 445. Tucker notes that Koltsov was shown Stalin's arrest order for Tal and so knew by this time that such things came directly from Stalin himself, rather than, as some people thought, from Stalin's underlings, who were imagined to be hiding things from Stalin!

48. Feuchtwanger, *Moscow 1937*, 135.

49. See *GW* 20:111ff. These notes were apparently written by Brecht for Walter Benjamin.

50. Cited in Arkady Vaksberg's harrowingly brilliant, *The Prosecutor, Andrei Vyshinsky and the Moscow Show Trials*, trans. Jan Butler (New York: Grove/Weidenfeld, 1991) 107. Hereafter: Vaksberg, *Vyshinsky*.

51. Vaksberg, *Vyshinsky*, 197.

Chapter 27

1. The democratically elected Spanish socialist government received virtually no recognition from countries other than the Soviet Union, whereas Hitler and Mussolini had already recognized Franco's "government" by 18 November 1936.

2. An English-language version of the book was published in Britain by the firm of Victor Gollanz.

3. This was the time at which the "Jewish Socialist Republic of Birobidchan" was created in an inhospitable region of the Soviet Far East.

4. Pike, *German Writers*, 179.
5. Stephan F. Cohen, *Bukharin and the Bolshevik Revolution* (New York: Knopf, 1973), 376. Cited in Pike, *German Writers*, 181.
6. Bukharina, *Nun*, 428.
7. MF, 262.
8. See Ehrenburg, *Memoirs*, 409.
9. BL, 328.
10. GW 8:252.
11. Details on Brecht's behavior in Hans Bunge interview with Ruth Berlau, 17 September 1959.
12. Bunge, *Lai-tu*, 156.
13. Author's interviews with Steffi Spira, Berlin, 1989 and 1990.
14. See BL, 338–42.
15. GW 9:781–82.
16. See Ernest Hemingway, *For Whom the Bell Tolls* (New York: Scribners, 1940), 228–35.
17. GW 9:586.
18. This version of the telephone conversation is given in Koltsov's memoirs, *Schlacht*, 306–7. The original Russian text of this book was published in 1938 but disappeared almost immediately as Koltsov was taken. By 1940, when Hemingway published *For Whom the Bell Tolls*, ironically, Koltsov had gone the way of "the murderous hyenas." See Ehrenburg, *Memoirs*, 378, for further details on Koltsov.
19. Ruth Fischer gives an account of this in *Stalin and German Communism* (Cambridge: Harvard University Press, 1948), 500. Ulbricht himself confirmed his presence in Spain at a meeting of Spanish Civil War veterans in Berlin in 1956. The war within the Spanish Civil War, as left destroyed left, is given in Deutscher, *Stalin*, 425.
20. See Pike, *German Writers*, 190–95.
21. See Arthur Koestler, *The God That Failed* (New York: The Macmillan Co., 1940), 21.
22. GW 12:392–93.
23. GW 12:394–96.
24. GW 12:376.
25. Alfred Forke's 1922 German translation of the philosophy of the fifth century B.C. Me-ti was one of the books Brecht carried with him into exile.
26. See Müller, *Säuberung*.
27. Sergei Tretiakov, *Gesichter der Avant-garde*, ed. Fritz Mierau (Berlin and Weimar: Aufbau, 1985).
28. Tucker, *Stalin*, 216–17.
29. Ehrenburg, *Memoirs*, 117ff., 420ff.
30. Medvedev, *Bukharin*, 161.
31. Cited in Nadezhda Mandelstam, *Hope against Hope*, trans. Max Hayward (New York: Atheneum, 1970), 11. Hereafter: Mandelstam, *Hope*.
32. Pike, *German Writers*, 339.
33. Given in a book published after Koltsov's posthumous rehabilitation, *Mikhail Koltsov: kakim on byl* (Moscow: Sovetskij pisaatel, 1965), 69–76. Incident is discussed in Pike, *German Writers*, 349–50. Hereafter: Koltsov, *kob*.

34. Vaksberg, *Vyshinsky*, 197–98.
35. Okljanskij, *POMS*, 311–12.
36. See Simone Barck, "Fragmentarisches über die Schriftstellerin Maria Osten," *Notate* 2 (April 1990).
37. Müller, *Säuberung*, 570–71.
38. A key problem in the book, and probably the real reason for its destruction, was the fact that Feuchtwanger cited "Lenin's Testament" in the book. He cited only a mildly critical remark of Lenin about Trotsky, but the "Testament" was not supposed to exist in the Soviet Union at that time. It had been suppressed because it contained damning remarks about Stalin.
39. *GW* 9:595. See also 594, 597, 688.
40. This terminology was widely used in the Brecht, Koltsov, Feuchtwanger circle. Koltsov says in *Schlacht* that Feuchtwanger was jealous about Koltsov's direct role in the Spanish struggle. Koltsov replied: "That's the naive jealousy of the artillerist looking at the infantry. From his bunker he shoots further and with greater force than ten men in the field with rifles" (518).
41. WBA. The archive contains sixty-seven pieces of correspondence from Steffin to Benjamin and eight replies from him.
42. Unpublished report made available to me by Dr. Morten Nielsen of Copenhagen.
43. Among the dozens who would regularly complain about this was the head of Malik Verlag, Wieland Herzfelde; Johannes R. Becher in Moscow; and Wreede in Berlin.
44. BL, 359.
45. See Børge Houmann, ed., *Breve fra Martin Andersen Nexø* 3 (Copenhagen: Gyldendal, 1952) 18–20.
46. BL, 370–71.

Chapter 28

1. A letter of Weigel from Paris confirms this. See Werner Hecht, *Bertolt Brecht* (Frankfurt am Main: Suhrkamp, 1978), 151. Hereafter: Hecht, *BB*.
2. Walter Benjamin, *Versuche über Brecht*, ed. Rolf Tiedemann (Frankfurt am Main: Suhrkamp, 1966), 134. Hereafter: Benjamin, *VüB*.
3. Benjamin, *VüB*, 128–35.
4. There had been a falling out between Brecht and Kurella in 1930 after Kurella's devastating analysis of *The Measures Taken*.
5. See Pike, *German Writers*, 293.
6. This copy of the journal with the scribbled marginal note had survived at the Brecht Archive until the late 1970s, but with no file number. When I last asked to see it in the mid-1980s, it had been lost.
7. BL, 302–3.
8. Cited by Pike in his essay, "Brecht and Stalin's Russia." In fact, we know that Brecht had apparently tried to ask Feuchtwanger to bring this up with Stalin, but Brecht's letter supposedly never got through to Feuchtwanger in Moscow.
9. Benjamin, *VüB*, 133.

10. Benjamin's wording rings true (*VüB*, 131), as it is the same wording Brentano quotes Brecht as using in Brentano's letter to Brecht of 23 January 1937. Document found (file number illegible) in Harvard Collection. Hereafter: HC.

11. *GW* 9:683–84.

12. A typical letter of complaint is one dated 14 December 36 from Wieland Herzfelde in London to Steffin in Denmark, where he comments, "For almost two years I have hardly had any letters from Brecht." He then says that Brecht has not responded when he has sent him a book by Agnes Smedley and books by other antifascist writers, asking Brecht to comment on them.

13. These works are now being published finally in Germany. See Steffin, *Konfutse*.

14. With the arrest of Koltsov and the closing down of the journals he was involved with, Steffin's translation of the Nexø memoirs, though firmly contracted for, was not allowed to appear. She could not collect her money for the work until 1941, when it would be used to save the entire exiled Brecht group.

15. *Das Wort* (1938) 1:66; 3:74; and 4:81. Steffin was credited as follows: "Authorized translation from the Norwegian by Margarete Steffin."

16. WBA, folder 23, date illegible.

17. See Antony Tatlow, *Brechts chinesischer Gedichte* (Frankfurt am Main: Suhrkamp, 1973).

18. Paula Hanssen shows that these are Hauptmann poems in her unpublished typescript "Elisabeth Hauptmann's Silent Collaboration with Brecht with the 'Chinesische Gedichte.' " Hereafter: Hanssen.

19. SA.

20. *Die Tageszeitung* (Berlin), 27 August 91, Kultur sec., 15.

21. *Süddeutsche Zeitung*, 30 November–1 December 1991, Kultur sec., 4.

22. Steffin, *Konfutse*, 119.

23. Bunge, *Lai-tu*, 273. Brecht's apology-poem is in *GW* 9:586.

24. See *GW* 9:739. Dated December 1938, Brecht's poem "The Crutches." Here the poet is a doctor who urges her to throw away her crutches.

25. The play, to the best of my knowledge, has never been produced and is completely ignored in Brecht scholarship, though it has as much claim to being a Brecht play as anything else collected in his aptly named, *Collected Works*.

26. This fine work was brought out in Danish in 1940 and in German in 1989.

27. People are still trying to cover up this incident in Copenhagen. Journalist Rudy Hassing asked me in 1991, "Do you really mean to name the doctor?" My answer was yes.

28. Excerpts from the letter where Berlau makes these charges are in Bunge, *Lai-tu*, 267–69.

29. James K. Lyon, *Bertolt Brecht's American Cicerone* (Bonn: Bouvier Verlag, 1978), 41. Hereafter: Lyon, *Cicerone*.

30. Ernst Schumacher argues in *Drama und Geschichte: Bertolt Brechts Leben des Galilei* (Berlin: Henschel, 1968), 110ff., that this is not so. Hereafter: Schumacher, *Geschichte*. Schumacher argues in vain, I think, against the Galileo-Bukharin connection that Deutscher points out so clearly in his three-volume Trotsky biography.

31. The work was issued in German under the title *Volkskommisariat für Justizwesen*

der UdSSR. Prozessbericht über die Strafsache des antisowjetischen "Blocks der Rechten und Trotzkisten" verhandelt vor dem Militäkollegium des obersten Gerichthofes der UdSSR vom 2.–13 März 1938 (nd., np.).

32. BBA 2071/07–08. See Mittenzwei's guarded but illuminating discussion of the Bukharin-Galileo connection in *Leben* 1:652–54.

33. See Medvedev, *Bukharin*, 152.

34. SA. See Guy Stern, "The Plight of the Exile," *Brecht Yearbook*, 1971, Fuegi et. al.

35. Crassus remembered being given one version of this play in 1937. If so, then obviously the 1938 version was not written from scratch in three weeks as Brecht claimed. The best account of the play's creation is that given in Schumacher, *Geschichte*. For close analysis of the classical structure of the play, see Fuegi, *Essential Brecht*, 161–79.

36. Bentley, *Seven Plays*, xxvi.

37. In a letter to Bentley cited in Bentley, *Memoir*, 35–36, Laughton, who had just played the lead role in *Galileo*, explicitly compares Brecht's greatness to that of Shakespeare.

38. BBA 275/14.

39. Richard Rhodes, *The Making of the Atomic Bomb* (New York: Simon & Schuster, 1986), 256ff.

40. Hans Christian Nørregaard, "Zur Entstehung von Brechts *Leben des Galilei*," in *Bertolt Brecht-die Wiedersprüche sind die Hoffnungen*, ed. Wucherpfennig and Schulte (Copenhagen and Munich: Wilhelm Fink Verlag, 1988), 65–86.

41. SA.

42. *AJ*, 1:36. The diary was begun in the middle of 1938 and maintained intermittently, very sporadically in the last years, until the middle of 1955.

43. Martin Esslin, "Letter to the Editor," *Encounter*, April 1978. Esslin's account was published while Walter Brecht was still alive.

44. Steffin's letters to Crassus were obtained by Rudy Hassing and made available to me by him; permission to publish them was granted by Steffin's heirs.

45. Engberg, *BaF*, 208. In describing the attraction Brecht so often exerted on those around him, Engberg speaks of "the erotic of the new sobriety" (201).

46. Georg Grosz, *Ein Kleines Ja und ein Grosses Nein* (Hamburg: Rowohlt, 1955), 182.

47. Cited in Engberg, *BaF*, 79.

48. See Steffin letter to Benjamin, *Konfutse*, 335.

49. See Steffin letter to Benjamin, *Konfutse*, 335.

50. See BBA 1396/79.

51. Crassus was still trying to clear up this case at the end of January 1940. Brecht was supposed to provide the struck child with 7,500 Danish kroner in damages, that is, the equivalent of the cost of a fairly large house in Skovsbostrand at that time. Details from Crassus letter to Brecht, 24 January 1940.

52. The Brecht Archive number on the Domke letter is 01/01. This means this was the very first document duplicated after Brecht's death in August 1956. Internal evidence strongly suggests that the very first items registered were of a highly personal and/or dangerously political nature, the things Brecht kept in his personal desk drawer. Needless to say, Brecht's letter to Domke is *not* in BL.

53. In a letter written to Felix Bloch Erben (FBE) on 12 November 1957 about this sale of *Happy End* in Paris in 1939, Hauptmann wrote, "I was in the USA at the time and knew nothing of the negotiations." FBE Files.

54. SA.

55. Kindly made available to me by the Kurt Weill Foundation. *Not* in BL.

56. Unpublished Habilitationsschrift, Hans Peter Neureuter, "Brecht in Finland" (University of Regensburg, 1987), documents sec., 207. Hereafter: Neureuter, "Finland." Cited Steffin letter notes three books of Agnes Smedley in Brecht's possession at the time. Smedley, a friend of Michaëlis, was recognized in the 1930s as a world authority on contemporary conditions in China.

57. Reported in Engberg, *BaF*, 239–40.

58. SA.

Chapter 29

1. See Jan E. Olsson, "Bertolt Brechts schwedisches Exil" (Ph.D. diss., University of Lund, Sweden 1969), 43, for exact details. Hereafter: Olsson, "Schwedisches Exil."

2. Olsson, "Schwedisches Exil," 36.

3. BL, 388.

4. Olsson, "Schwedisches Exil," 47.

5. AJ, 1:54.

6. Bertolt Brecht, *Svendborger Gedichte.* In the book itself, it is printed that it is published in London by Malik Verlag in 1939. Actually, as we know, it was published by Steffin and Berlau in Copenhagen in 1939. This particular passage is found on page 83.

7. See Engberg, *BaF*, 72.

8. Wifstrand's remarks cited in Olsson, "Schwedisches Exil," 91. Olsson confirms that Brecht and Weigel brought with them lots of furniture (43).

9. See, for instance, BBA 911/17. Gustav Hartung's letter to Brecht, 26 June 1939.

10. BBA 911/62.

11. SA.

12. Without Steffin's heirs having been consulted and without even a mention of Steffin's name, the first section of the work was published in GW 7:2964–84.

13. When published in the *Collected Works of Bertolt Brecht*, no mention was made of Berlau's role in the play's creation.

14. Völker, *Chronik*, 77.

15. See German edition of Völker biography, *Brecht*, for a number of these photos.

16. Olsson, "Schwedisches Exil," sec. 3, 28.

17. Olsson, "Schwedisches Exil," sec. 3, 20.

18. For a detailed examination of the relationship of the play to its forerunners, see, Fuegi, *Essential Brecht*, chap. 5.

19. See BBA 490.

20. In "Schwedisches Exil," Olsson says flatly of this typescript (BBA 1989) that it is "nicht von Brecht" (108).

21. Bentley, *Seven Plays*, xii.

22. In AJ, 1:205, Brecht muses, reflexively, on an imagined Shakespeare collective, "I find only that purely technically the plays are so constructed that I believe

I recognize the work of a collective." He then goes on, "The collective did not need always to be made up of the same people; it could have worked in a very loose way. Shakespeare could have been the decisive personality; he could have periodically had co-workers, etc."

23. Letter of Englind to his agent in New York, 2 November 1959.
24. The secret protocols of this agreement are finally being recognized in the former Soviet Union.
25. AJ, 1:62, 9 September 1939.
26. Louis Rapoport, *Stalin's War against the Jews* (New York: The Free Press, 1990), 58. Hereafter: *Stalin's War.*
27. BBA 525/13. The scene is dated 16 September [1939].
28. GW 10:833–38. John Willett suggests (correctly, I think) that the poem was written not in Scandinavia at the time of the outbreak of World War II but in America in 1941.
29. Greid claimed to have appeared in Berlin with Weigel in *Peer Gynt.* However, in no Weigel source have I found reference to her appearing in Berlin in this play.
30. Greid's reflections are still unpublished but cited in Olsson's dissertation.
31. AJ, 1:79.
32. GW 12:476–78.
33. Olsson has carefully researched Swedish police files and has interviewed a number of people who were part of the Brecht circle during the period spent in Sweden.
34. Anticipating that this would be the case, she asked (the first time she had made such a request of him) her husband, Juul, to sleep with her before she left Copenhagen. He refused.
35. BBA 1644/14–19.
36. *Washington Post,* 19 October 1992, A20, based on documents released by Boris Yeltsin.
37. After they left, the Lidingö villa was taken by Edmund Demaitre, Stockholm correspondent of the *Daily Express.* While living there, Demaitre raided Brecht's library and stole Brecht's copy of *Das Kapital.* The book is now in the McKeldin Library, University of Maryland, College Park.
38. *Not* given in BL. Text was read aloud at Berlau's burial by her dear friend Hans Bunge, who had earlier been fired from his job as head of the Brecht Archive. The Bunge Collection kindly made it available to me.
39. Berlau may or may not have noticed that much of the declaration was psychologically "distanced" by the use of Danish and of mere initials instead of the full phrase "I love you."

Chapter 30

1. See Neureuter, "Finland," 43. Neureuter gives four examples of prominent Brecht scholars (including, surprisingly, Ernst Schumacher and Klaus Völker, who are often among the most accurate people working in the field of Brecht studies) who, even though Brecht names the Tölö area in his diary (AJ, 1:96 6 May 1940), still persist in accepting the fantasy that Brecht lived in an "Arbeiterbezirk." This kind of scholarly carelessness in accepting

Brecht's stylizations as fact, which Neureuter points to here, is by no means an exception but the rule. The sad situation is that, with only a few dozen exceptions, among thousands of publications on Brecht, the mechanical acceptance of Brecht's often made-up "facts," rather than cross-checking them against other sources, is ubiquitous in the Brecht literature in virtually all countries, socialist or nonsocialist.

2. Neureuter, "Finland," 43.
3. GW 9:819.
4. GW 10:844.
5. Cited in an unpublished letter of Maria Osten.
6. Neureuter, "Finland," 59.
7. SA.
8. SA.
9. SA.
10. SA.
11. BBA 160/1–222. The postwar typescript (as originally submitted to the printer) has the notation "Mitarbeiter R. Berlau und M. Steffin." See BBA 1408/03; and AJ, 1:100. Date of AJ entry is 11 June 1940.
12. Oscar Mandel, "Brecht's Unheroes and Heroines," in Medieval Epic to the 'Epic Theater' of Brecht, ed. Rosario P. Armato and John M. Spalek (Los Angeles: University of Southern California Press, 1968), 239. Hereafter: Mandel, "Heroines."
13. The names of a number of characters were still undergoing changes at this time.
14. Berlau registered, as she was obliged to do, with the Finnish police on 20 May 1940.
15. Neureuter, "Finland," 64. Personal interview with Tove Nilson-Olsoni.
16. SA.
17. Wuolijoki's account of these evenings is given in Neureuter, "Finland," 128–32.
18. "Sauna und Beischlaf," Brecht, Gül, 199.
19. BBA 1793/60. Not in BL.
20. Brecht mentions such a meeting in a letter to Berlau. BL, 512–13.
21. Cited in Neureuter, "Finland," 129.
22. See Neureuter, "Finland," sec. 3, 139. Diary of Sylvi-Kyllikki Kilpi.
23. See Hella Wuolijoki and Bertolt Brecht, Soja Laul, Das Estonische Kriegslied, Hans Peter Neureuter, ed. (Stuttgart: Klett Cotta, 1984). Hereafter: Neureuter, Klett.
24. Steffin letter to Crassus, between Christmas Day and 31 December 1940.
25. AJ, 1:233.
26. Hauptmann letter is held by the Kurt Weill Foundation. Weill cabled $100 to Brecht.
27. For this and countless other valuable details see Neureuter, "Finland."
28. Details on Danish police records from Nørregaard.
29. Müller, KoS, 227.
30. AJ, 242–43. Neither Suhrkamp Verlag nor Brecht's heirs obtained permission from Steffin's heirs to publish her writing, and no effort was ever made to directly provide them with even a tiny portion of royalties that have earned them seven-figure sums.

31. These usually appear under Brecht's and Steffin's name even though Brecht knew virtually no Danish despite years spent in Denmark.
32. Several of these letters (see letters of 1 July & 27 July 1940, for instance) are *not* in BL. Xerox copies of the complete file were kindly provided to me by CSALA, in cooperation with the Moscow Central Economic and Mathematical Institute, whose guest I was at the time.
33. The details on this transaction turn up in Brecht's FBI file as obtained under FOIA.
34. For further details, see JW and Manheim, Letter no. 424x and note, p. 623. Willett here seeks to supplement the appallingly tendentious original German editing job. However, for all his efforts, the translated volume does not translate a pig's ear into a silk purse.
35. Brecht FBI file.
36. Full text of the agreement is given in Neureuter, "Finland," 108. "Das Stück Herr Puntila und sein Knecht Matti ist in Zussamenarbeit von Hella Wuolijoki und Bertolt Brecht entstanden. Die beiden Verfasser teilen alle Einnahmen zu gleichen Teilen."
37. Neureuter, "Finland," document sec., 150.
38. SA.

Chapter 31

1. For further details on Finnish-German joint military planning, see Neureuter, "Finland."
2. Fest, *Hitler*, 649.
3. Fest, *Hitler*, 650.
4. Fest, *Hitler*, 650.
5. Mader, Stuchlik, Pehnert, *Sorge Funkt*, 156. This entire book almost seems designed to confirm the importance of Bersin's network and what a disaster its unwarranted destruction was. Clearly, if this book is any guide, at least the GDR military understood that the Soviet Union under Stalin had made massive intelligence and military errors that cost hundreds of thousands of military and civilian lives.
6. Mader, Stuchlik, Pehnert, *Sorge Funkt*, 169.
7. Text of the telegram in Okljanskij, POMS, 316.
8. Brecht obviously lied to Velichkin. He had showed the American consul in Helsinki $1,000 for each member of the traveling party.
9. See Ehrenburg, *Memoirs* 505; Mandelstam, *Hope*, 377; Medvedev, *On Stalin*, 148; and Julius Hay, *Geboren 1900* (Hamburg: Christian Wegner Verlag, 1971), 245–46.
10. Tucker, *Stalin*, 449–50.
11. Okljanskij, POMS, 323.
12. Reich's account of this meeting appeared in a Soviet edition and in a GDR edition *(Im Wettlauf mit der Zeit)* in 1970. Many incidents included in the GDR edition were cut from the Soviet version.
13. For further details on Osten, see Koltsov, *kob*, 69–76.
14. Eugenia Semyonovna Ginzburg, *Journey into the Whirlwind*, trans. Paul Stevenson and Max Hayward (New York: Harcourt Brace Jovanovich, 1967), 192. Hereafter: Ginzburg, *Journey*.

15. Ginzburg, *Journey*, 192.
16. Buber-Neumann, *Gefangene*, 164.
17. See Schebera, "Carola Neher."
18. Drawn from CSALA files. *Not* in BL.
19. Bunge interview with Berlau, 15 September 1959.
20. See Lyon, *BinA*, 241.
21. See Anatoly Smeliansky, "The Last Decade: Stanislavsky and Stalinism," *Theater* (Spring 1991).
22. Okljanskij, *POMS*, 294–95.
23. Okljanskij, *POMS*, 294–95.
24. Though this claim is made by Okljanskij, in BL, 434, Brecht proposes the name "Karl Kinner"—too close to "Keuner" perhaps to be accidental.
25. AJ, 1:385, 433.
26. Brecht's notes on the trip in the ambulance and his visits to the hospital are in AJ 3:40–41.
27. Okljanskij, *POMS*, 299. A transcript of Okljanskij's interview with Dr. Shatkan conducted in 1964.
28. AJ 3:41.
29. In an interview with me, Marta Feuchtwanger confirmed this money was paid to Brecht from her husband's Moscow account.
30. AJ 3:41.
31. Bunge, *Lai-tu*, 135.
32. Bunge interview with Berlau, 15 September 1959.
33. Osten's notes on Steffin's last days have survived, and I draw on these, together with the recollections of Dr. Shatkan, for details on the last days and hours (CSALA).
34. See BBA 286/28.
35. Telegram is given in Schumacher, *LB*, 160.
36. Bunge, *Lai-tu*, 114. See also BBA 974/06, where Berlau tells Brecht she remembers Weigel saying of Grete's death and Berlau's fears of the effect this will have on his ability to write: "Na, das geht auch ohne ihr—er vergiest [*sic*] dass [*sic*] schnell" (Well, it will happen even without her—he will soon forget). The voice of Berlau reporting this can be heard in the film *Red Ruth*, where she says that Weigel said: "Warum, das vergisst er schnell?" (Why? He will soon forget.) The discrepancy between these two accounts does not seem unusual for recollections of stressful events occurring some eighteen years before.
37. The daughter of Sergei and Olga Tretiakov, whom I interviewed in 1991 in Moscow, claimed the arrest of Osten came on 23 June 1941. Other sources claim the arrest came in August.
38. The rehabilitation of Koltsov in 1965 was recognized with the publication of *Mikhail Koltsov: kakim on byl (kob)*.
39. File cited in Dirk Krüger, "Maria Osten: Spanienkämpferin und Stalinopfer," *Unsere Zeit* (Berlin), 8 September 1989, 10. Hereafter: Krüger, "Maria Osten."
40. Bunge, *Lai-tu*, 114.
41. Bunge interview with Berlau, 17 September 1959.
42. See Robert Conquest, *Kolyma: The Arctic Death Camps* (Oxford: Oxford Uni-

versity Press, 1979). Hereafter: Conquest, *Kolyma*. Ironically, after Conquest's work was for years denounced in the Soviet Union as CIA fabrications, as of 1989 Conquest began to regularly publish in the old Soviet Union.

43. Quoted in Conquest, *Kolyma*, from Elinor Lipper's personal account, *Eleven Years in Soviet Prison Camps* (Chicago: Henry Regnery Company, 1951).

44. See the memoir, Nicolas, *Viele Tausend*.

45. See Mittenzwei, *Leben* 1:739.

46. BL, 433–34.

47. Lyon, *BinA*, 315.

48. Details of the voyage given in Bunge's interviews with Berlau.

49. Major Akhmedov defected in 1953 and provided extraordinarily extensive and reliable early information on Stalin's massive intelligence failures up to and including World War II. For details, see Gilles Perrault, *The Red Orchestra*, trans. Peter Wiles (New York: Simon and Schuster, 1969), 46. Hereafter: Perrault, *Red Orchestra*.

50. Perrault, *Red Orchestra*, 46.

51. Cited in Vaksberg, *Vyshinsky*, 220, from material drawn from NKVD archives.

52. Bronnen, *P*, 384–85. Bronnen's Aryan status, on which more than his career depended, had been officially confirmed by Nazi courts on 5 May 1941.

53. Bronnen's friend Ernst von Salamon places him at this time at a cocktail party of the Berlin Red Orchestra, a.k.a the Fourth Channel group, where the talk of sabotage of the Nazi war effort was far too open for von Salamon's conspiratorial taste. See Ernst von Salamon, *Fragebogen: The Questionnaire*, trans. Constantine FitzGibbon (Garden City, New York: Doubleday, 1954).

54. The Harnacks and Schulze-Boysen remain almost completely unknown names to this day even though they were the earliest and most successful part of an otherwise radically incapable German resistance movement. See Perrault, *Red Orchestra*, 220. The Berlin group was discovered by the Gestapo as a direct result of a careless en clair transmission of names and residences over the clandestine Moscow-run shortwave radio network.

55. Fest, *Hitler*, 648.

56. See Vaksberg, *Vyshinsky*, 221ff., for typical details.

57. For documents of the period, see Ilya Ehrenburg's and Vasily Grossman's chilling and long suppressed in the Soviet Union *The Black Book*, trans. John Glad and James S. Levine (New York: Holocaust Library, 1981), 298–307. Hereafter: Ehrenburg and Grossman, *Black Book*.

58. Ehrenburg and Grossman, *Black Book*, 3–12.

59. Ehrenburg and Grossman, *Black Book*, 5.

60. Martin Gilbert provides these details in *The Holocaust* (New York: Henry Holt and Company, 1985), 206. Gilbert gives a figure of 33,771 deaths over a two-day period in the very famous massacre at Babi Yar. In the *Black Book* (5), we are told the death total was over 100,000 people (mainly Jews) for the whole German occupation period in the Babi Yar vicinity. Hereafter: Gilbert, *Holocaust*.

61. Gilbert reports that deaths in the Russian Black Sea ports of Nikolayev and Kherson, with their heavy Jewish populations, ran even higher in the early days of the invasion than those at Babi Yar.

62. See Gunnar Müller-Waldek, "Maria Osten zum Gedenken," *Notate* (April 1990), 14–15.
63. Mader, Stuchlik, Pehnert, *Sorge Funkt*, 282.
64. Fest, *Hitler*, 652–53.
65. Lyon, BinA, 315.

Chapter 32

1. Bunge interviews with Berlau, 14, 15, 17, 18, 21, 22 September and 12 October 1959.
2. BL, 455. The remark is made in a letter to Karl Korsch.
3. FBI files obtained under FOIA.
4. Lyon, *BinA*, 229, quotes both Oskar Homolka and Salka Viertel as describing Brecht's treatment of Weigel in these terms.
5. AJ, 1:291.
6. AJ, 1:293.
7. AJ, 1:325.
8. AJ, 1:325.
9. The parallels to the German attack on the Soviet Union are striking. The United States had broken the Japanese Code Purple in August 1940. See John Ranelagh, *The Agency: The Rise and Decline of the CIA* (New York: Simon and Schuster, 1986), 54–55. Hereafter: Ranelagh, *Agency*. Ranelagh claims that intercepted and decoded Japanese signals were in hand, however, "no one had put the information together and analyzed it accurately."
10. The acquaintance-informer is, as usual, not identified in the heavily censored Berlau file made available to me under FOIA.
11. AJ, 1:378.
12. GW 10:857.
13. AJ, 1:340.
14. AJ, 1:340.
15. Davies, *Mission*, 315.
16. The French film adaptation, "La Ronde" (1950), was directed by Max Ophuls, who knew Brecht in Hollywood.
17. For detailed and reliable information on Reyher and his relationship to Brecht, see Lyon, *Cicerone*.
18. The idea of doing another version of the Joan of Arc story had surfaced in Finland in 1940. In the Bunge interviews, Berlau claims she wrote the first version of the new play in California. This was confirmed by Marta Feuchtwanger, who was present during the play's creation. See Bruce Cook, *Brecht in Exile* (New York: Holt, Rinehart and Winston, 1982). Hereafter: Cook, *Exile*. Berlau's name appears on no published version of it, even though the legal contract specifies a 20 percent share for her in all earnings from the work.
19. This original document was made available to me by Berlau's executor, Johannes Hoffmann, in East Berlin. Another part of the puzzle confirming Berlau's original role in creating *Machard* came from documents provided to me by Dr. Harold von Hofe of the Feuchtwanger Library at the University of Southern California.

20. Lyon points out in *BinA*, 106, that the only way Brecht found he could conceive of Simone's patriotism and heroism was to suggest she be played by a child or that she be described as retarded.

21. Cited in Einem and Melchinger, *Caspar Neher*, 204.

22. When Brecht got word of Ihering's appointment, made by a ministry controlled by Joseph Goebbels, he bent over backward to explain, at least to himself, that this did not make Ihering a "Naziintendant." *AJ*, 2:555.

23. Claude Lanzmann, *Shoah, an Oral History of the Holocaust* (New York: Pantheon, 1985), 84. Hereafter: Lanzmann, *Shoah*.

24. See David S. Wyman, *The Abandonment of the Jews* (New York: Pantheon Books, 1984). Hereafter: Wyman, *Abandonment of the Jews*.

25. When Treblinka first opened as a death factory, it did not fulfill its norms. Kinks in the conveyor belt of death were removed by Kurt Franz and Franz Suchomel. See Lanzmann, *Shoah*, 107, where it is claimed that Treblinka could kill 18,000 a day. At his trial, Suchomel said he thought the top figure reached was 15,000 a day.

26. See Gilbert, *Holocaust*, 206.

27. See Wyman, *Abandonment of the Jews*.

28. The only (and that very modest) recognition of guilt about Steffin that I know of is contained in a fall 1937 poem where Brecht says he feels guilty because he has not written her enough letters. *GW* 9:589.

29. The day after his mother died he wrote: "Nobody loves me. I can die like a dog." *GW* 8:79.

30. See Völker, *Chronik*, 92–93.

31. *GW* 10:848. Original version with word "geduldig" crossed out in BBA 16/72.

32. Berlau claims (Bunge, *Lai-tu*, 162) that this provision was put in her divorce agreement at Weigel's suggestion.

33. In 1990, when I went with the film crew to shoot the documentary film *Red Ruth*, the building was vacant and deteriorating, with the windows of Ruth's old fourth-floor flat broken and open to the elements.

34. Berlau Collection. See also BBA 974/74.

35. See, for example, "Ruth," in *GW* 10:862. Title of poem dropped in *GW* as edited by Hauptmann.

36. See, for instance, telegram dated 26 December 1942, where Brecht belatedly asks Hauptmann to go and buy something for Ruth on his behalf.

37. A very faded Brecht note with no date but expressing these sentiments is in the Harvard Collection but *not* (like well over nine hundred other known Brecht letters and notes to Berlau) in BL.

Chapter 33

1. Bunge, *Lai-tu*, 13.

2. Many of the following details are from the OSS files obtained under FOIA.

3. See the preface to Dorothy Thompson, *Listen, Hans* (Cambridge: The Riverside Press, 1942), where she speaks proudly of Horst von Bärensprung's involvement with her on propaganda broadcasts to Germany.

4. OSS memo dated 16 October 1943, from Emmy C. Rado to Weston Howland, praises the quality of the information obtained from Bärensprung. As a result of this endorsement, Rado herself was placed under observation.

5. Bärensprung was almost certainly recruited by Maria Deutsch, who also lived at

243 Riverside Drive. Maria Deutsch was Rado's assistant at OSS. Maria Deutsch happened to have Soviet connections through her husband, Julius, who had served as a general in the Soviet-led anti-Franco forces in Spain.

6. Materials on Bärensprung from FBI files as released to me under FOIA contain repeated references to the MOCASE. From documents recently released to me, it seems that this case is still an open one. It is worth noting that after the fall of the GDR, CIA Director William Reynolds announced that the agency had gained access to the files of the East German secret police, the Stasi, and that, as he stated to the Washington Post, 9 October 1990, "we've learned a lot about some notorious cases."

7. See Pozner's own account of his relationship with Oppenheimer and Brecht in Vladimir Pozner erinnert sich (Leipzig: Verlag Philipp Reclam jun., 1986). Hereafter: Pozner, Vladimir Pozner.

8. See Athan Theoharis, From the Secret Files of J. Edgar Hoover (Chicago: Ivan R. Dee, 1991), 60ff. Hereafter: Theoharis, J. Edgar Hoover.

9. As usual, he was trying to hide his income from Weigel, Berlau, and the tax authorities.

10. Bentley, Memoir, 14.

11. Author's interview with Bernard Frizell, Paris, 1985.

12. My analysis of the FBI files has been materially helped by personal consultations with FBI authority Professor Athan Theoharis, who has kindly answered several questions.

13. For information on the New York field office itself, see the account of ex-agent Robert J. Lamphere in his FBI-vetted book, The FBI-KGB War: A Special Agent's Story (New York: Random House, 1986). Hereafter: Lamphere, FBI-KGB War. The main FBI office is on Foley Square in lower Manhattan. In the late World War II period, about one thousand agents worked out of this location with about sixty of them assigned to the Soviet Espionage Squad. As of 1945, Lamphere was put in charge of the Gerhart Eisler case.

14. Cited in JW, BinC, 98–99.

15. Poem recited in Norbert Bunge's 1989 film My Name Is Bertolt Brecht: Exile in America.

16. AJ, 2:567.

17. John Houseman, Front and Center (New York: Simon and Schuster, 1979), 58. Hereafter: Houseman, Front.

18. Bunge conversations with Berlau, Berun: September/October 1959.

19. See Lyon, Cicerone, for the complete story.

20. In the Militärverlag der Deutschen Demokratischen Republik book—Mader, Stuchlik, Pehnert, Sorge Funkt—the claim is made by apparently Eisler himself that he was "the organizer and commentator on the illegal German-language broadcasting station in the USA from 29/8/41 to 1949." According to FBI records, they never caught on that Eisler was running a secret transmitter from his apartment in Queens. If, as Lamphere says, an FBI-KGB war was fought in the United States in the midforties, it is clear that every major battle was lost by the FBI at that time. They never caught a single active nuclear spy prior to the Soviets exploding, to the almost total surprise of the Western "intelligence" community, their first atomic weapon in September 1949.

21. BL, 464–65. In a 30 June 1943 letter to Berlau, Brecht refers disparagingly to Piscator's "projudische Sache."

22. The revealing Weill-Lenya correspondence was kindly made available to me by the Kurt Weill Foundation.
23. BL, 457.
24. AJ, 2:569.
25. GW 12:375–76.
26. AJ, 2:569.
27. Pozner, *Vladimir Pozner*, 17.
28. Pozner, *Vladimir Pozner*, 19.
29. BL, 463–64.
30. GW 10:888.

Chapter 34

1. An account that accepts Brecht's views of this meeting is given in Christopher Hampton's teleplay *Tales from Hollywood*. Regrettably, what Hampton presents is a radically ill-informed, wholly cliché view both of Thomas Mann and of Brecht.
2. AJ, 2:602.
3. Privately, however, Mann could sometimes act no better than Brecht. See details of Mann's cynically exploitative relationship with the wealthy American Agnes Meyer in Hans R. Vaget, ed., *Thomas Mann/Agnes E. Meyer Briefwechsel* (Frankfurt am Main: Fischer, 1992). While praising Ms. Meyer in his letters to her, and repeatedly asking for large sums of money, calling her his "princess," he said in his diary that he found her silly, disgusting, stupid, and hysterical.
4. Berlau FBI file.
5. Bunge interviews with Berlau, East Berlin, September/October 1959.
6. Cited in Sanders, *Days Grow Short*, 320.
7. BL, 481.
8. A copy of this agreement was kindly provided by Dr. Harold von Hofe.
9. Cited (perhaps for copyright reasons) in single quotes by Völker, *Brecht*, 301. Völker publishes his work on Brecht in much the way the Brecht heirs have treated those who contributed so much to Brecht's work—without first clearing citations with the heirs or with Suhrkamp.
10. GW 12:585.
11. HC. *Not* in BL. Many of the Harvard photocopies are so badly faded that whole sections of text and identifying file numbers are illegible. Among the key Berlau folders are: 168, 171, 974, 1187, 1188, 1189, 1795, 1796, 1797, 1799, 1959, 2200, 2201. There are over 500 Brecht letters to Berlau in HC, approximately half the known total.
12. HC. *Not* in BL.
13. HC. *Not* in BL.
14. Bunge interviews with Berlau, East Berlin, September/October 1959.
15. Brecht said he would get it re-etched as his penknife was apparently not enough to do a permanent job, and pen and ink tended to get worn right away. See BL, 481.
16. AJ 2:622. For a discussion of the metaphor of surgeon as used by Brecht and by various Stalinists, see Michael Rohrwasser's superb essay, "Ist also

Schweigen das Beste? Brechts Schreibtisch-Schublade und das Messer des Chirurgen," in *Text und Kritik. Macht Apparat Literatur. Literatur und Stalinismus*, ed. H. L. Arnold (Munich: edition text und kritik, 1990), 38–47.

17. Nielsen, "Freundschaft," 20.
18. Nielsen, "Freundschaft," 22.
19. Nielsen, "Freundschaft," 21.
20. AJ 2:636.
21. Letter preserved in Brecht FBI file.
22. BL, 484.
23. See Aufricht, 259–60.
24. Aufricht, 259–60.
25. As Brecht is a literary ecologist, one is not surprised to find that several of the songs are recycled material. They are dependent on the style and actual verses from the Estonian folktale "The Poem of War," which Wuolijoki and the dying Steffin worked on together (with, as far as I know, no input from Brecht) in the winter of 1940–41.
26. See Werner Hecht, ed., *Materialien zu Brechts 'Der kaukasische Kreidekreis'* (Frankfurt am Main: Suhrkamp, 1968), 20. Hereafter: Hecht, 'Kreidekreis.'
27. Lion Feuchtwanger, *Briefwechsel mit Freunden 1933–58*, ed. Harold von Hofe and Sigrid Washburn (Berlin: Aufbau, 1991). Hereafter: Feuchtwanger, L.
28. Document kindly provided by Dr. Harold von Hofe, Feuchtwanger Library, University of Southern California.
29. Berlau first learned in 1955 how much money was involved with the sale of *Simone Machard*. She said in a 1955 letter that she could have lived very comfortably had Brecht given her but 1 percent of the proceeds from the works she contributed to, virtually every play from late 1933 on. However, when she asked for a regular income rather than handouts, he said she was "being a Shylock trying to cash in on old debts." BBA 1451/28–33.
30. Lyon, BinA, 79.
31. The Feuchtwanger villa was bought in 1943 for $9,000.
32. For confirmation, see Feuchtwanger's secretary, Hilda Waldo, in the film *Red Ruth*. Weigel's spending her own money on the house is claimed by Mari Barbara Brecht-Schall in a 20 September 1993 letter to Nordsk Film.
33. See Lyon, BinA, 229.
34. Text included in the film *Red Ruth*.
35. See Charles Higham, *Charles Laughton, an Intimate Biography* (Garden City, New York: Doubleday & Company, 1976).
36. Higham, *Charles Laughton*.
37. Hear Berlau's own voice in the German version of the film *Red Ruth*.
38. See Bunge, *Lai-tu*, 317.

Chapter 35

1. Berlau and Brecht FBI files.
2. Unpublished January 1946 communication of Hauptmann to Brecht on Berlau's condition, HC (illegible file number).
3. Details from FBI files.
4. From FBI transcript of the broadcast as found in Berlau's FBI file, which I obtained under FOIA.

5. Bentley, *Memoir*, 22.
6. Bentley, *Memoir*, 22.
7. Bentley, *Memoir*, 22.
8. Bentley, *Memoir*, 88.
9. Cited in Lyon, *BinA*, 136.
10. A good discussion of Viertel's ideas is in Hans Christof Wächter, *Theater im Exil* (Munich: Carl Hanser Verlag, 1973), 167–69.
11. Houseman, *Front*, 56.
12. Peter Kurth, *American Cassandra: The Life of Dorothy Thompson* (Boston/Toronto/London: Little Brown & Company, 1990), 300.
13. Los Angeles Office FBI report to J. Edgar Hoover, dated 17 September 1945.
14. HC, undated. *Not* in BL.
15. BL, 512–13.
16. *GW* 10:935.
17. *GW* 10:939–40.
18. *GW* 10:933.
19. *GW* 10:945.
20. Völker, *Brecht*, 311.
21. American rights to key plays were still in Englind's hands in 1959.
22. BBA 1763/20.
23. Hogan's letter is in the Brecht Archive under the number 1185/17. *Not* in BL.
24. For an account of the Fischer family's view of Suhrkamp's behavior, see "Nach Hause Sind Wir Nie Zurückgekehrt," *Der Spiegel*, no. 1, 1987, 96–103. I believe no legal challenge was mounted against the damning facts brought out in that interview with Brigitte and Bermann Fischer, conducted by *Spiegel* editors Harold Wieser and Peter Suhrovsky.
25. For its first years of existence, the letterhead of the firm read: "Suhrkamp Verlag vorm. S. Fischer Verlag" (Suhrkamp Press formerly S. Fischer Press).
26. The book is titled *Emil Jannings* and was published in the Third Reich in 1941. The book speaks, for instance, of "Hitler's national socialist elevation," and of the National Socialist seizure of Danzig by arms as the "freeing" of Danzig.
27. Bentley, *Memoir*, 27.
28. Bentley to Laughlin. Original held by Bentley.
29. Leopold Lindtberg, *Reden und Aufsätze* (Zurich: Atlantis, 1972), 121.
30. Bentley, *Memoir*, 21.
31. *AJ*, 2:768
32. *AJ*, 2:768.
33. The unpublished report by Ida Bachmann is dated 11 January 1946. See BBA 286/04-10.
34. This and subsequent quotations in following paragraphs from Ida Bachmann's report on her friend's condition in late 1945. BBA 286/04–10.
35. Given in Lyon, *Cicerone*, 183. *Not* in BL.
36. See Paul Alexander, *Rough Magic, a Biography of Sylvia Plath* (New York: Viking, 1991), 118ff.
37. BL, 518.
38. This letter is BBA 01/04. *Not* in BL.

Chapter 36

1. The *New York Times*, 6 February 1946, quotes Laughton as saying that Brecht had not yet arrived but was expected soon. However, an FBI note (as is so often the case, not a reliable one) claims Brecht got to New York 1 February.
2. A possible source for the money could have been a sale to MGM around this time of the film rights to *Mother Courage*, which was not legal, as we know, because Englind in Sweden held the American rights to *Courage* until 1959. Whatever the source of the money, it is highly doubtful Weigel saw much of it. James K. Lyon has told me that Weigel claimed in a 1970 interview with him that she only had small amounts of household money to work with throughout the exile years in America.
3. As both sender and recipient were in New York City, the use of a letter is worthy of note. Hauptmann was still trying to resist Brecht's allure and at that time only used the deliberately distancing, formal "Sie" form of address and insisted on the same from him.
4. Lyon, *BinA*, 142.
5. Lyon, *BinA*, 238.
6. BBA 1798/48.
7. Johannes Hoffmann's Berlau collection as kindly made available to me by Hoffmann. Currently held by Copenhagen's Royal Library.
8. Lyon, *BinA*, 227.
9. Interview with Rhoda "Ricki" Pecker (Riker) in Bunge film *My Name Is Bertolt Brecht*.
10. Unpublished note, Rhoda Riker to Eric Bentley, 20 May 1967. Letter shared with me by Bentley.
11. Lyon, *BinA*, 244.
12. Interview with Pecker (Riker) in Bunge film *My Name Is Bertolt Brecht*.
13. Lyon, *BinA*, 179.
14. Lyon, *Cicerone*, 105.
15. Lyon, *Cicerone*, 106.
16. Lyon, *Cicerone*, 74.
17. Nielsen, "Freundschaft," 33.
18. Cited in JW, "Bacon?" 132.
19. Edith Schloss, "A Poet in Exile: Notes on Brecht in New York," *International Herald Tribune*, 6 July 1984, 7.
20. Lamphere, *FBI-KGB War*, 291.
21. Cited in Gary Wills, *Reagan's America, Innocents at Home* (Garden City, New York: Doubleday & Company, 1987), 245. Hereafter: Wills, *Reagan*.
22. Wills, *Reagan*, 252.
23. See Theoharis, *J. Edgar Hoover*, 115.
24. Kenneth O'Reily, *Hoover and the Unamericans: The FBI, HUAC, and the Red Menace* (Philadelphia: Temple University Press, 1983), 92.
25. My account of the hearings draws frequently on Eric Bentley, *Thirty Years of Treason* (New York, Viking, 1971). Hereafter: Bentley, *Treason*.
26. Bentley, *Treason*, 57.
27. Bentley, *Treason*, 61.
28. Bentley, *Treason*, 36.

29. *J. Edgar Hoover*, Theoharis, 114–16.
30. Houseman, *Front*, 235.
31. Bentley, *Memoir*, 36.
32. Author's and Rudy Hassing interview with Bentley, New York City, 10 November 1990.
33. Some of this historical footage is included in the film *Red Ruth*.
34. Bunge interview with Berlau, East Berlin, 21 September 1959.
35. Bentley, *Memoir*, 30.
36. For many excellent further details, see Lyon, *BinA*, chap. 19.
37. Lyon, *BinA*, 315.
38. Lyon, *BinA*, 316.
39. Eisler's testimony in Bentley, *Treason*, 73–107.
40. Text of the letter in Bentley, *Treason*, 107.
41. Bentley, *Treason*, 107–8.

Chapter 37

1. Cited in Gordon Kahn, *Hollywood on Trial* (New York: Boni & Gaer, 1948), v. Hereafter: Kahn, *Hollywood*.
2. Cited in Bentley, *Treason*, 668.
3. In *BinA*, Lyon reports that of those he interviewed who had attended the Shrine rally, none remembered seeing Brecht there.
4. Though the testimony was supposed to be presented exactly as rehearsed, Reagan complained to the FBI later that HUAC's chief counsel sometimes departed from the prepared scenario. See Wills, *Reagan*, 429.
5. Bentley, *Treason*, 147.
6. Bentley, *Treason*, 147.
7. Lyon, *BinA*, 322.
8. Personal communication to the author from Eric Bentley.
9. Lyon, *BinA*, 320.
10. See BBA 03/06–9, where Brecht gives his own self-serving account of HUAC.
11. Cited in Lyon, *BinA*, 327.
12. Cited in Kahn, *Hollywood*, 114.
13. Brecht's entire testimony is given in Bentley, *Treason*; and in Peter Demetz, *Brecht, a Collection of Critical Essays* (Englewood Cliffs, N.J.: Prentice-Hall, 1962), 30–42. A recording of the testimony has been issued by Bentley on Folkways FD 5531. A GDR (German Democratic Republic) record of the testimony cuts out crucial words of denial by Brecht that were, for those in East Germany, rather like Peter's denial of Christ.
14. Portions of Brecht's HUAC appearance can be seen and heard in the film *Red Ruth*.
15. For Cole's recollections, see Cook, *Exile*, 197–98. Other useful details on Brecht and HUAC are given in Lyon, *BinA*, 314–37.
16. Lyon, *BinA*, 289.
17. Lyon, *BinA*, 11.
18. Berlau discusses this in her recorded conversations with Bunge, East Berlin, 1959.
19. BL, 559.

20. For an example of Moscow Central's cold shoulder for broken discipline, see Ruth Werner, *Sonjas Rapport* (Berlin: Verlag Neues Leben, 1977). "Sonja" worked with Dr. Sorge in the Far East and then "ran" Klaus Fuchs for awhile while he was in Britain.
21. AJ, 2:787.
22. AJ, 2:788.
23. The best book on the CIA is Ranelagh, *Agency*. For a discussion of the need to create the CIA because of the manifest inabilities of the FBI and for the work of the first CIA director, Admiral Hillenkoeter, see Ranelagh, *Agency*, 112.

Chapter 38

1. BL, 516–17.
2. AJ, 2:789.
3. BL, 557.
4. Cited in JW, CN, 126.
5. Caspar Neher Diary, 5 November 1947.
6. George F. Kennan, *Memoirs 1925–50* (New York: Pantheon Books, 1967), 550.
7. CIA document, cited in Ranelagh, *Agency*, 177.
8. Völker, *Chronik*, 117.
9. The CIA, as requested by the FBI, immediately got on Brecht's trail in Zurich as a CIA cleartext (ie, uncoded) transmission of 12 December 1947 reveals.
10. The letter with its telling notations by Berlau is in HC, *not* in BL.
11. The apt phrase "versified invective," which I borrow here for its appropriateness, is used in Lyon, *BinA*, 270.
12. GW 10:967.
13. JW, CN, 66.
14. For a detailed analysis of *Antigone* in Chur, see Fuegi, CAP, 101–7.
15. See Neureuter, "Finland," for the full text of this legally binding agreement.
16. On 28 August 1948, Brecht wrote a letter (BL, 570) to his Munich agent, Jacob Geis, giving his own explanation of why the name was omitted. If the charge of stealing material from Wuolijoki was allowed to stand, it was doubtful Desch would have been willing to pay the 2,500 mark advance for *Puntila* that Geis was negotiating. See also Geis letter to Brecht: BBA 01/016. The same week, 24 August 1948, the then Soviet-controlled German film company DEFA committed themselves (see BBA 01/039) to pay 10,000 Swiss francs to Brecht for a film treatment of the 14th-century folk story "Till Eulenspiegel."
17. BL, 564.
18. Letter (summer of 1948) HC. *Not* in BL.
19. Bentley, *Memoir*.
20. Same letter as in preceding note, HC.
21. For a good solid essay on the gulf between early Brecht theory and the later plays, see Hans-Dieter Zimmermann, "Die Last der Lehre. Fünf Thesen zu den späten Stücken Bertolt Brechts," in *Beyond Brecht*.
22. Bentley, *Memoir*, 89ff.
23. "Verfremdung" is an oxymoronic term conveying both the meaning "rendering the strange familiar" and "rendering the familiar strange." Berlin actors who worked with Brecht have repeatedly confirmed that these terms were

rarely used in their actual theater practice with Brecht in the post–World War II years.

24. Mollie Panter-Downes, *The New Yorker*, 29 December 1980, 57.

25. Bentley, *Memoir*, 92.

26. Bentley, *Memoir*, 94.

27. Cited in Bentley, *Memoir*, 70.

28. Bentley, *Memoir*, 96.

29. Max Frisch, "Diary 1948," in *Brecht As They Knew Him*, 112.

30. AJ, 2:833.

31. See Bunge interviews with Berlau, East Berlin, 15 September 1959.

32. AJ, 2:828.

33. Letter, Friedrich Wolf to Piscator, 17 March 1947, Piscator Papers. In this letter, Wolf proposes that Piscator come to Berlin for the winter of 1947–48 to serve as a guest director at the Soviet Sector Volksbühne.

34. See letter, Friedrich Wolf to Piscator, 23 May 1947, cited in Thea Kirfel-Lenk, *Erwin Piscator im Exil in den USA 1939–51* (Berlin: Henschel Verlag, 1984), 214.

35. Details given by Max Frisch in an interview in *Literaturnaya gazeta* (Moscow), no. 52, 7 August 1985.

36. Cited in Christopher Innes, *Erwin Piscator's Political Theatre* (Cambridge: Cambridge University Press, 1972), 89.

37. Alexander Dymschitz, *Dramaturgische Blätter*, no. 1 (1947); and Alexander Dymschitz, *Dramaturgische Blätter*, no. 2 (1947).

38. BBA 01/017–018; HC.

39. Under considerable pressure from Wuolijoki, who was being pressed by Finnish, British, and American friends to go public about the continued deception, Brecht did sign a change in the Desch agreement for *Puntila* on 10 June 1949, recognizing Wuolijoki's legal rights. However, this ended up doing her no good as Desch then pointed out that they had already paid Brecht, and she would need to collect her share directly from him. He never did pay her her money. On 3 September 1953, Brecht, again with no mention of Wuolijoki, collected 60,000 Austrian schillings for *Puntila* from Wien Film (for contract, see BBA 1085/51). She, the former millionaire, who had rescued the entire Brecht group in 1940–41, died in poverty. See Neureuter, "Finland," for a rather desperate 1951 letter of Wuolijoki to Weigel asking Weigel to help her collect her money. As far as I can determine, Weigel did not intervene.

40. BL, 573–74.

Chapter 39

1. Always with a sense of drama, Brecht generally staged his scenes of arrival and departure.

2. AJ, 2:847.

3. AJ, 2:964–65.

4. AJ, 2:848.

5. Details given in author's interview with Angelika Hurwicz, Scheveningen, Holland, November 1984.

6. AJ, 2:849.

7. See Müller, *KoS*, 63, for an account of how his father was strong-armed by the Russians to go along with the creation of the SED.

8. *AJ*, 2:857.

9. *AJ*, 2:864.

10. The comment was made by Curt Riess and is cited in Mittenzwei, *Leben* 2:325.

11. Engel, like Caspar Neher and Herbert Ihering, had stayed on in the Third Reich. Engel's position, however, as he was defined technically by the Nazis as a "half-Jew," was a strange anomaly as he was continuously employed in theater and film throughout the Goebbels-Hitler years.

12. *AJ*, 2:883.

13. *AJ*, 2:889.

14. Ronald Hayman, *Writing Against: A Biography of Sartre* (London: Weidenfeld & Nicolson, 1987) 254.

15. The mass graves of KGB victims in Germany began to be opened and examined as of late 1990. Estimates of the dead in KGB camps on German territory are about 87,000, or, to put this in some perspective, two-and-half times one major estimate of the slayings by the Nazis at Babi Yar.

16. A more detailed account of this production in Fuegi, *Essential Brecht*, 81–97.

17. Bentley, *Memoir*, 54–55.

18. Bentley, *Seven Plays*, xiii.

19. Boris Sachawa, "Stärken und Schwächen des Brecht Theater," *Kunst und Literatur* 5 (1957): 1369.

20. George Steiner, *The Death of Tragedy* (New York: Knopf, 1958), 353–54.

21. The story was related to John Willett by Elisabeth Hauptmann in 1956. See JW, *BinC*, 238.

22. Albrecht Schöne, "Bertolt Brecht, Theatertheorie und dramatische Dichtung," *Euphorion* 52, no. 3 (1958): 290.

23. Brecht, *SPG* 6:131.

24. Brecht, *SPG* 6:133–34. Though included in the 1964 *SPG*, this text is not in recent editions of Brecht.

25. Brecht, *SPG* 6:161.

26. Cited in JW, *Eight Aspects*, 185.

27. Both Meyerhold and Tairov, the real originators of the "cold" style of acting, had known from the outset—Meyerhold in 1905 and Tairov by 1920—that cold acting often led to hotter audience reactions than could be obtained by conventional hot means.

28. Cited in Völker, *Brecht*, 333.

29. Fritz Erpenbeck, "Einige Bemerkungen zu Brechts 'Mutter Courage,'" *Die Weltbühne*, February 1949, 101.

30. Wolfgang Harich, *Die Weltbühne*, June 1949, 315.

Chapter 40

1. Alexander Dymschitz's accounts of his conversations with Brecht are found in *Ein unvergesslicher Frühling. Literarische Portraits und Erinnerungen* (Berlin: Aufbau, 1970), 309ff. Hereafter: Dymschitz, *Literarische Portraits*.

2. Dymschitz's first published work was a positive appraisal of Mayakovsky.

3. These Bentley comments on Berlau may be seen and heard in the film *Red Ruth*.

4. BBA 1398/01.
5. Unpublished portion of Bunge interview with Berlau, East Berlin, 12 October 1959.
6. Bunge interviews with Berlau, East Berlin, 1959.
7. Bentley, *Memoir*, 94.
8. BL, 587–89.
9. See Mittenzwei *Leben* 2:382 for details on Brecht urging Weigel to buy the house. *Not* in BL.
10. BBA 654/111.
11. This letter to Weigel, together with literally thousands of pages of contracts, has not been published before.
12. Though Manfred Wekwerth bent over backward to be helpful in providing me with details on the early history of the Berliner Ensemble, the actual records at the Schiffbauerdamm are scant and one must rely on personal contracts held by individuals.
13. Confirming receipt of Steffin's belongings, see Brecht diary entry for Whitsunday, 1949 (AJ, 2:900). More of Steffin's Moscow possessions were placed in Weigel's hands in 1961, but she made no effort to place them in the hands of Steffin's heirs.
14. Hauptmann claims, in JoR, 227, that in her first years in Berlin she lived "in einem Kleinen Loch von einem Zimmer."
15. Bunge interview with Berlau, East Berlin, 21 September 1959. Berlau also told Bunge that Hauptmann was treated very badly by Brecht when she returned to Berlin in 1949.
16. Peter Elsass, *Strategies for Survival*, trans. Fran Hopenwasser (New York: New York University Press, 1992), 128. Hereafter: Elsass, *Strategies*.
17. Müller, *KoS*, 83.
18. BL, 551–53. Herta Hanisch told me that the letters published here and supposedly sent by Brecht to Frau Hanisch and her mother, Johanna Steffin, in June–July 1947, if sent, never arrived.
19. Berlau was present when this question was asked. Bunge interview with Berlau, East Berlin, 15 September 1959. Grete's things have still not been returned to her heirs.
20. Details given in author's interview with Herta Hanisch, 17 December 1987.
21. Hauptmann's letters complaining about the way her adaptations had been taken over without acknowledgment were routinely ignored.
22. See Jacob Geis letter to Brecht, 25 May 1949, BBA 1646/13–14.
23. This account was given to me by Dr. Christoph Köhler of Felix Bloch Erben on my visit to the firm on 15 October 1984. Dr. Köhler kindly made all archival holdings of the firm relating to Hauptmann, Bronnen, and Brecht freely available to me to photocopy and examine at my leisure.
24. For details, see BBA 1183/55.

Chapter 41

1. In choosing this car, as with earlier attempts to get his hands on a Mercedes, Brecht paid no attention to the behavior of these companies during the Nazi years.

2. BL, 615–16.
3. Author's interview with Angelika Hurwicz at her home, Scheveningen, Holland, November 1982.
4. AJ, 2:908.
5. Originally cited in *Neues Deutschland*, July 1952, as cited in *Der Spiegel*, May 1992, 76.
6. For a history of the Stasi, see Lienhard Wawrzyn, *Der Blaue. Das Spitzelsystem der DDR* (Berlin: Wagenbach, 1990).
7. Letter is cited in Mittenzwei, *Leben* 2:376. *Not* in BL.
8. The letter is found in Neureuter, "Finland," Document 332.
9. See Hanssen for clear evidence of Hauptmann's dominant role in the creation of the Chinese poems.
10. JW, *Brecht Poems*, xx.
11. Though Picasso was committed to the French Communist party, his work was not accepted in socialist countries.
12. BBA 971/72.
13. BL, 627.
14. BL, 590.
15. See, for instance, the newest volume of Brecht, *Werke*, volume nine of the plays, published as a joint undertaking of Suhrkamp Verlag and the former East German Aufbau Verlag. The texts, though primarily by Hauptmann (as the editors admit in a tiny note on page 417ff.), still have Brecht's name written large on the cover. This is wholly typical. The editors fail to address the question in a way accessible to a general reader as to what in this Brecht edition was written by Brecht, and what was actually written by others such as Hauptmann, Steffin, Berlau, Besson, Pohl, Ottwalt, and others.
16. I first began drawing public attention to this fact in my essay "Whodunit: Brecht's Adaptation of Molière's Don Juan," *Comparative Literature Studies* 11, no. 2 (June 1974). Hereafter: Fuegi, "Whodunit." None of the facts I presented there have ever been disproven. Likewise, my essay on the scam involved with *The Threepenny Opera* has been in print since 1986 in English and since 1988 in German, and also has not been disproven.
17. Bunge interviews with Berlau, East Berlin, 1959.
18. Details that follow given in a meeting I had with Käthe Reichel at her Berlin apartment, 16 December 1987.
19. See BBA 1186/55. Here Brecht says, "I need a spy; I must know how you are doing."
20. BBA 1186/52.
21. BBA 974/49–50.
22. BBA 974/01–03.
23. She uses the expression "Magig" (a kind of telescoping of *magic* in English and *machtig* [powerful] in German), BBA 1186/24.
24. BBA 974/23. Brecht's proposal of weekly visits is strikingly like that of Macheath's of visiting Jenny every Thursday.
25. BBA 974/28–30.
26. Bentley, *Memoir*, 57.
27. Ehrenburg, *Memoirs*, 206–7.
28. For supporting details, see Medvedev, *On Stalin*, 146–48; and Louis Rapoport,

Stalin's War. For the overall dimensions of Stalin's crimes against his own people, see Stephen F. Cohen's observations that "Stalin's policies caused a Soviet hocaust, from his collectivization 'pogrom' against the peasantry in 1929–33 through the relentless mass terror that continued until his death in March 1953" (Cohen, preface to Antonov-Ovseyenko, *Portrait*). Cohen believes that a death total of twenty million, exclusive of World War II, should be laid at Stalin's door.

29. See Medvedev, *On Stalin*, 148. For a variant account, see Martin Bauml Duberman, *Paul Robeson* (New York: Ballantine Books, 1989), 352–53, where Feffer tells Robeson in sign language that Mikhoels had been murdered. If this is true, Robeson concealed this information when he returned to the West, revealing it only to his son and pledging him to silence. Tellingly, Fadayev committed suicide in 1956 after Khrushchev revealed details of Stalin's, and by direct association, Fadayev's, and a host of others' crimes.

30. Bentley's copy of the play has detailed notes on cuts and changes that were made in performance.

31. Bentley, *Memoir*, 67.

32. Bentley, *Memoir*, 59–63.

33. Bentley, *Memoir*, 62.

34. Bentley, *Memoir*, 68. Listening to the tapes made of Brecht's rehearsals in the 50s, one hears how apt is Bentley's comparison of Brecht's tirades to those of Hitler. Heiner Müller makes the same point in *KoS*, 228.

35. Müller, *KoS*, 228.

36. Bentley, *Memoir*, 69.

37. BL, 645.

38. A typical CIA document on Brecht, dated 11 September 1950 and labeled "Routine," says, "RUMOR CIRCULATING BRLN CLAIMS BERT BRECHT IN MUNICH TO STAY. PLS QUESTION [GAP IN CENSORED TEXT] AND ADVISE."

39. So far, I have seen records of American intelligence interest in Brecht and members of the circle from OSS, the CIA, the FBI, the United States Air Force, and the United States Diplomatic Service.

40. For further details see Lyon, *Cicerone*, 147–49.

41. Lyon, *Cicerone*, 147–49.

42. Lyon, *Cicerone*, 147–49.

43. See Völker, *Brecht*, 347.

44. See BBA 1186/68.

45. See Völker, *Brecht*, 347. *Not* in BL.

46. Brecht would turn fifty-three on 10 February 1951. Bunge gives the incorrect date of 1952 in *Lai-tu*, 274.

47. Suhrkamp did not bring the book out.

48. Excerpts from this letter are given in Bunge, *Lai-tu*, 267–69.

49. Bunge, *Lai-tu*, 272.

50. Copies of the checks Brecht personally wrote on his own account are in HC, thus giving a direct lie to what was told Berlau.

51. Berlau to Brecht, 10 March 1951.

Chapter 42

1. Cited in Mittenzwei, *Leben* 2:425.
2. Cited in Mittenzwei, *Leben* 2:425.
3. See Joachim Luchessi, *Das Verhör in der Oper* (Berlin: Basisdruck, 1993).
4. Mittenzwei, *Leben* 2:436.
5. BBA 971/62–63.
6. Bentley, *Memoir*, 89.
7. Müller, *KoS*, 227.
8. BBA 973/89, dated 19 March 1952.
9. BBA 973/91.
10. *JoR*, 230.
11. *JoR*, 230.
12. BBA 698/48–49.
13. *JoR*, 226–27.
14. For a solid general discussion, see both the collection of original documents, *Schauprozesse unter Stalin 1932–52*, trans. from Russian by Hilde Ettinger and Gottfried Holdt (Berlin: Dietz, 1990); and Georg Hermann Hodos, *Schauprozesse: Stalinische Säberungen in Osteuropa 1948–54* (Frankfurt/New York: Campus Verlag, 1988). Hereafter: Hodos, *Schauprozesse*.
15. Hodos, *Schauprozesse*, 177.
16. Ulbricht, like Stalin, was known for his extraordinary memory. Ulbricht is unlikely to have forgotten either Walcher's close, personal connection with the subsequently denigrated Rosa Luxemburg or the fact that Walcher had been one of those who had sent a blunt letter to Ulbricht on 1 October 1937 (as Ulbricht was busy decimating the ranks of those Stalin wanted liquidated in western Europe). The letter charged Ulbricht, "You are weakening the popular front movement at a time when its establishment within and outside Germany is more necessary than ever before" (cited in Pike, *German Writers*, 191).
17. See Medvedev, *On Stalin*, 159. In the same book, page 148, Medvedev deliberately uses the expression "final solution" to describe Stalin's treatment of Jews.
18. Müller, *KoS*, 226.
19. Martin Pohl and Ulrich Panndorf, *Memorial* (Berlin: Mariannenpresse, 1986), 31.
20. An extensive section of this interview with Martin Pohl is included in the film *Red Ruth*.
21. Given in Tax, *Fleisser*, 200.
22. See BBA 1186/21–22, for instance.
23. This and other reviews are given in Bernd Mahl, *Brechts und Monks 'Urfaust' Inszenierung* (Stuttgart and Zurich: Belser Verlag, 1986), 188. Hereafter: Mahl, *'Urfaust.'*
24. Mahl, *'Urfaust,'* 189–90.
25. Letter in JW, *CN*, 75–76.
26. BBA 838/95. *Not* in BL.
27. Brecht's self-serving reply is, of course, included in BL, 696. Though the editor claims to have excluded business correspondence, it is clear that some business correspondence is more equal than others.
28. An excellent discussion of Pohl's relationship to Brecht is given by Stephan

Bock, "Die Tage des Busching. Brechts 'Garbe'—Ein Deutsches Lehrstück," in *Dramatik der DDR*, ed. Ulrich Profitlich (Frankfurt am Main: Suhrkamp, 1987) 19–39. See also Pohl's own account, "Zum Beispiel: Martin Pohl," in *Nach Brecht*, ed. Inge Gellert (Berlin: Argon, 1992). Additional details were given to me directly in my interview with Pohl, Berlin, 28 September 1990.

29. Fuegi, interview with Martin Pohl, 28 September 1990. See also Brown.

30. A solid account of some aspects of her work with Brecht is given in Käthe Rülicke-Weiler, *Die Dramaturgie Brechts* (Berlin: Henschel Verlag, 1966). Additional details were given to me in three interviews I conducted with Rülicke-Weiler in Berlin, 15 February and 5 December 1985 and 22 February 1989.

31. See BBA 1186/68, where Reichel refers to Rülicke as "diese Hitlerjugendmädchen."

32. Author's interview with Käthe Rülicke-Weiler, Berlin, 22 February 1989.

33. BBA 676/08.

34. BBA 676/10.

35. Bentley, *Memoir*, 31

36. Bentley personal files, letter dated November 1954. *Not* in BL.

37. Author's interview with Angelika Hurwicz at her home, Scheveningen, Holland, 1984.

38. BBA 1644/37.

39. Cited in Ehrenburg, *Memoirs*, 295.

40. See *Der Slansky-Prozess* (Prague: 1953) 253ff.

41. BBA 1298/31.

42. Bunge, *Lai-tu*, 233–34.

43. BBA 1827/10. *Not* in BL. Was this letter excluded because the editor considered it a business letter?

44. Cited in Bentley, *Memoir*, 70.

45. AJ, 2:1008.

46. SuF, 2d, 9.

47. Mahl, *'Urfaust,'* 190.

48. For excellent details on this production, see Hans Bunge, *Die Debatte um Hanns Eislers 'Johann Faustus'* (Berlin: BasisDruck, 1991).

49. Mahl, *'Urfaust,'* 199–200.

50. *Not* in BL. HC.

51. Lev Kopelev, *Ease My Sorrows*, trans. Antonia W. Bouis (New York: Random House, 1983), 205. Hereafter: Kopelev, *Sorrows*.

52. BL, 692–93.

53. Robert Havemann, *Fragen Antworten Fragen. Aus der Biographie eines Deutsches Marxisten* (Munich: Piper, 1970), 132–48. Hereafter: Havemann, *Fragen*.

54. Havemann, *Memoirs*, 135.

55. Havemann, *Memoirs*, 137.

56. Havemann, *Memoirs*, 140.

57. See Christopher Andrew and Oleg Gordevsky, *KGB. The Inside Story of Its Operations from Lenin to Gorbachev* (New York: Harper/Collins, 1990), 423. Hereafter: Andrew and Gordevsky, *KGB*.

58. *Not* in BL. HC.

59. BL, 694.

60. BL, 693–94.

61. Müller, *KoS*, 132. See also Brecht's and Reich's similar observations on Hitler in the early 1920s. There, also, the organizing and protecting metaphor was "the theater." There is an obvious aversion factor at work in all these instances.

62. Manfred Wekwerth, *Schriften: Arbeit mit Brecht* (Berlin: Henschelverlag, 1973), 64.

Chapter 43

1. The facts given in this paragraph are taken from the official, though still unpublished, fifteen-page transcript of the Berliner Ensemble meeting. Collection of the author.

2. Gody Suter, "Brecht," *Tagesanzeiger* (Zurich), 1 September 1956.

3. Suter, "Brecht."

4. *SuF*, 2d, 341.

5. *Neues Deutschland*, 23 June 1953.

6. BL, 695–97.

7. BBA 559/01–02.

8. *AJ*, 2:1017.

9. GW 10:1009.

10. *Berliner Zeitung*, 15 July 1953.

11. GW 10:1009–10. Circulated privately at the time it was written, the poem was first published in 1967.

12. See Magdalena Heider and Kerstin Thöns, eds., *SED und Intellektuelle in der DDR der fünfziger Jahre. Kulturbund Protokolle* (Cologne: Edition Deutschland Archiv, 1990), 10. Hereafter: Heider and Thöns, *SED*.

13. BBA 676/49–53. The conversations were written down by Käthe Rülicke.

14. Rosa Luxemburg's frequently negative views of the Soviet Revolution and its aftermath were set down in a text called "The Russian Revolution." Attempts were made by Radek, Bukharin, and Zetkin to have this text destroyed after Luxemburg's murder in early 1919. However, her executor, Paul Levi, published it verbatim in 1921. East German and Soviet editions of Luxemburg's work excluded this prescient text, where she foretold how a revolution from above would fail. In January 1949, West Berlin radio broadcast the full text of "The Russian Revolution" and thereby caused a considerable stir in the East.

15. It is quite possible that Professor Mittenzwei, writing as he did in preglasnost days, did not see the full text of the Buckow conversations. He often said to me about such texts, "Go ahead and publish them, John, then we too can use them."

16. GW 10:1011–12.

17. See Walter Janka's devastating and, I believe, accurate portrait of Becher's (and Anna Segher's) behavior and of the cultural minister's luxurious personal standard of living in Walter Janka, *Schwierigkeiten mit der Wahrheit* (Reinbek bei Hamburg: Rowohlt, 1989), 9–65. Hereafter: Janka, *SmdW*.

18. Bunge, *Lai-tu*, 318; and Mittenzwei, *Leben* 2:549ff.

19. BL, 698–99.

20. BBA 972/20.

21. Undated manuscript found among Berlau's papers after her mysterious death by fire. Made available to me by Johannes Hoffmann.
22. The first of my interviews with Isot Kilian (kindly arranged by Manfred Wekwerth) was conducted at her Berlin apartment, 16 October 1984.
23. Völker, *Brecht*, 349.
24. Kilian's account of the incident is given in an interview with Matthias Braun in *Sonntag* 33 (1986): 3.
25. Isot Kilian claimed this in an interview with me in East Berlin, 16 February 1985, shortly before her death in 1986.
26. Author's interviews with Hans Bunge, East Berlin, 26 February 1982 and 8 December 1984.
27. See BBA 1085/51.
28. A person who saw inside the "Gruppe Ulbricht" was Wolfgang Leonhard. See his observations on faking workers' statistics in the Soviet Union and the GDR in *Die Revolution entlässt ihre Kinder* (Cologne: Kiepenheuer and Witsch, 1955), 466–67. Hereafter: Leonhard, *Kinder*.
29. Cited in Knopf, *BHT*, 342.
30. Published in 1982 in *GW*, sup. vol. 2:413.
31. BBA 796/31.
32. BBA 797/13.
33. This note of Berlau is found in BBA 971/37–38.
34. BBA 972/58–59. See also BBA 971/100, signed, "your creature [or *creation*]-Ute-Whore-Ruth."
35. Author's interview with Benno Besson, Berlin, 28 November 1966. See also André Müller's book containing interviews with Besson, *Der Regisseur Benno Besson* (Berlin: Henschelverlag, 1967). What Besson told me was not only that Brecht had very little to do with *Don Juan* at any stage but that Brecht had even less to do with the translation and production of *Trumpets and Drums* from Farquhar's *The Recruiting Officer*, a project that Besson did entirely with Hauptmann.
36. See Fuegi, "Whodunit." For evidence that at least one of the editors of the new Brecht edition knows this is not a Brecht play, see Knopf, *BHT*, 321, where he accepts my conclusions as to authorship but fails thereafter to reassign authorship of the play in the *Collected Works*.
37. BBA 972/75–76.

Chapter 44

1. See BBA 772/75–76.
2. BBA 1186/69.
3. BBA 1186/106.
4. Völker, *Brecht*, 41.
5. Diary 1920–54, 237–38.
6. See *Das Magazin* (Berlin), February 1978, 16.
7. Rehearsal transcripts kindly supplied to me by Hans Bunge and Manfred Wekwerth.
8. Given in Bentley, *Memoir*, 78.
9. See Hecht, '*Kreidekreis*,' 64.

10. Gerda Goedhart and Angelika Hurwicz, *Brecht Inszeniert 'Der kaukasische Krei-dekreis'* (Velber bei Hannover: Friedrich Verlag, 1964), unnumbered. Here-after: Goedhart and Hurwicz, *KKInszeniert.* This marvelous little book has more to say about staging Brecht than the volumes of theory written on the subject.

11. Bunge, *Lai-tu,* 275–76.

12. Bunge, *Lai-tu,* 277–80.

13. The phrase is central to what I feel is Berlau's best sustained long piece of writing, her linked set of short stories published in Danish in 1940, *Ethvert dyr kan det* (Copenhagen: Arthur Jensens Forlag, 1940).

14. BBA 1083/25.

15. BBA 1083/24.

Chapter 45

1. BBA 656/68.

2. Carola Neher's friend Erich Wollenberg escaped and published his memoirs, *Der Apparat: Stalins Fünfte Kolonne* (Bonn: Bundesministerium für gesamt-deutsche Fragen, 1951). Wollenberg had been close to Zinoviev, who is supposed to have told him bluntly at one time, "Apart from the German Social Democrats, Stalin bears the main responsibility for Hitler's victory." Cited in Deutscher, *Prophet* 3:166.

3. See Buber-Neumann, *Gefangene.*

4. BL, 728. This prize alone would make Brecht a GDR millionaire.

5. BBA 1644/46.

6. See Mittenzwei, *Leben* 2:611, for the account of Brecht's conversation.

7. BL, 744.

8. See, for instance, BBA 1186/21.

9. Bunge, *Lai-tu,* 293–94.

10. See the film *Red Ruth* for the text of this note.

11. Another example of blatantly tendentious selection. Brecht letters to Berlau of 24 April and 7 May are given, but the letter of 1 May 1955 is *not* in BL.

12. BL, 745.

13. Rülicke-Weiler's account of her Moscow trip with Brecht and Weigel is given in "Seitdem hat die Welt ihre Hoffnung," *Neue Deutsche Literatur* 2 (February 1968). Hereafter: Rülicke-Weiler, "Hoffnung." An English version of this account is given in Witt, *Brecht As They Knew Him.*

14. For details see Reich, *W,* 381.

15. BL, 747.

16. The name of the group is taken from a collection of stories by E. T. A. Hoffmann.

17. For instance, at the height of the purges, Tikhonov was sent to the 1937 Writers' Congress in Paris, where he denounced erstwhile friends who had meanwhile been arrested in the Soviet Union, and lied repeatedly about conditions of intellectual and physical freedom in the Soviet Union.

18. See Rülicke-Weiler, "Hoffnung."

19. GW 20:343–44. Bertolt Brecht.

20. See Asja Lazis, *Revolutionär im Beruf,* 77.

21. BBA 717/17.
22. I was shown through this apartment in 1972.
23. BBA 715/18. *Not* in BL.
24. Spoto, *Lenya*, 213–14.
25. Spoto, *Lenya*, 213–14.
26. The shop is still operating at this location.
27. Pozner in Witt, *Brecht As They Knew Him*, 170–84.
28. A less frank account is given by Mittenzwei, *Leben* 2:581–83.
29. BBA 757/11. *Not* in BL.
30. BBA 757/31. *Not* in BL.
31. BBA 766/34. *Not* in BL.
32. BBA 834/39. *Not* in BL.
33. Details provided to me by Käthe Rülicke-Weiler, Berlin, October 1984.
34. The most sensitive account is in Tax, *Fleisser.*
35. Given in Tax, *Fleisser*, 207–8.
36. *GW.* 2:307. Marieluise Fleisser.
37. Cited in Tax, *Fleisser*, 210–11.
38. BBA 1826/01–02.
39. BL, 766.
40. BL, 769.
41. This point was originally acknowledged to Steffin in 1938 as the group in Svendborg realized that Bukharin's trial was faked and based on "evidence" extracted, as with Galileo, under threat of torture or torture itself.
42. *GW* 3:1340–41.
43. The person who provided this detailed description was the head of the photo lab at the Berliner Ensemble, Vera Tenschert. Author's interview with Tenschert, Berlin, 5 June 1985.
44. See BBA 757/35.
45. BBA 767/77. *Not* in BL.
46. Diary 1920–54, 237.
47. See Mittenzwei, *Leben* 2:638–40.
48. BL, 774.
49. BBA 717/35.
50. BBA 718/37.
51. HC. *Not* in BL.
52. BL, 778.
53. BL, 776.
54. BL, 781–82.
55. See Walter Janka, *Spuren eines Lebens* (Berlin: Rowohlt, 1991), 258. Hereafter: Janka, *SeL.*
56. See protocol of Stasi interrogation of Wolfgang Harich in Ingke Brodersen ed., *Der Prozess gegen Walter Janka und andere* (Reinbek bei Hamburg: Rowohlt, 1990), 56. Hereafter: Brodersen, *Prozess.*
57. Janka, *SeL*, 294.
58. BBA 1826/01–02.
59. That Brecht had treatment privileges at the Regierungskrankenhaus is verified in BBA 754/27.
60. Weigel, as head of the Berliner Ensemble, dealt with contracts every day but

nevertheless styled herself in a letter to Lion Feuchtwanger dated 13 July 1957 as "a lost lamb." Later that month, she wrote to Lion Feuchtwanger to bemoan the fact that Ruth Berlau was claiming her percentage of *Simone Machard*. Feuchtwanger explicitly confirmed that Berlau was legally entitled to 20 percent. Despite this, Berlau was never given her legal share either by Suhrkamp Verlag or by Weigel. In 1962, with Suhrkamp then run by Siegfried Unseld, Unseld's office again denied Berlau's claim despite having had the original contract sent to Germany from California. Though the work has been played from Tel Aviv to Hong Kong, neither Berlau nor her heir has collected their legal share of the royalties. The actual royalty documents, including the original contract naming Berlau, are shown in the film *Red Ruth*.

61. BBA 761/23; and BL, 788.
62. BBA 791/01.
63. BBA 791/09.
64. The statement was made to Manfred Hertwig, who reports on his relationship with Harich and other members of the anti-Ulbricht forces in Reinhard Crusius and Manfred Wilke, eds., *Entstalinisierung. Der XX. Parteitag der KPdSU und seine Folgen* (Frankfurt am Main: Suhrkamp, 1977), 479. Hereafter: Crusius and Wilke, *Folgen*.
65. Crusius and Wilke, *Folgen*, 479.
66. See eyewitness account in, Walter Janka, *SeL*, 294.

Chapter 46

1. See Tucker, *Stalin*, 449–50; and Vaksberg, *Vyshinsky*, 355.
2. The party meeting at the Humboldt University is described in Havemann, *Fragen*, 107–13.
3. Hans Mayer cited in Crusius and Wilke, *Folgen*, 431–55.
4. The parallel to the Soviet trips made by Steffin in the 1930s is obvious.
5. Bentley, *Memoir*, 76.
6. Bentley, *Memoir*, 78.
7. Bentley, *Memoir*, 79.
8. Bentley, *Memoir*, 80.
9. Peter Hacks interview with Brecht in Mittenzwei, *Leben* 2:650.
10. Rohrwasser, "Ist also Schweigen das Beste?" 45.
11. Rohrwasser, "Ist also Schweigen das Beste?" 45.
12. Brecht, Diary 1920–54, 32.
13. Brecht, Diary 1920–54, 57.
14. Brecht, SPG 2:253.
15. See Martin Esslin, *Brecht: The Man and His Work* (Garden City, New York: Doubleday, 1961), 191; but also see BBA 29/14.
16. BBA 7/11. *Not* in BL.
17. See JW, *BinC*, 238.
18. JW, *BinC*, 240.
19. BBA 761/14.
20. Cited in Martin Jänicke, *Der Dritte Weg. Die antistalinistische Opposition gegen Ulbricht seit 1953* (Cologne: Neuer Deutscher Verlag, 1964). Hereafter: Jänicke, *DDW*.

21. A version of Kantorowicz's book with the missing details restored was published in what was then West Germany as *Spanisches Kriegstagebuch* (Cologne: Verlag Wissenschaft und Politik, 1966), 14. Hereafter: Kantorowicz, *SK*.
22. Kantorowicz, *SK*, 407–8.
23. BBA 655/01–04.
24. Letter cited in Völker, *Chronik*, 156. *Not* in BL.
25. Walter Janka shared this letter with Jorge Semprun, who then shared it with me. See Janka, *SmdW*, 67, where he recounts that his first Stasi interrogation was conducted in 1957 under a gigantic portrait of Stalín.
26. Wekwerth, *Schriften*, 76.
27. Wekwerth, *Schriften*, 78.
28. Wekwerth, *Schriften*, 78.
29. BBA 768/43.
30. BBA 791/74.
31. BBA 1826/03–04.
32. BL, 789.
33. See Medvedev, *On Stalin*, 86.
34. BBA 771/110.
35. BBA 771/112.
36. BBA 768/64.
37. BBA 1826/03–04.
38. BBA 655/59; and HC. *Not* in BL.
39. BBA 1646/48.
40. Piscator Papers.
41. Pozner, *Vladimir Pozner*, 105.
42. Author's interview with Gerhart Thieme, Berlin, 22 February 1989.
43. Hans Mayer, cited in Crusius and Wilke, *Folgen*, 451.
44. GW 6:2666.
45. Cited in Crusius and Wilke, *Folgen*.

Chapter 47

1. Janka, *SmdW*, 28ff.
2. Janka, *SeL*, 276.
3. See Brodersen, *Prozess*.
4. Cited in Brigitte Klump, *Das rote Kloster* (Hamburg: Hoffmann and Campe, 1978), 352. Hereafter: Klump, *Kloster*.
5. Author's interview with Hans Mayer, Frankfurt am Main, February 1978.
6. CIA file on Bertolt Brecht.
7. For one apparent exception, see Klump, *Kloster*, 316.
8. See Müller, *KoS*, 178–79, 407–10.
9. Personal letter to author from Jan Knopf, 20 January 1987; and in author's conversation with Knopf, Roskilde, Denmark, 3 October 1986.
10. The correspondence between Bunge and Brecht-Schall was provided to me by Hans Bunge before his death. The correspondence makes clear that Brecht-Schall used her influence within the Honecker state to prevent for several years the publication of Bunge's research on Ruth Berlau.

11. See John Fuegi, "Brechtian Characters in Search of Their Author," *Annals of Scholarship: On Character in Modern Drama* 9, no. 3 (1993).

12. Author's interview with Elisabeth Hauptmann, Berlin, 9 November 1970.

13. Sergei Tretiakov, "Bert Brecht," in Demetz, *Brecht: Twentieth Century Views*, 21.

14. Yuri Galanskov, who died in the gulag in 1972, cited in Conquest, *Kolyma*, 214.

Photo Credits

Given here (where known) are the names of the photographer, the copyright holder, and the special collection.

Frontispiece (clockwise from top): Hauptmann family, St. Louis; Berlau Collection, Berlin; Ernst Schumacher, Berlin; Steffin family, Berlin
1. Konrad Ressler Collection/Munich Photo Museum
2. Konrad Ressler Collection/Munich Photo Museum
3. Georg Birzele, Augsburg
4. Photographer unknown
5. Ernst Becker, Berlin
6. Photographer unknown
7. Photographer unknown
8. Marietta Rotter, Augsburg
9. Photographer unknown
10. Paula Banholzer Gross, Augsburg
11. Marie Rose Elgen, Augsburg
12. Heiner Hagg, Augsburg
13. Paula Banholzer Gross, Augsburg
14. Photographer unknown
15. Sketch by Caspar Neher
16. Ullstein Bilderdienst
17. Zander & Labisch
18. Ernst Schumacher, Berlin
19. Theaterwissenschaftliches Archiv Dr. Steinfeld
20. Central State Archive for Literature and Art, Moscow
21. Hans Christian Nørrregaard, Copenhagen
22. Hauptmann family, St. Louis
23. Ullstein Bilderdienst
24. Theaterwissenschaftliches Archiv Dr. Steinfeld
25. Fleisser
26. Theaterwissenschaftliches Archiv Dr. Steinfeld
27. Photographer unknown
28. Photographer unknown
29. Hauptmann family, St. Louis
30. Ullstein Bilderdienst
31. Photographer unknown
32. Cologne University Theater Museum

33. Hauptmann family, St. Louis
34. Ullstein Bilderdienst
35. Photographer unknown
36. Photographer unknown
37. Academy of Arts, Berlin
38. Photo in possession of Otto Hopf
39. Photographer unknown
40. Theaterwissenschaftliches Archiv Dr. Steinfeld
41. Steffin family, Berlin
42. Steffin family, Berlin
43. Markisches Museum, Berlin
45. Photographer unknown
46. Stadtsbibliothek, Berlin
47. Photographer unknown
48. Stadtsbibliothek, Berlin
49. Berlau Collection, Berlin
50. Berlau Collection, Berlin
51. Berlau Collection, Berlin
52. Berlau Collection, Berlin
53. Photographer unknown
54. Steffin Collection, Berlin
55. Berlau Collection, Berlin
56. Hauptmann family, St. Louis
57. Hauptmann family, St. Louis
58 and 59. *Pravda*
60. Photographer unknown
61. Photographer unknown
62. Berlau Collection, Berlin
63. Steffin Collection, Berlin
64. Photographer unknown
65. Berlau Collection, Berlin
66. Photographer unknown
67. Photographer unknown
68. Photographer unknown
69. Photographer unknown
70. Berlau Collection, Berlin
71. Feuchtwanger Archive, Los Angeles
72. Eric Bentley, New York
73. Gerda Goedhart, Holland
74. Hobby Hollywood
75. Paula Banholzer Gross, Augsburg
76. Berlau Collection, Berlin
77. Hauptmann family, St. Louis
78. Berlau Collection, Berlin
79. Berlau Collection, Berlin
80. Fuegi Collection, Washington
81. Berlau Collection, Berlin
82. Berlau photo, Eric Bentley, New York

83. Photographer Unknown
84. Berlau Collection, Berlin
85. Berlau Collection, Berlin
86. Berlau Collection, Berlin
87. Photographer Unknown
88. Theaterwissenschaftliches Archiv Dr. Steinfeld
89. Berliner Ensemble, Berlin
90. Willi Saeger, Berlin
91. Berliner Ensemble, Berlin
92. Berliner Ensemble, Berlin
93. Academy of Arts, Berlin/Christian Kraushaar
94. Gerda Goedhart, Holland
95. Photographer unknown
96. This version of death mask in Fuegi Collection
97. Hauptmann family, St. Louis
98. Berlau Collection, Berlin. Stasi photo.

Index